HOW SHALL THEY HEAR
WITHOUT A PREACHER?

The Life of Ernest Fremont Tittle

Photograph by Wesley Bowman Studio, Inc.

First Methodist Church, Evanston, Illinois

Photograph by J. D. Toloff.

Earnest Fremont Tittle

HOW SHALL THEY HEAR
WITHOUT A PREACHER?

The Life of Ernest Fremont Tittle

by Robert Moats Miller

The University of North Carolina Press / *Chapel Hill*

Manufactured in the United States of America.
Printed by The Seeman Printery, Durham, North Carolina.
ISBN 0-8078-1173-4.
Library of Congress Catalog Card Number 74-149031.

For Carol

CONTENTS

PREFACE

I would not wish to be guilty of promising more or something different in this brief preface than the following pages deliver. Certainly I would not wish any prospective reader to be gulled into thinking that here is one of those moist memorials or effusive reminiscences or quaint anecdotal accounts that frequently masquerade as religious biography. Surely those in search of pious refreshment will not find this book their cup of tea. I have intended this to be a serious study of a serious (but not dour) man who was profoundly involved in matters of ultimate concern to men and nations. The volume is for those who hunger to encounter an authentic person grappling with authentic issues and who have the stomach for substantial (although not, I trust, tough) fare. Ernest Fremont Tittle was such a person and, perhaps, to know him through these pages will assuage that hunger.

But to know Tittle will not bring peace of mind. He was the burdened minister of a real church with real and therefore flawed parishioners, not the unflawed pastor of that perfect and conveniently "invisible" Church fantasied by some seminary scholars. He was a man under authority commissioned to proclaim the word of God. The awfulness (and the presumption) of this commission was never long absent from his consciousness, for as he cautioned a class of young seminarians, "The prophet is not a man before a microphone saying: 'I predict'; he is a man declaring: 'Thus saith the Lord.' " He came to know the meaning of Paul's anguished cry: "For necessity is laid upon me. Woe to me if I do not preach the gospel." For Tittle preaching the gospel meant placing under judgment all of man's disorders—war, racial pride, exploitation, injustice, and all the other demoniac consequences of man's overweening egoism—thwarting God's design. It meant afflicting the comfortable even as he comforted the afflicted broken by the terror and contingency of life. Men in every age have been displeased to be told that God is not mocked, yet for thirty-one years from the pulpit of First Methodist Church, Evanston, Illinois—the "Cathedral of Methodism" and perhaps Methodism's most strategic parish—Tittle so declared, and though he bore the stripes of which Paul writes, it was death and not the muffling hands of men that in 1949 finally silenced his prophetic voice. Tittle comprehended, however, that we do not have death to fear, but the living God. Time and again he echoed Luther's affirmation: "Here I stand. I cannot do otherwise. God help me." Happily, Tittle's oak-hearted congregation stood fast in their support, thereby writing one of the fine chapters in the history of the "free pulpit" in America.

In all American Protestantism in the first half of the twentieth century no man exceeded in greatness Ernest Fremont Tittle in the totality of the quintuple roles of priest, pastor, preacher, prophet, and denominational and interdenominational leader. To be sure, there were more brilliant theologians than Tittle, and more powerful ecclesiastical statesmen and more popular evangelists and more burning mystics and more fiery crusaders and more saintly "Fools-for-Christ," but there were no "working" ministers greater than he. The significance of Tittle's prophecy lies precisely in the fact that he shared the responsibilities and vulnerability of Methodism's burdened band of parish ministers, and that at the time of his death he was acknowledged by that band as their leader. A fledgling minister once bitterly lamented: "Bravely and boldly the professors tell young seminarians to preach a realistic gospel—and wave good-bye to them from their bomb-proof dugout as the young hopefuls go out to the battle." But Tittle did not live in a bomb-proof dugout, and this is why I believe that no man's career more clearly illuminates than his the travails—theological, liturgical, institutional, and psychological—of modern American Protestantism. That these are large and bold assertions I quite comprehend. I like to think that those readers who see this volume through will at the last judge them comprehensible.

It is said we live today in a post-Protestant—if not, indeed, post-religious—era, and that the religious situation of only yesterday—Tittle's day—is beyond recovery. This assertion may very possibly be true. Yet it does not follow that our concern is merely antiquarian. For one thing, those issues challenging and shivering American society today were earlier confronted by Tittle; indeed, it is astonishing how closely the conflicts of our time, from the war in the jungles of Vietnam to the war in the streets of the United States, are a continuation of those faced by Tittle. "Relevant" is the most hackneyed word in our current vocabulary, yet no other word suggests itself to describe the meaning of Tittle's life for today. The conditions of the parish ministry and the structure of the institutional church have changed radically in the second half of the century, but those things that ultimately concerned Tittle are of ultimate concern today—in truth, are timeless. For another thing, there are few more fruitful ways to come to an understanding of American culture than through a study of American religious history. Tittle's career leads us to a larger perception of religion in American life and this perception in turn leads us to a deeper knowledge of American society at large. I have not written primarily for an audience of historians, but possibly historians will judge these pages to be a legitimate chapter in twentieth-century social history. (The truth is I have not written for *any* particular audience. I suppose this is a strategic error, but I cannot think that Tittle belongs exclusively to any special group of readers.)

The book is long and there are lengthy passages in Tittle's own words. In both regards the decision was a conscious one. I have said what I thought needed to be said, neither more nor less; and I have permitted Tittle's voice to be heard on the assumption that to do so is not inappropriate in a biography of a preacher.

Finally, to set the record straight here and now: I did not personally know Tittle and this is not an authorized biography commissioned by the Tittle family. The study was conceived by me and written on my terms. Having said this, let it immediately be added that the Tittle family has been warmly cooperative and wonderfully patient during my twelve years of labor. Not once have they attempted to influence my judgments or censor my words. My gratitude, therefore, to Ernest Fremont Tittle's widow, Glenna Myers Tittle, and to his sons, John Myers Tittle and William Myers Tittle, and to his daughter, Mrs. Elizabeth Poston, is enormous. Although the study was not initiated by the Tittles, it could never have been completed without their generous support.

Incomplete and inadequate recognition is given in the footnotes to the scores of individuals whose assistance sustained the enterprise. Here it is possible to acknowledge by name only five persons: Joseph Thomas, Roland Wolseley, Mrs. Roland Wolseley, John E. Semonche, and Donald G. Mathews. They read the manuscript from far different angles of vision, but they shared one thing in common: a critical and questioning eye. If the study possesses some merit, not a little of the credit goes to them. If after their readings the study remains flawed, doubtless it is because I was too mulish to accept *all* their suggestions. Ultimately, therefore, all errors of fact and interpretation are mine alone.

The Faculty Research Council of the University of North Carolina at Chapel Hill partially underwrote the costs of research travel to Colorado, Georgia, Illinois, and Ohio. The University of North Carolina History Department generously granted me a semester's leave at that crucial time when it was necessary to turn from research to the actual writing. And from the University of North Carolina—Duke University Cooperative Program in the Humanities I received a Summer Research Award to free me from summer teaching in order to bring the long labor to a close.

The dedication to my wife, Carol Herter Miller, comes from a grateful heart.

R. M. M.

HOW SHALL THEY HEAR
WITHOUT A PREACHER?

The Life of Ernest Fremont Tittle

1. *YOUNG MAN TITTLE*

I

It was Recognition Day at Ohio Wesleyan University, Wednesday, June 20, 1906. Though the dizzying twentieth-century winds of change then touched only lightly the pleasant little village of Delaware, Ohio, the young man who marched forward in Gray Chapel to be graduated magna cum laude and receive Wesleyan's highest award for classical scholarship, the Slocum Prize, knew that his own life was at an end and a beginning.[1] Because commencement is a time of introspection and because this serious lad of twenty had committed his life to the ministry, perhaps on this day the words of Saint Paul haunted his mind, "When I was a child, I spake as a child, I understood as a child, I thought as a child: but when I became a man, I put away childish things." Though the schoolboy was to become a man and put away childish things, though he was doomed, as all men, to be free and to make himself by his own engagement in choices, he could not erase what had gone before. "The child is the father of the man" is an incontrovertible insight. If we are to understand the forty-three years of increasing greatness that lay ahead for Wesleyan's proud senior, we must first probe those twenty years of existence that lay behind.

The task is not simple. There is much in the infancy and youth of Ernest Fremont Tittle that is unknown and indeed unknowable. When Agnellus, the ninth-century Bishop of Ravenna, undertook to write a complete series of lives of his predecessors, he was undaunted by lack of source material on one of his subjects and composed the life himself

1. *Ohio Wesleyan Transcript,* XL (June 20, 1906), 26.

"with the help of God and the prayers of his brethren." Unhappily, modern biographers are of less sturdy faith; they dare not venture much beyond the tether of their sources. A sketch of young man Tittle necessarily must be fragmented and tentative, an impression, not a photograph.

II

The physical appearance of the Slocum Prize winner excited little comment from the chapel audience, except perhaps for the observation that he seemed more youthful than his fellow seniors. The face was open, even innocent, strikingly boyish for a "sophisticated" senior. Yet it was a strong face: the chin so resolute as to win for him the nickname "Bulldog"; the lips firm; the nose blunt; the hair brown, light in texture, combed flat on the right side; the eyes dark, piercing, intense, dominating the entire face. Altogether it was a good face, suggesting steadiness and seriousness and resolve but little playfulness. The lad's body was trim and muscular, that of a welterweight boxer rather than a football lineman, and if he did not star in sports, he relished rough-and-tumble contact, both in school and later as a young pastor and YMCA secretary. Biographers often quite properly make much of the relationship between appearance and personality. Try to imagine Washington as a dwarf or John F. Kennedy as grotesque. In the case of young Tittle, however, no inspired relationship can be established. Free from facial scarring or bodily deformity, his appearance did not repel. Yet he was not so strikingly handsome as to flutter the hearts of all women and he was not so commanding of visage and figure as to awe the spirits of men. At twenty Tittle's looks gave him little reason to be either vain or cringing.

III

As the young man's physical endowment did not unconditionally shape his view of the world, so also it might be surmised that only tangentially did his ancestry determine his angle of vision. The mature Tittle displayed a yawning indifference to the subject of genealogy, and on several occasions confessed almost total ignorance of his forebears. To be sure, no one can escape totally his blood inheritance. Yet at the psychological level inheritance is significant only if the individual *thinks* it is significant, and Tittle shared the nonchalance of Jefferson, who once remarked dryly of his people, "They trace their pedigree far back in England and Scotland, to which let everyone ascribe the faith and merit he chooses."

The lad was descended from pioneering stock dating at least in part from colonial times, and hence he could count himself among the respected senior partners in the American enterprise. It was, however, a background undistinguished by great wealth or learning, fame or power. His forebears were little noted nor long remembered. In brief, Ernest's credentials were proper but hardly prestigious. Such was the briskness of his movements that his college comrades dubbed him "Zip." Yet he did not run for quite the same reason as Sammy Glick or Bigger Thomas, for no one had hurled at him the epithets "Christ-killer" or "Black boy." He had been careful to select ancestors whose faith was Christian and whose faces were white. Because young Tittle was not a Jew, Negro, or immigrant, his view of things was unclouded by anger or alienation; and because he was not an Adams or Apley or Compson, his view was neither misted by patrician pride nor distorted by aristocratic estrangement.

The truth is that the young man did not trouble to peer into the family past. He possessed a name. It was not the name of one of the nation's disinherited racial or ethnic minorities. He was under no compulsion to prove his right to membership in the national club. And unlike the scions of New England brahmins or Southern cavaliers he was under no strain to uphold a name honored by association with the Mayflower Band or Bonnie Prince Charlie. Perhaps he was aware at this graduation time that any glory or any shame that came to be associated with his name would be the consequence of what he, Ernest Fremont Tittle, might do or leave undone. His unconcern with his own ancestry was to find reflection in his indifference to the pedigree of others. The mature Tittle held no man in contempt or in awe because of his family, applying to ancestry the lines of Robert Burns, "The rank is but the guinea's stamp / The man's the gowd for a' that."[2]

2. In our attempt to know young man Tittle it is comforting to think that ancestry is not destiny, for despite much time-consuming (though scarcely passionate) research, much concerning his forebears remains a mystery. A first cousin, Mr. Walter Tittle, the noted artist, generously shared his genealogical investigations, and I am much in his debt. Alas, his findings are incomplete and inconclusive. The picture is somewhat filled out by personal interviews with Ernest Fremont Tittle's brother, widow, and children, and also with individuals who were childhood neighbors and schoolmates. An examination of Clark County birth, marriage, and death records proved helpful, as did a scrutiny of Springfield newspapers, street directories, and gravestone inscriptions. Tittle himself stated the little he knew about his ancestors in letters to Mrs. Eugene Field Eckel, September 14, 1933, and W. F. Tittle, June 2, 1942. (Tittle Collection, now housed at The University of North Carolina at Chapel Hill and soon to be deposited in the Garrett Theological Seminary Library, Evanston, Ill.; hereafter, unless otherwise indicated, all correspondence cited is in this collection.)

Clayton Darius Tittle, the father, was born in Hummelstown, Pennsylvania, on November 25, 1865. The first Tittles had migrated to America from England and northern Ireland in the mid-eighteenth century, settling originally on the Maryland border where they built blockhouses and took out land warrants. Elements of the clan then drifted into the area of Hummelstown and Harrisburg. Some of these Tittles, including grandfather Levi, married Pennsylvania Dutch girls, and thus a strain of German was added to the English and Scotch-Irish blood of Ernest's paternal ancestors. Ernest's mother was Elizabeth May (or Mary) Henry. She was born somewhere in Ohio in 1865.[3] Nothing is known about the Henry lineage, although family tradition has it (quite naturally) that Patrick Henry was a distant relation.

As young Tittle was not a stranger in America, so he was not an outsider in the land of Ohio, for he had been born in Springfield, only some fifty miles from where the graduation exercises were under way. A cluster of Tittles had migrated from Pennsylvania to Springfield in the 1870's, and in 1876, for the first time, the town directory carried the name Tittle, listing two uncles and grandfather Levi. The father's name, Clayton, was not added until 1881-82.[4] Clayton married Elizabeth Henry on November 18, 1884, and the following October 21 a son was born to them in their home.[5]

IV

In that year Geronimo was still terrorizing the Southwest, the Sioux were yet to be finally crushed in the Ghost Dance War, the "Boomers" were only now flooding the Oklahoma District, and not for five years was the United States Census director to announce "there can hardly be said to be a frontier line." But the frontier line long since had been erased in Ohio. Tittle the man recalled that as a boy it seemed to him that "God, Buffalo Bill, and Frances Willard were the three most

3. The gravestone in Fernlawn Cemetery does not give the middle name; the marriage certificate, state of Ohio, Clark County Probate Court, gives only the initial *M;* and the spelling of the middle name on the death certificate, Register of Deaths, No. 1, Springfield Board of Health, has been obscured so that the name could be either May or Mary. Neither the marriage certificate nor death certificate state the exact place and date of her birth.

4. Tittle was mistaken when he wrote, "My people came to Ohio from Hummelstown, Dolphin [sic] County, Pennsylvania, sometime before the Civil War." Letter from Tittle to W. F. Tittle, June 2, 1942.

5. Presumably the birth took place at home for the Springfield hospital was not built until 1887. See Benjamin F. Prince, *A Standard History of Springfield and Clark County, Ohio,* 2 vols. (New York and Chicago: American Historical Society, 1922), I, 427.

wonderful people on the earth."[6] Only in some happier world than this, however, would the boy have Buffalo Bill's opportunity to scalp an Indian; there simply was an acute shortage of savage redmen in Ohio in 1885. After all, the center of population in the United States was, according to the 1880 Census, eight miles west by south of Cincinnati, Ohio. Ohio Wesleyan's most honored senior was clearly no rawboned, roughhewn product of a primitive frontier society.

Less self-evident but equally incontrovertible is the fact that here was no barefooted, tan-cheeked farm boy blessed by birth in a bucolic paradise. Ohio was no longer the Garden of the World (as it once had been in myth if not in reality) peopled by sturdy yeomen only slightly less innocent than the first Adam. To be sure, when *Huckleberry Finn* appeared in 1885, many Americans still were able to identify with Twain's evocation of agrarian, mid-century life; and reading James Whitcomb Riley permitted them to pay (as Richard Hofstadter suggests) a kind of homage to the fancied innocence of their origins. Yet even as men sang the songs of Stephen Foster, recited the lines of Whittier, and read the smiling words of Riley they sensed the old order slipping away. Rural America was a stag at bay with the hounds of industry, technology, and urbanization moving in for the kill. Revealingly, the Census of 1890 states that the center of all manufacturing in the United States was at a point eight and a half miles west of Canton, Ohio.

Thus Tittle was not a product of the passing rural order, but neither was he a child of the emerging urban culture. Rather, he was a town boy—and an Ohio town boy at that—and he knew an environment not unlike that of millions of Americans born at the turn of the century. Perhaps, however, such a statement really does not help our understanding very much. After all, it makes considerable difference whether town culture is described by Booth Tarkington or Edward Howe, Thornton Wilder or Sinclair Lewis. Sherwood Anderson's *Winesburg, Ohio* and Helen Santmyer's *Ohio Town* are set in the same state in the same general period of time; they might as well be located on different planets, so dissimilar are they. If a generalization may be made, most autobiographical accounts of town life are warm and appreciative, most sociological studies are mordant and deprecative. Perhaps the only hope to approximate the "truth" about Tittle as a young man is to sketch Springfield at the turn of the century and place what little is known about Tittle's early years in that setting.

6. "Frances Willard," typed MS, a sermon preached October 1, 1939, Tittle Collection; all unpublished sermons hereafter cited are in this collection.

To begin with, to be a town boy in nineteenth-century America did not necessarily mean imprisonment in a world of asphalt, cement, and glass, cut off completely from the mystery and majesty of nature. Doubtless the nineteenth-century town had its nightmarish aspects, but within loping distance there were green fields, dark woods, and clear streams. In later years Tittle was constantly to find renewal of spirit and body climbing a mountain in Washington, whipping a trout stream in Colorado or paddling on a quiet Minnesota lake. Surely it was as a boy in the country surrounding Springfield, a gentle rolling land laced with streams and blanketed with groves of trees, that he first came to love the outdoors, and the odds are at least even that something of the green Ohio countryside went into his making.

Although at home in fields and woods, Tittle was nonetheless a town boy. Springfield, wrote an observer in 1846, "is noted for the morality and intelligence of its inhabitants, and, by many, is considered the most beautiful village within the limits of Ohio."[7] Forty years later, however, Springfield was described as a "famous manufacturing city of 35,000 to 40,000 people," "one of the most commercially solid and prosperous, as it is certainly one of the most beautiful inland cities of America."[8] Springfield dominated Clark County, possessing in the mid-1880's over half the county's total population. Industry dominated Springfield, in the mid-1880's one-fourth of the town's population being employed in manufacturing, especially in the great network of factories collectively called the "Champion works" that made Springfield a world leader in the manufacturing of agricultural machinery. In 1887 disaster overtook this promising industrial complex. Enterprises were plunged into receivership. Banks failed. A stiff-kneed management resisted the attempts of the Knights of Labor to unionize a major factory, resulting in strife and ultimately, in 1891, the closing of a plant employing two thousand hands. The jobless multiplied. Unrest mounted. Community leaders of substance were wiped out. When the depression of 1893 swept the nation, it was said that "Springfield had not yet recovered from a panic of its own. . . ."[9] "Good times" returned to Springfield at the very end of the decade, but the permanent passing of leadership in the

7. Quoted in Henry Howe, *Historical Collections of Ohio* (Cincinnati: State of Ohio, 1902), I, 397.

8. Quoted in *ibid.,* p. 399. Other sources suggest the population of Springfield in the mid-1880's to be 26,000. See especially *Springfield and Clark County Ohio: Compiled by Workers of the Writers' Program of the Work Projects Administration in the State of Ohio* (Springfield, Ohio: Springfield Tribune Printing Co., 1941), p. 33. This figure agrees with the United States Census statistics: 20,730 inhabitants in 1880; 31,895 inhabitants in 1890.

9. Prince, *Standard History,* p. 247.

manufacturing of agricultural machinery left a void only partially filled by new industry. The depression of '93, the harshest of the century, racked the entire nation. But because Springfield could date its economic troubles back to 1887, the impact was unusually severe and the effect lasting.

Tittle was very young during this time of trouble. He was only two when the first blow fell and under fifteen when the crisis passed, and maybe it all escaped his consciousness. Perhaps, however, something of the mood of anger and frustration reflected in the drawn faces of adults and in the bitter tone of their overheard conversations touched the lad. Tittle the man never considered the American economic system sacrosanct; it is possible (though not provable) that his early childhood memories sharpened his critical sense.

Unlike many American towns undergoing industrialization, Springfield attracted relatively few immigrants, the Census of 1900 placing the number at only 3,302 of a total population of 38,258. Consequently, Springfield's population remained basically homogeneous—basically English, German, and Scotch-Irish. The one considerable stream of new immigration came not from eastern and southern Europe, but from the American South. Negroes were attracted to Springfield because "no colored line had been drawn against them in the shops and in the pursuit of other avocations."[10] The schools were integrated, but if Tittle had close classroom and playground black friends, it is certain that these chums did not enter the Tittle home.[11] In 1904 and again in 1906 racial tensions in Springfield erupted in violence, and the memory of these riots may have contributed to the color blindness of the mature Tittle.

Tittle's boyhood was consequently passed in an attractive town set in a lovely countryside; it was, however, a town that had lost its innocence. The harsh facts of life in an industrial society were being painfully learned even as the boy himself grew to adolescence. Springfield shared with much of the United States the wrenchings that accompanied the passing of the older agrarian order. Its citizens knew the meaning of racism, poverty, unemployment, class conflict, and the anxiety of struggling in a Spencerian industrial jungle where the weak were ruthlessly weeded out and only the fittest survived.

10. William M. Rockel (ed.), *20th Century History of Springfield and Clark County, Ohio, and Representative Citizens* (Chicago: Biographical Publishing Co., 1908), p. 137.

11. Author's interview with Stern Tittle, Thomasville, Ga., April 18-19, 1960.

V

It is not quite sufficient to say that young Tittle was a product of an Ohio town at the turn of the century, for although class lines were not drawn as unconscionably as in some seaboard cities and some southern sections, it assuredly made a difference whether one's father worked in a bank or in a foundry; whether one's home was a mansion on upper High Street or in a soiled rooming house in that section of town revealingly called "the Jungles." The Tittles were neither the brightest nor the dullest stars in the Springfield galaxy. They belonged to what was termed in colonial America the middling class and to what sociologists today, with their fine precision, probably call something like the upper lower middle class. It is frequently held that Ernest Fremont Tittle's life is in the classic Samuel Smiles and Horatio Alger tradition, that of a poor boy who rose from rags to riches, or rather more exactly in Ernest's case, from rags to renown. This is not quite true. (In fact it is not quite true of Alger's young heroes, who achieved respectability, not great wealth.)

Clayton Tittle found steady employment as a clothing salesman, being associated with one firm during most of Ernest's boyhood. The numerous members of the Tittle clan are listed in the Springfield directories as clerk, salesman, superintendent of lighting company, pattern maker, meterman, gas fitter, printer, traveling salesman, plumber, foreman in pattern room, foreman in casting room, molder, traveling agent, canvasser, driver, lithographer. These Tittles were ambitious, industrious, capable men, and the fragmentary evidence suggests that most of them or their sons in time scrambled up the ladder of success to upper middle-class status.

Clayton Tittle did not own his own home and he moved his family from residence to residence, at least four and possibly five times during Ernest's youth. This peripatetic existence need not have scarred the boy with a sense of rootlessness. All of the houses were within a radius of a few blocks. None of them were in shanty neighborhoods. Usually the prior occupants were Tittles, for the clan seems to have done a good deal of exchanging of homes. The two houses that survive today, while uninspired architectually, are not hovels.[12] In the Tittle home, as in millions of middling households, thrift was more a necessity than a virtue, and probably grocery string was carefully saved, one pinch of tea sufficed for three cups, teeth were brushed with salt and baking soda, slivers of soap were pressed together to make a large cake, chewing gum

12. I am grateful to Miss Carrie Clarke and Mrs. Robert S. Shaw (the former Nell Clarke) for guiding me on June 15, 1960, to the Tittle homes.

was left on the boys' bedposts overnight, and, in general, the family lived by the stern motto "Use it up, wear it out; make it do, or do without."

Like countless other lads of his class and generation, Ernest held down a series of jobs. While in grammar school he lit city gas lamps, turning them on at nine in the evening and off at five the next morning. During high-school summer vacations he labored in an iron foundry—for five dollars a week. In college he waited tables, served as a professor's assistant, and taught several high-school classes.[13] Before entering the ministry Tittle already knew what it was to earn bread by the sweat of the brow.

But all this does not spell poverty. For one thing, Tittle himself never referred to a poverty-stricken childhood. For another, his brother does not recall serious deprivation. For a third, men and women who were then neighboring children and schoolmates deny that the Clayton Tittles were considered poor. After all, for a time they had a maid. Ernest took violin lessons and played with the church choir and in concerts; years later when the *Springfield News-Sun* reported on Tittle's career, it flung a banner headline across all eight columns of one page: "Former Local Musician Observes Anniversary of Pastorate."[14] The Tittle Christmas tree ornaments were considered the most elaborate in the neighborhood. Ernest, as befitting the son of a clothing salesman, dressed rather more neatly than Tom, Dick, and Harry. And in the home were paint brushes and boxes, the lad being almost as talented at drawing as in music.

It is clear that Tittle came from a scrambling, tight, but not destitute economic background, and he was not scarred. Tittle ran hard all his life, but what he sought at the end of the rainbow was not a pot of gold. Had money been his goal in life, he would have possessed it, for he commanded the brains, ability, and drive to make his way successfully in the business world. Instead, his decision, already reached by this June day in 1906, was to enter the Methodist ministry, where his first annual compensation was to be $800 and a broken-down house.[15]

VI

A few days after Tittle's death, his friend Paul Hutchinson of the *Christian Century* affirmed: "It is not often that I meet a preacher who

13. Unsigned, undated note in Tittle's handwriting in Tittle Collection. Perhaps he also delivered bakery goods in a horse-drawn wagon, as his brother vaguely remembers.

14. Paul Hutchinson, "Portrait of a Preacher," foreword to Tittle, *A Mighty Fortress* (New York: Harper & Brothers, 1949), p. xi.

15. Letter from Tittle to N. C. Nagler, March 7, 1932.

seems to me to have been foreordained to that high calling from his mother's womb. Most prominent ministers suggest the eminence they might have attained in other pursuits: 'What a great jurist he would have made!' Or 'what a great corporation promoter!' Or 'what a great actor!' But it was never possible for me to think of Ernest Tittle as anything but a Christian preacher. For this he was born, predestined, foreordained—and let his Methodist brethren make of such Calvinism what they please."[16]

Hutchinson is persuasive, but not entirely convincing. To be sure, it is not possible to imagine Tittle as a Valentino, Gable, or Brando, or as a Vanderbilt, Gould, or Morgan. It is permissible, however, to hold that he might well have been a "great jurist," not perhaps a Holmes or Brandeis, but very possibly a Charles Evans Hughes or Earl Warren. Indeed, his brother and childhood friends dimly recollect that at one time Ernest seriously considered the legal profession. He might have been a public servant, not perhaps a Franklin D. Roosevelt, but very possibly a Henry L. Stimson or George Norris. Nor does it strain credibility to imagine him as a teacher, doctor, engineer, or even a warrior in the mold of Omar Bradley or George C. Marshall. In point of fact, he came within a heartbeat of entering West Point. "During my senior year at Springfield High School," Tittle remembered, "I made application for admission to West Point. At that time, admission was secured by congressional appointment, the appointment being made once in two years. When I heard that the appointment for our congressional district had just been made and that I would need to wait another two years, I gave up the idea and decided to go to college instead."[17]

William Temple, whom Tittle much admired and frequently quoted, once said that the greatest single transgression against God that a young person could make was to choose his lifework (where there was a choice) on purely selfish grounds. That the young Wesleyan senior wanted to be *somebody* is beyond debate. His ambition, as William Herndon said of his law partner, Lincoln, was a little engine that knew no rest, but it was an engine fueled by a passion to serve, not by a drive for wealth or power. The point of disagreement with Hutchinson is that the ministry was not the only calling open to a young man committed to a life of

16. "A Word About a Friend," *Christian Century*, LXVI (August 17, 1949), 958.

17. Neither Joseph M. O'Donnell, assistant archivist, United States Military Academy, nor Major General R. V. Lee, Office of the Adjutant General, were able to locate Tittle's name in their files. This does not mean, they explained, that Tittle's account is not true. Letters to author, June 24, 1959, and July 13, 1959. Tittle's statement is in a letter to Edward L. Rice, April 1, 1940.

service. It is unthinkable to imagine Tittle as a huckster. (It is also unthinkable to imagine him as a monk contemplating in solitude the dazzling mystery of God.) We need not conclude, however, that he was "born, predestined, foreordained" for a single career, that of "Christian preacher."

Why, then, did Tittle elect the ministry? Hutchinson holds that it "would be hard to say," and after suggesting the influence of Ohio Wesleyan, he concludes: "I am inclined to think that he was caught up in a tendency so general that he would himself have found it hard to put his finger on the time and place of his decision."[18] This is a sensible statement. In all truth, an authoritative answer is beyond the biographer's grasp; yet the search must be made.

In 1912 the bishops of Northern Methodism stated, "No man has ever been lawfully inducted into holy orders under Methodist sanction without first declaring that he was called by the Holy Ghost to that office and work."[19] Yet Tittle experienced no burning bushes, blinding flashes on a Damascus road, dramatic readings of Paul's Epistle to the Romans, or hearts strangely warmed at Aldersgate. There is no evidence that he heard a call, faced a moment of truth, and made a climactic decision to commit his life to Christ. "When I went to Drew Theological Seminary I had but very little in the way of religious experience," he was later to remember. "I had, however, a growing desire to be a minister."[20]

Why this growing desire? Undoubtedly some men enter the ministry in order to reconcile, as George Eliot sneered, "small ability with great ambition, superficial knowledge with the prestige of erudition, a middling morals with a high reputation for sanctity." Veblen, Mencken, and company have suggested even more ignoble motivations, depicting clergymen as "ipso facto frauds" consumed in the "fabrication of vendible imponderables," epicene individuals to be carefully watched, "especially when young girls or young boys were about."

The motivation of aspiring ministers has now become the subject of considerable psychological investigation, and increasingly seminarians are required to undergo psychological examination. The conspicuous social dignity of the ministry, psychology suggests, attracts young men who have suffered in their childhoods from feelings of inferiority. Persuasive also is the insight that the ministry provides a psychological

18. Hutchinson, "Portrait," p. x.
19. *The Daily Christian Advocate,* Methodist Episcopal Church, May 4, 1912, p. 100.
20. Letter from Tittle to Sam Napolitan, December 6, 1943.

security to those who experienced a loveless home life and for whom the church means "being at home in my father's house." Then, too, sensitive, aesthetic lads often seek refuge in the church from the storms of "real" existence in the secular world; "those who can do, those who can't preach." Further, in American culture the ministry (and priesthood) represents one of the few occupations that permits a man to participate without embarrassment or apology in emotional experiences mediated by aesthetic forms.

Let us now place these generalizations against the fragmentary knowledge we have of Tittle as a young man in the hope of illuminating the motives compelling him to the ministry. Elizabeth Tittle, the mother, was a devout Christian woman who attended the St. Paul Methodist Episcopal Church, though illness prevented extensive participation in parish activities.[21] Religion was a part of her very being. Burdened with asthma and other afflictions no less agonizing because they were possibly psychosomatic in origin, by pain sentenced to bed many days of the year, increasingly broken to a condition of semi-invalidism, grieved by the death in 1891 of her infant daughter, this frail woman found in her religion strength, solace, and the promise of final victory. The boy revered his mother, and his thoughts must have been with her this graduation day, for she was not present. Two years earlier, on April 1, 1904, death had come to her in the cruel form of chronic nephritis at the cruelly premature age of thirty-nine. Ernest was eighteen at the time, not an age when a sensitive boy can bear lightly the loss of an adored and adoring mother. Years later Tittle recalled that his mother's death "after a long and painful illness" was "to me a terrific blow."[22]

Elizabeth Tittle wanted her sons "to have the best and be the best."[23] Consistent with her piety, she coveted for them a good name and an honorable life. The ministry would have provided the status she aspired for her sons. It is possible that she expressed this hope to Ernest, perhaps for the last time in the moments before her death. In this hour of shock and sorrow, he may have made his commitment to the ministry.

21. The St. Paul minister Ira P. Benton informed me (October 30, 1959): "There is no record that the family of Dr. Tittle ever joined the church, while some of the older members are of the opinion that his mother was a member." Despite the silent record, I believe Elizabeth Tittle was a St. Paul member. This is the memory of several individuals close to the Tittles in Springfield, and it is also the memory of the younger son, Stern.

22. Letter from Tittle to Mrs. Daniel Taylor Hinckley, February 11, 1941.

23. Author's interview with Miss Carrie Clarke and Mrs. Robert S. Shaw (the former Nell Clarke), Springfield, Ohio, June 15, 1960; letters from Mrs. Robert S. Shaw to author, August 11, 1959, and November 3, 1959; letter from Mrs. Charlotte Margileth to author, October 30, 1959.

Of course, this is conjecture. It is certain, however, that the mother influenced her older son toward a career of service, if not toward the ministry itself.

Clayton Tittle, the father, was not a man of ostensible piety. If he attended church, it was but rarely, and it is improbable that he was a St. Paul member.[24] Unlike many nineteenth-century Methodist fathers, he did not read aloud from the Bible, establish a family altar, or lead in family prayer. Those who remember this early period are in agreement that Clayton Tittle did not share in the religious passion of his wife or, to phrase it more charitably, if he possessed such a passion, it was not made known in faithful public worship or professions of piety. Indeed, Clayton Tittle took his sorrows to another sanctuary. He loved the bottle not wisely but too well. In his long, gallant struggle with an implacable foe he was ultimately victorious, but not before alcohol had won a number of fearful battles in the long war. Why he drank heavily is unknown. The explanation may be simple. As a salesman in a clothing store, he was expected to treat his customers to a toddy in the saloon next door and perhaps he too took a sociable (and profitable) drink. The mid-twentieth-century expense-account pre-luncheon martini is simply a continuation of the practice of nineteenth-century "Springfield merchants [who] kept a jug of whiskey by the water pitcher for the free use of all. . . ."[25] By the end of the century the custom was to step next door. In this manner perhaps he slowly, insensibly, lost his self-mastery. It is fashionable to view alcoholism as a disease comparable to, say, diabetes. The difference is that *every* man is a *potential* alcoholic. Every man who drinks runs the risk of slipping beyond the point of no return; he needs only to consume enough liquor over a long enough period of time. Perhaps this was Clayton's commonplace but nonetheless tragic fate— a fate, however, not beyond volitional control. Perhaps the explanation for his drinking is more complex. Perhaps he found in the bottle a companionship his semi-invalid wife could not always give him. Perhaps whiskey eased the sexual tensions that almost inevitably would rack a vigorous man in the prime of life who found himself married to a chronically ill woman. Perhaps only in liquor could he find momentary release from the double strain of being breadwinner and, because Eliza-

24. This is the judgment of his younger son, Stern, and several other individuals. As noted earlier, the St. Paul records do not prove or disprove this point. At the time of his death, however, he was a member of the Central Methodist Church, Springfield, according to the obituary in the *Springfield Daily News,* March 29, 1946.

25. Prince, *Standard History,* I, 442.

beth was so often bedridden, homemaker. In any case, Clayton Tittle drank—and drank hard.

Yet he was not a sodden brute nor was he a helpless lush. The little children in the neighborhood regarded him as a kind man who often cooked the family dinners, baked cakes, made ice cream, fixed toys, imaginatively decorated Christmas trees, and enjoyed picnics. They knew him as "a most likeable man, very jolly, keen, with a quick mind," a man "very considerate to everyone." He "tried to do the things she [his wife] wasn't able to do."[26] More significantly, the younger son, Stern, remembers his father with affection, as a kind and generous father, who after a visit to the saloon retired quietly to his room and did not bully his family.[27] Thus there are those who saw Clayton Tittle as a good man, faithful husband, and gentle father, whose only flaw was a weakness regarding liquor, a weakness that can be understood if not condoned.

The wife of Clayton's stepson remembers Clayton Tittle in an importantly different light.[28] In her eyes, he was a good man but also a strong man; a man of forceful personality, capable of anger, with the will to conquer his ancient foe. The fact that he lived to be eighty proves that he did not go to an alcoholic's early grave. A snapshot taken about the time of Ernest's graduation reveals a sturdily built man, broad-shouldered and full-chested, with a commanding face. It is hardly a picture of a weak, ineffectual fellow.

Though these views are significant, the crucial image of the man is, of course, the one held by his older son. The papers of Ernest Fremont Tittle are silent on this point. There is extant not a single letter either to or from his father. Not once in his sermons does the son refer to him, either in love or bitterness. One volume from Ernest's pen, *A World That Cannot Be Shaken,* is dedicated "To My Father." Yet the inferential evidence points to a strained relationship between father and son, especially as the son grew to manhood.

Here was a lad who revered his fragile mother. As this good Christian woman's heart was wounded by the excessive drinking of her husband, so Ernest must have shared in his mother's pain. It does not

26. Author's interview with Miss Carrie Clarke and Mrs. Robert S. Shaw (the former Nell Clarke), Springfield, Ohio, June 15, 1960; letters from Mrs. Robert S. Shaw to author, August 11, 1959, and November 3, 1959.

27. Author's interview with Stern Tittle, Thomasville, Ga., April 18-19, 1960.

28. Author's interview with Mrs. Orville E. Kiser, Springfield, Ohio, June 16, 1960. As shall be seen, after the death of Elizabeth, Clayton remarried. His second wife, a divorcee, Rosie E. Buckles Kiser, had a son, Orville, by her first marriage. After Rosie's death, Clayton made his home for some time with Orville and his wife. Thus her testimony bears great weight.

matter that the man never struck his wife or sons in drunken rage. It was sufficient that Elizabeth Tittle should spend many long, empty evening hours in the knowledge that her husband preferred the saloon to her company. Perhaps Ernest shared in this knowledge, for it is probable that she poured out her bitterness to the only available listener, her older boy. Here was a lad of propriety who knew the shame of searching saloons for a father too blind with drink to make his way home alone.[29] Here was a lad of sensitivity who too often watched his father stagger up the front walk, aware that the neighbors were also at their windows. Here was a lad of ambition whose father never achieved more than middling success as a clothing salesman. Here was a lad who even as a schoolboy sweated to earn money while his father pushed countless dollars over the bar. Here was an extraordinarily conscientious youngster who, being five years older than his only brother, must have felt a sense of responsibility that the younger boy did not know; and consequently it is not to be wondered that the younger son should remember the father's kindness and the older the father's irresponsibility. And when only two years after Elizabeth Tittle died Clayton remarried a divorced woman, it is understandable (particularly in that era of stern morality) that Ernest could not bring himself to love his stepmother as he could not bring himself to forgive his father. A gulf now separated the father and son that was never to be completely bridged.[30] Is it not possible that Ernest sought in the church a psychological security he did not know at home; that he sought in the ministry a prestige that would wipe out the inner shame of being a drinking man's son; that he sought a Father to substitute for the natural father who failed him? Erik Erikson in his study of young man Luther makes brilliant use of George Bernard Shaw's confession, "I work as my father drank." These words might have been uttered by the young Tittle.

The *Ohio Wesleyan Transcript* for June 20, 1906, described Ernest's "Previous Condition of Servitude" as "Engaged," his "Tendencies Developed" as "Matrimony," and his "Favorite Study" as the "Ladies' Home Journal." There is more than a casual relationship between his commitment to matrimony and his commitment to the ministry, for the girl to whom Tittle was betrothed powerfully influenced him toward a career in the Methodist Church. Glenna Myers was born on May 2, 1881, in North Hampton, Ohio, a little village ten miles northwest of

29. Mrs. Robert S. Shaw's words are: "During those years, Ernest would often go and get his father out of a saloon, and I know it made him very bitter." Letter to author, August 11, 1959.

30. Author's interview with Mr. and Mrs. John M. Tittle, Winnetka, Ill., August 4, 1959.

Springfield. Her parents, who were of German and Swiss stock, moved to Springfield when she was very young where they soon established themselves as citizens of enterprise, civic responsibility, and Methodist piety. Although neither the wealthiest nor most prestigious of Springfield's citizens, they were clearly a rung or two higher on the social ladder than the Clayton Tittles.[31] Methodism's concern for the nurture of her youth rather than "destiny" brought Glenna and Ernest together, for they met when she was president and he vice-president of the St. Paul Epworth League. This was in 1903-4, a year after her graduation from Ohio Wesleyan and his freshman year at Wittenberg College in Springfield. Tittle later joked that his initial subordinate position remained unchanged after marriage.[32]

Attempting to judge the "style" of a person from her picture in a college yearbook is a hazardous enterprise. In the Ohio Wesleyan *The Bijou* above the name of Glenna Myers, class of 1902, is the face of an attractive young lady: deep set, penetrating eyes, hair abundant in the fashion of the time, good cheek bones and chin, finely proportioned nose, moderately full lips. Her expression is grave. It is a face appropriate to the verbal descriptions given by those who knew her in this period. Testimony is in agreement that Glenna Myers was a splendid young woman: pretty of feature, trim of figure, neat of dress, gracious of manner, proper of morals, alert of mind, and above all, in religion most devout. Not only a leader of youth groups in St. Paul Church, she was also active in YWCA work at Ohio Wesleyan and then went on to become assistant state secretary of the Young Women's Christian Association for Ohio Colleges.

Attempting to judge why young people fall in love and marry is also a hazardous enterprise. Perhaps Ernest was interested in the Myers's moderate wealth. This explanation must be rejected, not because it is cynical (after all, hundreds of great Americans have married women of affluence), but because it does not agree with the facts. Glenna brought much to the young man she adored, but she did not bring money. Perhaps Ernest saw in Glenna a symbol of the propriety for which he hungred and in marriage to her both an act of atonement for being a drinking man's son and a reassurance of his own respectability. The difficulty with the hypothesis that Tittle was driven by psychic needs into the arms of Miss Myers is that it is unsupported by either direct or

31. Prince, *Standard History*, II, 396-97.
32. Author's interviews with Glenna Myers Tittle, Evanston, Ill., July 27 and 31 and August 14 and 28, 1959. Though Mrs. Tittle was exceedingly gracious and on some points informative, she did no more than touch on her courtship with Ernest. See also letter from Ira P. Benton to author, October 30, 1959.

circumstantial evidence. To be sure, there was some social distance between the Clayton Tittles and the William Myers, but it simply was not a case of a Snopes marrying a Compson. Perhaps Ernest saw in Glenna a mother image. She was, after all, more than four years his senior. Moreover, someone (though not Ernest or Glenna, for the hand is not theirs) penciled on their marriage certificate in the Clark County Probate Court, "Please don't take ages." It is true that Ernest was deeply attached to his mother, but there is no evidence that in his adult life this attachment crippled him emotionally. It is true that there existed an unusual age differential between the couple and this fact *might* be psychologically relevant. But again, there is nothing in their marriage relationship to suggest, much less *prove,* that the marriage would have been any more or any less happy had the ages of the partners been different. For a man of twenty-two to marry a woman of twenty-seven invites invidious speculation. Yet if it proves to be a good marriage that endures for forty-three years—as long as a lifetime—must not then the theories give way to the record of those forty-three years? In any case, a cursory check of the marriages of American leaders suggest that great men rather often marry older women. Perhaps Ernest leaped into marriage, as, unhappily, a lot of youngsters do, because the urgency of his passions gave him no peace. Yet he did not rush to the nupital bed. Engaged in 1906, he and his beloved prudently agreed not to marry until he finished his theological training, in 1908. Perhaps— just perhaps—Ernest Tittle proposed to Glenna Myers because he was in love. And he was in love because the girl of his choice was pretty, personable, intelligent, spirited, sensible, and shared his religious view of life and hopes for the future; and because, not the least, she obviously had her cap tipped for him. The major point is that any doubts that the young man might have had about entering the ministry were resolved, not compounded, by the encouraging attitude of the girl with whom he had fallen in love.

Thus far an attempt has been made to suggest the possible influence of Tittle's mother and father and betrothed on his decision to enter the ministry. It is now time to return to Paul Hutchinson's thoughtful conjecture that Tittle "was caught up in a tendency so general that he would himself have found it hard to put his finger on the time and place of his decision."

What, then, was this tendency so general? To begin with, Ernest was born at a time when Methodism was the largest and strongest Protestant denomination in the nation and in a state where Methodists boasted twice the membership of the next largest denomination (Presbyterian) and in a town where Methodists led.[33] Thus no laws of probability were violated when he attended Sunday School and in 1894 was received from probation into membership in the St. Paul Methodist Episcopal Church, perhaps following a revival.[34] As a boy and young man Ernest took an active part in the life of St. Paul, playing the violin in the choir and assuming leadership of the young peoples' groups. Christian nurture was the explicit purpose of the Sunday School; it was also an implicit aim of the public schools as late as the turn of the century. To be sure, it was no longer quite true to say that the public schools were an unofficial auxiliary of evangelical Protestantism. To be sure, as the century drew to a close secularization had triumphed partially over piety in the schools of Ohio. Bible study, daily Bible reading, acts of worship, formal courses in religion and morality, all these and more were being nudged from the classroom. Even the strictly religious content of the reading books in Ohio schools dropped to only 2 to 4 percent by 1891. Yet the losses (as most Protestant churchmen viewed them) were relative, not absolute. Particularly persistent was the custom of conducting opening exercises of five to fifteen minutes, consisting of scriptural readings, prayers, and hymns. In any event, the president of the Ohio Teachers Association stated in 1886 that if teachers were not to introduce formal religious ceremonies in their classes, they were nonetheless "to make all their teaching glow with a general faith, hope and charity."[35]

The transition from the public schools to college was not a spiritually painful experience for Ernest. At Wittenberg and Ohio Wesleyan he encountered no shattering spirit of skepticism. Wittenberg, located in Springfield, first opening its doors in 1845, was a Lutheran school founded by the Synod of Ohio to train young men for the ministry. Broadening into a coeducational liberal arts college, it retained nevertheless a powerful and pervasive religious orientation.[36]

When in the fall of 1904 Ernest transferred from Wittenberg College to Ohio Wesleyan University he merely moved from an atmosphere of

33. See Benjamin William Arnett, "The North-West Territory," *Ohio Archaeological and Historical Society Publications*, VIII (1900), 452-57.

34. This is the memory of Mrs. Robert S. Shaw. There exist in the St. Paul archives no records for baptisms before 1898.

35. See Bernard Mandel, "Religion and the Public Schools of Ohio," *Ohio Archaeological and Historical Quarterly*, LVIII (April, 1949), 185-206. Several fine recent studies conclusively demonstrate the high content of piety (and patriotism) in nineteenth-century public schools and schoolbooks.

36. See *The Wittenberg Bulletin*, Vol. 1, No. 1, 58th annual catalogue (Springfield, 1904) and Harold H. Lentz, *A History of Wittenberg College (1845-1945)* (Springfield, Ohio: The Wittenberg Press, 1946), p. 200 and *passim*.

Lutheran piety to one of Methodist zeal. It was here, Hutchinson believes, that Tittle most certainly made his final decision to enter the ministry, and Hutchinson is right. This should occasion small surprise. Since 1844 Ohio Wesleyan had produced a host of ministers and missionaries; indeed, its list of graduates reads much like a *Who's Who* of American Methodism. The first years of the twentieth century witnessed a swelling of the stream of young men and women pouring out of Delaware, Ohio, committed (in the watchward of the day) to the "evangelization of the world in this generation." With reason the school became known as the "West Point of missions." In 1900 President James Whitford Bashford (who became Bishop Bashford and who, in truth, "was not just a bishop; he was a contagion") set forth the purposes of Ohio Wesleyan as the "development of all one's faculties to their highest power and their consecration to the highest service of mankind."[37]

Daily chapel "genuinely and unashamedly religious in purpose and program."[38] Prescribed Sunday attendance at a Delaware church. An annual day of prayer when the students met by classes and indeed prayed. Gospel teams organized by the students to spread the "good news" during vacation periods. Bible study. Revivals. A vigorous Student Volunteer Band. An active YMCA and YWCA. Drinking, smoking, dancing banned from the campus. How could the atmosphere of Ohio Wesleyan have been other than evangelical and missionary? How could a lad, already inclined to be reverential of spirit and sober of character, have remained uninfluenced by this godly environment? Writing to a friend many years later, Tittle made this assessment of the mood of the school of his youth: "I have been thinking a good deal of late about Ohio Wesleyan—past and present. As undergraduates you and I were indeed exposed to a certain kind of idealism, yet as I now view it it was a little sticky with sentimentalism. At any rate, it did not come to grips with the political or economic situation at home or abroad. Would it be going too far to say that it was almost wholly devoid of social insight? It was largely 'missionary,' that is, a compound of

37. *The Daily Christian Advocate*, Methodist Episcopal Church, May 16, 1900, p. 20ff.

38. Henry Clyde Hubbart, *Ohio Wesleyan's First Hundred Years* (Delaware: Ohio Wesleyan University, 1943), p. 115. (Hereafter cited as Hubbart, *Ohio Wesleyan*.) Hubbart quotes (p. 318) an account of a 1903 campus revival: ". . . a wave of something we would now think was akin to sentimentalism swept over the college . . . . Toward the end of the meetings Dr. Bashford called for testimonies. The students got to their feet in droves, ten or a dozen at a time. I think 476 testified in about an hour. I doubt if anything like it was ever seen before or since."

unselfish devotion and spiritual pride."[39] This is a harsh judgment but it confirms rather than refutes President Bashford's assertion that Ohio Wesleyan was then the "most noted revival and missionary center in Methodism." It must be emphasized, however, that compared to many church schools the religious spirit of O.W. was broad and generous, not narrowly sectarian or fundamentalist. The findings of science—Lyell, Darwin, the Higher Criticism—were not proscribed. In fact, Christian liberalism, theological and social, was staunchly championed, not the least by President Herbert Welch, who came to the helm during Ernest's senior year. Regular visitors to the campus included not only John R. Mott and Robert E. Speer with their message of evangelism, but also Jane Addams, Walter Rauschenbusch, Booker T. Washington, Washington Gladden, Graham Taylor, Jacob Riis, and others with their message of social Christianity.

In addition to the general temper of the school and in addition to the formal courses he carried in English Bible, religions, philosophy, and Hebrew, young Tittle came under the specific tutelage of several older men who influenced his decision to give his life to the service of God and humanity. One mentor was Richard T. Stevenson, professor of American history, ordained minister, and a leader in Methodism at large. Popular with students, respected by colleagues, erudite, eloquent, urbane in bearing and dress, Stevenson saw in Ernest a youth of "rare gifts and purpose to be encouraged and fostered."[40] The relationship between teacher and pupil became intimate; during his senior year Ernest served as Stevenson's assistant in the history department. The older man urged the lad to transfer his ambitions from "Y" work to larger and deeper service in the church. "The church needs you," he entreated, and no plea could have been more persuasive than this, for the youth was already inclined to a career of service. The friendship then formed endured for a lifetime. "The idea that I should consider the ministry as a vocation was put into my mind by Professor Richard T. Stevenson," Tittle later recalled.[41]

A second lasting friendship was made with President Herbert Welch. Throughout his career Tittle was to turn to Welch for guidance, addressing him as "Dear Prexy" or, when writing to Mrs. Welch as well, "Dearly Beloved." Tittle warmly acknowledged in his letters to Welch

39. Letter from Tittle to Harry Gorrell, November 13, 1935.

40. Letter from Miss Sarah C. Stevenson (Dr. Stevenson's daughter) to author, November 27, 1959.

41. Letter from Tittle to Sam Napolitan, December 6, 1943. Also Hutchinson, "Portrait," p. x; author's interview with Glenna Myers Tittle, Evanston, Ill., August 14, 1959.

that Welch was "largely responsible" for his entering the ministry. "The belief that I might find joy in the ministry," Tittle replied to an inquiry, "came through contact with Bishop Herbert Welch, who was then president of Ohio Wesleyan."[42] Welch was a commanding personality, one of the giants of American Methodism, serving the church in many capacities and ultimately being elected to the episcopacy in 1916. A small man of large character, Welch was (in the phrase then fashionable) a "splendid force making for good."

William E. Smyser, professor of the English language and literature, was a third mentor to guide the young undergraduate. Well-knit, immaculate, unselfconscious, much at home in nineteenth-century English literature, Smyser stood, said Tittle, for a humane, civilized existence. He gave to his students not only an inspired introduction to Arnold, Tennyson, and Browning, but also a philosophy that made them very sure of the existence of God.[43] He, too, counted Tittle his friend for life, and he, too, encouraged the young man to consider the ministry.

If Ernest's professors were convinced that he was a promising candidate for the church, their evaluation rested in part on his enthusiastic participation in the religious life of the campus and finally on his leadership in this area. Tittle was chairman of Bible study work. He participated in a practice known as morning watch, consisting of Bible reading, meditations, and prayer. Looking back upon it, he could "see that it left many human needs unsatisfied, owing to the ideas we brought to it—ideas of God, of the Bible, of prayer, of the world and life that were, to say the least, inadequate. Yet I feel bound to suppose that this 'morning watch' rendered an all-essential service; for it did serve to keep us in the way of the highest we then saw, the best we then knew."[44] And he was active in the YMCA, becoming president in 1905-6. Under his aggressive leadership the "Y" retained its position as the largest and most commanding student fellowship, having "more influence on the life and work of this college than all other organizations combined."[45]

Ernest was one of the delegates representing Ohio Wesleyan at the International Convention of the Student Volunteer Movement, held in Nashville, Tennessee, in January, 1906, a meeting of "four thousand of

42. Letter from Tittle to Sam Napolitan, December 6, 1943. In expressing his gratitude to Welch in a letter dated January 17, 1940, Tittle also stressed the influence of "Stevie"—most certainly Professor Stevenson.

43. Tittle, "William Emory Smyser," *Ohio Wesleyan Magazine* (June, 1935), p. 108, an extraordinarily moving memorial tribute. It is revealing that Tittle was also asked to preach the memorial sermon at the death of Professor Stevenson.

44. Tittle, "On Becoming Our Best," *The First Church Pulpit*, Vol. II, No. 10, a sermon preached January 8, 1939.

45. Hubbart, *Ohio Wesleyan*, p. 319.

the choicest individuals of the choicest class of American young people," many of whom had "already declared their purpose of giving their lives to the great and generous enterprise of evangelizing the world." At this convention, "the whole weight of the appeal to young Christians to give their lives to service, if need be in some foreign field, was based on a simple statement of the claims of Christ as Lord and of the need of the world. These two mighty considerations were stressed by constant and simple iteration till they were more compelling than any sensational stirring of youthful emotions. Never [was] the appalling condition of a sinful world put, in quiet, sympathetic, simple words, more vividly and more appealingly."[46] Years later Tittle recalled: "I shall never forget the hush which came over that great student conference in Nashville when Robert E. Speer stood before us with watch in hand and told us, minute after minute, how many human beings in Asia and in Africa were passing into eternity without hope. If only we had been there with our saving gospel before they died! Before the conference adjourned many of us had volunteered to go, many more of us returned to our homes feeling selfish and cowardly, condemning ourselves because we had not volunteered."[47] If Tittle, at the conclusion of the conference, did not volunteer for missionary duty in "Ceylon's isle" where "every prospect pleases" and "only man is vile," it may nevertheless be conjectured that the exhortation of Speer strengthened his determination to pursue a career of service. After all, at this moment when idealism in the United States knew one of its finest hours, thousands of sturdy young men on every campus were making the same commitment. Tittle was later to remember, "such students commanded the unqualified respect of their several colleges. In not a few cases they were accorded a hero-worship which today is given only to stars of the gridiron."[48] The Student Volunteer movement and the Laymen's Missionary movement in particular and missionary and settlement work in general tapped the same reservoir of moral idealism in the era of Teddy Roosevelt that the Peace Corps was to tap in the era of John F. Kennedy.

Moreover, in Tittle's boyhood clergymen continued to enjoy much prestige, being regarded, according to the perceptive Lord Bryce, as the nation's "first Citizens," exercising "an influence often wider and more powerful than that of any laymen." For example, Phillips Brooks brought international renown to the pulpit of Trinity Church, Boston.

46. *Nashville Christian Advocate*, LXVII (March 8, 1906), 5-7.
47. Tittle, *A World That Cannot Be Shaken* (New York and London: Harper & Brothers, 1933), p. 50.
48. *Ibid.*, p. 49.

Such was Brooks's charisma that upon his death in 1893 Bryce reported that not since Lincoln had there been an American "so warmly admired and so widely mourned." In Philadelphia Russell Conwell made Baptist Temple the largest Protestant congregation in the country. His "Acres of Diamonds" address (delivered more than six thousand times) was memorized by the nation. Henry Ward Beecher (that magnificent weathervane of respectable opinion and on some issues an aboriginal Brooklyn Dodger, to borrow Sidney E. Mead's delightful characterization) drew weekly audiences averaging twenty-five hundred to his Plymouth Congregational Church, Brooklyn. So extraordinary was Beecher's popularity he was importuned to write testimonials for Pear's Soap, an honor later generations were to reserve for Hollywood actresses and professional ball players. (The Reverend Mr. Beecher explained, "Cleanliness is next to Godliness. Soap must be considered as a means of grace and a clergyman who recommends moral things—should be willing to recommend soap.") Beecher's successor at Plymouth Church was the less ebullient Lyman Abbott, who won a wide following and enjoyed national influence, especially in his capacity as editor of the *Outlook* and as associate of Theodore Roosevelt. But Beecher's reputation as America's most popular pulpit orator probably passed to Thomas DeWitt Talmage, who held important Presbyterian pastorates in Philadelphia, Brooklyn, and Washington, D.C. If some Americans became "nauseated with this silver-tongued orator preaching," to quote the complaint of Dwight L. Moody, they could find a sterner message in the revivalism of Moody himself, for he continued his evangelical work until the last year of the century. Moody's successors were also to know fame, though in the case of such men as Samuel P. Jones, Rodney (Gypsy) Smith, and William (Billy) A. Sunday, fame and notoriety met in uneasy symbiosis. If Beecher and Talmage were too slick and Smith and Sunday too flamboyant to compel universal admiration, there were a host of Protestant preachers revered by the godly, righteous, and sober: George A. Gordon, David James Burrell, Washington Gladden, Frank W. Gunsalus, Charles A. Parkhurst, George W. Truett, Charles M. Sheldon, and such enormously prestigious church leaders as John R. Mott and Robert E. Speer.

It was Ernest's ambition to join this honored band. To enter the Protestant ministry in the United States at the turn of the century required making grievous sacrifices in terms of luxury, ease, worldly pleasures, and even bodily health. It was not a commitment to be made frivolously. But it was a profession that still retained a large measure of dignity; the preacher was still a man of influence in his community, and the pulpit continued to speak with authority. Tittle hungered for recognition. Here was a career that would have pleased his devout mother. Here was a profession that would atone for the intemperance of his father. Here was a calling urged upon him by his adored Glenna. Here was the path pointed out by his college mentors. Here was a fitting climax to a serious, earnest boyhood.

VII

The name Ernest is singularly appropriate to the youth's character. To begin with, he was infinitely dutiful. Though it was Robert E. Lee who said the word "duty" was the sublimest in the English language, the statement might have been made by young Tittle. Years later he was to inquire, "If any one of us were asked to choose between mediocrity, accompanied by happiness, and greatness, accompanied by pain, in any hour when he was most himself which choice would he probably make?"[49] His own answer is suggested by the sentence he checked and heavily underscored in his copy of William James's *The Will to Believe and Other Essays in Popular Philosophy:* "Are we not bound to take some suffering upon ourselves, to do some self-denying service with our lives, in return for all those lives upon which ours are built." Many youngsters of the late nineteenth century learned the lines, "Do your duty that is best and leave unto the Lord the rest." Ernest lived these lines just as surely as did Washington, Lee, Rowan, the hero of Elbert Hubbard's *The Message to Garcia,* all the lads in Horatio Alger's 119 novels, and all the gallants of American history known to all schoolboys, from Captain Parker and Nathan Hale to David Farragut and "Pap" Thomas to Dewey and Gridley of the late "splendid little war" with Spain. In point of fact, for Tittle duty was the sublimest word in the English language. In this, he was a true son of Middle America, a true product of William Holmes McGuffey's *Readers,*[50] a true personification of the Chautauqua spirit, and, not the least, a true disciple of John Wesley.

Industry was a second notable aspect of Ernest's character. He did not view life as a sinecure. "Work for the night is coming." "Sweat and be saved." "The devil has work for idle hands." "Root, hog, or die." "Fish, cut bait, or row home." "He who does not work does not eat." "Leisure is the time for doing something useful." "Life is real, life is earnest." "Let us be up and doing." These phrases, too vital to be

49. Tittle, *In Quest of Peace,* a sermon preached March 16, 1930 (pamphlet).
50. Tittle recalls studying McGuffey's *Readers* in "Symbol and Sacrament," typed MS, a sermon preached May 11, 1941.

trite, were embedded in the boy's consciousness. He would have agreed with Harriet Martineau's observation that America is the only country in the world where one is ashamed of having nothing to do. He memorized the McGuffey command, "If at first you don't succeed, try, try again." And he knew the fate of "Lazy Ned," who owned a fine new sled but who was too indolent to climb the hill in order to race his fellows down the slope:

> Thus, he would never take the pains
> To seek the prize that labor gains,
>   Until the time had passed;
> For, all his life, he dreaded still
> The silly bugbear of *up hill*
>   And died a dunce at last.

Young Tittle took the pains to seek the prize that labor gains. His prodigious industry may have stemmed from the Protestant Ethic or from the historic frontier experiences of the American people. It may have been a reflection of the competitive, acquisitive, feverish, hard-driving temper of the Gilded Age in which he grew to manhood. Or it may have been rooted in personal, subjective factors, the desire of his mother for him to be *somebody*, the failure of his father to climb many rungs up the ladder of success. Perhaps his intense activity was both a rational method of attacking anxieties and an irrational method of escaping them, to borrow Walter Houghton's insight into the Victorian mind. Whatever the reason, Tittle drove himself hard.

Closely allied to dutifulness and industry are the attributes of self-denial and self-control. Ernest was, to paraphrase David Riesman, an inner-directed boy. The words "flinty," "resolute," "independent," "craggy" best describe his character even as a lad. Relentlessly disciplining his will and body, ordering his waking hours as carefully as Wesley, denying himself the silly and frivolous as well as the sinful, he was a moral athlete. On several instances later in life he confessed to a grave disposition and a violent temper; indeed, as a youth his temper was "almost ungovernable."[51] Yet he did not surrender himself to a bleak, enervating (and delicious) pessimism fashionable among undergraduates in every generation, and his quick temper was usually sufficiently reined to prevent many disastrous explosions.

His body was trim and hard, suggesting much exercise and manual labor and an avoidance of that most pervasive of teenage vices—gluttony. It is almost certain that he did not use tobacco or liquor and that

51. Author's interview with Mrs. Bernice Wolseley, Evanston, Ill., July 13, 1960.

he was chaste. Most middle-class American lads in that ancient age were chaste, and Tittle was much too ambitious to jeopardize his community and school standing by dallying with what were then euphemistically called "chippies." Also, his courtship of Glenna assured him of the subliminating companionship of a lovely and proper girl.

The conscience that monitored his conduct never slept. He examined the state of his soul much as a small boy tends a garden, daily pulling up the carrot to check the health of the roots. Yet it is at least possible that his intense activity—study, work, YMCA leadership—represented attempted flight from this self-torturing introspection. Despite the many surface manifestations to the contrary, he was a lonely boy, burdened with responsibilities he neither could nor would lay aside, pricked by an implacable conscience, driven to climb toward the goal of high recognition.

His massive integrity brought him the respect and admiration of his peers and superiors. He knew a measure of popularity as well, for he was president of his senior class in high school and president of the Ohio Wesleyan YMCA. One has the hunch, however, that Tittle the grown man was a more lovable person than Tittle the young man. He displayed certain rather unattractive traits as a youth that diminished or disappeared with a mellowing maturity. His temper was explosive. A certain stubbornness sometimes shaded into rigidity. He could not easily take a ribbing. He was a bit of a "sobersides." He was not an ordinary boy, and alas, he knew it. His vaulting ambition was ill-disguised. Others apparently found his rectitude a trifle grating. The *Ohio Wesleyan Transcript* said of him, "Future dignity prophesied."[52] Another sketch concludes, "*Ambition . . . Be dignified*."[53] He could be somewhat prudish. To the question asked by a *Transcript* reporter, "Would you be willing to have a truthful account of your convention trip told in the *Transcript?*" Tittle replied: "Yes, so far as I am concerned, but for the sake of another, don't."[54] Though some called him "Zip" or "Bulldog," it is revealing (because so unusual) that the yearbook mentions no nickname for him. All in all, the young Tittle reminds one considerably of Freeman's portrait of the young Washington: ambitious, conscientious, dignified, proper, hot-tempered, serious, rather humorless, but withal, about him the promise of future greatness.

52. XL (February 21, 1906), 355.
53. XL (June 20, 1906), 11.
54. XL (March 7, 1906), 395.

VIII

Did Ernest have the mind to sustain him in his march toward high recognition? Were his intellectual assets comparable to his resources of energy and will? Did he train and discipline his mental powers as he did his character? Was his education adequate to the tasks ahead? Some men in history have risen to prominence without impressive intellectual credentials just as some men without character have done so. Particularly has it been assumed that an educated mind is not a prerequisite to success in the Protestant ministry in America, least of all in Methodism, a denomination notorious in the nineteenth century for its nonintellectual (some would say anti-intellectual) temper.

The grade school Ernest attended was separated from the Tittle home on Dibert street only by a vacant lot. Constructed of red brick and substantial in size, it enrolled approximately three hundred. Here Ernest was introduced to the McGuffey *Readers*. Here he learned his Three R's. Here he was inculcated with the virtues of honesty, thrift, charity, courage, diligence, sobriety, patriotism, and piety. Here he was warned against the vices of selfishness, greed, sloth, lying, and smoking, drinking, gambling. No report cards exist to prove that he was a diligent junior scholar, but a half-century later a beloved teacher wrote him: "Many years ago when you went to the Dibert School in Springfield, Ohio, you were my pupil in second grade. I was very fond of the child with the broad brow, earnest eyes and perfect lessons."[55] And it is the recollection of school chums that he was an omnivorous reader even as a small boy.

The high-school academic record rests on a firmer factual basis. During Ernest's freshman year he carried Latin, English, algebra, physiology, and botany, scoring respectively 93, 90, 89, 91, and 95, for an average of 90.9, sufficient for his report card to bear the accolade "cum laude." (Physiology and botany were half-year courses.) During his sophomore year he carried algebra, civics, English, Greek, and Latin, scoring respectively 92, 98, 95, 96, 96, for an average of 95, and now the card read "magna cum laude." His junior year he carried geometry, Greek, history, Latin, English, and elocution (for only two months), scoring respectively 96, 95, 99, 96, 95, and 95, for an average of 96.2, again "magna cum laude." His senior year he carried English literature, geometry, Greek, Latin, and physics, scoring respectively 96, 95, 97, 95, and 94, for an average of 95.4, "magna cum laude."[56]

Manifestly this is a splendid record. If the curriculum seems narrow by mid-twentieth-century standards, it was not necessarily a sterile pro-

55. Letter from Mrs. Daniel Taylor Hinckley to Tittle, February 6, 1941.
56. The report cards are in the Tittle Collection.

gram of study. Let the worst be assumed: that the science was obsolete; that the mathematics was elementary and unrelated to the image of the universe held by Einstein; that the one course in history and the one in civics were less than an adequate introduction to the social sciences; that the literature was limited to a few accepted English and American authors and was generally genteel. All this is probably true. Yet not even the most wretched teaching can wring all excitement and relevance from Hawthorne, Dickens, Goldsmith, Addison, Longfellow, Milton, and Tennyson, or from Caesar, Cicero, Virgil, Xenophon, and Homer. As for the textbook authors, Meiklejohn, Kittredge, Channing and company were not without scholarly status.[57] Tittle's high-school education might be compared to a Scotsman's supper: plain, simple, and without hors d' oeuvres, wines, or pastry, but nourishing once gotten down. Ernest did his best by what he was served.

There is little in the sources beyond the report cards with which to assess Ernest's high-school record.[58] He was absent from classes ten times in four years, five times as a sophomore and five as a senior. He was often tardy: thirty-nine times. Perhaps his gas light job had something to do with this; perhaps conditions at home are the explanation. He was senior class president. In a larger sense, however, "popularity" was not as central to school life as in a later era. The notion that the school should be a social center was beyond consideration. The term "well adjusted" was unknown. Few were the social clubs, even fewer the organized athletic teams. Proms were of course proscribed. Botanizing, fossil-hunting, and hickory-nutting expeditions were about the only legitimate activities. Homework assignments were heavy. Generally a student went home after the last bell—and studied.

Upon graduation from high school and after the negative decision concerning West Point, Ernest entered Wittenberg College where he was to study only one year. Perhaps Wittenberg, then with 325 students and 14 professors, was his choice because he won a handsome scholarship. Perhaps family considerations—his mother's ill health and his father's drinking—were a factor, for Wittenberg was located in Springfield and matriculation there permitted him to live at home. During the fall term

57. The certificate of graduation forwarded from the high school to Ohio Wesleyan describes the textbooks and readings for each course.

58. A rather diligent search failed to turn up a yearbook or school newspaper for these years. It is the memory of Mr. Clarence Smith, schoolmate of Tittle's and for fifty years a teacher in the Springfield high schools, that at the turn of the century these publications simply did not exist. Author's interview with Clarence Smith, Springfield, Ohio, June 16, 1960. This corroborates the opinion of the present school librarians.

Ernest carried Greek, Latin, English, French, mathematics, and "Biological Sciences"; the winter term, Greek, history, Latin, English, French, and mathematics; and the spring term, Greek, history, Latin, English, French, and mathematics. He won straight A's.[59] The extent of his participation in extracurricular activities is unknown. Probably he engaged in "Y" work. It is certain that he was initiated in the Ohio Beta chapter of Phi Kappa Psi, since he later recalled the "days in Wittenberg College and, in particular, a certain evening in the Phi Kappa Psi house when, under the direction of Reese [*sic*] Tullos, I received 'the works' as a Greek letter neophyte. 'The works' included a vigorous use of barrel staves on bare skin and a more or less merciful use of plenty of cold water as means of revival."[60]

In the fall of 1904 Ernest transferred to Ohio Wesleyan preceded by a letter from President Heckert describing him as "a young man of exceptional ability and a gentleman in every respect."[61] The precise reasons for the move to Ohio Wesleyan are unknown. Perhaps the death of his mother in April freed him from the obligation of remaining in Springfield. Perhaps Glenna Myers persuaded him to attend her Alma Mater. Perhaps it was his desire to be associated with a Methodist institution, for already he was probing the possibility of a career in the Methodist ministry. Perhaps the decision was based on the objective fact that Ohio Wesleyan enjoyed a somewhat higher academic reputation than did the Lutheran school.

Ernest's record at Ohio Wesleyan was splendid. He fulfilled the requirements for graduation in only two years. In June, 1906, it was clear that he merited magna cum laude, Phi Beta Kappa honors, and the Slocum Prize, the highest award for classical scholarship. His grade-point average was 2.99 out of a possible 3.0. On the surface, at least, the courses he carried were neither trivial in content nor undemanding of effort: chemistry (9 hours), English (15), Bible (15), geology (4), German (15), Greek (15), Hebrew (9), history (6), Latin (3), mathematics (6), oratory (7), religions (6), philosophy (5), zoology (3) and military and gymnasium for which no grades were given. Additionally, he received 6 hours credit by certificate in English, 9 in French, 12 in Greek, 2 in history, 12 in Latin, 12 in mathematics, 3 in zoology, and 9 in electives. In his second term of chemistry he received a B. This is the

59. Photostatic copies of the three reports are in the author's possession.
60. Letter from Tittle to Carl W. Mitchell, January 20, 1942. Rees Edgar Tulloss later became an outstanding president of Wittenberg. See also the 1903-4 file of *The Wittenberger*.
61. Letter from Charles G. Heckert to the Faculty, Ohio Wesleyan University, September 21, 1904, copy in author's possession.

only mark below A ("high-honor grade") in the entire Ohio Wesleyan record—or Wittenberg record.

Patently these grades become meaningful only when placed in the context of the caliber of the institution awarding them. In later years Tittle was to confide to his wife and intimates that his formal education had ill-prepared him intellectually for the challenges he was to face in his ministerial career.[62] He felt even more strongly about the inadequacy of his seminary training. Throughout his adult life he continued to be a student, digging hard on his own, attempting to plug the holes and strengthen the foundations of what he deemed to be his rickety education. It is the curious custom of many great Americans to denigrate their formal schooling and count themselves self-made men intellectually. In holding this affectation Tittle was in impressive company, but this does not mean he was entirely right.

To be sure, Ohio Wesleyan University was not a university at all but a college, then possessing merely the College of Liberal Arts, the School of Music, the School of Oratory, the School of Business, the School of Fine Arts, and a tenuous and soon-to-be-terminated relationship with the Cleveland College of Physicians and Surgeons. (There was also a preparatory academy connected with the school, soon to be discontinued.) The faculty numbered 44 and the student enrollment in the college itself was 930. To be sure, the faculty was overworked and underpaid, having little time or energy for original research; and consequently the emphasis was on the transmission of inherited knowledge rather than the search for new knowledge. The faculty without exception viewed the universe from a theistic angle of vision and the students were overwhelmingly Christian, indeed evangelical Protestant; consequently there was little abrasive confrontation of antagonistic minds. The cultivation of piety and the disciplining of character were recognized aims and this contributed to an unrecognized diminishment of the claims of the intellect. Undoubtedly the curriculum was too limited, especially in the area of the social sciences, the teaching too often authoritarian, and the recitation technique tedious.

There were in fact, then, serious deficiencies in the education provided by a school such as Ohio Wesleyan at the turn of the century. These flaws should not be obscured by the romantic myths surrounding Mark Hopkins and the student on that long log. They should not be minimized in a wave of nostalgia engendered by disenchantment over

62. Author's interview with Glenna Myers Tittle, Evanston, Ill., August 14, 1959; Hutchinson, "Portrait," p. xi; and numerous comments scattered throughout Tittle's correspondence.

the failures of modern, mid-century, multi-university education. When Tittle said his formal schooling was inadequate and much remained to be learned on his own after graduation he was not being entirely prideful.

But neither was he being entirely fair. As Daniel Webster said of Dartmouth, Ohio Wesleyan was only a small school, but there were those who loved it—and respected it. In the academic year 1905-6 Ohio Wesleyan stood first among the colleges of the United States in the number of alumni doing graduate work at Harvard University, and the following year it stood second. In 1905 and 1909 its students were appointed Rhodes Scholars. Under the leadership of President Bashford (1889-1904) an impressive building program was successfully undertaken, including increasing the library holdings to fifty-five thousand volumes. Bashford also brought to Delaware a band of young, vigorous teachers carrying impressive credentials of advanced study in leading American and European universities. The most incontestable evidence of Ohio Wesleyan's quality, however, is the number of her graduates who went on to leadership in medicine, law, scholarship, public life, and the ministry.

Ernest was not engaged in a plethora of campus activities. The hours in the day were too few and pre-empted by studies, table waiting, assisting Professor Stevenson, and teaching in the high school. He did not enter into varsity sports. If the yearbook is correct, he took little if any interest in the affairs of Phi Kappa Psi. He was initiated into Chrestomathean, the men's literary society, though he did not become an officer. He debated. But the YMCA represented his one major extracurricular interest.

What conclusions, then, can be drawn concerning the education of Ernest Fremont Tittle? Did it prepare him for life in the twentieth century? In one obvious and fundamental sense the answer can only be no. It did not prepare him to comprehend the stunning new conceptions hypothesized by twentieth-century science or the chilling new insights into human behavior and social organization hypothesized by twentieth-century social sciences. It did not prepare him to comprehend the shattering new forms in art, drama, literature, and music, creations based on subjective concepts of reality without apparent order, progression, logic, meaning, or religious inspiration or moral value. It did not prepare him to comprehend the liberating yet terrifying forces of anticolonialism and anticapitalism about to sweep the globe, for who in the United States before 1906 knew the names of Gandhi or Lenin? It did not prepare him to comprehend the ferocious power of the modern totalitarian state, for after all Hitler was four years his junior and Mussolini and Stalin only two and six years his senior; and if he thought of a Leviathan state it most probably was in terms of Edward Bellamy's utopian dream, not George Orwell's nightmare. As for Verdun and Tannenberg Forest, Coventry and Hiroshima, indeed what education could possibly have prepared a young American emerging to manhood at the turn of the century for these enormities? Let it again be remembered that Tittle was born the year Ulysses S. Grant died of cancer and General "Chinese" Gordon of the spears of the Mahdi Mohammed Ahmed at Khartum, a year when Queen Victoria continued to reign serenely and when the accumulation of a large surplus in the United States treasury proved to be an embarrassment to the *Democratic* president, Grover Cleveland. It was a long time ago.

Although Tittle's education failed to prepare him completely for life in the twentieth century, it was not a total waste. To begin with, he acquired the habit of hard, sustained, systematic study. This is not an inconsiderable asset for a young man to possess and it was never to be lost. His education fired him with intellectual curiosity. He coveted knowledge. He never ceased to be a student. Graduation was not for him the end of learning. Tittle's schooling ill-armed him with the information necessary to understand the twentieth century, but it did not make him contemptuous of the life of the mind. Quite the contrary. Somehow the Springfield public schools, Wittenberg College, and Ohio Wesleyan University infused him with a passion for learning. This is a fact that is as indisputable as perhaps it is inexplicable.

In the second place, education in that age had as a fundamental purpose the development of character. No one can seriously maintain that the schools failed in this purpose in the case of Ernest Fremont Tittle. He emerged from his schooling a man; there was nothing foppish about him. He emerged a gentleman; there was nothing vulgar about him. He had respect for his fellow men and a sense of responsibility toward them; they were not to be exploited or manipulated. His social consciousness was lively. He felt concern for the issues of the day, and if he misjudged their nature or solution, he at least recognized the commitment to become involved. He was not cursed with the affliction common among the university-bred: contempt for the "masses" and indifference to their welfare. The training of the intellect and the cultivation of character are not necessarily antimonies; in the education of Tittle they were not.

When Tittle said farewell to college in 1906 he was not an unflawed youngster or a fully informed one, but he was well on his way to becoming an authentic, whole man.

2. *THE EARLY MINISTRY*

I

Daniel Drew, said Ernest Fremont Tittle in 1936, was "probably the most pious pirate who ever scuttled a stock market."[1] Exactly thirty years earlier, Tittle, with a B.A. degree from Ohio Wesleyan tucked under his academic belt, traveled to Madison, New Jersey, to enter the theological seminary named for this pious pirate. He was to complete the three-year program in only two years, just as he had completed his undergraduate work in a year less than customary, and in 1908 he was awarded the Bachelor of Divinity degree from Drew Theological Seminary. It was a long two years, anxious as he was to test himself in the world and determined as he and Glenna were not to marry until he had completed his training.

II

Though Harvard College was founded in 1636 by the Puritan saints who dreaded "to leave an illiterate ministry to the churches when our present ministers shall lie in the dust," though higher education in colonial America was intimately (and as was then believed, properly) related to religion, though denominational schools and seminaries proliferated in early nineteenth-century America (in part, alas, because of sectarian rivalry), it cannot be claimed that American Methodism led in this integration of the life of the mind with the life of the spirit. When the Methodist Episcopal Church was organized in 1784-85, it is doubtful whether any of its preachers (excepting only Bishop Thomas

1. *Evanston Daily News-Index,* June 15, 1936, p. 12.

Coke) had seen the inside of a college, and during the first half-century of Methodism in America there were no Methodist colleges of note or permanence. The early Methodist circuit riders were generally men of limited formal education. They preached to frontiersmen who were mostly untutored. This does not mean, however, that either group was witless. These rough-voiced ministers and rough-handed laymen joyously and fiercely wrestled with hard theological questions—questions that were for them quite literally ones of life and death. And their minds were sharpened in defending their Arminian beliefs against the many contenders ranging from Unitarians on the left to Old School Presbyterians on the right. It is a mistake to equate the anti-intellectualism of twentieth-century fundamentalism with nineteenth-century evangelicalism. It is an error to underestimate American Protestantism's (and Methodism's) concern with theology. To be sure, these early Methodist laymen were unschooled. Some of them certainly preferred an unschooled preacher such as Peter Cartwright to a seminary trained scholar, complete with "cabalistic initials" tacked after his name. But frontier Methodists were unschooled because of circumstances, not through choice.

As the nineteenth century deepened, as the frontier was tamed, as the sons of the pioneers became settled farmers, village merchants, middle-class entrepreneurs and professional men, the Peter Cartwrights became increasingly anachronistic. Wesleyan University opened its doors in 1831, the first permanent Methodist college, and within two decades with typical Methodist zeal and energy thirty-four colleges were established. It was now imperative to provide ministers capable of serving an educated laity. Thus quite unlike the Presbyterians, Congregationalists, and Episcopalians, an educated Methodist ministry had to wait on the creation of an educated Methodist laity. The alacrity with which Methodists threw themselves into the establishment of schools and other educational ventures suggests that for the followers of Wesley (an Oxford graduate) there was no necessary antagonism between piety and learning. However, the fact that the two Methodist seminaries opened before the Civil War were carefully named Biblical Institutes suggests a continuing Methodist doubt that the truth that makes men free could be grasped by the intellect alone or that theological expertise could in itself bring men to a knowledge of God's love and purposes.

III

Drew Theological Seminary was the third Methodist institution founded for the purpose of training young men for the ministry but the first to call itself a theological seminary rather than a Biblical Institute.[2] When Ernest entered on September 19, 1906, he was one of 167 students, most of whom came from the mid-Atlantic states and Ohio—in fact, Ohio Wesleyan contributed more graduates than any other school, 13.[3]

The seminary stated as its purpose the training of "young men to be effective preachers of the gospel and to fit them by scholarly attainments for any service which the Church may require at their hands. While theology in all its branches is carefully taught, the art of preaching is assiduously cultivated."[4] It further sought "to give suitable prominence to the instruction which is needed by students proposing to go as Missionaries to foreign countries and by Ministers at home, who ought always to have an intelligent sympathy with their brethren in the foreign field, and a fixed purpose to promote the conversion of the world."[5] To accomplish these aims an impressive faculty had by 1906 been assembled, augmented by a ninety-five-thousand-volume library said to rank among the first four theological libraries in America.

As at Wittenberg and Ohio Wesleyan, Ernest's academic record at Drew was brilliant. He romped through the three-year program in two years. In every course scored with an alphabetical grade he won an "E" or "Excellent." In every course scored with a numerical grade he won 97.5 or higher.[6] He was one of five Newman Scholars. He was also awarded the coveted Easton Scholarship for 1907-8, an honor "given to that member of the Junior class on the basis of high rank as a scholar, preacher, and man of affairs."[7]

Ernest carried Biblical hermeneutics under Professor Charles Fremont Sitterly. A second course, Christian ethics, was taught by President Henry Anson Buttz. One of American Methodism's unspectacular workhorses, a capable administrator and able scholar, Butts was perhaps not the best man to teach a course in Christian ethics—at least not to young seminarians aflame with social passion. Years later Tittle was to say that

2. See Ezra Squier Tipple, *Drew Theological Seminary, 1867-1917* (New York and Cincinnati, Ohio: The Methodist Book Concern, 1917), *passim.* See also Charles Fremont Sitterly, *The Building of Drew University* (New York; Cincinnati, Ohio; and Chicago: The Methodist Book Concern, 1938), *passim.*

3. *Year Book of Drew Theological Seminary of the Methodist Episcopal Church, 1906-1907* (Madison, N. J., 1907), pp. 26ff.

4. *Catalogue of Drew Theological Seminary of the Methodist Episcopal Church, Fortieth Year, 1907-1908* (n.p., n.d.), p. 40.

5. *Year Book of Drew, 1906-1907*, p. 48.

6. Copy of Drew Theological Seminary Examination Certificate, August 28, 1908, signed by W. C. Noble, registrar, in Tittle Collection.

7. *Catalogue of Drew, 1907-1908*, pp. 10, 50.

he took no real work in social ethics and that "Drew in that period was not very much concerned with this important subject."[8] Tittle was similarly unimpressed by his courses in homiletics, recalling that from them he "received absolutely nothing of value."[9] Exegetical studies in the prophets and the psalms was the province of Professor Robert William Rogers, as was the Old Testament seminar. Rogers's main principle was "not so much to teach things about the Old Testament as to teach the books themselves, by wide, sympathetic, and enthusiastic reading of them."[10] If few students shared the "Rabbi's" passion for Hebrew, all stood in awe of his immense learning. President Buttz was again Ernest's mentor in exegetical studies in the Greek Gospel, praxis in Greek manuscripts, and the New Testament. His teaching was methodical, meticulous, and microscopic. "He led his students to accuracy, rather than to broad, superficial conclusions. They may have missed the sweep of the forest, but at least they learned something at close range about the trees!"[11] Tittle deeply regretted missing that "sweep of the forest." For systematic theology Ernest engaged in mind-to-mind confrontation with Professor Olin Alfred Curtis. Catholic in his interests, passionate in his convictions, enthusiastic in his teaching, Curtis was one of Methodism's leading theologians and his courses were considered the heart of the Drew curriculum. The basic text was John Miley's *Systematic Theology,* "one of the most substantial and well-knit statements of Arminian theology produced in the nineteenth century."[12] In this course Tittle encountered the liberalism of the German Ritschl and the philosophic idealism of Borden Parker Bowne, the "vagaries" (to use the wording of the catalogue description) of Christian Science and Spiritualism, the relationship of evolution and socialism to religion, and other modern intellectual developments. Work in the history of the Christian Church under the staunch theological conservative John Alfred Faulkner completed Ernest's academic program at Drew.[13]

Tittle did not hold in high regard his training at Drew. In later years he expressed the wish that he had attended another seminary, more

8. Letter from Tittle to Howard P. Weatherbee, December 11, 1940.

9. Letter from Tittle to Joseph Fort Newton, March 8, 1935.

10. *Year Book of Drew, 1906-1907,* p. 36.

11. James Richard Joy (ed.), *The Teachers of Drew, 1867-1942* (Madison, N. J.: Drew University, 1942), p. 56.

12. *Ibid.,* p. 88.

13. Tittle of course carried such additional standard work as Biblical Geography and Discipline of the Methodist Episcopal Church. A helpful volume sketching Drew teachers and students is William Pearson Tolley (ed.), *Alumni Record of Drew Theological Seminary, Madison, New Jersey, 1867-1925* (Madison, N. J.: Drew Theological Seminary, 1926). The sketch of Tittle, however, is not accurate.

particularly Union or Boston or Garrett, and he sometimes wondered if he should not have taken postgraduate study in a secular university. The reasons for his disenchantment with Drew are not clear. After all, Drew was an established and respected institution. Its faculty was impressive and in the case of two or three men quite distinguished. Its buildings and grounds were handsome and its library excellent. Many of its graduates went on to achieve renown in American church life. In brief, Drew was certainly among the top eight or ten seminaries in the country in the opening years of the century.

Tittle's disenchantment could not have stemmed from a bitter feeling that Drew had not properly recognized his abilities. Indeed, it awarded him as a student high honors and financial assistance, and in later years invited him back to lecture; and faculty friends persistently hoped that he would return as a teacher.

Perhaps Tittle's memories of Drew were dark because while there he desperately overworked himself, becoming physically and psychically drained as he completed the three-year program in two years. Perhaps he was homesick for Ohio, for this was his first prolonged absence from familiar surroundings. Perhaps the young man's sexual energies were not completely sublimated in study and he ached with unadmitted longings. Drew may have been viewed as an enemy to be overcome because it separated him from his beloved Glenna. (Jacob toiled seven years for the opportunity of wedding Rachel, and these many years, we are told, "seemed unto him but a few days, for the love he had to her." Surely Jacob was an exceptional young man.) Moreover, Tittle was anxious to prove himself in the world and Drew was as much a hurdle as a stepping-stone. These, of course, are all subjective factors having little relationship to the objective quality of the training offered by Drew, but they may have been the unconscious basis of his criticism. More probably, however, his disappointment with Drew stemmed from the later realization that came to him Saturday evening after Saturday evening that what he had learned was not so much "wrong" as it was irrelevant to the preparation of living sermons to be preached Sunday morning after Sunday morning.

Tittle attended Drew at a time of raging theological storms. The findings of modern science and scholarship struck with hurricane force, smashing the old orthodoxies. Nineteenth-century geology had destroyed confidence in the Mosaic cosmogony and, as Henry Adams remarked, "completely wrecked the Garden of Eden." "Gentlemen," Louis Agassiz informed his Harvard classes, "the world is older than we have been taught to think. Its age is as if one were gently to rub a silk handkerchief across Plymouth Rock once a year until it were reduced to rubble." For many of the faithful, it was simply impossible to reconcile the age of rocks with the Rock of Ages. The implications of Darwinism seemed even more stunning. If organic evolution were accepted, the distinction between the animal kingdom and the human realm would break down altogether; man had not fallen from an elevated estate, but had ascended almost imperceptibly from simple animal origins. Moreover, if man evolved through natural selection, if survival and adaption, variation and struggle governed the course of development, what then was left of the belief that God had presided over a single act of creation, and, indeed, of the assurance that God had created man in His own image? For many of the faithful, the issue was clear-cut: God or gorilla? The findings of Biblical scholarship, especially the Higher Criticism associated with Germany, proved more disturbing to many Protestants than Darwinism. If accepted, the Biblical literalists believed, the dogma of the inerrancy of the Scriptures could not endure. President Cleveland spoke for millions of the agonized faithful when he said: "The Bible is good enough for me: just the old book under which I was brought up. I do not want notes or criticism, or explanations about authorship or origin, or even cross-references. I do not need or understand them, and they confuse me." And the great evangelist Dwight L. Moody spoke measuredly and soberly: "I have said that ministers of the Gospel who are cutting up the Bible in this way, denying Moses today and Isaiah tomorrow, and Daniel the next day and Jonah the next, are doing great injury to the Church; and I stand by what I have said. I don't say they are bad men. They may be good men, but that makes the results of their work all the worse. . . . They are emptying the churches and driving the young men of this generation into infidelity."

The names of Darwin and Lyell, Spencer and Huxley, Ritschl and Schleiermacher, Harnack and Ingersoll, James Freeman Clarke and William Newton Clarke, Draper and White, Gladden and Bowne, Nietzsche and James excited debate in every seminary in the opening years of the twentieth century. Also debated were the recent heresy trials of Charles A. Briggs and Arthur Cushman McGiffert, Presbyterian professors at Union Seminary, and that of Professor Henry Preserved Smith of Lane Seminary. Every major denomination was racked by theological warfare. Methodism, though not much given to inquisitions and generally generous in the freedom permitted in the area of doctrine, found itself involved in two ugly episodes. In 1904 Professor Borden Parker Bowne, the most distinguished member of the faculty of Boston University, was brought to trial by his conference for heresy. He was acquitted. At that same time the bishops refused to confirm H. G. Mitchell as professor of Old Testament in the Boston University School of Theology because of his acceptance of the Higher Criticism. The matter was finally carried to the 1908 General Conference, which pronounced in favor of Mitchell. Tittle was caught up in these intense theological battles; and being Ernest Fremont Tittle, he chose sides and committed himself.

The memories of Ernest's fellow theologues are revealing. Edwin Lewis, class of '08 and one of modern Methodism's leading theologians, recalled: "I was in at least two seminars with him—one in the O.T. with Dr. R. W. Rogers, and one in Sys. Theo. with Dr. Olin A. Curtis. In both of these, Tittle had the reputation of being outspoken in his criticisms, and inclined to take what to-day would be called the 'modernistic' side, especially in theology. I am not quite sure, but my memory is that in the Theology Seminar he read a paper on The New Social Emphases in Theology. As you will realize, this was an anticipation of his later directions. He was generally regarded in the student body as marked for high preaching success. This was based partly on his 'chapel sermon'— at that time a requirement of every senior. The 'senior chapel sermon' was subject to criticism from the floor of the chapel, and I remember that Tittle's friends were present in force, on the supposition that he would be subjected to sharp criticism from some of the more conservative members of the student body and they were prepared to defend him."[14] Arlo Ayres Brown remembered being with Tittle in the Browning Literary Society where he "was an excellent student and we predicted great things for him." Later when Brown became president of Drew he invited Tittle, "a very modest, friendly, and brilliant man," to become professor of homiletics, an honor declined.[15] Lynn Harold Hough, another Drew graduate to know fame in Methodism, recollected: "I can say something definite as regards the sort of person he was as a student at Drew. He was a young man of vigorous and independent mind. He judged everything including the administration of the school in a fearless individual fashion. He was a young man of much personal charm and drew people toward him quite unconsciously." "There was something firm and dependable about him under all judgments," Hough continued, having in mind Tittle the man as well as the student. "I remember once saying to him: 'Ernest, I can think of places where I would disagree with your opinion, but I could not possibly disagree with

14. Letter from Edwin Lewis to author, July 20, 1959.
15. Letter from Arlo Ayres Brown to author, July 7, 1959.

you."[16] Tittle himself recalled having heated arguments with fellow students of conservative theological convictions, adding ruefully, "I might have discovered then and there the utter futility of arguing with a man whose ideas are fixed."[17]

At Drew the young Tittle manifested many of the attributes of mind and personality that were to characterize his later great ministry: an enthusiastic embracement of the new liberalizing and liberating movements in theology; a passion to make religion relevant to life; a stubborn independence of mind; a critical and questioning attitude toward the established order of things; and withal a personal charm that marked him, without conscious effort on his part, as a leader of men.

IV

Upon the completion of his seminary studies, Ernest and Glenna were married on June 11, 1908. Their vows were solemnized by the Reverend W. D. Gilliland, pastor of St. Paul Methodist Episcopal Church, Springfield. It was a rather elegant wedding, but the couple did not have a formal honeymoon for there was no money for such a luxury.[18] For a while they lived with Clayton Tittle and his second wife. It could not have been a tension-free time—for any of them.

In September the appointing powers of Methodism in their inscrutable wisdom sent Tittle to a four-point country circuit where he embarked upon his career as faithful minister of Jesus Christ.[19] It was not an auspicious beginning. Though Christiansburg, Ohio, is less than fifty miles from Springfield on the map, it seemed a foreign land to the town-bred, college-educated, seminary-trained Tittle. And doubtless the good villagers and farm folk viewed their new young parson, with his fancy degrees, with suspicion. It was to be a two-year purgatorial experience, comparable to John Wesley's lot at the little hamlet of Wroote. Tittle later commented that Christiansburg was misnamed, "because there is little about the place that can be called Christian, though it is somewhat of a burg."[20] Yet these were not necessarily lost years. Purgatory has its purposes. Even the Christiansburg flock had need of a shepherd. And Methodists know that "God moves in a mys-

16. Letter from Lynn Harold Hough to author, July 10, 1959.
17. Tittle, *A World That Cannot Be Shaken* (New York and London: Harper & Brothers, 1933), p. 51.
18. Author's interview with Glenna Myers Tittle, Evanston, Ill., August 28, 1959.
19. Tittle had been received on trial by the Cincinnati Annual Conference, and on November 14, 1908, was licensed to solemnize marriages by the Probate Court, Troy, Ohio. The minister's license is in the Tittle Collection.
20. *Evanston News-Index,* November 30, 1918, p. 1.

terious way / His wonders to proclaim." It is very possible that Tittle emerged from this ordeal with his little four-point country circuit a wiser and humbler man.

The four little churches composing Tittle's first pastoral charge were less than imposing in size and vitality. The church in the village itself boasted one male member, lending credence to the lament of the Methodist bishops that in "many congregations there are twice as many women as men."[21] Two of the churches located in the country were not merely dead; rigor mortis had set in. Here is Tittle's memory of one of them: "It boasted a membership of seven. Its worshippers sometimes numbered as many as thirteen! The organist was a young woman who meant well and did the best she could, but who managed to draw something very new and strange out of the hymns of the ages. The choir consisted of two incorrigible bachelors who possessed the extraordinary power to fall into a deep slumber as soon as the preliminary service was over."[22] The fourth church, also located in the open country, was "rather nice,"[23] though far from grand.

In these difficult circumstances the young parson did the only thing thinkable for him: he bit the bullet. In order to serve his scattered parishioners he purchased a horse and buggy. "Shine" was a big, old, former race horse who did not much respect his master's town-clumsy touch of the reins. But Shine's spiritedness was matched by his master's mulishness, and in time he learned to behave himself. One day Shine dropped dead in the harness and Tittle continued to church on foot. He then purchased a bicycle, a triumph of experience over hope, unlike second marriages. He joined the volunteer fire department. He deposited $200 in the bank (and this on an annual support of $800). Both gestures were unusual for a rural Methodist minister and both were designed to increase his community stature. He complied with a request to conduct a two-week revival. No one attended the services the first week. When he inquired concerning the nonattendance one lady responded, "We are waiting for you to get warmed up." Apparently Tittle "warmed up" the second week for a woman prostrated herself on the church floor, seized by a hysterial conversion. A somewhat discomforted young preacher could think of nothing more appropriate to say

21. *The Daily Christian Advocate,* Methodist Episcopal Church, May 6, 1904, p. 36.

22. Tittle, "Some Religious Editorials," *First Church Review,* II (June, 1925), 3.

23. Author's interview with Glenna Myers Tittle, Evanston, Ill., July 27, 1959. Paul Hutchinson fails to suggest this in "Portrait of a Preacher," foreword to Tittle, *A Mighty Fortress* (New York: Harper & Brothers, 1949), p. xii.

than, "Come, now, madam, this is not as bad as you think!" When asked in a tone of complaint why he did not preach more on the devil, Tittle gently replied, "I am not very well acquainted with him."[24]

Ernest and Glenna lived in a decrepit, paintless house built in 1854. "During that first winter," he recalled, "the snow came through the chink in the clapboards and we found it on various floors in the morning. Under such conditions our first baby was born. Then I told my district superintendent that unless the saints could provide me a decent place to house my family he had my resignation. The saints did provide a decent home within a year, and we are still in the ministry."[25]

The weeks passed into months. It was not really a bad time for Glenna. She had her beloved husband and a fine new son named John Myers. The countryside was familiar. She already knew some of the people from her girlhood days in North Hampton. She and Ernest made new friends. The parishioners warmed to their vigorous young pastor and his wife. Attendance at the services increased a bit.[26]

Yet increasingly it was a bad time for Ernest. "Try as he might, he could not adjust to the pettiness and 'sotness' of villages which had not changed from time out of mind and did not intend to change now."[27] He wondered if he might not be stuck there indefinitely and in his frustration he considered leaving the Methodist Church with its connectional system for a denomination with a congregational polity.[28] On one occasion he was accused of calling upon persons who were not Methodists. The accusation was brought at a Quarterly Conference presided over by the district superintendent. "Fortunately," Tittle remembered, "I had with me a copy of the New Testament from which I proceeded to read at some length. The charge was dropped."[29] On another instance he opened a sermon on Jonah with the words, "Once upon a time," and was sharply reminded that the Good Book was not *that* imprecise. Because he talked with villagers on the street corner, on the

24. These little stories concerning Christiansburg were told me by Mrs. Tittle. But they are also rather common knowledge. Tittle liked to relate them, especially in informal chats with students and young preachers. It warmed and encouraged them to learn that one of America's great ministers had started his career under discouraging circumstances.

25. Letter from Tittle to N. C. Nagler, March 7, 1932.

26. Glenna's memories are not bitter. The *Dayton Daily News*, September 5, 1910, p. 7, reported that at Christiansburg Tittle "advanced his congregation noticeably by reasons of his endeavors." Thomas A. Stafford believes that Tittle's Christiansburg ministry was under the circumstances remarkably successful. Author's interview with Thomas A. Stafford, Denver, Col., May 1, 1960.

27. Hutchinson, "Portrait," p. xii.

28. Author's interview with Glenna Myers Tittle, Evanston, Ill., July 31, 1959.

29. Letter from Tittle to J. E. Harlow, July 3, 1944.

steps of the general store, and in the barber shop, he was again charged before the Quarterly Conference of "associating with the men of the town"—a charge which, as Paul Hutchinson observed, while probably unique in Methodist annals, was not without its New Testament overtones. Tittle was to remember another unhappy experience: "Years ago in a little country church, one of the four which I was then serving during a protracted meeting (if you know what I mean, which most of you, probably, do not) an earnest layman, in my behalf, offered up to heaven's throne a very earnest prayer. Apparently he was troubled by something in me or in my preaching. (There were many things in me and in my preaching which might have troubled him.) But apparently, also, he was not able to make clear to himself just what it was; so he asked God in his mercy to save me from the fate of the rich man in the parable, who, he reminded God and the congregation and me, was sent to perdition (he used another simpler, shorter word) and, he added, 'Why, O Lord, the Good Book does not say.' "[30]

Tittle's discouragement deepened, but he was saved from total despair by the inspiration of the great Baptist Walter Rauschenbusch, unquestionably the most searching and theologically grounded of all the early Social Gospel prophets. Tittle remembered: "I am inclined to think that the one book which has most powerfully influenced my own life is Walter Rauschenbusch's prophetic volume entitled 'Christianity and the Social Crisis.' It appeared in 1908 [1907] and I read it in the fall of that year just after I had gone to my first church with the miserable feeling that I had nothing to say that was worth saying. In this volume I found a gospel, good news, which I tried to pass on to my people. To me as a young and inexperienced preacher it proved to be a godsend. Even now when I dip into it I find myself stimulated and refreshed."[31] Yet not even the sustaining message of Rauschenbusch could make Christiansburg endurable much longer. The little four-point circuit

30. "Christianity and Wealth," typed MS, a sermon preached February 2, 1936. Tittle was to repeat this tale with slight variations in other sermons.

31. Letter from Tittle to Lew Sarett, September 24, 1934. In a letter to Mrs. Walter Rauschenbusch, April 10, 1942, Tittle acknowledged that *Christianity and the Social Crisis* "has done more for me than any other [book], save the New Testament, which I have read.' See also the tribute paid by Tittle to the great Baptist in "To Them That Love God," typed MS, a sermon preached June 2, 1935. In that year he went to visit Mrs. Rauschenbusch in Rochester, as to a shrine. As we shall see below, Rauschenbusch's influence was enormous outside as well as inside the church. Said Norman Thomas: "Insofar as any one man or any one book, or series of books made me a Socialist, it was probably Walter Rauschenbusch and his writings."

world was too small for this young man, driven as he was by the compulsion to "be somebody."[32]

V

It was, then, with joy that Tittle in early September, 1910, received the news that he had been appointed to the Riverdale Methodist Episcopal Church in Dayton, Ohio. Though pleased, he could not have considered the Dayton appointment a leap to the top. The members of his new flock were not very numerous, perhaps only two hundred or so. They were mostly lower-middle-class folk and except for a doctor and a dentist without college education.[33] Because it was not an affluent congregation, Ernest's support was modest, and he and Glenna (and son John) continued to live just over the bright side of the line of genuine hardship. They rented their home until 1913 when the saints "purchased a new parsonage for Rev. Tittle on Warder street, outlaying almost $6,000."[34] Ernest dreamed of an automobile as he peddled his bike up the hilly streets of suburban Dayton, but the dream did not become a reality.

Glenna remembers these as being good years. And one has the feeling that they were good years for Ernest as well. Now in his mid-twenties, his health was bouyant, his energy inexhaustible. His wife was dear to him and his young son a delight. The currents of theological liberalism and the Social Gospel were running clear and strong and in these Tittle found a bracing pulpit message. The nation was at peace, as was the world for a last moment. Progressivism gave the promise that poverty and injustice would soon be banished from American life. If Riverdale was not a grand parish, it beat those country miles of circuit riding in Christiansburg. Above all, the future seemed open.

In 1910, having passed his two-year probationary period, the Cincinnati Conference received Tittle into full membership and he was ordained to the office of deacon. The following year, on Sunday afternoon, September 3, in the Grace Methodist Church in Dayton, Bishop David H. Moore set Tittle apart for the office of an elder in the Methodist Episcopal Church, and he thereby became "a proper person to administer the Sacraments and Ordinances, and to Feed the Flock of Christ." It was an impressive ceremony. Bishop Moore propounded the questions to the candidates and then, after receiving affirmative answers,

32. On rare instances in later years Tittle received letters from his old Christiansburg flock. His replies were affectionate and humble, expressing regret for his immaturity and his appreciation for their patience with him.

33. Letter from Florence Peterson to author, October 4, 1959.

34. *Dayton Daily News,* October 7, 1913, p. 17.

he and the district superintendents laid their hands in benediction upon the heads of the young men. Bishop William F. McDowell, who "was just about the last word in grace of bearing and of speech,"[35] concluded the service with a peroration on the glory of the Christian ministry.[36]

Tittle evolved a full church program for his congregation. A typical Sunday included the following: 9:15, Bible School; 10:30, morning worship; 2:30, Junior League; 6:30, Epworth League; 7:30, evening worship. Wednesday evening, of course, was set aside for prayer service. From time to time, "evangelistic services" were "held every night during the week except Saturday." Riverdale M.E. Church participated in an eight-day campaign conducted by the Men and Religion Forward movement. It cooperated in a series of union meetings with five other Protestant congregations. Visiting speakers warned presumably attentive audiences of the perils of "The Liquor Traffic" and "The White Slave Trade." A boys' club was formed, meeting in the basement of the church, which Tittle had equipped with athletic gear.[37] And Tittle remembered "hilarious parties (perfectly proper, of course) which a number of us youngsters threw on Sunday nights after the evening service as a means of securing some needed relaxation and also a means of becoming better acquainted with one another."[38] It was not all fun and games, however, for Tittle proposed that the congregation increase its benevolent giving fivefold at a time when there was not enough money to pay the church coal bill.[39]

Tittle's pulpit message at Riverdale continued to draw heavily on the prophetic social passion of Rauschenbusch. Though no file of the minister's sermons exists for this period,[40] their content may be inferred from the titles as announced in the Dayton newspapers: "The Social Awakening of the Modern Church," "The Lord's Prayer: Its Social Meaning," "The Christian, a Man Who Serves," and the like. Moreover, Riverdale members were to recall that even in these early years Tittle stressed the social application of the Gospel. His interests and energies involved him in the wider religious and civic life of the city; he especially extended

35. Francis J. McConnell, *By the Way: An Autobiography* (New York and Nashville, Tenn.: Abingdon-Cokesbury Press, 1952), p. 231.

36. *Dayton Daily News,* September 4, 1911, p. 1.

37. A close and tedious examination of the *Dayton Daily News,* August, 1910-October, 1913, provided the basis for this survey of Riverdale's activities under Tittle. See also letter from Charles F. Sullivan to Tittle, December 7, 1942.

38. Letter from Tittle to C. R. Williamson, September 26, 1932.

39. *Ibid.*

40. I am indebted to the Reverend Warren R. Powell, now pastor of Riverdale, for his cooperation in an unsuccessful attempt to track down Tittle's early sermons.

himself for the community for a sleepless week at the time of the fearful 1913 flood.[41]

Ernest Fremont Tittle, only in his mid-twenties and looking eighteen, was a real shepherd to his little Riverdale flock. It is important to remember (for it is so often forgotten) that he was a faithful minister of Jesus Christ long before he became nationally famous as the great preacher of "The Cathedral of Methodism" in Evanston. Though Tittle was ambitious, he was no cheat. He did not reserve his energies and talents for later, greater undertakings. He did not hoard his gifts, waiting for better opportunities to bestow them. He gave all of himself fully and freely to his rather unimpressive Riverdale flock. And they knew it —and loved him for it.

"As I look back now," remembers one parishioner, "I can appreciate the qualities in Mr. Tittle which made him so beloved and respected. He did not talk down to his audience with trite jokes and commonplace remarks as so many young ministers would have done to a congregation like ours. He was able to make people with limited backgrounds *want* to have their visions broadened and thoughts enlarged. Instead of smug condescension he met people at their level and prodded them forward." The parishioner continued: "Although he often said his first name was very appropriate, he had a lively sense of humor and often joined in the frolics of the young folks which he seemed to *enjoy*. We never felt he was joining in our activities out of a sense of duty." This is a significant assessment, for although Tittle was by nature grave, he was not pompous or joyless, and, moreover, he now seemed a warmer person than he appeared as an undergraduate. "He was devoted to his wife and his gallant treatment of her made some of the women a bit envious—they were not accustomed to having husbands show the deference and little courtesies he showed his wife." Here is another clue that Ernest and Glenna had a good marriage. The parishioner then went on to make a point that a later age was largely to forget: "In his theology and social attitudes he was what in those days one called a liberal. The theological controversy centered on 'higher criticism' versus the literal interpretation of the Bible and most of his congregation had been brought up on the latter. Since I was approaching the age of questioning and skepticism, I have always felt that it was Mr. Tittle's interpretation of religious ideas in those crucial years of my life which kept me from becoming what in those days was labelled 'atheism.' " It is sobering to be reminded that tens of thousands of men and women early in the century owed

41. This statement is based on an examination of the news columns of the *Dayton Daily News*.

their very religious lives to a liberal theology which mediated between a fundamentalist obscurantism and a bleak agnosticism. The parishioner concluded her reminiscence: "After I finished college I did not see him much but he continued to mean a great deal to me, and that is something which is hard to put into words. He remained always a reassuring presence and whenever I had a difficult question or hard problem to resolve, always in the back of my mind was, 'How would Dr. Tittle answer this?' "[42]

VI

Almost exactly six months after the flood the *Dayton Daily News* reported that members of the Riverdale Church "are indignant over the sudden removal of their pastor, Rev. E. F. Tittle. The announcement by Bishop Anderson of Cincinnati that he is to take up his duties at the William Street M. E. Church at Delaware, O., was made after the conference held at Chillicothe."[43] Delaware's minister, Thomas Housel, had died without warning, and it was imperative that Bishop Anderson act at once to fill the pulpit of this strategic church.

Tittle and his new church were perfectly mated. The three years in Dayton had been good. The three years he was to spend in Delaware were better. For the first time he was now minister of a major church, one with almost a century's history of importance in Ohio Methodism. The building itself, constructed in 1887, was an imposing edifice, modified Gothic in design, built of brick, stone, and sandstone, capped by a slate roof and three towers, the central tower handsome with its six stained-glass windows. The interior was commodious, and beautifully appointed with three large stained windows, carefully executed frescoing, impressive chandeliers, pulpit, and communion table, fine organ and choir loft seating thirty.[44] Tittle had a reverence for beauty and the church must have been particularly satisfying to him after the five aesthetically barren years at Christiansburg and Dayton. But it was the congregation itself that was most satisfying, heavily peppered as it was with Ohio Wesleyan students and faculty. He was now for the first time

42. Letter from Florence Peterson to author, October 4, 1959. Similar testimony was given in letters to the author from Mrs. Herbert L. Henderson, Josephine A. Sheeler, Wilbur A. Vorhis, and Eva M. Lowe.

43. October 7, 1913, p. 17. "The Riverdale church was never in better shape than at present," reported the paper (October 16, 1913, p. 8) at the end of Tittle's pastorate.

44. A detailed and loving description of the church is given in Thomas Dickson Graham, *An Historical Sketch of the William Street Methodist Church, Delaware, Ohio, 1818-1958* (Delaware, Ohio: William Street Methodist Church, 1958), pp. 50-54.

challenged with exciting the minds and quickening the spirits of college men and women. He was now for the first time confronted by men in the pews more learned than he, many of whom were his former teachers and leaders of American Methodism. And he now preached in the awareness that his words would be carried throughout the reaches of world Methodism.

These were good years. Delaware was a lovely little town and, of course, its scenes were familiar to Ernest and Glenna from their undergraduate days. Here their second child and first daughter, Elizabeth Ann, was born. Students and professors crowded to hear Tittle preach, his pastorate being the "most successful" the church had ever known, "especially in the way of increasing membership."[45] He kept in touch with the larger Church by attending conferences and addressing religious groups. He knew the immense satisfaction of being wanted elsewhere. "Tell me what we will have to do to get you down here," read one invitation, "and I will see that it is done."[46] He sealed important friendships with such figures as Herbert Welch, president of Ohio Wesleyan, and came to know intimately Bishop William Fraser McDowell and his wife, "Auntie Mac," as Tittle affectionately called her. The old, large parsonage was always open to students and Glenna prepared plates of cookies and pitchers of milk and lemonade to welcome them. Somehow the bills were paid, though Tittle's annual support was only $2,000.

Tittle's sermons continued to be characterized by clarity, directness, and earnestness, "especially those on social and industrial problems, in which he is intensely interested."[47] It may be doubted, however, if this early preaching plumbed the depths later reached. The local newspaper carried rather too many announcements of sermons with such titles as "The World's Debt to Mother" and "Abraham Lincoln."

His associations with Ohio Wesleyan were of course close and his services to the university were many, as President Welch repeatedly acknowledged. Indeed, in 1916, when Tittle was only thirty, the trustees of Ohio Wesleyan came within one vote of electing him president to succeed Welch. Instead, the nod went to Dr. John Washington Hoffman, then pastor of the First Methodist Episcopal Church in Duluth. Interestingly, the third top contender for the post was Harris Franklin Rall, later to be one of Tittle's most intimate friends and closest adviser

45. *Delaware Daily Gazette,* August 4, 1916, p. 8.
46. Letter from W. D. Gilliland to Tittle, September 1, 1915.
47. *Delaware Daily Gazette,* August 4, 1916, p. 8. I am indebted to Mrs. Donald Butman, now William Street Church secretary, for her cooperation in an unsuccessful attempt to track down Tittle's early sermons.

on matters of theology. Edmund D. Soper and Lynn Harold Hough were also under consideration and their careers were curiously interwoven with Tittle's. Hutchinson comments regarding the election: "If West Point was the first, that may be counted the second of his narrow escapes."[48] From the perspective of Tittle's later preaching career, this evaluation is undoubtedly correct. Yet it can be hazarded that at the time Tittle was deeply wounded. He was not so constituted as to lightly suffer defeat. And there are elusive hints in the record that the contest for the presidency of Ohio Wesleyan in 1916, decided against Tittle, left scars that were slow in healing. In spite of—or perhaps because of—this defeat, the following year O.W. honored him with the degree of Doctor of Divinity. The citation accompanying the degree was typically innocuous: "Ernest Fremont Tittle, B.A., '06; B.D. A leader of men. An apostle to the Modern City. A preacher of social righteousness whose work already is meeting with the strong approval of the church."[49]

VII

To receive the honorary degree Tittle had traveled to Delaware from Columbus, Ohio, for since September, 1916, he had been pastor of the Broad Street Methodist Episcopal Church in the capital city. It is possible that his decision to leave Delaware and accept the Columbus call was influenced by his failure to win the presidency of Ohio Wesleyan. In any case the two events were curiously related. John W. Hoffman had been the Broad Street Church's first choice for its new pastor, and with his election to the leadership of the university, the church then turned to Tittle. Perhaps the hand of Dr. Rollin H. Walker may be discerned in the matter. A close friend of Tittle's, this Wesleyan professor had long been a powerful force in the Broad Street Church, and he recommended Tittle as "a young man of simplicity, directness, brevity and earnestness and in every way an exceedingly strong preacher, who has an intense interest in social and industrial problems."[50] The call came in August. The circumstances were unusual, at least for Methodism in that era. Negotiations between the church and the candidate were conducted independently of the Ohio Annual Conference, which was not scheduled to meet until September, and Bishop Anderson confirmed the contract in advance of the formal appointment by the conference.[51] Thus, though technically an appointment as required by

48. Hutchinson, "Portrait," p. xiii.
49. Copy in author's possession. I am much indebted to Dean Allan C. Ingraham for his cooperation in all matters pertaining to Ohio Wesleyan.
50. Unidentified, undated newspaper clipping in Tittle Collection.
51. *Columbus Evening Dispatch,* September 22, 1916, p. 1.

Methodist discipline, it was in fact a call, a practice to become increasingly common in American Methodism.

Tittle was on the eve of his thirty-first birthday when he preached his first sermon from the pulpit of the Broad Street Church on Sunday, September 24, 1916. He was the youngest minister in the history of the church, a tribute to his growing reputation "as one of the most brilliant and promising men in Methodism"[52] and "one of the coming young men of Ohio Methodism."[53] Most clergymen would have considered a call to the Broad Street pulpit a distinguished climax to a long career in the ministry, and surely Tittle was aware of the honor being accorded to him only eight years after his graduation from Drew.

In these years Columbus had the largest Methodist membership for its population of any city in the United States.[54] It boasted twenty-six Methodist congregations.[55] And of these, Broad Street was outstanding. Indeed, it was one of the oldest and most eminent churches in all Methodism. The present structure had been consecrated the year of Tittle's birth. It was considered a noble Gothic edifice. Only recently a new recreation hall had been completed. In all, it was a large, modern, splendidly equipped church with property and buildings valued at several hundred thousands of dollars.[56] It was situated in what was then one of Columbus's most exclusive residential areas, a neighborhood noted for its lovely homes and affluent citizenry, yet within sight of the state capitol. The congregation counted several millionaires among its twelve hundred members. No visitor, of course, was permitted to remain uninformed of the fact that many Ohio notables had worshipped there, including governors McKinley and Foraker.[57]

It is almost gratuitous to mention that Tittle threw himself into the new post with energy and devotion. For the first time his talents as an administrator were taxed. He was now the head of an "institutional" church. It was now his responsibility to supervise a rather considerable staff, including an assistant minister, oversee a large physical plant, raise substantial sums of money, and conduct an active and varied church program ministering not only to the needs of his immediate congregation

52. *Delaware Daily Gazette,* August 4, 1916, p. 8.
53. *Columbus Evening Dispatch,* September 23, 1916, p. 3.
54. *Nashville Christian Advocate,* LXXV (September 25, 1914), 8.
55. *Columbus Evening Dispatch,* January 6, 1917, p. 5.
56. See Harriett Daily Collins, *Endless Splendor: A History of Broad Street Methodist Church, Columbus, Ohio, 1874-1959* (Columbus, Ohio: Broad Street Methodist Church, 1959), *passim.* See also various news items in the *Columbus Evening Dispatch,* August, 1916-June, 1918.
57. Author's interview with Harriett Daily Collins, Columbus, Ohio, June 14, 1960; author's interview with Mrs. Russell Beck, Columbus, Ohio, June 16, 1960.

sending you this note to assure you of the love which I have for
d Street Church and its people. I came to them when I was but
y years of age and they were long-suffering and kind. Long-suffer-
they needed to be, and kind they choose to be. You can well under-
d, therefore, how deep is my affection for them and how profound
appreciation."[59] Tittle gave of his best to his Columbus flock. His
y nature would not permit him to give less. Yet events compelled him
depart in less than two years under circumstances that did indeed
quire the Broad Street people to be long-suffering.

59. Letter from Tittle to Dr. John Taylor Alton, September 24, 1934.

but also to the city at large. This experience wa
years ahead. But the commitment he made in
disembodied future congregation, it was to the
that moment in time.

The muscular Christianity of the era, the inten
is reflected in the Broad Street stationery heading:
Day in the Week xxx Gymnasium Classes, Games ai
Church Activities, Five Afternoons and Evenings An
Each Week xxx Competent Leaders in Charge xxx
itual Efficiency Is Best Achieved Through Sound E
always to believe with Theodore Parker in a religion
morning and works all day. Perhaps, however, he l
recognition that much of the pre–World War I empl
activity represented an attempt to compensate for the l
Protestantism of spiritual direction.

Judging from the fragmentary evidence, there was
Columbus preaching to foreshadow the great Evanst
attempted to demonstrate to a conservative congregation
mentalist the relevance and rightness of the new libe
"Fundamental facts on which religious experience is ba
change," he explained. "But they do need to be reinterp
language in which our fathers expressed their faith is not tl
in which we can express our faith with naturalness and sinc
old faith must be restated in forms which are vital to modern
this series of sermons an attempt to do this will be mad
attempted to awaken also a congregation largely conservative
and economic thought to the complexities and brutalities of ii
America; to remind them in this new steel-hard era of the distan
of Amos, "Let justice roll down as water and righteousness as a
stream"; to invoke them to do battle with the new kings of cap
who "beat my people to pieces, and grind the face of the poor."
in Columbus Tittle came to know Washington Gladden who, thoug
retirement, preached from Tittle's pulpit. As Tittle was indebteo
Rauschenbusch, so he drew from the social passion of Gladden
carried on the prophetic tradition of both men.

Years later Tittle was invited to return to Broad Street for a vis
and he replied: "Unable as I am to be present at the great anniversar

58. *Columbus Evening Dispatch,* December 30, 1916, p. 6. I am indebted to
Mrs. Harriett Daily Collins, Broad Street historian, and Mrs. Russell Beck, Broad
Street secretary, for their cooperation in an unsuccessful attempt to track down
Tittle's early sermons.

3. THE CALL TO EVANSTON
AND THE CALL TO THE COLORS

I

On September 28, 1916, the officials of First Methodist Episcopal Church in Evanston, Illinois, for the twelfth consecutive year requested the presiding bishop and district superintendent to return Dr. Timothy Prescott Frost to them, for "that he has been wise and faithful; loving and discreet; loyal and true to his Divine Master and to the people he has served, is equally convincing and irresistible."[1] But Timothy Frost, who had reached the age of sixty-six, was soon to announce to his devoted congregation that he had reached an age at which he wished to retire to the hills of his native Vermont, and that this must be his terminal year as their minister.

Consequently, on November 14, the Official Board authorized a Committee of Seven to "take up the matter of selecting a new Pastor."[2] The seven were William A. Dyche, chairman, Frank P. Crandon, Edwin S. Mills, James F. Oates, Henry W. Price, John C. Shaffer, and Charles N. Stevens. To say that the group was impressive is an understatement. These were men of great ability holding positions of national prominence in industry, banking, publishing, merchandising, and education, and, with perhaps one or two exceptions, they possessed much wealth. The

1. Unsigned letter attached to Minutes of the Fourth Quarterly Conference, First Church, September 28, 1916. I wish to express my gratitude to First Church for generously granting me full and free access to its records. Not a single restriction was placed on my research. To my knowledge, not a single document was withheld from my examination. The First Church archives are voluminous, completely occupying a very large room.

2. Minutes of the Official Board, First Church, November 14, 1916.

searchers proceeded to the business at hand. In December Dyche received a communication from Thomas Nicholson, presiding bishop of the Rock River Annual Conference. This bearded, angular leader was acutely conscious of the importance of First Church to American Methodism, for he had studied at Garrett Biblical Institute and Northwestern University, both located in Evanston and both associated historically with First Church. He wrote:

> From all I can learn, the Rev. E. F. Tipple [*sic*] of Columbus, Ohio is one of the men you should investigate with great care. I have had track of him for three or four years. . . . He is clearly one of the men in the class; but he has just gone this year to Broad Street, Columbus, and I know from [David S.] Gray, the Nestor of that church, that it is their habit to have a tacit understanding (a sort of gentleman's agreement) with any man who goes to Broad Street that it is a five-year arrangement and that unless, for most exceptional causes, it is necessary, neither party is to raise the question until the end of five years, and then they either make a change or make an agreement for another five years. I therefore doubt whether we could pull Dr. Tipple away, but it is worth trying.[3]

As it happened, Edwin S. Mills had a brother who was a member of the Broad Street congregation and he confirmed the report of "a definite contract or understanding for a five year pastorate from which Dr. Tittle would not be able to secure release if indeed he could be induced to consider such a suggestion."[4]

Nevertheless, though Tittle seemed fixed in Columbus and though many other ministers throughout the nation came under consideration, his name was not scratched from the list of possibilities. And he had the inestimable asset of being backed by Bishop William Fraser McDowell, a towering figure in Methodism, who both knew the Evanston situation and liked Tittle. Early in March four First Church men traveled to Columbus to "size him up" and "sound him out." As they entered the Broad Street Church to hear Tittle preach, Dyche, the leader of the quartet, ordered James Alton James to assess Tittle's history; Mills, his economics; and Oates, his theology. Dyche added dryly, "I'll see if he can keep me awake forty-five minutes." None of the visitors napped that morning—or that afternoon, for after lunch they met with eight members of the Broad Street Official Board at the Deshler Hotel. Amity was not the dominant mood. The Columbus people did not intend to sur-

3. Letter from Bishop Thomas Nicholson to William A. Dyche, December 23, 1916.
4. Letter from Edwin S. Mills to William A. Dyche, January 8, 1917.

render their pastor to Dyche's marauders. But they did make one crucial concession: Tittle was at least to be informed that he was under consideration by First Church. The meeting adjourned, the Evanston four heard Tittle preach an evening sermon, and then departed for Illinois knowing that the Broad Street leaders felt "much bitterness" toward them. They knew too that Tittle was the man they wanted![5]

But desire alone was not enough. The proposed transfer of course required the approval of Tittle's episcopal superior in Ohio, Bishop William F. Anderson. And so Dyche wrote Anderson, concluding his plea with the prescient statement: "We in Evanston have learned of the advantages of a long pastorate. We hope to have a man who is capable of giving us such a pastorate. In other words, Dr. Frost's successor has the prospect of staying here as long as he can sustain himself—ten or fifteen or twenty years."[6] Bishop Anderson was naturally reluctant to lose one of his most promising ministers and he declined an invitation to meet with Tittle, Bishop Nicholson, and Dyche's committee in Chicago in mid-March. It was a crucial meeting. After lunch at the University Club Tittle was motored along the beautiful Lake Michigan shore to the elegant suburb of Evanston. There he saw First Church, the imposing edifice that had been dedicated in 1911. Not only did Bishop Anderson not attend the meeting, he wrote Bishop Nicholson in protest, pointing out that Broad Street was "probably the most important church in our State" and that though "The Kingdom of God *is* important in Evanston . . . my dear and trusted friend, we have the Kingdom over here in Ohio too." He then related an interview with Tittle in which Tittle allegedly stated he was perfectly willing to leave the decision up to his episcopal superiors and "absolutely satisfied and happy to remain" in Columbus.[7]

"Absolutely satisfied and happy to remain" is hardly an accurate reflection of Tittle's true feelings. In his perplexity he turned for guidance to his old and trusted mentor Bishop McDowell. The fundamental question, Tittle believed, was whether the Kingdom of God should be built up in Evanston at the expense of tearing it down in Columbus. As he explained, "Broad Street church *has* reached a crisis in its history. It has become a down-town church. Its substantial members are moving to the suburbs. Its leaders are old men. Only by hard and heroic work

5. Author's interview with James Alton James, Evanston, Ill., July 23, 1960; letter from William A. Dyche to Bishop William F. McDowell, March 17, 1917.

6. Letter from William A. Dyche to Bishop William F. Anderson, March 9, 1917.

7. Letter from Bishop William F. Anderson to Bishop Thomas Nicholson, March 29, 1917. In later years Tittle exchanged many cordial letters with Bishop Anderson, and in his correspondence he always spoke highly of his former bishop.

can its reputation be sustained. Just now, we are having a 'good time.' People are coming from all parts of the city. Whether they can be kept coming is another question. But our official members think they can if there is no change of pastorate."[8] Moreover, in his opinion Columbus was grievously overstocked with Methodist churches. It is not cynical to observe that in addition to the question of the advancement of the Kingdom of God there was the question of the future of Ernest Fremont Tittle. In 1917 he sensed what was later to become a reality: the decline of Broad Street as one of Methodism's great churches with the decay of its exclusive residential surroundings.

Meanwhile, Dyche also continued to seek the assistance of Bishop McDowell, a man persistent in his own right. (When taxed with having preached the same baccalaureate sermon five times to successive Northwestern classes, McDowell is supposed to have answered, "Yes, why not? They haven't begun to put what I've preached into practice yet. When they do, it will be time enough to get a new sermon.") After slyly commenting on the bishop's golf game, Dyche wondered, "Is there any way by which the difference of opinion between Bishops Nicholson and Anderson can be arbitrated? Some brother bishop who is a good golf-player would suit us first rate as the arbiter, but I suppose if he had once lived in Evanston, that would disqualify him."[9]

One April 22 at a special meeting of the First Church Official Board it was resolved unanimously to extend a call to Tittle.[10] The following day the message was dispatched.[11] Two weeks later Tittle replied to Dyche in a brief, longhand note: "May I not have until the middle of next week to consider this *so* difficult question? Why doesn't Bishop Anderson write? I have not had a line from him."[12]

8. Letter from Tittle to Bishop William F. McDowell, April 10, 1917. Although the First Church offer more than doubled his Broad Street salary, there is not the slightest hint in the record to suggest that financial considerations figured prominently in Tittle's decision. Nor did he succumb to pressure from Glenna, who, as a matter of fact, did not wish to leave Columbus.

9. Letter from William A. Dyche to Bishop William F. McDowell, April 9, 1917. Bishop McDowell once said that the secret to his administrative success was that he was born lazy. He never did any more work than absolutely necessary, being happy to delegate responsibility to his subordinates, thus freeing him for more time on the golf links. He further mused that some of his colleagues in the episcopacy—who need not be named—might well increase their efficiency by following his example.

10. Minutes of Special Meeting of the Official Board, First Church, April 22, 1917. James Alton James, *From Log Schoolhouse to Church Tower: A History of the First Methodist Church, Evanston, Illinois* (n.p., n.d.), p. 33, states that this resolution was adopted on May 13, 1917. This is an error.

11. Letter from William A. Dyche to Tittle, April 23, 1917.

12. Letter from Tittle to William A. Dyche, May 5, 1917.

It was a sticky situation and surely a sleepless time for Tittle, cleft as he was by desire and duty—and indeed by an honest doubt concerning where his duty lay. It was perhaps late at night when a weary, troubled Tittle sat down at his desk to write Dyche these lines: ". . . it would be impossible for me to remain here if there was anything like a formal agreement that I was to leave in the fall of 1918. Psychologically impossible. I am sure that a psychological situation would result in which neither the congregation nor I myself could labor efficiently. The certainty of my leaving would be as a dark shadow following me every day; not that I do not want to go, but I do not want to know so long in advance that I am certain to go. I fear the effect of such knowledge upon my own inner attitude. It is for this reason that I am asking you to withdraw the present invitation and hold yourselves free to invite someone else to become your pastor. Should you do this I could say to Broad Street and to Bishop Anderson and to anyone else found to be curious 'First Church has withdrawn its invitation' and I could say also to myself 'It is not certain that you will be given another invitation and it may be that they will desire a handsomer man.' A totally different psychological situation will result. . . . I cannot persuade myself that I am the best man you could get for your pulpit but if after further investigation you still feel that you want and need me, tell me so some time during the month of June, 1918. I shall say "Thank you very much for the invitation. I shall be pleased to accept it.' "[13] Dyche reported the substance of this letter to the Official Board on May 13. The Board voted to officially withdraw the invitation, but if another man was not secured by "one year from now," then a second call would be extended to Tittle.[14] The following day Tittle was formally notified of the withdrawal of the invitation.[15]

A tense year passed. Tittle and Dyche wanted to keep their "understanding" confidential, but this was obviously hopeless. Dyche's committee continued to go through the motions of finding another man, but nearly everyone knew the "search" to be a charade. In Columbus curses were increasingly heard, not loud, perhaps, but deep. On April 28, 1918, First Church renewed its invitation, and on May 13 Tittle telegraphed his affirmative reply, after steeling himself to inform the Broad Street leaders of the news. In a covering letter he revealed the anguish

13. This letter is not in the Tittle Collection or First Church archives. It is quoted by Dyche in a letter to Lynn Harold Hough, May 14, 1917.

14. Minutes of the Official Board, First Church, May 13, 1917. Dyche's report is in the Official Board Scrapbook.

15. Letter from William A. Dyche to Tittle, May 14, 1917.

of the decision: "You will understand, but only in part, what it has cost us to leave here. Our affection for these people is very great, and their affection for us has made our decision to leave them seem a very grave one. We can only hope that it will prove to be good and wise."[16] At this juncture Dyche requested a picture of Tittle for the Evanston papers. Tittle replied laconically, "I cannot locate a photograph, and would advise you not to prejudice the situation by using one."[17]

The road to Evanston was now open, but Tittle was diamond-hard in his determination to first make a longer journey to France. Securing a YMCA secretaryship and the reluctant permission of Dyche to postpone until December his First Church duties, he boarded the troopship S.S. *Walmar Castle* on June 19 to participate in President Wilson's Great Crusade. (A chaplaincy had been considered but vetoed because it involved such a long and indefinite commitment.) Why did the man soon to emerge as Methodism's most passionate pacifist respond so ardently to his nation's call to the colors in 1917?

II

In August, 1914, Great Britain decided to draw the sword against Imperial Germany. Mrs. Asquith, the wife of the prime minister, remembered that at that moment "I got up and leaned my head against his, and we could not speak for tears." All humanity had cause to weep. Europe was now a gigantic Golgotha. For sixty-three months of unutterable agony mankind was to hang on the cross of war. Who willed this terrible thing? King George V pleaded to the American ambassador, "My God, Mr. Page, what else could we do?" This plea might have come from the throats of other rulers, too. It is for the diplomatic historians to assess the candor or hypocrisy of these exculpations and to weigh the relative responsibilities of the Great Powers in the shattering of peace—and the debate rages as intensely today as in the 1920s and 1930s. Here it is needful to observe only that war is a normal occurrence in any system of independent and proximate states, and that international life itself, with its commercialized nationalisms, imperialistic rivalries, contending ideologies, and competing wills to power, bears war within itself as the sea bears the tempest. Skillful diplomacy might have postponed the Great War (as it had done for many years in crisis after crisis), but sooner or later even skilled diplomats must play their last card, and in 1914 the nation-state system was too powerful and civilization too sick to keep the peace.

16. Letter from Tittle to William A. Dyche, May 15, 1918.
17. Letter from Tittle to William A. Dyche, May 15, 1918.

Most Americans early in the twentieth century rather prided themselves on their exceptionalism, thanking the Lord (or their lucky stars) that they were not like other warring Asian, African, Latin American, and European peoples. They somehow viewed as aberrations from the norm of peace the events of 1775 (not to mention the colonial wars), 1812, 1846, 1861, and 1898. Viewed as aberrations also or now almost forgotten were the Indian wars and the undeclared naval war with France, the Barbary Pirate wars, the invasion of Spanish Florida, the Canadian border skirmishing, the nineteenth-century bombardments of Chinese, Korean, and Japanese territory, the Philippine Insurrection, the Boxer Rebellion, and the military expeditions to the Caribbean. If it is true that the United States had not been a particularly warlike nation—and it *is* true—then could there be a more devastating indictment of the modern world?

But Americans had an inordinate capacity to banish from their collective memory these earlier wars or if remembered, to glorify and rationalize them. As Bishop Henry W. Warren, in defending the acquisition of the Philippines, explained: "Taking them was a tremendous responsibility. But twice in our history God has intrusted to us the care of inferior races, and despite some results of infirmities of human nature, we had treated the Indians and Negroes in a way that led Him to intrust us with the redemption of Cuba and the Philippines."[18] In any case, these struggles belonged to the past. The new century was to be an age of treaties rather than an age of wars, as the secretary of the Church Peace Union phrased it. "War," affirmed a Methodist editor in 1910, "is soon to become so preposterous and so unpopular that it will cease."[19] And another Methodist leader declared in 1908, "On this ninth anniversary of the first Hague Conference the General Conference of the Methodist Episcopal Church views with gratitude the absence of any occasion or prospect of war."[20]

Yet it is possible to overstate the utopianism of these pre-1914 Americans. To be sure, they shared a faith in the rational perfectability of mankind impossible to reconcile with the brutalities of history. They shared a faith in the capacity of moral men animated by pure love and the example of Jesus of Nazareth to convert wicked men to righteousness. All this and more has been pointed out unmercifully by mid-century critics. Nevertheless, thoughtful Americans read the newspapers and

18. *New York Christian Advocate*, LXXIX (December 15, 1904), 2032.
19. *Nashville Christian Advocate*, LXXI (January 14, 1910), 4.
20. *The Daily Christian Advocate*, Methodist Episcopal Church, May 19, 1908, p. 2.

knew of the "minor" wars raging on every continent. They knew, too, of the deadly rivalry between the Great Powers, which threatened the world as it had not been threatened since the Age of Napoleon. They comprehended that "Every nation of Europe today is armed to the teeth, standing ready to maintain 'the balance of power' by rushing into human battle. . . ."[21] The American people in 1914 were not purblind, and when war came to Europe they were shocked but not totally surprised.

The British foreign minister, Sir Edward Grey, at that agonizing moment in history stared into the gathering London dusk and murmured, "The lamps are going out all over Europe; we shall not see them lit again in our lifetime." American Methodists in 1914 and indeed up to the opening months of 1917 were, with only a few exceptions, convinced it was the duty of the United States to remain at peace, tending the lamps of civilization so that at the last the Old World might rekindle her lamps from those that remained burning in the New. "Every man who really loves America," President Wilson appealed at the outbreak of hostilities, "will act and speak in the true spirit of neutrality, which is the spirit of impartiality and fairness and friendliness to all concerned." The United States, he asserted, "must be neutral in fact as well as in name . . . impartial in thought as well as in action." Wilson, of course, was asking the impossible, and Methodists, like all citizens, felt greater sympathy for one or another of the belligerents; and as the months passed sympathy for the Allies mounted.

Nevertheless most Methodists were in agreement with the *Nashville Christian Advocate* when it editorialized: "Every patriotic American citizen would have his government be of real service to all involved and, if possible, have some part in bringing the conflict to an early close. The government at Washington can render such service only by maintaining an attitude of strict neutrality."[22] In 1916 the Northern bishops declared in their Episcopal Address, "Never have so many millions of people been 'scattered and peeled' by the shameless perfidies and terrifying cruelties of an utterly lawless war." The bishops did not single out Germany for condemnation or the Allies for praise.[23] Methodists continued to be grateful that their country was at peace, but by 1916 they were less prideful in their exceptionalism. A Fraternal Messenger from Southern

21. Report No. 1 of the Committee on International and Industrial Peace, *The Daily Christian Advocate,* Methodist Episcopal Church, May 19, 1904, p. 221.
22. LXXV (August 21, 1914), 5.
23. *The Daily Christian Advocate,* Methodist Episcopal Church, May 3, 1916, p. 39.

Methodism, Edwin B. Chappell, spoke these sober words to the 1916 General Conference of Northern Methodism: "We are by no means so self-satisfied and so cocksure about ourselves as we were two years ago . . . . We mourn over the sad plight of Europe and the gloomy outlook that is before her, but what about our own land? Let us not beguile ourselves with the pleasing thought that we in this great Western republic, separated by oceans from the nations of the Old World, are in a measure free from the vices that afflict them and the dangers that threaten them."[24]

The words were prophetic. In April, 1917, after thirty-two months of attempted neutrality, America entered the Great War. The world's agony was now her agony also. Whatever the causes for American intervention, it is certain that President Wilson sought to carry the American people with him by appealing to their loftiest motives and noblest ideals, by subsuming the national interests in a great crusade to make the world safe for democracy. "We have no selfish ends to serve. We desire no conquest, no dominion. We seek no indemnities for ourselves, no material compensation for the sacrifices we shall freely make. We are but one of the champions of the rights of mankind."

III

To read President Wilson's imperishable words is to comprehend the response of the young, idealistic minister Ernest Fremont Tittle. To believe without a flicker of doubt that his country was embarking on a righteous crusade was for Tittle nothing less than an absolute psychological necessity. He had to believe this. Yet, there is much to suggest that Tittle should have been a reluctant recruit in Wilson's crusading army. To begin with, he was reared in Ohio, and as a Mid-American it is not illogical to guess that he shared in that section's isolationist and pacifistic temper. For a second thing, Tittle's paternal grandmother was of German stock and both she and her son, Ernest's father, spoke the language fluently. Moreover, there were not a few respected German families in Springfield and in that section of Columbus near the Broad Street Church.[25] To shout "To hell with the Hun" does not come quite so easily under such circumstances because it does not seem true to one's experience. Thirdly, the man to whom Tittle acknowledged the greatest intellectual and spiritual debt, Walter Rauschenbusch, refused to bless the war; and another hero, Washington Gladden, was until the early

24. *Ibid.*, May 12, 1916, p. 203.
25. Author's interview with Harriett Daily Collins, Columbus, Ohio, June 14, 1960.

spring of 1917 strongly anti-interventionist. Furthermore, his beloved mentor at Ohio Wesleyan, Professor Richard T. Stevenson, authored a volume entitled, *Missions versus Militarism,* "a strong appeal for the destruction of Militarism through the strengthening of the opposing force—Missions."[26] Nor is it without possible relevance that the Merrick lectures at Ohio Wesleyan delivered by the famous Charles E. Jefferson, were strongly pacifistic in tone, and Tittle probably heard them. Finally, the Social Gospel was permeated with pacifism even in the pre-1914 years and his early preaching, insofar as the fragmentary evidence permits a judgment, was infused with social passion. Therefore it would be plausible to conclude that even before his experiences in France Tittle was inclined toward pacifism.

This hypothesis is exploded by the discovery of a single sermon preached by Tittle in May, 1916, in recognition of Memorial Day. The sermon, printed in the *Delaware Semi-Weekly Gazette,* May 30, 1916, p. 4, is entitled, "Are We Worthy of the Men Who Fought at Gettysburg and at Valley Forge?" Tittle begins by wondering what would have been the history of America if Patrick Henry and George Washington and Lincoln had been "too proud to fight." He then meditates on the popular song "I Didn't Raise My Boy to Be a Soldier," the popular slogan "Safety First," and the popular demand "especially here in the Middle West," for "peace at any price." He describes in lurid language the atrocities, including rape, committed in Mexico against American citizens. He tells of "American men, women, children, and babies whose lives were lost when the ships on which they were peaceably traveling had been torpedoed without warning." He relates the fate of the Armenians at the hands of the Turks,

> how their wives and children had been led away to die of starvation and neglect or to live a life far worse than a hundred deaths; how at one place the officer in charge of the Turkish troops had told his men openly that they might do what they chose with their women captives. And when I reflected that not even then had America spoken a clear, brave, strong word in behalf of right and justice and ordinary humanity, I began to wonder whether we, the sons, were worthy of our fathers; whether the present generation of American men and women were worthy of the generations that had lived before them. Certainly it is difficult to discover the spirit of the men who fought at Gettysburg and at

26. See advertisements in *The Daily Christian Advocate,* Methodist Episcopal Church, May 1, 1916, p. 6, and *New York Christian Advocate,* XCI (April 20, 1916), 547.

Valley Forge in the men of today who would refuse to lift even a finger to remove the burden that rests upon the backs of oppressed peoples. And it is difficult to discover that spirit of the women who sent their sons to fight under Washington and under Meade who when their own sex is being brutally outraged, are applauding the sentiment of the song, "I Didn't Raise My Boy to be a Soldier." It never occurs to these unthinking women that if they don't raise their sons to be soldiers when there is need of soldiers they may raise their daughters to be victims of an alien soldiery. Now there are two all too popular statements that have a right to be challenged. They are: "That war is wicked, always wicked, necessarily wicked," and the other is that "Peace is noble, always noble, and necessarily noble." Some day it will become apparent that the slogan, "Safety first," is not altogether a creditable slogan. When you are dealing with material values it is very good. In every mill, railroad, shop, in every factory and plant, you see that motto. But, when you are dealing with moral values, the slogan is bad and sometimes it is contemptible. In a national crisis the motto should be not "safety first" but "duty first" and "honor first." It is true that since the Civil War we have been lying in a sheltered valley. We have been making money, we have piled up wealth, we have become fat with prosperity. And in the midst of our sheltered valley and in the midst of our great prosperity we have become too fat, too indulgent, too soft and too unselfish. Will it become necessary for God to permit some great calamity to befall us, a calamity that will scourage us to an elevation where we can see the great everlasting things that really matter for a nation, or will we, of our own will and accord, lay aside the sins that hamper us and climb high enough to see the great demands of duty, of honor, of patriotism.

This sermon is worthy of Theodore Roosevelt. It is worthy of the battalion of patrician warriors who since the 1890's had been preaching duty and destiny and national honor to justify war with Spain, the acquisition of an overseas empire, intervention in the Carribbean, involvement in the Far East, and the punishment of Mexico. It is unworthy of the later Tittle. At the time Randolph Bourne suggested that American intellectuals followed Wilson unhesitatingly into war out of an "unanalyzable feeling" that this was a war in which they had to participate. And in retrospect Christopher Lasch speculated of these intellectuals: "Logic may have dictated nonintervention, but something deeper than logic dictated war. The thirst for action, the craving for involvement, the longing to commit themselves to the onward march of events—these things dictated war." And Lasch added in words perhaps pertinent to Tittle, they "feared isolation not only for America but for themselves."[27]

Tittle responded in April, 1917, to the call to colors with all the intensity of his nature. At that moment he remembered, "I fully believed that everything that America stood for was in danger" and "that everything I cared for was at stake."[28] He "knew next to nothing about the underlying causes of the World War, had no suspicion that idealistic slogans were a shining concealment of brutal facts." He swallowed everything "told by Caesar's propagandists."[29] He was of course not alone in his ardent support of the war. In truth, save for a pitifully small, stubborn remnant, preachers presented arms with a zeal unsurpassed by any group in the nation. As Harry Emerson Fosdick, who like Tittle became a "Y" worker, asserted, "The wolf has come and we must be shepherds and not hirelings."[30]

Tittle's Ohio Annual Conference resolved that America had unsheathed the sword in defense of faith, honor, and justice, and in Columbus itself the churches' support of the war could not have been more feverish. Week after week the newspapers announced that the Reverend Mr. Thus-and-So had exchanged his pastorate for a chaplaincy or "Y" secretaryship or other wartime service. The Reverend Dr. George W. Benn confessed at a Rotary Club luncheon that he had once been a pacifist, but that he had asked God to forgive him and now sought propitiation by offering his sons to his country. Prudence as well as patriotism may have dictated Dr. Benn's *mea culpa* for over in Henry County they were tarring and feathering antiwar pastors prior to formal dismissal by their congregations.[31] Indeed, throughout the State of Ohio love of country was wondrously manifested in hatred of all things German. The Ohio legislature passed a bill outlawing the teaching of German below the eighth grade to erase a "direct menace to Americanism." The president of Baldwin-Wallace College, a Methodist institution, was fired because of doubts about his loyalty. The German Methodist press was severely proscribed, German singing societies suppressed, and Ger-

27. Christopher Lasch, *The New Radicalism in America*, (New York: Random House, Vintage Books, 1967), p. 223.

28. *The Daily Christian Advocate*, The Methodist Church, May 2, 1940, p. 413.

29. Review by Tittle of Ray H. Abrams, *Preachers Present Arms* in *Religion in Life*, III (Winter, 1934), 139.

30. Harry Emerson Fosdick, *The Challenge of the Present Crisis* (New York: Association Press, 1917), p. 34.

31. See Martha L. Edwards, "Ohio's Religious Organizations and the War," *Ohio Archaeological and Historical Publications*, XXVIII (1919), 214 and *passim*.

man composers and authors blacklisted. The denouement to all this was too dangerous to be ludicrous: pretzels banned from saloon counters, German fried potatoes deleted from hotel menus, sauerkraut renamed "liberty cabbage," frankfurters renamed "hot dogs," and dachshunds renamed "liberty pups." Luckily it was discovered in time that Limburger cheese really was introduced to mankind by Belgium.[32]

In Illinois patriotism burned no less brightly. " 'Unconditional surrender' is the Christian ultimatum as we face civilization's foe," resolved Rock River Methodists in annual conference.[33] At First Church the Official Board ordered the display of two American flags in the sanctuary and charged the acting minister "to have a distinctive patriotic hymn sung at each Sunday Morning Service."[34] Garrett Biblical Institute went "over the top" on the fourth Liberty Loan with one hundred per cent participation by faculty and students.[35]

All this is of course a twice-told tale and need not be explicated once again. Two points merit comment, however. In the first place, historians have tended to overstress the uniqueness of the hysteria of the First World War era. The American people had long been susceptible to mass emotionalism and irrationalism; their darker instincts had often broken loose from the moorings of decency to smash and shatter madly. What happened in 1917 was not something new in the American experience. Alas, neither was it to be something forever buried with the coming of peace. In their hysteria, intolerance, vigilantism, and thirst for violence these World War I Americans may not be viewed simply as aberrations from the all-American norm of sweet reasonableness. Secondly, although Methodists have much of which to be contrite concerning the war, they may also remember without shame their church's ministry to the boys in service, to their families at home, and to the victims of war in Europe and America. The National War Council of Northern Methodism, the War-Work Commission of Southern Methodism, and the War-Work Commission of the Methodist Protestant Church all creditably attempted to meet the spiritual hunger and physical need of youngsters in camps and trenches, bored lads on transports, and pain-racked boys in hospitals. Approximately 325 Methodist chaplains served with the colors and at least 500 Methodist ministers were engaged in

32. See Carl Wittke, "Ohio's German-Language Press and the War," *Ohio Archaeological and Historical Publications,* XXVIII (1919), 82-95. See also the many well-known monographs dealing with the suppression of civil liberties during the First World War.
33. *Minutes* of the Rock River Annual Conference (1918), p. 61.
34. Minutes of the Official Board, First Church, October 22, 1917.
35. *Evanston News-Index,* October 19, 1918, p. 81.

"Y" work. Nor did the labor cease when the Western Front stilled, for disbanded soldiers, including Negro servicemen, and European refugees and American influenza victims were succored.

Shortly after Congress declared war, Tittle informed his Broad Street congregation, "If America would save her own life, she should be willing to lay it down in the cause of common humanity."[36] "There is something more important than peace," he believed. "Truth and right, justice and honor and freedom—these are more important than peace. Without them, life ceases to be worth living. It becomes brutish and vain. Shame on us if we stand by and do nothing, when they are imperiled. Shame on us if we refuse to fight for them. We should not allow ourselves to hate the German people; they, too, are victims of the furious and brutal madness of their government. But we should count no sacrifice too great to destroy the power of their military masters and thus to deliver them, as well as ourselves and our children, from the awful danger that now threatens the world."[37] In the months that followed he preached on such subjects as "Can We Hate and Be Christians?," "A League to Enforce Peace," "The Sword of Righteousness," "War and Religion," "The World War—An Attempt at Interpretation," "Democracy on the March," "Culture and Kultur," "The Causes of the War," "Is the World's Night Passing?" He spoke also before Columbus audiences at various bond and recruiting rallies.[38]

The Broad Street Church flung itself into the Great Crusade. Its young men volunteered for duty, Its recreational director resigned to work with the "Y," as did his successor. Liberty Loan drives were supported. Funds were raised for European relief work. Boxes of food and clothing were sent to the boys in camp. Recreation programs were instituted for soldiers stationed in the area.[39] Though Tittle did not himself preach venomous sermons, the Broad Street pulpit was opened to speakers who betrayed the noble idealism set forth by President Wilson. "The German, the unspeakable German," cried one visiting evangelist, is "a barbarian from nature and a savage by inbreeding since the days of

36. *Columbus Evening Dispatch,* April 16, 1917, p. 9.
37. Tittle quoting himself in "On Being Neutral," typed MS, a sermon preached May 30, 1937.
38. This information is drawn from news items in the *Columbus Evening Dispatch.*
39. Harriet Daily Collins, *Endless Splendor: A History of Broad Street Methodist Church, Columbus, Ohio, 1814-1959* (Columbus, Ohio: Broad Street Methodist Church, 1959), pp. 50-51. Various news items in the *Columbus Evening Dispatch.*

Attila. . . ." And when the evangelist declared the war might last for three or even ten years, the audience interrupted with applause.[40]

Having heard the beat of Wilson's drum, nothing could hold Tittle in the pulpit, not even his love of preaching. In August, 1917, he wrangled a leave of absence to serve as religious work director of the YMCA at Camp Sheridan, Alabama. The Official Board was reluctant to grant the furlough. But Tittle would not be denied. For the period of his absence he forfeited his salary. He carefully left behind a program of worship, study, and recreation to be followed by his assistant.[41]

Camp Sheridan occupied about two thousand acres of former tobacco, peanut, and cotton fields five miles due south of Montgomery, the Confederacy's first capital. There in the late summer of 1917 twenty-three thousand enlisted men and fifteen hundred officers, most of whom were volunteer members of the Ohio National Guard, prepared with blessedly dull imaginations for what lay ahead in France. The monotony of training was relieved by swimming and fishing in the Alabama, Tallapoosa, and Cossa rivers; by recklessly experimenting with Southern cooking ("highly seasoned and swimming in gravy of all sorts," Tittle reported); and by futilely attempting to ferret out Montgomery's bars and bordellos, both types of establishments being effectively sealed—or so Ohio newspaper readers were assured. Some lucky Yankee lads were invited to take Sunday supper in Montgomery homes; a few, if they were as handsome as F. Scott Fitzgerald (and officers), met spirited Southern belles like Zelda. All of them choked on the clouds of red dust and all except the exceedingly pious cursed the rains that turned the dust to red mud. All except the most compassionate felt a twinge of Nietzschean pride as Montgomery's "darkies" removed their hats and removed themselves entirely from the sidewalks as the white soldiers passed.[42]

But they were mostly wretchedly homesick, like all soldier boys in all the basic training camps in all the warring nations. And to these lonely lads the "Y" endeavored to minister. Tittle did his part. He read letters for the illiterates and helped compose replies. He held for safekeeping soldiers' pay or arranged for it to be sent home. He umpired baseball games, organized amateur theatricals, led in song fests, and played

40. *Columbus Evening Dispatch,* February 8, 1918, p. 3.
41. Collins, *Endless Splendor,* p. 51.
42. This paragraph is reconstructed from news items in the *Columbus Evening Dispatch;* letter from Tittle to William S. Smith, February 2, 1943; letter from Tittle to Glenna, undated; memorandum in Tittle's hand written on Camp Sheridan YMCA stationery, undated; and standard histories of the United States Army in World War I.

checkers or pingpong with shy boys. He counseled the perplexed, cheered the discouraged, calmed the frightened. Also, "We do a little preaching now & then—on Wednesday nights & on Sunday nights and on Sunday morning."[43] Tittle recounted a typical Wednesday night: The tent is crowded. Some men are writing letters, others playing checkers or chess or reading. Some are smoking. Some cursing. Tittle mounts the platform: "Men, we are going to have a religious service." The soldiers promptly become quiet. A hymn is sung. A scripture passage is read. Tittle comments briefly on the passage. He prays. There is a final hymn. The Wednesday evening service is over. The letter writing, reading, and games resume. "But," Tittle believed, "there is no more cursing. The service has lasted just fifteen minutes. It is long enough to change the atmosphere."[44]

Tittle had no illusions concerning the transforming power of his preaching. He knew and resented the fact that sometimes commanding officers ordered their men to attend his services.[45] He ruefully confessed that some of the lads remained awake during his little sermons only because the wooden benches were "sufficiently uncomfortable." He was aware that a "Y" hut was no substitute for home, but he hoped the atmosphere provided at least a "touch of home." And he remembered what so many churchmen forgot: the "Y" secretary's job was not to try to reform the soldiers, but to endeavor "to keep alive in these boys the goodness that is already there."[46]

In many ways the soldiers returned to Tittle as much as they received and Camp Sheridan was an educational experience comparable to that four-point circuit in Christiansburg. For one thing, he worked with Catholics and Jews, a rather unfamiliar experience for a Methodist minister in those days. Indeed, he became friends with a certain Father O'Conner and assisted him (in the capacity of usher, to be sure) in the Mass; and on another occasion he spoke in a Montgomery synagogue, bringing tears to the eyes of his audience.[47] For another, he encountered a type of boy largely absent from Ohio Epworth League circles: immigrant lads and city "toughs" whose vocabulary was as profane as it was

43. Memorandum in Tittle's handwriting on Camp Sheridan YMCA stationery, undated.

44. Memorandum in Tittle's handwriting on Broad Street Church stationery, undated.

45. "Lest We Forget," longhand MS, undated sermon.

46. Memorandum in Tittle's handwriting on Camp Sheridan YMCA stationery, undated.

47. Tittle, *The Church in the New Day,* a sermon preached January 12, 1919 (pamphlet); Tittle, *What Must the Church Do to Be Saved?* (New York and Cincinnati, Ohio: Abingdon Press, 1921), pp. 33-34.

colorful. "But I still insist," Tittle observed in a slightly mugwumpish tone, "that these poor fellows are feeling for something better." They display great "shrewdness—I can scarcely say intelligence."[48] For a third, Tittle came into contact with another equally strange breed: Southerners, and Alabamians at that. "They are," he reported, "a fine lot."[49]

It is to Tittle's credit that he did not attempt to seal himself off from these unfamiliar influences. To the contrary, he purposefully ate with the enlisted men rather than sharing the more elegant fare of the officers' mess, and he also deliberately sought acquaintanceship with the people of Montgomery. Rather too consciously, perhaps, he coveted the reputation of a "regular fellow." After mentioning passing a group of enlisted men playing ball on Sunday, he commented in a letter to Glenna: "But pshaw! they all mean well and in their own way are seeking after the more abundant life. I looked on the game for a few minutes just to show my 'unprofessional' interest and live up to my reputation. For be it known unto you that I am advertised by the club leader as follows: 'Doctor Tittle of Columbus will speak. 'Doc' is one of the boys. Pat him on the shoulder if you like. He'll stand for it.' "[50] Tittle was not by nature an "other-directed" man. The easy spirit of camaraderie that comes so effortlessly to some men was not in his makeup. Yet he made himself assume a free and easy manner—and he carried it off.

"Believe me, we missed you at the 'Y,' " wrote one Camp Sheridan soldier. "Your successor is a fine man, but he's too dignified and preachified to suit me. Really, Doc, associating with you has aroused new ambitions in me to take up the ministry as a profession. There are so many poor men in the ministry, and I came across so many during the last few months before coming down South, that I almost reached the point where I thot I didn't care to be classed with them. Meeting a preacher who was still an all around good scout, in every respect a red-blooded man, was a delight and an inspiration."[51]

The clearest indication of Tittle's attitude toward the war while stationed at Camp Sheridan is revealed in a sermon he delivered before a "large crowd of Montgomerians together with many Ohio and Alabama soldiers" at union services in the city auditorium. Though the

48. Letter from Tittle to Glenna, undated.
49. Letter from Tittle to Glenna, undated.
50. Letter from Tittle to Glenna, undated.
51. Letter from Hubert Kimmel to Tittle, December 8, 1917. Another soldier who remembered Tittle's thoughtfulness is quoted in Henry Clyde Hubbart, *Ohio Wesleyan's First Hundred Years* (Delaware: Ohio Wesleyan University, 1943), p. 131.

reporters judged it a "very forceful sermon," impressing the listeners with its "earnestness and clear logic," the idealism seems strained and even shrill to a later generation. After stressing the point that Christianity is a social religion and that we are our brother's keeper, Tittle inquired: "Do we say that the Belgian peasant is not our brother? When his uprooted country is ruthlessly invaded, his son mutilated, his daughter ravished, do we refuse to utter so much as a single word of protest?" He continued to beat upon the theme of service, concluding with the peroration:

> And America? Well, America has entered the war in a spirit splendidly unselfish. We are not fighting for ourselves alone. We are contending for the common rights of all mankind. Once more we have highly resolved that the dead shall have not died in vain, that seven millions of youths whose poor broken bodies have enriched the soil of Europe, and whose death-defying spirits have enriched the soul of the race, that these noble boys shall not have died in vain; but that, under God, the whole world shall have a new birth of freedom, and government of the people, by the people, for the people, shall not perish from the earth. And if America remains true to her first purpose, she will not lose her life, she will save it. Aye, even though like heroic France she be bled white in battle, she shall stand forth cleansed, uplifted, unconquered in spirit, splendidly endowed with all that makes a nation truly great.[52]

In early November Tittle left Camp Sheridan to return to Columbus. The following June, having completed the Evanston negotiations, he sailed for Europe, confident in the conviction that his decision to leave wife and children and participate in the war was "right and proper,"[53] and happy in the expectation that as a "Y" secretary without rank, rather than as a chaplain, he would be able to "get closer to the men and be of greater service to them."[54] On shipboard Tittle served the

52. Unidentified, undated newspaper clipping in Tittle Collection.
53. Letter from Tittle to Robert O. Bright, July 1, 1942.
54. Letter from Tittle to Edward L. Rice, April 1, 1940. The official records of the YMCA contain only five brief sentences about Tittle's work, stating without elaboration his date of departure, date of return, disposition of passport, date of service at Camp Sheridan, and nature of service as traveling speaker, hut secretary, and organizer. Letter from Mrs. Virginia Downes, Librarian, YMCA Historical Library, New York, to author, June 7, 1959.
Much of what follows in this chapter rests upon letters written by Tittle to Glenna. He was a faithful correspondent, writing almost every day except for a period in France when circumstances made it impossible to do so. These letters were in the personal possession of Mrs. Tittle and were not on deposit in the Tittle Collection. In the summer of 1959 Mrs. Tittle turned them over to me. Before doing so, however, she severely censored them. In doing this, of course,

soldiers in varied ways from conducting religious services to refereeing
boxing and wrestling matches. He found the enlisted men "splendid"
fellows, enjoyed their association, and was grateful for their appreciation.

On July 1 land was sighted and by July 3 he was in London. He
fell in love with the city: Westminister Abbey, the Tower, St. Paul's,
Buckingham Palace, the Houses of Parliament. In charming letters to
Glenna and the children he described his excitement at visiting these
historic places. On July 4 he heard a "most eloquent" address, one "in
every respect worthy of the occasion," by Winston Churchill. Yet he was
as American as Plymouth Rock. "And what shall I say of the emotion
that an American feels over here when he sees the flag, or hears the
anthem, or passes a lad in khaki? I know now the full meaning of that
ancient phrase, 'The love of country.' "[55] While in London he spoke to
soldiers at the "Y" center, at a British hospital, and at a Red Cross
hospital.

Within a week, however, he was off on a tour of American bases in
England, Scotland, and Ireland, hiking and hitch-hiking from camp to
camp accompanied by a singer. "In the morning I walked the four miles
to the next camp through a driving rain, and felt 'bully' upon my
arrival," he related to Glenna.[56] At each camp he would speak a bit,
more often on the war than on specifically religious themes. After
marching as far north as Inverness he returned to London and then
departed for Ireland. On the crossing he attempted to persuade a Sinn
Feiner that Ireland must "think in world terms instead of purely local
terms," for only by losing her life could she save it. After the war the
United States would see to it that Ireland received justice. His listener
remained "quite unconvinced."[57]

Back in London by the first of August, he spoke in the great City
Temple before a large congregation. "I had gone expecting to preach

she had a perfect right. Yet letter after letter was so mutilated by Mrs. Tittle's
scissors as to be virtually unintelligible. It is my guess that the deleted portions
did not deal with personal, family matters, but rather with Tittle's opinions of the
war, politics, and diplomacy, and in light of his later pacifist career, Mrs. Tittle
deemed it prudent to suppress some of his wartime thoughts. If I am wrong in
this conjecture and if I have misjudged Tittle's attitudes in 1918, is it ungallant
to suggest that the responsibility be shared by Mrs. Tittle's scissors? In one undated letter Tittle made the request: "Will you save the letters? I write them
just as I feel at the time, and the epistles, poor tho they are from a literary viewpoint, will preserve moods and impressions which I may want to recall. In a
word, they will become sort of a diary."

55. Letter from Tittle to Glenna, July 4, 1918.
56. Letter from Tittle to Glenna, July 11, 1918.
57. Letter from Tittle to Glenna, page with date missing.

a sermon, but discovered that a discussion of the war from the American viewpoint would be much appreciated; so I straightway forgot the sermon and adopted my war talk to the audience before me. I had, for me, a good time, and found it easier to speak in City Temple than in any other place to which I have been sent in England."[58] At this moment there was developing in his mind the conviction that "the world's one hope for future welfare, with justice and peace, is the recognition and application of the principle of 'self-determination,' and the serious endeavor to effect a League of Nations to maintain worldwide peace 'on the basis of common right and justice.' "[59]

London now seemed less thrilling than in those initial days when every historic spot was fresh to his eyes. His little hotel room became "just about the loneliest place I can imagine."[60] He missed his children enormously and wrote them wonderfully sweet letters. He longed for his beloved Glenna. He was a vigorous man in his early thirties and two months had passed since he had held his wife in his arms. Racked by mounting tensions, it was probably on a sleepless night in his bleak London room that he penned the lines to Glenna: "Some of our dear secretaries are having a damned good time. Lonely? Not they! They make me feel sick and bitter."[61] Yet he never expressed regret concerning his decision to serve overseas. In less than a week he would cross the channel for the Great Adventure, "and," he exclaimed, "I shall be glad, glad, glad to be in France."[62]

The crossing was made on August 6 while Tittle slept peacefully and by the 8th he was in Paris. He was bewitched by the city. "Paris is a dream," he reported in the words of so many Americans before and after him. He shared a hotel room with a Yale man, "a bully good fellow." His mood was ebullient—and rather sanctimonious: "Poor Walt! Poor Hargroves! Poor Clarence! Really, I have stopped condemning them, and only pity them. They will have no part in the future. They cannot tell their sons—'I've seen the darkness put to flight; I've seen the morning break.' God, how I pity them. They will save their bodies—and lose their souls."[63] Undoubtedly his spirits were chipper not only because he was at last in France, but also because there

58. Letter from Tittle to Glenna, August 5, 1918.
59. Letter from Tittle to Glenna, August 4, 1918.
60. Letter from Tittle to Glenna, July 30, 1918.
61. *Ibid.*
62. Letter from Tittle to Glenna, July 23, 1918.
63. Letter from Tittle to Glenna, August 9, 1918. I imagine "Walt" refers to his first cousin and "Clarence" to Clarence Smith, an old Springfield friend, but I cannot even guess the identity of "Hargroves."

awaited him in Paris thirteen letters from Glenna. "Oh what joy was mine. . . . But think dear: two months nearly without a line."[64] Any man long separated from his wife knows what a sense of relief must have flooded over Tittle at this moment. Inefficient mail service, not Glenna's indifference, he now knew, accounted for the agonizingly long silence.

For the next two weeks Tittle addressed groups of American and French soldiers in the vicinity of Paris, the talk that "went over biggest" being one he had prepared on Abraham Lincoln. Unlike many dough-boys, he came to be fond of the French people, finding them "thoroughly and delightfully human." He lived in a French home "in which no single word of English is ever spoken." A snapshot he received of Glenna and the children drew a warm and very human response: "You cannot realize how much this picture means to me. It represents the great, best part of me. . . ." In the same letter he returned to a conviction much in his thoughts: "I see now, even more clearly than I saw in America, that any one who hopes to preach to the coming generations will be terribly handicapped if he has not had this experience. The churchmen of the future are all here, or coming here, and how can one hope to talk to them intelligently unless he has discovered by actual observation and. . . ."[65] The next page is missing, but one can conjecture its contents, for repeatedly he spoke of "my wonderful experience in France," an experience that "can be capitalized in America."

The third week in August he was transferred from the lecture circuit to a large base hospital at Chaumont to relieve a "Y" secretary who had not had a break for seven months. He welcomed this new experience. "It is a positive relief," he recounted, "to sell cigarettes, canned goods etc. over the counter. I believe that much can be accomplishd by 'The foolishness of preaching;' on the other hand I sometimes become weary of listening to my own voice."[66] And from this hospital he wrote, "You ought to see me selling cigars etc."[67] It is a well-known secret that Tittle in his Evanston years was an inveterate cigar smoker. No one seems to remember precisely when he acquired the habit. It is at least possible that he smoked his first cigar in the late summer of 1918 in France. Kipling to the contrary, because Tittle found a cigar a darn good smoke, he did not subscribe to the thesis that a "woman is only a woman." His letters to Glenna often closed, "I *love* you, old pal." Only

64. Letter from Tittle to Glenna, August 9, 1918.
65. Letter from Tittle to Glenna, August 16, 1918.
66. Letter from Tittle to Glenna, August 27, 1918.
67. Letter from Tittle to Glenna, August 30, 1918.

a wife of many years perhaps could appreciate the affection implicit in this epistolary termination. Perhaps only a man who has served overseas could catch the significance of this lament: "Have I told you that I have received no letters from Columbus, and none from father, Stern, or anyone else save Hough, 'Newby,' and Anne?"[68] Even the most self-sufficient man values the affection of his father and brother and presumed friends, and it is not difficult to share Tittle's sense of hurt when these individuals did not trouble to write.

At this time Tittle introduced a thought that was to remain a constant in his thinking: "I discover, among other things, that hatred increases exactly in proportion to one's distance from the trenches. The real fighters, i.e., sufferers, do not hate. They merely do their duities like heroes."[69] On September 8 Tittle cryptically informed Glenna that he was off on a "most interesting trip" to do "a little speaking, and a little selling, and a little investigating, etc. etc."[70] He was not to write again for more than a week. The Saint Mihiel offensive commanded his entire energies. It was to be his closest acquaintanceship with the total hell that is modern war.

The Saint Mihiel Salient immediately below Verdun and sixty miles north of Chaumont, Pershing's headquarters, was (to use Tittle's imagery in turn borrowed from the French) "a hernia in the Allies' front, a hernia that had to be removed."[71] The American armies were given the responsibility of performing the operation. The deed was done swiftly and by the brutal standards of the Great War painlessly, the Germans prudently deciding on an early withdrawal to the interior positions of the Michel Stellung area. It was all "so easy that afterwards the St. Mihiel Salient was referred to as the sector in which the Americans relieved the Germans," commented one historian.[72] The green American doughboys involved in the battle would not have agreed with the historian's nonchalant assessment. Their eight thousand casualties were trivial in that abattoir called the Western Front, but the figure was high by innocent New World measurement. Indeed, almost twice as many Yanks were killed as were slain by enemy bullets in the entire Spanish-American war.

68. Letter from Tittle to Glenna, September 4, 1918. "Stern" was of course his brother; "Hough" was a Drew man, Methodist leader, and First Church member; "Anne" perhaps refers to the daughter of Bishop McDowell; "Newby" is an unfamiliar name to me.

69. Letter from Tittle to Glenna, September 4, 1918.

70. Letter from Tittle to Glenna, September 8, 1918.

71. *Evanston News-Index,* November 30, 1918, p. 1.

72. Barrie Pitt, *1918: The Last Act* (New York: W. W. Norton & Company, 1962), p. 231.

At 1:00 A.M. on September 12, 2,971 French and British guns opened a four-hour bombardment of the German trenches. Tittle, together with three other "Y" men and one woman "Y" worker, watched the "show" from a little evacuated village three miles behind the front lines. Tittle had persuaded his chief that "I would never be happy again if he did not permit me to go to the front." At 5:00 A.M. the infantry went "over the top." At 11:30 German prisoners and American wounded began to return from the front. For twenty hours a day for the next days Tittle was to do his bit pouring cups of hot chocolate for exhausted lads, offering lighted cigarettes to boys shaking with fear, loading cassionettes with supplies for the front, helping as best he could at the dressing stations. "It is hard to see men suffer," he wrote, "as I saw them that day and many another day after that. The face cases are the worst—to look at; but there were leg and gas cases that were bad enough, God knows. And yet what heroism—what quiet, patient, and cheerful endurance of pain."[73] After the drive had spent its initial force Tittle spent several days attempting to perform in the triple capacity of "Y" hut secretary, hospital secretary, and warehouse secretary. "I nearly worked my fool head off, and then 'blew' two jobs and kept one—the warehouse secretaryship."[74] It was a tough assignment and he continued to work around the clock, but the Saint Mihiel experience was over.

It was an experience the young, idealistic crusader much meditated and long remembered. Two decades later he recalled: "One night in France when big guns were belching shrapnel all over the place; and Very lights were providing sudden illumination in which terrible things could be seen; and poor fellows, badly wounded, were being brought to the field hospital where I was stationed; and we ran out of anesthetics, so that emergency operations were performed under conditions that even now I dread to recall, I stepped out for a moment, feeling the need of fresh air, and, looking up at the sky, I bitterly reflected upon the apparent indifference of those distant, silent stars. Just what I expected them to do I hardly know, but evidently something primitive and irrational in me supposed that they were the dwelling-place of the Most High and so wondered why from that quarter no celestial battalions came to put an end to such infernal business as was going on that night."[75] Saint Mihiel did not drive Tittle to pacifism, but it did strip from war all romance and reveal its stark horror. "One terrible night in 1918 during

73. Undated longhand notebook MS in Tittle Collection.
74. Letter from Tittle to Glenna, September 30, 1918.
75. "Where Is God in the World Today?" typed MS, a sermon preached February 12, 1939.

the battle of St. Mihiel," he later related, "when I was lifting horribly wounded men out of ambulances, I registered a vow that if I were permitted to live I would devote the rest of my life to the cause of peace. I am not sure that I made this vow to God. I am obliged to confess that all the time I was at the front I found it very difficult, even so much as to think of God. But I did make it to myself. I am sure of that. I made a vow that I would devote the rest of my life to the cause of peace, and I see no reason today why I should renounce that vow. On the contrary, I see every reason why I should be true to it. I have no doubt that I would be everlastingly damned if I should be untrue to it."[76] And in a letter to a friend he testified: "During the battle of St. Mihiel, I made a vow that, should my life be spared, I would spend the rest of it working against war and for peace."[77] As we shall see, Tittle did not become an "instant pacifist" in September, 1918; nor was he instantly disillusioned about the rightness and righteousness of the Great Crusade. But Saint Mihiel is the key to Tittle's later unconditional, absolute opposition to war.

A final point to be made concerning Tittle's war experience is that he made a splendid "Y" secretary. It is almost gratuitous to point out that he was conscientious, untiring, faithful, efficient, uncomplaining, manly, thoughtful, kind, a true shepherd to his doughboy flock. Never in his entire career did Tittle give less than his total being to his people, and never did he make a fuller commitment than to the Yanks in France. W. W. Gethmann, YMCA regional director, 7th Region, reported to Bishop Luther B. Wilson, Religious Work Department, YMCA:

> I have been so much impressed with the kind of work Dr. E. F. Tittle has been doing in the 7th and other Regions that I cannot refrain from calling his work and his methods to your attention. Contrary to so many men of Dr. Tittle's capacity he has seen fit to get out into the field and to make himself a real part of whatever organization he goes out to serve. All through the St. Mihiel drive he was attached to the 90th Division, doing the most menial service at the hot drink stations, at the dressing stations and for that matter at any other point where men needed attention of any kind whatsoever. Having shared the hardships of the men with the men he was able to give the men of that Division under those trying conditions the kind of spiritual assistance which would not have been received from him had he approached them in any other way. Since his return to the 7th

76. *God and Peace,* a sermon preached November 11, 1934 (pamphlet). See also "On Making Vows," *The First Church Pulpit,* Vol. VIII, No. 8, a sermon preached January 6, 1946.
77. Letter from Tittle to Edward L. Rice, April 1, 1940.

Region he has for the second time taken complete charge of the Association work for entire regiments. In so doing he has accepted responsibility for an enormous amount of real physical work but he has in every case been able to render a maximum service along spiritual and religious lines. May I not suggest that some so-called spiritual experts who come out to do religious work with men be instructed to adopt the tactics used so effectively by Dr. Tittle. The men in the ranks are assuming a more and more critical attitude towards those members of our Association who come out to do them good by merely talking to them or at them. We have had both types in our region, and I can assure you from careful observation that only the working or service type of preacher has made any real impression or left any lasting friends in the field of his activities. I honestly believe that Dr. Tittle has proved himself the most powerful, the most effective and the most loved preacher who has come to us in the past ten months, and I sincerely hope that you will find it possible to send us more men of his type and spirit.[78]

After his arduous warehouse duties Tittle volunteered to establish a canteen at a new camp some seventy or eighty miles behind the lines to serve "seventeen white officers who promise to treat me like a prince, and fifteen hundred negroes, who will give me some interesting if not valuable experience."[79] At this moment he had not heard from Glenna for almost a month. The sublimating excitement of Saint Mihiel was past. The homesickness returned with redoubled intensity. "Have I thought of you?," he wrote his wife. "God knows I have, with anguish sometimes; and I have longed for you so much that I dared not let the longing find words, but forced myself to think cheerfully."[80] Poignant also were the expressions of love for his children. The work dragged. "Sometimes in my sleep I *dream* that I am selling chocolate, cigarettes and cookies. 'How long, O Lord, how long?' "[81]

In later years Negroes came to count Tittle as their champion as he valiantly labored to break the fetters of caste in church and society. His letters from France, however, covering the two weeks he served with black troopers do not reveal a keen sensitivity to or a burning rage over the Negro's fate. To be sure, he volunteered for this duty and it is certain that he gave of his best, as always. Indeed, he confessed shortly after assuming his new assignment, "I am having a great time with the

78. Copy of letter from W. W. Gethmann to Bishop Luther B. Wilson, October 24, 1918, in Tittle Collection.
79. Letter from Tittle to Glenna, September 30, 1918.
80. *Ibid.*
81. Letter from Tittle to Glenna, page with date missing.

negroes."[82] In no letter did he express even so much as a hint of racial hatred. On no occasion did he display feelings of naked bigotry. Yet if he accurately and objectively described the actions of the black soldiers, it was without any apparent attempt to understand why they were as they were, and without any awareness of society's responsibility for their being childlike. In sum, his attitude toward "Uncle Sam's black soldiers" and "my darkies" was sympathetic but superficial and condescending. For example:

> Last night we managed to show a "movie" to our colored audience. The appreciation was audible and voluble. Tomorrow afternoon, Sunday, we shall organize a football team and get a match going between two company organizations. In the morning, we may hold a song service; but there will be no preaching by *me*. I think I can sell these Southern negroes cakes and tobacco, but preach to them—never. They have the minds of children; forty per cent of them are illiterate; and for them religion means singing and shouting and using controversial phrases. But they are wonderfully interesting, for all that, and are learning with surprising quickness the art of war. They have no sense of responsibility as regards money, and will eagerly spend all they have (which is considerable) for something to eat. The major tells me that most of them are married, but that in many cases their wives have left them.

He added, after describing the difficulty of explaining to the men the relative value of French and American money, "I have also to hold on to my patience with both hands."[83] He was finally compelled to admit, "I shall be glad to be with white troops again."[84] The point to be underscored is not that Tittle's descriptions are inaccurate or infused with bigotry, but simply that in 1918 he did not manifest the sensitivity that later characterized his understanding of the Negro's ordeal.

Two concluding comments concerning Tittle's "Y" work: First, it angered him to read or hear the criticisms of the YMCA that became so prevalent in the months following the Armistice. As far as he was concerned the "Y" did a magnificent job in serving the doughboys and he was proud of his association with it. Time and again he defended the "Y" against what he considered false and unfair charges. Second, Tittle never had much to say (at least as far as can be ascertained from the fragmentary record) about the moral conduct of the American soldiers. Cursing, gambling, boozing, whoring—these activities were of course of

82. Letter from Tittle to Glenna, October 2, 1918.
83. Letter from Tittle to Glenna, October 5, 1918.
84. Letter from Tittle to Glenna, page with date missing.

grave and proper concern to churchmen in general and chaplains and
"Y" secretaries in particular, but they did not elicit much comment from
Tittle. One comes away from a reading of wartime sermons, church
press editorials and articles, committee reports, and conference resolutions and addresses saddened by the repeated argument that "our
boys" must remain clean and pure, unstained by liquor and illicit sex,
in order that they might more efficiently kill Huns. "Men who are clean
of life and of good moral character make the best fighters," observed the
superintendent of Army Work of Southern Methodism in Texas.[85]
Bishop James Cannon, Jr., wired President Wilson: "The mothers and
fathers of our country . . . insist that while their sons are in the army,
the navy, or the training camp, they be protected from the liquor and
vice traffic. They fear the possibiilty of moral and physical evil in the
army, navy and camp life more than they fear physical wounding and
death by German bullets."[86] And when Bishop Cannon reported to the
1918 General Conference of Southern Methodism on his overseas experiences his message centered on just that point, and he seemed immeasur-
ably more disturbed about the corruption of American lads in Paris
bordellos than about their obliteration in Western Front trenches. Even
such a worldly clergyman as Episcopal Bishop Charles H. Brent, chief
chaplain at Pershing's headquarters, was deeply distressed by the sexual
promiscuity of the doughboys.[87] Many American churchmen apparently
held it a greater sin to make love to a French girl than to kill a German boy; indeed, "our boys" must avoid French girls (and French wine)
in order that they might visit death upon a greater number of the Boche.
To be sure, the Christian has no more license to violate his own integrity
or exploit another's body in time of war than in time of peace. What is
dispiriting is to find Christian ministers unaware of the terrible ambiguity
involved in their twin injunctions to the soldier boys: remain "morally"
unstained while about the bloody duty of killing well. The slogan "Make
love, not war," is ambiguous, but surely no more so than "make war,
not love."

Finally, though Tittle harbored no vindictiveness toward the German
people and though he did not favor a Carthaginian peace, he did insist
that the war be pushed to total victory; and in the months immediately
following the Armistice he continued to defend Wilson's decision to

85. *Nashville Christian Advocate,* LXXIX (March 1, 1918), 22.
86. Telegram from James Cannon, Jr., to the Honorable Woodrow Wilson,
April 26, 1917, Cannon Papers, Duke University, Durham, N. C.
87. See Brent Papers, typescript diaries, Box 3, Library of Congress, Washington, D. C.

intervene. In a letter written from France to someone he called "You dear heathen," Tittle argued that annihilation was not the solution. He continued: "You ask me what I think about the 'Love your enemies,' as it applies to the German nation. Well, I believe that if we really love the German nation, we will do our d——dest to deliver it from the curse of its present government; and furthermore, that the only way to accomplish this is utterly to discredit the present government by a decisive military defeat. In brief, I cry 'Bravo' to President Wilson when he demands the unconditional surrender of the Kaiser and his crowd. On the other hand, I am with him too when he holds out a hand of hope to the German people. . . . There *are* people in Germany—we have no means of ascertaining their number, but have reason to believe that it is considerable—who are tragically disillusioned and dissatisfied with their present government; and it seems to me that a wise statesmanship would do precisely what Wilson has done, give them all possible encouragement in their struggle for democracy. It would be poor statesmanship utterly to dishearten them by a merciless annihilation policy."[88] This is a reasonable statement, but not that of a new convert to pacifism. And in a letter to Glenna written on October 10 he outlined a peace settlement quite similar to Wilson's Fourteen Points. It did not let Germany off lightly, but neither was it Draconian.

Shortly after the Armistice Tittle delivered a speech so impassioned, so patriotic, so idealistic that it simply could not have been prepared by a man who had been wholly shattered by disenchantment at Saint Mihiel. The "soul of mankind would have perished" had the "Potsdam gang" been victorious, he began. Bull dog Tommies "added a new glory to the Anglo-Saxon race" when "they stayed the advance of the German horde." Heroic France fought gallantly "since that fateful day in August when a treacherous foe struck at her thru Belgium—in the back." "The women of France—are they good? Are they pure? As good and as pure as the women of America." After Chateau Thierry all doubt vanished from French minds and all fear was banished from French hearts. "America had come in—come really in—and ooh-la-la how those Yanks could fight!" Tittle then described in detail his experiences at the front. He had seen with his own eyes that war was hell. He concludes: "I hate war and fervently pray that shamed and enlightened consciences of mankind will turn upon it to destroy it! I have never been, nor am I now, a pacifist. I have never subscribed, nor do I now subscribe, to the Tolstoian doctrine of nonresistance. Not to resist evil is to encourage evil. Not Luxemburg but Belgium has added to the moral treasures of

88. Letter from Tittle, address and date unknown, first and last pages missing.

the race. Not Holland but America has quickened man's faith in the goodness of God. There are cir' [cumstances] under which yet again I would vote for war—but I hate war."[89]

In late October Tittle journeyed to Paris, purchased little gifts for his family, and on November 10 wired Glenna that he was waiting at the port to sail home. On November 21 William A. Dyche received a telegram informing him that the "handsome man" from Columbus had arrived in the United States and planned to preach his first sermon from the First Church pulpit on December 1.[90]

The great adventure in France was behind Tittle. A greater adventure lay ahead in Evanston.

89. Undated longhand notebook MS in Tittle Collection.
90. *Evanston News-Index,* November 21, 1918, p. 1.

4. HUSBAND, FATHER, AND FRIEND

I

"Ernest Fremont Tittle is the greatest preacher I have ever heard." This oft-repeated testimony is susceptible of rough proof. It can be checked against the several ratings of Protestant preachers conducted in Tittle's lifetime. It can be supported by reference to the many honors and accolades that were bestowed on him. Less tractable is the statement, "Ernest Fremont Tittle is the greatest man I have ever known," for of course such a tribute is beyond objective measurement. Yet the two assessments are indivisible. Tittle was a great preacher because he was first a great man. His life gives force to Phillips Brooks's famous aphorism, "preaching is personality." Indeed, what was said of Brooks can be said of Tittle: his "supreme contribution to this country was himself."

To be sure, in assessing a man it is often necessary to radically divide his private from his public life, making appropriate a critical judgment in one area and a praiseful one in another. Yet the life of a preacher cannot be so compartmentalized. If he is esteemed, it is first because of what he *is* and only secondarily because of what he *says*. The man cannot be divorced from his pulpit proclamation. He cannot effectively and steadily preach the love of God without hungering to know that love in his own life, and without the congregation's sensing its shepherd's hunger. He cannot effectively and steadily preach the judgment of God without the humbling awareness that he, too, is under that judgment, and without the congregation's sensing its shepherd's awe. Ministers are not made less dizzy than others by man's condition of radical freedom. But it is the minister's fate that other men always should ask of him the ancient question of Chaucer's: "If gold rust, what then will iron do?" It is a fair question.

II

Time magazine described Tittle as a big, powerful man who spoke out of the side of his mouth.[1] Though objectively this picture is false, curiously it suggests a key truth: he was a man's man. "Ernest Tittle is the strongest man I have ever known," said a top Standard Oil executive.[2] During his Evanston years Tittle was in constant and close association with men of large affairs—big men in business, finance, railroading, publishing, government, education, and the Church. Though he did not always win their support, without exception he commanded their respect, and he impressed them with his strength.

This impression was derived in part from his physical appearance. It was not that he was a giant, for he stood only about 5 feet, 9 inches and weighed less than 170 pounds. But there was about the cut of his jib the suggestion of strength: solid body, broad shoulders, bulldog jaw, wide brow, penetrating dark eyes, blunt nose, square hands, deep voice (though he did not speak out of the side of his mouth). At the age of thirty he looked twenty, but his youthful appearance did not long survive the strains of the Evanston ministry. As he approached fifty his hair thinned and grayed, his eyes required spectacles, tired lines etched his face, and no longer were his shoulders thrown back quite so erectly. About this time someone suggested he looked like a "spiritualized prize fighter"—grimly determined to hang on fifteen rounds. Tittle's face aged well. If it lost its early innocence, it also lost its touch of youthful arrogance. Yet it did not become a cynical countenance. And the strength that was there in early manhood was not corrupted by slackness or puffiness. It had always been a good face. In middle age it became a fine face: strong, resolute, and now for the first time, compassionate.

There was about the style of the man a vigorous masculinity. His movements were decisive, his walk brisk. For this a few friends dubbed him "Zip," unaware that this also had been his nickname in college.[3] Though Stephen A. Douglas's sobriquet "steam engine in breeches" is

1. March 27, 1933, p. 19.
2. Amos Ball, as quoted in author's interview with Joseph Thomas, Evanston, Ill., July 29, 1959.
3. Much of what follows in this chapter is based on interviews with Tittle's family, friends, staff, congregation, students, and colleagues and on letters to the author from them. Unless the point being made is especially unusual, controversial, or damaging, it does not seem necessary to cite the source. Indeed, in most instances the information was derived from more than one individual.

appropriate to Tittle, though his being was charged with great vitality, there was nothing nervous, fretful, or flighty about his bearing. He was not a twitcher. But he was a rocker. Almost every room in his house was equipped with a rocking chair and while traveling he petitioned the hotel keepers to provide him with one, giving point to the old explanation for the popularity of the rocker in America: it is the one chair that permits a man to sit and move at the same time, thus escaping a sinful feeling of idleness.

According to his own testimony, he was capable of tremendous anger, but it was not his custom to throw infantile temper tantrums in the fashion of Andrew Jackson—or more recent presidents. When he laughed he laughed as a man should—heartily, with head thrown back. He was not a giggler. He could be impatient. Once in a hurry to obtain his robe from the sacristy he discovered he had forgotten the key. He pulled the lock off the door. Mostly he kept a tight rein on his temper and impetuosity. There was a turbulent, restless, raging side to his nature and this wildness was tamed at a psychic cost known only to his family and a handful of perceptive friends.

As he had dressed neatly as a boy, so he continued to do so as a man. In those days, all Methodist ministers wore businessmen's suits rather than the distinctive clerical garb now increasingly fashionable even in evangelical denominations. Though meticulously groomed in public, he was not a dandy, and in the privacy of his study he preferred corduroy pants and a khaki shirt. His fishing hats were notoriously battered.

He shared many of the prejudices common to his sex, at least in America in his generation. He disliked things tepid. Food supposed to be hot was to be piping hot; beverages designed to be hot were to be scalding; and cold meant ice cold. Casserole was a fighting word: even if the ingredients could be identified they were too jumbled together. Tittle was not a fussy eater and certainly not a gourmet, but he enjoyed food well enough, especially if it was pungent rather than bland, crunchy rather than soft (except for lemon cream pie). Parsnips were a favorite, which only readers over sixty will comprehend. Coffee he downed by the gallon: hot, strong, undefiled by cream or sugar. He conducted a lifelong crusade to convert all coffee lovers to taking it black. One lady dining companion confessed to him that he had been successful in persuading her to forsake sugar but that, alas, she still took a little cream. "Madam," he replied gallantly, "if all my people followed half the advice I give them I would be satisfied." He disliked pastel hues, preferring bold, identifiable colors. His conversation was peppered with an occasional "hell" and "damn," more so immediately following his return from France than in later years. He did not permit himself the use of the grosser functional words. He neither told bawdy stories nor found pleasure in hearing them. "Some words are not acceptable in the sight of God," he believed. "Ribald words, foul talk, stories that are risqué— these violate the sanctities of life. They are an affront to God, an insult to man."[4] From time to time he and a companion or two would join fishing or mountain-climbing groups. It was not advertised that he was a clergyman. He was readily accepted by these fraternities of out- doorsmen. Yet in a day or so the other men when in the presence of Tittle (still unaware of his clerical status) would instinctively temper their smoking-car language and leave untold their more obscene stories.[5] "Self-respect involves that a man will be himself and make no pretense of being someone else," Tittle maintained. "If he is a clergyman, he will try to think and speak and act in a way agreeable with his calling; he will not try in any company to appear as an ultra-sophisticated man of the world."[6]

Being an American male born in 1885, he viewed with suspicion the growing masculinity of the American female. "I can only say," he explained without much logic, "that I thoroughly dislike a manish woman and devoutly hope that something essentially and uniquely feminine will always remain in this world." Tittle made this statement to a young lady who had inquired about the propriety of her smoking. Yet he admitted that it was "hard to justify a dual standard which says that it is right for men to smoke and wrong for women to smoke."[7] He, of course, smoked cigars and a pipe and "when I am tired and nervous . . . I smoke like a house afire."[8] He was appreciative when friends pre- sented him with a box of his favorites, as they frequently did. "The Robert Burns cigars arrived just in time," he wrote in one "thank you" note, "for Mrs. Tittle was almost ready to have me forcibly removed from the house by reason of the unbearable odor of the cheap cigars which I have been smoking. You have, therefore, rendered a real service not only to me but to her, for deep down in my heart I cannot believe

4. "Acceptable Words," *The First Church Pulpit,* Vol. X, No. 5, a sermon preached February 24, 1946.
5. Author's interview with Herbert Stoetzel, Lake Forest, Ill., August 31, 1959. Inasmuch as Mr. Stoetzel was one of Tittle's fishing companions, he speaks with authority on this point.
6. "Self-Respect," *The First Church Pulpit,* Vol. VIII, No. 14, a sermon preached March 17, 1946.
7. Letter from Tittle to Marjorie Pearson, April 21, 1932.
8. Letter from Tittle to Luther A. Weigle, March 22, 1932.

that she would allow me to remain long out of doors."[9] Quite understandably, he did not smoke in public. In fact, he felt free to "light up"
only in the privacy of his study or in the presence of his family, secretaries, and close friends. "I am somewhat flabbergasted by the news of
your decision to go to Grand Forks," he wrote a Methodist colleague,
for "there will be one less Methodist preacher in this part of the world
with whom I may smoke and before whom I may on occasion say,
Damn."[10]

Naturally, many church leaders found this habit distressing. One
president of Garrett Biblical Institute periodically admonished his seminarians, "Endeavor to emulate Dr. Tittle in all things save his smoking."
And it was a Garrett student who inquired of Tittle, "Did you not sign
an agreement not to smoke?" "Yes, but I was young when I took that
vow." "Well," returned the student pointedly, "how old were you when
you got married?"[11] Tittle could only plead in extenuation that Lady
Nicotine had cast a spell over him. In the last years of his life and under
stern orders from his doctors he gave up cigars. Doubtless it is a matter
of regret that Tittle should have acquired the smoking habit. Yet it can
scarcely be termed a fatal flaw in character. Moreover, if his smoking
suggests a certain fraility of the flesh it also indicates an independence
of spirit and a manly refusal to be bound by a querulous legalism.

Tittle did not use spirits, not even wine or beer. In a later chapter
his views on the prohibition question will be set forth. Here it need
only be said that not only did he not drink himself, he attempted by
word to persuade and even more forcefully by example to demonstrate
to the teenage boys and girls of Evanston, the Northwestern students,
and the young married couples in First Church that it was possible to
have jolly times without recourse to the stimulation of liquor. Tittle
knew from his father's experiences that the companionship of John
Barleycorn was not without peril.

Someone once termed courage the noblest of virtues because it sustains all others. Tittle was a man of courage. This quality shines
brighter than any of the many other high attributes he possessed, saving
only that most luminous one of all, his industry. Repeatedly in his career
Tittle was confronted with the choice of being brave or flinching, and in
no crucial instance (insofar as the record speaks) did he fail the test.
Even his opponents acknowledged his massive moral courage. As to his

9. Letter from Tittle to H. Haddon MacLean, March 21, 1934.
10. Letter from Tittle to the Reverend Theodore Leonard, September 13, 1933.
11. Author's interview with Bishop J. Ralph Magee, Evanston, Ill., August
31, 1959. The prohibition on smoking was first placed in the *Discipline* of the
Methodist Episcopal Church in 1880. It remained there until after Tittle's death.

physical bravery, there is not much in the documentation to go on. Certainly it takes physical courage to climb mountains as he did. And on one occasion in Colorado he laced up his boots, bit his old brier pipe, and resolutely set about the task of clearing out underbrush thought to be crawling with rattlesnakes. The one recorded failure of nerve suffered by Tittle came when he ordered a fifty-dollar fly rod and anxiously awaited the reaction of Glenna—an understanding woman but nonetheless a wife. This is not to say that he did not know fear. Quite the contrary. He confessed to being always "scared stiff" before rising to give an address.[12] Rather, it is to state that he did not permit his fear to freeze him in inaction or to cause him to emulate Bunyon's Mr. Facing-Both-Ways. Courage was for Tittle fear that had said its prayers.

"Almost invariably I have a strange experience whenever I talk about Dr. Tittle. I find myself choking up."[13] This expression of deep affection suggests something about Tittle known to only a few. He was a sensitive, lonely, vulnerable person who was nagged by self-doubt. And he was gentle. Often his little acts of kindness had no formal relation to his job: a note to the widow of the mailman; a check to the hotel clerk who had unwittingly undercharged him; a refusal to prosecute the burglar apprehended in the parsonage while the Tittles were vacationing; stopping to chat with the church janitors or having a cup of coffee with the commissary dishwashers; quickly looking away in order to avoid embarrassment to the neighbor lady secretly snipping lilacs in his yard. These little acts are characteristic of the man.

He was on occasion capable of curtness to his peers and superiors, but never did he cut those weaker than he or those society termed his inferiors. And invariably he was gallant to women. Indeed, despite his masculinity he was at ease with ladies and they, perhaps because of his manliness, were attracted to him, and he inspired in them a quite extraordinary intensity of devotion. He paid them the compliment of treating them as intellectual equals and many a woman found it stimulating and flattering to be seriously engaged in serious conversation.

Generally the world saw Tittle as a ruggedly independent, self-contained, inner-directed individual. His family and intimate friends knew him to be a lonely man hungry for affection. He was lonely in part because his was a lonely job. A good pastor gives so fully, freely, and impartially of himself that he has neither the time nor the energy to nurture many close friendships in daily association. Then, too, some found his massive integrity intimidating. We all know individuals whom

12. Author's interview with Thomas Stafford, Denver, Col., May 1, 1960.
13. Letter from G. Eugene Durham to author, September 8, 1959.

we admire and indeed love but whom we find it difficult to slap on the back or call by their first names. It is not a question of age or rank or wealth. It is a question of personality. Tittle commanded respect with an effortlessness reminiscent of Robert E. Lee. He hoped that his congregation would call him Ernest, but save for a few they insisted on addressing him as "Dr. Tittle."[14] "Chief" and "dominie" were titles often employed by his secretaries and assistants. He wounded easily, but was too courageous (or too proud) to seek to avoid being wounded. He dreaded the arrival of mail early in the week for all too often there were letters bitingly critical of his Sunday morning pulpit proclamations on social issues. Some of the epistles were so scatological that they were kept from Glenna's eyes. In fact Tittle's devoted secretaries screened the most vile communications from Tittle himself.[15] Yet he would not halt these criticisms by the quite simple measure of blunting the sharpness of his witness to the truth as the truth was revealed to him. Tittle was and remained essentially an innocent man, and to be innocent is to be vulnerable, for truly innocent people never learn. Consequently they are perpetually surprised when others act as they themselves would never dream of acting—or rather, as they would act only in their dreams. Tittle's visage was rugged, but his skin was thin. He was a strong man who knew the respect of all. Yet it was his gentleness, sensitivity, and vulnerabiltiy that caused men to say, "You could not help loving him."[16]

If Tittle was a lonely man he was not blameless in the matter, for though some knew his essential humanity, others counted him reserved and much withdrawn within himself. Not even Tittle's warmest admirers presume to insist that he was a jovial chap and not even his sternest critics dare charge that he was a frivolous fellow. He admitted to a gloomy temperment. Though he possessed a massive will, he could not will himself into a perpetually happy mood. He had that quality the Romans called *gravitas*. It is a manner that Americans associate with Washington, Lee, Henry L. Stimson, and George C. Marshall. Contrariwise, Tittle was short on that sunny quality that Americans associate with Henry Clay, Al Smith, and FDR. His dominant spirit was serious rather than blithe, sober rather than gay.

Though he dutifully attended hundreds of Methodist and interdenominational conferences, he was not much of a convention man. Hearty backslaps and hollow smiles in hotel lobbies, feckless jokes and

14. Author's interview with Mr. and Mrs. Murray Leiffer, Denver, Col., May 2, 1960.

15. Author's interview with Mrs. Bernice Wolseley, Evanston, Ill., July 13, 1960.

16. Author's interview with Thomas Stafford, Denver, Col., May 1, 1960.

fey gossip in hotel rooms left him bored. Even wholesome comaraderie could not ease his longing to return rapidly to the things he loved: his congregation, pulpit, books, and family. When he spoke to a question, whether at a General Conference or Evanston ministerial association meeting, men listened with respect. But he did not much contribute to a spirit of fellowship at these gatherings. Generally it was his custom to stay only as long as was absolutely necessary to conclude the business matters; he could not bring himself to fritter away precious hours in social intercourse. He lived an efficient life—the near total concentration of his time, energy, and talent on that which he judged worthwhile.

It was just this sense of the preciousness of time that caused some of his colleagues to regard him as brusque. The most signal instance of this brusqueness occured one Saturday afternoon in 1924. Tittle had been on a speaking tour most of the week. He was at home in his upstairs study desperately attempting to complete his Sunday sermon. Bishop and Mrs. Edwin Holt Hughes, who had just been assigned to the Chicago area, came to the door to call. Glenna went upstairs to inform her husband of their visitors. It became her painful duty to explain to the bishop (one of Methodism's most prestigious figures) and his wife that Tittle simply could not break away from his sermon preparation to greet his unexpected guests.[17]

Bishop Hughes was not the only man made to feel that he could not be spared Tittle's time. It is necessary to insist, however, that in allotting his hours Tittle gave no preference to the high and mighty over the low and lost. In fact, there seems to have been an almost inverse correlation between one's station in life and one's chances of commanding an appointment. Moreover, a number of individuals believe that Tittle was excessively protected by his wife and secretaries and that often the decision not to interrupt him was made without his knowledge.

Yet the fundamental fact remains that small talk bored him. If the conversation did not contain ideas, he withdrew into silence. Sometimes at a dinner party or social gathering, if he deemed the talk inconse-

17. Author's interview with Glenna Myers Tittle, Evanston, Ill., July 31, 1959. Bishop Hughes in his autobiography significantly makes no mention of Tittle, though First Church was the greatest church under his jurisdiction. He hints at some difficulty in these sentences: "Yet the Area was amazingly loyal. The anti-official obsession was not vigorous enough to make wide disturbance." *I Was Made a Minister* (New York and Nashville, Tenn.: Abingdon, Cokesbury Press, 1943), p. 127. It must be added that this event became a rather well known secret. Several individuals believe that Glenna made the decision not to disturb her husband, and that not until later did Tittle learn of the bishop's visit. Author's interviews with Horace G. Smith, Evanston, Ill., August 17, 1959, and Bishop Ralph Magee, Evanston, Ill., August 31, 1959.

quential he would remain mute until a subject arose that interested him. "Why," he once asked, "should intelligent people spend an entire afternoon or evening talking twaddle, not to mention gossip?"[18] To be sure, there was much to preoccupy his mind, and like many who live in the house of intellect he was so often absorbed in his thoughts as to be oblivious to the words swirling about him. As Paul Hutchinson puts it, "He could sit at the table, seemingly taking in what was being said, even replying from time to time to questions tossed at him, and afterwards not remember a word."[19] "To chatter was to silence him," remembered one fiercely loyal parishioner. Yet far from being offended, she rejoiced in "the great friendly silences."[20]

If there was a reserve about Tittle that some found difficult to penetrate, he was neither pompous nor dour. He would have agreed with Wesley's admonition, "Sour godliness is the devil's religion." And all those who have testified concerning Tittle's personality cite his engaging sense of humor, a reflection of his essential humility. The familiar barbs hurled at clergymen miss Tittle by a country mile. There was nothing buffoonishly bluff and falsely hearty about him. It was unnecessary for him to affect the tweedy dress, sonorous voice, and Rotarian manner of those ministers who are unconsciously unsure of their masculinity. On the other hand, he was free of that unctuous piety, sniveling sanctimoniousness, and Uriah Heap self-depreciation that in some quarters passes for godliness. There was not a milligram of cant or sham in his being.

Once when corrected on a Biblical point by a scholar, he wrote back in mock anger, "You know too d—— much!"[21] On another occasion he remarked to a young lady painter: "Thanks for the pencil portrait, which shows unusual skill in drawing. But is it a likeness? My first impulse was to exclaim, 'I'll be hanged if I look like that!' On reflection, however, I merely felt disposed to remark, 'If I do look like that I ought to be hanged.' "[22] He was embarrassed when individuals requested of him an autographed picture and only infrequently and late in his career did he comply. He would refer to "my ugly mug" and say "I am as common looking as an old shoe." He was not unaware of a growing baldness, writing on one occasion, "I am blushing to the roots of the few

18. *The Power of Words,* a sermon preached July 8, 1934 (pamphlet).
19. "Portrait of a Preacher," foreword to Tittle, *A Mighty Fortress* (New York: Harper & Brothers, 1949), p. xxxi.
20. Author's interview with Mrs. Roscoe Page, Evanston, Ill., August 10, 1959.
21. Letter from Tittle to James Taft Hatfield, July 28, 1942.
22. Letter from Tittle to Jean Wallace, June 24, 1935.

hairs left on my head."[23] In a letter to the president of Garrett he prefaced a critical comment with the disarming words, "Being an incorrigible offerer of suggestions (wise and unwise), I am venturing to express the belief that. . . ."[24]

Tittle repeatedly confessed that he was an "impatient mortal who cannot wait"[25] and that he was "not, to tell the truth, a good waiter."[26] This tendency tried Glenna's patience. She could not break him of the horrendous habit of opening presents in advance of Christmas day or his birthday. Her only recourse was to hide the packages. It was the custom of his brother, Stern, to send a box of Georgia pecans at Christmas. One year Tittle spied the box, imagined the contents, and mailed a thank you note. The contents turned out to be tangerines. He flashed a second note reading, "I'm nuts!"

Tittle of course possessed a proper self-regard. But he was not arrogant. And in reviewing his life one arrives at the unmistakable conclusion that his modesty increased with the passing of the years and that at the height of his Evanston fame he was less prideful than in his younger days. He came to know the truth of the French proverb: "Experience teaches us that we must sooner or later bend the knee, and it is before God that it is least humiliating to bow." Tittle's copy of William Inge's *Labels & Libels* is marked at this passage: "But I believe there are many people with whom the inferiority complex has been the secret of their success in life. It has made them grim fighters and furious workers. The naturally contented seldom do much in the world. They have what they want already." Tittle penciled the laconic marginal note, "I have to work harder, all right!"

III

It is of course possible for a man to be admired without being loved, and this truism gives force to the old observation that we like our friends despite their many virtues. Adult male friendships in America are rare because they rest upon experiences shared, and grown men, unlike schoolboys and soldiers, rarely share together highly personal experiences revealing of their true selves. Most men have been too bruised by life to permit others to see their nakedness, and they are too proud, also. Considering the many barriers to the formation of adult male friendships, barriers even higher for ministers than for laymen, it is really

23. Letter from Tittle to Eward Scribner Ames, January 11, 1934.
24. Letter from Tittle to Horace G. Smith, January 16, 1941.
25. Letter from Tittle to Ada Nate McIntosh, December 19, 1933.
26. Letter from Tittle to George W. Eddy, December 22, 1933.

quite wondrous that Tittle should have won so many friends. It is true that he was a lonely man, but it is not an unusual paradox for a man to be lonely though blessed with a crowd of friends.

Although it is neither possible nor prudent to list the roll of Tittle's friendships, several generalizations are permissible. For one thing, his friends were a variagated group not confined to one social, economic, or professional class. For another, they included an unusual percentage of younger people; Tittle successfully bridged that much-deplored "generation gap." Thirdly, friendships once sealed were seldom broken, not even when there was intense disagreement on public issues. Finally, as mentioned earlier, Tittle knew the friendship of women, and this in a society that assumes that every male-female relationship necessarily is romantic or sexual.

Garrett professor Harris Franklin Rall was his theological mentor, Tittle often remarking "I preach the gospel according to Rall." *Christian Century* editor Paul Hutchinson was his mentor in matters of Methodist polity, and many times the two men talked late into the night, filling the air with blue cigar smoke and blunt words. William A. Dyche, business manager of Northwestern University and an important figure in the life of Evanston, remained until his death in 1936 the strongest pillar in First Church. The admiration the two men felt for each other deepened with the years, Tittle testifying that Dyche was the "man to whom Northwestern University owes most; and to whom the city of Evanston owes more than to anyone who has ever lived in it."[27] Among Evanston ministers, the Congregationalist Hugh Elmer Brown provided splendid companionship. Among Northwestern professors Dean James Alton James, Dean Raymond A. Kent, Dean Peter Lutkin, Dean Ralph B. Dennis, Dean Thomas F. Holgate, and Paul Schilpp were especially close. In Methodism at large Tittle rejoiced in the friendship of Halford Luccock (who Tittle correctly believed wrote with the most witty pen in Methodism) and Bishops McConnell, Welch, and McDowell, among a galaxy of others. The First Church staff adored their "chief"; above all he had the total admiration of his secretary, Mrs. Bernice Wolseley, who said with fierce devotion, "Ernest Fremont Tittle was the finest man I have ever known."[28] Many other individuals echoed these words, but if I continue to cite names I will be compiling a list of all his friends, a project manifestly impossible here.

27. *Evanston Daily News-Index,* February 19, 1936, p. 12.
28. Author's interview with Mrs. Bernice Wolseley, Evanston, Ill., July 13, 1960. Her husband, a Northwestern professor before going to Syracuse University, shared this admiration. Revealingly, Tittle dedicated a major book, *A Way to Life* (New York: Henry Holt & Co., 1935) to Roland and Bernice Wolseley.

Did the years bring a reconciliation between Tittle and his father? The answer must be no. It was not that they quarreled bitterly, but worse, that they lived in almost total isolation, rarely visiting together, rarely writing, the alienation being virtually total. Ernest left undone those things that a good son ought to have done, and when Clayton Tittle died he was buried by the side of his second wife, Rosie Kiser, far distant from where the other Tittles lie in the cemetery. Such are the contingencies of human relationships that we may agree that the father was a good man (though in the eyes of his son not a good father) and the son a great man (though in the eyes of the father not a good son) and yet accept without judgment the fact of their estrangement.[29]

Ernest's relationship with his only brother was not sufficiently warm to compensate for the coolness between him and his father. Stern Tittle, five years Ernest's junior, is remembered as a jolly, friendly, fun-loving youngster, fond of a good time and not overly impressed with the merits of hard study. After attending Ohio Wesleyan (supported financially in part by his brother), he knocked about the world free as a whistle, happy as a porpoise, and as directionless as a leaky hose. Finally in his middle years he settled down in Thomasville, Georgia, as the very responsible and capable manager of a large plantation. He married a lovely woman whom death called tragically all too soon. They had no children. It would take an acute psychologist to explain the far different life paths traveled by the two brothers, but common sense is sufficient to the task of observing that they viewed the world from such different angles of vision that it was almost literally impossible for them to communicate with each other. They were both independent souls, but one was a prophet and the other a maverick.[30]

It remains only to add that Tittle corresponded warmly with his first cousin Walter, the noted artist, and sweetly with several nieces. Apparently his relationship with Glenna's parents, who lived at the manse for a time, was not inharmonious. But all in all, it cannot be maintained that Tittle knew the blessing of close kinship.

IV

The epigram "America has no honors list except the tax list" is not

29. Authors' interview with Mrs. Orville E. Kiser, Springfield, Ohio, June 16, 1960. A personal examination was made of the location of the gravestones.

30. On April 18-19, 1960, I was the house guest of Stern Tittle at the Sinkola Plantation. I liked and admired him immediately and intuitively. The talk ranged widely over many subjects and though I often disagreed with his position (on every point more conservative than that of his brother), he was a thoughtful host and pleasant companion.

supported by the career of Ernest Fremont Tittle, nor is his life a testimony to the mordant observation of Will Rogers, "Americans are united by a common impulse for the same buck." After Tittle came to Evanston it was his great good fortune to be free from severe personal financial worries. (Of course he was intensely concerned with the financial problems of First Church.) His income was now roughly adequate to the needs of his family, though it hardly permitted luxurious living. Because he was not an avaricious man, he was content with an income that provided his family with some protection and modest comfort. Because he was not an insecure man, he did not hunger each year always to earn more than the year before. Because he knew that his congregation loved him, he did not demand that they show their love in annual salary raises. Finally, he heeded the hard words of Jesus concerning the perils to the spirit of acquisitiveness.

A closer evaluation of this subject must begin with a few figures.[31] Tittle's initial salary at First Church was $5,000. The following year it was raised to $6,000 and in 1927 to $10,000. It was never again to be that high. In the depression years it was slashed back, at his insistence, to $7,000. Not until 1943 was it raised to $7,250 and finally to $8,000 at the time of his death.

This base salary was significantly supplemented in several ways. For one thing, First Church supplied Tittle with a parsonage, freeing him of the expense of home ownership. During the initial two years in Evanston the church rented for Tittle the old James A. Patton residence and onetime home of Northwestern University presidents. Then in 1920 the church purchased for $26,515 for use as a parsonage a large residence at 1810 Hinman Avenue, where Tittle was to live for the rest of his life. It was not an ideal house, but First Church voted funds to help in the furnishing and over the years paid many thousands of dollars for repairs and improvements. Moreover, Tittle himself was spared the payment of a property tax, which in Evanston is a staggering sum. In brief, the parsonage was easily equivalent to several thousand dollars annually in cash. Then, too, during most years Tittle added about $1,000 to his income from speaking engagements, book royalties, and magazine articles. From time to time, also, he was the beneficiary of little gifts of cash, and on at least two occasions he was presented with a new car, once by the church membership and once by John C. Shaffer, the pub-

31. The information that follows is drawn from the Minutes of the Official Board, First Church, and income tax returns and other memorandum in the Tittle Collection.

lisher and editor.[32] Tittle's more affluent parishioners further invited him as their guest to functions and places that otherwise would have been financially "off limits" to a parson, and somehow he was made a member of two country clubs (which he almost never patronized) at almost no expense to himself. Finally, at the time of his illnesses First Church partially underwrote the heavy medical expenses.

Manifestly Tittle won a living wage. His income, including the aggregate of fringe benefits, was sufficient to provide his family with security and some measure of comfort. Indeed, most Methodist ministers would have deemed such an income princely—and a few of them bitterly informed Tittle of the disparity between their remuneration and his.[33] In the very year that Tittle came to First Church the average annual salary (excluding house rent) of Rock River Conference pastors was $1,440.[34] And this figure was some $400 more than the average received by all ministers in the Methodist Episcopal Church. In fact, in 1916, 60 percent of Methodist preachers received less than $1,000 per year, including house rent![35]

Precisely because Tittle received a handsome salary by comparative, ministerial standards he was the subject of critical comment in some Methodist circles. Once he was driven to reply:

> Inasmuch as your letter appears to be critical of me, I may, perhaps, be permitted to say a word in my own behalf. My salary, thanks to three successive reductions which I myself initiated, is no longer one of the top salaries paid to Methodist preachers. However, it is still too high in relation to the salaries paid to the majority of Methodist preachers. This year I refused an increase of a thousand dollars which the Finance Committee of the church insisted upon providing for me. I insisted that it should be used, instead, to increase the salaries of other members of the church staff. Some years ago . . . I sponsored a plan I still think was feasible to raise the minimum salary paid to pastors in my own conference. This plan was actually adopted by the conference, but was later "torpedoed" by certain laymen and also, I have been told, by certain of our district superintendents. I agree with you that the time has come for the church to set its own house in order, and I propose to lend a hand to the job. I am not myself

32. "You have given me the biggest surprise of my life. The car is a beauty. Stop. Right size, excellent taste. I have no words adequate to express my appreciation." Day letter from Tittle to John C. Shaffer, October 21, 1935.

33. Tittle was quite aware that his comrades thought his situation comparable to "a pig in clover." Letter from Tittle to Theodore Miner, November 30, 1931.

34. *Minutes* of the Rock River Annual Conference (1919).

35. *The Daily Christian Advocate,* Methodist Episcopal Church, May 6, 1916, p. 90.

committed to the idea of one salary for all preachers. Even Russia, under Soviet direction, has felt obliged to adopt a wage differential. But I am committed to the idea of lessening the gap which now exists between the top and the bottom salaries of Methodism.[36]

Earlier in his career he had stated a profound truth in speaking to another parson, "After all, none of us does anything more than make a living at this business."[37]

At the time of his death Tittle owned not a foot of real estate. Glenna was left quite literally shelterless. After all, the lot at 1810 Hinman and the house on it, had simply been on loan from First Church. Nor was there more than a modest sum in cash and stocks. Tittle's primary effort to hedge against the future was to carry $65,000 in life insurance.[38] Thus, these insurance policies, a pocketful of cash, a few stocks, an automobile, a bit of furniture, a cluster of old fishing poles, and several thousand worn books (willed to a Negro seminary) were Ernest Fremont Tittle's worldly possessions after a life of unremitting toil. He was not an acquisitive man. He stood squarely in the tradition of John Wesley.

A final point in assessing Tittle's income is this: he lived in a community of great wealth, one "reported to be the second largest income-tax paying city in the United States, on a per capita basis."[39] Many of the members of First Church were affluent, not a few were wealthy, and several were millionaires. If Tittle had lived in a lower class or slum area, it would have been unseemly for him to have exacted from his parishioners a salary far exceeding their own incomes, at great sacrifice to them. In Evanston, however, it would have been bemeaning to him and a disgrace to his calling if he had been compelled to live in a shabby gentility. A congregation that pampers itself while sentencing its shepherd to a barren existence without books, travel, leisure time, a few of the amenities, much less mere financial security, deserves exactly what it is most likely to get—a tired, uninformed, narrow, fawning, pitiable person, broken in spirit and drained of enthusiasm. First Church had the good sense to pay Tittle a good wage. But it was not a corrupting wage. In the land of the blind the one-eyed man is king, and in ministerial circles Tittle was a well-to-do man. Evanston, however, was a

36. Letter from Tittle to David Simpson, February 18, 1941.
37. Letter from Wilbur A. Vorhis to author, August 24, 1959.
38. See memorandum drawn up by John Tittle, probably about June, 1946, in the Tittle Collection.
39. *Evanston Review,* September 28, 1933, p. 1.

land of three-eyed people, and in North Shore circles Tittle's income was unremarkable.

V

Ernest Fremont Tittle once confided to a close family friend, "There is no other experience comparable to being married to the same woman all one's life, to know and love her more deeply with each passing year."[40] The Tittle marriage was a good one. Glenna gave Ernest love, comfort, honor, and kept him in sickness and in health, forsaking all others, as long as they both lived. And after death parted her from her husband, she cherished his memory.

Because for Ernest there were never enough hours in the day, Glenna doubled as his research assistant, daily reading newspapers and magazines, clipping items for his attention. Because of Ernest's preoccupation with his thoughts he made a lackadaisical automobile driver, and so Glenna became his chauffeur. Because her husband's burdens were heavy, she sometimes called on afflicted parishioners for him. Because Ernest loved to hike and fish, Glenna became an outdoorswoman, though at what cost to her patience only a wife who has been required to sit *silently* for hours in a row boat while her man refused to call it a day can comprehend. Because Ernest suffered sickness, Glenna became a nurse who watched him (as he put it) "like a hawk or better, like a dear hen (mustn't say old)."[41] Because Tittle's life was his work, Glenna was forced to share her husband with countless others, and rare was the evening when they could be alone, perhaps to play Russian Bank or cribbage or to sneak off to a movie together. And when Tittle was home after supper usually he was upstairs in his study, locked in thought; and of necessity Glenna was thrown much on her own resources. She was called "Buzzy" by her husband and intimate friends, not because she was a chatterer, but because when she became excited the verbal sparks flew. Her tongue was not sharp, but her wit did have an edge. She was liked by the women of First Church, perhaps because she made no attempt to dominate the ladies' groups. She wore well. This is fortunate, for thirty-one years with one flock is a longer period for the shepherd's wife than for the shepherd himself. It is revealing that the people of First Church should name a beautiful new parlor "Glenna Hall." In 1934 she was elected president of the Rock River Conference ministers' wives association, but generally she had no interest in becoming a powerful figure in

40. Letter from Mrs. Roscoe Page to author, undated.
41. Letter from Tittle to Mrs. Paul Hutchinson, December 30, 1946.

the Methodist Establishment and she held no high office in the Church at large.

The fundamental truth of this marriage is that Glenna devoted herself to the untiring care and comfort of her husband and completely melded her life with his. She was an ever-present help in time of trouble and in time of triumph. According to some authorities on the "Feminine Mystique" Glenna must have been, consequently, rather a turnip. To the contrary, she was a spirited, intelligent, independent-minded human being, both physically and psychically healthy; and because she did not despise herself she was capable of loving her husband. For these qualities, Ernest's love for her was deep. "After twenty-five years," he said of their marriage, "we find ourselves more completely at one than ever before, and mightily rejoicing in the fact that we have each other and the three kids."[42]

Glenna and Ernest were blessed with three fine children. The oldest, John Myers, attended the Evanston public schools and in 1930 was graduated from the Northwestern University School of Commerce (after a brief stint at Antioch College). In that bleak year he entered the investment business—and in time prospered. In 1931 he knew a triumph of a different sort: he met, wooed, and won a lovely girl, Phyllis Fox. Their marriage was enduring and Tittle rejoiced in his three fine grandchildren. As the years passed, increasingly the father came to depend on his oldest son. John (and the name is appropriate) was a rock of steadiness. Insurance, tax, and other financial problems were turned over to him. Moreover, after a long, hard Sunday it was heaven for the father to be able to unwind in the evening at John's and Phyllis's home, proudly eyeing his grandchildren and savoring his favorite lemon pie. John was the sort of oldest son that every father dreams of claiming. It is revealing that Phyllis remembers her father-in-law with an affection transparently sincere. It cannot be documented (though it has been suggested by individuals close to the family), but it is entirely convincing to say that one reason Tittle remained at First Church was that he could not bear the thought of being separated from the comforting presence of John and John's wife and children.

Elizabeth Ann was the second child, the first and only daughter. After attending Roycemore, a private school for girls in Evanston, she went on to DePauw, a Methodist university in Indiana, and then to Smith. In 1937 she married David Gray Poston of Kentucky. David was, Ernest and Glenna believed, a fine husband for their beloved Betsy,

42. Letter from Tittle to Mrs. Arthur Margileth, June 15, 1932.

"all we could hope for."[43] David took his bride to Shanghai, where under orders of the Board of Foreign Missions of the Protestant Episcopal Church he taught history at St. John's University. It was an anxious time for the Tittles for Japan was then on the march. Though they trusted the good judgment of David, it was with relief that they welcomed their daughter's return from the war zone early in 1941. After graduate study at the University of Chicago David Poston taught at Montana State College and then at the University of Redlands. It was with real joy that Ernest and Glenna occasionally visited with the Postons in Montana and California. It is trite but nonetheless true to say that Betsy was and always remained the apple of her father's eye.

William Myers was the third and last child. (It is perhaps revealing of the family relationships that both boys were given as their middle name their mother's maiden name.) After winning honors at North Shore Country Day (a scholarship covered almost all costs at this outstanding prep school), Bill went on to Northwestern. In 1942 he married an exceptionally attractive girl, Mary Rosetta Stewart, whom Tittle deemed "a great person and one grand gal."[44] Almost immediately Bill was faced with the rugged decision of shouldering a gun or serving his country in a Civilian Public Service Camp. He honored the pacifist position of his father at a price only other conscientious objectors can comprehend. Though unlike his father physically, being long-limbed and rawboned, Bill possessed the Tittle qualities of integrity, strength, and independence of spirit. As his father said of him, "son of mine though he is, he has lots of good stuff in him."[45]

In truth, all the children became as adults fine individuals. This is somewhat surprising. For one thing, that the children of great men turn out badly seems to apply rather more frequently than the law of averages would seem to decree. For another, the sons and daughters of clergymen have a proclivity for trodding primrose paths (or such is the wisdom of folklore). Finally, it is difficult to pinpoint in just what respects Tittle was a good father. Though most companionable with college students, he was rather inept with little children. He did not much enjoy playing with them. He did not understand them. It is quite possible that they bored him. After all, tots are not much good at the exchange of ideas.[46] Even more to the point, as his wife and children admit, he simply did

43. Letter from Tittle to J. N. Lott, August 10, 1937.
44. Letter from Tittle to Donald R. Stewart, June 27, 1944.
45. Letter from Tittle to Arthur Anderson, November 30, 1937.
46. Author's interview with Mr. and Mrs. Murray Leiffer, Denver, Col., May 2, 1960.

not have the time to devote to John, Betsy, and Bill. Few were the minutes, even fewer the hours, and almost nonexistent the days when he could romp or read with them. Yet, such are the mysteries of parenthood all three children turned out splendidly. All three hold the memory of their father in reverence—and more significantly, in affection. Apparently Tittle was one of the few fathers to successfully get away with practicing that absurd piece of child guidance, "Set your children a good example and then leave them alone."

The parsonage at 1810 Hinman Street was within an easy walk of First Church. It was an old, tall, narrow, commodious, comfortable gray stucco structure fronted by a delightful double porch adorned with four Greek pillars. Its lines were awkward to modern eyes, its heating and plumbing plants antiquated, its three stories necessitated much stair climbing, and it did not lend itself to efficient housekeeping. Yet it was livable. There was enough space for each child "to do his thing." The large handsome dining room and finished basement made it possible to entertain First Church groups. Tittle's upstairs book-lined study was a quiet sanctuary. The porches caught the breezes off Lake Michigan and were a delight on summer evenings; long winter nights were thawed by the four cozy fireplaces. When the infirmities of old age threatened the house, Raymond C. Wieboldt of First Church got his workmen to patch, paint, and repair. Fortunately for Ernest, he was not handy with tools or garden equipment (or was this only a clever ruse?), and Glenna soon learned not to depend on her husband to fix things about the house or tidy up the yard. And fortunately for Glenna, she had sufficient help to make it possible for her to manage without her husband's assistance, though it was not always easy.

And so the parsonage became a home, a home in which Tittle was king despite the fact that he affectionately termed Glenna "chief" and "boss." But Tittle was not a tyrant. As he said at one time, "For the chance of intellectual and spiritual comradeship with his wife and with his grown sons and daughters a man can well afford to surrender the legal right to be a tyrant in his own home."[47] Naturally there were times in their marriage when both he and Glenna might have subscribed to James Thurber's "Smallhousen Theory"—namely, *every* house, regardless of physical size, at times becomes too small to hold a man and a woman simultaneously. "I have lived long enough to suspect that no home, not even the happiest, is entirely free from friction," Tittle once stated.[48]

47. "The Christian Home," typed MS, a sermon preached December 7, 1941.
48. "The Meaning and Way of Salvation," *The First Church Pulpit,* Vol. IX, No. 18, a sermon preached March 21, 1948.

In summing up, it may again be underscored that Glenna was a fiercely loyal, utterly devoted, unflaggingly protective, unfailingly helpful wife. She did not compete—or feel the need to compete—with her husband. She unchained Ernest from all domestic anxieties so that he might soar in his calling. She gave him the assurance that he was loved and esteemed, an assurance that all men (but none more than Tittle) need. The one possible ingredient missing from the marriage was an element of Dionysian joy, a dash of wackiness. Both Ernest and Glenna had senses of humor, but both were fundamentally sober, serious individuals. This common angle of vision gave to their marriage a firm, enduring foundation. But it also made it impossible for Tittle ever to cut loose in a completely swinging mood in the company of a lilting—even silly— woman. This is not a criticism of Glenna, because she could no more will herself into being frivolous than Ernest could will himself into playing the clown.[49]

VI

Tittle died years before the actuarial tables decreed, and perhaps one explanation is that he echoed too faithfully Wesley's confession, "Leisure and I have parted company." It is an irony of life that intense individuals who most need to learn to relax are the very ones least capable of mastering that lesson. Tittle drove himself mercilessly. Even his nights were too often sleepless. Work was his passion. As with all unchecked passions, it became, in terms of his health, a vice. The compulsion to be somebody did not disappear with maturity. He ran hard his entire life. Consequently his life was shortened. It would have been further shortened if First Church had now awarded him generous annual vacations. Except for speaking engagements, conferences, and other duty-dictated trips that left him more fatigued than refreshed, Tittle was locked in Evanston most of the year. The wild dunes of Indiana, the lovely parks of central Illinois, the game-filled woods and fish-brimming lakes of Wisconsin were within easy weekend reach of Chicago-area residents, but for Tittle eleven o'clock Sunday morning was the moment of truth, and every Saturday a day of hard preparation for that moment.[50] Thus for Tittle Evanston was a prison, an attractive prison, to

49. I prefer not to cite the names of the individuals who made this observation about the marriage, although, as far as I could judge, they spoke not in malice but in love for both Glenna and Ernest.

50. Knowledgeable Chicago area citizens will recognize that this is a description of these recreation areas as they existed in the 1920's and 1930's, not as they are today.

be sure, but one that afforded few recreational opportunities, or to phrase it more accurately, few that were his cup of tea.

He did not as an adult swim (save on two occasions when his fishing boat tipped over and he had reason to be thankful that he *could* swim) or sail. Consequently Lake Michigan was appreciated solely for its beauty and breezes. (To picture Tittle spending hours stretched out on an Evanston beach sunbathing confounds the imagination.) He did not ice-skate or play tennis or squash. There were no true woods nearby for hiking. On his arrival in Evanston some First Church members talked him into taking up golf. It was a mistake he promptly rectified by the simple expedient of throwing away his clubs. "Golf . . . I thoroughly dislike," he growled.[51] And to his congregation he confessed, "Let God be thanked, it isn't necessary for everybody to play golf!"[52] He belonged to two country clubs, but in time resigned with the explanation that neither he nor his children ever made use of the clubs' facilities. Yet he was not incapable of joining in sports contests. At church outings he pitched horseshoes with the best of them. He occasionally tossed a baseball with his sons, to the articulate consternation of a leading First Church member who observed the male Tittles in this activity one Sunday afternoon. Once in his middle years at a Saturday Methodist student picnic he competed vigorously in a hop, skip, and jump contest. "Today," he ruefully confessed after the Sunday service, "was the most miserable hour I ever spent in the pulpit."[53]

Circumstantial evidence suggests that he was not much interested in spectator sports. In a sermon preached July 9, 1933, he referred to a man at the radio listening to the Chicago Cubs playing the Chicago Bears. This is a slip that not even Freud could explain on grounds other than Tittle's indifference to Chicago's (then) great baseball and football teams. In a letter to the Northwestern football coach, Lynn Waldorf (the son of Tittle's bishop), he congratulated him on Saturday's victory, but admitted that it was the first game he had seen in several years.

Tittle's contempt for bridge was monumental. To be sure, on an occasional evening he played two-handed card games with Glenna. But his heart was not in these encounters. In fact, the only way to compel him to leave his study and play a hand or two before bedtime was to threaten to inform his doctors that he was not behaving.[54] He did not

51. Letter from Tittle to Edgar De Witt Jones, January 16, 1933.
52. *Keeping Up One's Morale,* a sermon preached July 15, 1934 (pamphlet).
53. Letter from Robert H. Hamill to author, September 14, 1959.
54. Author's interview with William and Mary Tittle, Chapel Hill, N. C., November 1, 1965.

collect coins or stamps or butterflies. The fact is, he was being truthful when he wrote to a man preparing a biographical sketch, "I am sorry to report that I have no hobby."[55]

Though Tittle was active in a host of religious, civic, reform, and civil libertarian organizations, as shall be seen, he was not the sort of joiner Will Rogers had in mind when he observed that two Americans could not meet each other on the street without one of them banging a gavel and calling the other to order. He was a Mason and admired the order's good works, but was hardly an active member. He was a charter member of the Evanston Rotary Club, vice-president in 1920-21, and was made honorary life member in 1940, but after the first years his participation was perfunctory. His old college fraternity surely gave up on him. Since he had no hobbies, in any meaningful sense he belonged to no fraternal lodges, and the one fellowship in Evanston he truly cherished was that of First Church.

What, then, did he do in the few moments stolen from his duties? Now and then he and Glenna went to the movies. On infrequent occasions (and always on Christmas Eve) he played the violin. He never entirely lost the skill he displayed as a boy. He also sketched, usually scenes of nature, another talent at which in his youth he showed much promise. He soon gave up trying his hand at poetry. "My few heroic attempts to use the poetic medium," he reported, "have been uniformly disastrous."[56] In this he resembled John C. Calhoun who, in his one effort at poetry, never got beyond the opening word, and that word was "whereas." When the pressures became unendurable, there were a few nearby country estates, owned by such friends as H. Haddon MacLean, where he might retire for a few days of perfect solitude.

The above represents a pretty limited recreational agenda. It must be remembered, however, that there were numerous aspects of his calling where pleasure was combined with business—that is, the many banquets, musical programs, holiday festivities, parties, and even dances sponsored by First Church at which the Tittles were often in attendance. Then, too, his date books reveal that he and Glenna were much in demand as dinner guests, and if the conversation was normally sober, this was quite to his liking.

One summer just prior to his vacation he wrote a friend, "I am myself utterly weary of listening to my own voice. At the moment, I feel like chucking preaching for all time. I, too, am weary, and looking forword with overwhelming eagerness to the first day of August, when I

55. Letter from Tittle to Edgar De Witt Jones, January 16, 1933.
56. Letter from Tittle to E. J. Moulton, June 27, 1938.

shall kick up my heels again."[57] One September at the conclusion of his summer vacation he informed a friend, "Mrs. Tittle and I had a glorious summer in the mountains. I have come back hard as nails and with a spirit that for the present at least feels able for anything; fortunately, it appears, for almost any damn thing is likely to come my way this year."[58] In a sermon he asked: "Who, being human, does not look forward to a vacation as to a taste of heaven? . . . Phillips Brooks once confessed that no sooner did one vacation come to an end than he began to look forward to the coming of another. And I may, I trust, without immodesty report that in this one respect, I myself, resemble Phillips Brooks."[59]

These three statements suggest how absolutely essential Tittle's summer vacations were to him, to his continuing effectiveness as a minister, and indeed to his very survival. And for him, a summer vacation meant mountain-climbing and above all fishing. He once confided to his congregation, "I speak as one who is not a good fisherman but only crazy about fishing and somewhat inventive when it comes to reporting the catch."[60] And he once explained to the Official Board, "My main job is to do what little I can to improve the *human* race. But occasionally I catch fish, so that they may learn to be more careful next time."[61] After his heart attacks his doctors naturally placed a ban on mountain-climbing and hiking, but until the very last he continued to fish, even though he could no longer row a boat or walk more than a block of shore line.

To Tittle, fishing meant casting, and best of all fly-casting for trout. Often he made his own flies, studding his battered old fishing hat with them. He carried a huge tackle box, and if one lure failed to bring a catch, he would replace it, and thus would begin an endless process of substitution until he hit upon a successful one. Like all true fishermen, he loved to eat fish and quite cheerfully cleaned his own catches. (Glenna was an adoring wife and happily cooked the fish, but drew the line at cleaning them.)[62]

For six or eight weeks every summer Tittle was granted a vacation. The Colorado ranch of John C. Shaffer was a favorite (and glorious)

57. Letter from Tittle to Georgia Harkness, July 16, 1940.
58. Letter from Tittle to Walter D. Warrick, September 17, 1935.
59. "A Well Proportioned Life," *First Church Review,* I (October, 1924), 3.
60. "Peace of Mind," *The First Church Pulpit,* Vol. IX, No. 22, a sermon preached July 24, 1948.
61. Letter from Tittle to the Official Board, December 2, 1940, in Official Board Letterbook.
62. The files of the *Evanston News-Index,* the *Evanston Review,* and the *First Church Review* are good sources of factual information concerning when and where Tittle vacationed.

spot for several summers in the 1920's. The Black Hills of South Dakota then beckoned for three consecutive years, and it was there in a cabin beneath Mt. Elkhorn that Tittle completed his famous 1931 Lyman Beecher Lectures. Earlier he had joined a group of rugged men in the great adventure of climbing Washington's Mt. Rainer, experiencing "a feeling of elation, a sense of triumph, a kind of spiritual exultation."[63] In 1924 Ernest and Glenna left the children and sailed for a two-month European tour, mostly of England and Italy. They soon found the tour too constrictive and set off on their own. Tittle had an enjoyable enough time in Europe, but it is indicative of a certain provincialism, an attitude that he could never quite shake, that "he was ready to start home several weeks before his schedule would allow."[64] Ill health in 1927 dictated a southern trip. Under doctors' orders, Tittle and young Betsy traveled down to the Gulf Coast, loafed (in Tittle's case a better word is fretted) in the Mississippi sun, and then cruised to Cuba. He was of course fearfully bored, ignored his doctors, and cut the trip short. Early in the 'thirties the summers were spent fishing at Basswood Lake on the Canadian border. If ever the quiet majesty of nature could refresh a man's body, revive his spirits, and restore his soul, it is this wooded lake country of northern Minnesota. The bass, pike, and muskie are as plentiful (and for a fisherman as lovely) as the houris in a Mussulman's heaven.[65]

In 1934 Tittle acquired his one piece of real estate, a ten-acre wooded tract high in the Rockies, about four miles south of Estes Park village in an area known locally as "Holy Hill." The cabin, comfortable but not plush, was in a clearing between two tracts of timber and commanded a magnificent view. It tells us much about the state of the American economy in the 1930's to learn that land, cabin, and furnishings cost Tittle no more than $3,000 and that annual maintenance, including the $40 tax, came to about $75. Here for four consecutive summers he vacationed, experiencing the happiest moments of his life. He climbed Long's Peak, and Pike's Peak, gazing down on beautiful white clouds that looked like whipped cream. He caught twelve-inch rainbow trout in Gem Lake, high, isolated, breathtaking with its sheer cliffs and huge boulders studding the banks. Four glorious summers—and then came the first heart attack. His doctors forbade him ever again to

63. *The Foolishness of Preaching* (New York: Henry Holt & Co., 1930), p. 267.

64. *First Church Review,* I (October, 1924), 3.

65. Anyhow this is how I felt when years ago my young son and I canoed the Basswood territory.

return. Surely it was with a heavy as well as wounded heart that he placed this precious possession up for sale—at $2,500.

The remaining summers Tittle mostly vacationed in the North Woods or visited with Betsy and David Poston in Montana and then California. As the years passed and claimed their toll, First Church granted him mid-winter and spring vacations. These generous leaves rested his tired heart; alas, they could not mend it.

VII

Immediately upon Tittle's arrival in Evanston a reporter interviewed the new pastor of First Church, and the description that appeared in the newspaper opened with these words: "Dr. Tittle is a very forceful appearing young man. He is but 33 years old, is clean shaved, has a fighter's chin and the sparkling eyes of an athlete."[66] The sketch continued in this vein. The reporter was neither the first nor last individual to come away from an initial meeting with Tittle convinced that here was a man of great physical vigor, inexhaustible vitality, robust health, and steel nerves. Yet as we know, Tittle was in fact intense, conscientious, ambitious, introspective, driven, sensitive to the point of being thin-skinned, and haunted by doubts concerning his ability. And because of his calling, he carried the sorrows of countless others in his heart and their burdens on his shoulders. The fact that he relentlessly curbed his monumental temper, that he bridled his turbulent nature and presented to the world a composed and controlled countenance, simply heightened his inner tension. As he entered middle age inevitably these stresses exacted a physiological toll. The first heavy blow fell in the mid-1920's when he was entering his forties.

Recalling that wretched period, he wrote Mrs. Walter Rauschenbusch, "Many thanks for your helpful information concerning the treatment of insomnia. For four long years I did not sleep a single night without the aid of drugs."[67] Again he remembered: "Ten years ago I myself was knocked out completely by a virulent streptococcus infection which hit my nerves and more or less incapacitated me for four years."[68] And again: "In fact, I was knocked out completely for an entire year, the cause being a streptococcus infection which played havoc with my whole nervous system."[69] In still other letters Tittle speaks of being so nervously exhausted as hardly to know his own mind.

66. *Evanston News-Index*, November 30, 1918, p. 1.
67. Letter from Tittle to Mrs. Walter Rauschenbusch, July 1, 1935.
68. Letter from Tittle to Charles A. Kent, November 17, 1936.
69. Letter from Tittle to Walter Tittle, January 4, 1937.

On Sunday, October 24, 1926, Tittle preached the morning sermon as usual. He was not again to enter the First Church pulpit until September 1, 1927. His massive will could no longer compel obedience from his racked body. In desperation, displaying symptoms of "extreme irritability, nervousness and colonic spasms of muscle,"[70] he turned to the Mayo Clinic. There Dr. Edward C. Rosenow discovered the source of the trouble: a number of dead teeth were infecting his entire system, torturing his nerves, denying him sleep. The necessary operations were performed. Tittle was thereafter to speak of Dr. Rosenow with the utmost gratitude. Yet the recovery was slow. In the late fall and winter the First Church Official Board periodically announced that Dr. Tittle was expected momentarily to return to his duties. The moment was much delayed. On May 2, 1927, the board definitely stated that its pastor would be on sick leave until September 1. It was during this time that Tittle and Betsy made the convalescent trip to the Gulf and Cuba.

Tittle himself always placed the responsibility for his tortured condition squarely on the infected teeth. This, of course, was Dr. Rosenow's continuing opinion. "Do not think," he wrote Tittle's Evanston physician "that I was unaware of the feelings of the men who saw Dr. Tittle at the Clinic. Indeed, two of them warned me not to promise anything nor to expect much result from eradication of foci in his case because it was a plain case of nervous breakdown demanding a long period of rest, etc."[71] On the other hand, Glenna is inclined to the belief that her husband suffered primarily from "nervous exhaustion," and that the infection merely aggravated the more fundamental source of his adversity.[72] One senses that Glenna is probably right. Evidence to support her thesis is found in letters Tittle was writing to friends only a few years later, especially in 1931-32, in which he states that he is on the verge of "another smash" and that somehow he must find release from the intolerable pressures.

The second week of November, 1937, was a fairly normal work week for Tittle, that is to say, a fiercely crowded one: an address at Carleton College, Northfield, Minnesota, on the 8th; an address at the University of Wisconsin on the 14th; speeches before Evanston and Chicago groups; two World Peace Commission meetings in Chicago; a Board of Foreign

70. Letter from Dr. Edward C. Rosenow to Dr. Mary G. McEwen, December 18, 1926. Dr. McEwen was at this time Tittle's family doctor in Evanston.

71. Letter from Dr. Edward C. Rosenow to Dr. Mary G. McEwen, January 21, 1927.

72. Author's interview with Glenna Myers Tittle, Evanston, Ill., August 14, 1959. The medical men with whom I reviewed the case tend to share Glenna's hunch.

Missions meeting, also downtown; a Board of Home Missions meeting in Evanston; a meeting of the Evanston Conference on Christian Faith and Life; a funeral service; a wedding rehearsal and bridal dinner; two social dinners; Sunday morning worship services on the 7th and 14th (the Wisconsin address was in the evening); sermon preparations; pastoral calling, correspondence; regular First Church administrative duties. All engagements for Friday the 19th were suddenly cancelled. The troublesome chest pains long warning him had become acute. On Sunday the assistant minister, Arthur T. Clark, read the following announcement to the disturbed congregation: "With very deep regret, which you will all share, I have to announce that Dr. Tittle must be absent from his pulpit for some time. Certain repeated attacks were diagnosed by the physicians as a form of heart trouble [angina pectoris] due to long continued and excessive work. The specialists who were consulted have insisted upon two or three weeks of rest and quiet followed by a few months of recuperation in a warmer climate. You will be glad to know, that a thorough examination of Dr. Tittle's heart shows that while it has been strained it has not been damaged and there is every reason to believe that sufficient rest will make it possible for him to enjoy many more years of Christian service."[73]

Monday night the Official Board drafted this message to their pastor: "The members of the Official Board, sitting in 'consultation' as lay doctors, have unanimously decided that you should get well soon,—but don't hurry! And to that end your prescription is as follows:—'Take a leave of absence for such time as may be necessary for your complete recovery; Take twice each month the usual salary check; CAUTION: Don't mix work with rest! And don't worry!' Our loyalty to the church is challenged to carry on in your absence. Be assured your people will not fail you. We will hold you in constant thought and affection, trusting that this separation may unite us all more closely in our common purpose."[74] The First Church fellowship also pressed a gift of $1,000 on their "dominie."

Tittle replied with transparent gratitude:

To All Members and Friends of First Church: I now know that a certain sum, fully adequate, has been deposited to my account; and that this has been done, thanks to your generosity and direction. What shall I say? My first impulse was to protest, which, in fact, I did; my thought being, But the *church* needs,

73. *Evanston Daily News-Index,* November 22, 1937, p. 1.
74. "A Message from the Official Board to Doctor Tittle," November 22, 1937, in Official Board Letterbook.

and should receive, this money. However, it was made abundantly clear to me—the speaker being a man who, on proper occasion, can and does speak forcibly—that it would be ungracious, not to say churlish, for me to refuse a gift so frought with good will and loving-kindness; and that, in any case, I would not be permitted, this time, to have my own way. (As if I were accustomed to have it!) So, with glad and thankful heart, I shall spend this money in an effort to get well; that I may again have the privilege and joy of being one of the active ministers of a church which, of all churches, is the one I would soonest serve. This week, Mrs. Tittle and I will go South, heartened by your many expressions of good will and thankful to God for every one of you.[75]

On December 15 Ernest and Glenna rolled southward to Miami aboard the *Seminole*. By January he was permitted to be out of bed four hours daily. By early February he was up most of the time, basking in the sun, walking a little, motoring along the beaches. In June the return was made to Evanston. July and August were continued months of rest. In mid-September Tittle was back in the pulpit, but for some time his activity was confined to the Sunday worship service, Mr. Clark carrying on the pastoral duties. More than a year later Tittle wrote a friend, "I am now making very real progress toward what promises to be a complete recovery. Nevertheless, I am bound to work within my physical limitations, which at the moment are rather considerable."[76]

Gradually nature worked her miracles of healing, gradually Tittle returned to a work schedule that to discerning observers seemed no lighter than before the attack. He took in stride even such a painful affliction as shingles, informing Bishop Charles Wesley Flint, "As for shingles, I feel bound to suppose that they are not data for the problem of evil but rather for the problem of good. The wonder is not that I have them but that a worse fate has not befallen me!"[77] Under doctors' orders he could no longer fly, but like every sensible man he had long preferred to travel by Pullman anyhow, finding on trainboard a rare opportunity to unwind. Also under doctors' orders he could no longer drive, but having a decent respect for the opinion (not to say safety) of mankind, he had long since turned that miserable chore over to Glenna.

75. *First Church Review*, XV (December 11, 1937), 1. Tittle also carried southward a check from a friend who observed from "personal experience" that when traveling "a little extra change in the pocket gives one a quiet feeling. . . . Please do not go to the trouble of answering this note. Conserve your strength and save your postage stamps." Letter from Haddon MacLean to Tittle, November 26, 1937.

76. Letter from Tittle to Thomas C. Clark, December 6, 1938.

77. Letter from Tittle to Bishop Charles Wesley Flint, March 20, 1942.

And from time to time he succumbed to that scourge of humanity, the "common" cold.

The years passed. There was the bother of taking thyroid tablets to raise his metabolism. And it was troublesome always to remember to carry those "T.N.T." pills should his heart again misbehave. And there was a minor rectal operation. Nevertheless, he could write to an old fishing pal in late 1945, "I am glad to report the best health I have had in ten years."[78] And he comforted a victim of heart disease: "Perhaps I may serve to demonstrate that an angina patient who *watches hi*⁻ *step* can not only last but can do as much work as he ever did. During the past two or three years I have been going the old gait."[79]

For a victim of angina he was too sanguine. In August, 1946, he was visiting Betsy and her family in Montana. He was alone. John, of course, was busy with his duties as breadwinner. Bill was concluding a long ordeal in a Civilian Public Service camp. Glenna, for the only time in her married life, was vacationing independently from her husband, in Mexico, with her sister. The fish in the Gallatin River were biting. Ernest wetted a line. He was an old pro at fishing—and at heart attacks. The warning signal thumped in his chest. He sat down on the bank. In time—and it must have seemed an eternity—his son-in-law came along. There were consultations with the local doctors. Shortly, the train carried him back to Evanston alone. The specialists called it a coronary occlusion. In only a few months he was back in the pulpit.

Mrs. Bernice Wolseley, his secretary for two decades and unquestionably the person closest to his thoughts, save only for Glenna, gave the following assessment of Tittle's attitude toward his health in the last years: "He faced his physical problems squarely, I am sure, as he did every fact with which he was confronted; he never tried to dodge the problem, was determined to carry on as long as he could, and made such concessions (in the way of avoiding physical strain, for example) as he felt he must to spin out his strength. The heart difficulty first appeared in 1937. . . . He made a remarkable recovery and got back to almost the old schedule for a number of years. He made a remarkable recovery, too, from an illness in the summer of 1946. In recent months he had known that his condition was not good; his reaction was the same as before—stay on the job. He was not afraid of the future. You can get that clearly by comparing his mood . . . with the knowledge he possessed concerning the progressing of his heart difficulty."[80] Shortly before the

78. Letter from Tittle to Harry C. Wilson, December 5, 1945.
79. Letter from Tittle to John L. Ferguson, July 5, 1945.
80. Letter from Mrs. Bernice Wolseley to Robert H. Hamill, October 4, 1949, quoted in letter from Hamill to author, September 14, 1959.

end, in a letter to a friend, he expressed an ageless hope: "As you may or may not know, I have heart trouble. I thought I had entirely recovered from the coronary occlusion of three years ago, but in May my 'ticker' began acting up again and by the first of June was cutting such capers that the doctor forbade me to leave town. . . . You will rejoice to know that a new drug which I am now taking is making a very real difference."[81] The new drug did not, after all, make a very real difference. In six weeks the final summons came.

Four days before his death, Tittle stood for the last time in the pulpit of First Church. In the course of the sermon, "Hope," he uttered a sentence as revealing as a mirror: "If I may be allowed a personal word, I may confess that I have learned more from three prolonged illnesses than I have ever been able to get from books."[82] Save only for his illnesses, in any objective sense Tittle's life had not been darkened by tragedy. He knew the love of a faithful, helpful, adoring woman who survived him. His three children were all physically and mentally healthy, who married happily and in turn had good families. There is no reason to suppose that John, Bill, or Betsy caused their father heartbreak or bitterness. Poverty did not scar Tittle and after 1918 never approached sufficiently close to scare him. Violence showed its face to him at only one moment in his life, at Saint Mihiel. He enjoyed honor, love, obedience, troops of friends. His star ascended steadily and it was at its zenith when he died. He escaped the darkness of old age. All that a man might reasonably hope for, he possessed. Thus, the tragic dimensions of life were revealed most fully to him in his illnesses—the nights when his tortured nerves denied him sleep, the sudden pain as though a giant hand were crushing his chest, the monotonous weeks of convalescence when he dared not stir, the sharp reminder that came to him when his hand accidentally brushed the box of glycerin pills in his pocket that all men die, and for him, no doubt, sooner rather than later. After his first attack, he said to Dr. Soper, "Ned, I'm not the same man you used to know. Now I've got some religion."[83] After his second attack he said to a friend, in attempting to explain the new depth of his preaching, "I had to get hold of something I could hang on to myself."[84] He wrote to a Methodist colleague: "I then decided [after an attack] that it was up to me to practice what I preached. So I did, one day, turn to God in trust, asking nothing for myself save only a continuing

81. Letter from Tittle to Frank J. Prout, June 22, 1949.
82. *A Mighty Fortress* (New York: Harper & Brothers, 1949), p. 174.
83. Author's interview with Edmund D. Soper, Evanston, Ill., August 5, 1959.
84. Author's interview with Horace G. Smith, Evanston, Ill., August 17, 1959.

sense of His nearness and the privilege of being used in some way as His servant. I did not undertake to inform the Lord that I ought to get well, or that I ought to be returned to the pulpit of the First Methodist Episcopal Church in Evanston. In fact (for the first time), I left all such details to Him. Today, though I cannot bring myself to tell anyone all that I have come to know and experience in consequence of this simple decision really to trust God, I may say to you that it has made a world of difference."[85] And even before his first heart attack, when in the traumatic years of the early 1930's he feared for his sanity and pressures threatened to overwhelm him, he "determined to find time every day, no matter how busy I might be, to 'practice the presence of God,' that is, to sit down, become quiet, and remind myself that God is; God, Christlike in character, slowly but surely working out his grand design; in his hands all I held dear safe, all that gives life meaning, all that is full of promise and glory, including every great cause in whose justice and importance I profoundly believe. . . . As many of you know, during the past two years I have enjoyed much better health than I have had in any period that I can remember. I have a peace of mind for which I have always striven and almost despaired of achieving. Here is a great discovery. This is the truth, and because I know now that it is the truth I could no sooner think of going without food or drink than I would of going without this daily practice of the presence of God. As a means of banishing fear, worry, a sense of stress and strain that becomes intolerable, as a means of maintaining courage and hope, there is just nothing comparable to it, at least in my experience."[86]

In an extraordinarily busy and useful life, perhaps it was in a moment of illness that Ernest Fremont Tittle first heard clearly the words, "Be still and know that I am God."

85. Letter from Tittle to Paul G. Perkins, January 20, 1942.
86. "The Great Physician," typed MS, a sermon preached March 17, 1935.

5. THE FIRST CHURCH FELLOWSHIP

I

On Sunday morning, December 1, 1918, Ernest Fremont Tittle preached his first sermon from the pulpit of the First Methodist Episcopal Church, Evanston, Illinois. It's title: "The New Day and the Men Who Make It."[1] The message of the buoyant, boyish-appearing new minister was one of challenge and confidence. Out of the night of world war there would dawn a new day bright with peace, brotherhood, and abundance, and he enjoined the congregation to work with God in fulfilling His will of a sweeter, fairer life for all mankind. On Sunday morning, July 31, 1949, Tittle preached his last sermon. It's title: "Hope." The message of the now aging, angina-afflicted veteran minister was yet one of triumph. "The servant of God may carry on in his day and generation in the quiet confidence that his labor is not in vain."[2] Must not one weep at the innocence of this man, smile at his fatuity, rage at his blindness? How could he speak of "hope" in 1949 when the new day promised in 1918 had been rather a long, dark, nightmare? How could he speak of "hope" when the men of his "day and generation" were new men only in the magnitude of their madness? How could he speak of "hope" after Hitler and Stalin, after Hiroshima and Nagasaki? And how could a generation that had both endured and inflicted an agony exceeding a million crucifixions listen to a proclamation of "hope" and not sigh, "Ah, the foolishness of preaching"? Above all, whence came the confidence that the labor of the servant of the Lord is not in vain?

1. *Evanston News-Index,* December 2, 1918, p. 1.
2. *A Mighty Fortress* (New York: Harper & Brothers, 1949), pp. 175-76.

It is important to seek to answer the last question first: does the servant of the Lord labor in vain? Let us draw the circle tighter: did Ernest Tittle labor in vain? And still tighter: did he labor in vain at First Church? To some readers, of course, the question will seem insignificant, for what difference does the fate of a few parishioners in a Chicago suburb make when our proper concern is "The Human Condition"? Should not the biographer omit the parochial, pastoral aspects of Tittle's ministry and concentrate on the large issues of economic justice, race relations, and world peace? Why bother with the lot of one congregation when our true interest is the Church Universal?

These are fair questions. Yet I am persuaded that if Tittle did not love the men and women in his own flock, his professions of love for broken humanity would be a mockery. If he had not faithfully ministered to his own people, his status as national church leader would be empty and his national honors tarnished. If love and justice were absent from the First Church fellowship, Tittle's prophetic preaching would be not so much foolish as monstrously hypocritical. The uniqueness and in large measure the greatness of Tittle's life lies in the fact that he was at once a prophet of towering national stature and also a working minister; and to grasp the significance of Tittle's witness to God's ever-coming Kingdom on earth it is first necessary to establish the authenticity of his pastoral ministry.

II

In this chapter we will attempt an imaginary reconstruction of the experiences of a boy and young man whose fortune it was to be in the First Church fellowship throughout the years of Tittle's ministry. Although this individual is fictitious, the experiences created for him were in fact those of First Church members; he is "true" to the extent that a composite picture is true.

In December, 1918, to a man and wife long members of First Church a son was born. Tittle was informed. He mounted his bike and peddled the chilly mile from First Church to the Evanston Hospital to visit the mother and child. He did not tire. The months in France had toughened his naturally muscular body. His mood was as ebullient as ever his sober temperment permitted. His new congregation had welcomed him warmly at official receptions and informally in their homes. Attendance at the services had been splendid. The newspapers reported that his initial sermons had "gone over big," and he was confident that his pulpit message was relevant to the new age. Moreover, Glenna, though originally opposed to leaving Columbus, now seemed happy with the move, and after an absence of six months it was heaven to be rejoined with her and John, Betsy, and Billy. To be sure, some of the older saints objected to what they deemed their pastor's undignified mode of transportation, but it was not until August, 1921, when his grateful congregation presented him with an automobile, that Tittle put his bike out to pasture. And it was not until 1924, when James V. Thompson became assistant minister, that he had someone to share the labors of pastoral calling, though earlier an old Dayton parishioner, Charles E. Lowe, had come to Evanston to assist in the capacity of executive secretary.

The mother welcomed the visit of her pastor, rejoicing in his little gift and in the handsome compliments he paid her infant son. Before leaving the hospital, Tittle made certain to drop in on several ailing parishioners. Returning to his office, he wrote several little notes. "Dear —— and ——," he greeted the happy parents, "Hurrah! Hurrah! Hurrah! Hurrah! Et cetera! And then some! Yours, now and evermore."[3] The infant also received a note of congratulations on his safe arrival in the world.

The birth of a child is a great moment in the life of a man and wife. Throughout Tittle's ministry couples were made aware of his involvement in their new happiness or, as sometimes happened when things went badly at the birth, in their grief. In later years his assistants often made the hospital visitations, but to the very end Tittle somehow found the time to pen a little note to the parents and perhaps to the infant and indeed occasionally to the grandparents.

The months passed. The infant grew. Palm Sunday approached and the parents were reminded of their duty to present their son for the sacrament of baptism, so that he might "be steadfast in faith, joyful through hope, and rooted in love, and may so overcome all evil that finally he may reign with thee, world without end, through Jesus Christ our Lord."[4] Tittle cut through the legalism surrounding the issue of

3. After much painful deliberation I have made the decision not to disclose in every case the names of those individuals to whom Tittle wrote and from whom he received letters touching on personal, private matters. I am persuaded that this decent veiling does not in a substantive sense violate the canons of scholarship. In no instance will a letter be altered or expurgated. Obviously in this chapter only a handful of the thousands of letters in the Tittle Collection will be quoted.

4. These words are from the old Methodist order for the administration of baptism to infants, the order followed by Tittle except for certain modifications, including the deletion of the phrase that the child may never run "into the evils of an unbridled appetite." This statement is based on a comparison of the order as it appears in Tittle's book of ritual and a typewritten manuscript entitled, "The Ritual used by Ernest Fremont Tittle," with the order as it appeared over the years in the Methodist *Discipline*. Moreover, Tittle wrote to Lester Auman,

baptism—a legalism he found appalling. "Think of Jesus saying," Tittle requested his congregation, " 'Suffer the little children to come unto me; forbid them not: for to such belongeth the kingdom of God.' Then think of a group of solemn-faced theologians and ecclesiastics deciding that a certain rite called baptism is so essential to the soul's eternal welfare that, unless it is administered, even innocent little babies will be forever damned. Would it ever have been possible for civilized persons to come to so grotesque a conclusion if only they had considered the implications of their own faith that God is like Jesus? How glad one is to learn that when, at last, a General Assembly was found with sufficient moral insight and moral courage to repudiate the doctrine of eternal damnation of unbaptized infants, one member rose up to move that the decision of the Assembly be made retroactive!"[5] Plainly Tittle did not hold baptism essential to salvation. He did, however, honor it as an outward and visible sign of an inward and spiritual grace, the entrance of the spirit of God into human life, and as an element in the larger design of Christian nurture whereby the child might be enabled to grow in grace. To Tittle, the presentation of a child for Christian baptism imposed upon the parents a solemn obligation. "Infant baptism," he wrote, "is an empty form unless parents thereby bind themselves to provide for the child a Christian home and instruction in 'things which a Christian ought to know and believe to his soul's health,' and unless 'the child is by baptism incorporated into the organism of the Church and made to share in its saving power.' "[6]

A day or so following the service he penned a note to the parents: "Dear——, It was an extraordinary pleasure for me to baptize——, who is certainly one of the sweetest packages that was ever brought into the world." And to the little child he wrote: "Dear——, This is to extend to you a most cordial invitation to come and discuss with me the foolishness of preaching or any other kind of foolishness that you have in

March 15, 1940, the following: "The baptismal service for children which we use at First Church, Evanston, is the one which appears in the old Discipline, changed, however, at the point where parents are told what is required of them. At this point, we use the text which appears in the new Discipline. The baptismal service which we use for adults is the last part (only) of the old and familiar service." In the early Evanston years it was Tittle's custom to baptize infants at the Palm Sunday morning worship service. Later this was done at a vesper service on Easter Sunday. Still later the sacrament was administered at a late afternoon service in the chapel on the last Sunday of each month.

5. *The Religion of the Spirit* (New York and Cincinnati, Ohio: Abingdon Press, 1928), pp. 45-46. See also "The God of Our Faith," *The First Church Pulpit*, Vol. IX, No. 14, a sermon preached February 22, 1948.

6. *The Gospel According To Luke* (New York: Harper & Brothers, 1951), p. 22.

or on or around your mind. I was delighted to be accorded the privilege of baptizing you, which gave me the rare joy of holding you in my arms for a minute. You were most gracious to allow me to do that and you gave me a moment of great happiness. You ask me whether I will be good enough to officiate at your wedding and I hasten to assure you that I am yours to command on that or any other occasion which is of importance to you." Although Tittle had been at First Church less than six months when he administered the sacrament of infant baptism on Palm Sunday, 1919, already the parents of the son born in December were reminded of Goldsmith's portrait of a preacher: "But in his duty prompt at every call, / He watched and wept and prayed and felt for all."

III

One of the scandals of modern American Protestantism is its failure to heed Saint Paul's injunction concerning children, "Bring them up in discipline and instruction of the Lord." Forced by historic circumstances to abandon revivalism as the prime means of bringing individuals to God, the evangelical churches largely botched the noble task of Christian nurture. It has been said that eleven o'clock Sunday morning is the most segregated hour in the week. With how much greater justice could it be said by those whose childhood memories are of the 1920's, 1930's, and 1940's that the Sunday School hour was for them the most wasted hour in the week—and this through no fault of their gentle teachers.

It is one of the glories of Tittle's ministry that a child reared in the First Church fellowship during these decades would immediately and perhaps angrily challenge this generalization, for his memories would be different. Church School at First Church (Tittle insisted that the term "Sunday School" give way to "Church School") was not simply a free baby-sitting service, though in fact one of Tittle's first actions was to institute a Cradle Roll Department to permit parents of infants to attend the morning worship service. Nor was it all picnics and hayrides and mid-winter sleigh rides, though in fact under church sponsorship the boys and girls had joyous times. Church School at First Church was anchored in a firmer foundation. "We wish our children and youth to have definite knowledge of the Christian faith and way of life, the Bible, Christian History, and the Church," stated the last of the several dedicated ministers of education to serve under Tittle. "We believe that religion is more than an inner attitude and a readiness to experiment; it involves knowledge and clear conviction, and without these we are not ready for life." We covet for our children, he continued, "a knowledge about Christianity, a personal life of fellowship with God, a genuinely Christian spirit and attitude in regard to personal goals and human relations, the achievement of the richest life . . . and a preparation for the largest service to others."[7]

One thing it meant to be a youngster in the First Church fellowship was to experience the corporate worship of God. Each age group had its own robed choir and its own worship committee. Encouragement was given to the composition of original prayers, hymns, and litanies. Throughout the later grades and high school, training was given in carrying out Orders of Worship; at least once each season Holy Communion was celebrated especially for them, the service being sung by the combined junior-high and high-school choirs. These choirs participated frequently in the worship of the total church—Palm Sunday, Easter, Pentecost, Christmas, Christmas Eve, New Year's Eve, Thanksgiving, and other special services, including Communion.

Another thing it meant was to acquire an objective knowledge of the Bible and the history of the Church and to move from that knowledge to commitment and from commitment to action. "To know about religion," declared a Church School bulletin, "has value only in order that we ourselves may know religion, that we may find the strength and confidence and courage for living which comes from God."[8]

A third thing it meant was to explore the meaning of Christian brotherhood. First Church children were not left unaware that poverty, exploitation, bigotry, and war blighted the world, nor of the Christian's responsibility to right these wrongs. They were expected to give to others—and give they did, $3,000 the last year of Tittle's ministry. (At this time, the child made a pledge and the amount he contributed became part of the total church budget.) And they stepped out of their little circle to worship and play with Negro and Jewish children in exchange programs extending over many years.

When the boy approached the age of decision he was placed in an instructional class for church membership, as Methodist discipline required. For several decades Tittle taught these classes, though toward the end this crucial duty was performed by an assistant. It was a solemn occasion when one Easter Sunday about his twelfth year the lad stood in the presence of the congregation, renewed his baptismal vow, confessed Jesus Christ his Lord and Savior, professed the Christian faith as contained in the New Testament, and pledged to uphold the Methodist

7. Charles H. Johnson, *First Church Review,* Special Activities Edition, October, 1948.
8. *Curriculum Outlines for the Church School,* undated typed MS, p. 3.

Episcopal Church. Perhaps he remembered (or more probably was reminded) of Wesley's statement that the children of Methodists are "the children of faith and of many prayers."

IV

In the mid-1920's the Dancing Masters' Association of America hoped to win Methodist approval for the Terpsichorean art by introducing a decorous step entitled the Wesleyan Waltz. According to the association, the partners were to follow a list of ten "don'ts." The editor of a Methodist paper added one more: "Don't dance."[9] The editor was voicing the official position of his church and the convictions of the overwhelming majority of Methodists in their middle years and older who had been reared in the nineteenth-century Methodist tradition of pietism and moralism. In 1930 the Official Board of First Church gave its approval to dancing by young people in the parish house. Paradoxically, the board in this action was both looking to the future in making an appeal to rising generations and also returning to the distant past and finding justification in the spirit of John Wesley's broad standard: the avoidance of only such diversions as cannot be taken in the name of the Lord Jesus.

The matter of dancing is, of course, only one facet of the larger issue: what diversions must a Christian avoid? Unhappily, the answer given by American Methodism until well into the twentieth century was as narrow as it was long. To be sure, it was right that a Christian be concerned with the question of how he employs his leisure. It was proper that he avoid brutalizing amusement. It was good that he enjoy recreation that re-creates rather than debilitates. It was fine that he not trifle away precious time. To be clean unto the Lord, to aspire to Christlikeness in thought, word, and deed are imperatives Methodism took seriously. Thus, when Methodists urged the avoidance of drinking, gambling, cockfighting, and prize fighting they were being true to a worthy heritage. However, when they proscribed such things as circuses, novel reading, the theater, all card games, and dancing, the result was a drab and dreary legalism as alien to Wesley's true intent as it was fatal to the future of Methodism.

A youngster raised in First Church worshiped, studied, served. He also played. In the church his body was exercised, his mind quickened, his morale lifted, his hunger for sheer fun fulfilled. He came to know in a quite literal sense the joy of Christian fellowship. First Church boys

9. See Robert Moats Miller, *American Protestantism and Social Issues, 1919-1939* (Chapel Hill: The University of North Carolina Press, 1958), pp. 18-20.

and girls regularly suppered together Sunday evenings. They picnicked and beach partied, they ice-skated and tobogganed, they sneezed on hayrides and froze on sleigh rides. They sang, staged dramatic productions, read and discussed novels, saw and analyzed serious movies, visited museums and art galleries. Talented youth found satisfaction in the junior orchestra. First Church had Boy and Girl Scout troops and boy and girl basketball, volleyball, and bowling teams. And finally in 1930 it became possible to dance and play cards in the parish house. This action is significant, not because these diversions are necessarily meritorious, but because in sanctioning them First Church broke from Methodism's rigid posture that had made it in the minds of many Americans synonymous with comstockery.

In answer to one of many letters of criticism, Tittle defended the relaxation of the rules:

> . . . let me ask you to consider the fact that the modern church is obliged to deal with a generation which almost universally indulges in such amusements as dancing and playing cards. Not only our boys and girls but our young married people and many of our middle-aged folk do, as a matter of fact, play cards in one another's homes and dance in such places as the Woman's Club of Evanston and in the hotels of Chicago. My own belief is that the time has come when the church, instead of taking merely a negative attitude toward such amusements ought boldly to undertake to see to it that they are indulged in under proper conditions. In doing so the church will not only retain the interest and affection of this present generation but render to it a very much needed service. The fundamental question is, of course, Are such amusements as dancing and playing of cards inherently wrong? If they are, the church cannot afford on any account to endorse them. If, however, they are not inherently wrong, the church can greatly help by controlling the conditions under which they are indulged in. My own belief is now and has for many years been that they are not inherently wrong but that they do need to be controlled and that the church, if only it has the wisdom and courage to do so, is of all organizations the best fitted to control them.[10]

Thereafter First Church teenagers, young adults, and young married couples held some lively parties. The most successful and significant ones were those held on New Year's Eve, beginning in 1939. These gala affairs annually attracted some five hundred young people. Beginning at 9:00 P.M. and ending at 2:00 A.M., the participants dined on a three-course turkey supper, danced to the music of a local orchestra, watched

10. Letter from Tittle to J. P. McLaughlin, January 26, 1931.

a gay show produced by First Church members, and at midnight engaged in a grand jollification of popping balloons, absurd noise makers, and a heartfelt singing of "Auld Lang Syne." Tittle explained the origin of the affair to a curious correspondent: "Some years ago I was besought by young people in our congregation for Pete's sake to do something about the New Year's Eve problem. They didn't have the ten or fifteen bucks needed to go to a Chicago hotel or night club, they told me, and, besides, they didn't like the drinking and obscenity which they found in such places. I therefore ventured to offer the kind of party I have described, the cost of which, in the first instance, I myself underwrote. (You will be interested to know that the party cost $490.10 and we took in $490.)"[11]

Though Tittle came in for his share of criticism in Methodist circles, many ministers faced with the problem of holding young people to the church were grateful for his example, saying, "Thank God for what First Church, Evanston, is doing."[12] The boy raised in the First Church fellowship might well have echoed this benediction. He loved his church for many reasons, not the least of them being that his church and his pastor did not insist that all joy be squeezed from boyhood.

V

The boy graduated from Evanston Township High School in 1936 and in the fall he entered Northwestern University located only a couple of blocks from First Church. As a member of the Methodist Student Foundation, on Sunday mornings he went to the John Evans Religious Center for breakfast and religious study. (College-age persons who were not Northwestern students met at First Church.) Then at eleven he walked to First Church. Like hundreds of his fellow students he continually experienced a sense of renewal when he entered the sanctuary. The beauty of the building, the majesty of the ritual, the power of the sermon came to have heightened meaning for him, living as he did the fervid and feverish life of an undergraduate.

Being a home-town boy he was not as lonesome as most, yet he thanked God for the fellowship afforded by First Church. He did not consider himself a Pecksniff, but because he did not drink and because he did not count chastity a curse, like-minded companions were not always easy to encounter on campus. And so on Sunday evenings he met with several hundred college-age young people (who were not necessarily

11. Letter from Tittle to J. A. Downey, September 11, 1944.
12. A Methodist minister quoted by Tittle in a letter to Golder Lawrence, February 26, 1943.

Methodists) in the church to dine, sing, debate, study, or worship. He looked forward keenly to the Friday night parties in the parish house and to the Saturday afternoon picnics followed by supper and songs and bull sessions around a blazing fire. It was fun to go with the gang downtown to an opera or play. It was good to work out with the First Church athletic teams. It was fine to blow the French horn in the First Church Little Symphony orchestra and to appear in dramatic productions and (perhaps best of all) to whisper in a pretty girl's ear at the church dances.

Over the thirty-one years of Tittle's pastorate thousands of Northwestern University students found in the First Church fellowship an escape from dispiriting loneliness and an alternative to the prevailing off-campus social life of booze and bundling. The young men and women in the First Church college fellowship not only were assured wholesome recreation but may possibly have experienced more joyous times than their allegedly sophisticated peers.

VI

One day during his senior year the young man called the First Church office to make an appointment through Mrs. Wolseley, the secretary, to see Tittle. He wished to consult with his pastor about a question that could no longer be dodged: "What shall I do with my life?" Mrs. Wolseley scheduled a late afternoon meeting. Later she informed "the chief" of his appointment on the private line between the church office and his home study where he generally spent his precious free hours. Having calls channeled through the office spared Tittle much seepage of time and was an even greater boon to Glenna, whose days prior to the private line were consumed in answering the relentlessly ringing telephone. Late afternoon was the customary hour for pastoral counseling, though Tittle firmly commanded his secretaries to make an immediate appointment if the matter was urgent.

The hour for the appointment arrived and Tittle endeavored to answer the youth's question. The answer was a distillation of what he had said (and was to continue to say) in innumerable sermons, lectures, addresses, and articles. To begin with, Tittle recognized that most men must labor hard to make their way in the world. "For the ordinary man life largely revolves around the problems of money," he said. "Earning a livelihood, making ends meet, providing for the contingencies of illness, accident and old age—these for the ordinary man are urgent matters not to be neglected except on pain of disaster for himself and his family. Jesus recognized this. A surprising amount of his teaching is devoted to the problems of money. And here as elsewhere what he has to say is of the greatest importance. Jesus does not belittle the material. We are to pray for daily bread as well as for forgiveness. He does not decry working, saving, looking ahead, the absence of which simply means that others will have to look out for us or our family."[13] Because most men spend most of their waking hours on the job or commuting to and from work, Tittle also pointed out that

> a man actually becomes what he seeks and does in daily work
> . . . . A man's primary obligation to society is to do well the
> work that is his to do. There are, to be sure, other ways in which
> he may serve. He may help to raise money for such community-
> serving agencies as schools, churches, hospitals, boys' clubs and
> social settlements. He may, perhaps, be accorded the opportunity
> of serving as a trustee of some university or philanthropic foun-
> dation. But his primary obligation is simple fidelity in daily
> work . . . . There was something wrong with the old Sunday-
> school story about the cobbler who, when asked what his business
> was, said: "My business is saving souls, but I mend shoes to
> pay expenses." A cobbler's first business is not saving souls. It
> is saving feet. Let him do a good job in mending shoes and he
> may, perhaps, be used of God to save somebody's soul; whereas if
> he bilks his customers with poor leather or poor workmanship
> his attempt to save their souls will be an impertinence which they
> may well resent.[14]

Thus the youth was warned that he could not hope to compartmentalize his life, following pagan practices in his work while holding fast to the Christian ethic in his private conduct.

This thought led Tittle to a discussion of a matter about which he felt intensely: One of the most terribly mistaken notions that has ever crept into human thinking is the notion that a few occupations are sacred and all others secular:

> At Christian student conferences some thirty years ago there was
> always at least one meeting devoted to the life-work question.
> The various choices were presented in a certain order: first busi-
> ness, then law, then medicine, then teaching, then the ministry,
> and finally the foreign missionary enterprise. This order of pre-
> sentation was deliberate and intentional. It was intended to sug-
> gest that if you chose business or law or medicine or teaching you
> might hope, even so, to do *some* good in the world, but not
> nearly as much good as you could have hoped to do had you
> chosen to enter the ministry or, better still, to go as a missionary

13. *Mighty Fortress*, p. 55.
14. *Ibid.*, pp. 127-28.

to some foreign field. Well, it is, I think, a sign of progress—and not the least—that this evaluation of human vocations has been challenged and repudiated by increasing numbers of people. We have come to see that what is of greatest importance is not the vocation we choose but the personal aims and ambitions with which we pursue our vocation, whatever it may be. In business, in law, in medicine, in teaching, a man may be a minister rendering valiant service to the community and, incidentally, getting a big kick out of it. Yes, and in the ministry a man may be a self-seeker, concerned chiefly with his own security, popularity, and advancement.[15]

At this point Tittle stated one of his deepest convictions: "The money standard of success is pitiful. It plays into the hands of pride, greed, selfishness, and snobbery. It condemns the multitude of men to a most bitter sense of frustration and inferiority; they have really no chance to succeed in a competitive struggle for money and power. And the relatively few who in such a struggle do manage to 'succeed' may hardly be listed among the truly great of their day and generation. Not to be envied is *he who lays up treasure for himself, and is not rich toward God.'* "[16] And again:

We do not fear death half so much as we fear failure. We can be reconciled to the certainty that we shall one day die, but never to the possibility that we will end up a failure. Well, there is, of course, no escape from the dread of failure so long as you think of success in terms of material wealth or of business or professional standing. We cannot all make a lot of money. We cannot all reach the top in the business or professional world. Moreover, the desire to outstrip others in the race for money and position has worked havoc in our society. It has played into the hands of greed, selfishness, and insincerity. It has infected children with false notions and standards. It has filled the world with fear, mistrust, cynicism, bitterness, and resentment. It has blocked the way to world order and peace. One thing now desperately needed is a different standard of success—the standard lifted up by Jesus when he said: "Whoever would be great among you must be your servant."[17]

Jesus bids us to pray for daily bread, said Tittle, "but it is bread that we are bidden to pray for, not cake."[18]

15. "What Do We Want?" in *Christian Vocation: A Series of Radio Sermons.* . . . . (Boston and Chicago: The Pilgrim Press, 1945), p. 54.
16. *Gospel According To Luke,* p. 137.
17. *Ibid.,* pp. 98-99.
18. *The Lord's Prayer* (New York and Nashville, Tenn.: Abingdon-Cokesbury, 1942), p. 80.

These were the thoughts Tittle shared with the young man who sought advice on what he should do with his life. Labor is an essential part of life; a man's job and how he performs it shapes the sort of person he becomes; all honest occupations, however menial, are honorable; the prevailing standard of success is false and cruel; the passionate pursuit of money is perilous to spiritual growth; great wealth does not bring happiness; nations as well as men have been brought to destruction through a lust for profits and power; he who would serve God must serve his fellow man. Though Tittle's thoughts were neither very original nor profound, they were nonetheless good, hard words. They were words that went against the grain of American life. They were words not easy to honor in a hard-driving society where a man's salary was the yardstick of his success. They were words that challenged the American Dream with a nobler vision.

Tittle's advice to the young man was, however, not fully relevant to the economic conditions of mid-century America. To assert that the sewer digger "derives no little satisfaction from the knowledge that 'his digging is a vital part of public health' " is fatuous.[19] Increasingly in a rationalized economy men found their jobs without meaning because they were in fact meaningless, devoid of challenge, variety, appeal to the instinct of craftsmanship, and, indeed, without social worth; increasingly the "dignity of labor" became a cant phrase. To maintain that hard work is meritorious is scarcely illuminating to men in an age of automation who are told that a thirty-hour work week is inevitable. Nowhere does Tittle face up to the fact that in modern society many men are doomed to leisure. Historically Americans had been defined and had defined themselves by their jobs. Tittle had little to say about the fact that technology was rendering this definition less and less valid.

VII

The young man graduated in June, found employment in Chicago (with Tittle's recommendation), and continued to live in Evanston; therefore First Church continued to be his church home. He joined the First Church Post Kollege Klub, first organized on Tittle's suggestion in 1933 (and later known as the Delta Club). Despite the too-cute spelling, the "Klub" was a source of much joy to the young unmarried adults of the North Shore, for the immediate post-college years can be as cold and lonely as the far side of the moon; old friends scatter and girls once available for a Saturday night date become suddenly and unaccountably

19. "Success," *The First Church Pulpit*, Vol. VIII, No. 12, a sermon preached February 10, 1946.

married. In the group he found companions who rejoiced in serious discussion, reveled in the encounter of ideas, and found the configuration of ice and skates more fun than that of ice and gin. The group met regularly for study, discussion, worship, and sheer play, happily blending high jinks with high purpose. In a sophisticated age and community, the Post Kollege Klub shone like a jewel in a toad's head. Tittle probably did not know the lines of Bertold Brecht, "If you crammed a ship full of human bodies til it burst, the loneliness inside it would be so great that they would turn to ice . . . so great is our isolation," but he did comprehend human loneliness and he strove to make First Church a warming fellowship melting the ice of human isolation.

Not the least of the reasons the young man found the club appealing was the presence of a number of personable members of the gentler sex. In truth, the club rather gained the reputation of a matrimonial bureau. One girl in particular charmed him. She was not a Methodist. Her first introduction to First Church had been through the Business and Professional Women's Group, another one of the many organizations instituted by Tittle to serve the community and answer a need. In fact, the first meeting of the society was held in the parsonage shortly after Tittle's arrival in Evanston, thereafter meeting regularly in the parish house. Composed of working women of all faith, it became one of the most vigorous and worthwhile civic clubs on the North Shore.

One day in the fall of 1940 Tittle noticed in *The Evanston Review* the announcement of the engagement of the two young people who had met in the Post Kollege Klub. Immediately he dictated a note to the lad: "Dear ——, I am rejoicing to learn of your engagement to that lovely girl. . . . You are, as you have always been, a lucky dog. God bless you!" Soon thereafter the pair made known to Tittle their wish to be married in the First Church chapel and their hope that he would perform the ceremony. In point of fact, they were unwilling to set the date until they received his assurance that he would be in town and able to act as officiating minister. The assurance was forthcoming: "Dear ——, I'll be there with bells on. Congratulations!" It is a tribute to Tittle's hold on the young people in his church that numbers of them, particularly the girls, would not consider being married by anyone other than he, and more than one wedding date was synchronized with his crowded schedule. (Tittle performed on the average about fifty or sixty weddings annually.)

Some weeks before the wedding Tittle called the couple to his office for a talk, as he endeavored to do with all young people planning marriage. His manner was grave; his words serious. For one thing, marriage was meant to be a permanent union of one man and one woman until death. "It is possible," he said, "to overstate the piety and morality of an era that looked upon divorce as a disgrace but countenanced no little cruelty in marital relations. It is also possible to overstate the enlightenment of an era in which divorce, so far from being looked upon as a disgrace, is coming to be regarded as one of those things, you know, which though doubtless to be regretted, really cannot be helped."[20] Nevertheless, Tittle did not place an absolute prohibition on divorce. "In some cases, divorce is almost certainly the lesser of two evils: to maintain a 'union' that has in fact ceased to exist would mean not only intense suffering but an intolerable violation of the sanctities of life, and might well mean serious illness, physical and mental."[21] And so in exceptional cases Tittle would solemnize the marriage of a divorced person as permitted under the laws of the Methodist Church. As he interpreted the Methodist discipline, "I do not marry divorced persons whose divorce has been obtained merely on the grounds of incompatibility. I do marry divorced persons in cases where the ground for divorce was actual (not legal) cruelty, or habitual drunkiness [sic] or adultery, or deliberate and prolonged desertion. I do not marry persons whose parents have not been informed of their intention to marry."[22]

Though no marriage was without some friction, Tittle believed that it was within the family relationship that a man could be his best self and know the purest love. Jesus' teaching, he pointed out, "is full of tender allusion to family life; and indeed, what he saw of life within the home largely determined his faith about God and man and human destiny. When he is asked to suggest a pattern for prayer, he advises, 'Pray like this: Our Father, who art in heaven.' When he undertakes to show forth the relation of God to men, he tells the story of a loving father dealing with a prodigal son. And it is in terms of family life that he envisages the relations among men that will obtain in the blessed kingdom of God. No higher tribute to the family could be paid than the value put upon it by Jesus."[23] Tittle shared in a widespread and oft-expressed judgment when he stated: "In the organization of the home there is nothing which stands in the way of life on the Christian level, nothing that makes it desperately difficult, if not impossible, to practice unselfishness and loving-kindness, nothing that prevents intelligent co-

20. "The Christian Home," typed MS, a sermon preached December 7, 1941.
21. *Gospel According to Luke,* p. 177.
22. In a personal letter in reply to a private inquiry.
23. "The Supreme Loyalty," *The First Church Pulpit,* Vol. IX, No. 9, a sermon preached March 2, 1947.

operation for the common good. For most of us it is far easier within
the home than it is outside the home to be a Christian."[24] It would seem
truer to say (although it is in fact seldom said) that it is far easier within
the home to be either a saint or a sinner. The home provides the opportunity and the setting for husbands, wives, and children to brutalize,
tyrannize, exploit, debase, and torture each other physically and mentally
as they would not dare to do outside the family. A child is beaten—not
by a stranger but by father or mother. A murder is committed—more
often in the home by the victim's spouse than on the streets by a
stranger. A woman is cursed obscenely—by her husband, not her neighbor. A man is emasculated—not by a surgeon's scalpel but by a wife's
scorn. It is often stated that in the brutal outside world a man must
become Mr. Hyde to survive, reverting to good Dr. Jekyll when he
returns to the bosom of his family. Yet it would seem that not infrequently the opposite is true: among neighbors, friends, and business
associates the man dons the mask of civility and repression, revealing
only to his family his naked savagery.

Regarding marriage, Tittle recognized, as not all Christian churchmen have done, that it was a union of whole persons; and consequently
he acknowledged the fact of human sexuality. He said, "If, being a
normal person, we crave the intimate companionship of marriage, body
and soul, then we must be quite frank about it in any conversation we
may have with ourselves and not try to make out that anything as
primitive as the sex urge could not possibly belong to us."[25] I have had
occasion to read thousands of sermons by scores of Protestant ministers
and know that regarding the subject of human sexuality some clergymen
remain prudishly silent, others reveal an interest suspiciously obsessive
and in fact prurient, and yet others affect a bluff breeziness and false
urbanity. None of these observations can justly be made of Tittle. It
cannot be maintained, however, that he advanced in his sermons and
writings a fully articulated philosophy of Christianity and sex, such as a
number of churchmen have attempted, especially in the 1950's and
1960's. Tittle refers to the subject on several dozen instances, but never
in detail or depth.

Tittle held that sexual intercourse could be legitimate only within the
context of marriage and could be meaningful only in the context of the
total love held by a man and wife for each other. It was an encounter

24. *Christianity and the Family,* a sermon preached November 24, 1935
(pamphlet).

25. "Self-Mastery," *The First Church Pulpit,* Vol. VIII, No. 15, a sermon
preached March 24, 1946.

between two persons involving their whole selves, not simply their physical selves. Unlike some Freudians who present an "orificial" view of man, Tittle saw the "whole" man. He firmly counseled premarital chastity. One of the major reasons he instituted for young people a full church program of worship, study, sports, and play was so that they might weather the sexual storms assailing them, storms made especially cruel because of the sex-saturated movies, magazines, books, and advertisements from which there was no place to hide. For youngsters to drink cokes and dance in the parish house was in modern America about the only alternative to their drinking from flasks in a parked and darkened car. More than any culture in all history, modern America permits the titilation of its youth (indeed, such are the profits involved that it encourages the excitation of its youth) without sanctioning any form of release. When a Northwestern co-ed wrote Tittle lamenting that there were no chaste and high-minded boys who were not also "drips," Tittle replied that this "simply is not true. I myself know literally scores of young men who have what the Bible beautifully calls clean hands and a pure heart, and they are from every standpoint the most desirable young men whom I know." He continued: "One thing to remember about promiscuity in sexual relationships is the fact that what it represents is not any great spiritual achievement but a very primitive and, indeed, animalistic phenomenon. It is not 'modern,' it is not in the way of progress. On the contrary, it is a throw-back to barbarism. . . . I am personally convinced that it will presently give way to a more intelligent, a more civilized conception. Meanwhile, it is, I think, incumbent upon all high-minded people to resist it in the name of what, deep down in our hearts, we all know represents a nobler and more satisfying relationship between the sexes."

As Tittle commended chastity before marriage, so he enjoined faithfulness after marriage. He did not insist that sexual intercourse be indulged in solely for the purpose of procreation. Indeed, with his denomination and Protestantism generally he endorsed family planning. Nowhere in his writings did he intimate that the act of love between man and wife was a base (but probably inevitable) surrender to the coarser instincts; he did not as so many clergymen of his generation view sex as an enemy. Rather, promiscuity was the enemy. "It leads only to disillusionment, boredom, and disgust. It did so yesterday. It does so today. It will do so tomorrow and evermore."[26] As to faithfulness, "Is that man-made morality and, as some insist, a harsh, ill-considered

26. *A Way To Life* (New York: Henry Holt & Co., 1935), p. 41.

attempt to impose upon human nature an unnatural obligation and restraint? On the contrary, it is not a discovery which, after centuries of experimentation and bitter disillusionment, man finally made concerning the one only relationship between the sexes that offers a real and lasting opportunity for stability, happiness, and spiritual development?"[27] Tittle was disturbed but not dismayed by the sexual revolution seemingly sweeping the Western world. "Moral law," he said, "does not depend for its existence on the number of people who recognize and obey it. If every man and woman on earth should one day decide that promiscuity in sex relations is 'all right,' that would not make it right, any more than an overwhelming vote to suspend or abolish gravitation would make it safe to leap from an eight story window. Moral law, no less than physical law, belongs to the nature of things, is something *given* in the very structure of life, something which we men and women can choose to disregard but cannot get away from nor disregard with impunity."[28]

In stating the case for faithfulness and against promiscuity Tittle might have probed more deeply. He displayed little understanding of the factors in modern life that made sex seem to be the one natural thing left in an artificial world; or how in an increasingly institutionalized, collectivized, mechanized, and externalized society a man might look to sex for reassurance that he was alive; or why in a faceless, nameless age a man having been robbed of his identity by the state, corporation, and computer might seek to discover himself in the one remaining area of individual freedom, his sex life. It was in a thoughtful mood that David Riesman termed sex "The Last Frontier." Furthermore, many mid-century men, once true believers, felt betrayed by the causes to which they had dedicated themselves, and in their new disenchantment (or wisdom, as they maintained) they turned to the quest for personal fulfillment, satisfaction, and happiness. The slogan, "Make love, not war," is really a commemoration to those millions of twentieth-century individuals who meaninglessly sacrificed themselves in the name of a larger loyalty—the party, the fatherland, the cause, the movement, the revolution, the crusade, the true faith. More and more the sexual revolution of today seems to be a way of getting even with an enslaving civilization. As Horace Walpole asked two centuries ago, "When will the world know that peace and propagation are the two most delightful things in it?"

27. *Ibid.*, pp. 41-42.
28. "Peace of Mind," *The First Church Pulpit,* Vol. IX, No. 22, a sermon preached July 25, 1948.

There is a final thing to be said concerning Tittle's view of human sexuality. The text is a passage from his first book: "Consider the case of a gently nurtured and fine-spirited woman who discovers, too late, that her husband is a beast. As he sits in her presence, dazed by liquor, or consumed by lust, every spiritual thing in him submerged, her soul writhes in anguish; she is *wounded* by his transgressions."[29] To repeat a point made earlier, Tittle did not view sex as an enemy; he would not prohibit the sexual act when conception was not the purpose. He repeatedly denied that Jesus was a frightened or embittered ascetic holding marriage merely a concession to the flesh. He repeatedly affirmed that one of Christianity's glorious achievements was to elevate women from the status of things to that of persons. He always held that sex is a gift of God, a good and natural impulse when fulfilled within the context of marriage. Nevertheless, Tittle's occasional sermonic references to husbands "consumed by lust" or following the "awful courses of lust and perversion" might have troubled a few of the husbands and wives seated together before him. Is it not possible that some husbands felt a heightened sense of shame for the intensity and urgency with which they approached the nuptial bed? Is it not possible that some wives, incapable themselves of finding joy in the sexual encounter, were confirmed in their suspicions that they were married to "beasts"? At precisely what temperature does a husband become "consumed by lust"? What precisely is the proper sexual response of a "gently nurtured" wife? Doubtless many marriages are wrecked on the shoals of lust, as Tittle warned. But Tittle had nothing to say about those other marriages made damp, gray, leaden, and sullen because in the bedroom the sun was never permitted to shine intensely, where instead a dispiriting drizzle prevailed.

Perhaps Tittle spoke of these things as he chatted with the couple in his office. He knew the young man well, of course, and as the conversation continued he became increasingly convinced that the lad had selected a splendid mate. It was clear that the two shared a common view of the universe. In considering a wife, Tittle often said in a paraphrase of G. K. Chesterton, the really important question is not, "Can you cook?" or "Are you a good housekeeper?" but, "What is your view of the universe?" And he was once again reminded of the dictum of Walter Rauschenbusch, "Nothing will shrivel the idealistic conceptions of life in a young man as thoroughly as love for a selfish woman." Manifestly the woman before him was not selfish, and the final plans for the wedding proceeded smoothly, save at one point where she wished slightly

---

29. *What Must the Church Do to Be Saved?* (New York and Cincinnati, Ohio: Abingdon Press, 1921), pp. 95-96.

to alter the Methodist ritual by the incorporation of parts of the Quaker ceremony; but Tittle dissuaded her, insisting that the Methodist service was virtually perfect as it stood and terming the old (1932) Order for the Solemnization of Matrimony "quite the most beautiful Order in existence."[30]

On Saturday afternoon several weeks later the wedding group assembled in the new First Church chapel, a Gothic gem of architectural award-winning loveliness. A major argument advanced by Tittle for the construction of a chapel was the fact that many couples who desired a simple wedding found the sanctuary too large and too expensive to decorate. The chapel was much in demand by Methodist and non-Methodist couples whose tastes did not require or whose checkbooks could not sustain an elaborate ceremony. A small group of close friends and relatives did not feel lost in a chapel seating 250; a couple of ushers could manage nicely; and a few simple flowers only were most appropriate.

It was in this setting that the young man and woman vowed to live together after God's ordinance in the holy estate of matrimony. Tittle administered the ceremony with solemnity. There could have been no doubt in the couple's mind that this was a most sacred moment. If at the conclusion the couple kissed, it was but lightly and briefly, for Tittle "objected to the kiss following the vows since this tended to subjugate the God-centered ceremony somewhat to the desires of man."[31]

VIII

After their honeymoon the bride and groom returned to Evanston where they eased into married life in one of the many new apartment buildings now crowding the proud old mansions and disfiguring once-lovely meadow lands. Sunday after Sunday they found continuing inspiration, courage, and comfort in the First Church worship service. And when they called First Church their church home they did so with affection and appreciation. One of the facts about Tittle's ministry most heartening is the esprit de corps of the young married couples of First Church. Many churches are blessed with loyal aged members. Many have a large middle-aged membership. Less common but not unknown are congregations with an active body of students. First Church, of course, could lay rightful claim to attracting all these age groups. But it is doubtful if any parish excelled the ability of First Church under Tittle

30. Letter from Tittle to Oscar T. Olson, August 8, 1941.
31. Letter from Mrs. Roscoe Page to author, undated. One of the Page's sons was married to a Quaker girl by Tittle.

to capture the hearts and command the devotion of men and women in their twenties, thirties, and early forties. Couple after couple now in their middle and late middle years have testified to the joy they found in the First Church fellowship during their early married life. The greenness of their memories is extraordinary. Friendships formed then lasted a lifetime. Somehow a spirit of camaraderie was generated that never entirely cooled. Somehow Tittle managed to create a magic mood among the young married couples in First Church that led many of them years later to say, "That was a good time in our lives."

From the very beginning of his Evanston pastorate Tittle made manifest his intense interest in the young married people, as indeed he had done in Ohio. Shortly after arriving he and Glenna held a party in the parsonage with the avowed purpose of bringing the young couples together. Tittle found some two hundred such couples claiming First Church as their home. Many of them had come from small towns to settle in the Chicago area. They were desperately lonely. And so a young married people's fellowship was formed taking several names over the years and ultimately becoming known as the Mr. and Mrs. Club. In the early days there were Bible classes, wiener roasts on the beach, mixed baseball games, and round-robin singing. As the decades passed the programs became more sophisticated, but even in 1949 there were picnics and beach parties, scavenger hunts and nickelodeons, progressive dinners and barn dances.

The group our young couple joined in 1940 was called the Fortnightly Forum. First conceived in 1933, Tittle believed the Forum to be "infinitely promising." The promise was fulfilled, Tittle considering it one of the key measures of his ministry. In the Fortnightly Forum the couples met in each other's homes on alternate Sunday evenings to consider the relevance of Christianity to modern life. At the meetings one or two couples who had made special preparation on a given theme led off the discussion, after which everyone joined in. "The Third Term," "Lend Lease," "Why Socialized Medicine?," "Progressive Education," "Latin America in 1940," "Social Security," were typical topics. Perhaps one of the reasons for the success of the Forum is the fact that although young people hunger for serious discussion, conversation in young married circles is generally governed by the motto, "Let's keep it innocuous." Moreover, many young adults rejoiced in the opportunity given by the Forum to face the question: "How may young married people, attempting 'to get a start in the world,' make a Christian impact upon that portion of the world which they meet in business, professional, and social relationships?"[32] The group further engaged in varied service work such as sending CARE packages to Europe, contributing time and money to the local Negro hospital, and establishing a cooperative store.

In addition to the Fortnightly Forum, the wife found companionship in the Junior Guild, the group in the Women's Union (after 1940 the Woman's Society of Christian Service) designed for all women of the church under thirty-five. In the Guild she participated in numerous service projects and enjoyed many social activities. For his part, the young husband found additional fellowship in the Men's Club (originally the Men's Union), a club long established but revitalized under Tittle.

The young married couples rejoiced in the many parties sponsored by First Church. Whether held in the parsonage, parish house, Evanston Women's Club, or homes of individual members, these parties were often imaginatively conceived, carefully planned, and joyfully consummated. The Olde Mediaeval Feaste and Yuletide Jollyte was an annual event at which a Lord of Misrule, with his Jesters, Minstrels, and Heralds, guided the evening's festivities following the traditional boar's head banquet. Each fall there was a Harvest Home party in Great Hall with much singing, square-dancing, and jollification. Each spring there was an all-church frolic with imaginative themes.

So it was that young married couples found in their First Church home those things which make for a true home—warmth, joy, companionship, laughter, love. And it is paradoxical but true to say that Tittle was a wonderful host. It is paradoxical because, as we know, his prevailing mood was serious and introspective, because his one passion was work, because he was a lonely and sensitive man. It is true because at church parties he was a genial fellow, radiating high spirits, ready to throw back his head to roar with laughter or belt out a song, and capable of such Keystone Comedy jinks as adorning a companion's face with a whole pie. And how he chuckled at one party when one of the female pillars of the church introduced herself to the new assistant minister, Arthur T. Clark, saying, "Mr. Clark, I am Mrs. Ulysses S. Grant." "Oh," came the reply, "well, then, I am Mr. Abraham Lincoln." "Young man," snapped Mrs. U. S. Grant, for such indeed was her name, "I *am* Mrs. Ulysses S. Grant!" "And I," insisted the new minister, "*am* Abraham Lincoln." This exchange went on for some time with growing heat until an excruciatingly embarrassed Mr. Clark was gently assured by Tittle that he *was* talking with Mrs. Grant.

The tempering of certain rules existing when Tittle came to Evanston contributed to the relaxed mood of the First Church social occasions and

32. Letter from Tittle to Mrs. Paul Gorby, October 18, 1933.

to their variety. For one thing, when the Official Board voted in 1930 to permit dancing in the parish house it also sanctioned card-playing in designated areas. Initially benefit card parties were disallowed, but this prohibition was raised by action of the Official Board on September 26, 1932. Needless to say, playing cards for stakes was not permitted. At the time the matters of dancing and cards were passed on, a motion to permit smoking in the basement recreation room was defeated by a two-to-one vote. However, after long consideration and much debate, on July 6, 1936, the Official Board approved, by a vote of twenty-six to eight, to allow smoking in one or two basement rooms, the dining room, and Great Hall on the occasion of a banquet. In this action the Board made it clear that it was not endorsing the smoking habit, but merely acknowledging the gloomy fact that some adults were addicted to tobacco.

One of Tittle's closest friends, Halford E. Luccock, in describing a fashionable, successful, institutional church, bit out the words: "Isn't it lovely? Such a church resembles nothing so much as a sun parlor of a large country club, or the perfumed rose room of a large hotel. It is the church with the engine lifted entirely out of it. It shows a remarkable lack of penetration into the real issues of life in the world today, to imagine that such a little esthetic paradise can ever speak healingly to the world's need and tragedy. . . . A pink-tea church will never do. . . . The world is not saved by 'pretty' religion. Jesus died on a Cross and men who have carried His spirit into the world are men who had a profound religion, based on the proclamation of great truths that went to the very center of life."[33] Because First Church was in fact an institutional church, and a very "successful" one at that, because in this chapter much has been said about the social aspects of the First Church fellowship, because dancing, bridge-playing, New Year's Eve parties, and Mediaeval Feastes have been mentioned, perhaps the impression has been given that Tittle's church was one of those "pink-tea" parishes with "the engine lifted entirely out of it." Not so! No man was more critical than Tittle of "churches that resemble nothing so much as a motion picture palace . . . trying to stimulate jaded appetites of weary worldlings by offering to them on Sundays the same sort of pabulum which they have set before them on week days"; no minister was more convinced than he that it was his duty to make known that "in our church there is to be public worship of God, and . . . everything we are going to do will be in the awestruck sense that he is there."[34] Tittle

33. New York *Christian Advocate,* CII (October 20, 1927), 1263.
34. *Evanston News-Index,* September 20, 1924, p. 1.

insisted only that in the First Church fellowship there be some time for sheer play and liberating joy.

IX

In 1941 the couple had their first child, a little girl. Because of mounting duties and his heart condition, Tittle no longer regularly visited new mothers in the hospital, this responsibility (and joy) being assumed by an assistant. However, Tittle did dictate a little note to the infant: "Dear Lynn Elizabeth——: What lovely names you have! Especially Elizabeth, which is the name my daughter bears, although she prefers to be called Betsy. But what, in this note, I want most to do is to congratulate you on the wisdom you have displayed in the selection of parents. Your father and mother are two of the dearest and finest people I know, and I have known them intimately. . . . You have everything in your favor—which means that there is resting upon you a certain obligation to do something worth while in the world. I am sure that you will not disappoint the many people who have earnestly prayed for your coming and who now rejoice in your presence. God bless you, little lady, now and always!" The grandmother also received a short message: "Dear ——: From grandparents to a grandparent, Congratulations! Mrs. Tittle and I are rejoicing with you in what we know is a great joy. What a privilege it is to live on not only in one's children but also in one's grandchildren!"

Even as the couple rejoiced in their new daughter, disaster struck. The man lost his job, the firm having to cut its labor force; unhappily, its products were not remotely associated with armaments. Tittle did what he could. The man was made to understand that he was not alone. Members of the congregation rallied around. The women of the church contributed gifts of food and clothing. The chairman of the finance committee ordered him to forget about his church pledge. Tittle had a special fund for emergency purposes and a loan was extended to meet the rent. It was hoped that the loan would be repaid when the man got back on his feet, but interest was not charged and no specific date was set for repayment. The check was accompanied by a note from Tittle: "I cannot begin to tell you how much I rejoice in the fact that the church . . . you . . . have so devotedly served for many years is now in a position to render this small service." A church committee on unemployment, established in 1930, attempted to find the man a job. The mother and baby received free medical care from a group of First Church physicians, these men donating their services to financially hard-pressed members of the congregation. Tittle made inquiries, by phone and letter, of friends in business, hoping that one of them might hire the man.

In this time of trouble for the young man, another blow fell. His father died after a cruel period of illness. In the terminal weeks, Tittle greatly comforted his stricken old parishioner. Though his schedule was intolerably crowded, though his doctors urged him to slacken his pace, to the very end of his ministry Tittle was at the bedside of the sick and the dying. The memorial service (Tittle was called on to conduct about forty annually) was simple yet not unstately; the spirit one of thanksgiving and triumph revealing of Tittle's faith in the Risen Lord.

Tittle's comforting of the bereaved did not end with the moment of burial. Rather, he continued to pen strengthening notes and to pay calls of encouragement. Knowing that the first Christmas after the loss of a husband is almost beyond endurance for the widow, on that day the Christian world counts most joyful, Tittle would drop in on lonely homes to comfort the women, play with the children, perhaps building on the floor a little farm made from old cigar boxes and match sticks. On these visitations, Tittle came armed with candy, fruit, fruit cake and other little gifts for the children. "Many people thought of Dr. Tittle only as a man of great intellect, profoundly interested in far-reaching causes," recalled a comforted widow. "He was that, to be sure, but some of us had occasion to know him on a very different basis—as someone who in simple and 'homely' ways helped us finally to discover that 'underneath *are* the everlasting arms'—and that side of the story needs to be told also."[35]

The day following the burial, the young man came to Tittle's office. Recognizing the depth of his despair, the secretary at once phoned the parsonage and Tittle hurried over, for this obviously was a pastoral conference that could not be placed on the calendar. Shivered by anxiety over the loss of his job, desolated by the death of his father, racked by nameless fears, the young man confessed that in the sleepless, predawn hours thoughts of suicide welled to his consciousness. Tittle calmed the desperate individual with the wisdom born of much experience. Unlike Harry Emerson Fosdick,[36] Tittle never undertook intensive formal training in counseling, never worked closely with psychiatrists, and never wrote volumes dealing with therapeutic themes. Yet he could do the one most needful thing—he could listen. And when he spoke his words

35. Letter from Mrs. Max Forrer to author, October 7, 1959.
36. Stated Fosdick, "I am commonly thought of as a preacher, but I should not put preaching central in my ministry. Personal counseling has been central." *The Living of These Days* (New York: Harper & Brothers, 1956), p. 214.

were informed by faith, hope, and love. If unable to "reach" the individual, he would recommend professional help. One has the feeling that Tittle at the start of his ministry had little understanding of psychiatry, but that as the years of counseling passed he came increasingly to the recognition that some burdened individuals required more aid than even the most understanding pastor could supply.

A few days after the conference between the young man and Tittle, war came to America. Though a husband and father, the young man immediately enlisted in one of the armed forces. He was not forgotten by his church or his pastor. A newsletter, "Salute," kept him informed of First Church activities. He was sent little gifts such as sewing kits, toilet articles, and candy, and Easter messages, Christmas cards, and autographed copies of printed sermons. If promoted, he was congratulated. If wounded or made prisoner, Tittle wrote wonderful letters of concern and comfort. He was remembered in prayer and vesper service. Above all, perhaps, his wife and child received the special solicitude of the First Church fellowship.

At last the war ended. The young man returned to Evanston. He received a warm welcome from his old church. Parties, "bull sessions" (so they were termed), and get-togethers of all sorts eased his adjustment to civilian life. He was further helped by a new committee composed of businessmen and, significantly, psychiatrists, created for the purpose of rendering any needed service to the returning warriors.

He found a job. He prospered. He was rejoined with his wife and daughter. In a year or so a son was born. In their gratitude, the couple named him Ernest Tittle. The tiny fellow soon received a letter: "Dear little Namesake: I am writing to express the extraordinary interest which I have in your appearance in this world. You and I, it appears, are to bear in part the same name. I earnestly hope that you will not regret the fact that it was attached to you by your adoring and adorable parents. If, however, you should do so, you may quite properly quote Shakespeare to the effect that that which we call a rose would by any other name smell as sweet. . . ." As the father read aloud this letter to his uncomprehending infant, he came anew to the understanding that he was a very lucky person to have been a member of the First Church fellowship; and he counted himself blessed to have had Tittle as his shepherd. In this mood of gratitude he wrote Tittle a note, concluding, "And so because of you, I can believe there is a God and have some idea of what he is like."

6. WORSHIP IN FIRST CHURCH UNDER TITTLE

I

The young man whose life in the First Church fellowship we are attempting to reconstruct placed his note of gratitude to Tittle in an envelope. Tittle received it on Saturday. He was at his desk, pencil in hand, "sweating blood" (to use his own term) over a sermon that already had received much refurbishing. He labored so that if men failed to encounter God at the Sunday worship service it could not be said that the senior minister's slothfulness had blocked the encounter.

Morning came. In a mood of expectancy the young couple made their way to First Church. Though careful to arrive thirty minutes early, already the sanctuary seating 1,750 was well filled, and many minutes before 11:00 few pews would be empty. On some Sundays, and always at Easter and Christmas, additional hundreds worshipped in the chapel, Great Hall, and Glenna Hall, the service being transmitted by public address system. About 80,000 persons came to worship in First Church in the course of a year. It was not necessary for Tittle to admonish his people to be prompt. Self-interest dictated that they be so. The fact that the congregation arrived early and eager, the fact that latecomers could not nonchalantly assume to find an empty seat waiting for them, generated an electric atmosphere that sparked the morale of clergy and laity alike. The old pew rental system had been abolished shortly after Tittle's arrival, in 1920. Though Tittle vigorously advocated the termination of the system, the spirit of the times dictated its demise. Everywhere in America it was being judged aristocratic and anachronistic, and in Evanston, according to the newspaper announcements,

Tittle's church was neither the only one nor the first to abolish it. At First Church the custom expired painlessly, save for a brief flurry of resentment when some Northwestern students deliberately (and no doubt mischievously) pre-empted the pews of some of the more venerable of the congregation.

II

Passing through the arched east portal, which bore a group of symbols representing the triumph of virtue over evil, the couple was guided to their seats by an usher elegantly garbed in morning suit, gloves, and carnation. The fact that John Tittle was for several years head usher suggests that at First Church the responsibility was not a frivolous one. As the couple prayed there was no distracting hum of conversation. Emerson's words, "I like the quiet church when the service begins," were quoted in First Church bulletins. Soon the man raised his head. The sight that met his eyes never failed to awaken a sense of awe and adoration. Under Tittle's teaching the people of First Church had been returned to the ancient truth that it was good to worship God in the beauty of architectural setting as well as the beauty of holiness. They came to the recognition that it was possible for modern man to draw inspiration from the grandeur of Gothic architecture without retreating to medieval dogma. Therefore, when the young man lifted his eyes it was to a sanctuary of far more stately beauty than the one in which he had been baptized in 1919, and he was grateful to his minister for the transformation. Tittle once explained to his staunch Methodist congregation:

> The ineffable requires the symbol. What cannot be said through the medium of words must be said through some other medium; hence, music and art. Sensitive spirits in every generation have felt that the deepest meanings of religion cannot be spoken. Men profoundly believe that there are realities other than those which can be seen and touched. Indeed, they believe that these invisible, intangible realities are the greatest and most enduring of all realities. But the moment they attempt to speak of them, they feel embarrassed. Their faith does not fail them, but their vocabulary does. They reach out for words which they cannot find, and those which they do find appear distressingly inadequate. The fact of the matter is that life's supreme realities cannot be expressed through the medium of words. For this reason, men have erected great cathedrals, whose flying buttresses, stately naves, soaring arches, and vaulted roofs have uttered the unutterable. For this reason, too, they have filled the windows of their cathedrals with colored glass. The deep justification of the stained glass window

is that it helps us to express the inexpressible. It says something which cannot be said from any pulpit, however eloquent. Before the great east window of Yorkminster, one stands awesomely *aware* of those greatest of all realities which no human tongue can pronounce.[1]

It was Tittle's task, in many such statements addressed to his people in the first decade after his arrival, to win their acceptance of architectural forms sinisterly strange to the eyes of good Methodists, forms shunned by their nineteenth-century ancestors whose plain meetinghouses were stripped of Romish adornment. The church inherited by Tittle was a Gothic structure of impressive proportions designed by a First Church member, the noted Thomas E. Tallmadge (of Tallmadge and Watson, Chicago). Completed in 1911 at great expense, it was considered at the time to be a noble edifice fully adequate to the needs of the congregation in the foreseeable future. Yet in less than a decade it was apparent that such was the growth of First Church's membership and such was the expansion of its program under Tittle that the 1911 building no longer sufficed. The church had to be enlarged, and Tittle was determined to enhance its beauty as well.

There were, however, two alternatives to enlargement, aside from doing nothing, a stagnating decision that most certainly would have driven Tittle from Evanston. One was to split into two churches, colonizing half the congregation elsewhere. This was rejected by the membership if for no other reason than that their beloved minister could not be thus neatly divided. Moreover, it is permissible to conjecture that Tittle's ambitions for First Church (and for the senior minister of First Church) made such surgery unthinkable. A second alternative was to raze the existing church, sell the valuable property, and build a great cathedral on a new location. This was Tittle's dream. In his dream he was supported by many of the strongest men in the congregation, most notably William A. Dyche and Raymond C. Wieboldt. The dream was given form by Ralph Adams Cram, the most distinguished architect of Gothic in all America if not in the modern world, who was commissioned to draft sketches of a glorious million-dollar structure.

A committee was appointed to survey the geographical center of the church population. A second committee surveyed possible sites, reporting the only satisfactory one to be on Northwestern University property, on Sheridan Road between Noyes Street and Dartmouth Place. An anonymous donor pledged $265,000 toward the project. Wieboldt personally bought the lot back of the Northwestern property in order to accommo-

1. *Stained Glass Windows,* a pamphlet published by First Church, undated.

date the large cathedral sketched by Cram. A straw vote was taken at a congregational meeting revealing strong sentiment for the move. Then the congregation was polled by secret ballot with 800 voting affirmatively and 223 negatively.[2] The matter was of course extensively discussed at Official Board meetings. It was much debated in the Evanston papers.[3] Undoubtedly it was the subject of much acrimonious conversation in the homes of First Church members. Despite Tittle's persuasion, a number of pillars, notably Fred Sargent, remained unconvinced of the wisdom of the new adventure. Ultimately the question was decided not by the First Church congregation but by the trustees of Northwestern University. Dyche, business manager of the university and a man of extraordinary influence in university affairs, was confident he could persuade the trustees to sell or lease the desired property. He was mistaken. On recommendation of two of its committees, the Committees on Evanston Campus and on Business, the Board of Trustees found "with great regret" that they could not "see their way clear to advise the Executive Committee to alienate the land."[4]

Tittle was deeply disappointed. He had burned with the dream of creating a great new church—a Ralph Adams Cram–inspired Gothic cathedral[5]—facing the Northwestern campus almost on the shores of Lake Michigan. Defeat did not come easily to him. Seated on the front pew of his existing church, his strong shoulders at an angle of dejection, he spoke in brooding tones to his companion, Wieboldt, "Well, Raymond, where do we go from here!"[6]

The answer, of course, was to pursue with renewed vigor the plans approved the previous October to enlarge and modernize the parish house, remodel the sanctuary, and erect a new community hall and a new chapel and cloister. Acquisition of the William D. Allen property just south of the existing structure made the expansion possible. Already a half-million dollars had been pledged to the program and before completion the expenditures would mount to over three-quarters of a millon

2. "Report of Tellers," Minutes of the Official Board, First Church, June 5, 1929. The Official Board might proceed only on the approval of a two-thirds majority of the congregation.

3. See the *Evanston News-Index,* May 27, 1929, p. 1, for a particularly forceful statement against the move made by N. M. Jones, a Garrett trustee and leading First Church member.

4. "Extract from the Minutes of the Meeting of the Executive Committee of Northwestern University Held June 11, 1929, at Which More Than a Quorum Was Present," in First Church archives.

5. I am aware that in a technical sense Methodism has no cathedrals.

6. Author's interview with Raymond C. Wieboldt, Evanston, Ill., August 6, 1959.

dollars.[7] Though Tittle liked to win, though the failure to acquire the Northwestern property was a hard blow, he did not long remain depressed. Rather, with energy, enthusiasm, and knowledge he set out to transform the old First Church plant into a magnificent House of the Lord. On Easter Sunday, 1931, 2,500 individuals came to First Church to worship the Risen Lord in the newly completed chapel, Great Hall, Glenna Hall, and remodeled sanctuary. It was a moment of triumph.

The triumph owed much, first of all and above all, to the members and friends of First Church. It was their loyalty that supported the high enterprise and their dollars that underwrote it. And it was they who as individuals donated the chimes, baptismal font, lectern, pulpit, stained-glass windows, organ, and other objects of loveliness and necessity.[8] Much, also, was owed to the creative genius of Thomas E. Tallmadge, the architect of the original structure, who was re-engaged; and to the consulting architects, the firm of Cram and Ferguson, of Boston. Raymond C. Wieboldt, of the firm bearing his name, was engaged as contractor, and to him belongs a share of the credit that perhaps Tittle alone could measure. Finally, there is the role of Tittle himself.

Testimony is unanimous that Tittle possessed an unerring sense of what was architectually meet and proper. As a boy, it will be remembered, he showed marked promise as an artist. As a man, he occasionally dabbled in water colors. Perhaps he was in fact endowed with an innate artistic sense. But this is only cloudy conjecture. What can be objectively proven is that Tittle spent hundred of hours reading books on art and architecture. He immersed himself in study. He pored over drafts and sketches and blueprints and engaged in intense conversation or correspondence with Tallmadge, Cram's firm, Wieboldt, and the craftsmen who designed and executed the windows, reredos, fountains, altar, lamps, and other objects of beauty in the transformed church.

Some hold that great cathedrals make a mockery of Jesus of Nazareth, agreeing with Auden's lines, "Cathedrals, Luxury liners laden with souls." The recast First Church would not have pleased them. And there are some living in the twentieth century who share Sir Henry

7. In 1954 Wieboldt estimated that to replace "this magnificent structure today would cost about $2,500,000." *One Hundred Years . . . and a Month, July 13, 1854-August 15, 1954: The Thrilling Story of a Great Christian Institution,* a booklet published by First Church.

8. Probably it would be unwise to attempt to list the individuals who contributed these objects, since the number is very large. Moreover, in some instances the donors preferred to remain anonymous.

Wotton's seventeenth-century opinion of Gothic: "This form, both for the natural imbecility of the sharp angle itself, and likewise for its very Uncomelinesse, ought to bee exiled from judicious eyes, and left to its first inventors, the Gothes or Lombards, amongst other Reliques of that barbarous age." The recast First Church would not have pleased them. But for those who believe it is good to worship God in a beautiful setting and who stubbornly cling to the notion that Gothic is a noble form, the recast First Church justly claims the title of "The Cathedral of Methodism." And it must be remembered (as James White has so brilliantly reminded us) that to many Protestant worshippers in Tittle's era, the admiration of Gothic was more than a notion, it was a conviction, reflecting as it did the powerful Anglo-American cultural currents of the late nineteenth and early twentieth centuries. The new chapel was lovely, with its turrets and slender tower to the south and serene cloister connecting with the sanctuary to the north. Great Hall, too, was grand in its medieval design, though totally modern in its functionalism. Functional and handsome were the new classrooms, parlors, offices, dining room, and kitchen. But it was the remodeled sanctuary that met the eyes of the young man on this Sunday morning.

The open chancel permits an unobstructed view of the white marble altar and of the cross resting upon it. Behind and flanking the altar the exquisitely carved oak reredos tower in majesty to a magnificent rose window, a window of vivid pattern and harmonious colors, made by Heinigke and Smith of New York and said to be one of the finest examples of its kind in America. The dominating figure depicted in the reredos is that of the resurrected Christ, surmounting the figures of an angel and a soldier guard. Below, Christ in the Garden of Gethsemane is presented. In the left-hand panel are the Nativity, the Baptism, and the Healing. In the right-hand panel are The Sermon on the Mount, The Transfiguration, and The Crucifixion. Groups of flanking figures at both sides are symbolic of the Great Voices of the Ages—Isaiah, Amos, Jeremiah, Paul, John, Origen, Augustine, St. Francis, Thomas Aquinas, Luther, Calvin, and Wesley. Above is the traditional symbol of the Church—a ship, carved upon a shield supported by two angels. This superb work was designed by Cram and Ferguson and executed by Irving and Casson, also of Boston.

The divided choir and the pulpit seats are at right angles to the altar, the cased Austin organ is to the left rear, and the organ pipes are high on both sides. The oak lectern trimmed with bands of carving is to the left; the pulpit, similarly adorned, is to the right, Tittle choosing to reverse the usual placing. The chancel floor is of marble.

The nave presents a rich and churchly appearance. The oak pews are arranged with a center aisle that puts the middle entrance on axis with the altar. Handsome large pendant lights of handwrought iron swing over the nave and gallery. Stained-glass windows heighten the sanctuary's glory. All save the Rose Window were designed by James H. Hogan of James P. Powell and Sons, London, made in England, shipped to America, and installed by glaziers. The south transept window carries the theme of the parables of Jesus, the north transept window the theme of the works of Jesus. The six windows beneath the transepts, three under each, portray the six acts of mercy enumerated by Jesus. The nave windows depict the Spread of Christianity and Great Christians, including the figures of Wesley, Asbury, Lincoln and Frances Willard. Opposite the Rose Window, at the other end of the sanctuary, is the East Window. Its theme is the great hymn of praise, "Te Deum." In the morning sunlight it is one of the glories of the church; indeed, of American Christianity. Running through the base of the design are the words, "We praise thee, O God, we acknowledge thee to be the Lord. Heaven and earth are full of thy glory." The central light contains the main theme of the Incarnation, the Crucifixion, and the glorified and ascended Christ, while the others represent the "glorious company of the apostles, the goodly fellowship of the prophets, the noble army of the martyrs." Tittle once said, "These walls and arches and vaulted roof and rose window have sacramental values. Through things that are made we see here the invisible things of God."[9]

III

It was, then, in this setting of rare beauty that the young man sat in prayer and quiet mediation. His mood of expectancy heightened. On Sunday morning something special happened: the public worship of God. Tittle did not denigrate private meditation, yet he always insisted that spiritual experience is more than the mystical "flight of the alone to the Alone." This morning—now—in First Church, Evanston, men and women had publicly assembled to adore, praise, and thank God, confess their sins and seek forgiveness, affirm their faith, and dedicate their lives. In offering opportunity for the public worship of God, the church, said Tittle, "is doing one thing which no other institution on earth is doing or may ever be expected to do unless it should itself become the church."[10] In truth, public worship "is the primary task of

9. *Life as a Sacrament,* an undated sermon (pamphlet).
10. "The Public Worship of God," *The First Church Pulpit,* Vol. IV, No. 1, a sermon preached October 20, 1940.

the church."[11] And as the man awaited, the quiet now broken by the organ prelude, perhaps the lines came to him:

> Lo, God is here! let us adore,
>   And own how dreadful is this place!
> Let all within us feel His power,
>   And silent bow before His face;
> Who knows His power, His grace who prove,
> Serve him with awe, with reverence love.[12]

Early nineteenth-century American Methodists had been proud of the unfettered freedom, stirring enthusiasm, intense individualism, and informal spontaneity of their worship services. They rejoiced in the extempore prayers concluded with ringing congregational "Amens," the fervent preaching punctuated with shouts of "Praise the Lord," the lusty singing of Gospel hymns. John Wesley had prepared for American Methodism *The Sunday Service of the Methodists in North America,* paralleling the *Book of Common Prayer* of the Church of England, containing orders of worship for Sunday, together with the ritual for sacraments, ordinations, and "various occasions." *The Sunday Service* was adopted by the Christmas Conference of 1784, at which the Methodist Episcopal Church was organized, as the ark and covenant for the Church. In fact, however, Wesley's guides for worship were soon ignored, or to use Jesse Lee's more gentle term, "laid aside."[13] For one thing, the smell of freedom was in the American air. As the Revolution meant political freedom from England, so it meant freedom from the formalism and sacerdotalism of the Church of England. "The rites and ceremonies of the ancient church," explained Bishop Nolan B. Harmon, "seemed to our fathers as grave-clothes constricting the living Spirit, and pristine Methodism threw these off almost spasmodically and went gloriously ahead making its own rules as it went."[14] For another, the austerity of the Puritan worship service, with its distrust of papish ceremonial, influenced Methodist thinking. Above all, American Methodists in laying aside Wesley's adaptation of the *Book of Common Prayer* were making a virtue of necessity. Many of them were illiterate, and for those

11. "God and the Church," *The First Church Pulpit,* Vol. IV, No. 6, a sermon preached July 20, 1941.

12. From Tersteegen, as quoted in John A. Bishop, *Methodist Worship in Relation To Free Church Worship* (London: The Epworth Press, 1950), p. 16.

13. Paul S. Sanders, "The Methodist Communion Order," *The Pastor,* XI (May, 1948), 25.

14. Nolan B. Harmon, "Uniform But Unfettered," *The Pastor,* XV (March, 1952), 19.

who could read, books were often unavailable. Moreover, a formal service seemed inappropriate to the primitive setting of open field, brush arbor, barn, or sail-loft. The itinerant circuit rider had no time to instruct his people in the amenities of a liturgical service, and his saddle bags scarcely had room for prayer books and the linens and embroidery of priestly vesture, crammed as they were with items of personal toiletry, tracts, and pamphlets. Finally, these saddle-bag preachers were themselves untrained in the administration of an orderly and sophisticated service.

The freedom and fervor that characterized these early Methodist worship services were purchased at a dear price. Too often a disdain for the "rags of ritualism" led to wild improvisation and bizarre vagaries. The services were further flawed by sentimentalism and didacticism. Above all, they were infused with a self-conscious subjectivism wherein the people were entertained, informed, and even "inspired," but they were not always brought into the "objective" or "real" presence of God. At their best these unfettered services made possible the perfect liberty of the individual to meet his God, but they also carried the peril of centering the thought of the worshipper on himself.

Often subsumed but never entirely extinguished in American Methodism was a countervailing determination that there be order, dignity, historicity, and uniformity in worship. John Wesley, after all, was a priest in the Church of England who advised his New World followers that there was "no Liturgy in the world, either in ancient or modern language, which breathes more of solid, Scriptural, rational piety than the Common Prayer of the Church of England."[15] He was a churchman, even a sacramentalist. The very name Method-ist suggests a strong desire to be uniform and regular, to preserve an established and historic order of worship. Thus, from the beginning the General Conferences of American Methodism prescribed well-wrought rules for the general conduct of public worship. And as the nineteenth century deepened and the twentieth century opened, increasingly in its worship practices Methodism moved from revivalism to ritual, from freedom to form. This "recovery of worship" was not instituted in one clean stroke. Its victory was never total. And there were some Methodists who not without justice found only shallow prettification and showy ornamentation in this liturgical revival. Tittle's ministry began just after the divisions of American Methodism had adopted in 1905 a common hymnal in which

15. Quoted in Nolan B. Harmon, "Methodist Worship: Practices and Ideals," in *Methodism,* ed. William K. Anderson (Cincinnati, Ohio: The Methodist Publishing House, 1957), p. 230.

there was conspicuously placed a formal order of worship. Shortly before his death a united Methodism published, in 1945, for the instruction of its people *The Book of Worship for Church and Home,* marking a resolution of the tension between freedom and form largely in favor of the latter.

Midway in his Evanston pastorate Tittle wrote a Methodist bishop expressing his thanksgiving that "our great church" is moving "in the direction of a more liturgical service."[16] For Tittle, a "more liturgical service" did not mean the clothing of a so-called "bare" service with quaint or pretty little liturgical odds and ends. Worship is not liturgical just because the minister wears a round collar and a Geneva gown, nor just because the choir is vested, voices responses and chants, and marches in and out. Neither does it result, as Paul Sanders observed, "from merely having regimented the choir, the ushers, the congregation (and perhaps even God) into a set pattern of procedure."[17] At First Church the worship service was not defined as a dramatic spectacle or an esthetically satisfying "production"; Tittle would not have been pleased by the characterization "liturgy craftsman." At First Church the spirit of the worship service is suggested by the words of a French peasant in answer to the question of why he spent so much time on his knees before the altar of the Presence: "I look at him and he looks at me." The people of First Church understood worship to be their bounden duty and solemn obligation, and also their richest privilege. There, on holy ground, they turned their broken and contrite hearts upward toward God instead of inward toward themselves, and they awaited in the expectation of being found by Him. And they were found. Harassed, haunted, and anxious men and women were cleansed, healed, and made whole again.

After Tittle's death, his people prepared a memorial statement in which they said: "Dr. Tittle was a leader of worship. The public service meant more to him than beautifully rendered music and an entertaining sermon; it meant that by hymn and Scripture and choir music, by prayer and sermon, men should be made to know God and feel his presence and join in his worship. So the public worship of our church has been for us all a time of inspiration and help and high fellowship."[18] After his death, also, Mrs. Tittle received a letter from a man in Burma

16. Letter from Tittle to Bishop Wilbur P. Thirkield, November 17, 1931.
17. Paul S. Saunders, "Drama—Not Dramatics," *The Pastor,* XVII December, 1935), 10.
18. *A Memorial To Ernest Fremont Tittle Prepared for the Official Board and Adopted Unanimously as an Expression of the Feeling of the 2500 Members of First Church, October 3, 1949,* a pamphlet published by First Church.

who spoke of the "inestimable privilege of worshipping God under the rare inspiration of your husband's gifted leadership. I am sure he would want us to have felt the experience in that order, worshipping God primarily, rather than going to hear Tittle preach. That, as I understood his message and ministry, was what he was striving to accomplish."[19]

Tittle would have agreed with John Bishop's dictum, "Worship is essentially formal and its forms are of the essence."[20] First Church services were highly structured, perfectly proportioned, meticulously planned, fusing form and function. They were conducted with majesty and solemnity so that men might know they were in the awful presence of the Eternal. No detail was too insignificant to command Tittle's attention. Nothing in the service was done carelessly or perfunctorily. New assistant ministers were required to practice speaking from the pulpit while Tittle sat in the back pew listening; in First Church there would be no inaudible mumblings to frustrate worshippers seated beyond the first rows. Assistants also were required to practice reading aloud prayers, scripture, lessons, responsive readings, and even announcements. Indeed, very few announcements were permitted to break the mood of reverence, and these announcements were brief and carefully written out in advance in order that no discordant or awkward phrase be uttered.

It had been necessary for Tittle to lead his people gradually, patiently, and gently to an appreciation of a more liturgical worship service. In truth, it is probably more accurate to state that Tittle himself only slowly awakened to the rightfulness of a formal service. Those whose memories run back to his Ohio pastorates commented without exception on the power of his sermons, but not, significantly, on the beauty of his worship services; and in the first Evanston years there was little that was distinctive or distinguished in Tittle's order of worship.

Yet his library contains a number of volumes written in the 1920's, such as those by Von Ogden Vogt and Willard Sperry, calling for a liturgical revival, and in 1922 a first step was taken, for the Minutes of the Official Board for December 12 read: "Moved and carried that the members of the Choir be permitted to wear gowns at the Sunday services."[21] In 1924 the question of the robing of the ministers was "discussed at length" by the Official Board, a committee investigated the sentiment of the membership, and finally on January 5, 1925, it was

19. Letter from Harry Harwood to Mrs. Tittle, August 27, 1949.
20. Bishop, *Methodist Worship*, p. 11.
21. The brochure, *Twenty Memorable Years . . . in the History of First Church,* celebrating the twentieth anniversary of Tittle's pastorate, must be mistaken in giving the year 1924 for the robing of the choir.

"Moved, after extended discussion, that the pastors be requested to wear gowns in the pulpit. Motion adopted unanimously." On April 6, 1931, again after "discussion," the Official Board resolved that the cross be placed on the altars of the church and chapel. On November 5, 1945, the Official Board authorized the use of candles on the altar. It was made clear to the membership that the lads who lit and extinguished the candles were not to be called "acolytes" but were to be regarded simply as "choir boys" performing a duty that might properly be considered a part of the choir's service. All of these innovations, taken so for granted in much of American Protestantism today, met with bitter opposition from many parishioners, who viewed them as ecclesiastical pomp and idolatrous foppery.[22] There was in fact a real danger that this liturgical revival would end only in sterile ritualism, and those who opposed Tittle were not simply being mulish. They were seeking to preserve the precious Methodist heritage of free and, as they maintained, vital worship. Yet in First Church the danger did not materialize. The formal service introduced by Tittle heightened the drama of man's encounter with God; it was not a matter of pretty dramatics.

IV

The place of music in this order of worship is significant. It will be remembered that as a lad Tittle enjoyed something of a reputation as a violinist. Though he now drew his bow only infrequently, music remained to him one of the richest joys of life. Under his leadership First Church came to support a minister of music, three or four organists, a chancel choir, a chapel choir, and four church-school choirs, an Oratorio society, and a symphony orchestra of some seventy musicians. This concern for music is appropriate, for Methodism was born singing, and Methodism's spread over the American continent was carried as much on the wings of Charles Wesley's hymns as on John Wesley's theology. In truth, the hymnal is "the layman's manual of theology,"[23] and nineteenth-century Methodists sang fervently of their sins and more thrillingly still of Jesus' redeeming love. Everywhere they were admired as a singing people. If their songs were laced with a strong tinge of subjectivism and if, alas, they were infected by an unbiblical sentimentalism, in raising

22. This opposition is mentioned explicitly by many individuals and runs as a thread through the Minutes of the Official Board.

23. Canon Charles Winfred Douglas, as quoted in Leonard Ellinwood, "Religious Music In America," *Religious Perspectives in American Culture,* Vol. II of *Religion in American Life,* ed. James Ward Smith and A. Leland Jamison (Princeton, N. J.: Princeton University Press, 1961), p. 309.

their voices these early Methodists nonetheless gave expression to a vital faith.

By the time of Tittle's arrival in Evanston, however, a sad transformation had taken place. In many respectable residential Methodist churches it was now fashionable for the congregation to remain virtually mute while paid quartets and professional soloists entertained them; and though the singing may have been technically skillful, it was without fire, for personal vainglory, not God's glory, inspired it. The decline of congregational participation was a sad loss, one that Tittle was determined to rectify. The paid quartet was replaced by a chancel choir of sixty voices, "of whom all but two gave their services without compensation."[24] This choir was blessed with the presence of a number of gifted artists of national fame, perhaps most notably Helen Hedges, Helen Hawk Carlisle, Raymund Koch, and Eugene Dressler. Great care was exercised so that the choir did not self-consciously call attention to itself. Its purpose was to aid in the worship of God, not to rivet thoughts on the merely esthetically satisfying. Music was to be integrated into the worship mood of confession and contrition, affirmation and adoration.

In 1935 the Methodist Episcopal Church, the Methodist Episcopal Church, South, and the Methodist Protestant Church cooperated in bringing out a new hymnal, the first revision since 1905. "My own distaste for the new Methodist Hymnal is profound," growled Tittle after a close examination.[25] He and his music director studied the book, as they had the old one, crossing out songs deemed musically impossible and rating the others according to merit.[26] It is revealing of Tittle's social passion that he could write: "The Church of today is particularly lacking in hymns of the kingdom of God. There are hymns in abundance— they cannot be too many—which proclaim a possible triumph of the human spirit over sin and fear and death, but all too few that declare the Christian faith that God is concerned with both the salvation of the individual and the redemption of the corporate life of the world."[27] In general, as Tittle moved toward a more liturgical worship service the music became increasingly majestic, antisentimental, objective, and "universal."

There were many musicians of distinction associated with First Church. To begin with, Tittle tapped the knowledge of Peter Christian

24. Letter from Tittle to Golder Lawrence, May 15, 1941.
25. Letter from Tittle to Edmund C. Wiley, January 27, 1936.
26. Author's interviews with Robert C. Teare, Evanston, Ill., August 28, 1959, and Mrs. Bernice Wolseley, Evanston, Ill., July 13, 1960.
27. *The Gospel According to Luke* (New York: Harper & Brothers, 1951), p. 6.

Lutkin, dean of the Northwestern School of Music, co-editor for music
of the famous 1905 Methodist hymnal, and until 1931 director of the
First Church Cappella Choir. On Lutkin's death Tittle wrote his widow,
"For me Dean Lutkin was not only a great man but a dear, good friend
who gave to me time and strength which I had no right to expect. He
has been, is, and will ever be a source of beautiful inspiration."[28] Leo
Sowerby, organist and choir director in the second half of the 1920's,
ranked high in the field of sacred music, winning in 1946 a Pulitzer
Prize for his cantata, "The Canticle of the Sun." LeRoy Wetzel served
as chief organist and choir director during the entire 1930's. An accomplished artist and conductor, Wetzel's reputation was international. In
1940 Emory Leland Gallup became minister of music and remained at
that post until his death in 1947. Gallup and Tittle found themselves
in perfect agreement and became warm personal friends. A gentleman,
an Episcopalian, and an artist of austere standards, when he played the
organ at Christian Science weddings, it was Gallup's custom to charge
extra to play the tunes of Mary Baker Eddy.[29] At a surprise birthday
party honoring Gallup, Tittle proposed the toast, "To Emory Gallup,
distinguished musician, great director of church music, cultured gentleman, good friend!"[30] There were, of course, many other individuals who
made possible a rich ministry of music at First Church, from Mrs. Kath-
erine Howard Ward, who in 1925 retired after twenty-five years as
organist, to the able Porter Heaps, who for four years served as organist
and music director, to John K. Christensen, who was minister of music
in Tittle's last years.

V

Nurtured in First Church, the young man had been led by Tittle to
the truth that prayer is the essence of worship. "Prayer is communion
with God. It is, therefore, the most important business we have to
attend to. Among all the things clamoring to be done in the course of
the day none ranks in importance with prayer. We can afford to go
without lunch if we are too busy to eat. We can never afford to go
through a day without prayer."[31] Prayer is honest speaking and honest
listening to God. It is recognizing one's dependence, as in the case of

28. Letter from Tittle to Mrs. Peter C. Lutkin, December 28, 1931.
29. Author's interview with Glenna Myers Tittle, Evanston, Ill., July 31, 1959.
30. Memorandum in Tittle Collection dated February 18, 1943.
31. "Prayer," *The First Church Pulpit,* Vol. VIII, No. 3, a sermon preached
January 20, 1946.

the Bretton fisherman who prayed, "O God, thy sea is so great and my boat is so small."[32]

Tittle was convinced that although some individuals cease to pray because they have become unsure of God, others have become unsure of God largely because they have ceased to pray. God soon fades out of the life of the man who does not pray. What chance would a sunset have to fill our minds with elevated thoughts if we never stopped long enough really to see the glorious afterglow of an evening sky? What chance would music have to soothe or inspire us if seldom or never did we listen to it? What chance would poetry have to stimulate our imaginations and enrich our lives if we never read it? What chance would friendship have to live and grow if we never sat down and conversed with a friend? Similarly, "What chance does God have to reveal himself to us if seldom or never do we pray?"[33] Tittle was not much concerned to defend the practice of prayer on logical or theoretical grounds. When invited to address a group on the subject, "Does Everyone Need to Pray?" he suggested that the topic might well be phrased, "Do People Need God—his forgiveness, his guidance and help?"[34] Long ago it was said, "Taste and see that the Lord is good." Well, argued Tittle, instead of waiting for a demonstration of the effectiveness of prayer that we shall never get unless and until we start praying, why not "taste and see that the Lord is good"? Tittle placed no ban on the pouring out of the heart before God. There are times when the heart has need to cry out its griefs, its fears, its hopes, its most earnest desires. Overwhelming emotion must find an outlet if it is not to work havoc, physical and mental. Hence, prayer commonly takes the form of petition. And the petition may be for anything that a man needs, or honestly thinks he needs:

> Jesus Himself made no such distinction of spiritual and material as His followers, in many cases, have undertaken to make. For Him, there would have been something strange, not to say offensive, in a so-called Christianity that was concerned for men's souls but not at all for their bodies, whether their stomachs were filled or empty, whether their backs were clothed or naked, whether they had a roof over their heads or not. As a matter of fact, this pietistic distinction of spiritual and material is not likely to be made by human beings who have not had enough to eat, much less to get an education, but only by persons who, being them-

32. "Prayer in the Name of Christ," *The First Church Pulpit*, Vol. IX, No. 2, a sermon preached March 23, 1947.
33. *The Need of Prayer*, a sermon preached November 29, 1931 (pamphlet).
34. "When You Pray," *The First Church Pulpit*, Vol. X, No. 15, a sermon preached April 3, 1949.

selves well-fed, well-clothed, and well-housed, can easily afford to say, "Let us talk about things spiritual." It is surely significant that the Lord's prayer contains a petition for daily bread as well as a petition for the forgiveness of sins.[35]

Prayer is also thanksgiving and adoration. It would indeed be strange if, in fellowship with God, human beings never felt moved to return thanks or to cry out, "Holy, Holy, Holy, Lord God of hosts, Heaven and earth are full of thy glory: Glory be to thee, O Lord Most High!" But in personal fellowship with God prayer is often petition, even on the lips of the greatest and best men. In the Lord's Prayer every utterance, from "Hallowed by thy name" to "Deliver us from evil," is a petition. And while we know but little concerning the content of Jesus' own prayers, we know that he, in extremis, prayed, "If it be possible, let this cup pass away from me." Unless God is regarded as an impersonal cosmic order to which human beings are left to adjust themselves as best they can, prayer is bound, on occasion, to be petition. It is but natural for us to seek guidance and help from our Father who is in heaven. It would be unnatural for us not to do so. True, "The cup from which Jesus prayed to be delivered was not taken away from him. It could not be. But, as he prayed, he was given strength for the ordeal which, in the situation that had developed, was inescapable. In the meaningful language of the New Testament, 'angels came and ministered unto him.' He who in a difficult situation cries for deliverance may or may not obtain the deliverance he asks for. But, in any event, he will be given strength to do what he may and endure what he must."[36]

Tittle taught his people to pray for others. Jesus prayed for others. God Himself prompts us to pray for others. "It is not, therefore, surprising that Christian prayer is often prayer for others and that, at its best, it knows no distinction of race or nation or class or creed—no, nor of friend and foe." He continued: "We are 'members one of another,' as the New Testament declares. We *must* live in relation with others if we are to be persons and not mere individuals of a species. There is no such thing as an isolated person. A human infant, if it were completely cut off from human fellowship, could not possibly become a person in the full sense, even if it managed somehow to survive. We become persons only in association with other persons. And what slightest chance would we have to become Christlike persons if we were left entirely to

35. *Prayer in Christian Faith,* a booklet published by the General Commission on Evangelism of The Methodist Church (Nashville, Tenn., n.d.), pp. 7-8.
36. "Prayer as Petition," *The First Church Pulpit,* Vol. IV, No. 11, a sermon preached April 26, 1942.

ourselves? We must live in fellowship with one another if anything comparable to the love of God is ever to appear on the stage of history." Consequently prayer for others does make a difference. Furthermore, "Christianity believes in the communion of saints, the resurrection of the dead, and the life everlasting. Hence, Christian prayer includes not only those who now live on earth but also those who live in a world that has no end. If those whom we love, no longer with us in the flesh, live with God for evermore, it is surely right and proper to pray for them; that, increasing in knowledge and love of God, they may advance in His service and therein find unending joy and peace."[37] And in a letter to a parishioner, Tittle explained: "Prayer for our beloved dead is, I think, regarded as orthodox. In any case, it is profoundly Christian. It follows quite naturally from the Christian faith that nothing, not even death, shall be able to separate us from the love of God."[38]

Thus it was that in the moments before the opening note of the processional our young man prayed in silence as he had been taught by his minister to do. The instruction had been by example as well as precept. In Tittle's prayers the young man had good models. Tittle was a great preacher. His sermons won for him national fame. The people of First Church, however, knew that their pastor's prayers matched his sermons. After his death many of his flock remembered his prayers with an intensity of gratitude exceeding even that felt for his sermons. Rereading Tittle's prayers today, one comes to the judgment of their enduring quality, and to a fresh understanding of why it was said that "Ernest Fremont Tittle is a great Christian minister."

Three years before his death Tittle wrote an essay entitled, "The Pastoral Prayer."[39] This essay merits extended quotation, so clearly does it illuminate Tittle's thinking. The essay begins: "The pastoral prayer, in all too many cases, is the most neglected part of the service. . . . Such neglect is something more than a pity; it is a disgrace. When the moment comes to say, 'Let us pray,' the minister has the opportunity of helping the people to 'draw boldly unto the throne of grace, that [they] may receive mercy and find grace to help [them] in time of need.' And what greater opportunity does the minister have during the entire course of the service? It is even arguable that the prayer may be of greater

37. "Prayer for Others," *The First Church Pulpit,* Vol. IV, No. 11, a sermon preached May 10, 1942.

38. Letter from Tittle to Mrs. J. P. MacMillan, April 15, 1942.

39. The essay first appeared in the Summer, 1946, issue of *Religion in Life.* It is reprinted in *A Book of Pastoral Prayers* (New York and Nashville, Tenn.: Abingdon Press, 1951), pp. 9-28. All quotations are taken from *A Book of Pastoral Prayers.*

value than the sermon." After underscoring this point, Tittle continues: "The minister in the nonliturgical church may sometimes wish he were free to dispense with 'free' prayer in favor of a liturgical order. The disciplines required for the preparation and delivery of sermons are persistent and exacting enough; but they are hardly to be compared to the disciplines called for by the pastoral prayer, whose purpose is to present before God the unspoken supplications of the people, whose language (ideally) is the language of poetry, and whose helpfulness cannot but be affected by the known character of the ministrant. To meet fully the demands of the pastoral prayer the minister would need to be at once priest, poet, and saint." He then examines extemporary prayer in the context of the old issue between liturgical and nonliturgical orders of worship. He finds much that is meritorious in formal prayer, holding that the reading or the recitation by heart of familiar words can be, and is, a means of grace. However, this "does not necessarily mean that the nonliturgical church should abandon the practice of free prayer. . . . Words and phrases become obsolete. Changes come over the face of the earth and the life of a people. New occasions arise, and new ideas, new concerns, new hopes. . . . Free prayer is immediately adaptable to a given situation. And, what is more, it admits of an intimacy not otherwise attainable, so that it may serve to beget in a worshipping congregation a most blessed sense of the reality and presence of God."

As both formal prayer and free prayer have their merits, so they have their dangers. "The danger of formal prayer is that it may become a parrotlike recitation of words whose meaning and intention go unrecognized. The danger of free prayer is that it may be woefully inadequate. Hence the historical alternation between liturgical and nonliturgical worship. Let formal prayer become lifeless, and there is a Puritan Revolution. Let free prayer become slovenly and thoughtless, and there is a demand for 'enrichment' of worship." Tittle is prepared to utilize the values of both traditions.

He then refers to a minister who, having in mind a bereaved family on whom he had just called, prayed: "Lord, we are a poor widow with six children." "That," comments Tittle, "was a real pastoral prayer. The minister in *public* prayer is a priest presenting before God the common need of forgiveness, of cleansing and comfort, of guidance and help, of self-commitment to the divine purpose, of faith and hope and courage and strength." The minister may not lightly undertake so great a responsibility. "Free prayer must not be free in the sense that it is offered on the spur of the moment without previous thought or only with such thought as may be given to it after the service begins. Who without previous preparation can present before God the unspoken supplications of the people, and this in words capable of directing attention toward God?" It is not unusual, Tittle admits, for him to spend as much as two hours in the preparation of a single prayer.

Tittle then makes a central point: "Public prayer no less than private should be addressed to God. This observation may seem superfluous but apparently it is not. I have myself heard or read prayers whose object, it would seem, was to inform or exhort the congregation."[40] He then cites examples of prayers that unfortunately are in reality lectures or arguments.

Several concrete suggestions follow. The pastoral prayer should not ramble. If it is more than three hundred words it is probably too long. Secondly, the choice of words is of the greatest importance. "Those words are suitable, and those alone, which serve to lift mind and heart toward God." The language of the classroom or the soapbox should be avoided. In general, Anglo-Saxon words are to be preferred to Greek or Latin derivatives. Words like "bread," "work," "light," and "truth" may more certainly be depended upon to lift mind and heart to God than words like "sustenance," "employment," "universe," "illumination," and "veracity," which have far less power to reach the depths of the soul. The use of technical words and controversial phrases such as "labor movement," "production for use," and "co-operative commonwealth" is improper. "Most unsuitable are forms of expression that call attention to the minister and provoke wonder at his eloquence or (as some may view it) his exhibitionism. If the minister in prayer alludes to 'the wave-tossed surface of our wind-driven life,' or to 'the last loving haven from the loneliness of life,' or to 'a morning glorious, alight with the brightness of resurrection and the promise of a day of opportunity,' then he may be sure that the people are thinking about *him,* though not entirely sure what they are thinking. Here the problem is not only intellectual but moral and spiritual as well. Basically it is the problem of self-forgetting." In this connection, the temptation to use numerous adjectives must be resisted. "They slow down a prayer whose true mission is to lead the people to the throne of grace. Worse still, they get in the way of the people's approach to God, attracting attention to themselves, like persons flashily dressed. . . . It is worthy of note that the

40. Elsewhere Tittle had said: "Public prayer should be addressed to God, not to the people. The pulpit prayer reported some years ago as the most eloquent ever addressed to a Boston audience was alas! not the last of its kind." "When You Pray," *The First Church Pulpit,* Vol. X, No. 15, a sermon preached April 3, 1949.

prayers of the ages contain but few adjectives—the greatest of all, only one."

Tittle continues:

> The native language of prayer is the language of poetry. Only the language of poetry can adequately convey the reality of eternal God: "Lord, thou hast been our dwelling place in all generations." Or the reality of human creatureship: "Know ye that the Lord he is God: it is he that hath made us, and not we ourselves; we are his people, and the sheep of his pasture." Or the soul's need and plea for forgiveness: "Create in me a clean heart, O God; and renew a right spirit within me." Or the confidence of the trusting soul: "Yea, though I walk through the valley of the shadow of death, I will fear no evil; for thou art with me." Or the soul's invincible surmise: "And he shall wipe away every tear from their eyes; and death shall be no more; neither shall there be mourning, nor crying, nor pain, any more: the former things are passed away." Not all God's preachers are poets. And what is one to do if one is not? Being myself a preacher who is not a poet or a poet's son, I have found it necessary and most helpful to steep my mind in the Psalms, in Isaiah, and in *The Book of Common Prayer*. This practice I recommend to anyone whose mental processes are similarly prosaic. It is not, of course, a substitute for the divine gift of poetry; but it may serve to induce the mood and to some extent even the manner of poetry, so that the prayer thus resulting will have some correspondence with what is true and good in the public worship of God.

He then discusses the art of making collects, "for the collect at its best has the virtue of unity, of conciseness, of enduring grace and strength." And the litany, "a prayer form of extraordinary promise." The essay concludes: "It would be easy for the minister in the nonliturgical church simply to 'lift' collects or litanies from a prayer book. But this would be a surrender to laziness and a deplorable repudiation of a great tradition. The church needs, in addition to the 'prayers of the ages,' prayers immediately relevant to the contemporary situation and voiced in the living language of the day. The minister in the nonliturgical church may well feel called of God to pay the price, intellectual and spiritual, of effective pastoral prayer."

Believing about prayer as he did, it is not a matter of astonishment that Tittle should painstakingly have worked out a group of prayers for the Sunday worship service, and for weddings, baptisms, and funerals, and for the sick, the dying, the bereaved, the departed, and for special subjects such as missions, peace, race relations, and for days in the Christian Year. It is sometimes asserted that the Social Gospel was nothing more than a gloss on Theodore Roosevelt's New Nationalism or Wood-row Wilson's New Freedom or Franklin D. Roosevelt's New Deal or Eugene Debs's and Norman Thomas's mild socialism couched in the language of piety; that, indeed, the Social Gospelites were merely secular reformers in clerical garb for whom God was no more of a reality than an oblong blur. The inaccuracy of this characterization is revealed to anyone who troubles to read the hymns of Washington Gladden and Frank Mason North or the prayers of Walter Rauschenbusch and England's William Temple. The characterization is totally challenged by the God-centered prayers of Ernest Fremont Tittle. And those who worshipped in First Church, including the young man whose First Church life we have been attempting to reconstruct, serve as our witnesses.

7. THE THEORY AND PRACTICE
OF PROPHETIC PREACHING

I

Writing to a friend in 1934 when he was under savage personal attack and the nation was stretched on the rack of depression, Tittle declared, "This is at once a great and terrible time to be a preacher, but . . . I am glad that preaching is my business."[1] There were others who had reason to rejoice that Tittle was in the "business" of preaching. Those who worshipped in First Church knew that Sunday after Sunday they were hearing great sermons; and they came to the more wonderful awareness that they were in the presence of a great Christian preacher. Tittle's people loved him as a pastor who counseled them in their trouble and comforted them in their grief and shared in their moments of joy. They revered him as a priest who led them in the worship of the living God in services of beauty and majesty. They admired him as a minister who nurtured the young and served the community. They honored him as an ecclesiarch whose attendance was coveted in the councils of Methodism and the larger Christian Church. And they respected him (perhaps grudgingly in some instances) for his championship of the disinherited in a host of secular reform movements. Yet primarily and preeminently, Ernest Fremont Tittle was a preacher. This is the judgment of those intimate with his ministry. It is Tittle's own understanding of his life and labor. He used the atmosphere of the cathedral to bring his hearers into the mysterious presence of God, and having brought them there as a worshiping unit, he preached the evangelistic messages that brought conviction to their souls.

1. Letter from Tittle to W. M. Lockett, Jr., January 2, 1934.

II

By the second quarter of the twentieth century the word "preacher" had been shorn of much of its former dignity. The American Protestant ministry knew a kind of Indian summer in the opening years of the new century, but by about 1925 a winter of discontent had settled down upon it. "Preacher" was not yet a tawdry word despite the obscenities of the Elmer Gantrys. It was not yet a ludicrous word despite the buffoonery of John Roach Stratton, J. Frank Norris, and Billy Sunday. It was not yet a sinister word despite the clergy-endorsed anti-evolution legislation threatening to blanket the schools of America or the mushrooming of the Ku Klux Klan with its corps of ministerial Kludds and Kleagles. But it was now a word without grandeur. And now when it was spoken, somehow one thought of timid little gray creatures or briskly efficient salesmen in clerical collars or hatchet-faced, lank-haired, kill-joys or booming-voiced, barrel-chested, chuckleheaded YMCA secretaries. To be sure, in one's more honest moments one admitted these images to be gross caricatures of the man living in the parsonage at Main and Elm. Nevertheless few Americans in the post–World War era could easily associate their preacher with the great tradition of Isaiah, Amos, Paul, Bernard, Wesley, Edwards, Parker, and Brooks.

Those who worshipped in First Church, however, made the association, for they deemed their preacher to be in the goodly fellowship of the prophets, a man under authority, commissioned to proclaim the will of God. They were made aware of ancient truths. Preaching is worship. Every true sermon is a sacramental act. There is no inevitable tension between gospel preaching and gospel sacraments, between pulpit and altar, between the sermon and the Eucharist. Christianity began not with a book but with preaching. Preaching is God's activity wherein He uses one to speak so that all, including the preacher, may listen in faith to His word. They did not lament the high place of honor accorded to the pulpit by Protestantism historically or scorn the old affection the people called Methodists had for the simple word "preacher." And they denied the familiar charge that in the modern world preaching was irrelevant, for if this were true then would not the Lord's commission to proclaim the Word be obsolete? To be sure, God would always break through to speak to men who listen in faith, but if the pulpit were mute, the encounter would be handicapped. "How shall they hear without a preacher?" In First Church when Tittle mounted the pulpit one comprehended that in one's need God did not remain silent. In First Church the Thirteenth of the Twenty-five Articles of Religion of the Methodist Episcopal Church was honored: "The visible church of Christ is a congregation of faithful men in which the *pure word of God is preached* and the sacraments duly administered."[2]

The awfulness (and the presumption) of his commission was never long absent from Tittle's consciousness. Replying to an inquiry from a woman whose son was contemplating the ministry as a career, Tittle began by saying that "I have never regretted my own choice. It has been a hard life but for me an endlessly interesting one." He then emphasized the "fact that the ministry makes extraordinary demands upon anyone who enters it. In order to do anything worth while in the Protestant ministry you must be an unusually able *preacher*, for Protestantism, as you know, is built around a pulpit, not around an altar. And if the pulpit has nothing to say Protestantism is doomed to die."[3] This is so because "the prophet is not a man before a microphone saying: 'I predict'; he is a man declaring: 'Thus saith the Lord.' "[4] And no conviction was dearer to Tittle than that the true preacher was a prophet. He explicitly stated this certitude a hundred times and it was implicit in all his sermons.

It is revealing that his first address to the students of Garrett Biblical Institute in March, 1919, was entitled, "Priest or Prophet?" and that his last Garrett baccalaureate sermon preached in June, 1949, was designated, "In the Prophetic Succession." In his earlier years Tittle tended to draw a sharp and invidious distinction between the priest and the prophet. "The great alternative," he initially believed, "before every minister of whatever church is just this: priest or prophet? Shall he be a priest apart from men or a prophet in the midst of men? Shall he be a priest upholding tradition or a prophet led on by faith?"[5] As he grew older, however, he saw that the priestly and prophetic elements of Christianity need not be mutually exclusive: "The preacher can be at once a priest and a prophet. Indeed, he *must* be both if he is to do at all adequately the work to which he is called."[6] As we know, increasingly he felt "a most urgent obligation to provide a service of worship in which men and women hard-beset may gain a sense of the reality of God."[7] And we know, too, that he did not neglect the pastoral ministry, "a ministry of

2. Italics added.

3. Letter from Tittle to Mrs. George Eckert, September 8, 1933.

4. "In the Prophetic Succession," *The First Church Pulpit,* Vol. X, No. 2, a Garrett baccalaureate sermon preached June 12, 1949.

5. *Priest or Prophet?* Garrett convocation address preached March 19, 1919 (pamphlet).

6. "Priest and Prophet," *The First Church Pulpit,* Vol. VII, No. 10, a Garrett baccalaureate sermon preached June 11, 1944.

7. *Ibid.*

encouragement and comfort, of warning and hope for troubled and harassed men and women."[8] In truth, Tittle was critical of the activism in American Protestantism, which "inclined to think that time spent in worship might have been better spent in earnest consideration of human problems waiting to be solved" and that "a devotional service was but a conventional introduction to the real business of the day." Its attitude, he lampooned, was, "Ask someone to read something from the Bible and offer a prayer, and tell him to make it snappy so we can get down to work."[9]

Though Tittle's appreciation of the priestly attributes of the ministry heightened with the years and though at no time in his carrer had he failed to be a faithful pastor, he nonetheless remained consistent in the conviction of the centrality of the prophetic pulpit in Protestantism. As he informed a class of seminarians, "Your work, my young colleagues, is cut out for you. You are called, in the words of Saint Paul, to 'do the work of an evangelist,' than which there is no work more exacting, more rewarding or more needed among men." The "essential and real meaning of evangelism is the preaching of the Gospel, the making known what God is and what he has done for us men and for our salvation, and what we must do to be saved."[10] Time and again Tittle voiced this conviction, but nowhere with more eloquence than in a sermon of 1930 entitled, "The Foolishness of Preaching."[11]

Tittle begins by reviewing the arguments advanced to prove that the "pulpit is an anachronism in the modern world" and that preaching is indeed foolishness. Roman Catholicism, he points out, need not worry about this indictment because that Church is built around the altar, not the pulpit; the priest is chiefly an instrument for the administration of the sacraments, the efficacy of which is held unaffected by the character of the man who administers them. "But," Tittle continues, "the Protestant church is an incarnation of the prophetic type of religion. It *is* built around a pulpit. The medium on which Protestantism most depends for the conveyance of truth and grace is personality. In Protestant theory, the personality of the preacher is of supreme importance. It is through him, not merely through properly administered sacraments,

8. "In the Prophetic Succession," *The First Church Pulpit,* Vol. X, No. 2, a Garrett baccalaureate sermon preached June 12, 1949.

9. "Religion As Commitment and Action," typed MS, a sermon preached February 4, 1940.

10. "The Work of an Evangelist," *The First Church Pulpit,* Vol. VIII, No. 21, a Garrett baccalaureate sermon preached June 16, 1946.

11. Reprinted in *The Foolishness of Preaching* (New York: Henry Holt & Co., 1930), pp. 301-14.

that the eternal God must be enabled to speak. And if through him, whether by reason of any moral or intellectual weakness, God is not able to speak, the Protestant church is badly handicapped."

After making this judgment (a judgment in which numerous Protestants of course could not concur), Tittle admits that "many Protestant churches today are half empty." He is positive, however, that whenever in a modern Protestant pulpit you find a strong man, "you do not find any considerable numbers of empty pews. The human heart today is as hungry for religion as ever it was. If the modern preacher has the bread of life to offer, people will come to get it. If he has anything vital to say about the great realities, the eternal values, people will come to hear it. This is not a theory, but fact, as is proved by every church which, even under such social conditions as now prevail, is filled Sunday after Sunday with eager worshippers." He hastens to make clear that by a "strong" man he does not necessarily mean a great man, and certainly not an eloquent man. The number of great preachers, like the number of great artists, musicians, scientists, and statesmen, has always been small and doubtless always will be. As for the number of eloquent preachers, if it is growing less, "let us all thank God and take courage. What the man on the street pronounces eloquence will kill any church in ten years." By a "strong" man he means "simply a man in whom to at least an average amount of intellectual ability is added a determination, at whatever cost, to have something to say that is worth saying Sunday after Sunday and who, moreover, is himself a living illustration of what he is attempting to preach."

If the minister of a strategically located church finds attendance lagging, he may persuade himself (and attempt to persuade his long-suffering wife) that the fault is not his but that of his lazy, religiously indifferent parishioners. Tittle suggests, however, that perhaps the minister should begin "to wonder whether there was not something seriously wrong with himself; whether he was working hard enough and living dangerously enough; whether he was giving himself with that gay and reckless kind of abandon which is required of a minister of the gospel of Christ?"

He then speaks some chilling words to his colleagues:

Too many preachers are lying down on the job. Oh, to be sure, they are keeping busy, busy as bees, but not in the study. There, they merely dabble and dawdle. The time which they do spend among their books, or, to speak more accurately, in the same room where their books are—what do they do with it? Mostly they kill it. Many a preacher has proudly boasted, "I spent four hours in my study this morning," when he ought to have confessed, "In my study this morning I wasted four mortal hours. Two of them I spent day-dreaming. The other two I spent scanning a few unimportant magazine articles and leafing the pages of some second-rate book." Such a man is lying down on the job, notwithstanding the number of calls he may be making, or the amount of committee work he may be doing, or even the number of speeches he may be delivering before chambers of commerce and eating clubs. Neither calling nor committee work nor luncheon club speaking is unimportant. Calling is essential, essential among other things to preaching. No man can preach effectively unless he knows the human heart, and no man can know the human heart unless he keeps in close touch with human lives. Nevertheless, a preacher who for any reason steps into his pulpit on Sunday morning unprepared to discharge his great prophetic function is lying down on the job. He is not giving to his congregation a square deal. He is not giving God a fair chance to speak to that congregation through him. Except in communities that are obviously and wickedly over-churched, and except also in those far too numerous instances where churches are poorly located, if the church is empty it is largely because the preacher is empty.

After citing a specific but anonymous example of an unprofitable pulpit ministry, Tittle goes on: "Both the Roman Catholic and the Protestant systems have their weaknesses. One great weakness of the Roman Catholic system is that it does not make adequate provision for the saving truth which may come through a luminous and inspiring personality. One great weakness of the Protestant system is that it stakes so much upon the appearance of truth-revealing personalities that when they fail to appear it is left almost impotent. In a Roman Catholic church, even though you get nothing at all from the sermon, you have a fairly good chance of getting at least something from the service. In a Protestant church, if you get nothing at all from the sermon, you are 'out of luck.' " He elaborates on this theme:

> It is, I suppose, hardly to be wondered at that many Protestant churches are attempting to "enrich" their service of worship, not only or chiefly because they are beginning at long last to recognize the value of worship, but because they are beginning to despair of getting and maintaining an adequate pulpit. There are laymen today, belonging to non-liturgical churches, who frankly admit that their one hope of holding their young people lies in the erection of a beautiful church edifice and the development of a beautiful service of worship. Now, the religious value of Gothic architecture is, in my judgment, beyond dispute, as is also the

religious value of a well-conducted service of worship. For both, even from the Protestant standpoint, there is a vast deal to be said; provided only that they are sought after as a supplement of prophetic preaching, not as a substitute for it. It will, I think, be nothing less than tragic if, because of an increasing dearth of prophets, the Protestant church begins more and more to subordinate the prophetic office and eventually to smother it with architecture and ritual. But when it comes to institutions, self-preservation is one of the recognized laws of life; and you can in any case hardly blame a group of earnest Protestants if, after years of listening to poor preaching and trying in vain to get their children to listen to it, they begin to hunger after the flesh pots of medievalism. The only way to keep prophetic religion and a prophetic church alive in the world is to go on producing prophets.

Tittle then bluntly denies the explanation that it is absurd to expect any man to have something worthwhile to say every Sunday morning, year in and year out, and that preachers might as well make the admission and give up the hopeless attempt. It is not asking too much, he insists:

It is undeniably asking a great deal, enough in fact to give any man pause, any man who is spiritually sensitive and not a conceited ass. But it is not asking too much. It is probably not asking more than is required of lawyers and editorial writers. What the preacher greatly needs to do is to stop pitying himself and get down to work. Let him resolve that never under any circumstances will he enter his pulpit unprepared, that at whatever cost of toil and tears he will be God's spokesman Sunday after Sunday. Even in that event he will not always be at his best. His sermons will not all be equally helpful. But after listening to him people will go away feeling that it has been worth while for them to have come to church. By the vision and passion of the preacher they will have been lifted up into the presence of God and been enabled to see a bit more clearly life's great realities, its supreme and enduring values. If this result is accomplished, people will go to church. They will go miles to church and in all kinds of weather. Spiritually helpful preaching is not passe, nor will it ever be. Nothing ever will or can take the place of it. For preaching is not only the presentation of truth, but the presentation of truth through personality. Truth may now be presented by means of print. It may be presented also by means of the radio. But never will it be presented with such uplifting power as when it comes through the lips of an inspiring and visible personality. . . . As long as personality endures and remains, as it seems destined to do, the great power in the world, nothing will take the place of spiritually helpful preaching.

But can even great preaching accomplish enough to justify the price the preacher must pay for it, Tittle then asks? Yes, because in every congregation there are "persons who are in truly desperate need of personal help—men who are terribly tempted, women whose hearts ache, young people who are rather dreadfully confused, all sorts of people who feel baffled and beaten and ready to give up." To give such individuals a new grip on life is well worth the preacher's supreme efforts. Yes, also, because the world is in desperate need to hear the redemptive word of God, and by proclamation of the word the preacher may "change the very fabric of human society."

Tittle continues, "Preaching becomes a power only when it is practiced." The impotence of many a pulpit is due quite as much to moral failure as to intellectual failure. Alas, however, goodness alone does not suffice. "I wish I could believe that it were enough for the preacher to live Christianity; but that apparently is not enough. When the congregation goes home Sunday after Sunday saying, 'He is a good man, but he cannot preach,' the church must get another preacher or go out of business!"

He concludes with a reaffirmation of the intimate relationship between Christian preaching and the Christian preacher. Can able preaching alone persuade a congregation that Jesus is the Way, the Truth, and the Life?

> I very much doubt that it can. To the able exposition of Christian principles must be added the convincing demonstration of Christian practice. People must not only hear a man say that they ought to love their enemies, they must actually see this man loving *his* enemies. They must not only hear a man say that they ought, in their several fields, to seek first the Kingdom of Heaven; they must actually see this man in his *own* field seeking first, not public applause nor ecclesiastical preferment, but the triumph of truth and the redemption of society. Nothing that is profoundly Christian is likely to be accomplished by a preacher who talks courage and acts cowardice, or who talks forgiveness and acts vindictiveness, or who talks spirituality and consecration and heroic unselfishness and then acts with an eye single to his own interests. Though I speak with the tongue of men and of angels and do not practice what I preach, I am become as sounding brass and a clanging cymbal, and this notwithstanding the fact that undiscerning persons may consider me a wonderful preacher. If all that was needed were to pack a church, it might be enough to preach Christianity in a brilliant fashion. But if what is needed is a new birth of faith and hope and love, Christianity will have to be lived by the preacher who proclaims it.

Thus it was that Tittle stoutly accorded the pulpit a place of high honor in Protestantism and counted his calling as preacher an honorable one. The proclamation of the will of God required above all that the preacher himself possess a steady and luminous sense of the reality of God. It also required wisdom, knowledge, judgment. Therefore, Tittle considered the "besetting sin of the ministry" to be "intellectual laziness."[12] Prophetic preaching further necessitated courage. Therefore Tittle deemed cowardice a second sin of the ministry.[13] He once delivered a sermon entitled, "The Field of the Pulpit—Life." He took as the province of preaching nothing less than "life" precisely because there was no area of life exempt from God's judgment and redemption.

The terms "crusader," "fighter," "liberal," and "reformer" fail utterly to describe Tittle the preacher. The term "Social Gospel" is too freighted with misunderstanding to get at the essence of his sermons. There is a terrible irony here. Fundamentalists raked him for not confining his pulpit message to the great and only gospel, "Christ—and Him crucified." But Christ and His sacrifice as the supreme revelation of God's love was central to all Tittle preached. Neo-orthodox (or crisis) theologians charged him with preaching a feckless liberalism in which (to quote H. Richard Niebuhr's biting words) "a God without wrath brought men without sin into a kingdom without judgment through the ministrations of a Christ without a Cross." But God as Lord of History was Tittle's supreme conviction. Secular reactionaries flayed him for meddling in political and economic matters when his duty was to seek the regeneration of individuals and not the reformation of society, to assist souls into heaven and not agitate for the Kingdom on earth. But it was exactly Tittle's concern for individuals that led inevitably to a critique of social conditions that crushed and degenerated men. Secular radicals sneered at his moralism and pacifism and refusal to bless violence, not even in the cause of class, racial, or political justice, indeed, not even in the name of the Four Freedoms. As a matter of fact, it was his loyalty to the God revealed in Jesus Christ that made it impossible for him to bow before the gods of Marx and Mars as did so many American liberals in the second and third quarters of the twentieth century.

Paul Hutchinson wrote these perceptive words upon Tittle's death:

Once in a while one heard it said that Dr. Tittle preached too much about war, or color discrimination, or slum clearance, or

12. Letter from Tittle to Edgar DeWitt Jones, January 16, 1933. See also Edgar DeWitt Jones, "Ernest Fremont Tittle," *American Preachers of To-Day* (Indianapolis: The Bobbs-Merrill Company, 1933), p. 88.
13. *Ibid.*

the other social issues of our day. As a matter of fact, he didn't preach about them at all. The only thing he preached about was theology—God, the Christian God as revealed in Jesus Christ. But in the course of preaching such a God he inevitably ran into such questions as his purposes for man, whether man could discover those purposes and what would happen if he did. That was when war and color and the slums and similar illustrations would get into his sermons, for he believed in facing the big issues. He never tried to evade the problems which really torment men. But he wasn't preaching sociology or a disguised political reformism. He was preaching the gospel. He began his sermon always with some aspect of the fact of God; he ended always with man at the moment of decision when confronted with the will of God.[14]

Harris Franklin Rall also recognized the deeply spiritual basis underlying Tittle's preaching. "He was not a crusader, looking for causes to promote; but he loved men and could not stand by in silence and inaction when they were wronged." His faith was not a set of ideas, but a "profound belief in God as the one that mattered in human life, and in Christ's way as the way out for a world in darkness and the way to peace and strength for each individual soul."[15] On the occasion of Tittle's twenty-fifth anniversary at First Church, his people expressed their gratitude that "Sunday after Sunday, by his preaching, he has brought us face to face with God and brought God down to our conditions and needs. He has always dealt with great themes and yet has always kept close to human life. We know that he is a master of the art of preaching, of clearness and vigor of thought, of fitness and beauty of diction. What has meant even more is the vision and courage and loyalty to his Lord with which he has spoken what God has given him."[16] His people's memorial at his death reiterates this gratitude: "The man came first. There was his integrity: we knew that in him the man and the message were one. There was deep conviction. He believed with all his heart in the Christian gospel. He believed that it had the answer to the needs of men and of nations. He brought to us its rich resources of truth, of comfort and courage and peace. He held before us its high demands. We listened to him expound some great theme, and then in the closing minutes bring its truth to bear on our own personal life. When

14. "A Word About a Friend," *Christian Century,* LXVI (August 17, 1949), 959.

15. "Ernest F. Tittle—Preacher," *The Garrett Tower,* XXIV (September, 1949), 9.

16. *A Quarter Century, 1918-1943,* a brochure published by First Church, February 21, 1944.

he ended, we did not think of the preacher and his eloquence; we thought of God and of what our life meant in his sight."[17] Tittle's preaching, observed Joseph Fort Newton, "is preaching open at both ends, toward man in his poignant need, and toward God in His abundant supply."[18] Tittle sought "to present timeless truth set in the boundaries of our time and world," insisted Halford E. Luccock.

> It can truly be said that he had one theme—God. That was increasingly so as the years went on. He had one dominant message, the God and Father of our Lord Jesus Christ. That was the sun around which every planet revolved. That in itself is remarkable when one remembers all the things in our whole social scene about which Dr. Tittle cared passionately and desperately. Dr. Tittle was an outstanding prophet of social righteousness. He had the courage of the specific, a passionate devotion to Christian social action, which made him a dependable leader and a fighter against the great social evils of the day. Yet, he was one of the most distinctively theological preachers of his day. He followed the injunction, "What God hath joined together, let no man put asunder." Again and again . . . he voices his conviction that Christian ethics and action stem from Christian faith. He brought the apostolic leverage to particular tasks, "I beseech you, brethren, *by the mercies of God.*" That deep theological basis gave and gives a permanence and power to his witness. In that he was in a truly apostolic succession, one that is frequently not noticed as it should be. It is worth much thought that many of the greatest leaders in the interpretation of the so-called (and inadequately called) "social gospel," were equally or more noteworthy in their interpretation of Christianity as a personal experience.[19]

It is unnecessary to continue to load supporting statement upon supporting statement to refute the impression that Tittle (like allegedly the other champions of twentieth-century religious liberalism) preached a truncated or secularized gospel. Men and women who heard Tittle's sermons knew that the will of God was being proclaimed and given dominion over all life. If they had not been possessed by this awareness, then Tittle's preaching would have fallen miserably short of his own concept of the field of the pulpit—"life." He set forth this concept so frequently and so forcefully that it is difficult to select from the many

17. *A Memorial To Ernest Fremont Tittle Prepared for the Official Board and Adopted unanimously as an Expression of the Feelings of the 2500 Members of First Church, October 3, 1949,* a pamphlet published by First Church.
18. Quoted by Halford E. Luccock in the foreword to *A World That Cannot Be Shaken* (New York and London: Harper & Brothers, 1933), p. ix.
19. Foreword to *The Gospel According to Luke* (New York: Harper & Brothers, 1951), pp. vi-vii.

statements. Perhaps, however, it is appropriate to turn first to a major declaration made by Tittle in 1939 in the *Christian Century*'s series, "How My Mind Has Changed in This Decade." It is revealing that Tittle's contribution is entitled, "A God-Centered Ministry."[20]

He begins with the admission that his early preaching was "mostly of the ethical type" and that he more than suspected that his early sermons left his congregations "religiously unfed." He continues:

> I now know that preaching must be God-centered if it is to carry conviction, stir conscience, afford guidance, sustain morale, and offer an enduring ground for hope of a better world. It is, therefore, most encouraging to find in myself a new sense of the reality of God. In recent years, an overwhelming recognition of the world's needs—and of my own—has led me to re-examine the grounds for belief in God. It also has led me to study the Christian faith experimentally, not merely intellectually—for homiletical purposes. Yet like many another who, walking in darkness, has finally seen a great light, I am convinced that such assurance as I now have was graciously given me by God himself, so that I can only wonder and be thankful.

He then asserts his new appreciation of the Christian faith in "the revelation of God in Christ," while holding fast to an old conviction:

> I still feel obliged to take seriously the teachings of Jesus. I cannot believe that Jesus Christ is God's supreme self-disclosure and, at the same time, suppose that the Jesus of history has little if anything to say to us. I am very distrustful of current interpretations of Christianity that belittle the Sermon on the Mount and stress, almost exclusively, the presence in Jesus of something "numinous" which, they would have us believe, is profoundly indicative of the nature of God, although not to be interpreted in rational or ethical terms. That there was something "numinous" in Jesus which profoundly impressed his disciples I am fully prepared to believe. What I am not prepared to believe is that it did not convey to them any impression of moral and spiritual grandeur but only of transcendent and incalculable power. Against this view, the letters of Saint Paul, not to mention the four Gospels, seem to me to be decisive. It is, I think, a travesty of Christianity to assert that the God of Christian faith is but transcendent and incalculable power. Moreover, such an assertion may be the expression not so much of a confident faith as of a secret and sickening doubt. (I do not say that it necessarily is but only that it may be.) Desperately wanting to believe in a God who is more than a match for intrenched and triumphant evil, and being none too sure that there is such a God, one may nervously proclaim the

20. *Christian Century*, LVI (June 21, 1939), 795-97.

transcendence of God in terms of sheer otherness and arbitrary, unlimited power. It is not, for me, a new conviction that God is (Christlike) love; or that the love of God is also the wisdom and the power of God. However, my present belief that it was God himself who gave 'the light of the knowledge of his glory in the face of Jesus Christ' has greatly strengthened this conviction that the love of God, far from being impotent, is the ultimate power in history.

This plea for a God-centered ministry and this defense of a faith both personal and social in its concern was made many times. Writing to a professor, Tittle stated:

> I am convinced that the field of the pulpit is in all of life. I should like, however, to state and emphasize a growing conviction that preaching, on whatever subject, should be distinctively religious and not merely the sort of thing that may be found in an editorial in such magazines as *The Nation* and *The New Republic*. Always, preaching should be God-centered. In especial, sermons on controversial subjects should bring out the relevance of the Christian idea of God to the political-economic order and to every relation of human beings to one another. This approach proclaims the preacher's right to speak on the subject under discussion and assures to him a hearing on the part of persons who, otherwise, may be inclined to think he is merely voicing his own opinions and this in relation to matters on which he has no competence to speak.[21]

Tittle once warned a young man contemplating the ministry as a career that the modern "preacher must be able to speak directly from the Christian viewpoint to the contemporaneous situation and all its manifold aspects, personal, political and social. But he must speak from a definitely religious standpoint, not merely from the standpoint of a secular journalism. Hence, his first and imperative need of thinking his way through to an intelligent and commanding conception of God. His conception of God should be the background of all his preaching on whatever theme. Otherwise, he will be speaking not with religious authority but only as a secular scribe."[22] On another occasion a young parson announced in the press his intention to preach a series of book sermons. Tittle flashed the plea: "As one who loves you like a father and believes that you have it in you to become a great preacher, may I venture to say, Don't do it. The preacher of book sermons is terribly tempted to depend upon other men's thinking and usually yields, after a

21. Letter from Tittle to Harry F. Baughman, July 29, 1943. For identical wording, see letter from Tittle to Lionel Crocker, January 2, 1947.
22. Letter from Tittle to Estel I. Odle, June 25, 1934.

while, to the temptation. It is so much easier to review a book than it is to produce a sermon which will set forth one's own interpretation of life, and you simply must not become a purveyor of homiletical hash! This bit of advice I give you gratis and you may do with it whatever you see fit to do."[23]

Indeed, the admonition hundreds of young seminarians and preachers received from Tittle was terse and unambiguous: "Don't be afraid to talk religion!" Bluntly and repeatedly he pronounced, "The function of preaching is to speak directly and concretely to human need, to tell live-able truth to people."[24] He had only sympathy for the discouraged lay-man who said of his rector, "If I should steal his Sunday morning newspaper, I do not know what he would preach about."[25] Repeatedly he made the observation that he did not know of a single instance where the preachers of merely topical or sensational sermons (preachers who tickled the ears of their congregation so that they might itch the more, to borrow from Saint Augustine) retained their popularity for more than a few years.

It did not follow, however, that the world revealed in the pages of the Sunday newspaper must be isolated from the word preached in the Sunday pulpit. Tittle knew that the truths of the gospel were no truths at all if they did not refer men eventually to the contemporary world. The necessary congruence between religion and life was at the very marrow of his pulpit proclamation. That there is no religion without righteousness was as self-evident a proposition to Tittle as to Amos.

Thus he frequently reflected upon the text: "If a man say, I love God, and hateth his brother, he is a liar: for he who loveth not his brother whom he sees cannot love God whom he hath not seen." And: "Let justice roll down as waters, and righteousness as a mighty stream." Yet even as his people were confronted with these stern words, they also received the assurance of the comfortable words: "God is our refuge and strength, a very present help in trouble." And: "Come unto me, all ye that labor and are heavy-laden, and I will give you rest." And: "This corruptible must put on incorruption, and this mortal must put on immortality. But when this corruptible shall have put on incorruption, and this mortal shall have put on immortality, then shall come to pass the saying that is written, Death is swallowed up in victory."[26] For Tittle

23. Letter from Tittle to Cecil Ristow, November 17, 1931.
24. Luccock's foreword to *A World That Cannot Be Shaken,* p. x.
25. *The Timely and the Timeless,* Garrett baccalaureate sermon preached June 7, 1936 (pamphlet).
26. For example, these passages are juxtaposed in *A Way to Life* (New York: Henry Holt & Co., 1935), pp. 65-78.

as for Martin Buber, religion was both a vertical relationship between man and God and a horizontal relationship between man and man. He knew what it meant to be told by Jesus that he must love God in order to love his neighbor, and he did not need the "clarifying" interpretation of a modern theologian, "Relatedness requires the vertical dimension to actualise the horizontal dimension." The tired debate between the Fundamentalists and Social Gospelites, said Tittle, serves mostly to obfuscate. The real distinction is not between a so-called personal religion and a so-called social religion, but between a truncated and whole faith. "The trouble, of course, with fundamentalism is that it is not fundamental enough. It leaves out of consideration very fundamental things of which the New Testament makes a good deal, as, for example, justice and mercy and integrity and loyalty to truth." The only religion there is or ever can be is personal religion. "Religion may be true or false. It may be ethical or unethical. It may be possessed or devoid of a sense of social responsibility. The one thing religion cannot be is non-personal. There is no disembodied faith. There is faith only in persons."[27]

To the question, Is not the proper function of the Church the salvation of souls? Tittle replied: "Yes, of course that is the purpose and the only concern of the Church; and for this very reason the Church cannot afford to be indifferent to social conditions. Consider child labor —what it does to the soul of a child. And mass unemployment—what it does to the soul of the unemployed. And the totalitarian state, under which the individual is denied every freedom that is essential for moral and spiritual development. If it be true, as it undoubtedly is, that the purpose, the sole concern of the Church is the salvation of human souls, it follows that the Church cannot possibly afford to be indifferent to political institutions, social customs, economic practices that condition the moral and spiritual life of men."[28] Thus, the true preacher must comfort the afflicted but also afflict the comfortable. "He must not cry, 'Peace, peace,' when there is no peace and can be none, inasmuch as there is no repentance, no turning to God, no recognition of the divine purpose in history. The preacher must set forth the conditions of real and enduring comfort. He must be God's servant in the bringing of men to God—bringing their social and political institutions and their own lives into conformity with the will of God—that they and their children

27. "Personal Religion," typed MS, a sermon preached July 23, 1939.
28. "The Upbuilding of the Body of Christ," typed MS, a sermon preached June 14, 1942.

may have life and not appalling death and destruction."[29] The true preacher fears God—but none besides. He fears to leave unuttered the word he is bidden to speak, that true and righteous and searching word which is "in his heart as a burning fire," that he must speak or else be consumed.

Tittle recalled that when he was a boy he often heard the complaint that preachers were forever talking about the Amalekites and the Jebusites to the neglect of matters of immediate concern. Nowadays, however, he heard exactly the opposite complaint, that preachers were forever talking about war and peace, politics and economics, to the neglect of matters of eternal concern (like the Amalekites and the Jebusites?). As great preaching must be at once individual and social, so it must be both timely and timeless; timely in the sense of being relevant to the contemporary condition of man, timeless in the sense that it is grounded in the eternal, in the nature of God and His purpose for mankind. "It must speak to the man who is a child of his time, caught in the meshes of the contemporary situation; *and* it must speak to the man who is a child *in* time, a finite creature who, as all other finite creatures of whatever time or place, must deal with the recalcitrant elements in his own nature and face the mystery and experience the vicissitudes of life. In order to be greatly effective, preaching must speak to these two men in every man; and this it can do only if it is at once timely and timeless."[30]

III

Tittle was determined to be innocent of Milton's withering arraignment of the Anglican clergy, "The hungry sheep look up and are not fed." He sought to sustain his people throughout the year with sermonic nourishment carefully proprotioned, varied, and appropriate to their hungers. Unlike many Protestant ministers of his generation, he observed the Christian calendar, preparing special sermons for All Saint's Day, the Sundays in Advent, Christmas, New Year's, Ash Wednesday, Lent, Palm Sunday, Maundy Thursday, Good Friday, Easter, the First Sunday after Easter, Whitsunday; and also for Thanksgiving, Race Relations Sunday, Children's Day, the Fourth of July, Memorial Day, Armistice Day. Naturally he was much importuned by vested groups to promote their particular interests: prohibition, education, conservation, Americanization, and the like. It was impossible to accommodate every request,

29. "Priest and Prophet," *The First Church Pulpit,* Vol. VII, No. 10, a Garrett baccalaureate sermon preached June 11, 1944.

30. "The Timely and the Timeless," Garrett baccalaureate sermon preached June 7, 1936 (pamphlet).

even when the cause was worthy. "If I should do so," he once ruefully observed, "I would find myself promoting somebody's interest practically every Sunday of the year. Not long ago I was invited by the pure milk companies in this county to preach a sermon on pure milk and was furnished biblical texts without number for such a discourse!"[31] In his later ministry, at least two series of sermons were included in the preaching year, one during Lent and the other during the Northwestern University summer session. A third series was often part of the autumn preaching calendar. Some of the themes of these series were "Finding Oneself," "The Christian Faith," "What Jesus Has to Say," "A Philosophy of Life," and "Ways of Life." From time to time he planned an additional series, for instance, on "God" or "Personal Salvation." The "great themes" he had no hesitation in discussing "year after year."[32]

Early in his career Tittle did not always preach from a scriptural text. As he informed Joseph Fort Newton, "I have such a violent distaste for anything perfunctory, especially in religion, that I refuse to 'take a text' merely because sermonizers are expected to do so. Incidentally, I have noted the fact that some preachers who always do take a text do not always allow the text to take them beyond the first paragraph. Furthermore, my personal belief that the living God has not been dumb since the Biblical canon was closed leads me to look for instances of extra-Biblical 'inspiration' and to make grateful use of them when I find them."[33] As the years passed, however, his preaching became increasingly Biblical and now only rarely did he fail to take a text. As he informed his Garrett class, "It is not easy to take a great text, or a poor text, and build an entire sermon on it. But it pays off in the end. The sermon is far less likely to be superficial and thin. And after its delivery the people though they may forget—they usually do—what you have said, may remember the text all the rest of their life and derive much benefit from it."[34]

IV

Ernest Fremont Tittle held a vision of prophetic preaching. He possessed the valor to sustain the vision. Convictions unsupported by courage, of course, are no convictions at all. But he also remembered Jesus' admonition: "Behold, I send you forth as sheep in the midst of

31. "Christianity and Race Relations," typed MS, a sermon preached February 24, 1935.

32. Letter from Tittle to Herbert J. Doran, January 15, 1942.

33. Letter from Tittle to Joseph Fort Newton, January 19, 1931.

34. Harold Arthur Brack, "Ernest Fremont Tittle's Theory and Practice of Preaching" (Ph.D. dissertation, Northwestern University, 1953), p. 143.

wolves: be ye therefore wise as serpents, and harmless as doves." For thirty-one years from the pulpit of First Church Tittle proclaimed God's will. This fact testifies to his courage, but it is equally a tribute to his carefully formulated strategy for a prophetic ministry.

It is necessary to understand that the significance of Tittle's prophecy lies precisely in the fact that he was a working minister with real parish responsibilities, priestly, pastoral, and administrative. Moreover, because he was a Methodist minister, he was accountable to denominational as well as congregational discipline. It is sobering to observe that almost all the outstanding champions of Protestant social passion in the twentieth century were bishops and executive secretaries, seminary professors, editors, officers in reform and civic agencies, peripatetic public speakers and pastors of community churches unfettered by a larger denominational loyalty. To be sure, he stood not absolutely alone, but in modern America the inheritors of the mantle of Amos and Isaiah were generally not parish parsons. A fledgling minister once bitterly lamented, "Bravely and boldly the professors tell young seminarians to preach a realistic gospel—and wave good-bye to them from their bomb-proof dugouts as the young hopefuls go out to the battle."[35] But Tittle did not live in a bomb-proof dugout. He too faced the tensions between preaching a gospel wherein the vast reaches of society were placed under God's judgment and at the same time ministering daily to anxious parishioners. He too knew the necessity of administering a church, a large multi-million-dollar institution. This meant the raising and distributing annually of enormous sums of money. Money placed on the altar may properly be termed "minted blood," but it is a fact of Protestant life that such blood is usually not forthcoming from an angry layman who, like Crevecoeur's "Low Dutchman" could conceive of "no other idea of a clergyman than that of a hired hand; if he does his work well he will pay him the stipulated sum; if not he will dismiss him, and do without his sermons, and let his church be shut up for years." Tittle too was commissioned to preach the truth, but if the consequences were not to be a mutinous flock, a sullen Official Board, and a censorious national Methodism, the truth somehow had to be spoken in love. How, then, did Tittle do this?

Tittle believed the prophet must aspire to two graces if he hoped to be heard (much less honored) : he must speak the truth *in love* and he must *be* what he preaches. Tittle once observed: "After much bitter experience brought on by myself I have learned that radicals get into trouble not so much by reason of what they say, if they tell the truth, as

35. *Christian Century*, LIV (August 4, 1937), 973.

by the spirit in which they say it. I have learned that if a preacher loves his people and gives them abundant reason to know that he does he can say anything to them that needs to be said. They will not always agree with him, but they will accord him full freedom of speech. And not only have I learned that truth spoken in love is effective, I am beginning to learn that love gives birth to insight and leads to the discovery of truth, that truth about human nature and human conduct which no preacher can afford not to know."[36] On another occasion he advised some young ministers: "Congress should make no law abridging the freedom of the pulpit, or the right of the pew peaceably to assemble and petition the ecclesiastical government for a redress of grievances. In and out of the church not a few radicals get into trouble not so much because they are radicals as because they are fools. Not even radicalism can or should make up for the absence of good judgment and fair play. . . . My own increasing conviction is that you can say anything that needs to be said to people whom you love and have reason to know that you love them."[37] Many a man of prophetic quality, said Tittle, has gotten into trouble, not so much by reason of what he has said, as by reason of the way in which he said it. After all, "It is not necessary to be rude in order to be honest."[38] It is foolish as well as unnecessary to be rude, to scold, nag, denounce, for such sermons rarely hit their intended target. As Tittle confided to his congregation, "In my early ministry, and if the whole truth must be told, rather late in my ministry, I indulged in the practice of denunciation. I denounced this and that. . . . I flattered myself in the belief that I was being very courageous when, as a matter of fact, I was merely displaying my callowness and inexperience. Eventually, however, I woke up to the fact that my ringing denunciations were not doing any good. They were applauded by people whom they did not hit and resented by people whom they did hit; resented, never considered."[39] Maybe Henry Ward Beecher had a point when he observed that the churches of America were filled with bald-headed sinners whose hair had grown thin and scant by reason of the sermons that had caromed off their skulls only to hit a brother in the pew behind. We have it on rather good authority that if a man says he loves God and hates his brother, he is a liar. Tittle was not a liar;

36. Letter from Tittle to Joseph Fort Newton, January 19, 1931.
37. "A Free and Effective Pulpit," *World Service News*, XVII (March, 1931), 2. See also, Paul H. Yourd, "Tittle of Evanston," *Church Management*, VIII (April, 1932), 480.
38. *Foolishness of Preaching*, p. 294.
39. *On Getting Rid of Evil Spirits*, a sermon preached February 2, 1930 (pamphlet).

he was not a counterfeit man. Preaching is foolishness unless the preacher practices the service of Christ, which is perfect freedom. It was Tittle's conviction that the freedom of the pulpit could never be suppressed from without unless within its possessor first betrayed his prophetic commission. Such a betrayal was unthinkable to Tittle, for he comprehended that we do not have death to fear, but God.

Yet if Tittle was loyal to his commission to preach the truth in love and live the truth he preached, he was not so arrogant as to presume that questions of tactics were beneath his consideration. To the contrary, he much meditated on what it meant to be as wise as serpents and harmless as doves. As a professional politician is rightly not contemptuous of the processes by which he must remain in office, so Tittle was not indifferent to how a preacher might best retain the ear of his people. A prophet without listeners is hardly less irrelevant than a politician without an office.

To begin with, Tittle had little love for controversy and no taste for martyrdom; and he was at once too humble and too self-possessed to be feisty. If his style was not that of a field mouse, neither was it that of a wolverine. Only when the danger was clear and present did he engage in public exchanges with his critics. Almost equally rare were his private letters of rebuttal. Let one example stand in illustration of this point. On December 15, 1938, Dr. Emory W. Luccock, minister of the First Presbyterian Church in Evanston, wrote Tittle sharply rebuking him for his pacifist position as set forth in a recent article. Tittle said nothing in reply. On February 8, 1939, Dr. Luccock somewhat petulantly wondered about Tittle's silence. At last Tittle's calm answer came: "Please try to believe me when I say that I honestly think your letter concerning my *Christian Century* article does not call for any reply. Long ago, acting on a hint from Dr. Lyman Abbott, I made it a rule never to reply to a purely personal attack. After an observance of thirty years, I am completely convinced that this is a wise rule to follow."[40]

Over the years, also, Tittle learned the wisdom of the old adage, "A soft answer turneth away wrath." To a disaffected parishioner, a man who would one day cancel his church membership but who never withdrew his friendship, Tittle wrote: "Dear Wilbur: You are good enough to say that I need not reply to your letter. Nevertheless I want you to know how much I appreciate your sending it to me and the fine spirit which it reveals in you. More than I can say I appreciate your tolerance and patience in listening to a preacher with whom you do not always

40. Letter from Tittle to Emory W. Luccock, February 10, 1939.

agree. For myself, I can only say that I am making an earnest effort to be at once intelligent and just in my moral judgments."[41] Another critic received this note: "I am very glad that you wrote to me as frankly as you did, and I cannot be thankful enough for the friendly spirit in which you have written. I cannot expect that everyone will agree with the positions which I venture to take. Neither can I venture to hope that all my positions will prove to be wisely taken. But as you know the alternative to making mistakes is to sit down and do nothing and the latter I simply cannot do. Please, therefore, try to bear with me as I attempt to furnish some sort of leadership in this time of crisis."[42] When a couple threatened to leave First Church because of Tittle's arraignment of police brutality during the 1937 steel strike on Chicago's South Side, he had only these plain words to say: "Naturally I regret to learn of your feeling that you should no longer attend the services of First Church. However, I, too, have my conscience to consider, and you will agree that I am morally bound to obey what I conceive to be the command of God, irrespective of the effect which such obedience on my part may have upon the conduct of some one member or attendant of First Church."[43] Perhaps, however, the spirit of Tittle's reaction to criticism is best captured in this wonderfully open epistle: "Dear Charley: Bully for you! I am referring, of course, to your excellently frank statement that Ernest Tittle was wrong. Of course, it doesn't follow that he is! But he would be glad to know why you think he is. So go to it."[44]

Because Tittle possessed the grace either to remain silent or to reply in softness to wrathful criticism he was able to keep old friendships that otherwise might have shattered. There is no more extraordinary chapter in his entire ministry than this. In instance after instance men reproached him for his pacifism or radicalism or color blindness, often threatening to withdraw from First Church and in fact occasionally doing so. Yet it was to Tittle they returned in moments of joy and despair, to marry their children and bury their dead. Tittle once confided to his secretary that he consciously sought to follow Lincoln's example of working with men even as they mocked him.[45] He was successful in his emulation because he, like Lincoln, possessed a humility born of self-acceptance.

A second tactical element in the prophetic preaching of Tittle was

41. Letter from Tittle to Wilbur Helm, May 31, 1934.
42. Letter from Tittle to W. E. Wahlman, July 1, 1932.
43. Letter from Tittle to William Forney Hovis, June 24, 1937.
44. Letter from Tittle to Charles Ward, July 11, 1936.
45. Author's interview with Mrs. Bernice Wolseley, Evanston, Ill., July 13, 1960.

an absolutely scrupulous respect for facts. Vulnerable is the minister who utilizes the pulpit to express his opinions on social issues when these opinions are unsupported by facts, for he then cannot reply to those in the pew who grumble about "windy fancies." Vulnerable, too, is the minister who presumes to speak authoritatively on technical matters when he has no technical knowledge. Tittle hammered this point home to his Garrett classes. It was the burden of his advice to scores of young liberals under fire in their pastorates. "Facts, facts, facts—you fought with facts," he once exclaimed to his secretary.[46] Tittle never ceased to be a student; he never lost his love of study. Consequently, he rarely was caught with his homework unprepared, and he entered the fray armored in rightness as well as righteousness. This is all the more remarkable because he was by nature passionate and impulsive, and the temptation must have been great to prophesy without fear—and without research. Uusually, however, his self-discipline and sense of responsibility enabled him to resist the temptation. In this he was aided by his faculty friends at Garrett and Northwestern, for it was to them he turned, over the phone or over coffee, for technical consultation. Advice was solicited not only in matters of theology, but also in history, political science, economics, sociology, law, medicine, the sciences in general, and music and art and philosophy; indeed, there was scarcely a department in Northwestern University with a member whose mind had not been tapped by Tittle.

Timing was another tactical element deemed important by Tittle. As he warned his Garrett students, Christmas Sunday is no day to preach on temperance. To be sure, there is the temptation to postpone action, to persuade oneself that this is no time to "rock the boat," that tomorrow will be a more propitious day for the moment of decision. The priest and the Levite in the parable of the Good Samaritan, Tittle often speculated, passed by on the other side probably because they were hurrying to Jerusalem to attend an "important" meeting of the Social Action Committee. Ultimately the bullet must be bitten, the unpopular stand taken, and the only thing the prophet can then do is " 'grin and bear it' with such help as he can get, and will get if he seeks it, from God."[47] Yet the wise prophet hewed to the main line and allowed no extraneous or untimely issues to jeopardize the prophetic enterprise. He tried to do in a given situation certainly not less but also not more than his best judgment indicated he had a fighting chance of carrying through. He

46. Letter from Mrs. Bernice Wolseley to author, May 28, 1961.
47. Letter from Tittle to Howard Ray Carey, September 16, 1943.

did not relinquish his convictions or deny his faith, but also he did not risk losing the war (no other word suggests itself) by insisting on fighting battles unnecessary and hopeless. For instance, in championing unsegregated hotel facilities in the key 1932 General Conference debate, he did not permit the issue to be deflected by an obstructive argument over miscegenation.

A kind of corollary to the admonition to be wise and harmless is another one found in Matthew 7:6: "Give not that which is holy unto the dogs, neither cast your pearls before swine, lest they trample them under their feet, and turn against and rend you." Tittle took this saying of Jesus to mean that there were concepts men were not yet ready to understand and accept, and that it was therefore necessary to lead them step by step to the truth, for without this gradual preparation the precious truth would go unrecognized as pearls cast before swine.[48]

Because Tittle was not vain he recognized the feeling of frustration that gripped laymen in the pews who Sunday after Sunday had to "take it" in silence, and because he was not a fool he understood the importance of affording them a chance for rebuttal. This is why at staff meetings he would read aloud critical letters, seeking from his assistants their evaluation of the legitimacy of the censure.[49] This is why at Official Board and other church meetings he was careful to see that everyone had an opportunity to speak his mind. And this is why, as he explained to a colleague, he saw to it "that the pulpit is supplemented by the forum, in which laymen have the opportunity to 'talk back.' In the church which it is my great privilege to serve we have learned to think and let think and to maintain our fellowship in Christ despite honest differences of opinion."[50]

Tittle also remembered what no Protestant minister should forget: the church he served was not his private property and he might not utilize the buildings for controversial purposes without first consulting the laity, just as he might not commit his congregation to a controversial position without their approval. In the course of his career Tittle signed hundreds of resolutions and petitions in the cause (as he believed) of social justice, and he served as officer, member, or sponsor of scores of reform organizations. But in doing so he strove to make clear that he was committing only himself, not the First Methodist Episcopal Church,

48. Letter from Mrs. Bernice Wolseley to author, May 28, 1961.
49. Author's interview with the Reverend Joseph Thomas, Evanston, Ill., July 29, 1959.
50. Letter from Tittle to Theodore W. Boltz, May 17, 1942.

Evanston. For example, he happily agreed to serve as sponsor of the Religion and Labor Institute providing his name alone was used, no reference being made to First Church. "This," he explained to the solicitor, "I am bound to say is only fair: my people are willing that I should personally sponsor any cause I believe in but they do not consider it proper for me to involve them without their knowledge or consent."[51] He also endorsed a resolution formulated by the Conference of Younger Churchmen in support of Norman Thomas and the Socialist Party in 1932 on one condition. "The condition is that no mention will be made of the church of which I am minister. I make this condition because of a long standing conviction that in cases of this sort a minister should speak and act as an individual, not as a representative of a group, many of whose members are not in sympathy with the position which he is taking. Please, therefore, use simply my name and make no mention of the church which I am serving."[52]

In later years he placed even severer restrictions on his political participation, now deeming it unwise to publicly endorse any given candidate for public office, or to become affiliated with any political organization whose purpose was party victory. He gave as his reasons: "A clergyman who feels bound, as I do, to preach a radical gospel cannot hope to be effective if he lays himself open to the charge of being a political partisan. This, after thirty years in the ministry, I now know to be true. I am, therefore, making it a rule never to endorse a candidate for public office even though, as in the case you mention, he has many things to commend him."[53] Again: ". . . it is unwise for a clergyman to become affiliated with any political organization, for it is then assumed by some, if not by many, of his hearers that his words are politically rather than religiously motivated. A clergyman, I am now convinced, must maintain, at any cost to himself, a position of religious objectivity, so that he seems to be, and actually is, a voice of the church and not of any other organization."[54] This is not to say that Tittle lacked the courage of the specific. It is not to say that he shied away from discussion of the political *issues* facing the nation. Nor is it to say that he believed ministers forfeited their rights as citizens. He of course voted and named his favorite candidates in private conversations. But the pulpit was not the place for a clergyman to extol the virtues of the Republican, Demo-

---

51. Letter from Tittle to W. B. Waltmire, December 27, 1938.
52. Letter from Tittle to Allan M. Fairbank, October 13, 1932.
53. Letter from Tittle to Jane Jungkunz, February 19, 1940.
54. Letter from Tittle to Albert Price, May 24, 1940.

cratic, Socialist, Prohibition or any other party; and the pulpit was not the place to announce support of Hoover or Roosevelt, Landon or Willkie.

Not all clergymen accept the legitimacy of Tittle's position. It is argued that the churchman has a moral obligation to support publicly the better candidate in a specific election and thereby guide his flock. Yet to do so is a dangerous game for the very reasons cited by Tittle, and as suggested by history as well. In 1928 was Hoover the better candidate (as the Protestant clergy maintained) or Smith (as the Catholic clergy believed)? Was the Federalist ministry wise in opposing Jefferson in 1800? Were the Whig theocrats prophetic in denouncing Jackson in 1828? And what can be said of Southern clerical hostility to Lincoln in 1860 or Northern ministerial endorsement of Grant in 1868?

As Tittle did not commit himself politically as minister of First Church, so the First Church fellowship did not commit itself as a congregation in specific elections. Candidates were not permitted the use of facilities to further their campaigns and a ban was placed on the distribution of campaign literature on the church premises. To be sure, scarcely a week passed that the parish house was not the scene of a debate, forum, or speech on social issues, and for this Tittle came under ugly attack. But even here a certain prudence was exercised, as Tittle attempted to explain to Willard E. Uphaus, executive director of the National Religion and Labor Foundation and editor of *Economic Justice*, a journal of Christian radicalism whose radicalism rather eclipsed the religious. "Personally," said Tittle, "I take the position that a preacher has a right, which must not be challenged, to say anything which he thinks should be said from his own pulpit. I also take the position that the preacher does not own the church building and has no right without consultation with his people to consent to its use for any purpose whatsoever other than the recognized services and activities of the church itself. In our case we have a committee on the use of the church. I see to it that it is a thoroughly representative committee. I appear before it and present my own views as to the action it should take. Then I abide by its decision. Laymen generally feel that a church building ought not to be used as a soapbox for any political party. Most of the members of our church are, I suspect, Hoover Republicans; and I am perfectly sure that no single one of them would be willing to have Herbert Hoover speak in any room in our church in behalf of the Republican Party."[55]

55. Letter from Tittle to Willard E. Uphaus, October 8, 1934.

When Ernest Fremont Tittle mounted the pulpit of First Church it was not an impertinence because he was conscious of the awfulness of his commission to preach the will of God, because his life did not give the lie to the words formed by his lips, because without being guilty of "inveterate amiability" he spoke the truth in love, and because he himself knew the perfect freedom of the service of God.

8. THE PREPARATION
AND PRESENTATION
OF PROPHETIC SERMONS

I

"I consider the besetting sin of the ministry is intellectual laziness."[1] These abrasive words were stated by Tittle in 1933. If uttered three hundred years earlier they would have been untrue, for the saints of colonial New England trained the minds of their ministers as carefully as space-age America trains its young astrophysicists. And in every age in the American past the words would have been unfair to the succession of preachers who cultivated their intellects as an integral element in Christian growth. The strain of anti-intellectualism in American Protestantism never totally triumphed because of a persistent countervailing respect for learning. The House of Intellect, after all, was inhabited by the heirs of the Reformation as well as of the Renaissance.

Nevertheless Tittle's diagnosis was essentially accurate. By the opening decades of the twentieth century American Protestantism was in a perilous condition because of its impaired intellectual foundations. The nineteenth-century evangelism of Finney and Lyman Beecher had degenerated into the obscurantist fideism of twentieth-century Fundamentalism, exemplified most shabbily by Billy Sunday and most poignantly by William Jennings Bryan. The early liberalism of Channing, Parker, and Bushnell had been drained of much of its intellectual rigor by a company of sentimental, moralistic, syncretistic "princes of the pulpit" from Henry Ward Beecher to Norman Vincent Peale, whose very rationalism, paradoxically, represented a retreat from thought.

1. Letter from Tittle to Edgar DeWitt Jones, January 16, 1933.

When in the 1920's a student paper carried the plea, "Please don't rattle the funnies during chapel, someone else might be studying," it was an expression of honest scorn as well as an exhibition of undergraduate high jinks. And much of the intellectual community roared at Mencken's story: "Once a Frenchman announced to an American friend that he was leaving the church of his fathers. The American asked what variety of Protestantism he proposed to patronize. 'I have lost my faith,' announced the Frenchman icily, 'but not my reason.'" Mencken continued: "So far as I am aware, no man of any genuine distinction in the world today is a Methodist; if I am in error, I apologize most humbly." Though Tittle marked this passage in his copy of *Treatise on the Gods*, it is conjectural that this underscoring signified assent.

Yet Tittle was fully aware of the low intellectual estate of the parish minister; no longer was he the wise man to whom the community turned for instruction. He was cognizant that increasingly the clergy and scholars lived in different camps, the bitterness of the clergy sharpened more by the indifference than by the criticism of the scholars. The revolution of thought in the natural and behavioral sciences and the revolutionary imaginative sensibilities of modern art and literature were either ignored on uncomprehended by much of the clergy. How could it be otherwise when (in the words of Perry Miller) the doctrine of justification by faith was interpreted as meaning justification by ignorance; and when (in the words of Heywood Broun) the ministry was the only learned profession in which a man might close his mind forever at the moment of ordination, and, indeed, when ordination required little rigorous training of the mind. Tittle was aware of these things because it was the burden of much secular investigation and because it was the lament of countless churchmen in articles, addresses, and discussion groups. Above all, his own experiences and observations bore witness to this sad condition.

II

If the prophet is given grace, if his vision is on rare occasions transcendent, soaring on the wings of inspiration, it is nevertheless to his intellect that he must finally return. Without the discipline of hard study, prophecy becomes raving. Without the wisdom that comes from sustained reflection, it becomes banal. And without abrasive encounter with science, history, philosophy, psychology, economics, it becomes irrelevant. That is why Tittle concurred in J. H. Jowett's oft-quoted warning, "If the study is a lounge, the pulpit is an impertinence." That is why in scores of letters and addresses he advised candidates for the ministry that their chosen vocation required of them, in addition to a commitment to God and moral courage, much intellectual toil. And that is why he himself engaged in a lifetime intellectual quest, always driven to seek new lands of knowledge. "Conceit," he once informed a university congregation, "can put an end to a man's education more quickly than anything else."[2]

Because Tittle took as the field of the pulpit all of life he drew not alone from the books in his study. The great preachers, with few exceptions, are those who have lived in the world and experienced that which the world both affords and inflicts. Hell may be other people, as Sartre claims, but to shelter oneself from human contacts is to attempt to escape from existence, and rare is the individual who can preach authentic words who has never known authentic human relationships. It may even be the requirement of great preaching that the minister shall have glimpsed hell at least once in his own life. It is therefore not a matter of astonishment that Tittle prepared for the pulpit by living, and because his human encounters were rich experiences his sermons were relevant. If the preacher refuses to rifle ideas from books he becomes guilty of solipsism; yet there is an aridity about ideas known only objectively, never existentially.

Tittle once explained: "I do not so much prepare sermons as let sermons prepare me. What I mean is that I lay hold of an idea and then give it a chance to lay hold of me. Not only do I live with it, I live it, or at least try to do so. If it proves liveable, I conclude that it is preachable and I find that I may be reasonably prepared to preach it." He continued:

> Where do I get ideas for sermons? I must confess that I steal them from people whom I meet in homes and hospitals, on street corners and in committee meetings. I used to take them from books, but in recent years almost without exception I have taken them from people, acting on the belief that the function of preaching is not so much to discuss subjects, which is, I take it, a task of the essayist, but rather to speak directly and concretely to human need. I still beg, borrow, or steal enough time to do a good deal of reading, but I read for the purpose of nourishing my mind, not in order to find sermonic subjects. These I find in all sorts of persons and places. I meet a modern Pharisee, and then preach on "Christianity and Respectability." I meet someone who is greatly upset by the realization that the bottom has dropped out of the old kind of religious authority, and then preach on "Spiritual Adventure." Discovering in my own con-

2. Quoted in Harris Franklin Rall, "Ernest Fremont Tittle—Preacher," *The Garrett Tower*, **XXIV** (September, 1949), 8.

gregation a lingering race prejudice, I preach on "The Modern Jonah." Someone reveals to me the fact that he or she has virtually stopped praying, so I preach "The Good of Prayer." A metropolitan newspaper undertakes to tell me what I should talk about, and especially what I should not talk about in the pulpit, and so I preach on "The Field of the Pulpit—Life." A man who has been hard-hit reveals to me an aching, discouraged heart, so I preach on "The Need of Courage" or "The Love of God." Are such sermons produced easily? In my own case they are not. I sweat no end of blood over them, for, as I have already suggested, I do not consider that an idea is preachable until I have discovered that it is livable. Furthermore, even when a livable idea gets hold of me, I do not find it easy to present in such fashion that it will get hold of other people. What are the words that will carry the thought, what the illustrations that will illuminate it, what the applications that will drive it home? I usually suffer a good deal before I find them.[3]

As the seeds of his sermons were watered by association with others in his capacity as pastor and priest, churchman and civic leader, so surely his more intimate experiences as friend, husband, and father further nourished his preaching. And as we know, a week before his death he confided that he had learned more from three prolonged illnesses than he had ever been able to get from books.

However necessary human association is to authentic existence (save perhaps on the rarest occasions), it is further true that a man's profoundest comprehension of life comes to him in moments of solitude. Such moments are infrequent, especially in the United States where activism is prized and contemplation ("navel-gazing" as the popular phraseology has it) scorned. The national motto might well be: "Let us be up and doing." In a land where all men are busy, it is axiomatic that some men will be more busy than others, and, ironically, these chosen men are clergymen. No vocation permits of less solitude than the Protestant ministry; no vocation so completely prides itself on the attributes of friendliness and usefulness (lest it be the ancillary one of undertaking). "Serviceability to the community"—this is the pearl of great price. To be sure, many parsons parade their everlasting busyness as a badge of honor, finding therein a seemingly legitimate reason to flee from the intolerable agony of intense and concentrated study. To be sure, most parsons' days (and nights) *are* filled with "doing good." Only a handful of charlatans would wish (and only a handful of miscreants would dare) to fritter away their hours playing pinochle or napping. Yet however worthy the enterprises that consume his time, the minister

3. Letter from Tittle to Joseph Fort Newton, January 19, 1931.

who permits himself to be eternally distracted is in fact betraying the vocation to which he has been called by God.

Ernest Tittle fought for his solitude as for his very life. His preaching life depended upon his wresting from a heavy schedule precious hours for contemplation and study. If necessary, he withdrew into his thoughts while physically remaining in a crowd. He sought isolation even at the risk of being deemed "unfriendly," in modern America that most damaging of accusations. In earlier chapters we noted the relationship between this need for solitude and his role as husband, father, friend, and churchman. He was not much of a convention man, and while he dutifully attended the necessary meetings, it was because of the urgency of the business at hand rather than the afforded companionship. He was not much of an automobile driver because his mind was preoccupied with problems other than those of the road. He was not always a congenial dinner partner because small talk bored him, "to chatter was to silence him," though those who loved him referred charitably to his "great, friendly silences." He did not merit the title of "pastoral director" because he did not permit (nor did his wife and secretaries) an uninterrupted flow of calls or callers into his office, and some who were halted were resentful, though the great majority of his people sought to protect him, knowing that when their need was great their shepherd would be at hand. He walked briskly, absorbed in thought, occasionally passing with sightless eyes an acquaintance who possibly hoped to engage him in a chat. Almost always he carried something in his pocket to read if an idle moment presented itself. He traveled by train and coveted the hours of privacy afforded by the Pullman. Even the dentist's chair doubled as a place of contemplation (if not relaxation).

Tittle's secretary reported: "He studied literally all the time when he was not obliged to be doing something else. By 'something else' I mean definite engagements: preaching, performing marriages, baptizing, conducting funerals, attending committee meetings, board meetings, functions of one kind or another inside of or out of the church, calling, counselling, what have you. Morning was always study time, except for unavoidable interruptions; but so were afternoon and evening if they were free for it."[4] Whenever possible, an entire weekday, from rising to

4. Letter from Mrs. Bernice Wolseley to Robert H. Hamill, October 4, 1949, as quoted in letter from Hamill to author, September 14, 1959. Regarding the mornings, Tittle reported: "Like all other preachers, I try to keep my mornings free for study, and like most of them I usually fail to do so." Letter from Tittle to Alfred L. Underhill, February 27, 1931.

bedtime, was set aside for study. Saturday was in theory reserved for polishing the Sunday sermon, though his engagement books reveal a number of duties on that day, especially weddings. The ministerial custom of counting Monday as a day of recreation was ignored.

Tittle did his hard studying at the parsonage rather than the church office, in a book-lined, spacious room on the second floor. Here he could be more easily shielded from callers by Glenna, who proved a very effective sentry, in fact probably more protective than Tittle realized. Here he could also be more easily shielded from phone calls, channeled as they were through the church office where Mrs. Wolseley and the other secretaries proved very effective monitors.

In his study he did not dawdle. His secretary recalled:

> He had an extraordinary capacity for sitting and thinking; it wasn't ruminative but an active and strenuous mental process. He remarked last summer that sermon preparation wouldn't have been so hard for him if he hadn't questioned everything. I think he said that apropos the beginning of the sermon on "Faith." He had started by writing that faith is the product of religion; the sentence finally read, "Faith has sometimes been represented as solely a requirement of religion." There were many erasures. He would make a generalization; then find himself asking whether it was true; then it would be necessary to take account of the exceptions, to make the qualifications which honesty and hard thought demanded. . . . I have had the experience of being forgotten when I was in the study for dictation, and I learned to sit quietly until he "came back" or, sometimes, just to make a quiet departure. A train of thought could be wrecked in two minutes by an interruption, with hours required to get it back on the track.[5]

Ralph W. Sockman reminisced that it was a common saying around Union Theological Seminary that Harry Emerson Fosdick spent one hour in sermon preparation for each minute of sermon delivery.[6] Appropriately (because the careers of Fosdick and Tittle so closely parallel), such also was the common saying around Garrett concerning Tittle. Indeed, far from being an exaggeration, this "scuttlebutt" understated the facts. Tittle's reading and preparation for sermons was more general than specific. Rarely did he "attempt to dig up material for 'next Sunday's sermon.' "[7] Rather, everything he read—and experienced—was grist for the sermonic mill. As Tittle reported to an inquirer, "In recent years I

5. Mrs. Bernice Wolseley, as quoted in Paul Hutchinson, "Portrait of a Preacher," foreword to Tittle, *A Mighty Fortress* (New York: Harper & Brothers, 1949), p. xxxi.
6. "Forty Years of Fosdick," *Religion In Life*, XXVI (Spring, 1957), 291.
7. Letter from Tittle to Harry F. Baughman, July 29, 1943.

have seldom read with reference to any specific subject which I was intending to discuss. My reading has been of a general nature, designed to feed my mind."[8] He once quoted to a Northwestern graduating class that deservedly famous stump speaker who said, "Fill yourself with your subject, then knock out the bung and let nature caper." "The reason why most of us do not say more," Tittle continued, "is just because we have nothing more to say. We cannot speak in public because we do not think in private."[9]

A generous friend once gave Tittle a check to purchase books and Tittle responded gratefully: "To me books are meat and drink. Not only are they the means of life; they are to a very large degree the joy and zest of life."[10] Again and again he declared his passion for books. His one extravagance was their purchase. Repeatedly he admonished his young colleagues of the cloth to sacrifice every luxury—almost every necessity—to the acquisition of a personal library.

Yet it is not quite accurate to characterize Tittle as a bibliomaniac. His passion for books was disciplined, controlled, even calculated. It is at once both a compliment and a criticism to observe that his attitude was more that of a bookworm than a book collector. The age, rarity, binding, design, print, paper of a volume did not much concern him. Books were to be read, not merely handled. His library was assembled not for prideful display, and there were few (if any) handsome volumes with uncut pages in it. Books were to him lovely in the manner that sharp, clean, bright surgical instruments are lovely to a physician. They were tools to be acquired, mastered, cared for, utilized, and appreciated for their usefulness. In sum, although Tittle claimed to find joy in books, it is doubtful that he sought relaxation or sheer fun in reading, and in the last analysis he valued books because they enabled him to more faithfully proclaim the Word of God.

Tittle possessed enormous powers of concentration. He was a hard reader. He never claimed the ability to devour a volume in a twinkling, yet he gave authors the sustained attention they merited. As he read, he noted key sentences with a small, neat check mark in the margin. Occasionally he marked passages for possible sermon use. Only rarely did he make extensive marginal comments; thus it is difficult to judge if a mark signifies agreement or disagreement with the author. He con-

8. Letter from Tittle to Alfred L. Underhill, February 27, 1931.
9. A commencement address delivered to the graduates of the Northwestern University School of Speech, June, 1924, reprinted in Alan H. Monroe, *Principles and Types of Speech* (New York: Scott, Foresman & Company, 1935), p. 228.
10. Letter from Tittle to Hadden MacLean, January 2, 1934.

fessed to having no method of gathering and keeping material. "I have tried various filing systems, but to no avail. I forget what I have filed and where I have filed it! I even forget that I have done any filing!"[11] Tittle was being too hard on himself. As Paul Hutchinson more fairly observed, while Tittle "never was able to assemble the sort of filing system which an efficiency expert would have approved, he had a way of being able to dive into the papers on his laden desk, or into his desk drawers, or into some spot on his study shelves and to come up with what he wanted that he had read and mentally filed 'for future use.' . . . And he followed hunches. Mulling over some problem universal to human experience he would say, 'Kagawa must have said something about that.' Whereupon he would take down a volume of the great Japanese Christian's poems and there, sure enough, he would find just what he was after."[12] It is to the point, furthermore, to observe that at his death the Tittle Collection was in good shape, revealing a certain respect for methodical order in his record-keeping.

Although the assistant ministers freed Tittle from many pastoral burdens, he did not have the services of a research assistant as such. The staff arrangement did not permit the secretaries to act in this capacity except occasionally for a specific bit of reference work. One person, however, was of immeasurable value in the preparation of sermons, and that person was of course Glenna. She read widely with an eye for sermonic material. She clipped the *New York Times*. She called attention to notices and reviews of recently published books. Tittle happily acknowledged his indebtedness to Glenna. Her labors saved him much reading time and, in fact, provided him with many of his most effective illustrations.[13]

Tittle subscribed to a fair number of periodicals, as the following incomplete listing suggests: *American Scholar, Asia, Christendom, Christian Century, Fellowship, Foreign Affairs, Fortune, Harper's, Headline Books, Manchester Guardian Weekly, Nation, New Republic, Social Frontiers, World Christianity, New York Times, Common Sense, The Call, Christian Newsletter, Christianity and Crisis, Motive, Life, Time, Saturday Review of Literature, Atlantic Monthly, Progressive, Outlook, Report to the Business Executive, Human Events, Religion in Life, World Tomorrow, Religion Today, Christian Advocate, Business Week, Reader's Digest, U.S. News and World Report,* and, of course, the Evanston and Chicago papers.

11. Letter from Tittle to Lionel Crocker, January 2, 1947.
12. Hutchinson, "Portrait," p. xxx.
13. Letter from Mrs. Bernice Wolseley to Elaine Williams, June 12, 1940.

In answer to an inquiry concerning his periodical reading, Tittle quite properly admitted that he read these publications "more or less," for it would have been absurd to pretend that there were enough hours in the week to permit a close scrutiny of some forty issues.[14] Nevertheless, the list is impressive for both its breadth and length, including as it does conservative, liberal, and socialist journals and a nice balance between the religious and secular. With few exceptions, however, the reading is sober: were there no moments for *The New Yorker*'s wit or the *National Geographic*'s romance? Also missing are the technical journals of the physical and social sciences and the more precious literary magazines. Yet the lacuna is not terribly great and on the whole Tittle could claim an acquaintanceship with the serious journalism of his generation.

What books did Tittle read, and how many? It is impossible to answer this question with precision. For one thing, he kept no close tabulation, and when queried would reply in such a general fashion as: "I read many books during the year but never keep count of the number."[15] For another, at his death his library was willed to Gammon Theological Seminary in Atlanta, founded in 1883 for the ministerial training of Negroes. The Gammon (now the Interdenominational Theological Center) librarians do not possess the acquisition list. Consequently, it would be necessary to remove every book from the shelves (and call in those signed out) and examine it for the Tittle bookmark in order to reconstruct his library. This seemed an impossible task and only a heavy sampling was undertaken, primarily to judge the manner in which Tittle "marked up" a volume while reading it. Nevertheless, if we may never know all that he read, a reasonably accurate conclusion can be reached based on his correspondence, several incomplete check lists in the Tittle Collection, and his sermon references.

Shortly before his death, after four decades of experience in and reflection about the ministry, Tittle advised a young preacher "to read books of sermons less and less and great books on philosophy and theology more and more."[16] It is true that Tittle possessed complete sets of the sermons of such major preachers as Phillips Brooks and it is true that he read with avidity the sermons of such prominent contemporaries as Harry Emerson Fosdick, but it is further true that he engaged in his own explorations of the nature of God and the destiny of man. Time and again he warned young seminarians to avoid those dreary and

14. Letter from Tittle to James H. Laird, January 3, 1947.
15. Letter from Tittle to Edmund H. Carlisle, January 8, 1942.
16. Letter from Tittle to Lionel Crocker, January 2, 1947.

wooden books, "canned" sermons, sermon outlines, sermonic "hints," designed to serve as crutches for impotent and lazy minds. Repeatedly he implored his fellow preachers to encounter at first hand the thoughts of the great minds. Especially did he urge the reading of philosophy, theology, history (including biography), psychology, economics, and general literature. Although this is the order in which he ranked the subjects in importance,[17] individuals close to Tittle believe that in fact his widest reading was in history and biography.[18] If history may be said to embrace current events—serious discussions of contemporary political, diplomatic, economic, and social problems—then this is probably a correct conjecture.

For Tittle books were tools and like all craftsmen he found some tools more indispensable than others. For instance, he advised a fledgling parson to "sell his shirt, if necessary," in order to acquire Hasting's *Encyclopedia of Religion and Ethics.*[19] Hasting's *Dictionary of the Bible* he also found essential, as he did the *Book of Common Prayer*, Peake's *Commentary*, the Abingdon *Commentary*, Moffatt's and Goodspeed's translations, concordances, and, of course, the *Encyclopaedia Britannica*.

The books that influenced his thinking in the areas of race, economics, foreign affairs, and theology will be the subject of assessment in later chapters, and it will be observed that despite sustained study there were imbalances in his reading program. Here, however, it is mandatory only to note the single most glaring omission: Tittle read little imaginative literature; post-Victorian literature, especially, being a strange and largely unvisited country. This is not to criticize him for not reading for fun or relaxation. There is no overriding reason why he should have. After all, why do we find it reassuring to learn that Presidents Roosevelt, Eisenhower, and Kennedy devoured mysteries, westerns, and James Bond thrillers, unless we seek justification for our own reading of trivia? Why do we assume that because a great scientist (or statesman or educator) reads light fiction that he is necessarily a more "human" person? "Reading maketh a full man," but the fullness of which Bacon speaks does not come from a reading of hollow works.

The point at issue is far more substantive. The world of much of modern literature and drama is opaque, dense, fragmented, contingent, absurd, without a final intelligibility. The world meditated upon by many

17. For example, see letters from Tittle to Estel I. Odle, June 25, 1934, and Edmund H. Carlisle, January 8, 1942.
18. Hutchinson, "Portrait," xxviii; author's interview with Mrs. Bernice Wolseley, Evanston, Ill., July 13, 1960.
19. Letter from Tittle to Alfred L. Underhill, February 27, 1931.

modern authors sees each man as solitary and unsheltered before his own death; thus the deep existential anguish of the suffering of being. Tittle's own perception of reality was transparent, coherent, ordered, purposeful —and his reading largely confirmed rather than challenged this confident, meaningful vision. To be fully relevant, Christian preaching in the twentieth century must not only continue to appropriate Milton and Bunyan, Tennyson and Longfellow, it must encounter Proust and Kafka, Joyce and Jeffers. Ernest Tittle's ignorance of modern literature was not total and his preference for the older writers was not unqualified, but the fact remains that he failed to draw as fully and as richly as, say, Paul Tillich, from the springs of twentieth-century culture.

III

The seed of a sermon was planted in his mind by the approach of an important day in the Christian calendar, by an idea encountered while reading, or, more commonly, by a conversation or experience. The seed was then permitted to ripen in his thinking, perhaps for weeks. As the seed germinated, he sometimes nourished it with specific reading, though this reading served only to augment his vast reserves of general knowledge. Slowly the sermon took form and when the time came to commit an outline to paper it was already logically structured in his mind. Perhaps then he would discuss the outline with an assistant or a comrade such as Rall or Hutchinson or with his trusted secretary or Glenna. If after such conversations he still thought he had something preachable, he would begin to write the sermon out in full, not because he found it easy to write but because he had discovered that for him "writing is the best way of clarifying thought."[20] So convinced of this was he that he urged all Methodist seminaries to institute courses in advanced literary composition and require their students to write out sermons for useful criticism. He often quoted the advice of Charles Edward Jefferson: "Gentlemen, write. Write out in full at least one sermon each week. In addition, write articles on all sort of subjects. You may never get them published but the writing will do you good. It will keep the cobwebs out of your mind. If you do not like to write, write anyhow. If you find it painful to write, write nevertheless. If it kills you to write, make yourself do it. Blessed are they who die in the Lord."[21]

Tittle took Jefferson's advice quite literally—he did not dictate his sermons nor pound them out on a typewriter. He wrote them in long-

20. Letter from Tittle to Joseph Fort Newton, January 19, 1931.
21. Jefferson, as quoted by Tittle in "The Way to Life," *The First Church Pulpit,* Vol. IX, No. 5, a sermon preached March 9, 1947.

hand in pencil on unlined 8½-by-11-inch sheets of paper, leaving a wide margin on the left. During the construction of the sermon he would refer to a worksheet on which earlier he had jotted relevant statistics, quotations, illustrations. When he had finished writing he began immediately to revise, for, as he confessed, he was an "incorrigible reviser." Was he using words accurately and precisely? Were his subject and his expression appropriate to the audience? Were the ideas sharply focused? Were they true? Were they so true as to be banal? Did the illustrations illustrate or merely adorn? Would the congregation at the conclusion of the sermon comprehend that they had been confronted with the word of God? And so the manuscript would be worked and reworked until marginal notations, interlineations, crossings out, and transposition of phrases made the original draft unintelligible to anyone but the veteran secretary.

If the writing was going according to schedule, at mid-week the manuscript would be put aside, to be looked at only in spare moments when the pressure of pastoral work eased, and remain aside until Saturday. The preparation of the sermon did not cease, however, for during the interval when the manuscript was in his desk the subject remained much in his mind. It was a time of brewing if his instincts told him it was a good sermon; of stewing if he sensed it was somehow flawed. On Saturday the sermon would be read aloud, revised, and reread until the thought sequence became familiar. Tittle did not deliberately commit it to memory, but by the end of the day the phraseology had "stuck." His secretary testified: "I have seen both the handwritten manuscript and the type-script made from the Sunday morning report, and there was astonishingly little difference between them."[22] Occasionally he would rip up the sheets and begin afresh, disgusted with the original effort. This did not happen often because a sermon prepared from scratch on Saturday gave him such an awful pain in his mind before and during delivery and such an even more awful pain in his heart after delivery that he hated the very thought of it, and he would vow "that never again will I preach unprepared—a vow which I fail to keep."[23]

The penultimate step was to compile a brief set of speaker's notes. This was done on a single sheet of 8½-by-11-inch paper which was folded in half, with the fold running parallel to the 8½-inch side. Writing on all four surfaces, which this folded paper provided, with the front

22. Letter from Mrs. Bernice Wolseley to Robert H. Hamill, October 4, 1949, as quoted in letter from Hamill to author, September 14, 1959.
23. Letter from Tittle to Joseph Fort Newton, January 19, 1931.

being page 1, the back page 2, and the inside pages 3 and 4, he used roman numerals to indicate the main points and arabic numbers the subpoints. Here he recorded key sentences, transition sentences, statistics, quotations, and proper names. The notes were typed to insure legibility. He once explained why he did not read from a full manuscript: "I am a poor reader and, besides, I find that standing in the pulpit with only the barest outline before me but with an attentive congregation to inspire me I can more effectively deliver my soul than I could were I to confine myself to a manuscript."[24]

On Sunday morning there was one final practice delivery from only the notes, and a limbering of the voice with exercises prescribed by Dean Dennis. Now the preacher was armed for his task. This task, as Tittle defined it, was to speak directly and concretely to human need, to tell livable truth to people.

IV

Tittle's sermonic style was complementary to this purpose. For one thing, the directness was there. "Every sermon," he affirmed, "has, or should have, a quite definite aim which may be stated in a few words."[25] This aim should be elucidated at the onset and firmly fixed in the congregation's mind, and it should be declared in such piercing fashion as to arrest attention, for if the preacher fails to alert his people in the first five minutes he "has no chance at all for they are all asleep."[26] From this starting point he went by a straight line to the point where he wanted to come out thirty minutes later. The march of thought kept his listeners on the *qui vive*. The vigor of thought commanded their concentration. And because his thinking did not ramble, their minds did not roam. A Tittle sermon, thus, was characterized by a central idea sharply delineated, logically developed, affirmatively resolved; and the idea was never trivial, marginal, or merely "interesting." Tittle preached for a decision. But he did not scold, because, as he explained, "I do not think that exhortation has ever done me much good."[27] Tittle's model might well have been the First Epistle of Saint John.

The chastity of prose contributed to the sermon's directness. Tittle did not covet the title, "Pulpit Prince." He was constantly on guard against indulging in empty rhetoric, flights of oratory, verbal adornment,

24. *Ibid.*
25. "The Meaning of Faith in God," typed MS, a sermon preached September 27, 1942.
26. "The Will To Excel," typed MS, a sermon preached May 19, 1929.
27. "The Forgiveness of Sins," typed MS, a sermon preached March 25, 1928.

literary preciousness. He used words honestly to express thoughts clearly and truly. He hated all sham or pretense. His scorn for pulpit showmanship was monumental. "I have been thinking of the sensational preachers of our denomination," he once confided. "Not a single one managed to maintain himself in one place for a single decade."[28]

Thus there was a Hemingwayesque quality about his style: taut, limpid, muscular. On entering the ministry he was advised not to use a long word if a short word would do, or a bookish word if a word from common speech would serve as well, and he honored the admonition.[29] He disliked preaching that was adjectival rather than verbal. As he explained, in such preaching the message was lost in a wilderness of words and though at the time the congregation might think the minister wonderful, "for the life of them" they would be "unable half an hour afterward to recall a single thing he said."[30] Tittle did not employ great descriptive powers to paint captivating word pictures as did the practitioners of conscious pulpit artistry, though he did make effective use of imagery. Almost never from the pulpit did he crack a joke as a rather appalling number of ministers feel compelled to do in order to retain attention or maintain their image as a hearty good fellow. Said Tittle: "In my judgment, humor should be used in preaching, but sparingly. Moreover, it should be spontaneous and never dragged in for the purpose of entertainment. If it comes, let it come. If it does not come, do not strive for it. The best example of humor in preaching that I know may be found in the sermons of Halford Luccock."[31] Tittle's own use of humor is reminiscent of Luccock's: pithy, dry, sometimes edged with irony, rarely sarcastic.

Tittle was master of the apposite quotation, a mastery enhanced by the fact that he used quotes judiciously, and invariably they were characterized by brevity. Paul Hutchinson pays handsome tribute to Tittle's employment of illustrations. "Those of us who sat in the congregation were continually astonished by the range he had covered in securing the illustrations which always—and here the wonder grew!—illustrated."[32] This accolade is merited only partially. A minor reservation is that a few favorite illustrations cropped up in sermon after sermon, though surely this repetition is more apparent to the reader of his collected works than to the worshipers who heard the sermons spaced over many years.

28. "The Long View," typed MS, a sermon preached April 29, 1928.
29. "On Being Made Whole," *The First Church Pulpit*, Vol. VIII, No. 4, a sermon preached October 28, 1945.
30. "Jesus Said: "Give," typed MS, a sermon preached October 26, 1947.
31. Letter from Tittle to Ralph Chapman, undated.
32. Hutchinson, "Portrait," pp. xxix-xxx.

A more serious reservation emanates from the gap in his reading habits already explicated: it is rare (though not absolutely unknown) to encounter in a Tittle sermon an illustration from the life or writings of those post-Enlightenment artists, poets, novelists, and philosophers whose vision was subversive of the traditional values of Western (that is, Christian) civilization. A final parenthetical observation concerning Tittle's use of illustrations is that he was seldom autobiographical; therefore, a reading of his sermons is not much help in reconstructing the external events of his life.

As Tittle's sermonic style was direct, so also was it concrete. He agreed with Cardinal Newman that "definiteness is the life of preaching." As he confessed to his congregation, "I never seem able to stop with a statement of general principle."[33] This concern with the specific, this harnessing of the abstraction, this sanding of the glitter so that the generalization might be inspected for its true properties, imparted to his sermons pungency and bite. In an age when much Protestant preaching seemed modeled on the vaporous speeches of Warren G. Harding, when the average sermon disintegrated in the memory like a snowman in the bright noonday sun, it is not inconsiderable that worshipers should say of Tittle: "The sermons of that man stick!"

Thus, when worshipers trailed out of First Church after the service the talk was about the sermon, not reflections on the Saturday-night party or speculations on the Sunday dinner ahead.[34] And when during the week the conversation returned to the sermon (as in fact it often did), they referred not to Tittle the orator but to the "livable truth" he preached. As a young student explained, Tittle's preaching gripped him because the "mock heroics are absent, and he has ideas."[35] Above all, Tittle's sermons "stuck" because the message and the man were one. In his copy of Washington Gladden's *Live and Learn*, published in 1914, Tittle underscored this passage: "Finally, let us remember that the great secret of clear expression is sincerity. If your deepest desire is to speak the truth, your utterance will have the beauty and the power which belong to sincere speech. Say the thing you know, the thing you heartily believe, and say nothing else."

V

As Tittle's sermonic style was complementary to his stated purpose

33. "The Goodness We Need," typed MS, a sermon preached January 12, 1947.
34. Author's interview with Kenneth F. Thompson, Wilmette, Ill., August 6, 1959.
35. Elmer A. Nichols, "Ernest Tittle, Apostle to Youth," unidentified magazine clipping in Tittle Collection.

so his delivery was appropriate to the style. If Lincoln in fact admired the preacher who looked like he was fighting a swarm of bees, he would not have been happy in First Church, for there was nothing eccentric about Tittle's pulpit manner. The gestures were few and restrained. For the most part his strong hands gripped the folds of his robe or the pulpit sides. Only infrequently did he lift a single arm to drive home a point of great moment. His piercing eyes maintained a very direct contact with the audience, conveying perceptibly his emotions, twinkling with humor, flashing with righteousness, softening with compassion. Standing in the pulpit with his erect carriage, muscular body, rugged visage, and steady gaze he seemed as indestructible as a sea captain scanning the ocean from high on the quarterdeck. The very steadiness of his bearing heightened the intense impression of disciplined power, restrained force.

Yet the power of Tittle's preaching would not have been much reduced for a blind man, for his voice was his greatest physical asset. He trained it with all the care of a Shakespearean actor until it became a marvelously disciplined and magnificently effective instrument. On arriving in Evanston Tittle went immediately to Dean Ralph B. Dennis of the Northwestern School of Speech and, as it happened, a member of First Church. The auditorium, then without an amplifying system, was much larger than anything Tittle had been accustomed to, and he was determined that his voice carry to every worshiper. For many Sundays he paid Dean Dennis five dollars to prepare a critique of his delivery. For many years he took voice lessons. And until his death he followed the voice exercises Dennis suggested.[36]

Tittle heeded John Wesley as well as Ralph Dennis. "Scream no more at the peril of your soul," the father of Methodism once warned a follower, believing "No man can be bullied into heaven, and never was." "Natural" is the most appropriate word to describe Tittle's speaking voice. He did not have the "holy-willy" voice, the sepulchral voice, sometimes equipped with tremolo stop, that has been described by some researchers as a refined form of ventriloquism. "For your information," Tittle informed a questioner, "I may say that I have always spoken in a conversational tone, as if I were talking to a very few people, the only difference being a conscious effort to speak loud enough to be heard by those farthest away in the congregation."[37] His voice was deep, soft but

36. Author's interview with Mrs. Glenna Myers Tittle, Evanston, Ill., July 27, 1959.
37. Letter from Tittle to Theodore W. Boltz, May 17, 1942.

penetrating, toned like a great bell, magnificently appropriate to proclaim the glory of God.

VI

Primarily and pre-eminently Ernest Fremont Tittle was a preacher.
The pastoral and priestly functions of his ministry were performed with
skill and devotion, but it was the preparation and presentation of sermons that commanded the fullest measure of his being. His sermons
won for him a widening fame until at last his eminence was matched by
none in all American Methodism and exceeded by few in all American
Protestantism. Applicable to Tittle is the tribute paid her minister by an
old Scottish woman: "Ye canna hear Matheson preach and live in a
cellar." Confessed a rugged businessman: "I remarked the other day,
'How Dr. Tittle has changed.' Then I caught myself and said, after
thinking about it for a minute, 'No, *I* have changed!' "[38]

Midway in his ministry a former First Church man, now living in
Iowa, wrote Tittle a letter of appreciation, closing with the words, "You
have made First Church a state of mind."[39] There is in this tribute a
hint of the danger stated bluntly by George Craig Stewart, rector of
Evanston's fashionable St. Luke's Episcopal Church and later bishop of
the Chicago diocese, "First Church is not a church but a congregation of
damned Tittleites!"[40] Such was the power of Tittle's preaching, so intimate was the relationship between his personality and his message, there
was in fact a real peril of idolatry. Men who came to First Church
to worship God in time and without conscious awareness came to worship Tittle. That this sometimes happened is, I think, incontestable.
And tragic. The Church does not live by its preachers, but by its Word.
Yet, "How shall they hear without a preacher?" The measure of Tittle's
greatness lies in the fact that for the overwhelming majority of First
Church parishioners his sermons were themselves acts of worship.

38. Hutchinson, "Portrait," p. xxxiv.
39. Letter from "Ed" to Tittle, September 28, 1936.
40. Author's interview with Robert C. Teare, Evanston, Ill., August 28, 1959.

9. TRIALS AND TRIUMPHS

I

However discouraged and weary Tittle sometimes felt, the thirty-one years of his First Church ministry were not moribund. Pain and pressure he experienced in bountiful measure, but of boredom there was only a dram. As he knew all too well, the stoning of prophets was not a thing of the past, yet in assessing the calling of the cloth his summation was triumphant: "To any man . . . who possesses the spirit of adventure, a prophetic ministry offers a most attractive opportunity. Such a ministry becomes a history-making force; and the man who participates in it is bound to get as much high and exciting fun out of life as an ordinary mortal has a right to expect."[1] Tittle's burdens did not permit him always to sustain this lilting characterization. He experienced moments of anxiety and depression, occasionally referring to himself as a "middle-aged gentleman who of late has felt very weary and just a little discouraged."[2] On another instance he admitted that "One trouble with me is just the fact that I am exceedingly weary, too weary to see life steadily and see it whole."[3] Once in a while he would confess to "feeling bruised and disgusted"[4] by some rancid piece of church politicking. And there is a note of bitterness in this lament: "When I myself am under attack, which is fairly often, I sometimes wonder why the noise is all

1. "Mirrors of the Ministry," *The Student Challenge,* III (December, 1924), 1-2.
2. Letter from Tittle to Mr. and Mrs. Roscoe A. Page, July 11, 1934.
3. Letter from Tittle to Thomas F. Holgate, April 6, 1934.
4. Letter from Tittle to James V. Thompson, June 14, 1932.

being made by those who are opposed to me—none of those who profess to be in sympathy with me."[5] Yet despair's victory was never total, and for Tittle the ministry remained a high calling. Perhaps nowhere is this conviction more finely expressed than in a letter to a colleague gripped by melancholy.

> One thing I hope you will not do: namely, allow yourself to suppose that your labor has been in vain. I now profoundly believe that no man who labors sincerely for a great cause labors in vain. He, to be sure, may be unable to see the results of his efforts, but there are results which God uses to promote the coming of His kingdom upon the earth. I have sometimes wished that I had become a physician instead of a preacher. The physician is able to see obvious and immediate results of his efforts, whereas the preacher can but sow a seed and hope that it will develop. But I observe that I have this feeling only when I am physically weary. When I am physically fit I can understand the parable of the sower and rejoice to think that no valiant sower sows in vain. Jesus himself when he died had but little to show for his efforts, yet behold what has come of the life he lived and the death he died![6]

It is of course impossible for us to note the daily pricks of irritation and the daily little joys experienced by Tittle during the long course of his Evanston ministry. Rather, our purpose in this chapter will be to recreate those moments only when his troubles seemed beyond human endurance and those moments only when his congregation most luminously made manifest their love and loyalty, to observe him, that is, in his greatest trials and greatest triumphs.

Before turning to this assignment, however, we should be reminded that American Protestants historically have accorded prior loyalty to their local church rather than to the Church Universal, the Body of Christ, or even to the larger denomination. Congregational tranquility, parochial peace, too often was purchased at the price of ethical faithlessness. The actual chumminess of the local congregation, Reinhold Niebuhr once commented, had invalidated the universal principle at the heart of the gospel. Moreover, the generalization is valid that the Protestant denominations are the lengthened shadows of their people, they are mostly democratically governed and reflect, however imperfectly, the views of their members. This is one of the glories of the heirs of the Reformation, but it may also be a source of misery. In America the Protestant minister has been a vulnerable figure precisely because of the

5. Letter from Tittle to Robert Morse Lovett, July 6, 1935.
6. Letter from Tittle to Charles A. Kent, November 17, 1936.

power of the pew in the democratically structured denominations and precisely because most laymen have identified their loyalty too exclusively with the local parish. The Protestant minister is alone in his confrontation with his congregation, lacking the security enjoyed by rabbi and priest. As Lyman Beecher observed long ago, "No minister can be forced upon his people, without their suffrage and voluntary support. Each pastor stands upon his own character and deeds, without anything to break the force of his responsibility to his people."

Historically, the result has been predictable. Too often the Protestant minister in America has been viewed by his people—as indeed he has viewed himself—as a hired hand, a consecrated functionary, a masseur of tired spirits, a master of ceremonies, indeed, anything but a man of authority commissioned to proclaim the will of God. Tittle demurred from the bemeaning American definition. To laymen he admonished, "The great need of the Christian Church is leadership in the pulpit— and the way to develop it is for the laymen to treat their preachers right."[7] And his advice to preachers might be summed up in the aphorism attributed to Harry S Truman: "If you can't stand the heat, get out of the kitchen."

Tittle remained in the "kitchen," he "sweated it out," largely because of his loyalty to the God revealed in Jesus Christ and partly, no doubt, because of a certain mulishness of character which adversity served merely to stiffen. But there was also another consideration in his refusal to turn tail and seek safety in academic or administrative posts, posts snug however burdensome. "I am really less concerned for myself," he wrote the editor of *Zion's Herald*, at the height of a fierce controversy, "than I am for other men, especially younger men, who having been in their present charges not more than two or three years may find it extremely difficult to meet successfully such opposition as I have encountered. My hope is that the action of my board will serve to stiffen the knees of other lay bodies and so to give to these younger preachers needed support and encouragement."[8] Two years later he declined a handsome academic appointment, in part, as he explained, because "I am led (by several persons whose judgment I trust) to believe that if I should leave now for any reason my going would cause no little consternation in the case of many preachers throughout the country (young fellows, especially) who would interpret it to mean that accumulating pressures had, at last, become too great for flesh and blood to stand.

7. Letter from Tittle to William A. Dyche, August 28, 1921.
8. Letter from Tittle to Louis O. Hartman, April 11, 1933.

. . ."[9] And again: "I cannot but believe, in view of what has been said to me by several persons who have intimate knowledge of the present religious situation in the United States, that my going would be generally misinterpreted. Preachers everywhere would assume that I had been forced to go by accumulating pressures and would, in consequence, themselves feel terribly insecure. As Bishop James Baker put it, this First Church, Evanston, has become a symbol of a free church, where the gospel may be preached without fear or favor—a symbol which has been most heartening to preachers of every denomination; so that my leaving here at a time as tense as this would almost certainly be misinterpreted and, therefore, utterly disheartening."[10]

These statements might be deemed prideful if it were not for the fact that Tittle spoke the truth. The First Church pulpit under Tittle *was* a standard around which the liberal preachers of Methodism, and, indeed, Protestantism, rallied. The working ministers of America, and most especially the younger rebels, recognized his vulnerability, and they saw in him a prophet who shared their burdens. As long as Tittle's voice remained unmuted there was hope for the free pulpit everywhere. In 1936 a disturbed lad wrote: "Time and again I have found courage in recalling your ability to maintain your convictions in the face of opposition with patience and fairness. You cannot but realize such leadership we young fellows so desperately need. . . . We may not amount to much—we young fellows—but it cannot but be a lasting source of pride to you as the years come and go, that you gave us able leadership. Again, thank you!"[11]

The fact that Tittle was the recipient of countless letters from beleaguered liberal preachers suggests hard truths about American society and American Protestantism in the 1920's, 1930's, and 1940's. In these years of alleged "normalcy" as well as of depression and war, Americans were a deeply anxious people, and although dark strains are discernible in every era in the nation's past, perhaps at no time—save the Civil War —was the trauma so severe. Made bewildered and fearful by the swift and surging forces reshaping "their" country, unwilling or unable to understand this strange new age, many Americans—and most especially the senior partners, the Protestants—longed for the return of yesterday, for in their fantasies they identified yesterday with a purer and nobler America. Thus it was that Tittle and every other liberal minister in every section of the country (and not only the "benighted South") came

9. Letter from Tittle to Halford Luccock, July 6, 1935.
10. Letter from Tittle to Luke I. Wilson, May 24, 1935.
11. Letter from Gordan C. Chapman to Tittle, January 10, 1936.

under relentless and murderous attacks for questioning the old orthodoxies of theological Fundamentalism, white supremacy, laissez-faire
capitalism, and militant nationalism. The attackers were not, save for
the psychotic or cynical few, moral monsters; rather, they were mediocre
men so terribly anxious to resist change that they sanctioned, ironically,
the employment of weapons Protestants always had associated with the
Medieval Church's Inquisition. The assaults on the liberal ministry came
from within as well as from without the churches. Indeed, conservatives
in every denomination banded together to resist the subversion of orthodoxy, and virtually every congregation had its strong men in the pew
who sought, through naked threats or subtle suggestion, to muzzle the
pulpit. Moreover, almost every secular organization that practiced
intimidation in the name of patriotism also laid claim to much piety.
Consequently, it took much courage for ministers to reply as did Harry
Emerson Fosdick to a group of inquisitors: "May I be permitted to suggest that these gentlemen have somewhat seriously misapprehended the
temper of the Christian ministry of America? I am speaking for multitudes of my brethren when I say, *'Before high God, not for sale!'* "[12]

Because of this idolatrous concern for the local church, because of
this historic (but unbiblical) conception of the minister as a paid functionary, because of this pervasive anxiety of modern Americans, and
because Tittle was "not for sale," inevitably he experienced the wrath
of powerful First Church laymen. And when it came to push-and-tug,
some members cut back on their pledges and others severed their congregational connections. The precise number of those who withdrew
from First Church because of disagreement with Tittle's theological or
social convictions is of course unknown, but even if the figure is not
quantitatively high, the emotional coin exacted from the parties involved
was great. How could it be otherwise in view of Tittle's essential sensitivity and the unquestioned sincerity of those who broke with him, and,
indeed, their personal affection for him?

II

A few years after his arrival in Evanston, Tittle was fearfully jolted
when Dr. John Scott, prestigious professor of classics and brother of the
president of Northwestern University, announced his transfer to the
First Presbyterian Church. Dr. Scott found Tittle's theology heretical
(charging that he denied the divinity of Christ) and the fact that a
Methodist minister should play ball with his two sons in the parsonage

12. *Social Service Bulletin,* June, 1921.

yard on Sunday afternoons horrendous.[13] Perhaps because Tittle was young and relatively unbloodied and perhaps because of Dr. Scott's exalted reputation, this incident was one of the most shattering in Tittle's entire career. There were other, often poignant, estrangements. "My resignation from the church," announced Tittle's old parishioner, Burt J. Denman, who became dismayed at the "radical" tendencies within Methodism, "was made more difficult by my friendship with Dr. Tittle," and we remain "warm personal friends."[14]

When wealthy men withdrew from First Church it meant, naturally, the loss of substantial annual subscriptions, in at least two instances as much as $5,000.[15] It is possible for a church to bleed to death like a living thing when the seepage of pledges is not replaced by new transfusions. Happily, the rank-and-file membership rallied to the church's support, providing with a large number of modest pledges a healthy financial base, and ultimately virtually every man, woman, and child in the fellowship contributed something, if only (and as much) as the widow's mite. This was much to Tittle's satisfaction and he often asserted that he would never again allow any layman to provide so large a proportion of the budget that a threatened withdrawal of support would cause apprehension in the Official Board.

Withdrawal was not the course taken by most of the disaffected. Yet their continued presence in the First Church fellowship was not pure gain for Tittle. Once when his dentist inquired concerning his pensive mood, Tittle replied, "You know, it isn't so bad fighting sin and wickedness, but it is awfully hard to live with a stubborn man on your Official Board."[16] But Tittle was himself a stubborn man and he refused to be driven from Evanston, the consequence being both agony and joy.

III

The first half-decade of the Evanston ministry was for Tittle a good time, and by the standards of the Protestant ministry a relatively tranquil time. His health held. His wife was contented. His children matured without serious physical or emotional trials. The early admiration and affection of many in his flock grew into adoration and love.

13. Author's interviews with Horace G. Smith, Evanston, Ill., August 17, 1959; James Alton James, Evanston, Ill., July 23, 1960; Raymond C. Wieboldt, Evanston, Ill., August 6, 1959; Glenna Myers Tittle, Evanston, Ill., July 27, 1959.
14. *Evanston Daily News-Index,* September 3, 1935, p. 3.
15. Author's interview with Glenna Myers Tittle, Evanston, Ill., July 27, 1959; Paul Hutchinson, "Portrait of a Preacher," foreword to Tittle, *A Mighty Fortress* (New York: Harper & Brothers, 1949), p. xxii.
16. Letter from Robert Hamill to author, September 14, 1959.

The morning mail increasingly carried letters of gratitude and praise. Membership in First Church mounted; the worship services were admirably attended; other activities were well supported. Beginning in September, 1919, and continuing without exception through the years, the Official Board requested the presiding bishop of the Rock River Conference that he reappoint Tittle to Evanston. In 1921 he was presented with an automobile by his people, and this was only the grandest of many gifts of appreciation. He rapidly became a community leader. He was coveted as speaker for and chairman of numerous local causes. The most prestigious North Shore homes vied for his presence. He was a force in the affairs of Garrett and Northwestern. His work and words, as a stone dropped in a pool, spread outward in ever-widening circles of influence in the Chicago area, in national Methodism, and, indeed, in American Protestantism. High schools, colleges, universities, denominational and interdenominational conferences and agencies coveted him as a speaker, and in 1921 his De Pauw University Mendenhall Lectures were published under the title, *What Must the Church Do to be Saved?*, his first book.

To be sure, his liberal theology scandalized some, and it was painful to see pillars such as Dr. Scott depart for more flinty doctrinal fields. To be sure, his first book brought censure as well as praise. And there was a flurry over the abolition of pew renting and Wednesday-evening prayer service and over the introduction of liturgical elements in worship. Moreover, when Tittle spoke kindly of Catholics and Jews, Negroes and aliens, labor organizers and pacifists, and when he placed under judgment those in high seats of ecclesiastical and financial power, angry mutterings were at least audible. These discordancies were like the spats of honeymooners, sharp and spirited, but not shattering to a generally joyous mood, and until 1924 Tittle's relationship with the people of First Church and of Evanston was mostly harmonious. In that year he received a signal honor. The *Christian Century* polled the Protestant ministry to discover its choice of the twenty-five outstanding American preachers. Tittle was among them, the youngest in the group. Such is the irony of life, in that year also the patriots of Evanston came perilously close to hounding him from the First Church pulpit.

The controversy must be placed in the context of the counterrevolutionary spirit of the early 1920's when tribalism was on the march and anxious men in the white dream robes of the Ku Klux Klan or the brave blue uniforms of the American Legion viewed with Manichaean eyes "their" country being defiled by radicalism and debilitated by pacifism. Such was the peril, heroic surgery was required and everywhere the patriots (the term "professional patriots" suggests a certain cynicism whereas in fact the very sincerity of these children of light undergirded their fanaticism) whetted their scalpels. In truth, by 1924 disenchantment with the Great Crusade of 1917 was growing, and among liberal Protestant churchmen the antiwar fever intensified. "Nineteen twenty-four was a vintage year of revisionism in the United States," asserts one scholar.[17] In thousands of sermons, resolutions, petitions, articles, books, addresses, and declarations Protestant churchmen said farewell to arms, making a general confession of the things they had done and left undone in 1917 and pledging never again to bless war. The ensuing clash between the red-blooded patriots and the "Red-tainted" pacifists was fierce.

The controversy must be placed also in the context of a series of local happenings in early 1924. For one thing, on New Year's Day the Student Volunteer movement met in Indianapolis to discuss problems of economics, race, and war, a number of Garrett and Northwestern students being in attendance. Stiff condemnations were made of war and the Garrett delegates formed a League for Peace. Evanston patriots were made uneasy and both President Walter Dill Scott of Northwestern University and President Charles M. Stuart of Garrett Biblical Institute were forcefully informed of the patriots' disquietude. Then on February 5 and 6, 147 Northwestern and Garrett students held a conference in First Church and heard such speakers as Reinhold Niebuhr and Paul Blanchard (and Tittle himself) score the existing social and international order. At the meeting's conclusion, 38 of the delegates pledged that "we as individuals refuse to participate in another war."[18] Disquietude in Evanston now approached alarm. Early in March a Northwestern student group invited a leading English pacifist to address them. At the last moment permission to utilize a university hall was withheld, the official justification being that the students had failed to secure prior approval of the meeting.[19] Meanwhile, the Chicago press tub-thumbed about the dangerous infiltration of the schools and churches by slackers and pacifists.

On Sunday morning, March 23, the *Chicago Tribune* carried a front-page cartoon depicting a "pacifist educator" being lifted away from his pacifist lectures by an angry Uncle Sam who is sternly pointing to the

17. Warren I. Cohen, *The American Revisionists: The Lessons of Intervention in World War I* (Chicago and London: University of Chicago Press, 1967), p. 60.

18. "Findings of the Northwestern Student Conference," a mimeographed statement in the Tittle Collection.

19. *Social Service Bulletin,* March 15, 1924.

American flag and saying, "It's your business to teach patriotism." On the editorial page was an item entitled, "Pacifica Praecox," wherein a Professor Usam Erican's "learned" researches into the nature of pacifists were reviewed. Male pacifists are duo-sexed, easily recognizable by their feminine voices and coquettish manners. Female pacifists are in the grip of a subconscious desire to weaken the warlike qualities of their husbands so that another more virile race will conquer and provide them with more agreeable, that is, virile, companionship, like the Trojan women and the warriors of Greece, and the Roman women and the conquering Goths and Vandals. Pacifism being patently a "psychological illness," "institutions should be provided for the segregation and treatment of these unfortunates."

As it happened, that very evening, Sunday, March 23, Brent Dow Allinson was scheduled to address the Epworth League in First Church on the subject, "The Youth Movement in Germany." A young idealist and conscientious objector, in 1918 Allinson had been found guilty before a General Court Martial of the technical charge of desertion and sentenced to confinement in Leavenworth at hard labor for fifteen years.[20] His release and earlier appearance in Evanston in 1920 had then touched off protests from patriotic and veterans' groups.[21] As the hour for the speech approached, Tittle knew there would be trouble. The previous day he had been visited by a delegation of angry American Legionnaires. Forty-five minutes before the meeting he received a communication from John H. Wigmore, dean of the Northwestern School of Law, asserting that Allinson was not only a slacker, but had been "dismissed by the Department of State for disloyal conduct while a sworn officer of the State Department abroad" and that "his acts were so pro-German that they became intolerable." "Would you," Wigmore inquired of Tittle, "knowingly invite a notorious bootlegger to tell your congregation about the anti-alcohol movement?"[22] Fifteen minutes later Tittle received a similar communication from Colonel Philip Fox, also a Northwestern professor. Significantly, Colonel Fox was scheduled to speak in the Epworth League series the following Sunday on the subject of "Preparedness," presumably in the affirmative, though he deemed it a "scant honor to follow such a delinquent" as Allinson.[23]

What was Tittle to do? There was of course no time to call a con-

---

20. *Brent Dow Allinson: Conscientious Objector to War*, a pamphlet published by The Amnesty Committee of Chicago, 1919.
21. *Evanston News-Index,* July 31, 1920, p. 1.
22. The communication from Wigmore to Tittle is in the Tittle Collection.
23. The communication from Fox to Tittle is in the Tittle Collection.

ference of the governing board of the church. He quickly consulted with
two Legion leaders and they advised cancellation of the address.[24] When
Allinson arrived, alone, at the church he found the building surrounded
by Legionnaires in uniform and in an ugly mood. Determined to prevent his speaking, they threatened him with lynching, to throw him
bodily into Lake Michigan. Despite the intimidation, Allinson entered
the church.[25]

Tittle met the situation with a cool and clear head. After a few
remarks reviewing the recent events and attempting to set forth as he
saw them the issues involved, he put the question of Allinson's speaking
to a vote of the members of the Epworth League and the members of
First Church present. The "outsiders," that is, the Legionnaires who
were not First Church members, were not permitted to vote. While
Allinson waited in a side room, the vote was counted by the president of
the Epworth League and a Legionnaire. It was a vote to permit the
scheduled speaker to be heard, 117 to 9.

When the handsome, smiling speaker took the platform, he was
heartily applauded by the Epworth Leaguers. The Legionnaires held
onto their patience with both hands, especially when Allinson made such
statements as "the United States is even now preparing for the next
war." At the conclusion of the address, Allinson was questioned from
the floor, Captain C. B. Hopkins repeatedly shouting that America had
never fought an unjust war. The Epworth League boys and girls
responded with boos and laughter. When Alan H. Monroe, president of
the Epworth League, declared the meeting closed, Captain John W.
Gorby, past commander of the Lake Forest Post of the American Legion,
stepped to the platform announcing his intention to deliver a talk on
Americanism, adding, "And I want an American flag on this platform!"
Presently a Legionnaire returned with the colors, sarcastically remarking
that "it is mighty hard to find a flag in this church." The Epworth
Leaguers booed, but it was the statement and not the flag that was
hooted. Nevertheless the following morning the *Chicago Tribune* headlined: "Hiss Flag—Cheer Slacker" with the sub-head "War Heroes
Booed in M.E. Church." And this despite the fact that at the conclusion
of Captain Gorby's talk, "America" was sung with zeal and the audience
rose to a man.[26]

24. Tittle's account of the events, as he related them to his congregation, is
found in the *Evanston News-Index,* March 31, 1924, p. 1.

25. Letter from Brent Dow Allinson to author, December 16, 1962.

26. In addition to the *Chicago Tribune* account, see especially the *Evanston
News-Index,* March 24, 1924, p. 1, and the *Daily Northwestern,* March 25, 1924,
pp. 1, 3.

The following week Evanston, indeed, the Chicago area, buzzed with excitement. Tittle was the recipient of a host of angry letters, phone calls, and visitations. Patriotic groups such as the Minute Men of the Constitution, the Daughters of the American Revolution, and veterans of the Civil War, Spanish-American War, and, naturally, the World War passed resolutions condemning the "treasonable doctrines" of pacifism and censuring church and school authorities for encouraging this "organized campaign" to break down respect for the flag. Although the Evanston press was temperate in its reporting, some Chicago newspapers fanned patriotic fears. Indeed, Glenna was driven to announce publicly that she had been misrepresented by "The World's Greatest Newspaper."[27] Most Northwestern students hastened to affirm their patriotism. Every fraternity hung out flags to show that the Greek heart was loyal still. Many Evanston clergymen, including the leading Episcopal and Baptist ministers, announced in the press their willingness to serve with the newly formed Citizen's Military Training Camp, and the rector of St. Mary's Roman Catholic Church asserted that pacifism was anarchism. Early in the week additional numbers of Garrett and Northwestern students pledged themselves never to participate in war, and early in the week also the American Legion made plans for a great patriotic rally to be held the following Sunday. For Tittle, the tension was murderous.[28]

On Sunday morning, March 30, from the pulpit of First Church Tittle made a "plain statement to the people called Methodists," as Wesley would have put it. "People who know this church know that it is as patriotic an organization as there is in this city, or in any other city," he began. "People who know me know that there is not a drop of disloyal blood in my body. I love my country as only a man can love her who has risked his life for her." He then denied that he was an absolute pacifist or had ever advised young men to refuse military service in time of war. He continued:

> I have said that war is a crime—the greatest of all crimes because including all. I have said that modern war is not only cruel but futile; that whatever evolutionary purpose war may have served in the past, in the future it will be only dreadful. I have said that another war on a large scale will be unspeakably hideous; that it will be a war not only of armies against armies, but of

27. For Glenna's public letter, see the *Evanston News-Index*, March 25, 1924, p. 1.

28. See the *Evanston-News Index*, the *Daily Northwestern*, and the *Chicago Tribune* for this week, and, of course, the many communications to Tittle in the Tittle Collection.

armies against civilian populations; I have said that in my judgment the supreme duty of living men and women is to strive in every possible way to avert another war. I have said that the Christian church ought to insist that war is wrong, and that the whole war system is wrong. I have said that I myself will never again maintain that war is glorious; that black is white! But if, in spite of all I can do to prevent it, America should be drawn into another war, I shall endeavor, in some way, and to the very limit of my ability, to serve my country.

He then reviewed the events leading to Allinson's address. "The invitation to Mr. Allinson to address our young people's forum was not extended by me. I will frankly state that knowing what I now know, I would not have extended the invitation. It was, I think, a mistake to invite Mr. Allinson to appear on our forum program. Of his war record I myself knew absolutely nothing until I was informed of it by certain members of the American Legion on the Saturday preceding the Sunday when he was to speak." Tittle, however, defended his decision to put the question to a vote as the fairest and most democratic course at the eleventh hour.[29]

This confession of error, for such the patriots interpreted it to be, was of course predicated on the assumption that Dean Wigmore's charges against Allinson were accurate; that is, that the young conscientious objector had also been pro-German and traitorous. Therefore, Tittle's statement must be interpreted not as a retreat under fire, but as an admission that Allinson's "true" record was unknown to him.

That afternoon at three o'clock five thousand Northwestern students and Evanstonians assembled in Northwestern's Patten Gymnasium in response to a call from the university and the American Legion. President Coolidge telegraphed his blessing to this "patriotic expression of devotion to America." The preamble to the constitution of the American Legion was given by the state chaplain, who also recited "Ode to the Flag." There followed a number of speeches by clergymen, Spanish-American War veterans, and American Legionnaires, one of whom avowed that the organization that permitted Allinson to speak "might have forgotten a plank of its platform and thrown him down the sewer with the rest of the Evanston sewerage." The most forceful address was by Brigadier General Nathan William MacChesney, president of the General Alumni Association and Northwestern trustee. Comparing Allinson and the thirty-eight student pacifists to Judas Iscariot and Benedict Arnold, the general held them indictable under the laws of the United States. Cer-

29. The statement is printed in the *Evanston News-Index,* March 31, 1924, p. 1.

tainly Northwestern University and decent society, he said, has no place for the man who would not defend his mother from assault or his sister from ravishment. The "infamous 38" blackened the fair name of Northwestern. MacChesney did not intend his school to become a platform for the preaching of personal immorality, contempt for the church, or treason to America, and it was his prayer that "Northwestern will again as before be found 100 per cent patriotic." President Walter Dill Scott was obviously in a precarious position and his speech, which he read from a prepared text in order to avoid possibility of misrepresentation, was a careful, cautious yet not cowardly statement. He reviewed the patriotic record of Northwestern students, faculty, and alumni. He reminded the audience that Northwestern University was a cosmopolitan institution of higher learning and not an elementary school, and that America was a democracy and not a monarchy. He stated his determination that freedom of speech and freedom of conscience should prevail on the campus "so far as I can exert my influence." Yet he held the pacifists to be mistaken and that in his judgment "the way to avoid future wars is to prepare for war." It is the duty of the university, therefore, to convert the pacifists by example and by precept, and not by persecution, so that should another war come "the students of Northwestern who are American citizens will one and all be found in patriotic service to the land which we have already supported in three wars."

The demonstration concluded with the audience facing east for thirty seconds in silent tribute to the soldiers who had made the supreme sacrifice, followed by a rousing singing of the "Star Spangled Banner." The *Evanston News-Index,* the *Chicago News,* and the *Chicago Herald-Examiner* all applauded. Even the *Tribune* was satisfied: "Patriotism blazed up with the fervor of war on Northwestern Campus yesterday, shattering all hopes of organized pacifists that they might get a foothold in the University." It was a moment of triumph for the patriots.[30]

The following Sunday, April 6, Tittle preached in First Church a magnificent sermon in which the triumph of the patriots was challenged. "Crown Him Lord of All" may be Tittle's greatest sermon; surely nothing he ever preached remains more relevant to later generations, for he examined the ancient and continuing tension between Caesar and Christ. In it Tittle asserted the claims of Christ against the insatiable demands of the state and the claims of Christ's church against the jealous pos-

30. The best accounts of the meeting are in the *Evanston News-Index,* March 31, 1924, p. 1, and the Northwestern University *Alumni News,* undated clipping in the Tittle Collection.

sessiveness of nationalism. And in the very preaching of such a sermon his own courage was illuminated.

The sermon was widely quoted and Tittle received numerous requests for copies, often for distribution by the dozens to study groups and conferences. Meanwhile, he conducted an intensive investigation into the career of Allinson to determine if Dean Wigmore's charges were correct. Carefully gathering evidence from New York and Washington, Tittle presented his findings in a letter to Wigmore dated April 23, which the *Evanston News-Index* printed in full on April 29. The tone of the letter was dispassionate, but the facts were devastating, and as law school dean and author of a well-known textbook on the rules of evidence, even Wigmore must have been impressed by Tittle's brief. The letter opened: "On March thirtieth I stated to my congregation that in my judgment a mistake had been made in inviting Mr. Allinson to speak under the auspices of our Epworth League. This judgment was *not* based on the fact that Mr. Allinson had been a conscientious objector and had served a term in Leavenworth. (There is, of course, no reason why a Christian church should refuse to listen to a man who, at considerable cost to himself, has remained loyal to his deepest convictions.) It was based upon the fact alleged by you in your letter to me that Mr. Allinson in 1917 was 'recalled and dismissed by the Department of State for disloyal conduct while a sworn officer of the State Department abroad.' " Therefore, Tittle continued, he had been led by Wigmore to believe that Allinson had been guilty of moral perfidy. Tittle then presented the evidence to prove that Allinson, while indeed a conscientious objector, had never been "recalled and dismissed by the Department for disloyal conduct while a sworn officer of the State Department abroad."[31] When it was maintained by the patriots that Allinson's pacifism was in itself sufficient to prove his disloyalty, Tittle replied that throughout history Christians who chose to follow the "higher law" had been charged with disloyalty, as for example the Pilgrim Fathers, the leaders of the Protestant Reformation, and "the early disciples of Jesus who were savagely persecuted by the Roman Empire because they refused to burn incense before the statue of the emperor." "Surely, then," Tittle concluded, "the Christian church in our time cannot afford to take a position that would stigmatize as 'traitors' the men and women who constitute its 'noble company of martyrs.' "[32]

In 1924 American Protestantism in general and Northern Methodism

31. Letter from Tittle to Wigmore, April 23, 1924; *Evanston News-Index,* April 29, 1924, p. 1.
32. Letter from Tittle to Homer H. Cooper, May 1, 1924.

in particular was thrown into great turmoil by the "war question." The General Conference, meeting in May, in its resolutions began its approach to an antiwar position almost indistinguishable from that of the historic peace churches. It is enormously revealing of Tittle's perilous status that six pillars—one can almost say *the* six pillars—of First Church, James F. Oates, Edwin S. Mills, William A. Dyche, George P. Merrick, Robert W. Campbell, and Arthur Anderson, on May 17 telegraphed the Rock River delegation in protest to the General Conference's drift toward pacifism and urging the delegation "to leave no stone unturned in opposition." The senders made certain Tittle received a copy.[33] The fact that 124 of the 125 students and faculty of Garrett telegraphed their endorsement of the Conference's antiwar temper and pledged themselves never to participate in another war hardly soothed the Evanston patriots.[34] Nor did Tittle calm things when at a meeting of Chicago area Methodist ministers on April 21 he assumed leadership of the antiwar forces, his utterances being quoted in the press.[35] Before the summer was out, Tittle was to be in the forefront of the opposition to the National Defense Test Day, and in the fall he helped ram an antiwar resolution through the Rock River Annual Conference. As a matter of fact, forty-five annual conferences of the Methodist Episcopal Church passed such resolutions in 1924.[36]

The crisis touched off by Allinson's appearance continued. Almost every American Legion post in Illinois passed condemnatory resolutions, forwarding copies to Tittle, as did DAR chapters and also the GAR and the United Spanish War Veterans. The torrent of critical letters did not cease to flow: "If your idea of a 'leader' is Allinson, a slacker and a convict—then I wish to say—The Methodist Church—is a damned poor church." "I believe it would be better for the country that the churches be sunken to the lowest depths of hell rather than to allow such unpatriotic wretches as Brent Dow Allinson to desecrate their places of worship. THREE CHEERS FOR OLD GLORY AND THE U.S.A." "You have proved yourself a traitor & yellow cur to the people of America. You will hereafter be referred to as the 'slacker preacher.' . . . All churches are laughing at you and all people are criticising you as a dirty yellow dog. How can Mrs. Tittle live with a thing like you. She should refuse

33. The copy is in the Tittle Collection.
34. *Evanston News-Index,* May 15, 1924, p. 1. See also Ray H. Abrams, *Preachers Present Arms* (New York: Round Table Press, 1933), p. 235.
35. *Evanston News-Index,* April 22, 1924, p. 1.
36. See James Marion De Vinney, "The Attitude of the Methodist Episcopal Church Toward War from 1910 to 1927" (M.A. thesis, Northwestern University, 1928).

to do so if she is half a woman. Better get out of town before you are tarred & feathered which is going to happen soon." The unknown author of this last communication identified himself proudly (but with what bravery?) as "An Army Officer."

It would be a grave misreading of the spirit of the 'twenties and a serious minimization of the strength of the patriots to suppose that Tittle's inquisitors were all paranoid professional soldiers or neurotic old ladies. If this were true, then surely Maine Township High School would not have canceled Tittle's engagement to deliver the commencement sermon. In notifying Tittle of the decision, the principal observed that the criticism was so intense that the cancellation was "for your sake as well as that of the school." He added rather helplessly, "It is needless to tell you, dear Dr. Tittle, that I am very much distressed over this."[37] Apparently the pressures on the high-school principal were no greater— or at least no more resistible—than those on the president of Northwestern University, for in June Tittle was denied the honor of preaching the baccalaureate sermon, such was the continuing trauma over the Allinson affair.[38] Though deeply wounded, Tittle was magnanimous enough to accept the invitation of his friend, Dean Dennis, to deliver the Northwestern School of Speech commencement address.

In the spring of 1924 Tittle's friends and lovers of freedom everywhere rallied to his defense. ". . . we all enjoyed that fine 'Wallop' which you gave Dean Wigmore," wrote one. "Your restraining from comment on the evidence which certainly convicted him, was a mark of your usual good sense."[39] "I am very proud of the way you handled the fools of the Wigmore type," cheered Bishop Francis J. McConnell.[40] G. Bromley Oxnam related the similar attacks he had suffered in California, concluding that "the men thruout the Church are with you, and . . . I hope you are not worrying too much about this."[41] Tittle's own people were overwhelmingly loyal. Referring to the sermon "Crown Him Lord of All," one parishioner held that it "was as much a prophetic utterance as anything in Isaiah." Referring to his answer to Wigmore, another parishioner pronounced the verdict, "That was as clean a knockout as I've ever seen." Not only individual members of First Church but such groups as the Women's Union honored him "for the candor, toler-

37. Letter from C. H. Himel to Tittle, May 19, 1924.
38. *New York Times,* August 3, 1949, p. 23; *Chicago Tribune,* August 4, 1949, p. 8.
39. Letter from W. D. Schermerhorn to Tittle, May 5, 1924.
40. Letter from Bishop Francis J. McConnell to Tittle, April 19, 1924.
41. Letter from G. Bromley Oxnam to Tittle, April 17, 1924.

ance, patience, and nobility of spirit" he displayed.[42] At long last the issue was removed from the realm of doubt when on September 8 the Official Board voted unanimously to request the presiding bishop to return Tittle to First Church for another year, thereby honoring "the desire of the membership" and fulfilling "the best interests of the parish."[43] And only a year later President Scott of Northwestern wrote Tittle a long and admiring letter, concluding: "In my judgment, as I have stated on several occasions, you are today the greatest preacher in America. In my desire to create a 'Greater Northwestern' I want you as the prophet and the friend of our student body."[44] Incidentally, although the Chicago newspapers reported "N.U. Faculty Makes War on Pacifist 'Bug' " and "May Expel 'Pinks' in a Body" and although there was much pressure to discipline the "infamous 38," President Scott staunchly promised, "The American Legion, irate alumni, and others have attempted to goad us on to persecution, but they will not be successful."[45]

The Allinson affair of 1924 was for Tittle a bruising ordeal. Individuals close to the event believe that he walked the knife edge of dismissal or forced resignation. Tittle himself recalled that he very nearly lost his job.[46] Yet by standing fast under intense patriotic fire it may be said that in 1924 Tittle fully entered the "goodly fellowship of the Prophets."

IV

If the spring of 1924 had been a desperate time for Tittle the fall of 1928 was a golden moment. For one thing, the prolonged period of wretched health and shredded nerves was now temporarily over. For another, his national fame continued to widen: many honors were coming his way, and he probably was now counted among America's leading dozen preachers. And for a third, affairs at First Church were booming, and the great building program was under way.

On the evening of November 14, 1928, five hundred parishioners crowded the Orrington Hotel ballroom to celebrate the first decade of Tittle's First Church ministry. The eulogies were as warm as they were numerous, compelling Tittle to respond in gratitude for the "greatest tribute that he and Mrs. Tittle had ever received in their entire minis-

42. For these and many other expressions of loyalty, see the Tittle Collection.
43. Minutes of the Official Board, First Church, September 8, 1924.
44. Letter from President Walter Dill Scott to Tittle, September 28, 1925.
45. Copy of letter from Walter Dill Scott to George A. Coe, April 10, 1924, in Tittle Collection.
46. Letter from Tittle to Howard R. Carey, September 16, 1943.

try."[47] A congratulatory telegram was read during the evening from the Board of Bishops signed by Bishops McDowell, Welch, Nicholson, and Hughes. Most significant of all, the First Church Official Board passed and presented to Tittle a handsome resolution of appreciation, high regard, and affection. His many services were enumerated, his many qualities of idealism, courage, and vision were extolled. But the crucial paragraph in the resolution read: "Resolved, that we hereby assure Dr. Tittle of our earnest desire that he will continue to regard the pulpit of this church as one in which he may freely preach according to his convictions."[48]

For the Official Board to uphold explicitly and publicly the freedom of the First Church pulpit was to Tittle enormously encouraging. During the first five years of his Evanston ministry he had been only peppered, but during the second five years (that is, since the Allinson affair) he had been continually bludgeoned. Even the bravest of prophets must find reassuring the support of those under the greatest pressure to betray him, and it is self-evident that the First Church Official Board was subjected to relentless pressure to muzzle or remove Tittle.

The resolution was also reassuring to liberal Protestants everywhere, for it was widely quoted in the religious press and was the subject of much editorial comment. As the *World Tomorrow,* a journal of Christian pacifism and socialism, stated, "The significance of this action cannot be appreciated apart from a knowledge of the fact that the Evanston Church is one of the richest and most powerful in all Methodism and that Ernest Tittle is one of the most radical and courageous of all Methodist ministers."[49] Yet Tittle continued to receive critical communications. "A lot is heard, just now," read one such letter, "about what we can fear if Mr. Al Smith, the booze-loving Catholic Tammany boss, should be elected president. I happen to be a dry, a 32° Mason and in favor of Republican principles, but would rather take a chance with Rome than with any anti-resistance outfit such as you seem to speak for." The letter was signed, "Once a Methodist NOW an American."[50] Nevertheless, for a moment it seemed that a First Church layman expressed a growing sentiment when he said: "With much my preacher says I am in disagreement. But I expect him to speak his mind and conscience. He is the only chance God has in that pulpit. If I should attempt to

47. *First Church Review,* VI (November 17, 1928), 1.
48. The Official Board resolution, dated only November, 1928, is in the Tittle Collection.
49. "World Tomorrow," January, 1929, a clipping in Tittle Collection.
50. Letter to Tittle, May 28, 1928.

shut his mouth, I run the risk of shutting God's mouth, and that I would not dare to do. It is in the hope of hearing God that I go to Church."[51]

V

It is well that in late 1928 First Church gave explicit expression of its devotion to Tittle, for shortly he was to enter a time of trouble as intense and even more prolonged than that resulting from the Allinson case. He was to need desperately this memory of earlier moral support. The woes of the Great Depression were in themselves staggering. He grappled with enormous problems of church finances and congregational morale. And he suffered heightened attacks from patriots, nativists, and racists. In 1924 Tittle's position on war was the overriding issue. In the early 1930's considerations of race and radicalism were added to those of pacifism, and the resulting clash was almost sufficient to confirm the theological doctrine of original sin or the psychoanalytical analogue of the doctrine of universal neurosis.

Every person close to Tittle remembers that the early 'thirties was a time when he drove himself without mercy and when the attacks on him were merciless. "Tension was the order of the day," recalled one loyal comrade.[52] It was during these years that his letters are dotted with expressions of "feeling bruised and disgusted," "exceedingly weary," "very weary and just a little discouraged," and "on the verge of another 'smash-up.'" In a letter to a friend he gave clear expression to his mood at the height of the controversy. "We, the Tittles, are all well but are living under considerable strain. All the patriotic organizations along the North Shore are now shooting at me with rigor and vigor. I am accused of being a Communist, an atheist, wolf in sheep's clothing, and other interesting things. So far our own church has stood by me loyally. But how long it will continue to do so I do not know. But here and now I give you full assurance that there will be no weakening on my part. Glenna and I have both decided that no matter what comes we shall stick to our guns."[53]

On December 5, 1930, the *Evanston News-Index* headlined: "Organize for Fight on Reds." There followed the story of the formation of a community-wide federation of "all patriotic and military groups" to declare "open warfare" against "communistic speakers in Evanston" and

51. Unidentified individual quoted in unidentified magazine clipping in Tittle Collection.
52. Author's interview with Raymond C. Wieboldt, Evanston, Ill., August 6, 1959.
53. Letter from Tittle to S. Raymond Thornburg, February 28, 1933.

"local teachers of communism" in "high position in church and university." Revealingly, Tittle's old adversaries, Dean (now emeritus) Wigmore and Colonel Fox (now director of the Max Adler planetarium) were among the prime movers. The immediate background to the crusade was the appearance of Karl Borders before the First Church college group. Borders, occasional lecturer at Northwestern and the University of Chicago and secretary of the Chicago Branch of the League for Industrial Democracy, originally had been scheduled to speak to the Westminster Fellowship of the First Presbyterian Church. The engagement was cancelled at the command of the American Legion. (The Legion put into practice its slogan, "service to the community," by providing a substitute speaker, Fred A. Busby, chairman of the Americanism Committee for the Illinois State Department of the American Legion, who spoke on the subject, "Enemies from Within"!) Whereupon, in December, First Church opened its doors to Borders, despite the Legion's stern warnings. "In consequence," Tittle reported, "I am now under fire and the Legion has declared that it will never stop until I have been forced to resign."[54] It is significant that in late November Tittle wrote both the Department of State and the Department of Justice for the official "facts" on Borders. Was he a Russian propagandist taking orders from Moscow, as the patriots charged? Both State and Justice replied it was not their policy to divulge such information.[55] In the immediate background, also, was Dean Wigmore's public attack on Roger N. Baldwin and the American Civil Liberties Union, for Tittle was a champion of the ACLU and First Church had housed its local meetings. Furthermore, Harry A. Jung, founder of the American Vigilance Intelligence Federation, had been busy alerting Evanstonians to the dangers of "pink parsons."[56]

More generally, for years the Daughters of the American Revolution had been taking time off from hunting up their ancestors to hunting down pacifists and sundry "radicals" and compiling black lists of such "subversives" as Jane Addams. Indeed, the individuals indicted by these "Dear Amazon Reactionaries" (as one clergyman termed the ladies) were so distinguished that Harry Emerson Fosdick pouted because he had been overlooked. And the DAR was strong in Evanston. More gener-

54. Letter from Tittle to Adelaide L. Reis, December 17, 1930; letter from Tittle to James V. Thompson, December 17, 1930.

55. Letter from Nugent Dodds, acting head of the Criminal Division, Department of Justice, to Tittle November 25, 1930; letter from Robert F. Kelly, chief, Division of Eastern European Affairs, Department of State, to Tittle, December 10, 1930.

56. See, for example, the *Evanston Review,* April 30, 1930, p. 10.

ally, too, for years the American Legion had blustered about pacifism and radicalism in the pulpit, and in annual convention in 1929 had slandered American Protestantism by the passage of a resolution demanding a Senate investigation of the Federal Council of Churches.[57] And the Legion was strong in Evanston, as were many other military societies.

In 1931 the tempo of the attack picked up. And well it might have, for even as the worsening depression fired the anxiety of the patriots, Tittle's own judgments on war and unfettered capitalism sharpened. Increasingly curses both loud and deep were heard. "Two hundred Legionnaires," reported the press under the headline "Legion Scores 'Red' Activity in Evanston," "received in awed silence last night the annual report of the national defense committee of the Evanston post as it reviewed the results of an investigation made into alleged communistic activities of the community. Floor leaders who are seldom at a loss to express themselves on affairs of the community confessed amazement at revelations made in the report." As might be expected, the specific point discussed was a meeting of alleged atheistic radicals held in First Church. It tells us something of the uses of piety made by patriots to learn that "A general discussion followed among the Legion men, *many of whom admitted no church affiliations, but professed a reverence for the objects of religion.*"[58]

In 1932 to the issues of pacifism and radicalism was added that of race. For years some Evanstonians had harbored well-founded suspicions about Tittle's color blindness. For years the large Negro population in the community had counted him a friend. Then at the 1932 General Conference Tittle introduced and successfully defended a resolution stipulating that hereafter the General Conference meet only where hotel services and facilities were unsegregated. American Methodism was convulsed, and from every section of the country letters of extraordinary repulsion poured in. Read one: "A bunch of realy white men ought to catch you and stick your nose in a damn niggers ass and hold it there until you smuthered to death."[59] In Evanston the Ku Klux Klan circulated handbills and even good citizens warned that Tittle was setting the stage for a race riot. He was flayed for encouraging miscegenation, especially after Negro students attended a First Church Young People's Fellowship dance. His enemies even charged him with hypocrisy when

57. See Robert Moats Miller, *American Protestantism and Social Issues, 1919-1939*, Chapel Hill: The University of North Carolina Press, 1958), pp. 146ff.
58. *Evanston News-Index,* June 12, 1931, p. 1. Italics added.
59. Unsigned, undated letter to Tittle in envelope postmarked Harriman, Tenn., May 24, 1932. See Chapter 12 for the full account of the reaction to Tittle's 1932 General Conference resolution.

they circulated the rumor that a Negro woman had been refused membership in First Church. This Tittle branded as "absolutely and libelously false," and a group of First Church officials signed a statement nailing the lie to the mast. Tittle expressed his own troubled soul to a friend: "I came away from Atlantic City [meeting place of the General Conference] feeling bruised and disgusted. I came home to find that the patrioteers are once more making war on me. The attack has been more vigorous than ever, but I am thankful to discover that my own people are for the most part holding steady. However, it is a bit disturbing to have people in the community in which you have lived for more than thirteen years believe you are attempting to undermine the Government."[60]

On Friday evening, June 10, 1932, Tittle became one of the prime targets of Mrs. Elizabeth Dilling, a kind of antiradical Carrie Nation. Born in Chicago in 1895, Elizabeth Kirkpatrick attended private schools and the University of Chicago before marrying an engineer, Mr. Albert W. Dilling. A resident of Kenilworth, the second suburb beyond Evanston, in 1932 she took unto herself the inspired task of alerting the North Shore to the menace of communism. She was also a vicious anti-Semite, and during the Second World War she was indicted for sedition against the United States government, but that is another story.[61] A willowly figure, dramatically sculptured face, enormous brown eyes, shrill laugh, rapid speech, quick mind, and burning zeal gave to her a certain charismatic quality. Originally speaking before various women's clubs, she was soon chilling (or thrilling) the males of Evanston with her alarums. On June 10, speaking under the sponsorship of the DAR and American Legion, she warned an audience of 450 patriots of those Evanston ministers and Northwestern professors who preached "parlor pink propaganda," pointedly referring to one Evanston preacher who "must chloroform his parishioners to make them believe that the A.C.L.U. is an organization not devoted to the furtherance of Communism," and who also encouraged racial unrest. As the audience departed each person was handed a pamphlet "exposing" with charts and "documentary" citations the tie-up between the ACLU, the League for Industrial Democracy, the Federal Council of Churches, the American Friends Service Committee, and the Garland Fund and international communism. The association of certain Evanstonians with these "subversive" organizations was made manifest, and Tittle's name was most

60. Letter from Tittle to James V. Thompson, June 14, 1932.
61. See Ralph Lord Roy, *Apostles of Discord* (Boston: Beacon Press, 1953), pp. 30ff.

prominently displayed on the pamphlet's cover.[62] Before the year was out Tittle informed a neighbor and dear friend: "I find that Mrs. Dilling has done me much harm, as Saint Paul would say. Several members of the congregation have become disaffected as a result of these outrageous tales concerning me that she and others of our super-patriots have put into circulation. But whatever comes I can only say, 'Here I stand. I cannot do otherwise. God help me.' "[63]

In 1934 Mrs. Dilling won national fame of sorts with the publication of *The Red Network*, subtitled "A 'Who's Who' and Handbook of Radicalism for Patriots." The book examines 460 organizations allegedly supporting "the Communist-Socialist world conspiracy with its four horsemen, Atheism, Immorality, Class Hatred, and Pacifism-for-the-Sake-of-Red-Revolution." Among Mrs. Dilling's prized targets were the Federal Council of Churches, numerous church-related groups, and "those present-day Moscow-loving intellectual ministers who rewrite the Bible and teach it in modernist style so as to leave faith in little besides its covers." The dossier on Tittle was shorter than that on Jane Addams but longer than that on Mrs. Eleanor Roosevelt. Perhaps it is enough to say that for her "documentation" Mrs. Dilling relied heavily on such rancid "authorities" as E. N. Sanctuary (author of the 1931 infamy, *Tainted Contracts*) and Harry Jung (Red-baiting, strike-breaking racketeer). In any case, she brings to mind Mr. Dooley's definition of a fanatic: "a man that does what he thinks th' Lord wud do if He only knew th' facts iv th' case."

Because Tittle was prominent in this unusual "Who's Who," and because he and Mrs. Dilling were North Shore neighbors, he received a number of inquiries from throughout the country concerning this latter-day Cassandra. Invariably he replied that although she was the source of much mischief, he could not identify the individuals or groups backing her financially. Her purpose, he was convinced, was the destruction of liberalism and not simply the exposure of communism.[64] Early in 1936 Tittle made public reply to Mrs. Dilling, who obstinately replied by reiterating the original accusations.[65] It was, however, in 1933, even before the publication of *The Red Network*, that Mrs. Dilling came

62. *Evanston News-Index,* June 11, 1932, p. 1; *Evanston Review,* June 16, 1932, p. 34. The pamphlet is in the Tittle Collection. For a contemporary sketch of Mrs. Dilling, see the *Evanston Daily News-Index,* January 18, 1936, p. 1.

63. Letter from Tittle to Mrs. Edwin S. Mills, October 25, 1932.

64. See, for example, a letter from Tittle to Samuel McCrae Cavert, Federal Council of Churches official, December 17, 1934.

65. The exchange is printed in the *Evanston Daily News-Index,* January 18, 1936, p. 12.

closest to achieving her goal of driving Tittle from Evanston. On Friday evening, January 13, 1933, the American Civil Liberties Union met in a rented hall of First Church. On hand to speak were Dean Thomas F. Holgate of Northwestern University, a First Church member and companion of Tittle's, the Reverend Raymond B. Bragg, ACLU official, and Carl Haessler, who in fact was a Communist Party functionary. Mrs. Catharine Waugh McCulloch, distinguished citizen and both DAR and ACLU member, presided. Inevitably, on hand too was Mrs. Dilling and a coterie of patriots. In the course of the evening, Holgate, Bragg, McCulloch, and Tittle made emphatically clear that they had no sympathy with communism and were anxious only to uphold the American principles of free speech and free assembly.

After the meeting, according to Mrs. Dilling, "There was a small group of us talking on the sidewalk, when suddenly a young man thrust everyone aside and walked up to us shouting about Russia. I naturally became angry and began upbraiding him. He stood listening for a while and then suddenly lifted his hand to slap my face. Several men standing nearby interfered. He broke away and ran through the crowd with them right behind in pursuit. I know that if the crowd could have laid hands on him they would have killed him." Mrs. McCulloch, however, denied that the alleged face-slapping incident occurred, saying rather that the meeting could not have been pleasanter and that afterwards people chatted on the sidewalk and congratulated her on what had been a quiet and educational evening.[66] "Radical Tries to Hit Woman Foe of Reds," growled the *Chicago Tribune.*[67] In the following issue the near-miss became a sockdolager: "A Blow Starts Evanston Battling Over the 'Pinks.' "[68]

Tittle stood firm. "Why shouldn't we rent the church hall to the union," he asked. "I belong to the union and I believe in free speech and a free press. Communism was not discussed at this meeting and Haessler was the only radical present. I shall not be bluffed by persons claiming to be super patriots. We don't want Russia; we want free speech."[69] A few days later he elaborated: "I am a member of the American Civil Liberties Union. I joined years ago. The organization is fighting to preserve our traditional American rights of freedom of speech, freedom of press and freedom of assembly. The accusations that have been made repeatedly against the union are untrue. Nor is there

66. For both accounts, see the *Evanston News-Index,* January 14, 1933, p. 1.
67. *Chicago Tribune,* January 14, 1933, p. 13.
68. *Ibid.,* January 15, 1933, p. 3.
69. *Ibid.*

any truth in the statement that the Garland Fund is distributed for Communistic progaganda. It is used to better the existing social order. The union has defended the right of Communists to speak. But let it be understood that to defend freedom of speech does not necessarily mean that the organization which takes this step is in sympathy with the views which they express. Time has proved that it is safest to let them be heard."[70]

Meanwhile, the North Shore buzzed with excitement and the patriots seethed with rage. The American Legion mapped a new drive, complete with the old spider-web charts, to ferret out subversives.[71] The wartime American Protective League, a government-sanctioned "undercover" group of private citizens enrolling 250,000 in 1918, was revived to "offer the citizens of Evanston, in concrete facts, information it received and verified relating to any organization which is Communistic."[72] Spearheading the attack, however, was a new group of patriots, booted and spurred and ready to ride—the Paul Reveres. At the organizational meeting in Glencoe, exclusive North Shore suburb seven miles north of Evanston, the principal speaker was the notorious Harry Jung. Colonel E. M. Hadley, author of "Sinister Shadows" and prominent publisher, was made president. In January Evanston got its chapter, headed by John A. Kappelman, insurance broker. Kappelman set out to accomplish the stated aims of spreading "accurate, dependable information about organizations and individuals whose activities would destroy our form of government."[73] He publicly asked, "Can it be that the pastors of churches in Evanston, who are allowing the meeting of the Godless, atheist Communists to meet in their edifices, are being hoodwinked? Or is it possible that the pastors are attempting to hoodwink their congregations? They are not succeeding. . . ."[74]

In February the Evanston chapter distributed to 18,500 North Shore homes and offices a sixteen-page pamphlet entitled, "Paul Revere Rides Again." It was an anonymous attack in that the name of not a single officer or member of the Paul Reveres was given anywhere in the publication. Readers were assured that the alert Paul Reveres knew:

WHY taxation has almost reached the point of confiscation.
WHY Einstein wishes to come to America and what is behind it.
WHY George Bernard Shaw has been able to pull the wool over the

70. *Evanston News-Index,* January 23, 1933, p. 2.
71. *Ibid.,* January 24, 1933, p. 1.
72. *Ibid.,* January 23, 1933, p. 1.
73. Mimeographed letter distributed by the Paul Reveres, undated, copy in the Tittle Collection; *Time* (March 27, 1933), p. 19.
74. *Evanston News-Index,* January 26, 1933, p. 1.

eyes of the credulous and what he has accomplished toward the dissolution of an empire by his guidance of the
Fabian Society.

WHY a minister on Riverside Drive in New York [Harry Emerson
Fosdick] has a statue of an infidel in his church.

WHY our children are being indoctrinated with loose moral ideas
by certain degenerate teachers.

WHY the average age of our criminals has been lowered ten years.

There was much more of this sort of inanity—or was it insanity? The
Evanstonians Catharine Waugh McCulloch, the Reverend Lester R.
Mondale, Unitarian pastor who had permitted the League for Industrial
Democracy to meet in his church, Dr. James M. Yard, director of
religious education at Northwestern, and (naturally) Tittle came in for
especially rough handling; indeed, Tittle's name was honored by capital
letters. The key paragraph read: "We cannot serve God and anti-God
organizations at the same time. Since the Rev. Dr. Tittle and the Rev.
Mr. Mondale, both teachers of morals and religion have hook-ups with
Socialism and Communism, how can they and other citizens and non-
Preparationists justify their position of receiving their livelihood from a
capitalistic society and at the same time support Atheist-Socialist-Com-
munistic movements subversive and opposed to and destructive of our
American system which educated and fed them better than in any other
country in the world? How can certain pastors be allowed to preach
Christ on Sunday morning and preach Atheists' doctrines on week days?"

The outside cover of the pamphlet carried a quaint poem. The
opening stanzas read as follows:

Tell us, tell us, Pastors Pink,
Since by training taught to think,
How you square your Pink connections
With your Holy-Ghost reflections?
How do Socialistic leanings
Measure with your Christian gleanings?[75]

Happily, the Evanston Review called for fair play, saying of "Tittle
and Company," "These Evanstonians are nationally recognized for their
unselfish devotion to high causes and for their genuine contributions to
the betterment of community and nation. They are patriots in the highest sense, though they may not wave a flag. These attacks cannot hurt
them either at home or in the nation. And yet as a matter of justice to
itself, Evanston cannot let this incident pass without voicing its em-

75. Three copies of the pamphlet are in the Tittle Collection.

phatic disapproval."[76] Even more hard-hitting was an editorial entitled "Paul Revere Wasn't A Coward," a response to the distribution of the anonymously written pamphlet. The editorial concluded: "Off-hand we can mention no act that is more distinctly un-American than an anonymous attack on character. Nor can we think of any greater insult to the intelligence and fairness of Evanstonians than an anonymous attack on some of their most highly respected fellow citizens."[77] Mr. Kappelman angrily informed the editors that "Belittling The Paul Reveres will not detract one tittle from the unchallenged facts clearly set forth which have not been descredited [sic] or disproved."[78] Replied a *Review* columnist nonchalantly, "If it's the same Tittle we've been thinking of we'll say he's darn hard to detract."[79] It is well that Tittle was indeed "hard to detract," for the attacks on him continued throughout the decade, and, in truth, throughout his life, until he came to count on them as one of the rare consistencies of life. Yet he also could count on consistent supporters, and it would be a distortion to ignore this side of the story.

VI

On Sunday morning, September 18, 1932, a time when the patriots were sharpening their knives, the First Church congregation was read a resolution authorized by the Official Board praising every aspect of Tittle's fourteen-year pastorate, expressing the desire that he return "for the next year and the years to come," and concluding, "We know how unsparingly he has given himself to this congregation in public work and in personal service; but we know, too, that his supreme loyalty has been given to God, and that it is as a servant of God that he has served us." The congregation rose as a body to express its concurrence in the statement. In responding to this action, Tittle said, before he began the morning sermon, "To say that I was taken off my feet by Mr. Dyche's all-too-generous statement would be to speak mildly. I was and am still completely bowled over by it. Furthermore, I am deeply appreciative of it. No words of mine can ever say what the confidence and, may I add, affection of this congregation means to me. If the decision remains with me, I can tell you now what it is. You are in no danger whatever— if it is a danger—of my going away. You are in terrible danger of my staying for twenty more years."[80]

76. *Evanston Review,* February 9, 1933, p. 3.
77. *Ibid.,* March 2, 1933, p. 3.
78. *Ibid.,* March 9, 1933, p. 28.
79. *Ibid.,* p. 3.
80. Scrapbook of the Official Board, First Church; *First Church Review,* X

One evening in early March, 1933, at the very height of the Legion-Dilling-Paul Reveres brouhaha, Ernest and Glenna were invited to supper at the home of their close friends, the Fred Wesley Sargents. Mr. Sargent was president of the Chicago & Northwestern Railway Co. His social and economic views were such as to permit him to oppose the New Deal and support the American Liberty League. A neighboring lady entered the parlor and, not recognizing the Tittles, began to rant about the "Red" pastor of First Church. The embarrassment of all was excruciating. This incident in his own home brought Sargent forcefully to a comprehension of the hysteria sweeping Evanston, for though he was no pacifist or socialist, First Church was his church and Tittle was his pastor and friend.[81] Only a few days earlier Tittle had called into his office a small group of the strongest men in the church, including Dyche, Wieboldt, and James F. Oates, and had put the question squarely to them: Would they back him to the limit? The reply was a hearty "yes!"[82]

Thus it came about that these men, now led by Sargent, joined with other key First Church members to draft a declaration affirming their devotion to Tittle and their dedication to a free pulpit. Garrett professor Harris Franklin Rall served as stylist and the actual wording is from his pen.[83] Twenty-one First Church pillars affixed their signatures in personal endorsement, and then on March 6 the declaration was presented to the Official Board (after Tittle left the room) and was promptly and enthusiastically adopted by the Board as the expresison of its own sentiment, and sixteen new signatures were added.[84] The complete statement reads:

> For some time a campaign of insinuation, misrepresentation, and slander, much of it anonymous, has been directed against our pastor, Dr. Ernest F. Tittle. We believe that we owe it to him and to our church and to this community to assert unmistakably our loyalty to him and our protest against such un-American and un-Christian procedure.

(September 24, 1932), 1; *Evanston News-Index,* September 19, 1932, p. 3; *Evanston Review,* September 22, 1932, p. 7.

81. Author's interview with Mrs. Bernice Wolseley, Evanston, Ill., July 13, 1960.

82. Author's interview with Raymond C. Wieboldt, Evanston, Ill., August 6, 1959.

83. For evidence that Rall wrote the actual text, see letter from Mrs. Bernice Wolseley to Edwin E. Voigt, May 18, 1937, in Tittle Collection. For further evidence of Sargent's crucial role, see author's interview with Mr. and Mrs. John M. Tittle, Winnetka, Ill., August 4, 1960.

84. Minutes of the Official Board, First Church, March 6, 1933.

After fourteen years of intimate association with Dr. Tittle as our minister, we would express our absolute confidence in his Christian character and his deep and unselfish devotion to his country, to the church, and to humanity. He is unalterably opposed to the methods of violence advocated by communism, and steadfastly committed to the orderly processes of democratic government.

We stand for a free pulpit and a free church. We do not expect or desire a minister simply to echo the opinions of the congregation, and we do not assert our individual agreement with all of our minister's utterances. But we vigorously resent the effort of outside organizations to dictate to the church or to prescribe its message.

We hold it peculiarly important in this day that the church should stand apart from all appeals to passion, prejudice, and partisanship, and that our nation should have in the Christian church a clear, strong voice rising above all divisions, speaking in the name of God for justice, mutual understanding, and good will. This statement is authorized by the governing board of the First Methodist Episcopal Church of Evanston. It is personally endorsed by those whose names appear below.

Fred W. Sargent, B. J. Denman, M. H. MacLean, Arthur Andersen, William A. Dyche, Charles W. Spofford, A. D. Bruce, James F. Oates, Wilbur Helm, William KixMiller, Joseph H. Beek, H. L. Davis, Earl J. Cooper, Chester D. Tripp, Annie H. Price, E. S. Mills, Andrew H. Phelps, R. C. Wieboldt, Thomas F. Holgate, W. H. Dunham, Harris Franklin Rall, James A. James, Frank M. McKibben, Harold A. Smith, Walter E. Schwind, Robert C. Teare, Edward S. Price, S. P. Whiteside, C. B. Carter, M. J. Newell, D. E. Winter, James G. Carr, Carrie H. Wilson, Marie V. Swanson, Jeane Haskins Colwell, Alec R. Allenson, and Bruce H. Corzine.[85]

This "free pulpit" resolution is one of the heroic landmarks in the history of American Protestantism. As Paul Hutchinson wrote, "The victory which Ernest Tittle won over as irrational and foul-fighting an opposition as any minister ever faced thus became in some measure a victory for all his prophetic breathren in the pulpit."[86]

Northwestern and Garrett students hailed this defense of the preacher who so influenced campus life, and their professors saw in the resolution a victory for free expression in the classroom as well as in the pulpit.

85. The original typed copy with the thirty-seven signatures is in the Tittle Collection. Tittle, apparently, for the writing is in his hand, made one change in the Rall draft. For Rall's words "self-styled patriots and self-appointed censors," Tittle substituted the less abrasive phrase "outside organizations." The members of the Social Service Board of the Women's Union requested the "privilege of adding their names to those personally endorsing the statement."

86. Hutchinson, "Portrait," p. xxv.

The Evanston Ministerial Association unanimously resolved its "allegiance to a free and unfettered pulpit" and rejoiced "in the noble ministry of Ernest Fremont Tittle which has won national recognition and which has been marked by prophetic insight, social passion, and courageous Christian utterance."[87] (A few weeks earlier the *Christian Century* had warned that if the ministers of Evanston knuckled under they would deserve nothing but the moral and intellectual slavery into which they had delivered themselves.) The Methodist ministers of Chicago expressed their confidence in Tittle and recorded as their judgment that "he is one of the great prophetic spirits of the age."[88] Liberal religious journals throughout the country hailed the action of First Church. Even the secular press sensed the momentousness of the event. Above all, Tittle received many letters from other burdened working ministers encouraging him to stand firm and thanking him for the moral strength he gave to them. "Nine years ago," wrote one such fellow preacher, "I took a stand in an Indianapolis pulpit against the heathen principles of the Ku Klux Klan and I know what it is to have the hounds turned loose. There is nothing they will not do once they are aroused. They will try to rob you of your pulpit, intimidate your loved ones and assassinate your character."[89] Time and again Tittle explained his own position to troubled or angry parishioners, but never more simply than in these words: "I am the minister of a Christian Church. I am supposed to be a follower of Jesus. Indeed, my ministerial credentials authorize and command me to preach the gospel. So far as I am able to understand his gospel I am preaching it, and that is the only crime of which I am guilty."[90] In their historic "free pulpit" declaration of March 6, the people of First Church made clear their own belief that this was in fact Tittle's only crime.

VII

The 1933 "free pulpit" declaration put an end to the possibility of Tittle's being driven from Evanston, but the irritating attacks continued, and there was always the possibility that Tittle might forsake Evanston. As his national reputation widened it was but natural that handsome offers should come his way to accept seminary professorships or prestigious pastorates elsewhere.[91] He seriously considered one of these offers,

87. *Christian Century*, L (May 10, 1933), 632; *Evanston Review*, May 4, 1933, p. 5; *First Church Review*, X (May 6, 1933), 1.
88. *Christian Century*, L (April 5, 1933), 472.
89. Letter from F. E. Davison to Tittle, March 21, 1933.
90. Letter from Tittle to George Merrick, February 23, 1933.
91. The numerous invitations are in the Tittle Collection.

the pastorate of the American Church in Shanghai for a year, but this he ultimately declined because he felt his absence from Evanston even temporarily might prove "very embarrassing if not disastrous."[92]

The most persistent and alluring attraction, however, was the chaplaincy of Yale University. The offer had been dangled first in 1931 by the noted dean of the Yale Divinity School, Luther A. Weigle.[93] Tittle declined, adding, "In this, of course, I may be badly mistaken. I may say to you confidentially that Mrs. Tittle thinks that I am and that I ought not to say, No, to you without full consideration of the great opportunity at Yale."[94] In 1935 Yale again sought Tittle. Sidney Lovett, Raymond Morris, and Halford Luccock, all of whom Tittle much admired, wrote persuasive pleas. "It is the most important position in the school," stated Morris.[95] For Tittle the temptation was great. Glenna, whose first concern was always her husband's well-being, hoped he would acquiesce. The pressures in Evanston were literally killing and in retrospect Mrs. Tittle believes that had the Yale invitation been accepted, Ernest might not have died at the age of sixty-three.[96] As Tittle wrote his old friend Luccock, "I am frank to say that she [Glenna] looks upon you as the voice of wisdom and upon me as the voice of folly."[97]

Yet before Tittle could bring himself to say yes or no to the Yale offer, he decided to take stock of things in Evanston and at First Church. A number of anxieties, objective and subjective, shadowed his life in 1935. For one thing, the patriots continued relentlessly to push the assault. Though there was now no chance that Tittle would be "fired," the patriots, like the Confederacy after Gettysburg, did not know they were defeated, and they were still capable of inflicting cruel if not mortal wounds. For another, a few of the men who had signed the "free pulpit" resolution subsequently broke with Tittle and transferred their memberships to less confounding churches. For a third, the formation of the Conference of Methodist Laymen was to Tittle a puzzle and a pain. On July 29, 1935, thirty-five Methodist laymen met at the Union League Club in Chicago to check the spread of radicalism within Methodism, to re-orient the pulpit along personal rather than social lines, and to bring about a "renewed emphasis on the spiritual phase of the life and work of the church." These men were disturbed by the growing hostility

92. Letter from Tittle to Bishop Herbert Welch, May 14, 1934.
93. Letters from Luther A. Weigle to Tittle, February 2 and 6, 1931.
94. Letter from Tittle to Luther A. Weigle, February 5, 1931.
95. Letter from Raymond P. Morris to Tittle, October 15, 1935.
96. Author's interview with Glenna Myers Tittle, Evanston, Ill., July 31, 1959.
97. Letter from Tittle to Halford E. Luccock, October 30, 1935.

toward capitalism evidenced by Methodist preachers, periodicals, agencies, and conferences; they were especially discomforted by the Marxist posture of the Methodist Federation for Social Service. "Ours is not a movement to 'muzzle the pulpit,'" they declared, "but it is a movement to preserve the original and vital message of Christianity." An unofficial group of Methodist laymen, they hoped their example would inspire laymen in other denominations to bank the seemingly endemic fires of anticapitalism.

The Conference of Methodist Laymen was a genuinely conservative but not a demifascist organization and its members were not cut from the same neurotic cloth as Mrs. Dilling or the same cynical cloth as Harry Jung. They were individuals who honestly believed in the rightness of "rugged" capitalism and who sincerely felt it was not the function of the church to pass upon "secular" matters.[98] In a very real sense, however, this made them an even greater threat to prophetic Christianity, for as a First Church member observed, "If the Christian minister is confined to the subject of 'spiritual realities' I am inclined to think that two or three sermons in all probability would exhaust the supply."[99]

Tittle was particularly hurt because most of the organization's leaders had for years been faithful worshippers at First Church. Henry S. Henschen, Winnetka citizen and president of the Chicago Bank of Commerce, was chairman. (In attacking the group, liberals inferred that the banking profession was only slightly less reprehensible than the world's oldest.) Only a few years earlier Tittle had thanked Mr. Henschen for his interest in First Church matters and had suggested they lunch "together for no reason in particular except to enjoy each other's society."[100] When a few years later Henschen died Tittle delivered a moving memorial tribute, and he also comforted Mrs. Henschen at the time of her heart attack. Wilbur Helm, businessman and president of the Illinois chapter of the Sons of the American Revolution, was secretary. Mr. Helm and his wife were devoted First Church members and he had been one of the signers of the "free pulpit" declaration. Moreover, in 1933 and 1934 he and Tittle had exchanged warm letters, Tittle expressing his gratitude for Helm's "tolerance and patience" and "fine spirit" and thanking God for his support.[101] Burt J. Denman, vice-president and general manager of the United Light and Power Company, was also active in the group's formation. He, too, had signed the

98. See Miller, *American Protestantism and Social Issues,* p. 125.
99. Letter from Clyde D. Foster to editors of *Evanston Daily News-Index,* August 14, 1935, pp. 1-2.
100. Letter from Tittle to Henry S. Henschen, January 14, 1931.
101. Letters from Tittle to Wilbur Helm, June 26, 1933, and May 31, 1934.

"free pulpit" declaration and held Tittle in high esteem. For his part, Tittle had nominated him for membership in the University Club of Chicago, testifying, "Mr. Denman is a leading layman in the church of which I am the minister and is altogether one of the finest men I have ever known. He is public spirited, extraordinarily generous, interested in art and, indeed, everything that pertains to the life of the spirit."[102] Very shortly Mr. Denman was to transfer his membership to the Presbyterian Church, though when doing so he assured Tittle "that I hold you in the same old affection and esteem."[103] Most disturbing of all, Fred Sargent, prime mover in the great 1933 defense of Tittle, participated in the organization of the conference. Altogether, the fact that so many of his own people were in the newly formed Conference of Methodist Laymen must have raised in Tittle's mind a doubt as to the effectiveness of his ministry. Furthermore, it could not have been comforting to Tittle to know that First Church leaders, including Sargent, Sewell L. Avery (of Montgomery Ward), and the beloved Dyche were in the newly formed American Liberty League, a national union of respectable reactionaries bound together by a common hatred of President Roosevelt.

Still another source of anxiety was John Tittle's defeat in an Evanston School Board election in early 1935, especially when the "radicalism" of his father was injected into the campaign; Tittle came to a bitter new comprehension of the manner in which the "sins" of a father could be passed on to his son.

A final possible source of Tittle's disturbed state in 1935 is perhaps less objective but no less real. In October he would face his fiftieth birthday. He had run hard his entire life. The financial problems burdening First Church were heavy, and he was tired. This bone-weariness may be discerned in the letters he wrote at the time. His doctor, Don C. Sutton, a First Church member, reported to the Official Board the opinion that under no circumstances could the church afford to lose Tittle, "But that now he is much too tired and should take a long rest before it is forced upon him. I would like to suggest that he be given a year's leave of absence with pay, knowing full well the church will be repaid in the future."[104] Tittle had been a minister since 1908. He had been minister of First Church since 1918. This is a long time for a man to be in one calling and a fearfully long time to have served in the same church. It may be that to a feeling of exhaustion was added a momen-

102. Letter from Tittle to Admissions Committee, University Club of Chicago, December 17, 1930.
103. Letter from Burt J. Denman to Tittle, July 16, 1936.
104. Letter from Don C. Sutton to the Official Board, May 20, 1935.

tary mood of boredom, though I am aware that this conjecture contradicts an earlier assertion that Tittle never lost his zest for his job. But surely no man escapes moments when he wishes he might try his hand at something new. Then, too, however much Glenna liked Evanston, she loved her husband and coveted for him a more peaceful life in the groves of academe (in the "good old days"), and her influence was thrown in the scales on the side of Yale.

Perhaps not even Tittle himself could have put his finger on the precise reasons why he stunned the Official Board, meeting May 6, with the announcement that he was considering leaving. He then requested the board to "determine the consensus of opinion of as many of the congregation as possible relative to their desire to retain him as minister."[105] Though his voice was quiet, it was apparent that he was under severe emotional strain. In essence, Tittle confronted his people with two questions: First, "Am I wanted?"; second, "Will you support personally and financially the program of the church which is certain to be carried on if I remain here?"[106]

At a special meeting of the Official Board on May 20, Dean James Alton James read the following resolution bearing the signatures of sixty-seven individuals:

> We are informed that you have under consideration a call to another position. As members of the Official Board, in special session, we wish to express the conviction that your going would constitute an irreparable loss to our church. While you are to make the ultimate decision, we wish to assure you, as a Board, that your leadership grows continually more satisfying to us. It is our firm belief that you are now in a position to profit from your untiring efforts in our behalf over a most difficult period. We hereby pledge to you as individuals our unqualified support in assisting you in carrying forward a program which will even further contribute to the growth of our Christian fellowship.

After much enthusiastic discussion, the resolution was seconded and unanimously approved. A committee of five, but actually consisting of about ten persons, was appointed to wait on and present the resolution to Tittle, "which was done that evening."[107]

Meanwhile, and continuing into the summer Tittle, and Glenna, too,

105. Minutes of the Official Board, First Church, May 6, 1935.
106. This is how Tittle summed it up in a letter to a dear friend, Luke I. Wilson, May 24, 1935.
107. Minutes of the Official Board, First Church, May 20, 1935. The original resolution, typed with the signatures in ink, is in the Tittle Collection.

received scores of letters. Some of them were group expressions, signed by as many as sixty-five persons. Some of them were dictated to secretaries and typed on business stationery, but the overwhelming majority were written in longhand by individuals or by couples. Some were only a few lines in length; others ran to six and eight pages. All of them expressed a sense of utter loss at the thought of Tittle's leaving First Church and all of them affirmed an abiding loyalty to him. Almost all of them acknowledged his contributions not only to First Church, but also to Garrett, Northwestern, Evanston, and Chicago. Many persons said Tittle was responsible for saving their spiritual lives. Several individuals confessed that in moments of despair his words and deeds had stayed their hands from the act of suicide—and only now were they revealing this to him. "I love you deeply, old top," wrote one man, expressing a common sentiment. "We may not deserve you—but we need you," wrote one woman, expressing a common plea.[108] "You have become something of a symbol throughout the country of the possibility of a free church and a free pulpit. Should you leave it would take the heart out of many a man fighting a hard battle these hard and bitterly difficult days," wrote Bishop James C. Baker, expressing a common conviction.[109]

Ernest Fremont Tittle was a great man, but he was a man, not a demigod. He could and did stand up to brutish punishment, but even as the blows fell he required cheers of encouragement to cushion them. More than most men he suffered vilification; as much as any man he needed love. Beyond question it was the overwhelming demonstration of love on the part of the people of First Church in the spring and summer of 1935 that led him to decline the Yale offer—and the many other offers continuing to come his way.

VIII

Thus the great crisis of 1935 was safely passed. Two years later Tittle suffered his first heart attack and, as we know, he was absent from the pulpit for almost a year. Once again his people rallied to his side, their expressions of loyalty both strengthening his body and his determination to preach the full gospel so long as breath remained. Wrote one supporter: "Don't, for pete's sake, fade out of the picture when so many of us draw so much from your faith and courage and

108. It would be possible to quote for many pages similar expressions drawn from letters in the Tittle Collection.
109. Letter from Jim Baker to Tittle, May 19, 1935.

spiritual insight without which we are nothing. . . . After all the best years of your life are just ahead. Claim them, Man, claim them."[110]

The year 1938 marked the twentieth anniversary of Tittle's First Church pastorate. This fact was not forgotten. On December 28 a commemorative banquet was held, Bishop Francis J. McConnell traveling from New York to address the celebrants. During the evening James F. Oates announced that a fund of $100,000 had been raised to insure the future of First Church and underwrite the broadened program Tittle had charted. "The raising of $100,000 in so short a time [less than two months] may look like a Herculean task," Mr. Oates reported. "It was not. Once the Committee had the campaign started, the spirit of this church and its people took hold and we had only to step back out of the way."[111] What finer tribute to Tittle's leadership after "Twenty Memorable Years" than this demonstration of congregational esprit de corps!

The following year total war descended upon Europe just as in the preceding year it had engulfed the Far East, and then in 1941 war came to the Western hemisphere also. Yet Tittle did not abandon his pacifism. It was no easy thing to swim against the tides of honest passion and genuine patriotism which understandably carried the American people along after December 7, and Tittle was once again to be made aware of the high cost of discipleship. Yet, though the old accusations were flung at him—"Nazi neouratic," "hypochrondaic and coward," "dirty yellow dog"—it is both surprising and wonderfully encouraging that Tittle's job was not in grave danger. He had weathered many storms, especially in 1924 and the early 1930's, and he might have gone under on these occasions, but by 1941 such was the commitment of First Church to the freedom of the pulpit and so securely was Tittle bound to the hearts of his people, that not even a war for survival could place his ministry in jeopardy. This fact tells us something not only about Tittle and First Church, but also about the temper in which the American people fought the Second World War. Surely if Tittle had been a pacifist in 1917 he would have suffered the loss of his Columbus pastorate, and perhaps his his entire career would have been ruined. The obverse side of Wilsonian moral idealism was a harsh fanaticism which brooked no dissent. In 1941, however, the American people went to war grimly determined to do a necessary, ugly job. And as they were less certain that they were engaged in a holy crusade, so they were less insistent that all clergymen give their cleansing benediction to the business at hand—the defeat of Nazi

110. Letter from F. Theodore Miner to Tittle, December 7, 1937.
111. *Twenty Memorable Years,* booklet published by First Church, n.p., n.d.

Germany and Imperial Japan. This is not to say that the wartime record of civil liberties and civil rights in World War II was untarnished but to assert that compared to the hysteria of the Great Crusade of 1917 the record is relatively clean. On reflection, maybe the explanation should be turned about. Perhaps precisely because the American people in 1917 harbored secret doubts concerning the wisdom of intervention they were compelled to silence all doubts; whereas in 1941 the enormity of the peril was so self-evident that the dissent of a few pacifists could be tolerated.

In any event, it is notable that on February 21, 1944, in the midst of total war, First Church judged it proper to celebrate the silver anniversary of its pacifist minister. Once again a grand program was arranged, with Bishop G. Bromley Oxnam on hand to speak for all Methodism. Once again substance was given to the tribute by the raising of $66,000 from 544 individuals in order to pay off the last dollar of First Church indebtedness, with James F. Oates, as in 1938, the key figure in the planning. And once again the people of First Church paid tributes to Tittle so fulsome as to be embarrassing were they not so sincere.[112]

In December, 1948, Tittle's thirty years in Evanston were acknowledged in many ways, not the least of these being an order from his Official Board to take a special mid-winter vacation of five weeks. With characteristic modesty Tittle replied, "We are especially pleased in the statement that you rejoice in our 'continued' service. We have the feeling, however, that a resolution of appreciation instead of coming from you to us should have gone from us to you. You are a long-suffering people! Your loving-kindness, like the peace of God, passes all understanding. God bless you."[113]

At the time of Tittle's death in August, 1949, the membership of First Church and a "host of other friends far and near" were "joining in an expression of their love for Dr. and Mrs. Tittle" by the presentation of a great "Tittle Testimonial Fund." On Tittle's insistence, this was not to be a personal fund nor was it to interfere with the regular church budget. Rather, it was to be used by the Tittles for such benevolences they might select to minister to the "needs of the poor and sick." Somehow the words of the committee seem especially fitting, written as they were on the very threshhold of Tittle's death: "Whatever comes of the testimonial fund, it will at best be a meager expression of the abiding devotion that our church has for Dr. and Mrs. Tittle. They

112. *A Quarter Century, 1918-1943,* booklet published by First Church, n.p., n.d.

113. *First Church Review,* XXVI (December 25, 1948), 4.

have healed the sick at heart, they have preached the gospel, they have given of themselves to others unstintingly in complete unselfishness, they have spiritually regenerated thousands and they have lived so near to the pattern of life prescribed by Jesus Christ that they have inspired us to know him better by watching them."[114]

114. *Ibid.* (May 7, 1949), 1.

10. FIRST CHURCH AND
THE EVANSTON COMMUNITY

I

"This church, thank God, is to serve the community."[1] "This church, let God be thanked, is a community center."[2] On a thousand instances Tittle voiced the conviction that the life of First Church should not be divorced from the life of the community. The Christian congregation, like the individual follower of Christ, is under a commission to serve others, and for a church to seek purity in isolation from a corrupt and corrupting society would be to pay the high price of irrelevance. The popular slogan of the 1960's, "The Church Is Mission," hardly represents a new idea. The First Methodist Episcopal Church was the first church in Evanston in date of founding. It was also the first church in Evanston in point of influence. Tittle was invited to First Church for the express purpose of continuing and widening this influence. The expectation was fulfilled. When death summoned Tittle thirty-one years later First Church occupied a central place in Evanston life and his own community position was towering. This is not to claim for Tittle's presence a transfiguring power. It is merely to state that he did as much as any mortal man possibly could to hold before the eyes of the citizens of Evanston the ancient vision of a "Citty vpon a Hill." That he did so was the testimony of hundreds. "I know of no man whose death could

1. "Not Apart From Us," a sermon preached November 19, 1944, reprinted in James Alton James, *From Log Schoolhouse to Church Tower: A History of the First Methodist Church, Evanston, Illinois* (n.p., n.d.).
2. *Evanston Review*, January 14, 1954, p. 38. Much of this issue is devoted to the celebration of the centennial of First Church.

leave such a void as Dr. Tittle's," stated the president of Northwestern University, J. Roscoe Miller. "He was one of Evanston's greatest citizens and had exerted a tremendous influence on this community."[3] This judgment was seconded by the vice-president of Northwestern, Harry L. Wells: "One of Evanston's truly great men left us yesterday and his passing leaves an irreparable loss in our midst. We at the university who have known and honored him share our sorrow with the world. Dr. Tittle was admired and held in the highest esteem by all who knew him, but I think the word which describes the feeling that all of us had for him was 'love'—for we idolized him for his sterling character, his fine mind, his gay and affectionate nature, and his high courage."[4]

When in 1918 Tittle assumed the pastorate of First Church American Protestantism anticipated marching forward with the high and confident step of a drum major. The new era, said the Northern Methodist bishops, would be "one, big, blooming, buzzing confusion,"[5] yet churchmen throughout the land burned with enthusiasm and quivered with the expectation of final triumph—the complete evangelization and consequent redemption of humanity. The "Hun" had been crushed; the world had been made safe for democracy; the war to end all wars had ended. With the passage of the Eighteenth Amendment Americans were freed from the bondage of liquor and soon the entire world would outlaw the evil. The national unity seemingly achieved in the Great Crusade, the spirit of self-sacrifice and self-discipline freely accepted during the war, and the idealism manifest in Wilsonian progressivism all contributed to the optimism with which the churches faced the future. Although every major denomination launched its own postwar crusade or co-operated in the grandiose Interchurch World Movement, none was more revealing of a self-assertive confidence than the Methodist's ambitious Centenary Movement.

When Tittle died in 1949 the United States was being bathed in a torrential post–World War II religious revival, and this surge of piety seemed to touch every segment of American life and unprecedented numbers of citizens. Church memberships soared, attendance at worship services became *au courant*, and vast sums were lavished on building programs. The Norman Vincent Peales spoke to millions who sought peace of mind, the Billy Grahams spoke to millions who sought peace of soul, and even intellectuals, once so yawningly indifferent to theology, listened when the Niebuhrs and Tillichs spoke their hard words. Pres-

3. *Chicago Daily News,* August 4, 1949, a clipping in the Tittle Collection.
4. *Evanston Review,* August 11, 1949, a clipping in the Tittle Collection.
5. *The Daily Christian Advocate,* Methodist Episcopal Church, May 3, 1920, p. 28. The bishops were of course quoting William James.

idents and disc jockeys "got religion." Book publishers, Hollywood producers, and recording companies discovered that the "Man Upstairs" handsomely rewarded those who sang His praises—and they continued to sing His praises all the way to the bank. The Pledge of Allegiance was amended to include the phrase "under God," a prayer room was installed in the national capitol, and the president of the United States and the presidents of mighty corporations attended prayer breakfasts. Small wonder that by 1957 more than 96 percent of the American people claimed a specific religious affiliation.[6]

If 1918 and 1949 were deemed vintage years by those in America who tended the Lord's vineyards, the intervening period was for American Protestantism mostly a time of blight. Far from becoming a decade of triumph, the 1920's saw, in the words of Robert T. Handy, a "religious depression" or, at the very least, in the words of Winthrop S. Hudson, a "religious recession." Church attendance, Sunday School enrollment, and missionary giving declined. Religious faith was taken as a sign of intellectual inbecility associated with the benighted Bible Belt, the fatuous Bruce Barton, or the fawning clergy and feckless laymen in the Lynds' Middletown. It is "a fairly safe generalization to say that no profession of men is so thoroughly emptly of dignity and grace as that of the Protestant ministry today," asserted a Presbyterian preacher at the end of the decade.[7] One clue in support of this assertion is the pitifully small wage commanded by the average Protestant parson, less than $1,000 annually. Another clue is the fact that in 1920 some 2,700 students volunteered for foreign-mission service, but by 1928 the number had dwindled to 252.[8] A third clue is the lampooning ministers received on stage and screen, in book and periodical, to say nothing of the chilling treatment accorded churchmen in intellectual and academic communities. Harold Stearns explained in 1922 that there was no article on religion in his famed symposium, *Civilization in the United States,* because he could find no intellectual interested in the topic. The most telling evidence, however, of organized religion's depressed estate, its low morale and declining status, is the alacrity with which many churchmen

6. Winthrop S. Hudson, *Religion in America* (New York: Charles Scribner's Sons, 1965), pp. 382-83.

7. The Reverend Ellis J. Hough, as quoted in Paul A. Carter, *The Decline and Revival of the Social Gospel: Social and Political Liberalism in American Protestant Churches, 1920-1940* (Ithaca, N. Y.: Cornell University Press, 1954), p. 70.

8. Robert T. Handy, "The American Religious Depression," *Church History,* XXIX (March, 1960), 4.

accepted the standards and goals of the prestigious business world and emulated the techniques and jargon of successful businessmen.[9]

Then came the Great Depression with its cruel consequences. Church membership cascaded downward like the Great Bull market itself. A people shorn of their material wealth did not, as was predicted, turn to God in their humbling destitution. The Methodist Episcopal, Methodist Episcopal, South, and Methodist Protestant churches had 15.4 percent fewer members in 1936 than in 1926, many of the losses being picked up by the Pentecostal and Holiness sects. Budgets were slashed, bishops as well as preachers suffered salary cuts, and administrative workers were reluctantly dismissed. Churches were abandoned, and benevolent and missionary enterprises set adrift or sadly curtailed.

Then in 1941 war came to America and the churches were confronted with another era of crisis and challenge.

The Evanston ministry of Ernest Fremont Tittle must be placed in the context of the total American religious situation between the end of World War I and the eve of the Korean War. It was a time when Protestant preachers faced enormous difficulties. It was a period when the very life of the organized church seemed threatened by internal blight and external assault. In brief, Tittle's triumphs are all the more remarkable because they were won in what was for American Protestantism in general a time of trouble.

II

Although it would be unhistorical to minimize the challenges facing Tittle as pastor of First Church, it would be ungenerous to leave unmentioned the impressive advantages immediately accruing to any man called to the pulpit of the First Methodist Episcopal Church of Evanston, Illinois. In 1854, in a one-room log schoolhouse, the first Methodist quarterly conference was organized in the new village of Evanston. The village was named after Dr. John Evans, who together with a small group of Methodist ministers and laymen had met in the Chicago law office of Judge Goodrich to lay the foundations of Northwestern University. It was also deemed wise to establish a biblical institute, Garrett, in Evanston, thus giving the promise that one day the little community would become the educational center of midwestern Methodism. In 1856 Evanston Methodists erected a small, flat, frame structure, painted white, and costing only $2,800. The First Methodist Episcopal Church of Evanston was the first house of worship in the village.

9. See Robert Moats Miller, *American Protestantism and Social Issues, 1919-1939* (Chapel Hill: The University of North Carolina Press, 1958), pp. 17-30.

From the beginning, First Church's relationship with Northwestern and Garrett was intimate, and though the advantages were reciprocal, it is not too much to say that the services rendered by the church to the university and seminary were extraordinary. From the beginning, also, the church provided moral, civic, and social leadership to the community. Until well into the twentieth century the membership rolls of First Church read much like a *Who's Who* of the community, and, indeed, because Evanston was the first suburb north of Chicago on the shore, of much of Chicago's leadership as well. Moreover, because many of the boards and agencies of the Methodist Episcopal Church were in Chicago, many national leaders of Methodism lived in Evanston and worshiped in First Church. In sum, when in December, 1918, Tittle embarked on his great Evanston pastorate it was not in the role of pioneer. He was the inheritor of an old and prestigious parish with unusually close ties with a major Methodist university and seminary. The congregation of about one thousand included a large percentage of the "power elite" in an affluent and strategically located suburban community. Indeed, a lesser minister might easily have become suffused with complacency.

III

The role Tittle coveted for First Church in the life of the community was rooted in his conception of the nature of the Church. For Tittle, the Church is not a voluntary association which men themselves have formed to minister to their religious needs, and only in a secondary and derivative sense is the Church a formal, ecclesiastical organization. "As a matter of history," Tittle held,

the first Christians did not come together and say, "Let us form a Christian fellowship and call it the church." They became aware of an existing fellowship constituted of men and women who had come under the influence of Jesus. It was not an ecclesiastical foundation, deliberately established, that created a Christian fellowship. It was a Christian fellowship already in existence that organized itself for the propagation of the Gospel, the instruction of neophytes, the conduct of worship, and the doing of good. The church, in the first instance, was a spiritual community which men did not create but discovered. It was the historical result of the life and death and resurrection of Christ. If it be true that God was in Christ reconciling the world unto Himself, it certainly is true that the church is a divine creation and not merely a human association. As European Christians say, the church is an extension of the incarnation. As Saint Paul declared, the church is the body of Christ—a unique fellowship in which the spirit of Christ lives and labors in history.[10]

Closely related to his conception of the Church as fellowship, or even inseparable from it, is the conception of the Church as a committed community. This community is not composed of perfect men and women, most certainly not of those who think themselves perfect. When Saint Paul called the early Christians saints, he did not mean that they were sanctified, but that they had committed themselves to Christ as Lord. It is this consecrated community, which includes the faithful who "have gone before" as well as the faithful who still live on earth, that is the true Church, the communion of saints. It is a communion (koinonia) of the Holy Spirit. For Tittle, the "communion of saints" meant not merely the historical and mystical and transcendent, but something vital and human, a fellowship in which people knew each other and helped each other in matters both spiritual and temporal.[11] Tittle called upon his people to so demonstrate their love, care, and concern for one another that it might again be said as it was said in the first century, "Behold how these Christians love one another." As Tittle repeatedly warned, "What shall it profit a church if it becomes enthusiastic about missions, but remains lukewarm toward brotherhood? We ought, of course, to love all men. But we are not likely to persuade all men that we do love them if they observe that we hardly know our fellow churchmen, and have reason to suspect that some of them we do not care to know."[12] If the "communion of saints" begins in the local church in daily face-to-face relationships, it does not end there. The Christian Church transcends every barrier of distance, language, and culture and every political frontier. On a hundred occasions Tittle insisted that the Christian fellowship reaches out toward the ends of the earth, and that this universal community is the one hope in an age of racial, political, economic, and ideological fragmentation.

Tittle's sense of the extension of the incarnation is not that the Church is Christ or become Christ, but that the Church is the body of Christ, a unique fellowship in which the spirit of Christ lives and labors in history. This transcendent reference is a reference of judgment, for the Church points beyond itself to a judgment which is not its own but God's, a judgment under which it stands and by which it is condemned.

10. "God and the Church," *The First Church Pulpit*, Vol. IV, No. 6, a sermon preached July 20, 1941.
11. See the sermon "The Communion of Saints," in *A Mighty Fortress* (New York: Harper & Brothers, 1949), pp. 28-36.
12. *Fellowship*, a booklet published by First Church, n.p., n.d.

So the transcendent reference of the Church does not lead to a doctrine of ecclesiastical infallibility and consequently to the sin of pride, but rather to a sense of humility and a realization of finiteness. Only as it has this sense of origin in God and of its own weakness without God can the Church really be the Church.[13]

The cry of the Oxford Conference, "Let the Church be the Church," was repeatedly echoed by Tittle: "The church is always tempted to be something other than the church. In some cases, it is tempted to be an association of the well-to-do for the purpose of maintaining a kind of religion that promises to satisfy certain spiritual cravings—and to leave the status quo undisturbed. In other cases, especially in this country, it is tempted to be but a slightly religious edition of America's Town Meeting of the Air. In all cases it is tempted to be but the voice of a secular culture, employing, to be sure, the language and forms of religion but standing for nothing that is distinctively Christian. In a time of national crisis, it is tempted to be the mouthpiece of the state, taking its direction not from Christ but from Caesar." Therefore, "unless the church deliberately stands in the presence of God and takes its direction from God and receives constant help from God, it cannot be the church, it can only be one of the voices of its time; it cannot be the voice and instrument of the Eternal, redeeming its time." Because the Church is the people of God it "may not stand in the presence of the secular community, or of the national state, asking, 'What should we say? What should we do? What are we permitted to say and to do?' The church, if it is to be the church, must stand in the presence of the Eternal asking, 'What is Thy will, O God?' "[14]

Tittle hammered home the point that the place for the local church to *start* ministering to others is the local community. There is such a thing, he said, as a devotion to the good of humanity that takes no note of immediate, concrete, on-the-spot opportunities to serve. There is something phony—something suggestive of sounding brass or a tinkling cymbal—about a professed devotion to suffering humanity that bypasses near-by opportunities to sacrifice and serve.

The charges leveled against the institutional church are numerous and often valid. There is a tendency for the minister of an active urban

13. For an elaboration of this point, see Henry Eugene Kolbe, "The Church: Its Nature and Its Function in Society: The Views of Reinhold Niebuhr, John C. Bennett, and Ernest Fremont Tittle" (M.A. thesis, Northwestern University, 1946), pp. 30-40.

14. "God and the Church," *The First Church Pulpit*, Vol. IV, No. 6, a sermon preached July 20, 1941. See also "The Voice of the Church at Oxford," *Religion In Life*, VII (Winter, 1938), 14-21.

or suburban parish to lose his priestly character and to become entirely a social functionary. There is a tendency for the primary purpose—the worship of God—to be lost in a welter of study classes, lectures, forums, entertainments, athletic contests, teas, and dinners, all supervised by secretaries and specialists, and all contributing to the alleged transformation of American Protestantism into the "Great Society of the Outstretched Hand." Though Tittle agreed with the partial justice of this indictment, he remained firm in the faith that as long as he was chief minister of First Church he would never permit it to be dark and deserted, tenanted six days a week by mice, silence, and gloom.

IV

The first way in which First Church served the community was by providing a church home for increasing numbers of Evanston and North Shore citizens. In 1918 First Church reported 1,097 full members and 118 nonresident members. In 1949 it reported 2,524 full members and 801 nonresident members. That is, under Tittle's leadership the total membership grew from 1,215 to 3,325.[15] This steady growth is a tribute to the solidity with which Tittle built and to the recognition that he was not a counterfeit man. A minister who was no more than a "Prince of the Pulpit" would have burned up his pyrotechnics and burned out his audiences long before the lapse of three decades. The signal thing about Tittle's ministry is less the statistics of membership than the fact that Sunday after Sunday congregations averaging 1,500 gathered for public worship. Any church that annually draws 80,000 persons to its doors for the Sunday service is not moribund, especially when each week some 5,500 men, women, and children gathered on days other than Sunday to worship, pray, study, and play.

Tittle would have agreed with Henry Sloane Coffin's lamentation that too many Protestant ministers in their concern for sheer size had ceased to be shepherds and had become ranchers. He comprehended that by methods of high-pressure salesmanship people might be hornswoggled into attending church, but that to form in them "the mind of Christ is another matter."[16] As it happens, Tittle's ministry spanned an

15. Henry Steele Commager once observed that church statistics attain an unreliability that would be a penal offense in a corporation. The observation is not unjust. For First Church membership I have used the figures reported in the *Minutes* of the Rock River Annual Conference, 1918-1949, inclusive, rather than those sometimes given in the Evanston press, publicity releases, memorandums, and so forth, though the discrepancies are not suspiciously large.

16. *The Gospel According to Luke* (New York: Harper & Brothers, 1951), p. 16.

era when huckstering churchmen were very much the vogue, taking as their slogan: "Early to bed and early to rise / Preach the gospel and advertise." Catchy sermon titles, peppy slogans, tawdry advertisements, hard-sell membership drives, sensational worship services—none of these things were new in the history of American Protestantism. Yet they achieved a unique level of vulgarity following the Great War, Jesus being depicted as a champion salesman and Moses as a shrewd real estate promoter. Indeed, when on entering a town one saw the billboard "Jesus Saves" one scarcely knew if it had been erected by a church or a bank.[17]

Tittle did not succumb to this spirit of commercialism. Doubtless he coveted new members for his church as much as the next minister, and surely it was (secretly) satisfying to his ego to review at the end of the year fattened membership rolls. Yet he was not a clerical buccaneer raiding the Church Main for booty. "I cannot withhold some word of delight over the fact that you and your sister are 'tottering on the brink' of Methodism," he once replied to a letter of inquiry. "I must refrain from pushing you over, for that would be considered a violation of the ethics of my profession. I can only offer up a little prayer that some gentle or, if need be, stiff breeze will blow you in our direction! In any case, I shall be comforted by your presence in church on Sunday mornings."[18] On another occasion he wrote: "As you doubtless know, I have carefully refrained from urging or even inviting you to unite with our church because I wanted to play fair with a sister church here in Evanston. I may say, however, that when the time comes for you properly to make the move your entrance into the fellowship of my church will afford me no end of delight."[19]

As a postscript, it is interesting to note that once an individual joined First Church he was not bombarded with pleas from the pulpit to attend worship service regularly. Only on one instance did Tittle make a blunt petition for increased church attendance. This was in 1934 at a time when the depression had broken the morale of some parishioners, individuals who because of despair or shame at having lost their jobs had ceased going to church. Tittle based his petition on this fact, and not on any peevish injury to his own self-esteem.[20]

V

It is not necessary to subscribe to Parkinson's mordant Law to

17. See Miller, *American Protestantism and Social Issues,* pp. 22-29.
18. Letter from Tittle to Elizabeth Knobel, copy sent to author by Miss Knobel, undated.
19. Letter from Tittle to Oliver R. Aspegren, April 17, 1931.
20. See the Minutes of the Official Board, First Church, June 4, 1934.

accept as inevitable the creation of a large staff as an accompaniment to First Church's membership growth and multiplying activities. When in December, 1918, Tittle arrived in Evanston he had the services of only one full-time assistant: an unpaid volunteer named Glenna. Not until March, 1919, did Charles R. Lowe, an old comrade from the Dayton days, join the First Church organization as executive secretary or (as he was sometimes called) "assistant to the pastor." He remained as Tittle's trusted helper until ill-health forced his resignation in 1924. During this early period Miss Grace Campbell supplied part-time and then full-time secretarial service.[21] By the end of Tittle's ministry First Church employed approximately twenty persons fulltime, including, in addition to the senior minister, two assistant ministers chiefly responsible for pastoral duties, a minister of education and his assistant, a minister of music, a housekeeper-commissary manager, an office manager, seven secretaries, three sextons, and a chef. Additionally, a galaxy of individuals gave of their talents on a part-time basis in such areas as the church school and choirs.

Broad as Tittle's shoulders were, he simply could not have survived without the help of a corps of capable and devoted assistant ministers. They were James Voorhees Thompson (1924-27), Ormal L. Miller (1927-32), Edwin Edgar Voigt (1932-36), Arthur T. Clark (1937-44), William C. Rasche, Jr. (1944-48), and Kenneth F. Thompson and Joseph Thomas, both "on the job" at the time of Tittle's death.[22]

One need not be either a Calvinist or a psychiatrist to realize that there must have been strains involved in the job of assistant minister under Tittle. For one thing, as Tittle drove himself hard, so he expected much from his assistants; the job was not a sinecure. As Tittle grew older, as his heart faltered, as First Church grew in size and complexity, inevitably more and more parish responsibilities were shouldered by his aides. For a second thing, their salaries, while not ungenerous in comparison to Tittle's or in comparison to ministerial wages elsewhere, were barely sufficient to the cost of living and the style of life of the North Shore. Finally, to work as the assistant to a great man is to live in his

21. Minutes of the Official Board, First Church, March 10, 1919, September 8, 1924, August 22, 1920; *Evanston News-Index*, December 31, 1920, p. 2-E; author's interviews with Mrs. Grace Campbell Dennis, Wilmette, Ill., July 31, 1959, and Glenna Myers Tittle, Evanston, Ill., July 31, 1959. For Tittle's affectionate tribute to Lowe, see *First Church Review*, I (October, 1924), 4.

22. Until 1936 the titles "assistant minister" and "associate minister" were used interchangeably. In that year, however, the Official Board decreed that the man be called an "assistant" and not an "associate." Between September, 1936, and March, 1937, Tittle was without an assistant, and he was driven night after night to working until 1:00, 2:00, and even 3:00 A.M.

shadow, and surely at some time at least some of the assistants must have felt a pang of jealously, or worse, self-doubt. Though the evidence is shadowy, it is probable that one of them worked himself to the edge of a nervous breakdown. This is not a judgmental statement. After all, it is often that the finest ministers "crack up," while the least sensitive, least involved, sail healthily on. In any event, the evidence is overwhelming that Tittle and First Church were served faithfully and well by a succession of assistant ministers, and that without exception they idolized their "chief." One suspects that not every prophet was so honored by his working associates.

VI

It has been rightly said that an examination of a man's check stubs is revealing of what he holds important in life. Similarly, the quality and intensity of a congregation's commitment to Christ is at least partially revealed in the answers given to certain financial questions. How much money does the congregation give? What does this sum mean in relation to the income of the parishioners? Who in the congregation gives—the few very wealthy or the great mass of the membership? What are the instrumentalities employed in raising funds? In what spirit is the money raised and in what spirit is it given? And, not the least, for what purposes is the money budgeted?

Let us attempt several general answers and then proceed to a more detailed examination of First Church finances. Under Tittle, the budget grew from $27,000 to $108,000. (These figures do *not* include major sums raised for nonbudget benevolences.) That is, the budget increase exceeded the impressive membership growth, though this statement does not take into account the declining purchasing power of the dollar.

Secondly, the affluence of the First Church membership is legendary, and, as in most legends, a kernel of truth is inflated into myth. Less than a year after his arrival, Tittle reported to the Quarterly Conference: "Throughout the Rock River Conference and even beyond its borders, First Church of Evanston enjoys, or, if you please, suffers the reputation of being a wealthy congregation. I do not know what an 'oodle' is, but I have been gravely if not correctly informed that we have 'oodles of money.' The number of millionaires in our membership is popularly supposed to be seventeen, tho why this number was selected I have not been able to discover. The fact of the matter seems to be first, that we have not as many members possessing great wealth as is generally supposed; and, second, that a large number of our members who are in a position to give something to the 'support of the Gospel and the various

benevolent enterprises of the church' are actually giving nothing at all."[23]
The First Church membership comprised a few people of great wealth,
many people of moderate affluence, but also a large number in modest
circumstances and for whom a church pledge meant real sacrifice.

Thirdly, Tittle was determined to broaden the financial base of the
church—and with good reason. In 1919, of the 526 contributing units
the membership of the church represented, only 287, or 53 percent, contributed to the budget. Of the 239 noncontributing units it was estimated
that fully 125 could make some contribution and would if properly
appealed to.[24] This situation was not long to continue. Tittle's determination was rewarded, for during his pastorate the number of subscribers
to the budget increased more than five times. A tangential consequence
was that he was now less vulnerable to the pressure of any wealthy
parishioner who might threaten to withdraw his subscription if Tittle
refused to mute his "radical" preaching.[25]

Fourthly, Tittle was true to his Methodist heritage in strongly opposing bingo parties, lotteries, prizes won on wager, and all the devious
gimmicks employed in some churches to raise funds. Indeed, First
Church imposed an official ban on them.[26] Tittle also opposed the
practice of pew renting, sanctioned by Methodism and most other
denominations in early American history. As he argued, "in a Christian
Church a member's position from the altar ought not to be determined
by the amount of money he can offer for a pew."[27] Therefore, as we
have already seen, in the spring of 1919 he instructed the ushers to fill
the rented pews if unoccupied by the hour of worship service and in the
fall of 1920 the pew rental system was terminated by action of the
Official Board. (By 1921, all the major Evanston churches, with the
exception of St. Luke's Episcopal, had abolished the pew rental system.[28])

In the fifth place, for Tittle Christian stewardship meant more than
the giving of money; it meant the dedication of one's life. He once said:
"The kingdom of God is not advanced on earth by any man who,

23. Report of Tittle to Fourth Quarterly Conference, September 25, 1919,
First Church archives.
24. *Ibid.*
25. Paul Hutchinson, "Portrait of a Preacher," foreword to Tittle, *A Mighty
Fortress* (New York: Harper & Brothers, 1949), p. xxii; author's interviews with
Glenna Myers Tittle, Evanston, Ill., August 14, 1959; Raymond C. Wieboldt,
Evanston, Ill., August 6, 1959; Mrs. Bernice Wolseley, Evanston, Ill., July 13,
1960.
26. *Gospel According to Luke,* p. 209; Minutes of the Official Board, First
Church, March 4, 1946.
27. Report of Tittle to Fourth Quarterly Conference, September 25, 1919,
First Church archives.
28. *Evanston News-Index,* April 15, 1921, p. 1.

because he is a 'big giver,' thinks he owns the Church. Nor is it advanced by any man who makes his money in ways that are an affront to God, even though he gives a pipe organ to the Church. Christian stewardship calls for nothing less than the dedication of oneself to God and his purpose for mankind. When God gets a man's life, he also gets all the money that that man can give. More than that, he gets money that is made in ways that are as honest and just as can be found in the existing order of society. Still more, he gets a devotion that is concerned with the finding of better ways of making money than society at present offers to any but a relatively few of its members."[29] In giving money every man and woman has at hand an immediate opportunity to do something fine and heroic and sacrificial, whereas to only a few Christians is the opportunity afforded to demonstrate their faith as missionaries or martyrs. The acid test is not how much is given but how much is retained, for in the eyes of Jesus a "big giver" is not necessarily one who makes a large contribution but one whose contribution, large or small, represents real sacrifice.[30] Give sacrificially, though it may be only a "cup of cold water" or as little as the widow's mite. And give gratefully, cheerfully, heedlessly, and without consideration of advantage to self.

When Tittle called for sacrificial giving, he did not place an idolatrous priority on the demands, or the needs, of the church. He once wrote a parishioner who, because of the prolonged illness of his wife and consequent heavy medical bills, could not meet his church pledge: "I should like to underscore Mr. Rasche's statement that you are to 'forget' the unpaid balance of your pledge to the church. Please let me know personally if you are in need of financial assistance. The Church has a fund—not large but most usable—on which I can draw in behalf of members of our fellowship who are in need of assistance."[31]

A final generalization. Tittle was determined that even as his people raised enormous sums of money to enlarge and enhance the beauty of First Church, they continue to honor their responsibilities to others; that even as facilities for the well-being of the congregation were expanded, services to the community be broadened. Under Tittle First Church was committed to the general rule of giving as much for work outside the parish as was spent on itself, in fact, in some years twice as much was given to benevolences. This was not sheer altruism. Tittle held no con-

29. *Christian Stewardship in the World of Today,* a pamphlet published by The United Stewardship Council, Hillsdale, Mich., 1943.
30. *Gospel According to Luke,* p. 223.
31. Letter from Tittle to a parishioner, November 3, 1944.

viction more firmly than that "the one sure way to raise money for work at home is to raise money for work abroad."[32] A congregation daring to lose its life for Christ's sake—daring to give to others without calculation —will discover it has found its life. A congregation unwilling to support benevolence work would soon become too listless to underwrite its own most parochial programs.

Once a proposed budget had been settled upon by the finance committee, in close consultation with Tittle and approved by the Official Board, all that remained was to secure from the membership pledges equal to the proposed expenditures. That is to say, the campaign— figuratively and literally—had just begun. Tittle did not believe people could be "lectured" into giving. "There is no use telling us that we ought to give," he explained. "We know it, but can always find plausible reasons for withholding. One thing only will avail, and that is whole-hearted acceptance of the principle of stewardship. Let a man come to regard his income as a trust fund to be administered for the glory of God and the good of man, and he will need no one to tell him that he ought to give or to suggest what would be an appropriate amount."[33] Unquestionably the most important role played by Tittle in the financial campaigns of First Church was in his pastoral care day after day and in his prophetic preaching Sunday after Sunday—in creating in the First Church membership a deep and sustained acceptance of the principle of stewardship.

The awesome majesty of the First Church worship services was not often interrupted by appeals from the pulpit for cash, a statement that cannot be made of every Protestant (much less Catholic) church in the land. Only reluctantly and rarely, usually at the beginning of a financial drive, did Tittle make such a petition from the pulpit. And this despite the arguments of the financial stewards that one word from him was worth "twenty teams of canvassers."[34]

Only occasionally did Tittle write personal letters to a few key subscribers, members, and friends of First Church who were tardy in pledging or contributing, and then a "soft sell" style prevailed: "Dear Fred: I have been 'roped in' by the Finance Committee of First Church to the extent of writing a few persons who, I am quite sure, fully intend to

32. *Give!*, a pamphlet published by the Methodist Episcopal World Service Commission, Chicago, n.d.

33. *Gospel According to Luke*, p. 223.

34. Author's interview with Raymond C. Wieboldt, Evanston, Ill., August 6, 1959.

subscribe to this year's budget but have, as yet, neglected to do so. 'Nuff said. I am enclosing a subscription card for your convenience."[35]

In 1926 First Church purchased the adjacent Allen property for $60,000 and in 1928 plans were approved for the major transformation of the sanctuary, the building of a new chapel, and the expansion of the parish house, including Great Hall and Glenna Hall. This massive physical reconstruction was completed in 1930, making First Church one of the handsomest structures in American Methodism, at a cost of $750,000. A decade later Tittle was to write generous friends thanking them for "helping us to remove the load of indebtedness which we have carried during ten extremely difficult years and which had nearly broken my own back."[36] Viewing as Tittle did the church debt as a personal obligation, we may be certain that in truth it nearly broke his back, especially when it is remembered that there could be no moratorium called on annually raising budgets for benevolences and regular operating expenses.

Although the initial building-fund campaign was enormously successful, there remained unpaid $300,000, an awesome figure in any period, a fearful sum in 1930. During the years that followed, First Church struggled to raise each year a budget which, while steadily shrinking, nevertheless provided for interest at predepression rates and a small payment on principal. In 1936, in an era of general repudiation of debt, the remaining balance of $260,000 was refinanced and a plan adopted that would clear the entire debt in twelve years. On his birthday in 1938, Tittle was handed three signed pledges totaling $15,000. These were the initial contributions to the Tittle Twentieth Anniversary Fund, and under the superb leadership of James F. Oates the sum of $101,633 was raised from 605 subscribers to be applied to the church's indebtedness, leaving $145,000 to be met. Finally, in 1943, again under the leadership of Oates, a "Clear the Debt Fund," of $68,000 was raised. Thus, in 1944—four years ahead of schedule and not once defaulting— the last penny of a huge commitment was paid off.[37] Perhaps this story reveals the fullness of the commitment of the First Church fellowship to "Christ and His Church." In any case, the burden of proof is on those who argue that Christianity can survive without the followers of Christ

35. Letter from Tittle to Frederick R. Bliss, October 31, 1945.
36. Letter from Tittle to Mrs. Luke I. Wilson, June 17, 1941. Mr. Wilson was also a dear friend.
37. In addition to the First Church records, see *Twenty Memorable Years* (1918-1938), a booklet published by First Church, n.p., n.d., and *A Quarter Century, 1918-1943,* a booklet published by First Church, n.p., n.d.

organizing into churches, or that churches, unlike all other institutions, can somehow survive without financial support.

VII

Equally revealing of this commitment is the free and full offering of time and talent to the task of operating such a large enterprise as First Church. As prescribed by Methodist discipline, the general management of First Church was in the hands of the Official Board, whose members, totaling eighty-five at the time of Tittle's death, were representative of all interests, ages, and points of view in the church. Nevertheless, it would confound common sense and falsify the record to claim that the First Church fellowship achieved a sort of Christian communism—a utopian classless society where status had withered away. The same names constantly crop up in key posts, especially as trustees, and in the 1920's in particular a small group of able, dedicated, strong laymen constituted a power elite in First Church affairs. These men generally saw things from the same angle of vision and consequently gave to the church an extraordinarily efficient lay leadership. They were generally men who held high executive positions in the business world or posts of power at Northwestern, and, with some exceptions, they were men of wealth.

It was a blessing to First Church to have a cluster of really big men as officers, but only because they were men of genuine dedication and only because Tittle was at the helm as captain—and no man was bigger than he. Testimony is unanimous that Tittle ran a "taut ship." As we already know, he was careful to see that all parties had an opportunity to express their views, and he could be diplomatic and was adept at the art of flattery. Yet ultimately Tittle made the major decisions and ultimately these decisions were based on what he judged to be the welfare of First Church and the will of God. Although the First Church fellowship was not sheep-like in its docility, for thirty-one years there was never any serious question concerning who was shepherd of the flock. The closeness of the relationship between Tittle and his Official Board is suggested by a letter he once wrote: "My main job is to do what little I can to improve the *human* race. But occasionally I catch fish, so that they may learn to be more careful next time. And tonight I am going to the International Stock Show in order to encourage the improvement of livestock. Also to see the Show. . . . I feel a little guilty in playing hookey from the Official Board meeting, but not too guilty to accept the Coopers' invitation. Have I your permission to do this? I am assuming that I have. At any rate, when you hear this read, you may next picture me as having one grand time at the International Stock Show."[38]

Lest it be assumed that these big men—the First Church leadership— were concerned only with momentous issues, it is needful to state what is obvious to anyone who has ever served as a church officer: the Official Board minutes are cluttered with commonplace matters and niggling debates over air in the sanctuary (too drafty or too close?), lighting (too bright or too dim?), stolen overcoats (should or should not the victim be indemnified?), noise issuing from the kitchen and Sunday School rooms, parking and traffic, lighting rods, etc.

One matter debated over several years was of more serious moment, namely, that of changing the name of First Church to "Christ Church" or "Christ's Church," just as the great Madison Avenue Methodist Episcopal Church in New York had adopted the name of Christ Church. Tittle supported the idea because the new name would more clearly indicate the fact that First Church served "all denominations in Evanston" and was "truly inter-denominational."[39] But congregational enthusiasm for the idea was less than warm and it was dropped.

More extreme was the suggestion, supported by such leaders as Wieboldt, that First Church sever its Methodist connections and strike out alone as an independent community church.[40] Tittle gave the suggestion sober thought, but he was uneasy about the future of the community church in America, stating, "I can only say that I myself would not care to cast in my lot with it. It is a baby without a parent and it remains to be seen whether it can live."[41] Moreover, his loyalty to Methodism increased rather than diminished with the passing of the years.

VIII

Setting aside for the moment the question of Northwestern and Garrett and reserving for a later chapter the question of the Negro in Evanston, let us now summarize the service of First Church to the community. The word "summarize" is used advisedly, for it would be impossible to describe at length the manifold activities of First Church; only a portion of them can even be listed. To begin with, every Sunday First Church provided a majestic worship service attended by hundreds

38. Letter from Tittle to Official Board, December 2, 1940.
39. Minutes of the Official Board, First Church, September 24, 1930, and September 7, 1931.
40. Author's interview with Raymond C. Wieboldt, Evanston, Ill., August 6, 1959.
41. Letter from Tittle to John A. Vollendwider, October 19, 1933.

who were not members and by scores who were not even Methodists. Moreover, the lovely chapel was made available for weddings and funerals to "persons of whatever creed or ecclesiastical affiliation." Year after year First Church sponsored public addresses by individuals of renown, and also pageants, plays, and musical offerings. In 1919 Evanston's first community performance of "The Messiah" was given in First Church and when in time the performances were transferred to Northwestern, Tittle continued as narrator. In 1939 the First Church Little Symphony Orchestra gave its first public concert.

The day-nursery school was open to the children of working mothers whether church members or not. The Post Kollege Klub provided a fellowship for all young professional and business people in the community. The Business and Professional Women's Club, though instigated by Tittle and meeting in First Church, was also without denominational restriction. The International Social Club met a particularly acute need for the scores of lonely women on the North Shore who worked as clerks and domestics. It is revealing that such diverse community groups as the Evanston Civic Orchestra and the Evanston YWCA were started in First Church. The three thousand items in the World Friendship Library, staffed and supported by First Church, were available to the public. Shortly after arriving in Evanston Tittle opened the church in the evenings to provide a meeting place for the teenagers of Evanston, and programs of supervised recreation were undertaken. It can almost be assumed that First Church housed such organizations as the Boy Scouts, Girl Scouts, Girl Reserves, YMCA, YWCA, and Cosmopolitan Club, but it was also the meeting place of the School of Foreign Affairs and the Institute of International Relations, and also of the Evanston Bureau of Recreation, Adult Education classes, and during the depression even the WPA. In sum, over the years as many as two hundred different community organizations, at no cost to themselves, utilized the facilities of First Church, and in any given year perhaps fifty or sixty such groups regularly met in Tittle's church.

Beginning in 1932 Tittle launched a community enterprise he pronounced the "greatest social experiment ever successfully put over in this church."[42] This was the nationally famous and widely copied "Church Night." On consecutive Tuesday nights in the fall and winter the people of the community were invited to First Church for a bountiful meal at the nominal cost of fifty cents. Great Hall was filled with tables spread for ten or twelve guests and at each a host or hostess proffered the hospitality of the church to strangers and friends alike. About

42. Minutes of the Official Board, First Church, December 5, 1932.

7:30 the dinner came to a close and the guests adjourned to the classrooms where they re-formed into eight or ten "interest groups" to
study art, music, drama, current affairs, theology, the Bible, literature,
science, economics, and numerous other subjects. Tittle was able to persuade a platoon of Chicago-area scholars, artists, business leaders, and
public officials to serve without compensation as group leaders. At nine
the participants returned to Great Hall for a final cup of coffee and
light refreshments while swapping with friends accounts of their studies.
Church Night attendance averaged five hundred in the first years;
occasionally on a given evening as many as eight hundred were on hand.
This meant that for eight years during the depression the citizens of the
North Shore were offered an opportunity to enjoy an evening of food,
fellowship, and study, the only cost being that of the meal—and even
this expense could be ducked because it was possible to join the study
groups without first having dined. The importance of Church Night to
the morale of hundreds of individuals may be judged by the fact that
fully as many men as women participated. First Church sources and the
Evanston press make clear that here was a noble experiment that everyone—the congregation, the community, and Tittle himself—deemed a
thumping success.

Hard upon the heels of the depression came the challenge of the
Second World War, and First Church responded with all the resources
at its disposal. Here reference is not to the ministry afforded its own
young men "with the colors," but rather to the care and comfort of
servicemen stationed in the Chicago area, especially those in the V-12
unit at Northwestern, the sailors at Great Lakes, and the soldiers at
Fort Sheridan. The lads who attended First Church on a Sunday morning were requested to register, and soon after they received invitations
to Sunday dinner in the homes of First Church members, to monthly
dinners in Great Hall, and to church-sponsored dances, musicals, and
parties. More than one hundred First Church girls, ages eighteen to
twenty-four, formed a Junior Hostess unit; without their presence,
naturally, the entire enterprise would have been futile. Moreover, regular trips were made to Fort Sheridan where First Church speakers and
soloists assisted in the chapel services and where First Church girls
assisted in the following social hour; for this a letter of commendation
from the post chaplain was sent to Tittle. On more than a thousand
instances Tittle wrote the parents of soldiers and sailors who worshiped
in First Church, at the request of their sons. "You will never know how
much it helps for a mother to have letters of the kind you write," read
one reply. "It is the little thoughtful acts on the part of people like

yourself that help us to bear the separation from our loved ones. He, like so many other boys in the service, is away from home for the first time in his life. We know your friendly welcome will help him keep faith in the church and his fellow men during these trying days."[43]

In summation, over the years First Church succored with money and volunteer workers a raft of community enterprises involving the sick, the aged, the infirm, the poor and orphaned, unwed mothers, and prisoners—all those intolerably burdened or broken by life. Over the years Tittle was much concerned with such community questions as schools, hospitals, recreation, zoning, and he threw his weight on the side of what would make Evanston (in his judgment) a sweeter and fairer city. As First Church was the first church of Evanston so its first responsibility to the establishment of the kingdom on earth was exactly where it found itself—in Evanston. Tittle recognized a truth denied to many reformers: a transcendent vision and a parochial concern are not mutually exclusive.

If First Church was indeed deeply concerned with local questions, this does not mean that its concern was confined to the boundaries of Evanston. Long before Tittle's arrival, First Church had contributed tens of thousands of dollars to the churches and social centers of Chicago Italians, most especially the famous Newberry Avenue Center (originally the Elizabeth E. Marcy Center); and also to the support of Chicago's Bohemian and Korean churches. Ernest and Glenna were tremendously interested in continuing this work—and so it was. This story merits a separate volume; it is possible to note here only that though it is fashionable to deprecate settlement work and depreciate the motives of social workers, the hand held out by the "WASP's" of First Church was a hand of assistance and not a clinched fist, and that the beneficiaries, the "new" immigrants, perhaps felt slightly less like "strangers in the land." Further evidence of Tittle's concern is the fact that he was one of the founders and first president of the Chicago Council Against Racial and Religious Discrimination and worked with some twenty agencies in Chicago dealing with civic problems.

First Church's ministry, in fact, was to the world, made manifest in an outpouring of money for mission and relief. Annually First Church budgeted about half its funds to benevolence work, but this does not tell the whole story, for annually large sums were raised for causes outside the budget. Especially impressive is the record of the women of

43. Among many items, the most convenient summary of First Church's wartime service is an undated special issue of the *First Church Review* entitled "The Work of the Service Men's Groups of First Church."

the church. Missionaries were supported in Korea, China, India, and South America. Relief was extended to suffering peoples in the Near East, Germany, and Japan and other areas wracked by war, natural disaster, and poverty, including communities in the United States. First Church's contribution to Methodist World Service and Rock River Conference benevolences consistently placed it near the top in American Methodism. Moreover, First Church gave handsomely to Methodism's special drives from the centenary following World War I to the Bishops' great "Crusade for Christ" following World War II.

IX

First Church and Garrett Biblical Institute entered the world together, and for the century preceding Tittle's death in 1949 their relationship, if not perhaps as intimate as Siamese twins, was surely as close as that of brothers, sustaining and nurturing each other, without, however, the normal sibling rivalry, because the church and the seminary complemented rather than competed with each other. The close historic ties between the two were tightened during Tittle's ministry. He once stated: "I, alas! am not a Garrett man, save only through adoption by the precarious means of an honorary degree. I am, however, a rooter for Garrett, its standards, its outlook on life, its teachers, and its students."[44] On numerous occasions he ranked Garrett with Yale and Union as the nation's leading seminaries. At the time when Tittle was seriously considering leaving Evanston, the president of Garrett, Horace G. Smith, expressed the "very great loss" his departure would mean to Garrett, pointed out that many students elected Garrett in the anticipation of hearing Tittle preach and of taking at least some classwork with him. "It is even more true," Smith continued, "that all the men [faculty and students alike] richly enjoy their contacts with you." Smith emphasized the "very significant place you hold in the life and work of Garrett" and hoped that the "opportunity to touch a group of two hundred and fifty potential ministers year after year might well turn the balance in favor of remaining at your post here."[45]

Tittle counted heavily on the wisdom, experience, and scholarship of the Garrett faculty. Not a few of his closest friends were Garrett professors as were not a few of the staunchest First Church members. For their part, exceedingly great was their gratitude. In 1938, for example,

44. Letter from Tittle to Ralph H. Richardson, May 14, 1937.
45. Letter from Horace G. Smith to Tittle, May 18, 1935. President Smith confirmed these judgments in an interview with the author, Evanston, Ill., August 17, 1959.

thirteen Garrett professors presented Tittle with a beautifully engrossed parchment, the scroll reading in part: "We have been proud to count you as a colleague and friend in the work of Garrett Biblical Institute, and are grateful that succeeding generations of students have had the privilege of your instruction in preaching as well as the example of your ministry. Hundreds of these, throughout this country and in foreign lands, are better ministers of Christ because they have known you."[46] Earlier, in 1930, Garrett had expressed its admiration and appreciation in awarding Tittle an honorary Doctor of Divinity degree. Moreover, frequently in the first decades and invariably in the last decade of his Evanston ministry, Tittle was invited by Garrett to preach at commencement.

Burdened though he was, in many years Tittle wrung from his schedule the time to teach a course at Garrett, usually dealing with some aspect of preaching. The gratitude of the Garrett students exceeded even that of the faculty. From time to time an entire class would draft a resolution of appreciation. He also received scores of letters from former Garrett students, some of them stating that but for his example they might have abandoned their plans for the ministry. "I respect you as a man & admire you as a Christian," read one such letter. "For what you are, for what you stand for, & for what you do, I love you above all men I know. . . . If we could only be blessed with more like you—. Words fail my thoughts; may prayer take their place. Your sincere disciple."[47]

Tittle understood the imperative need for seminaries of quality. As he argued before the 1948 General Conference in opposition to a proposed lowering of educational standards so that "supply pastors" might be eligible for admission into the annual conferences, "In my opinion, a well-trained ministry is a necessary condition of survival of Protestant Christianity of the United States in our time." We have striven for years to raise the standards of the Methodist ministry, he continued, and if we allow increasing numbers of relatively untrained men to come into our ranks, it will be impossible to persuade the best men in college to choose the ministry as a vocation.[48] It was Tittle's conviction that seminaries must aspire to the high academic standards of the best graduate schools, and that in failing to appropriate the money to make this possible, Methodism—indeed, American Protestantism—was making a fatal miscalculation.

46. The document, dated December 28, 1938, is in the Tittle Collection.
47. Letter from Bob Hamill to Tittle, dated only "Sunday evening."
48. *The Daily Christian Advocate,* The Methodist Church, May 10, 1948, p. 354.

Early in Tittle's Evanston ministry President Walter Dill Scott termed Tittle the "greatest preacher in America" and in his desire to create a "Greater Northwestern" Scott wanted Tittle to continue "as the prophet and the friend of our student body."[49] Scott's successor, President Franklyn Bliss Snyder, testified: "Dr. Tittle was one of those rare men who have the mark of greatness on them. Whatever he did, he did with distinction, and all America knew and honored him. I am sorry that the university will no longer have the benefit of his wise and understanding counsel, and that our young people cannot hear him in his pulpit."[50] And Snyder's successor, President J. Roscoe Miller, declared: "Northwestern university mourns the great loss of Dr. Ernest Fremont Tittle, whose spiritual impact on the community was matched by his 29 years of selfless service as a member of the university's board of trustees. All Northwestern men and women, present and future, will lead richer lives because of Dr. Tittle's lasting influence."[51] These quotations suggest the uniquely close historic relationship between First Church and Northwestern. They suggest also that although each year saw a growing secularization erode the Methodist foundations of Northwestern, because of Tittle's presence in Evanston the claims of faith to a place in the life of a great university were not without a champion.

The school's charter provided that a majority of its trustees be Methodists and that eight of the trustees actually be elected by the four annual conferences of Rock River, Central Illinois, Michigan, and Detroit. Beginning in 1921 and continuing to his death, save only for the year 1934, Tittle was annually one of the trustees elected by the Rock River Conference. He regularly served as a member of the Educational Policies Committee and as chairman of the Religious Activities Committee of the Board of Trustees. He was respected for his knowledgeability and concern. Almost inevitably he was appointed to the governing body of such groups as the Northwestern Board of Religion and the Methodist Student Foundation. Almost inevitably, also, he found himself a frequent guest lecturer in Northwestern classrooms, and infrequently he offered courses for credit, particularly to students taking work in the Department of Religious Education. In 1919 he preached the baccalaureate sermon and later graduating classes so honored him. The inaugurations of Northwestern presidents were held in First Church.

It is altogether possible, however, that Tittle's greatest services to Northwestern were not as trustee and on the campus but as pastor of

49. Letter from Walter Dill Scott to Tittle, September 28, 1925.
50. *Evanston Review*, August 18, 1949, clipping in Tittle Collection.
51. *Ibid.*, August 11, 1949, clipping in Tittle Collection.

First Church and in First Church. "I reached Evanston one Saturday night and was desperately homesick," remembered one freshman from Great Falls, Montana. "I did not know a soul in this town. I went to the First Methodist Church on Sunday morning and heard Dr. Tittle preach. When he had finished his sermon my homesickness had left me. I said to myself, 'Evanston's all right. If I can hear Dr. Tittle preach every Sunday morning nothing else will matter much.' "[52] It was customary at the start of the school year for Tittle to address the freshman class assembled in First Church, and many of these new students, including some who were not Methodists, returned to worship Sunday after Sunday for four years. They found in the activities of First Church and in the Methodist Student Foundation, with headquarters at the John Evans Religious Center, a fellowship that warmed their lonely lives. Surely, then, it was as pastor of First Church even more than as Northwestern trustee that Tittle touched the lives of the student body.

Because Tittle was above all else a preacher rather than philosopher, educator, psychologist, or theologian, of necessity he commented on many areas of life without formulating fully and expressing in depth his judgments in all these areas. From time to time, in sermons, articles, and addresses, he had something to say concerning education, but it cannot therefore be concluded that he was an American Rousseau or Cardinal Newman, or a Horace Mann or John Dewey. From his pen there came no massive, memorable statement of educational philosophy. He did, however, possess certain convictions which constantly cropped up in his utterances. For one thing, he held that the Christian is under the obligation to be intelligent. "Thou shalt love the Lord thy God with all thy heart and with *all thy mind*." A man of burning piety but of slothful intellect is like a boiler with no connection to the engine. Idealism unsupported by hard intelligence is bound to peter out, or worse still, to linger on as a kind of gushy, impotent sentimentalism.[53]

Second, the Christian is a man of faith unafraid to pursue truth wherever it might lead. He steps out from his little circle of light into the vast darkness, not knowing what he will find there, but trusting that the God of light is the God also of darkness. He dares to assume that the truth will be worth knowing, whatever it is, and he has the courage to surrender if necessary much that had seemed of value in exchange for new truths that will prove to be of even greater value. Even if in the end he is stripped of all faith and left with nothing to

52. Letter from Anna A. Gordon to Tittle, January 28, 1921.
53. *The Obligation to Be Intelligent*, pamphlet reprint of a sermon preached January 12, 1930.

cling to but his own grit, it is better to be an unsheltered man than a contented swine. "I find," said Tittle, "that I simply cannot escape the conviction that light, however disturbing, is better than darkness, however comforting. If I am alone in the universe with nobody to turn to save my fellow humans, I would rather know it than go on uttering pathetic and futile prayers to a God who does not exist." Yet surely religion would survive any and every discovery the future had in store. The time would never come when an intelligent man might not believe in God.[54]

Third, Tittle held that intelligence uncontrolled by moral purpose will result in a race of moral eunuchs, and if the schools train the mind and neglect the character of the young, society will pay a justly high price.[55] Tittle agreed with Bertrand Russell's description of the "good life" as one "inspired by love and guided by knowledge." The career of Napoleon, he observed, is a striking example of the peril of knowledge without love, and the career of William Jennings Bryan an almost equally striking example of the peril of love without knowledge. The peril of knowledge without love is selfishness and cynicism. The peril of love without knowledge is sentimentalism and ineffectiveness.[56]

Tittle further held education to be one of the glories of the human race. When Hitler boasted, "We Germans think with our blood," he spoke for the forces of anti-intellectualism rampant in modern times. Tittle's faith in controlled intelligence as an instrument for the solving of great human problems was not as absolute as that, say, of John Dewey, but to extol instinct and passion in place of reason would spell the death of all "humane and civilized culture."[57]

Tittle was contemptuous of an education that fitted a man to become a financial giant but left him an intellectual, cultural, and moral midget. Our colleges and universities graduate by the thousands individuals trained in a narrow, vocational sense, but who "think that Gene Stratton Porter is a great novelist; and that Eddie Guest writes poetry; and that Henry Cabot Lodge is a statesman; and that the Ku Klux Klan is a patriotic organization." "Is it not time," he inquired, "for us to swing back a bit to the older idea of education which held that the primary purpose of education is not to enable a man to MAKE more, but rather

54. *Ibid.*
55. "What Service Alumni," a commencement address delivered at Ohio Wesleyan University, June 16, 1929, typed MS in Tittle Collection.
56. *The Obligation to Be Intelligent,* a sermon preached January 12, 1930 (pamphlet).
57. "Education and Religion," *The First Church Pulpit,* Vol. I, No. 9, a sermon preached October 4, 1936.

to enable a man to BE more? Unless we want to become a nation of 'Babbitts,' must we not go in for the sort of education that will cause the breadth of life to become equal to the length of it?"[58]

As a kind of capstone to these propositions, Tittle believed that the ultimate purpose of all education was to prepare young men and women mentally and morally for a life of service—youths "who, in intelligent and loyal efforts to serve their own community, their own nation, and the world at large, would themselves achieve intellectual and moral distinction."[59]

X

The citizens of Evanston were fond of asserting that their city "began in a prayer meeting" and it is true that the founding fathers turned to God in prayer for guidance in their plans to establish a great Methodist university north of Chicago. Evanston citizens also took pride in the sobriquet, "The Church Going City," and in the oft-quoted statement that "more people go regularly to church on Sunday in Evanston than any other city of its size in the country."[60] For many decades Evanston bore the stamp of its religious origins, of the fact that it was the home of Northwestern and Garrett, and also the home of a galaxy of noted preachers, bishops, missionaries, and lay leaders such as Frances Willard, Judson, Simpson, Haven, Hinman, Noyes, Foster, Hamlin, Lyon, Demptster, McDowell, Lunt, Evans. When in 1918 Tittle arrived in Evanston the religious aura of the community was still pervasive. As the years passed, as the mansions gave way to apartments, as the downtown area expanded with large department stores, as industry edged the western districts, inevitably the character of the city changed and the old piety was eroded by the new secularism. Yet the transformation was not total. In 1940-41, forty Evanston churches co-operated in the compiling of a religious census. The investigation revealed that 72.1 percent of the population claimed some affiliation with a religious organization. Methodists, Episcopalians, and Presbyterians showed the largest numbers among the 33,000 who adhered to the Protestant faith. Almost 13,000 were Roman Catholics. About 5 percent of the population reported being Jewish and about 5 percent Christian Scientists.[61]

58. "A Well Proportioned Life," *First Church Review,* I (October, 1924), 11.
59. "Education and the Public Welfare," *Educational Trends,* VI (October-November, 1937), 9.
60. See, for example, the *Evanston News-Index,* December 31, 1920, p. 3-A, and October 21, 1921, p. 1.
61. See the *Evanston Daily News-Index,* January 22, 1941, p. 1, and March 12, 1941, p. 1; and the *Evanston Review,* October 24, 1940, p. 16-b.

Thus it was that Tittle found himself pastor of a Methodist church in a community supporting some forty churches, including eight other Methodist churches (counting two African Methodist Episcopal congregations). The fragmentation of religion in America has been the source of much critical comment. In particular, the competition between Protestant bodies has been declared scandalous. Doubtless in Evanston rivalry existed, the shepherds jealously counting the neighboring flocks. Some neighborhoods were over-churched, and over the years some churches simply faded away. In brief, it would confound common sense to presume that the Christians of Evanston always lived in kindly affection one to another. Yet the fragmentary evidence does not support the view that Tittle's thirty-year ministry was analogous to the Thirty Years' War.

From time to time Tittle co-operated with other ministers in the holding of union services. He was ardent in his support of such agencies as the Evanston Council of Religious Education and the YMCA and YWCA. He was one of the founders of the Evanston Ministerial Association in 1924 and when the group made its initial appearance as guests of the Rotary Club, it was Tittle who as a member of Rotary introduced the clerics. He was chairman of the North Shore Fellowship of Faith. Toward the end of his life he strongly urged the creation of an Evanston Council of Churches, believing "it is high time that members of the Protestant churches come to know one another and learn to work together for a great end."[62] It is clear that First Church under Tittle did not live in splendid isolation from the other churches of the community.

Tittle, however, was not a man to cluster with other ministers for comfortable (and comforting) fellowship. He had no clerical golfing or poker cronies. He did not court popularity with his peers. In the last years he missed not a few meetings of the Ministerial Association. Some comrades of the cloth found him too absorbed in his own thoughts to be congenial company.[63] He was not aloof in the sense of being snobbish, but such was his intense consciousness of the preciousness of time he ill-concealed his impatience with aimless chatter and purposeless committee meetings. It is probable that he had the respect of almost the entire Evanston clergy and the adoration of many, especially the younger liberals, but that only a handful could claim him as a pal.

Moreover, beyond question there were those clerics who respected his integrity but profoundly disagreed with his views. One suspects, for

62. Letter from Tittle to Frank H. West, March 25, 1946.
63. Author's interview with Horace G. Smith, Evanston, Ill., August 17, 1959.

example, that Tittle's economic philosophy was anathema to Paul Austin Wolfe, the very able and very conservative minister called in 1931 to the First Presbyterian Church. One suspects that the Anglo-Catholicism of George Craig Stewart (later Bishop Stewart), rector of St. Luke's Episcopal Church, and a figure of towering prestige in Evanston, went against the grain of Tittle.[64] And one knows from the letters in Tittle's files that more than one Evanston clergyman (Protestant and Catholic) found his pacifism abhorrent, if not treasonable.

Nevertheless, despite much honest difference of judgment on theological and social matters, despite a natural spirit of competition, despite even an inevitable tincture of ugly envy, it is possible to conclude that Tittle's relations with his Evanston peers were good. At Tittle's death, David Jones, pastor emeritus of the First Presbyterian Church, testified, "I am profoundly grieved. He was a great friend. All who ever came in touch with him loved and honored him."[65] The minister of the Unitarian church, Homer Jack, also testified, "Some of us younger men looked up to him for strength and courage more than he . . . could ever know. Now that he is gone his memory will be an inspiration for those of us who seek to combine a socially militant ministry with personal gentleness."[66]

More revealing of Tittle the man, perhaps, than testimonials to him is the tribute he paid to Hugh Elmer Brown, beloved pastor of the First Congregational Church: "He has been a blessing to every church in Evanston, having stimulated all of them and robbed none of them. . . . He has the mind of a poet and the insight of a prophet. He has the courage and devotion of a true spokesman of God. He has a personality which lights up a room and enriches everyone whom it touches. He is good for whatever ails you. His laughter is medicine, restoring the soul. His loving-kindness, like the mercy of God, is fresh every morning."[67]

XI

In 1943 the *Chicago Sun-Times* presented Tittle with a Certificate of Honor for Meritorious Service "as a symbol of appreciation for your contribution to the making of a better community."[68] Six years later

64. But Bishop Stewart wrote Tittle a very warm letter at the time of the first heart attack, November 22, 1937.

65. *Chicago Daily News,* August 4, 1949, clipping in Tittle Collection.

66. *Evanston Review,* August 11, 1949, clipping in Tittle Collection.

67. Letter from Tittle to "The First Congregational Church, Evanston," October 5, 1938. Earlier, on October 19, 1933, Tittle had written Brown: "In you more than any other clergyman I have found a man of kindred spirit. I have looked to you for leadership and you have never failed me. God bless you!"

68. The award, signed by Marshall Field, is in the Tittle Collection.

Paul Arthur Schilpp, a philosopher of enormous distinction whom Tittle had helped to bring to Northwestern, said: "Dr. Tittle was the greatest progressive voice in American Protestantism, a great preacher, fighter for great causes, an indomitable spirit. He served God by serving humanity. His death is the greatest loss Evanston has had in a generation."[69]

69. *Chicago Sun-Times,* August 4, 1949, clipping in Tittle Collection.

11. NATIONAL LEADER

I

Biographers are advised to demonstrate rather than merely to assert their subject's significance. But how does one honor this sound rule in writing the life of Ernest Fremont Tittle? He founded no new church, sparked no reformation or counter-reformation, published no *summa theologiae* or massive work of scholarship, wielded no great official power by virtue of holding high ecclesiastical office, edited no prestigious journal, lighted no dark continent through missionary labors, suffered no martyr's death at the hands of a Nero or Henry II or Hitler; indeed, no revivals, no armies or converts can be credited to his preaching as are ascribed to a Whitefield, Moody, or Graham. Artistic and intellectual genius may be explicated in terms of the enduring painting, poem, score, novel, treatise, theory, or equation. Political and military leadership may be evaluated on the basis of nations founded, wars won, legislation enacted, parties formed, reforms instituted, power exercised, or institutions reshaped. The business tycoon knows a kind of immortality in the corporation he founds, the explorer in the region he discovers, the scientist in the "law" bearing his name. But how can the significance of a minister's life be "proved"? That he touches and transforms individual lives is difficult to demonstrate, but it is not impossible, because witnesses can be called to testify to their transformation. In this respect, a good minister is like a good teacher. And that Tittle did in fact inspire the lives of numbers of his parishioners and Evanstonians and Garrett and Northwestern students has largely been the burden of our story thus far. However, that the minister is a force beyond the boundaries of his parish, that he has influence in the larger affairs of the nation, is beyond objective proof. We may guess that this is one reason few historians have elected to write the biographies of Protestant ministers, and this despite the fact that increasingly historians have acknowledged the centrality of religion in American life. In the case of Tittle, we know that his passionate concerns were not parochial and that his influence extended beyond the boundaries of Evanston, however conjectural must remain the precise measurement of that influence.

II

An early clue to Tittle's mounting national reputation, at least within the circles of Methodism, was his appointment at the age of thirty to Columbus's historic Broad Street Church. Shortly thereafter the call to First Church, Evanston, confirmed the fact of his prestige among Wesley's followers. Then in 1924 the *Christian Century* polled the Protestant ministry to discover its choice of the twenty-five outstanding American preachers, the results appearing in the December 15 issue. Tittle was among them, the youngest in the group. Though not yet forty, his brother ministers of all denominations placed him in the dizzying company of Harry Emerson Fosdick, Henry Sloane Coffin, George A. Gordon, Francis J. McConnell, Robert E. Speer, and (truth to tell) William A. Sunday. Ten years later *Pulpit* magazine conducted a similar poll and Tittle was voted one of the nation's seven outstanding preachers. Various polls taken later substantiated the admiration of his peers.

If it is held that polls serve only to refute the dictum that "you can't fool all of the people all of the time," there is available other evidence to suggest Tittle's national stature. During his lifetime and also at the time of his death, a host of religious and secular leaders declared their esteem. Bishop Oxnam regarded him "as the ablest of the preachers of Methodism"[1] and "the greatest preacher in the church."[2] Other Methodist bishops seconded this judgment, and this despite Tittle's blunt criticisms of the episcopacy. As we know, Northwestern's presidents and professors sang his praises, Dean James ranking him as "one of the greatest preachers in Protestantism, if not the leading figure in the Protestant church,"[3] and Dean James McLeod declaring him to be "one of the greatest leaders of Protestantism of our time."[4] The president of

1. Letter from Bishop G. Bromely Oxnam to Tittle, October 13, 1943.
2. *Evanston Review,* August 18, 1949, clipping in the Tittle Collection.
3. *Chicago Daily News,* August 4, 1949, clipping in the Tittle Collection.
4. *Ibid.*

Garrett, Horace G. Smith, testified that at the peak of Tittle's career no other Methodist minister enjoyed comparable prestige and that the Methodist clergy held him in "sheer adulation."[5] President Harold C. Case of Boston University employed almost the same terms in his estimation of Tittle's influence.[6] The editor of the *Christian Century* declared in 1943: "Among Protestant ministers in this country in all communions, there is no man regarded with more respect, listened to with more attention, or followed with more hope than Ernest Fremont Tittle."[7] Theologian Harris Franklin Rall quite naturally accorded Tittle stellar ranking (considering Tittle's admiration for Rall's theology),[8] but so did Harold Paul Sloan, Edwin Lewis, Lynn Harold Hough, Arlo Ayres Brown, and many others whose views did not agree with Tittle's.[9] Federal Council leader Walter Van Kirk and World Council leader Henry Smith Leiper paid warm tributes at the time of Tittle's death, as did such secular leaders as Senator Paul Douglas and Senator John Foster Dulles. Even men who were in profound disagreement with Tittle's pacifism, such as Reinhold Niebuhr and Daniel Poling, acknowledged his integrity.

If it is held that these tributes must be discounted because of the notorious "back scratching" engaged in by prestigious people, there remains a final, irrefutable body of testimony to Tittle's high place in the national life of American Protestantism: namely, the expressions of affection and admiration voiced by the rank-and-file clergy. More than any other man in Methodism and as much as any other man in all American Protestantism, he was the standard around whom the social and theological liberals—and most especially the younger ones—rallied. As the younger radicals dubbed Reinhold Niebuhr "Mr. Judgment Day in Breeches," so the younger liberals called Tittle "My dear Father in the Gospel." In the words of Harold Case, Tittle was a "gutty and great" example precisely because he was a fellow working minister and therefore a leader with whom they could intimately identify as they could never identify with a bishop or seminary professor or executive secretary.[10] First Church became a symbol of a church that was at once enormously "successful" and fearlessly prophetic. Tittle's death left a

5. Author's interview with Horace G. Smith, Evanston, Ill., August 17, 1959.
6. Author's interview with Harold C. Case, Denver, Col., May 2, 1960.
7. Paul Hutchinson in undated, typed MS in the Tittle Collection on the occasion of the dinner honoring Tittle's twenty-fifth anniversary.
8. Author's interview with Dr. and Mrs. Harris Franklin Rall, Evanston, Ill., August 24, 1959.
9. In letters to the author from these men.
10. Author's interview with Harold C. Case, Denver, Col., May 2, 1960.

void in Methodism that no one in the succeeding decades has come forward to fill.

In the Tittle files there are hundreds of worshipful letters from ministers throughout the land and of every denomination. Some of them contain admissions of plagiarism, that most flattering of tributes. "I am not ashamed to confess," admitted one rookie preacher, "that I found some of your sermons worth repeating to my congregation, and I found others doing the same."[11] Another wrote: "We younger ministers banter about the fact that you can get $10,000 out of your sermons, while we are able to earn only $1,000 on them."[12] And Tittle's admirers are certain that some of his sermons found their way into the most famous pulpits in the land. The sermons were printed and made widely available in pamphlet form, at first irregularly and then systematically under the title, *The First Church Pulpit*. More than a million copies of *The First Church Pulpit* were printed and in this manner alone 250 sermons were distributed throughout the country.[13] A decade after Tittle's death a church leader remembered his early friendship with him, and uttered the poignant words: "Almost invariably I have a strange experience whenever I talk about Dr. Tittle. I find myself choking up."[14] But this "strange experience" was in fact an experience common to numbers of ministers with memories of association, casual as well as intimate, with Ernest Fremont Tittle.

III

Methodists are fond of asserting that there is no institution like the Annual Conference. They may be right. For Bishop Nolan B. Harmon it is "the most solid, irreducible unit of a solid irreducible church."[15] For the editors of the *Christian Advocate,* it is "the FATHER of the General Conference."[16] Borden P. Bowne's assessment is more mordant: "Undoubtedly the Grace of God is operative everywhere, but it often seems less evident in an Annual Conference."[17] Irrespective of the presence of the Grace of God, the Annual Conference is the linchpin of the Methodist system; withdraw it and the entire organizational structure would collapse.

11. Letter from F. A. Laxamana to Tittle, January 14, 1936.
12. Letter from Harold Darling to Tittle, December 8, 1936.
13. *First Church Review,* special memorial issue, September 10, 1949.
14. Letter from G. Eugene Durham to author, September 8, 1959.
15. *The Organization of the Methodist Church,* rev. ed. (Nashville, Tenn.: The Methodist Publishing House, 1953), p. 141.
16. *New York Christian Advocate,* LXXXVII (March 28, 1912), 415.
17. Quoted in John Paul Williams, *What Americans Believe and How They Worship* (New York: Harper & Brothers, 1952), p. 285.

Tittle was received into the Rock River Annual Conference in October, 1918, First Church being in the Chicago Northern District of that conference. Rock River is one of Methodism's notable conferences, embracing numerous members, strong churches, valuable properties, and important denominational institutions. It is also famed, together with the New York East and New England Conferences, for its historic social concern and crusading spirit. Tittle rapidly emerged as a conference leader and within a few years "stood head and shoulders above the other members."[18] This is remarkable because Rock River was blessed with many outstanding men and also because, as we already know, Tittle was not much of a convention man. He was acutely aware of the preciousness of time and jealous of every hour that took him away from his people and his books. He did not look upon conferences as social or diplomatic affairs at which one caught up on the gossip, made alliances, patched fences, wooed friends, and sought to influence people. Usually he was on hand only as long as it was necessary to present a report, guide a debate, defend a resolution, or cast a crucial vote. Yet such was the integrity of his character, the force of his personality, the rigor of his thought, and the clarity of his speaking, that more than any other individual, save, of course, the presiding bishop, he dominated the sessions.

In later chapters we shall examine in detail Tittle's leadership on specific matters. It is enough to say here that he served on and often chaired important committees, especially those dealing with social service, public policy, and world peace. As early as 1921 he was elected trustee of Northwestern University. In 1927 he received the highest number of votes as delegate to the 1928 General Conference and invariably thereafter he headed the Rock River delegation to the national quadrennial. From time to time, beginning in 1920, he delivered conference lectures, and in 1932 he gave the induction address to the laymen who for the first time were admitted to equal membership with the clergy. He was largely responsible for persuading the conference to adopt the position that every church should give its minister one full month off each year to do as he pleased. He consistently sought to raise the educational standards and also the salaries of the clergy, advocating a minimum annual clerical wage.[19]

18. Author's interview with Kenneth F. Thompson, Wilmette, Ill., August 6, 1959.

19. This section is based on an examination of the *Journal and Year Book of the Rock River Annual Conference,* 1918-1949, inclusive, and also on news items appearing in the Methodist and Evanston press. Throughout this study I have used the shortened citation, *Minutes* of the Rock River Annual Conference.

IV

As the leader of the Rock River delegation to the General Conferences of 1928, 1932, 1936, 1940, 1944, and 1948, Tittle's national stature was further enhanced. But to make an assessment of his General Conference role meaningful, it is necessary first to discover his general attitude toward the Methodist Church, and most especially toward that unique institution, the Methodist episcopacy. Here we tread very treacherous ground, for not only is the subject emotion-freighted, the evidence is ambiguous and even contradictory. We may immediately cut to the heart of the matter by asking, Was Tittle a good Methodist? Bishop J. Ralph Magee, resident bishop of the Chicago area during the last six years of Tittle's life, both admired and liked him. Yet in Magee's judgment Tittle was not a loyal soldier in the army of Methodism. Tittle obeyed only those orders that pleased him to obey and co-operated in only those denomination-wide programs that he judged significant. Though First Church bore the name Methodist, it was to a considerable degree independent of denominational discipline and pretty much marched to the beat of its own drum; and if it sometimes found itself in step with the national church, this was a matter of voluntary rather than coerced harmony.[20] Strong circumstantial evidence indicates that Magee's predecessors, especially Bishop Waldorf and Bishop Hughes, also found it impossible to break Tittle into harness. Moreover, as we already know, Tittle revised Methodist ritual to suit his own convictions and accorded the Methodist *Discipline* somewhat less obedience than the term suggests. Such was the muscle of First Church that for thirty consecutive years no bishop dared to deny its request to reappoint Tittle, and this despite the vaunted Methodist ideal of itinerancy and despite an average tenure of three and one-half years for Rock River pastors.[21] It has been noted already that Tittle favored legally changing the name of First Methodist Church to Christ Church and at least a few leading laymen advocated taking the final step of severing all ties with Methodism.

Tittle was a stiff-kneed man. There was a strong anti-authoritarian, anti-institutional strain in his makeup. His bulldog jaw accurately suggests the element of stubbornness in his personality. Although he rode his own turbulent nature with a tight rein, he did not take to discipline imposed externally. Doubtless these attributes of character contributed to his refusal to permit First Church to be melded completely into the purposes of the larger church. But there is also a more compelling expla-

20. Author's interview with Bishop J. Ralph Magee, Evanston, Ill., August 31, 1959.
21. *Minutes* of the Rock River Annual Conference (1937), p. 61.

nation which he stated succinctly in a note to a critic: "I am indeed sorry if I gave the impression that I am first of all a Methodist. My most earnest hope is that I am first of all a Christian."[22] If Tittle's fidelity to the Methodist Church was less than absolute, it was because of his unconditional commitment to a yet higher loyalty, the God who most fully revealed Himself in Jesus Christ. Therefore, when Tittle refused to obey an episcopal directive, when he declined to participate in a denominational program, when he expressed criticism of General Conference action, it was because he feared being a "bad" Christian more than he coveted the reputation of being a "good" Methodist.

When Bishop Magee gave his critique of Tittle's relationship to Methodism he noted a qualification. Magee was a key leader of the mighty and magnificently successful "Crusade for Christ" launched by the Methodist bishops in 1943, and he admitted that Tittle's cooperation was unqualified. Indeed it was. Tittle preached a fervent sermon explaining the enterprise to his flock.[23] First Church responded by contributing generously. He spoke in major cities throughout the Middle West under the sponsorship of the Crusade. In these and other ways his contribution to this movement of a now united Methodism was signal. If this were the only example of Tittle's denominational cooperation then it might properly be dismissed as a curious footnote to the general soundness of Magee's judgment. But there is much additional evidence to suggest Tittle's loyalty to Methodism—a loyalty on the one hand never total but on the other hand never trivial.

Bishop T. Otto Nall, one-time editor of the *Christian Advocate*, offered this estimate: "Dr. Tittle gave a good deal of time to the Methodist Church as a whole, serving on a number of important committees and as a member of several General Conferences. . . . I noticed that as he grew older his contacts with the leadership of the denomination became stronger and stronger, and his church became more and more of a truly Methodist church. This was an important aspect of his ministry in a community that prides itself on its ecumenical interest. Of course, Dr. Tittle added greatly to those ecumenical concerns but I think it may truly be said that he believed many of the important contributions of the Methodist Church should be made through its Methodist tradition, insights, and experience."[24]

Over the years Tittle wrote a number of articles and delivered a number of addresses dealing with Methodist history, Methodist ideals,

22. Letter from Tittle to Miss M. Frances McElroy, April 3, 1944.
23. *A Modern Crusade,* a sermon preached January 21, 1945 (pamphlet).
24. Letter from T. Otto Nall to author, September 9, 1959.

and Methodist conceptions of the church, and his judgments are over-whelmingly favorable. We may be certain that had he been commissioned to write a history of Methodism the tone would have been firmly positive. He expressed publicly and privately appreciation of and loyalty to the Methodist heritage. The 1928 General Conference, his first, filled him with admiration. He characterized the 1936 General Conference as "outstanding, both in its intelligent grasp of the issues presented and its moral and religious attitudes."[25] The 1940 General Conference was "a revelation of the present insight and potential power of American Methodism. I came away more thankful than ever for my own membership in the Methodist Church."[26] In 1940 also he wrote a comrade: "Please do not feel discouraged about present trends in The Methodist Church. I am myself more than ever convinced that The Methodist Church, with all its imperfections, offers to God the best instrument He now has for the kind of work which He is doing in the world. I can assure you that in the Middle West, where I live and have all my life lived, Methodism is not lacking either in Christian understanding or in Christian devotion. At any rate, there are many Methodists in this part of the world for whom I personally thank God."[27] And a year before his death he reported to his people on the 1948 General Conference: "I can state that I came away from Boston feeling not a little heartened. I had seen a great Church, a Church with many weaknesses, but still a great Church, face up to the realities of the world situation; concerned necessarily with its own organization, but viewing that as a means only, not as an end in itself; concerned with the sufferings, the fears, the hopes, the deepest needs of human beings all around the world; concerned above all to know and declare the will of God and to mediate a divine mercy and redemption to the children of men that a world in sore distress and dreadful peril might have a new birth of life and peace."[28]

His deeds gave substance to the words. He gave of his time, talents, and coin to a cluster of Methodist agencies such as the World Peace Commission, the Methodist Federation for Social Service (Action), and the National Council of Methodist Youth. He participated in scores of assemblies (aside from the Annual and General Conferences) concerned with various aspects of American and world Methodism. He was invited to address innumerable groups of Methodist clergymen and laymen convened in seminar and institute. He was a frequent contributor

25. Letter from Tittle to Harry W. Knowles, June 9, 1936; *Evanston Daily News-Index,* May 20, 1936, p. 7.

26. Letter from Tittle to Mrs. U. S. Grant, September 14, 1940.

27. Letter from Tittle to W. A. Rice, September 14, 1940.

28. "A Great Church Speaks Out," typed MS, a sermon preached June 6, 1948.

to the Methodist press. And First Church housed a succession of local, regional, national, and international Methodist gatherings. In sum, the question, Was Tittle a good Methodist? does not have a simple answer after all, for it depends on one's meaning of the term "good Methodist." Anyhow, the denomination that suffers "mavericks" such as Tittle has little about which to complain and still less about which to worry.

One might complain, however, if one were a member of a denomination with an episcopal polity and one happened to be a bishop. The single constant criticism of the Methodist Church made by Tittle—made, his opponents charged, with the monotonous refrain of the whippoorwill —was that the bishops regarded themselves as a "privileged order." It is unnecessary to review the history of the Methodist episcopacy to understand that it has been the traditional storm center of the whole Methodist organization. It is unnecessary to quote the ten thousand limericks, stories, jokes, and puns lampooning Methodist electioneering for episcopal office to acknowledge that such vast clouds of smoke must have origin in at least a tiny fire of tawdry fact. It is also unnecessary to observe that if all bishops were erased from the history of American Methodism the story would be not only less stormy but also less impressive.

Tittle's critical attitude was not born of "sour grapes." He was repeatedly importuned to permit his name to be presented for episcopal election. On one such occasion Bishop Wilbur E. Hammaker pressed him to flash a green signal to his supporters, warning, however, that there are "folks who definitely would not like to see you in the Episcopacy," and closing murkily, "You know there are wheels within wheels always in these matters."[29] In rare instances Tittle was sufficiently tempted to sound out his intimate friends. If they were true friends, they replied as did Paul Hutchinson: "I simply cannot think of a job in which you would be more unhappy or accomplish less of importance to the Kingdom of God than in the Methodist bishopric."[30] Usually, however, Tittle did not hesitate in tersely dissuading his persuaders. "I myself have no desire to be a bishop on any kind of tenure or, indeed, under any circumstances whatsoever," he declared.[31] Again: "I have just told the representatives of a group here in the Middle West that under no circumstances would I consent to an election even though by some

29. Letter from Bishop Wilbur E. Hammaker to Tittle, January 4, 1944. See also the letter from Hammaker to Tittle, January 17, 1944.
30. Letter from Paul Hutchinson to Tittle, October 6, 1943.
31. Letter from Tittle to Frank D. Sheets, November 31, 1931.

miracle it should be offered me."[32] His family, friends, and associates are in agreement that he did not covet the office of bishop. And the evidence is irrefutable that had he made the slightest effort on his own behalf, the ballots would have fallen into his lap like autumn leaves. There is only one slight reservation to this statement. In his very last years he might have accepted election had he been guaranteed the Chicago area assignment. Such election would not have necessitated a move from Evanston. And he knew the pastors and the people. But such an assignment was out of the question, for there were many veteran bishops with long tenure who were anxious to have the Chicago plum. And that was that.[33]

Although the origins of Tittle's critical attitude toward the Methodist episcopacy are obscure, we may guess that they are rooted in his early life and reveal something of Tittle as well as episcopal imperfections. We have repeatedly observed his anti-authoritarian temper. We know that as a divinity student he was considered something of a rebel. While in France, he met a "bully good fellow," adding: "It is quite refreshing to find a real man among candidates for the episcopacy. He, as you know, is in line for that exalted ? position."[34] Thus, as early as 1918 he had reservations about the office of bishop and the men who occupied it. Perhaps the headaches involved in transferring from Columbus to Evanston contributed to his critical attitude, though the bishops involved —Anderson, Bristol, McDowell, and Nicholson—all had his respect. In 1924 the eminent Edwin Holt Hughes assumed leadership of the Chicago area. As we learned earlier, when Bishop and Mrs. Hughes called at the parsonage Tittle found himself unable to break off the preparation of a sermon to greet them and there resulted a wounded relationship that never completely healed. Hughes's successor in 1932, Bishop Ernest Lynn Waldorf, was not close to Tittle, and again it is not possible to absolve Tittle of all responsibility for the estrangement. On one occasion, Tittle administered a severe tongue-lashing to the bishop ("laid him out in a man to man talk" is the phrasing of Tittle's secretary) because Tittle believed the bishop had unfairly emasculated a strong pacifist report drafted by Tittle.[35] Before this incident, Tittle had written concerning Bishop Waldorf: "Unfortunately, I cannot control the utterances of my bishop. But only once in four years is he invited to appear in the pulpit

32. Letter from Tittle to Morris W. Ehmes, October 20, 1931.
33. Author's interview with Joseph Thomas, Evanston, Ill., July 29, 1959.
34. Letter from Tittle to Glenna, September 24, 1918.
35. Author's interview with Mrs. Bernice Wolseley, Evanston, Ill., June 13, 1960.

of the First Methodist Church of Evanston, and on that occasion intelligent persons such as you may profitably bring with them to church some good book to read while the bishop speaks."[36]

It was at the 1932 General Conference that Tittle first gave public voice to his strong feelings about the bishops of Methodism. The delegates assembled in Atlantic City in an angry mood. Anti-episcopal sentiment, mounting for months, had now reached the boiling point. The rank-and-file pastors of Methodism, bewildered and bruised by the depression, were determined to make their will felt. This was to be "the pastors' conference." And in their frustration, they turned on their bishops, a natural target, though in 1932 the bishops were themselves a badly vexed and perplexed group. Open rebellion did not materialize, but rarely in Methodist history has the "episcopacy question" so racked a General Conference.

On May 14 Tittle spoke to a motion to return a retired bishop "to that Annual Conference in which his membership, held in suspension, while he was in the Episcopal office, rests." That is, retired bishops would receive their pensions from their Annual Conferences, not the General Conference, *at the same rate as retired preachers.* "To my mind," said Tittle in arguing that bishops receive the same retirement treatment as "some of the rest of us," "it is perfectly clear that we have got to make a choice here between maintaining the social position that has been acquired by men who have been in high office; and, on the other hand, maintaining interests that advance the Kingdom of God."[37] Four days later Tittle spoke in support of a motion to limit the tenure of bishops rather than to continue to elect them for life, concluding with the intemperate words:

> Complaint has been made that we are heckling our Bishops. I feel, as a Methodist preacher, humiliated every time anybody does heckle the Bishops. But what I deplore, even more than that, is the situation that calls forth the heckling.
>
> Why is it so many of us are distressed? When you find that you have an economic order under which it is impossible to secure justice and the welfare of mankind, you begin to assume that there is something wrong with the order. When you produce an ecclesiastical order that invites as much heckling as has occurred on the floor of this Conference, is it not a reasonable assumption there is something wrong with the ecclesiastical order?
>
> I for one believe that human nature is never equal to a privileged order. We assumed that when we founded our nation, in

36. Letter from Tittle to Bjarne J. Olson, June 22, 1936.
37. *The Daily Christian Advocate,* Methodist Episcopal Church, May 14, 1932, pp. 277-80.

which we did not create a kingship, but a democracy. There are any number of men here, today; and any number of men in the United States of America, in and out of the Christian Church, who believe that human nature is not kindly to the kind of an economic privileged order that we have at the present time. And we are seriously proposing—and the proposition is coming from some people who have profited by that order, but whose consciences are now disturbed by the situation in which they find themselves—that we change our privileged economic order in the interests of the welfare of mankind.

I believe that the time has come to make a change in a privileged ecclesiastical order in the name of the welfare of our Church, and in the name of the welfare of mankind. We are standing on the brink of a precipice, as a civilization. If we find that we cannot, as a Church, make a great pronouncement that will be the Christian message to the world, without having it toned down by men who are spoiled by a privileged ecclesiastical order, then I believe that we owe it to mankind to change the system that spoils the man.

I am a hero-worshipper, too. I have been cut to the heart by seeing too many of my heroes spoiled by a system in which they become victims. I believe that a limited tenure making this an administrative office would give us a profounder spiritual leadership and a more courageous spiritual leadership, a humbler, more Christ-like spiritual leadership, than we can hope to get in most cases under the present system.[38]

The motion received 407 yeas and 395 nays, short of the required two-thirds majority for passage. After Tittle's speech the bishops trooped back to their hotel, the Dennis, wrathful. Legend has it that only Bishops McConnell and Blake were smiling.[39] By any measurement, the utterance was immoderate. Even some of Tittle's friends believe the wording was unfortunate. However, in the following months Tittle received a number of letters from fellow preachers thanking him for administering such a "roasting" to the bishops, those "self-seeking peanut politicians" who enjoy a "vicious unbroken circle of power." For his part, Tittle never expressed contrition. "Do not be disturbed by any report concerning the treatment which was accorded me at Atlantic City," he reassured a concerned admirer. "I did speak with amazing frankness but I do not regret anything that I said, and a rough guess is

38. *Ibid.*, May 18, 1932, pp. 381-82.
39. Author's interviews with Kenneth F. Thompson, Wilmette, Ill., August 6, 1959; Thomas Stafford, Denver, Col., May 1, 1960; Horace G. Smith, Evanston, Ill., August 17, 1959; Bishop Ralph Magee, Evanston, Ill., August 31, 1959; and letter from Edwin Lewis to author, July 20, 1959.

that as many people agreed with me as disagreed."⁴⁰ Nevertheless, "Such petty politics I never expected to find in the Methodist Church."⁴¹

Toward the close of the 1936 General Conference a purge was made of the important Board of Education, the bishops voting to replace Bishop Blake with Bishop Adna Leonard, an ultraconservative, as its head; and Leonard then proceeded to request the resignations of Owen Geer and Blaine Kirkpatrick, two young avowed Socialists who had given vigorous leadership to the Youth Department. This and other actions of the bishops in 1936 caused Tittle to growl, "I certainly . . . hope that the skulduggery practiced by our reactionary bishops at the close of the General Conference will sound the death knell of the life tenure of the episcopacy."⁴² A few weeks later he was in a calmer frame of mind: "Replying to your letter . . . all I have to say is, Cheer up! The Christian church has always had the institutional mind to contend with. However, it has managed in spite of it to live for nineteen stormy centuries and to make a very considerable contribution to the welfare of the human race. I have myself decided not to let the frailties of the episcopacy 'get my goat.' From now on they are to be 'just one of those things.' I shall go ahead, trusting God and working like the devil in order to defeat the devil."⁴³ Following the 1940 General Conference Tittle took hope in the thought that the "present Council of Bishops" was not identical with The Methodist Church. "Indeed, it would not be going too far, I think, to say that, with a few notable exceptions, it is unrepresentative of contemporary Methodism at its best."⁴⁴ At his last General Conference he spoke against a motion to permit retired bishops to continue to vote at meetings of the Council of Bishops.⁴⁵ At his last North Central Jurisdictional Conference he shared in the election of bishops and "the maneuvering which had accompanied that struggle for high churchly office seemed to sicken him and to drain him of vitality. . . ."⁴⁶

As he approached the height of his career, a time when he was the focus of much controversy, he unburdened himself in a letter to Dan B. Brummitt, editor of the *Northwestern Christian Advocate*, and then penciled out the most candid sentence. The deleted words read: "I frankly

40. Letter from Tittle to Gilbert Loveland, June 27, 1932.
41. Letter from Tittle to "Dear Raymond" [Thornburg?], July 5, 1932.
42. Letter from Tittle to Amy Blanche Greene, September 14, 1936.
43. Letter from Tittle to Harry W. Knowles, October 13, 1936.
44. Letter from Tittle to Mrs. U. S. Grant, September 14, 1940.
45. *The Daily Christian Advocate*, The Methodist Church, May 7, 1948, p. 254.
46. Paul Hutchinson, "Portrait of a Preacher," foreword to Tittle, *A Mighty Fortress* (New York: Harper & Brothers, 1949), pp. xxxiii-xxxiv.

confess that I have become very sensitive to the attitude of near hostility that is taken toward me by the leaders of the Methodist Episcopal Church."[47] If by "leaders" he meant "bishops," then he probably was gauging with rough accuracy their sentiments in 1933. But it is imperative to remember that Tittle always admired and was in turn admired by many of the greatest bishops, including almost all of a progressive character: Francis J. McConnell, G. Bromley Oxnam, Edgar Blake, Herbert Welch, James C. Baker, Charles Wesley Flint, Wilbur E. Hammaker, William F. McDowell, Lewis O. Hartman, and others, to say nothing of many younger men who were elevated to the office after his death.[48]

V

A Methodist member of the United States Congress once said, "All I know about politics I learned at General Conference." Having read the *Journal* and the even more illuminating *Daily Christian Advocate* for every General Conference of the Methodist Episcopal Church and the Methodist Episcopal Church, South, and then The Methodist Church for the period 1898-1948; having examined in less thorough fashion nineteenth-century General Conferences; and having attended personally the sessions of one General Conference (1960), there have been moments when the congressman's cynical appraisal seemed just to me. But I am an outsider, and it may well be that Bishop McConnell was essentially right when in his autobiography he defended the General Conference as an effective, representative, democratic, progressive instrument of Methodism.

In any event, there can be no meaningful understanding of American Methodism without reference to the General Conferences, and for the years 1928-48 there can be no complete analysis of General Conference action without recognition of Tittle's role. He served on major committees, especially the key Committee on the State of the Church, and was its chairman in 1940, 1944, and 1948. In debate he excelled. His effectiveness as a spokesman was enhanced by the fact that he was not always leaping to his feet shouting "Mr. Chairman!" Nor was he

47. Letter from Tittle to Dan B. Brummitt, March 6, 1933.
48. This statement is based largely on letters to and from Tittle in the Tittle Collection. Tittle's affection for such older men as Welch is transparent, but among the bishops his greatest hero is McConnell, for "there is in the whole Christian church of this age no man with a greater vision or a more apostolic fervor." To Tittle, McConnell was a "continuous source of inspiration" and an "invisible guide for my thinking and doing." See *First Church Review*, V (May 5, 1928), 1, and letter from Tittle to McConnell, April 13, 1937.

windy when granted recognition. Save for his 1932 outburst against the bishops, he invariably spoke measuredly, clearly, and above all earnestly. He might have been dubbed "Mr. Root-of-the-Matter." His speeches possessed much the same qualities as his sermons. When he spoke the Conference listened. His admirers assert that no man enjoyed a more commanding respect. It is abundantly clear that the liberal clergy looked to him for leadership in committee meetings and floor debate. Only Glenna, who accompanied him, knew fully the fearful physical and psychic price exacted by these exhausting yet crucial Conferences.[49]

VI

At 11:00 a.m., Sunday, August 15, 1954, the organ of the First Methodist Church, Evanston, Illinois, played the stirring Reformation chorale "A Mighty Fortress Is Our God" as a great procession of Christian churchmen from many lands garbed in stunning variety moved through the doors. Thus opened the second Assembly of the World Council of Churches, the most momentous religious gathering ever to be held in America.[50] The 1,298 "official participants" came together to give witness to "Christ—the Hope of the World," surely an appropriate theme for a "fellowship of Churches which accept our Lord Jesus Christ as God and Saviour," the definition formulated at Amsterdam in 1948.

It is heartbreaking that Tittle's great heart failed to permit him to live to witness this mighty event in the community he served so long and to see the university he served, Northwestern, as the setting of the Council's deliberations and his beloved First Church as the scene of the Council's worship services. Tittle preached, prayed, and fought to bring about those things that had not, at the time of his death, come about: a warless world, a casteless and color-blind world, a world freed from the damnation of poverty and the bondage of ignorance. There was, however, one great dream Tittle cherished which the intractability of history had not totally frustrated—the cause of Christian unity. And though he did not live to see the fulfillments of the 1950's and 1960's, he did thrill to the final formation of the World Council of Churches in 1948, to the earnest pledge of those Christians assembled in Amsterdam, "We intend to stay together," and to the thoughtful evaluation of the Cambridge historian Ernest Barker: "Our century has its sad features,

49. Author's interview with Glenna Myers Tittle, Evanston, Ill., July 31, 1959. Needless to say, Tittle was a leader of the three sessions he attended of the North Central Jurisdictional Conference.

50. W. A. Visser 't Hooft (ed.), The Evanston Report: The Second Assembly of the World Council of Churches, 1954 (New York: Harper & Brothers, 1955), pp. 17-19.

but there is one feature in its history which is not sad. That is the gathering tide of Christian union."

Although confirmation of the site of the Second Assembly was not made until July, 1950, at Toronto,[51] it was in First Church in March, 1949, that the very first meeting of the American Conference of Member Churches of the World Council of Churches convened.[52] Dr. Paul G. Macy, program director, Committee of 100, Second Assembly of the World Council of Churches, judged that the way in which First Church "played host to that conference . . . had much to do with the choosing of Evanston as the place in which to hold the second assembly. . . ."[53] There was a certain happy propriety in the selection of Evanston. After all, a towering figure in the modern ecumenical movement was John R. Mott, American Methodist layman; the president of the World Council was G. Bromley Oxnam, American Methodist bishop; Dean James Alton James of Northwestern and First Church had labored to bring about the realization of the dream, held since he was a delegate to Lousanne in 1927, of hosting an ecumenical conference; and Tittle himself had long championed the idea of Christian unity.

To say that Tittle championed the idea is not, however, to claim that he led, or was one of the influential leaders, of the twentieth-century ecumenical movement. Many names spring easily to mind before his. What may properly be advanced in Tittle's case is to repeat the point that is the very heart of our story: few if any working ministers—burdened men with weekly preaching duties, pastoral calls, counseling, and pesky parish administrative responsibilities—did more to advance the ecumenical ideal among the rank-and-file of American Protestantism. As almost invariably happens in the reading of church history, one comes away from a review of the literature dealing with the modern ecumenical movement almost persuaded that it was entirely the work of archbishops and bishops, theologians and professors, evangelists and executive secretaries, editors and scholars, and even lawyers and businessmen; and that somehow it is possible and permissible to write about this growing tide of Christian fellowship without reference to those shepherds who most intimately instructed their flocks in the meaning of that fellowship. Tittle did not make the ideal of Christian unity a fact, but without

51. *Minutes and Reports of the Fourth Meeting of the Central Committee of the World Council of Churches Rolle (Switzerland) August 4-11, 1951* (Geneva, 1951), p. 81.

52. David P. Gaines, *The World Council of Churches: A Study of Its Background and History* (Peterborough, N. H.: Richard R. Smith Noone House, 1966), p. 549.

53. *Evanston Review,* January 14, 1954, p. 3.

thousands of working ministers like him, William Temple could never have written, "Almost incidentally the great world fellowship has arisen; it is the great new fact of our era."

One little, concrete thing Tittle did was to bring First Church into affiliation with the Evanston Council of Churches, the Church Federation of Greater Chicago, the Federal Council of Churches (the National Council was not formed until 1950), and the World Council of Churches. He was instrumental in the formation of the Evanston Council and he contributed much to the effectiveness of the Chicago Federation, the executive vice-president, Dr. John W. Harms, testifying to Tittle's "consuming passion for the cause of Christian unity" and his "inspiration to the churches of Greater Chicago."[54] In 1946 he was elected chairman of the Chicago and Midwest Regional Committee for the World Council of Churches.

This "consuming passion" is abundantly documented in the record. Indeed, there is no more urgent and persistent theme in his writings and utterances over the years than that of church union, save only that of world peace, and in fact for Tittle the two were intimately linked. In his first book he asserted that denominationalism was anachronistic, that the day is "almost certainly coming" when it would no longer be, for the tragedy of denominationalism lies in the fact "that a disunited Christendom is unable to speak with a united voice even when, as in August, 1914, the fate of a world hangs in the balance."[55] And among the very last words from his pen were these: ". . . there is coming into being a world Christian community transcending every physical, every political, every racial and cultural barrier. The existence of this world-wide Christian fellowship offers the opportunity of world order and peace established on the basis of a common faith, a common ethic, a mutual trust and interest and devotion."[56]

Tittle once preached a sermon interpretating for his congregation the words of St. Paul: "All belongs to you; Paul, Apollos, Cephas, the world, life, death, the present, and the future—all belongs to you; and you belong to Christ, and Christ to God." "And if Paul were alive today," Tittle asked,

> what would he be saying to the sectarians of our time? Do you not think that he would be saying, "Why bind yourself to Martin Luther, or to John Calvin, or to John Wesley, or to George Fox?

54. *Chicago Sun-Times,* August 4, 1949, clipping in the Tittle Collection.
55. *What Must the Church Do to Be Saved?* (New York and Cincinnati, Ohio: Abingdon Press, 1921), p. 37.
56. *The Gospel According to Luke* (New York: Harper & Brothers, 1951), p. 272.

Why take all your orders from Canterbury or from Rome? The glorious pagentry of the Roman Catholic church, the beautiful liturgy of the Episcopal church, the intellectual honesty of the Unitarian church, the social passion of the Methodist church, the moral vigor of the Congregational church, the democracy of the Baptist church, the spiritual insight and moral courage of the Society of Friends—it all belongs to you." In the face of all the difficulties, real and imaginary, that stand in the way, I am personally convinced that it might all belong to us. Religious pageantry as beautiful and inspiring as any ever produced in Rome; an order of worship as impressive and helpful as any followed in Canterbury; an intellectual honesty of which no scientist could feel ashamed; a social passion such as dwelt in the heart of Wesley and fired the soul of Walter Rauschenbusch; a spiritual insight and moral courage equal to the high and hard demands of a transitional time; the faith of saints; the courage of pioneers; and a mystical awareness of the presence of God—it all belongs to us, or at least it might belong to us. And how splendid it would be if you and I this morning should resolve that some day it shall belong to us![57]

Though Tittle could be caustic regarding certain types of churchmen, such was his irenic spirit that only rarely did he criticize entire denominations, even regarding the Unitarian Church as being within the Christian fold.[58] He believed it most appropriate for Methodists to seek union with the Congregationalists, though admittedly this would require revision of the Methodist episcopacy.[59] He did, however, dislike "high" Episcopalians for their leaning toward Rome, their excessive fondness of pomp and circumstance, their pride and theological conservativism. He could have been happy as rector of a "broad" Episcopal church.[60] The Oxford Movement he judged "one of the most dangerous religious symptoms of these troubled times."[61]

It is both an indication of Tittle's ecumenical concern and a gauge of his national stature that he should have been invited to participate in the work of the Federal Council of the Churches of Christ in America. At one time he was a member of the Council's Department of International Justice and Goodwill; at another a member of a special Council committee on "The State of the Church"; and significantly he was the only "working minister" on the Council's important Commission on the

57. *All Things Are Yours,* a sermon preached September 30, 1928 (pamphlet).
58. Letter from Tittle to Ward R. Clarke, September 5, 1933.
59. Letter from Tittle to Frank A. Horne, May 29, 1934.
60. Letter from Tittle to Lawrence K. Brown, September 11, 1933.
61. Letter from Tittle to S. R. Dunham, March 13, 1933.

Relation of the Church to the War in the Light of the Christian Faith.[62] Moreover, in 1940 the Council appointed a Commission to Study the Bases of a Just and Durable Peace under the chairmanship of a Presbyterian layman, John Foster Dulles. Tittle was a member of the executive committee. At the crucial Delaware, Ohio meeting of the Commission in 1942, attended by 377 delegates representing thirty-one communions and thirty-nine religious organizations and agencies, Tittle (together with President Charles J. Turck of Macalester College) headed the section on "The Economic Aspects of a Just and Durable Peace" and he was instrumental in drafting the Commission's statement on the church and the economic order. In the summer of 1943 the Commission held a major conference at Princeton attended by churchmen from twelve countries and Tittle participated. He further participated in the Christian Mission on World Order sponsored by the Commission, speaking in six cities in Arkansas, Tennessee, and Kentucky in the fall of 1943. In fact, Tittle continued to be deeply implicated in the labors of the Commission to Study the Bases of a Just and Durable Peace, and these labors were important in helping to formulate not only church attitudes, but public opinion in general, regarding the postwar settlements.

Another gauge of Tittle's ecumenical concern and national stature is evidenced by his invitation to the momentous Oxford Conference on Church, Community and State in 1937, the sequel to the first Life and Work Conference held at Stockholm in 1925. His judgment that Oxford spoke with "the voice of authentic Christianity" is surely correct, for it was Oxford that gave to world Christianity the exhortation, "Let the Church be the Church." His judgment that not since the Council of Nicea in 325 A.D. had there convened a more important gathering of Christians, unless it was the Edinburgh Conference immediately following, the sequel to the first Faith and Order Conference held at Lausanne in 1927, is possibly correct. Both Oxford and Edinburgh stand as majestic peaks in the often flat and bleak landscape of Christian church history, and from a confluence of these conferences there ultimately was born the World Council of Churches.[63]

62. Tittle once described a meeting of the Commission "consisting of a number of very distinguished theologians and one lone pastor." At first he felt ignored and isolated, but when he mustered the courage to initiate a conversation he discovered the theologians to be most humble and companionable human beings. See "The Problem of Loneliness," *The First Church Pulpit*, Vol. VI, No. 9, a sermon preached October 31, 1943.

63. For Tittle's accounts of Oxford, see "The Voice of the Church at Ox-

At Oxford Tittle belonged to study groups dealing with the church and the economic order and the church and the world of nations.[64] It cannot be asserted that he was a dominating figure in the Oxford deliberations. If his pen drafted any important statement, if his voice swayed any major session, the evidence remains buried. That he was in attendance, that he was attentive to the business at hand, that he impressed those with whom he met, we may be certain. But that he significantly influenced the official proceedings is a proposition that may be entertained but scarcely maintained. On the other hand, that Oxford profoundly influenced him is beyond dispute.

Unlike many of the Oxford delegates, including the Evanstonians James Alton James and George Craig Stewart, Tittle did not go on to Edinburgh. It may be that First Church duties hastened his return, but then it may be, as Dean James believes, that Tittle's interests were in Oxford's Life and Work more than in Edinburgh's Faith and Order emphasis.[65] In any event, shortly after his return Tittle helped organize an Evanston Conference on Christian Life and Faith, modeled on the meetings in the British Isles, and sponsored by the Evanston Ministerial Association, some four hundred delegates attending the four sessions.[66] The press hailed the conference as the most important religious event in twenty-five years of Evanston history and inquiries were received from church groups throughout the nation requesting information concerning how to organize their own conference. Thereafter, Tittle's support of a World Council of Churches was unstinted, and there is comfort in the thought that he lived to see the great consummation at Amsterdam in 1948 if not the great confirming event in 1954.

It would be possible to draft a complete list of all the interdenominational and interfaith conferences Tittle attended and all such commissions he joined but it would be a fairly long list. What is most striking is that often, as, for example with the National Interseminary Commit-

---

ford," *Religion In Life*, VII (Winter, 1938), 14-21. This article is reprinted in *The First Church Pulpit*, Vol. I, No. 11. See also "The Oxford Conference," typed MS, a sermon preached September 19, 1937.

64. See J. H. Oldham, *The Oxford Conference (Official Report)* (Chicago and New York: Willett, Clark & Co., 1937) and Henry Smith Leiper, *World Chaos or World Christianity: A Popular Interpretation of Oxford and Edinburgh, 1937* (Chicago and New York: Willett, Clark & Co., 1937).

65. Author's interview with Dean James Alton James, Evanston, Ill., July 23, 1960.

66. *Evanston Daily News-Index*, November 6, 1937, p. 6; November 10, 1937, p. 1; November 17, 1937, p. 1; and December 10, 1937, p. 1; and *Evanston Review*, October 7, 1937, p. 5.

tee,[67] his is the only (or almost only) name of a working minister in a roster of prestigious theologians, professors, and ecclesiastical officials.

VII

There was in Tittle's thinking no divorce between the movement for Christian unity and Christian missions. Agreeing with Emil Brunner that "the Church exists by missions as fire exists by burning," he wholeheartedly supported the Christian missionary thrust. He once concluded a sermon with the affirmation, "There is simply no one else who is able to do for all men what Jesus Christ is able to do, either in respect of their vision and experience of God or in respect of their hunger and thirst after righteousness, their longing for moral triumph and spiritual peace. How, then, can we withhold Him from the world? Giving Him a chance to speak to the heart of the world, as also to our own heart; giving His spirit a chance to prevail in the world, as also in our own life, we shall, in my judgment, be doing all we can possibly do to redeem the world and our own souls. And with God be the rest."[68] There was nothing prideful, patronizing, or possessive in his defense of the missionary enterprise. "I am myself entirely convinced that Christianity has a mission to the world," he once told his congregation.

> I should like to have it understood, however, that what I mean is just that: it has a mission to the world. I do not think that it has a peculiar mission to the Orient; as if the military mind in Japan were anything different from the military mind in Italy or France or the United States; as if the Japanese idea of a God-Emperor were essentially different from the German idea of a God-Fuhrer; as if the slums of Shanghai were worse than the slums of Chicago; or as if the lot of a coolie in Canton were more pitiable than the lot of a share-cropper in Arkansas. So far as Christianity today is concerned, I can see no essential difference between foreign missions and home missions, nor am I able to think of home missions merely as the establishment of churches and Sunday schools in communities where they do not now exist. As I see it, Christianity has a mission to the world considered as a whole, including governments and people nominally Christian, not merely to countries whose religion is officially something other than Christianity, not merely to countries which officially, as Russia and Turkey, have repudiated all religion, and not merely to lands that are regarded as backward lands because . . . they have coal mines and oil wells but not battleships. As I see it,

67. See Clarence Tucker Craig (ed.), *The Challenge of Our Culture* (New York and London: Harper & Brothers, 1946), p. iii.
68. *Good News for the World*, a sermon preached March 15, 1936 (pamphlet).

Christianity has something to say which the world needs to hear, and quite as much in Waukegan as in Soochow.[69]

On another instance, Tittle declared: "We of this generation do not and cannot believe that ignorance of Jesus Christ closes inevitably and forever the gates of heaven, the door of hope. We have too much respect for God to believe that, the God revealed in Jesus. Neither can we believe that other peoples are dwelling in a total darkness, unrelieved by any native insight. How can we believe that in the presence of a Gandhi or a Tagore? So great, indeed, is our appreciation of the best in the East and our dissatisfaction with the worst in the West that we are not so sure as our fathers were that it would greatly benefit the East to exchange its civilization for ours." However, Tittle denied a favorite thesis of cultural anthropologists. "It is simply absurd to say that one religion is as good as another. And if you know what you are talking about it is nothing short of cruelty to say that other peoples' religions are as good for them as Christianity is, or at least might be, for us." He further maintained that the East and West are bound to mingle and that the East should know not only the West's movies and weapons, but the West's missionary idealism. He concluded by quoting Jesus' assertion that he came not to destroy but to fulfill. "At its own best that is precisely what Christianity may say concerning every other religious culture. At its own best Christianity goes today into Africa or into Asia not to destroy but rather to fulfill anything of value in an existing culture."[70]

VIII

A paradox in Tittle's career is the continuing flow of invitations to speak on high school, college, and university campuses, for his Evanston ministry spanned a period when scholarship, science, and the arts largely had decreed the absurdity of faith with the corollary the foolishness of preaching. Though often billed as a lecturer, Tittle in fact never lectured, he preached. Yet throughout America's "religious depression" the invitations continued to clog his mail, sometimes coming from administration and faculty, sometimes from student groups. Mindful of his responsibilities to First Church, he accepted only a fraction of these invitations. Nevertheless, that fraction represented several score commitments annually, exacting a considerable amount of time and returning

69. "The World Needs Christianity," typed MS, a sermon preached March 7, 1937.

70. *A World That Cannot Be Shaken* (New York and London: Harper & Brothers, 1933), pp. 52-57.

only a dribble of income.[71] He sought, whenever possible, to conserve his energy by requesting that he be lodged in a hotel rather than in a private home.

Everyone who lives in a university community knows how frequently outside speakers appear on the scene, how blasé is the reception accorded even the most famous of them, how small in relation to the total university population are their audiences, and how quickly the visitor is forgotten. Tittle was no exception. He did not and could not sweep the campuses lighting fires of belief in faith-parched forests of students. Over the years his preaching reached the ears of tens of thousands of students, and if perhaps only a few hundred hearts were pierced by the proclaimed word of God, must we conclude therefore he was engaged in a futile enterprise? During his school life a student is subjected to a barrage of words and if he heard Tittle preach once or twice, what possible difference could the encounter have made? How does one measure the unmeasurable? We do know that Tittle's preaching with its intellectual clarity, ethical rigor, social passion, and unambiguous conception of God carried a special appeal to students. We also know that students across the land wrote him in gratitude. And we know that year after year he was invited to return to the same campuses, a fact suggestive of the enduring freshness of his preaching.[72]

Though Tittle preached on many campuses, he probably counted as most important his annual engagements at Chicago, Harvard, Yale, Princeton, and Cornell, though this does not necessarily mean that he took lightly his commitments to small colleges, high schools, and prep schools. He also fulfilled a number of special lectureships including the Merrick Foundation lectures at Ohio Wesleyan, the Ayer Foundation lectures at Colgate-Rochester, the Earl Foundation lectures at the Pacific School of Religion, the Gates Memorial Foundation lectures at Grinnell, the Russell Foundation lectures at Auburn, the Wilkin Foundation lectures at the University of Illinois, the Mendenhall Foundation lectures at DePauw, the Shaffer Foundation lectures at Northwestern.

Beyond question, one of the great moments in Tittle's life came when he received an invitation from Dean Luther A. Weigle of the Yale Divinity School to deliver the Lyman Beecher Lectures on Preaching. Dean Weigle wrote: "Our Faculty is unanimous in its desire to have you

71. For example, in January, 1934, Tittle filled nineteen speaking engagements in sixteen days, from Massachusetts to California.

72. In 1928, after speaking at the University of Iowa, several thousand good Iowans signed a petition declaring Tittle "an Anti-Christian" and demanding that he not again be permitted to corrupt the youth of Iowa with his modernistic theology. See unidentified newspaper clipping in Title Scrapbook.

give these lectures. We have had you in mind for a good while and your sermon in Battell Chapel last Sunday clinched our decision that now is the time to invite you."[73] Tittle replied "You ask me whether I will accept an invitation to deliver the Lyman Beecher Lectures on Preaching in the spring of 1932. It is as though you had asked a mouse whether he would be willing to eat a choice bit of cheese. My very prompt answer is that with profound appreciation I accept the invitation."[74] In 1940 Canon Charles E. Raven was to have been the Lyman Beecher lecturer, but he was obliged to cancel the engagement because of England's involvement in war, and Dean Weigle then asked six American ministers, including Tittle, each to give one lecture. Thus, Tittle twice was accorded the highest honor that can come to a preacher—an invitation to deliver the Beecher Lectures at Yale.

Tittle's popularity as a campus preacher is illuminated by a letter he once received from the Methodist editor John W. Langdale: "I have just come back from the Student Conference at Northfield. There I heard a conference between Sperry of Harvard, Wicks of Princeton and Elmore McKee of Yale. They agreed that Fosdick could probably secure a little larger hearing than any other minister because it is somewhat of a stunt to listen to him but, without knowing that I was interested in you at all, they agreed that you had left the most abiding and strengthening impression of any minister. Due, they said in response to my inquiry, to your thinking capacity and your fearless attitude."[75]

IX

Most sketches of Tittle refer to his "huge literary productivity" and the "tireless labor demanded by his literary undertakings." He was in fact the author of twelve volumes, three of them being published posthumously. Yet primarily and pre-eminently he was a preacher and not an author, his books being an extension of his preaching—and indeed they had, with one exception, first gone through his pulpit. If Tittle's books are long remembered it will be because of the timelessness of his preaching.

We know that he "sweated blood" over the preparation of sermons. Further blood was exacted in preparing the sermons for publication, for he revised the manuscripts three and four times before sending them off to the press.[76] It was hard work. He once reported to his secretary that

73. Letter from Dean Luther A. Weigle to Tittle, March 6, 1931.
74. Letter from Tittle to Dean Luther A. Weigle, March 10, 1931.
75. Letter from John W. Langdale to Tittle, undated.
76. See letter from Tittle to William Holmes Borders, May 15, 1939.

he and Glenna "like the rich man in the parable . . . are now in torment: I, because the dog gone sermons on the Lord's Prayer are not as hot as I hoped they were; GMT, because of my unhappy condition." He further warned that "the book will be ready for dictation and you will have one——of a time when I get back."[77]

The royalties from the books were unspectacular but this did not embitter him because he held no great expectations. As he informed a young associate. "There is no money to be got from writing on religious subjects. There is, however, no end of fun, provided only that you do not write for money."[78] But if he was not much concerned with profits, like every author, he kept an eye on the publicity accorded his books, and at least two of them, in his judgment, were awarded feeble advertising by the publishers. Such was his disgust, he even considered paying for advertisements out of his own pocket.[79] And also like every author, he was sensitive to reviews. There are no letters in the Tittle files lambasting reviewers for their critical judgments, but there are several thanking reviewers for their kind words. "You are far too generous in your review of my book," he wrote on one instance. "However, you have given me needed comfort. Whenever my stuff appears in print, I feel like crawling into a hole. This time I had the feeling that a very small hole would suffice to receive me. So I am returning heartfelt thanks and saying deep down, 'God bless Versteeg for his loving-kindness and tender mercies.' "[80]

Even sermons of great force take on a certain opaqueness in print. Written for the ear, they are now perceived through the eye. Moreover, a sermon is part of worship, is itself worship. As George A. Buttrick reminds us, "A sermon is an 'offering' on an altar. Perhaps it ought to be ephemeral. Perhaps it ought to perish in that sabbath's sacrifice. Perhaps no man had the right to draw it back, saying, 'I want to print it.' "[81] Yet individuals who regularly heard Tittle preach do not believe his sermons suffered any grievous loss of impact when reduced to cold type. He was one of those rare preachers whose words were not deprived of life when placed between book covers. Of course, the beauty of the sanctuary, the contagion of public worship, the commanding presence of the preacher, the compelling voice and direct gaze are of necessity absent from the books. Nevertheless, the essence of Tittle the preacher may be

77. Letter from Tittle to Mr. and Mrs. Roland E. Wolseley, August 29, 1941.
78. Letter from Tittle to G. MacDonald Jones, January 20, 1939.
79. Letter from Tittle to Halford E. Luccock, February 28, 1933.
80. Letter from Tittle to John M. Versteeg, April 3, 1942.
81. George A. Buttrick, *Sermons Preached in a University Church* (New York and Nashville, Tenn.: Abingdon Press, 1959), p. 9.

found in his books. Yet, because Tittle's preaching has and will continue to be the subject of our examination, it would be repetitious to accord his books detailed separate treatment.

X

A final measure of Tittle's national stature is the fact that he was awarded the honorary degree of Doctor of Divinity by Ohio Wesleyan, Garrett, and Yale and the honorary degree of Doctor of Laws by Wittenberg. The tributes uttered at these occasions need not be quoted; they are, naturally, quite flattering.

It is not, however, extravagant to conclude that Tittle was one of the very few working ministers of his generation whose name was known and honored beyond the boundaries of his parish, city, and state.

12. *THE PASSING OF PROTESTANT AMERICA*

I

If life were logical, surely Ernest Fremont Tittle's life would be para-
digmatic of those citizens who called themselves proudly (and variously)
"pioneers," "patricians," "old-stock Americans," "true and good Americans" and who later in the twentieth century have been called in turn
(and invidiously) "WASPs." There is a certain irony in the fact that
only by the accident of birth was it possible for a man to claim the
former badge or to bear the later stigma. In the very transformation of
the old-stock Protestant from senior partner in the American enterprise
to the status of a defensive though vital copartner in a pluralistic society
much of the history of modern America is disclosed.

Tittle was, of course, a white man of pioneer Protestant ancestry
born in 1885 in that most American of towns, Springfield, Ohio. He was
a Methodist—and a Methodist preacher at that—and as presidents,
publicists, and scholars agree, if the United States has had an "all-
American church," it is the Methodist Church. Moreover, to the end of
his days he retained many of the old-fashioned manners and morals of
the McKinley era of his boyhood. In sum, his credentials as a WASP
are impeccable. At the best he logically would seem to incarnate mug-
wumpery; at the worst, nativism.

Logically, also, First Church, Evanston, would seem to be paradig-
matic of the "suburban captivity of the churches," an exclusive white-
collar and professional upper-middle-class congregation located in a snug,
green, quiet community; a sterile, narrow, insulated fellowship cut off
from the turbulent forces of urbanization, industrialization, immigration,

and integration reshaping American society; a fellowship finding refuge in its lovely Gothic sanctuary from the stormy facts of modern life. Though the factories and stockyards, bars and brothels of Chicago lay almost within walking distance of First Church, after five o'clock in the evening—when the men had returned from their offices and the women from their shopping—a curtain dropped between the city and the suburb.

"My country in 1900 is something totally different from my own country of 1860," lamented Henry Adams. "I am wholly a stranger in it." Had Adams been born in 1885, as was Tittle, and lived to 1949, his sense of estrangement might well have been even more complete, for by mid-century the old Protestant America had become as "obsolete as the side-wheel showboat, the cigar-store Indian, or the Fourth of July oration."[1] In this chapter it will be our purpose to examine how one old-stock Protestant responded to the erosion of the Protestant culture which seemed so securely triumphant in 1885 and how he reacted to those "new" citizens flooding the country who would (if they could) roughly retire the senior partners from the seats of power. And perhaps in our examination of this man, Ernest Tittle, we shall learn anew that logic may betray us if we assume some monolithic, deterministic response on the part of all older Americans to the new century. Perhaps, too, we shall comprehend that a suburban church's bondage to middle-class culture need not be total.

II

Historians at last have come to the realization that the prohibition movement sharply illuminates the stresses and struggles attending America's coming of age, and that in its larger outlines prohibition reflects and reveals the older Protestant America's hopes and fears, powers and weaknesses, for inextricably enmeshed in the battle over booze were issues of rural-urban strain, immigrant tension, Protestant-Catholic power, church-state relationship, economic and class divisions, New World–Old World mores and morals, and, indeed, anthropology, eschatology, and ecclesiology. And a few historians have come to understand the ambivalent nature of the movement.

For one thing, prohibition was an integral element in progressivism in general and the Social Gospel in particular, of the dream of a sweeter and fairer land, of the approximation of the Kingdom of God in history. With the exception of the Protestant Episcopal, all the churches that had

1. Martin E. Marty, *The New Shape of American Religion* (New York: Harper & Brothers, 1958), p. 72.

been permeated by the Social Gospel were also officially committed to prohibition. "Thus if one does not posit an element of left-wing, populistic, social-reform feeling in their prohibitionism," wrote Paul Carter, "one would have considerable difficulty in explaining how the Social Gospel could have arisen in these churches at all."[2] For another, not all prohibitionists were hatchet-faced, blue-nosed, sour-visaged, kill-joys weaned on grape juice and teethed on persimmons, or their wives mustachioed matrons who somehow attained formidable proportions on a diet of water-cress sandwiches and sugarless lemonade—old ladies of both sexes haunted, as Mencken sneered, by the fear that someone, somewhere might be happy. To be sure, some were indeed cranky professional moralists, village vigilantes, local busybodies, or prudish Pecksniffs who threw themselves into the crusade against "sin" to ease subjective psychic tensions, especially sexual tensions. But many also were warmhearted, sweet-tempered, joyous individuals who fought liquor, as the Northern Methodist bishops said, not because it had made men happy, but because it had made them unhappy. All that many of us need do is to glance across the room or down the corridor of memory to realize that the cartoon caricature of the fanatical dry is just that—a caricature far removed from the reality of loving and beloved human beings. Moreover, the greatest of the early twentieth-century Protestant prophets— Rauschenbusch, Gladden, North, and the rest—supported prohibition for the same reason they supported child-labor legislation, minimum-wage and maximum-hour laws, antilynching measures, and safety and sanitary codes. Liquor thwarted God's purposes for men. Scarred personalities, rotted bodies, wasted lives, blighted homes—how God must weep, they believed, to see this end to beings of eternal dignity and worth, created in His image and called to be His sons. Faithful to the injunction to be their brothers' brothers, they saw drinking as a fearful social evil, and like all reformers they saw no invasion of personal liberty in seeking to place the evil under state control. Paraphrasing Reinbold Niebuhr's famous aphorism, they held that man's capacity for virtue made prohibition possible, but his inclination to license made it necessary. Therefore, it is a blurring of reality to term prohibition, as Richard Hofstadter has done, a "ludicrous caricature of the reforming impulse, of the Yankee-Protestant notion that it is both possible and desirable to moralize private life through public action." It was, asserts Hofstadter, a

2. Paul A. Carter, *The Decline and Revival of the Social Gospel: Social and Political Liberalism in American Protestant Churches, 1920-1940* (Ithaca, N. Y.: Cornell University Press, 1956), p. 33.

"psuedo-reform, a pinched, parochial substitute for reform which had a widespread appeal to a certain type of crusading mind."[3]

Yet it is equally disturbing that three distinguished Methodist scholars could without qualification praise the movement as "the *characteristic* Methodist battle of the century, the one which most fully enlisted the interest and enthusiasm of the church and the one in which Methodism rendered one of its largest services to the nation."[4] Ironically, this admiring statement unconsciously reveals some of the flaws of prohibition.

In the first place, the Eighteenth Amendment seemed a stunning vindication of the conviction that what was good for evangelical Protestantism was good for the country and that Protestants still could count upon their historic position as the leaders of the nation. It was a reassuring sign that the United States was moving toward the Protestant vision of a redeemed society and that the reins of power and hence control of direction still remained in Protestant hands. In prohibition the Protestant ethos and the American creed met in prideful identification. But the pride was premature. Already historic processes were at work to bring about repeal. As the Eighteenth Amendment symbolized Protestant power, the Twenty-First Amendment signaled the emergence of a pluralistic society in which Catholics and Jews knew equal identification with the American Way of Life. The passing of Protestant domination carried inevitable tensions, but these tensions were exacerbated by the prohibition issue. The Drys were overwhelmingly evangelical Protestants, old-line Americans, farmers and villagers or solid middle-class city folk. The Wets, on the other hand, were mostly Catholics, Jews, secularists, of recent immigrant background, concentrated in the working-class districts of the great cities, joined by men of corporate power who feared prohibition would heighten both taxes and governmental authority and by libertarians disinclined to permit the state (or Bishop Cannon) to dictate their personal habits and by those who lived in the rarefied and exhilarating atmosphere of "high society." (And by those who simply liked to drink, a group difficult to pigeonhole and hence ignored by sociologists and historians.) As the Dry cause was symbolized by the sturdy Yankee yeoman in field or village green, unspoiled by the urban world, the Wet incubus was symbolized by the superstitious, sensual immigrant proletarian slouched in factory or saloon or confessional. As it

3. Richard Hofstadter, *The Age of Reform* (New York: Alfred A. Knopf, 1955), p. 287.
4. Halford E. Luccock, Paul Hutchinson, and Robert W. Goodloe, *The Story of Methodism*, 2nd ed. (Nashville, Tenn.: Abingdon Press, 1949), p. 465. Italics added.

happened, the noble experiment was launched when the tides of population, power, and prestige were running heavily to the city and its "new" immigrant inhabitants. The legislative superintendent of the Anti-Saloon League warned in 1917 that the Eighteenth Amendment had to pass before 1920, because "when 1920 comes and reapportionment is here, forty new wet Congressmen will come from the great wet centers with their rapidly increasing population."[5] In this sense, prohibition was enacted at the last possible moment in American history. In another sense, it was enacted too late to receive the overwhelming support necessary to enforcement. In any event, prohibition was the most divisive issue of the opening decades of the twentieth century, tearing still wider apart an already dangerously splintered people.

Furthermore, if the crusade was rooted in a humanitarian concern for the victims of drink, it was also tinged with unconscious anxiety, unlovely pride, and un-Christlike vindictiveness. The vocabulary of the crusaders was militant, even vicious. The Wet "monsters of iniquity" would be "crushed" by the Dry "soldiers of righteousness." The association of a hog was preferable to that of a winebibber. The legal poisoning of industrial alcohol with the foreknowledge that men would die from drinking it was defended, for such was the reasonable fate of "scofflaws." "I had to lie, bribe, and drink to put over prohibition in America," confessed William E. ("Pussyfoot") Johnson.[6] Indeed, not a few zealots succumbed to the rationalization of tarnished methods. When "extremism was hardly a possibility on this subject,"[7] then is it really surprising that extreme means were sometimes employed? It is unnecessary to comment on the dangerous pragmatism lurking in the advice of a 1908 Northern Methodist General Conference speaker: "Wisdom requires the adoption of a plan which will secure to that end [prohibition] the cooperation of every man who desires that thing, REGARDLESS OF WHAT HE THINKS ABOUT ANYTHING ELSE."[8] And a bishop boasted: "So intense is the conviction of the Methodist preacher concerning the rum abomination, and so susceptible is he to an emotional appeal, that the dullest official speech-maker, failing to arouse interest in behalf of his cause, is sure to turn aside temporarily to the temperance question, and seldom fails to start a tempest of enthusiasm which carries him

5. Quoted in Carter, *Decline and Rise of the Social Gospel,* p. 37.
6. Quoted in Virginius Dabney, *Dry Messiah: The Life of Bishop Cannon* (New York: Alfred A. Knopf, 1949), p. 136.
7. *The Daily Christian Advocate,* Methodist Episcopal Church, South, May 9, 1902, p. 6.
8. *The Daily Christian Advocate,* Methodist Episcopal Church, May 13, 1908, p. 4. Capitalization in original.

triumphantly across the barren spot in his discourse, and makes his effort a rhetorical success."[9]

These statements suggest the greatest flaw in the prohibition movement and the one wreaking the greatest harm to the Protestant churches, and especially Methodism. Originally an element in the social passion of idealists, it became for some the only component in social Christianity; it evolved from one worthy cause among many to *the* cause. To borrow an allusion from the free-silver movement, prohibition became a cowbird nudging other reforms from the Social Gospel nest. It is tragic that no other crusade, not even those to end poverty, war, or segregation, compelled such universal dedication from so many good Christians. Prohibition was a jealous mistress. It demanded total commitment. It tolerated no halfheartedness. It lured men away from other reforms. It involved ministers in dangerous political games, most notably in elections when the liquor question transcended all others.

The prohibition movement is an essential chapter in the passing of Protestant America. Methodism was clearly the leading denomination in the movement (this despite the claims made for the Baptists), and Northern Methodism was as deeply implicated as Southern Methodism[10] (though this is not generally realized). First Church was among the most prestigious Methodist parishes, and Evanston was the home of Frances E. Willard (a First Church member) and the national headquarters of the Woman's Christian Temperance Union. Thus Tittle's attitude toward liquor is a matter of moment.

In 1932 Tittle's old mentor Bishop William F. Anderson importuned him to comment critically on the draft of a speech. After accepting the assignment, Tittle replied: "I am inclined to think that you have devoted a disproportionate amount of space to a discussion of temperance and, further, that instead of giving it the climactic position in your discussion you should deal with it before you deal with industry and peace. This, of course, represents my own personal feeling of its relative importance and may not be in accord with the actual situation."[11] Here is the essence of Tittle's position. He practiced and preached abstinence, initially supported the Eighteenth Amendment, fought to keep Evanston dry after repeal, and in a host of ways sought to sweep back the flood of liquor engulfing the land. But he did not extol abstinence as the crown

9. *Ibid.,* May 11, 1916, p. 177.

10. For an elaboration of this point, see Robert Moats Miller, "Methodism and American Society, 1900-1939," in *The History of American Methodism,* 3 vols., ed. Emory Stevens Bucke (New York and Nashville, Tenn.: Abingdon Press, 1964), Vol. III, chap. xxxi.

11. Letter from Tittle to Bishop William F. Anderson, February 19, 1932.

of Christian virtues, he did not view drinking as the world's most dangerous social ill, he did not permit prohibition to become a surrogate for
broader reform, and he did not sanction the tarnished tactics of the
extremists, most notably certain Anti-Saloon League leaders.

Any boy who knows the repeated experience of searching saloons for
a missing father and then guiding the besotted parent home has existential knowledge that liquor is not life, but the enemy of life. Any boy
raised by a strict Methodist mother in Ohio in the late nineteenth century might well have believed that "God, Buffalo Bill, and Frances Willard were the three most wonderful people on the earth."[12] Tittle was
such a boy. Small wonder, then, that as a man and Methodist minister
he labored for an America unstained by alcohol.

For one thing, he occasionally (but only occasionally) referred to the
liquor question in sermons and on exceedingly rare instances he devoted
an entire sermon to it. One such sermon, preached in 1929, was also
delivered as a radio talk and printed in the newspapers, and he received
many letters praising him for presenting "the very best case for prohibition." It was in fact a dispassionate, logically compelling justification
of prohibition and a plea to all citizens that it "be given a sporting
chance to show what it can do."[13]

For another thing, as a key member of the Rock River Annual Conference he had a hand in drafting the reports of the Committee on
Public Policy terming the Eighteenth Amendment "one of the greatest
moral achievements of the American people."[14] Moreover, the reports of
the General Conference's Committee on the State of the Church under
Tittle's chairmanship contained strong and cogent arguments supporting
abstinence. At the 1944 North Central Jurisdictional Conference he
introduced a resolution to petition the president to free chaplains from
the duty of arranging for the provision of alcoholic beverages for men
in the service. And he personally wired the Senate Committee on Military Affairs urging that liquor be barred from all military camps.

From time to time he addressed local groups on the subject and on
at least one occasion he spoke before the ladies of the National WCTU
headquarters in Evanston. He was a member of the National Honorary
Committee of the National Temperance Education Fund. Undoubtedly
much closer to his heart was the work of Alcoholics Anonymous. He

12. "Frances Willard," typed MS, a sermon preached October 1, 1939.
13. *The Prohibition Problem,* a sermon preached January 13, 1929 (pamphlet). This sermon is also reprinted in *The Foolishness of Preaching* (New York:
Henry Holt & Co., 1930).
14. *Minutes* of the Rock River Annual Conference (1922), p. 69.

co-operated closely with the Evanston unit, advised troubled parishioners of its existence, attended meetings, and praised the group highly in sermons, observing that church members might well emulate the AA's spirit of concerned, selfless, sacrificial fellowship.[15]

"There is small likelihood that the Eighteenth Amendment will ever be repealed," Tittle predicted in 1929.[16] As the likelihood swiftly mounted in the following years, he did what he could. With other civic leaders, he addressed a mass meeting in Chicago's Orchestra Hall in the hope of persuading the Democratic Party to pledge support of the Eighteenth Amendment. He communicated his views to Congress: "Chiefly on economic grounds I am vigorously opposed to any attempt to repeal or seriously modify the Eighteenth Amendment. . . . I cannot see how money spent for light wines or beer would give to our people more money to spend for bread, and it is bread we desperately need."[17] He reminded his parishioners that the "law which decrees that if you get drunk on Saturday night you will have a fierce headache on Sunday morning never would be repealed."[18] And in his private letters he urged continued support of the noble experiment, though "with both more intelligence and more sincerity than have yet been displayed."[19]

After repeal, as Evanston's most respected citizen he probably was as responsible as any man for the continued exclusion of bars and liquor stores from the community. Repeatedly he reminded the voters: "Evanston need not choose between a legal saloon and an illegal speakeasy. There may be communities in which such a choice will have to be made. But Evanston is not one of them. Evanston could say, 'In this community there shall be neither saloons nor speakeasies,' and, having said it, Evanston could drive out the bootlegger whenever he appears. Why, then, should we tolerate a legal saloon?"[20] To this day, Evanstonians may not drink in public places.

Yet it is clear that growing numbers of citizens indulged in alcoholic beverages in their homes and in the clubs bordering Evanston. In 1945 Tittle received a communication from thirty-two First Church ladies "concerned about the growth of cocktail drinking among our church members" and petitioning him to preach on the subject. "We feel that silence just now is giving aid to the enemy and we unite in asking your

15. Author's interview with Mr. and Mrs. John M. Tittle, Winnetka, Ill., August 4, 1959; *A Mighty Fortress* (New York: Harper & Brothers, 1949), p. 32.
16. *The Prohibition Problem,* a sermon preached January 13, 1929 (pamphlet).
17. Letter from Tittle to the Honorable Carl Chindblom, December 21, 1932.
18. *Foolishness of Preaching,* p. 88.
19. Letter from Tittle to Evans A. Worthy, February 5, 1931.
20. *Evanston Review,* March 29, 1934, p. 4.

help to combat this evil."[21] And a year earlier Tittle had written a First Church parishioner, "I rejoice to know that you do not drink. I wish as much could be said of every other member of First Church."[22] There is every reason why staunch Methodist abstainers everywhere should feel apprehensive, for by mid-century 31.5 percent of American Methodists felt free to drink moderately without reference to religious scruples and only 8.8 percent believed it their Christian duty to work for prohibition.[23]

Despite his efforts, such was the zeal of the prohibitionists that Tittle was periodically charged with lack of enthusiasm for the Dry cause, a serious accusation in Methodist circles. On one instance he sharply spiked rumors that he and John Barleycorn were friends: "I must now . . . tell you that you are quite mistaken in your belief that I am not opposed to the liquor traffic. I am opposed to it, and always will be. I should be most happy to have you remember this if and when you undertake to represent my position on the subject."[24] On another instance, Tittle was more puzzled than pleased when after preaching a rare sermon on prohibition the congregation burst into applause. Although he always preached for a verdict, the applause on this one occasion alone suggested that his people felt more deeply about the horrors of alcohol than of war or poverty or segregation.[25]

Perhaps the professional prohibitionists judged Tittle rightly. In the 1920's the Official Board denied the First Church pulpit to Anti-Saloon League speakers because "of our present lack of confidence in the moral judgment and leadership of the Anti-Saloon League." In one case permission was granted but with the condition that Wayne B. Wheeler be the speaker.[26] Though Tittle supported the Eighteenth Amendment and though he believed it was not given a fair trial, he ultimately held that "the way to prohibit the use of intoxicating liquors is not everlastingly to call attention to the thing prohibited but rather to call attention to what would be the moral and economic gains of a nation whose brains were clear."[27] To this end, he argued for the reintroduction of temperance

21. Letter from Mary D. Schemmerhorn and thirty-one others to Tittle, dated only "1945."

22. Letter from Tittle to Oliver R. Aspegren, June 13, 1944.

23. Walter G. Muelder, *Methodism and Society in the Twentieth Century* (New York and Nashville, Tenn.: Abingdon Press, 1961), pp. 339ff.

24. Letter from Tittle to Oliver R. Aspegren, March 5, 1945.

25. Author's interview with Mrs. Bernice Wolseley, Evanston, Ill., July 13, 1960.

26. See Minutes of the Official Board, First Church, September 8, 1924, and November 7, 1927; letter from George D. Safford, state superintendent, Anti-Saloon League of Illinois, to Official Board, undated.

27. *On Getting Rid of Evil Spirits,* a sermon preached February 2, 1930 (pamphlet).

education in the public schools and in the home. He finally concluded that a determined local citizenry could protect its community from invasion by liquor irrespective of the fate of national prohibition by following the example of Evanston.[28]

Indulgence in alcoholic beverages was not the only diversion proscribed by American Methodism or elements of American Methodism. In addition to cigarette smoking, Coca-Cola guzzling, card-playing, and novel reading, a delegate to the 1900 General Conference offered the following admittedly incomplete list of sinful activities: dancing, opera, grand opera, living pictures, tableaux, charades, prize fights, bull fights, dog fights, cock fights, yachting, roller skating, football, baseball, curling, backgammon, billiards, checkers, chess, dice, croquet, polo, pool, golf, lawn tennis, cricket, one o'cat, shinney, la crossee, old sow, pillow, Denmark, blindman's buff, prison goal, tug of war, crokinole, matadore, raffling, crap shooting, pitching quoits, archery, ten pins, shuffle board, bicycling, grab-bags, basket ball, house ball, hand-up, baltie collie, crack about, over the barn, house over or hally over, corner ball, black-baby, marbles, the game of authors, and that dangerous game of chance of casting lots for seats of General Conference delegates.[29] Presumably the delegate was being facetious, but it is sobering to remember that at that very General Conference the question of amusements provided "The Hottest Contest of the Session," evoking "strong emotion," "earnest debate," "intense personal feeling," and a "veritable storm."[30] Indeed, throughout the span of Tittle's ministry the subjects of diversions, sexual morality, and the Christian Sabbath occupied a curious paramountcy in Methodist thought as an examination of the Methodist press, sermons, and General Conference and Annual Conference minutes makes appallingly clear. Where Wesley would have said, "The sanctified person will not indulge in such trifles," his followers in the United States tended by a slight but momentous inversion to say: "Those who avoid such things are the sanctified, and the only sanctified persons."[31]

Tittle was in many ways an old-fashioned man. He opposed Sunday theater going. He favored federal censorship of "obscene" motion pictures and literature. Narcotics and prostitution were to be placed under the ban of law. But he was also a great believer in wholesome recreation

28. For a fuller exposition of Methodism and Prohibition, see Miller, "Methodism and American Society."

29. *The Daily Christian Advocate,* Methodist Episcopal Church, May 28, 1900, p. 356. I have followed the original spelling.

30. *Ibid.,* p. 353.

31. Richard M. Cameron, *Methodism and Society in Historical Perspective* (New York and Nashville, Tenn.: Abingdon Press, 1961), p. 218.

for youth and under his leadership First Church broke with Methodist legalism, attempting to provide a program of play mediating between the old repressive order and the new hedonism. In this he was well in advance of the general line held by Methodism; whether he would have joined, had he lived, the fashionable clerical advocates of "situational ethics" is, however, doubtful. In any case, the passing of Protestant America may partially be traced through the changing amusement habits of the American people in the twentieth century. It is not necessary to defend the old blue laws in order to sense some dismay at the new dispensation.

III

Not all prohibitionists were members of the revived Ku Klux Klan, but most Klansmen claimed to be as dry as a powder flask, and the Klan movement, like the prohibition movement, is enormously revealing of the tensions attending America's entrance into the new century. The Klan of the 1920's is a study in anxiety rather than in abnormality. To dismiss these three, four, or five million hooded Americans as peculiarly depraved is to blink away the banality of evil. The Klan illuminates the need of mediocre men to flee to the mysticism of the primitive collectively as it also illuminates the persistency of dark strains in American history, strains that have been eased but never entirely erased by faithfulness to the countervailing ideals of decency and fair play. Fragmented and amorphous, really a congeries of many virtually autonomous local units, it was yet a fellowship of belief, knitted together by a shared anxiety about tomorrow and a shared longing for the return of yesterday. Perhaps, after all, there was only one great enemy: change. Made bewildered and fearful by the swift and surging forces reshaping "their" country, unwilling or unable to understand this strange, new century, men banded to offer resistance. Essentially, then, the Klan was a counterrevoluntionary movement. Its core appeal was to those Americans who, through considerations of rational self-interest or unconscious emotional needs, dreamed that the clock might be stopped, and who, as they donned their white dream robes, knew a momentary identification with a fanciful older and purer community. If spawned in Europe, this secret, hooded order would have carried the designation "fascist."

The older and purer community of the Klansman's dream was, of course, a white man's community in which the black man must be kept in his place, if necessary by digging his grave. The Klan's founder, Colonel William Joseph Simmons, was an Alabamian who with a band of Georgians on Thanksgiving night, 1915, ascended Stone Mountain near

Atlanta to call "from its slumber of half a century" that Invisible Empire which once had saved the prostrate South from "mongrelization." After repeatedly viewing (on salvaged passes) that tarnishd epic, *The Birth of a Nation*, Simmons decided to combat the pretentions of the "darkies" who were "getting pretty uppity." It is therefore not surprising that all prospective Knights vowed to "faithfully strive for the eternal maintenance of white supremacy." Nor is it a matter of astonishment that when Simmons was euchered from control, his successor, Hiram Wesley Evans, reaffirmed the ancient dogma that "God Almighty never intended social equality for Negro and white man," and who, with a coterie of Dallas disciples, implemented the Almighty's wishes by branding with acid the initials KKK across the forehead of a Negro bellhop.

If many Americans were made fearful by the rising tide of color, it is possible that an ever greater number sweated blood over the menace of Rome. The shadow of the Pope seemed even darker than that of the Negro, and anti-Catholicism is the key to the Klan's growth in the far West and Midwest and, though not initially, perhaps in the South as well. Although Colonel Simmons dreamed of resurrecting the Reconstruction Klan, he in fact touched to life two other resistance movements, the Know-Nothings of the 1840's and 1850's and the American Protective Association of the 1880's and 1890's. If the conquest of America by Rome seemed a frightening possibility to nineteenth-century Protestants, to their twentieth-century sons it was an imminent probability and, in the great northern cities, an actuality. The power, the prestige, the "arrogance" of Catholicism seemed everywhere evident in American life, and when Alfred Emanuel Smith made his first bid for the presidency in 1924, the last, worst fear of Protestants was at hand: the "Dago of the Tiber" (to borrow a Klansman's characterization of the Pope) would now take up residence on the Potomac. The Ohio Klan leader was expressing the conviction of millions who identified Americanism with Protestantism when he cried, "We want the country ruled by the sort of people who settled it. This is *our* country and we alone are responsible for it." Therefore the Klan attracted patriots as well as bigots, appealing to nationalist loyalties as well as to religious prejudices, men who took sincerely the pledge to the "Klan verse" of the New Testament: "I beseech you therefore, brethren, by the mercies of God, that ye present your bodies a living sacrifice, holy, acceptable unto God, which is your reasonable service." (Romans 12:1) The very name *Roman* Catholic Church was suggestive of sinister foreign influence, underscoring the essential Americanism of the Protestant denominations.

The very militancy of Catholicism transmuted Protestant tolerance from a virtue to a weakness. And the very authoritarianism of the Church of Rome sharpened the revelation of Protestantism's fragmentation, rendering efforts to quench the conflagration of Catholicism sweeping the land as feeble and ill-directed as the spray from a leaky hose. The Klan carried the hope of Protestant unity and the promise of Protestant militancy. At long last God-fearing men could know, as they assembled around the blazing hillside cross, identification with a mighty supradenominational movement. Like all crusaders, these Klansmen without conscious hypocrisy could cry, "For God and country," and in their righteousness sense no shame as they battled the enemies of their faith and nation. "I've attended a lot of church gatherings and conventions," remarked an Exalted Cyclops after the Klan's 1924 national convention, "but I never attended one where the revival spirit was as pronounced as it was at the Klan Klonvocation." It is crucial to understand, however, that the Protestant denominations did not call forth the Klan; rather the Klan sought desperately to become identified by Protestants as an ally, and it did so by tapping the historic anti-Catholic bias learned by Protestant children in cradle and conventicle and by exploiting the prideful Protestant assumption that they were the darlings of American history.

The Klan made the identification in many ways. Its symbol was a cross, and "The Old Rugged Cross" became almost the official hymn, sometimes with the alteration, "I will cherish the bright Fiery Cross. . . ." Its Kreed "reverentially" acknowledged the majesty of God. Its code of conduct was drawn from the Ten Commandments. The *Kloran* declared that "the living Christ is a Klansman's criterion of character," and Klan pamphlets bore such titles as "Christ and Other Klansmen." Every Klavern had a chaplain called a Kludd, who opened each meeting with a prayer and closed with a benediction. The fervent religiosity of the meeting reached a crescendo as the Knights gathered before the altar to sing the "Kloxology." And perhaps as they marched from the Klavern to burn a warning cross atop a nearby hill, their voices broke forth in the militant "Onward, Christian Soldiers." Perhaps, too, a few thoughtful members quieted their troubled consciences with the words from another much loved hymn, "God moves in mysterious ways, His wonders to proclaim."

The Klan also reflected the sense of estrangement felt by the older Americans as they witnessed "their" land being flooded by a sea of new immigrants. Historians of immigration make much of the shock of alienation experienced by the "uprooted" as they migrated from the womblike warmth and psychological security of their familiar European villages to the unknown New World. These insights are altogether valid, for the immigrant's ordeal was seldom physically easy and never emotionally trivial. The obverse side of the coin, however, has been turned by fewer students. How does one accustomed to power and prestige respond when strangers enter the land to dethrone him? The fact that the dethronement is only in the imagination does not lessen the fear. Between the year William McKinley enlisted as a private in the 23rd Ohio Volunteer Infantry in the Civil War and his assassination at the hands of a twenty-eight-year-old Polish-American with the "sinister" name of Czolgosz, fourteen million people came to the United States, "new" immigrants from Southern and Eastern Europe accounting for over 50 per cent of the total by 1900. In the opening fourteen years of the new century the torrent accelerated rather than slackened, an average of one million entering annually, and now the "new" immigrants accounted for 72 per cent. The impulse was temporarily stemmed by the war, but with the coming of peace it was renewed. From June, 1920, to June, 1921, more than 800,000 individuals entered, and consuls in Europe reported that additional millions were planning to leave. Then, in one of the most momentous enactments in American history, Congress virtually closed the gates, and the Statue of Liberty lost all relevance save for returning tourists and a handful of immigrants. (Probably the whole twenty-five year period after 1925 saw fewer immigrants to the United States than the single year 1907).

There was more than a casual relationship between this surge of immigration and the resurgence of the Ku Klux Klan. These "new" immigrants, these "beaten men of beaten races," these mongrel worshippers of Bacchus or Baal or Marx seemed no less threatening to the cherished America of yesteryear than insolent blacks and arrogant Romans. Colonel Simmons in explaining the growth of the Klan inquired: "What were the dangers which the white man saw threatening to crush and overwhelm Anglo-Saxon civilization? The dangers were in the tremendous influx of foreign immigration, tutored in alien dogmas and alien creeds, flowing in from all climes and slowly pushing the native-born white American population into the center of the country, there to be ultimately overwhelmed and smothered." The Colonel's successor, Evans, elaborated: "When the Klan first appeared the nation was in the confusion of sudden awakening from the lovely dream of the melting pot, disorganized and helpless before the invasion of aliens and alien ideas. After ten years of the Klan it arms for defense."

It is again necessary to insist on a hard point. As the Klan tapped rather than created Negrophobia and anti-Catholicism, so it did not so much inspire as reflect a pervasive Anglo-Saxon racism. The Klan can be understood only in the context of the tribalism of the times: the lynching of Leo Frank and the judicial execution of Sacco and Vanzetti; the subtle anti-Semitic discrimination instituted by Eastern clubs, resorts, and universities and the crude slanders leveled at Jews by Henry Ford; the superman notions of Jack London and the elitest concepts of Irving Babbitt; the "Yellow Peril" warnings of Homer Lea and the anti-Japanese practices of native Californians; the findings prideful to Anglo-Saxons and diminishing to other "races" of the army intelligence tests administered during the war and the conclusions implicit in "objective" sociological studies; and the consensus seemingly reached by geneticists such as Osborn, geographers such as Huntington, psychologists such as McDougall and a host of pseudoscholars such as Madison Grant that the American grain was being choked by alien chaff.

Moreover, following the First World War the stereotype of the immigrant radical knew its most tarnished hour. During the war all Americans, irrespective of race or religion or ethnic background, had rallied 'round the flag, save only for some socialists, Wobblies, and other elements of the left wing. Thus radicalism was equated with wartime treason, the dissenter identified with the Hun. Scarcely had the United States been saved, despite the radicals' fifth-column activities, than the menace of bolshevism appeared. And in America the advance agents of the Comintern were quite obviously aliens who somehow owed a double allegiance to Germany and Russia. Surely alien agitators were responsible for the massive labor unrest, the Seattle General Strike, the Boston Police Strike, the Great Steel Strike, and the thousands of additional strikes involving millions of workers in 1919 and 1920. Surely no true American laborer, unless deranged by bolshevik propaganda, would march in May Day parades or shout "to hell with the United States" or join the new Communist and Communist-Labor parties. And certainly only foreigners were capable of the bombings and attempted assassinations of public officials which seemed proof positive of a vast revolutionary conspiracy.

Such was the peril, it was not enough to bar future immigration or patiently instruct foreigners in the meaning of Americanism. Heroic surgery was immediately required to cut out the cancerous growth. The "Great Red Scare" was a time of unparralled intimidation, suppression, imprisonment, deportation—at the local, state, and federal level—because at no time in American history, either before or since, had the American people been seized by such a collective failure of nerve. It is therefore altogether fitting that the most feared nativist movement in American history, the revived Ku Klux Klan, should date its take-off point from the "Great Red Scare." The Klan never articulated an economic program and capitalism is not mentioned in its constitution, but it is evident that the Klan saw Americanism and radicalism in unreconcilable tension, and that at least some elements in the business community supported the order as an ally in the war against all forms of radicalism, including, as it happens, labor unions.

Still another color of the chameleon-like Klan was its moral authoritarianism, its vigilantism, and its sadism. In the 1920's a social and moral revolution, already apparent before the war, seemed to be dislocating the old nineteenth-century Victorian structure. The acids of modernity seemed to be dissolving the old verities of piety, patriotism, and moral purity and reverence for church, country, and home. To many Americans, this revolution was as menacing as the rising tide of Negroes, Catholics, aliens, and radicals. Indeed, the strangers in the land (together with the proverbially sexually depraved blacks) had introduced these evils into a formerly chaste society, and now, obviously, even the sons and daughters of frontier camp meetings were being infected. Although the evidence is fragmentary, it is quite possible that the majority of individuals flogged, tarred and feathered, branded, emasculated, and otherwise tortured and intimidated by the Klan were those who had in some way transgressed morally. In America vigilantism had an old and not always dishonorable tradition. It is, after all, as much a sign of a desire for law and order as it is a manifestation of lawlessness. Naturally the hooded Knights, who took as their motto "Not for self, but for others" regarded themselves as perfect knights, *sans peur et sans reproche*, and therefore the proper guardians of public virtue and private morality. "Perhaps, in the pageant of American history," suggested Professor John Higham, "the white-robed Klansman should stand in the place of Santayana's genteel New England as the Last Puritan."

Paradoxically, even as the Klan attracted men anxious to preserve the purity of America, it sucked into its membership thousands made desperately bored by the repressions of middle-class society. Ennui, intellectual sterility, cultural vacuity, stringent recreational restrictions, and muffled sexuality exacted a fearful psychic toll from those who had known the "good old days." The Klan was the circus coming to town. It was a revival conducted by Billy Sunday or Gipsy Smith. It was a scandal involving the preacher and the married organist. It was news that war had been declared. It was a lynching. It was Halloween and the Fourth of July and the county fair. A Klan newspaper appealed to prospective members with the banner: "Just to Pep up the Game. This Slow Life Is Killing Me." To countless men, citizenship in the Invisible Empire gave assurance that they were still alive. "It is," Jean-Paul Sartre reminds us, *"fun* to be an anti-Semite."

The Klan also embodied another characteristic that if not uniquely American is surely identified with the Yankee style: huckstering. In our more cynical moments the revived Klan's ancestors appear to be less convent-burning Know-Nothings, night-riding ex-Confederates, or bigoted soldiers in the army of the American Protective Association than the Connecticut peddlers of wooden nutmegs, the slippery Simon Suggs, who took as his motto, "It pays to be shifty in a new country," the outrageous P. T. Barnum, and the fatuous Colonel Beriah Sellers. And in these moments of disenchantment, the Klan seems appropriate to the mood of the 1920's less because it was a time of trouble than because it was the decade of Barton and Babbitt, Gantry and Coué. On reflection, these four men were themselves anxious and pitched their appeals to insecure people whether selling advertising or real estate, salvation or mental health, thus suggesting the many faces of anxiety. In any case, at least some Klan leaders in opening a promotional meeting might well have borrowed the salutation of the night club empresario Texas Guinan, "Hello, suckers!" At least some might have taken to their hearts the admonition of W. C. Fields, "Never give a sucker an even break." And others might have substituted for the motto, "Not for self, but for others," the warning, "Caveat emptor." Professing to do good, the Klan leaders did well—Simmons, Evans, Edward Young Clarke, Mrs. Elizabeth Tyler, David C. Stephenson, and the other prissy and profane, platitudinous and shrewd, gross and tough, scabrous and salacious leaders of the Klan. Luckily, unlike the fascist movements in Europe, the Klan threw up no charismatic Mussolini or Hitler.

Despite the charlatans at the helm, the Klan cannot be dismissed as some gigantic bunko game. Far from being a uniquely reprehensible episode in an otherwise sunny American pageant, it was the archetype of nativist themes flowing from the distant American past. Far from being an isolated, ugly phenomenon in an age of wonderful nonsense, it reflected the tensions of an age of revolution and embodied the anxieties of a people convulsed by change. Far from being a membership entirely of society's failures, it embraced many citizens who historically had enjoyed power and prestige, the prerogatives of the nation's older stock. The Klan may best be understood as a counterrevolutionary movement called into being by sober individuals to resist a world they neither made nor admired—nor understood. The Klan adopted as one of its mottos the command attributed to George Washington: "Put none but Americans on guard tonight!" Alas, Klansmen would not acknowledge—indeed, could not bear to acknowledge—that Negroes, Catholics, immigrants, radicals, internationalists, modernists, Sabbath desecraters, evolutionists, imbibers, and fornicators had any rightful claim to the coveted title "American."[32]

In attempting to assess Tittle's stand on the Klan, two things must be kept in mind. First, the Klan was not an official instrument of American Protestantism in the sense, say, that the Inquisition was of the Medieval Church. On the contrary, the national leadership of Protestantism, including many ministers of fame, denounced the hooded order, as did almost every national governing body of the major denominations and also the bulk of the religious press. Specifically regarding Methodism, the *Northwestern Christian Advocate* termed the Klan an abnormal and vicious organization. The Klan, according to the *New York Christian Advocate*, was neither Christian nor American. Ministers approached by the bed-sheeted knights with bribes of money should cry, "Thy money perish with thee." The editors considered "The K.K.K. No Per Cent American." It was a "group which hides its very face from the light of day, and pursues its ends by the method of the mask, the black hand, and the poison pen." The *Nashville Christian Advocate* devoted less space to the Klan, yet several contributors denounced the group, and the editors said: "We sincerely trust that there may be found in the South only a few who have any sympathy whatever with the revived Ku-Klux organizations." The *North Carolina Christian Advocate*, the *Western Christian Advocate*, the *Pacific Christian Advocate*, *Zion's Herald*, the *Epworth Herald*, and the *Social Service Bulletin* of the Methodist Federation for Social Service all warned against the Klan. The *Wesleyan Christian Advocate* could not believe that "any considerable number of our people will identify secret methods, sectionalism, partisanism, and racial hatred with American democracy," and admonished its readers to resist the "Un-American and undemocratic order." Even the conservative *Arkansas Methodist*, while not always disapproving of the Klan's aims, condemned its methods as dangerous, saying, "Let us have none of it." A rather close examination does not reveal a single endorsement of the Klan in Methodist journals. More-

32. For an elaboration of my views on the revived Klan, see my essay, "The Ku Klux Klan," in *Change and Continuity in Twentieth-Century America: The 1920's,* ed. John Braeman, Robert H. Bremner, and David Brody (Columbus: Ohio State University Press, 1968), pp. 215-55.

over, the Northern General Conference and the Social Service Commission of Southern Methodism condemned the masked and hooded society. Among Methodist leaders who forcefully took the measure of the Klan in unmeasured terms were Ralph Sockman, Lynn Harold Hough, Rodney Roundy, Ralph B. Urmay, Harry F. Ward, and Bishops William Anderson, Luther Wilson, William McMurray, Francis J. McConnell, Edwin Mouzon, William Thirkield, and Edwin Holt Hughes. In some cases, such as that of Bishop McMurray, this meant an exchange of physical blows.

A second point to keep in mind is that although it took courage for a bishop or metropolitan pastor to oppose the Klan, the true heroes of the Klan war were unremembered, obscure rural and village parsons, for it was they who faced the greatest pressure and, in fact, physical danger. A Methodist preacher in Kentucky spoke for many when he wrote a friend in Texas: "I have been minister and teacher for more than 40 years, and have always opposed all such organizations whose slogan was 'to hate somebody.' I shall not approve such, nor meddling in my church affairs, whether they want me to persecute Jews and Catholics, or whether they ask me to fight Swedes and Baptists." This same minister received a letter from a colleague in Kansas who, after describing a flogging by the Klan, affirmed: "Such things make my blood boil. Many good men have been drawn into this movement; but I am no prophet if within the next year or so they do not repent in dust and ashes. They have not publicly presented me with a purse of money, nor *will* they do so." But not every Methodist parson possessed this courage or understanding. Unhappily, it is a fair guess that hundreds of Methodist ministers and thousands of Methodist laymen actively joined the Klan or gave it their tacit support; and additional thousands were placed under extreme pressure to do so.[33]

In 1930 Tittle recalled, "A few years ago, when I was leaving a meeting where I had vigorously denounced that ill-conceived organization known as the Ku Klux Klan, I was accosted by three of its enthusiastic members who were not unnaturally indignant at what I said. They proceeded to inform me that every week no less than thirty-five thousand men were joining the Klan and that nothing could stay its triumphant advance, certainly nothing so feeble as the piffling speech

33. For an elaboration of my views on the relationship between Methodism and the Klan (and also for documentation) see "A Note on the Relationship Between the Protestant Churches and the Revived Ku Klux Klan," *Journal of Southern History*, XXII (August, 1956) and *American Protestantism and Social Issues, 1919-1939* (Chapel Hill: The University of North Carolina Press, 1958), chap. x.

which I had just made. But these enthusiastic Klansmen apparently spoke in utter ignorance of the final fate of two similar movements [the Know-Nothing Party and the American Protective Association]."[34] Perhaps Tittle knew all along that the Klan would hang itself, but in the early twenties he must have experienced moments of doubt. "Not long ago," he reported in 1924, "I repeated the deservedly famous story of the merchant who hung out a sign reading, 'I am a One Hundred Per Cent American: I hate Jews, Catholics, negroes, and foreigners'; whereupon his competitor across the street hung out a sign reading, 'I am a Two Hundred Per Cent American: I hate everybody.' At the close of the meeting, an ardent member of the local Ku Klux Klan came forward and warmly congratulated me!" Tittle ruefully confessed that apparently he had not gotten his point across.[35]

To my knowledge, Tittle never devoted an entire sermon to the Klan, but from time to time in his preaching he did refer to its "brutal absurdities." And in an article in the *Epworth Herald* he warned against the issuing "from the womb of illiterate prejudice that hideous caricature of true Americanism, the Ku Klux Klan, with its ignorant and ferocious hatred of the Catholic, the Jew, the Negro, and the foreign-born."[36]

Unquestionably Tittle's most bruising encounters with Klansmen or at least Klan supporters occurred at the annual meetings of the Rock River Conference early in the decade. Unlike the *Daily Christian Advocates* covering the sessions of the General Conferences, the journals of the Annual Conferences do not carry the debates; therefore, it is largely through the newspapers that we learn that the Klan was the subject of "prolonged and spirited discussion" at the Rock River meetings. In 1922 Tittle's Public Policy Committee reported, "We view with intense disapproval any such organization as the Ku Klux Klan, with its masked irresponsibility, and its spirit of intolerance in relation to certain religious, social and cultural groups."[37] But by a vote of 119 to 41 the delegates expunged from the record this condemnation.[38] Tittle's final report, however, did condemn lynching, endorse federal antilynching

34. *Living in History,* a sermon preached May 11, 1930 (pamphlet).

35. A commencement address delivered to the graduates of the Northwestern School of Speech, June, 1924, reprinted in Alan H. Monroe, *Principles and Types of Speech* (New York: Scott, Foresman & Company, 1935), p. 230.

36. *Epworth Herald,* XXXIII (September 30, 1922), 6-7.

37. *Ibid.* (October 21, 1922), 1006.

38. *Shrevesport Times,* October 10, 1922, clipping in files of American Civil Liberties Union (Box 204). When I examined the files of the Union they were then on deposit in the New York Public Library. They are now at Princeton University.

legislation, and warn Methodists to shun groups preaching intolerance and suspicion toward people of other races or religions and who in the name of patriotism take the law into their own hands.[39]

The following year Tittle led the anti-Klan forces in a two-hour debate. "The arguments of those who favor the Ku Klux Klan," said Tittle, "seem to be about this: The Knights of Columbus have done certain things we do not like, therefore, organize the Ku Klux Klan. This is the doctrine of an eye for an eye, and a tooth for a tooth. To fight fire with fire is to produce a conflagration." The Klan endorsers advanced many appeals, most notably: "The Ku Klux Klan exists because public officials have failed to do their duty. If you condemn the Klan you are condemning some of the noblest men in this country and among them many of your own ministers."[40] Ultimately two sections of Tittle's Public Policy Committee report were deleted. But two relevant statements remained: *"We cannot look with favor upon any effort to enforce law and execute justice either by individual action or through organizations which ignore the constituted authorities and the regular channels of law enforcement."* And: *"Appeals to racial and religious prejudices and hatreds merit the condemnation of all honest and righteous men.* When made in a country which, like the United States, possesses millions of people of many diverse lands and races not yet welded into national homogeneity, who must live and work together, such accusations become the most dangerous form of treason. Whoever propagates in this country antagonism to any race or creed represented in our citizenship whether it be against Jews, Poles, Germans, Japanese, Chinese or Negroes, or against Judaism, Catholicsm or Protestantism *assails the very foundation of our most cherished and characteristic American institutions."*[41]

The Klan issue also proved divisive at the 1924 Rock River meeting, but by 1925 the debate was muted. In that year the hooded movement crested and soon membership began melting away like butter on hot cakes. There are many reasons for this rapid disintegration, not the least being that official American Protestantism with increasing firmness rejected the Klan's representation of itself as a great, militant, supra-denominational Protestant army. It is impossible to credit any one Protestant leader with rolling back this tide of intolerance. It is permissible to conclude that Ernest Fremont Tittle, fearing as always God

39. *Minutes* of the Rock River Annual Conference (1922), p. 71.
40. *Evanston News-Index,* October 9, 1923, p. 2.
41. *Minutes* of the Rock River Annual Conference (1923), pp. 66, 70. Italics in original.

and not men, did what he could to thwart the most powerful and dangerous nativist movement in American history.

Shadows just as dark, if not so lengthened, were also cast by a host of apostles of discord in the 1930's. The Black Legion, the Silver Shirt Legion of America, the Christian Frontists and the Christian Mobilizers were only a few of those groups professing in the name of piety (and with the exception of Father Charles Coughlin's followers, Protestant piety) and patriotism to save America from atheistic-communistic-Jewish subversion. Tittle's friend, Halford E. Luccock, punctured the pretentions of the patriots in one withering sentence: "Any American who can't be patriotic until he has paid ten dollars to a gabby racketeer and put on a trick shirt couldn't save a wide place in the road from an invasion of domestic ducks."[42] Again, Tittle did what was necessary and within his power in sermon, report, letter and petition to sound the alarm.[43] As we know, however, he himself faced the severest assaults not from such tub-thumpers of hate as Gerald Winrod, Gerald L. K. Smith, William Dudley Pelley, and Fritz Kuhn, but from such respectable societies as the American Legion and the Daughters of the American Revolution and from local patriotic bands composed not only of the Elizabeth Dillings, but also of solid North Shore citizens, including a few First Church pillars.

IV

Though some prohibitionists were Kluxers and most Klansmen claimed to be enemies of alcohol, the two movements were by no means identical; and though virtually all Klansmen—aside from the obvious charlatans—were Fundamentalist in their religious beliefs, not all Fundamentalists were Klan members, and it is erroneous to equate the two. Recent scholarship sees the Fundamentalist movement as very complex, many-sided, and not totally discreditable—a movement that cannot in fairness be symbolized by the Dayton "Monkey Trial" of 1925. Indeed, scholars now picture the Fundamentalists as sincere, courageous, not infrequently intelligent Christians, resisting in the name of "the faith once delivered to the saints" the new gods of scientism and secularism which ultimately left modern man shelterless. Nevertheless, in my judgment, the Ku Klux Klan–Fundamentalist syndrome is one that withstands the most sophisticated demythologizing. Most Fundamentalists and most Klansmen were mated in their anti-intellectualism, their mor-

42. *Northwestern Christian Advocate,* LXXXI (November 9, 1933), 1060.
43. See, for example, the American Civil Liberties Union *Bulletin,* June 17, 1936.

bid compulsion to suppress that which they could not understand, their resistance to economic and social reform, and their fear of the future. One may acknowledge that the Fundamentalists were men of unquestioning faith, utter conviction, total commitment, and self-sacrificial spirit. But it is one thing to recognize that they were not (and are not) villians, and another to see them as they saw themselves—the only true defenders of the faith.

In any case, the Fundamentalist movement and the ancillary anti-evolution crusade is still another revelation of the agony endured by older Protestant Americans in passing from the nineteenth to the twentieth century. Tittle was deeply implicated in this bitter, internecine Fundamentalist-Modernist war, as we shall see in a later chapter. Here it is necessary only to remember that it is a major chapter in the story of the "passing of Protestant America."

V

The presidential election of 1928 between Governor Alfred Emanuel Smith of New York and Herbert Hoover is also both symbol and watershed of a changing America. In that year and in that election all the tensions between the Wet, urban, Catholic "new"-stock America and Dry, rural, village, and suburb, Protestant, old-stock America came to a head. Al Smith was a test case of how far an Irish Catholic city boy of recent immigrant background could go, and how soon.

The 1928 campaign was foreshadowed at the 1924 Democratic Convention assembled at Madison Square Garden. There in the midst of a withering heat wave the delegates battled for seventeen days before they could agree on a platform and a candidate. There the lines were drawn between the older and newer America. The Texas delegates had to be dissuaded from burning a firey cross while, on the other hand, the Tammany Hall braves booed and shouted down southern and western speakers. So closely was the convention divided that a resolution to censure the Klan by name in the Democratic platform was defeated after acrimonious debate by a vote of 543 and 3/20ths to 542 and 3/20ths. The convention also divided on a candidate, William G. McAdoo, Wilson's son-in-law, being the choice of the South and West and Smith being the urban and eastern hero. After nine hot days of deadlock the favorites withdrew by agreement and a compromise darkhouse, John W. Davis, was nominated on the 103rd ballot. In November, of course, Calvin Coolidge, the Republican candidate, swept the country with fifteen million votes; Davis was second with the unbelievably low total of eight million; and Robert M. LaFollette, running on the Progressive ticket, trailed with less than five million votes. It was clear that many of Smith's followers boycotted the polls, refusing to vote because their champion had been repudiated. It was also clear that Smith could not be denied the Democratic nomination in 1928.

Protestantism's most dangerous and misguided commitment to damming the tides running against its historic domination in America came in 1928. Methodism (to confine our attention to Tittle's denomination) for the only time in the twentieth century officially, openly, and unequivocally committed itself to the defeat of a presidential candidate. Both the Northern and Southern General Conferences specifically served notice that they would fight any candidate whose record and attitude were hostile to prohibition—and that meant Smith. Methodist agencies and leaders actively entered the campaign. In mid-July, 1928, Bishop James Cannon, Jr., was elected chairman of the anti-Smith Democrats at a conference of Drys from every southern state held at Asheville, North Carolina. A week later three other Southern Methodist bishops— Edwin D. Mouzon, John M. Moore, and Horace M. Du Bose—joined Cannon in issuing a signed statement affirming their intention to wage a militant fight against Smith on the grounds that America should not elect (to quote Cannon) a "wet cocktail President." These "Four Horsemen of the Apocalypse" (again to use Cannon's phrasing) rode through the South carrying the alarm. Although Bishop Warren A. Candler (a conservative who opposed the church taking a stand on any social, economic, racial, or political issue) and Bishop Collins Denny and eighty-three Southern Methodist laymen decried the "dragging of our beloved church into politics," the Cannon forces prevailed. Without exception the Southern Methodist press supported Hoover, and according to Bishop Du Bose, out of 8,500 Southern Methodist preachers, only 4 failed to do so. Though Du Bose's figure is beyond proof, all authorities agree that Southern Methodism was overwhelmingly against Smith and several scholars credit (if such is the word) Bishop Cannon as the man most responsible for enabling Hoover to crack the "Solid South."

Northern Methodism was not less militant, a fact not always recognized. The General Conferences of 1924 and 1928 were blunt in their utterances. The Board of Temperance, Prohibition and Public Morals did yeoman work in opposing the Wet candidate. Without exception the Northern Methodist press also opposed Smith, including the *Northwestern Christian Advocate* in Tittle's area and *Zion's Herald,* the most liberal Methodist journal. Bishop Cannon could warn Southern Methodist Democrats not to support Smith because "the Scriptures positively forbid the working together of an ox and an ass," but Bishop Francis J.

McConnell, without employing similar terminology, was equally emphatic in his warnings to the Northern clergy.

Methodists avowed that they entered the political arena because the fate of the "noble experiment" hung in the balance. It is not necessary to take a cynical view of this explanation, to hold that prohibition was a mask for religious bigotry, as many commentators have done. As we have seen, many Methodists sincerely believed the crusade to free America from the bondage of liquor was the greatest moral issue facing the nation. It is hardly to be expected, then, that men and women who had devoted a lifetime to fighting the liquor traffic, who saw in the Eighteenth Amendment the greatest victory over evil since the abolition of slavery, would remain indifferent when that victory was jeopardized. In this connection it is significant that many Methodist spokesmen pubicly stated they found no objection to the Democrats' nominating Senator Thomas J. Walsh of Montana, a Roman Catholic but also a Dry. Though loyalty to prohibition explains in large measure Methodist intervention in the election of 1928, it does not justify such political action. Rather, it simply underscores a point made earlier: Methodist prohibitionists permitted this single question to override all others and in their zeal they engaged in imprudent tactics—tactics extremely damaging to the good name of the Church.

Moreover, the evidence that Methodists attacked Smith not solely because he was a Wet, but also because he was one of the "new" Americans, a stranger in the land owing primary allegiance to alien popes and alien ideas, is damaging. In 1928 many Methodists were simply unable to bring themselves to vote for a Roman Catholic, an Irishman at that, who had spent his boyhood on the sidewalks of New York.

Smith symbolized the world of Jimmy Walker and jazz, Al Jolson and Al Capone, cabarets and call girls, beer halls and Tammany Hall. Smith had not been born in a log cabin and to his great credit he did not pretend that he had, faking folksy rural mannerisms. His spats, brown derby, cigars, accent, and even his theme song, "The Sidewalks of New York," marked him as an outlander. As Walter Lippmann observed, "Quite apart even from the severe opposition of the prohibitionists, the objection to Tammany, the sectional objection to New York, there is an opposition to Smith which is as authentic, and, it seems to me, as poignant as his support. It is inspired by the feeling that the clamorous life of the city should not be acknowledged as the American ideal."

Moreover, Smith was seen as the champion of the immigrant, of the Jew, and indeed (without much justification) of the Negro. His election would encourage "mongrelization" and miscegenation. George Fort Milton, Tennessee editor and historian, wrote that Smith's appeal was to "the aliens, who feel that the older America, the America of the Anglo-Saxon stock, is a hateful thing which must be overturned and humiliated; to the northern negroes, who lust for social equality and racial dominance; to the Catholics who have been made to believe that they are entitled to the White House, and to the Jews who likewise are to be instilled with the feeling that this is the time for God's chosen people to chastise America. . . . As great as have been my doubts about Hoover, he is sprung from American soil and stock."

Finally, Smith was a Roman Catholic. Many Methodists apparently believed with Philip Guedalla that any stigma would do to beat a dogma and the old pious pornography of the Know-Nothing era was revived in a scurrilous whispering campaign. Many Methodists, too, stated in a frank and open fashion their objective reservations about elevating a Catholic to the presidency, honestly believing there was an irreconcilable difference between the authoritarian Church of Rome and American democratic institutions; and it may be bluntly stated that such an opinion was more tenable in the days of Pope Pious XI than in the era of Pope John XXIII—and his successors, it is hoped.

Though victory was claimed by the anti-Smith forces, the election of 1928 was the Indian summer of Anglo-Saxon, Protestant, town-and-country domination in the United States. Within five years prohibition was repealed and within less than thirty-five years an Irish Catholic resided in the White House. In the free and fluid society of America, it was not intolerably long, at least by historic, comparative standards, before the "beaten men of beaten races" emerged as fully equal citizens in a land where only recently their fathers had been strangers.[44]

In 1928 Tittle voted for Norman Thomas.[45] There is nothing in the record to show that he joined the crusade against Smith. It is a measure of his courage and common sense and sense of perspective that he refused to march with his Methodist brethren—or with his parishioners

44. For an elaboration of my views on the relationship between Methodism and the election of 1928 (and also for documentation), see "A Footnote to the Role of the Protestant Churches in the Election of 1928," *Church History, XXV* (June, 1956) and *American Protestantism and Social Issues*, chap. iv.

45. In a letter to Quentin Ogren, November 15, 1932, Tittle wrote: "Dear Comrade: You are right! I voted for Norman Thomas both in 1932 and 1928." Incidentally, the Report of the Public Policy Committee of the Rock River Annual Conference in 1928 opposed Smith, but in that year Tittle was not a member of the committee. *Minutes* of the Rock River Annual Conference (1928), p. 60.

and fellow citizens, for in Evanston, a solidly Republican community in any case, Hoover rolled up a more than four-to-one margin over his opponent.[46]

VI

"If the Jew did not exist, the anti-Semite would invent him."[47] In this sentence Sartre capsules the findings of those scholars, especially social psychologists, who discern the roots of bigotry in the bigot himself, in the structure of his "authoritarian personality." In this view, anti-Semitism fulfills a generic need to hate. It will manifest itself as long as men burdened with irrational anxieties passionately seek scapegoats to explain their own sense of failure. Other scholars, mostly, as it happens, historians, are inclined to interpret group prejudices as functions of specific conflicts, rooted in particular historical situations; that is, the objective conditions in American culture at a given moment provide a more meaningful explanation of anti-Semitism in the United States than the subjective pathology of the anti-Semite. "Thus," writes Professor John Higham, "the problem of anti-Semitism in America ultimately needs to be viewed in relation to mass immigration."[48] It was part of the responsive pattern of older Americans to the difficulties of integrating large numbers of first- and second-generation immigrants and differed only in degree from the reception accorded Irish, Italians, Japanese, Mexicans, and other transplanted minorities. This explains why the "Jewish question" was virtually invisible in early America and why in recent years anti-Semitism in all its forms has massively declined in the United States. In the thirty-five years prior to World War I, however, some two million Jews entered the country from Europe—an exodus then paralleled only by the great dispersion following the destruction of Jerusalem by Rome. Partly because they were often "foreign" in manner and appearance, partly because their hard-driving pursuit of economic and social advancement made their foreignness especially salient, they encountered discrimination and prejudice. Anti-Semitism in the United States, therefore, knew its most virulent and vicious hour in the last decades of the nineteenth and opening decades of the twentieth centuries, a time when millions of strangers were entering the land—and none seemed more strange in the eyes of the older Americans

46. *Evanston Review,* November 8, 1928, p. 1.
47. Jean-Paul Sartre, *Anti-Semite and Jew* (New York: Shocken Books, paperback edition, 1965), p. 13.
48. John Higham, "American Anti-Semitism Historically Reconsidered," in *Jews in the Mind of America,* ed. Charles Herbert Stember *et al.* (New York and London: Basic Books, 1966), p. 251.

than the Jews, especially those from Eastern Europe. Probably Higham is right in viewing anti-Semitism in America as a consequence of mass migration and its attendant tensions. Probably Will Herberg is right in conceiving of America at mid-century as one great community divided into three great subcommunities religiously defined—Protestant, Catholic, Jew—all equally American in their identification with the American Way of Life. But one is haunted by Sartre's warning that anti-Semitism is not an "opinion," it is a *passion*. And passion long repressed may suddenly break forth in violent form or manifest itself in ugly disguises.

If by some black miracle anti-Semitism in America had not ebbed but rather had mounted to a monstrous climax of pogroms and genocide, we may be as certain as the rising of the morning sun that Ernest Tittle would have gone to his death with the Jews. It is unthinkable that he would have accepted any fate other than that of Dietrich Bonhoeffer in Nazi Germany. Though never confronted with the ultimate decision, Tittle as a faithful minister of Jesus Christ did what he could to atone for the centuries of persecution inflicted on Jews "all in the name of Christ."

For one thing, not infrequently the rabbi of a neighboring Jewish congregation in Chicago to the south or Glencoe to the north was invited to occupy the First Church pulpit on Sunday morning, and Jewish speakers also addressed various First Church study groups. On occasion, the young people of the church would gather for fellowship with Jewish youngsters. In 1931 the Official Board extended an invitation to the Jewish students of Northwestern, then having no suitable place for their own, to freely use the facilities of First Church.[49] For his part, Tittle occasionally spoke before Jewish congregations, such as North Shore Congregation Israel in Glencoe.

For another thing, Tittle was on warm terms with Jewish leaders in the area. After a dreadful act of vandalism, he wrote Dr. Charles E. Shulman, rabbi of North Shore Congregation Israel, "I want to express my grief and shame over the defacement of your Temple. I am ashamed because this was the act of a Gentile, and I am grieved because it has hurt you and your dear people. I can but pledge you to do all I can to fight anti-Semitism and to develop the spirit of brotherhood, without which we are all destined to perish."[50] At the time of his death, Tittle was paid this tribute by Dr. Morton M. Berman, president of the Chicago Rabbinical Association: "The passing of Dr. Tittle comes as a great shock to all who respected him for his magnificent, selfless devo-

49. Minutes of the Official Board, First Church, April 6, 1931.
50. Letter from Tittle to Charles E. Shulman, July 12, 1946.

tion to every humanitarian cause."[51] And Rabbi Edgar E. Siskin of Glencoe declared: "Men of all faiths will miss his comradeship, his understanding, his brotherliness. The community, the nation, the world of spiritually like-minded men and women are infinitely the poorer for his passing. We had much need of him. Four Sundays ago, I came to the First Methodist church in order to participate in one of those services which his presence made such a thrilling experience. He preached on humility that morning. The message remains with me as a choice possession. It comforts me to know that I had the privilege of hearing his prophetic words before his eyes were closed in eternal sleep."[52]

Then too, at the Rock River, North Central Jurisdictional, and General conferences Tittle had a hand in drafting and defending innumerable reports and resolutions placing Methodism on record in its utter condemnation of anti-Semitism.

He was also involved in several organizations designed to combat prejudice. He was one of the founders and first chairman of the Chicago Council Against Racial and Religious Discrimination. He was one of the founders and first chairman of the North Shore Fellowship of Faith (Rabbi Shulman was vice-chairman), the first meeting of the group taking place in First Church. And he was much concerned with the work of the National Conference of Christians and Jews, participating in and speaking before its regional conference.

As early as 1933 he signed a petition protesting the Jewish persecutions in Germany.[53] He also protested the holding of the 1936 Olympics in Berlin. More significantly, in Annual, Jurisdictional, and General Conferences he urged the lifting of restriction barriers so as to permit the victims of Hitler's wrath to find asylum in America. In the teeth of the Second World War he wrote in contrition to a rabbi, stating "that the fate of Jews in Europe is a matter of the gravest concern to all mankind. Something must be done to relieve their desperate plight. We owe it to ourselves as well as to them to take immediate steps for their relief. Failure to do so would be for us an everlasting disgrace." The very least we can do, he closed, is to "make provision for the bringing to this country of large numbers of Jewish children."[54] In fact, Tittle repeatedly argued that more displaced persons be admitted to the United States.[55] In 1947 he advocated that Americans do more for the harried

51. *Chicago Sun-Times,* August 4, 1949, clipping in Tittle Collection.
52. *Evanston Review,* August 18, 1949, clipping in Tittle Collection.
53. *New York Times,* May 26, 1933, p. 13.
54. Letter from Tittle to Rabbi George Fox, April 6, 1943.
55. See "The Christian Man in an Unchristian World," typed MS, a sermon preached July 13, 1947.

Jews than to tell the Arabs and the British that they should immediately make room for them in little Palestine.[56] These may strike us as modest proposals until we recall that in 1943, eight out of ten Americans were opposed to increasing immigration quotas for political refugees from Germany, Austria, and other countries that had come under Nazi rule.[57]

Finally, in sermon after sermon Tittle returned to the theme of racial pride in general and anti-Semitism in particular, referring to "the curious mentality of those superpatriotic wearers of shirts, brown and silver, who appear to think that the Almighty had a special fondness for Gentiles, a special dislike of Jews, notwithstanding the fact that according to a generally accepted report the saviour of the world was a Jew."[58] With withering satire and a cool marshaling of the evidence of science, in a famous early sermon entitled "The Modern Jonah" Tittle harpooned the racists. God cares for the Jew and foreign-born and yellow man, and the brown, and the black, he said: "The love of God is broader than the measure of prejudiced people's minds. The concern of God reaches farther than hooded klansmen suppose."[59] He once informed an audience of students that "Christians may be very sure that anti-Semitism is an 'abomination' unto God." To "be despised, snubbed, and excluded for no reason at all except the fact that one belongs to a race that has produced Isaiah, Spinoza, and Einstein—such is the present fate of many a high-grade and sensitive person in a world that is torn by prejudices that are as irrational as they are cruel." But lest the undergraduates assume that Tittle is referring only to the situation in Nazi Germany, they might reflect upon the social situation that obtains on their own campus. For example, do they know of any "Christian" Greek-letter fraternity that has ever invited a Jewish student to join it?[60]

At the beginning of his Evanston ministry Tittle, having in mind the myriad Americans troubled by the influx of immigrant Jews, wrote an article entitled "What If Abraham Had Been Abraham Levinsky?" asking if he too would be excluded from our shores.[61] Near the end of Tittle's life he preached a famous sermon entitled "All God's Children," concluding: "We Americans, just for the reason that we are not a homogeneous people but a vast mixture of races, nationalities and creeds, now have an opportunity to do something creative and redemptive. We

56. *Ways to Peace,* a sermon preached November 9, 1947 (pamphlet).

57. Stember, *Jews in the Mind of America,* p. 9.

58. "Ridicule and Reverence," typed MS, a sermon preached June 24, 1934.

59. Reprinted in *Foolishness of Preaching,* chap. xiii.

60. *Christians in an Unchristian Society* (New York: Association Press, 1940), pp. 19-20.

61. *Epworth Herald* (December 24, 1921), p. 1269.

cannot prevent the spread of communism or totalitarianism by bitter denunciation, or by economic or military threat. We cannot force democracy on Russia or China or any other people. But this we can do: Among ourselves and before all the world, we can demonstrate that democracy is a workable idea—a democracy that knows no distinction of race, creed, color or national origin; that holds all human beings in respect and seeks for all the opportunity of a good life. Let us do that, and we shall make a very great contribution to the cause of human freedom and of world order and peace."[62] In yet another sermon Tittle bitterly observed that even after the Nazi terror had decimated European Jewry, there could be seen in America signs before hotels and resorts bearing the noxious words, "Christian Establishment." And though the United States urged the Arabs and English to admit homeless Jews into Palestine, America itself saw fit to open its doors to only "a mere handful of these desperate people. More than one nation today must confess cencerning the Jew: 'He is wounded for our transgressions.' "[63]

VII

For one year only, 1899, the federal immigration authorities compiled a record of the religious affiliation of immigrants. Protestants numbered 18.5 percent of the total and Roman Catholics 52.1 percent. If this year was typical, it is little wonder that the Roman Catholic Church gained in membership 114.1 percent from 1890 to 1916, and that in 1920 there were almost eighteen million baptized members; that is, every sixth American and every third church member was a Roman Catholic. Anti-Catholicism has been a persistent theme in the history of American nativism, in fact it has been termed the anti-Semitism of nineteenth-century America. Protestant-Catholic tensions continued into the twentieth century, both sides displaying much bigotry, but more significantly, both sides being honestly concerned about objective differences of belief and public policy. To dismiss religious conflict in modern America as sheer intolerance is a fancy of secularists which no devout Protestant, however irenic, would accept, and no loyal Catholic either, if he were candid. As a Protestant minister, Tittle doubtless heard many false and ugly charges hurled at Catholicism. As a citizen of the Chicago area, he was not left in doubt as to the zeal and power of the Catholic

62. "All God's Children," *The First Church Pulpit,* Vol. VIII, No. 24, a sermon preached January 26, 1947.
63. "On Belonging to a Minority," *The First Church Pulpit,* Vol. IX, No. 12, a sermon preached July 20, 1947.

population—a zeal that occasionally approached fanaticism and a power that occasionally bordered on arrogance.

Tittle's posture in the controversy was poised. "In this country," he counseled, "I would urge that intolerance on the part of Roman Catholics be met with patience and tolerance on the part of Protestants." "As a Protestant I would go more than half way in the direction of a friendly gesture toward the Roman Catholics of my own community."[64] Early in his ministry, he preached a sermon that attracted much attention. "I have known of you a long while," wrote one correspondent, "thru a famous sermon of yours in Ohio where you spoke tolerantly and kindly of Catholics."[65] As we know, Tittle as a "Y" man worked harmoniously with Catholic chaplains. He denounced the anti-Catholic fulminations of the Klan and he did not join the Protestant crusade against Al Smith. And he solicited funds for the Catholic hospital in Evanston.

But he was not blind to the drive for power of the Catholic hierachy and he was not intimidated by the prospects of being branded a bigot. And so he did sign an appeal to the Catholic leaders of Spain at the time of the Civil War urging that the Church dissociate itself from Franco. He did lament the proscriptions of freedom of worship in Latin America. He did uphold the rights of the Jehovah's Witnesses, a group understandably offensive to Catholics. Moreover, as chairman of the Rock River Peace Committee and the General Conference Committee on the State of the Church he drafted statements urging President Truman not to appoint a personal representative, with the rank of Ambassador, to His Holiness the Pope.[66] And here is his reply to a young man who inquired about the wisdom of marrying a Catholic girl: "Marrying a Roman Catholic is something of an adventure. If you are married by a Roman Catholic priest, you are required to sign a statement saying that any children born of the marriage will be brought up in the Roman Catholic faith. The Catholic partner to the marriage is, moreover, required to sign a statement saying that he or she will do all that is possible to bring the Protestant partner into the Roman Catholic Church. This, as you can well believe, does not always make for mutual understanding and trust. If children *are* born of the marriage, the situation may become acute since almost any Protestant is reluctant to have his children indoctrinated by the Roman Catholic Church before they are old enough to know what it is all about."[67]

64. Letter from Tittle to Clarence L. Oelfke, February 18, 1935.
65. Letter from P. J. O'Keefe to Tittle, April 9, 1921.
66. See *Minutes* of the Rock River Annual Conference (1946), p. 51, and *The Daily Christian Advocate,* Methodist Church, May 7, 1948, p. 278.
67. Letter from Tittle to Fred R. Bliss, September 24, 1948.

On balance, there was much that Tittle found admirable in the Church of Rome, but "its static theology, its mechanistic 'succession,' its moral casuistry and political expediency often leave us intellectually and morally uninspired."[68] Ultimately, Tittle's concern was in making good Protestants—he would have said good Christians—and not in ferreting out the faults of Catholicism.

VIII

The passing of Protestant America is manifested in the prohibition crusade, the revived Klan, the Fundamentalist controversy, the election of 1928, the growth of anti-Semitism, and Protestant-Catholic tensions. These manifestations are all subsumed in the epic mass migrations to America in the late nineteenth and early twentieth centuries. In 1922 Tittle calmly reminded the older Americans gripped by hysteria:

> In Europe, under favorable conditions, and sometimes even under wretchedly unfavorable conditions, the man whom we call a "dago" develops into a Garibaldi, a Mazzni, a Cavour. The man whom we call a "sheeny" develops into a Disraeli, a Gambetta, a Spinoza. The man whom we call a "Hunkie"—shamelessly ignorant of whether he is a Bohemian, a Lithuanian, a Croation, a Czech, or a Slovene—develops into a Huss, a Dvorak, a Masaryk. The man whom we despise as a Pole develops into a Copernicus, a Chopin, a Paderewski. And the man whom we call a "Wop" [sic] becomes a Gorki, a Turgenev, a Tschaikowsky. Who, then, will dare to say that the Italian, the Balkan Jew, the Bohemian, the Czech, the Pole, or the Russian are inferior peoples? Backward many of them may be, but by no means inferior! If only we could see ourselves as others see us, perhaps the foreign-born man or woman would not appear utterly backward even in America. A Slovene woman with a shawl over her head—what a sight! But is she, after all, so very much more of a "sight" than an American woman whose whole costume might have been made of that Slovene woman's shawl?"[69]

A year earlier Tittle reported to his Methodist brethren: "In respect of Americanization, we believe that the best results will be obtained by meeting the foreign-born with justice and sympathy and brotherly kindness. In the nineteenth chapter of Leviticus it is written: 'If a stranger sojourn with thee in your land, ye shall not do him wrong. The stranger that sojourneth with you shall be unto you as the home-born among you, and thou shalt love him as thyself; for ye were sojourners in the land of

68. *The Religion We Need,* a sermon preached January 25, 1931 (pamphlet).
69. "Interior [Inferior?] or Backward?" *Woman's Home Missions,* XXXIX (July, 1922), 4.

Egypt: I am Jehovah your God.' We believe that this famous passage contains a suggestion for better methods of Americanization than some of the rough and ready ones that are commonly employed."[70]

IX

If life were logical, as an old-stock Methodist minister Ernest Fremont Tittle should have been a fanatical Dry, a Klan Kludd, an opponent of Al Smith, an anxious anti-Semite, an apostle of anti-Popery, and a terror to the alien. But the God whom Tittle worshipped was no respecter of persons; consequently, Tittle was freed from the bondage of prejudice which burdened so many older Americans.

70. *Minutes* of the Rock River Annual Conference (1921), pp. 66-67.

13. RACIAL JUSTICE

I

Tittle's first summer at First Church is remembered by American Negroes as "The Red Summer"—a summer when the land was drenched in the blood of blacks. Twenty-six race riots shattered those long hot days and nights of 1919, the fiercest erupting on Chicago's South Side, only miles from "The Cathedral of Methodism." And in that year eighty-three Negro men, women, and youngsters were lynched, eleven enduring lingering deaths at the stake. These words are being written in the summer of 1967, the summer when "whitey's" blood mixed with that of Negroes in the gutters of Newark and Detroit and other northern cities and when the flaming stores of "honky" illuminated the terrifying night scene of firemen being picked off by black snipers and National Guardsmen gunning down teenagers clutching six-pack cartons of looted beer. The summer of 1967 mocks those men of good will who had looked back to 1919 and thought they discerned a half century of irreversible progress in race relations. The summer of 1967 makes Jeremiahs of us all. Yet if podsnappery is no longer possible, a closer comparison of 1919 and 1967 saves us from total despair. No black man and only white supremacists would wish to turn the clock back to that earlier date. The study of history gives us (if nothing else) the long view. And in this long view, during the twentieth century American Protestantism in general and Methodism in particular increasingly comprehended that the Kingdom of God is a kingdom without caste and that the churches as institutions and churchmen as individuals are under the stern judgment of that Kingdom.

Our purpose in this chapter is not to attempt an assessment of Protestantism and the Negro in modern times, or even to relate the total racial record of Methodism. Rather, ours is the account of how one man sought to overcome pride in his own heart and segregation in his own church—a man of good hope who knew that God is not mocked even as he recognized that his hopes for a color-blind world were doomed in his own lifetime. Tittle engaged in no freedom marches. He never stared into the muzzle of a redneck's shotgun or shared a jail cell with lunch-counter demonstrators. Unlike a sacrificial few, he did not resign his suburban pastorate in order to embark on a ministry to Negro slum-dwellers. Yet if it may be said that the true revolution in race relations rests in the changed hearts and minds of men, then perhaps the undramatic labors of Tittle were not in vain. Starting where he was, doing what he could, he sought to make it impossible for Negro leaders to continue in fairness to say (as one spokesman asserted in 1925) : "Of all the groups devoted to social uplift, I have the least hope in the white Christian ministers." Years after Tittle's death, James Baldwin declared: "It is not too much to say that whoever wishes to become a truly moral human being . . . must first divorce himself from the prohibitions, crimes and hypocrisies of the Christian Church. If the concept of God has any validity or any use, it can only be to make us larger, freer and more loving. If God cannot do this, then it is time to get rid of him." Tittle would have agreed that the Christian Church was guilty of "prohibitions, crimes and hypocrisies," but he would not have blamed the failures of the institutional church on God. The answer to man's disorder lay not in the flaws of God's design, but rather in the corruption of men— including Ernest Fremont Tittle and James Baldwin. Tittle labored to rid his parish, community, denomination, and nation from the sin of racial pride, and he sought to do so not by getting rid of God but by confronting men with His will.

II

The facts concerning Tittle's early contacts with Negroes are, alas, few, and even this scant information is open to differing interpretation. Springfield, Ohio, at the turn of the century had a sizable Negro population, a conservative estimate placing the figure at just under five thousand.[1] In young Ernest's grade school, Dibert, perhaps 35

1. August Mier and Elliott Rudwick, "Early Boycotts of Segregated Schools: The Case of Springfield, Ohio, 1922-23," *American Quarterly,* XX (Winter, 1968), 746. But Benjamin F. Prince, *A Standard History of Springfield and Clark County, Ohio,* 2 vols. (New York and Chicago: American Historical So-

percent of the pupils were Negroes, and in his high school though the percentage was smaller it was nonetheless considerable.[2] Yet apparently Ernest had no particularly close Negro pals, at least none close enough to be invited into the Tittle home.[3] In 1904 and 1906 (as earlier in 1868 and later in 1921) race riots broke out in Springfield, and though loss of life was slight, Negro areas were burned and soldiers were called in to restore order. If in later years Tittle ever referred to these trage- dies, the evidence has vanished from the record. We may be certain, however, that as a young man he was not unaware of the racial tension in America.

At Wittenberg in Tittle's day there was a sprinkling of Negro stu- dents, one of whom ran for the first touchdown scored on Zimmerman Field. Though the debating society favorably resolved that the blacks should not be colonized, how Tittle felt about this question we do not know.[4] Nor do we know anything about his racial attitudes while at Ohio Wesleyan. If the segregation of Negro student delegates at the great Student Volunteer Convention in Cincinnati in 1906, attended by Tittle, disturbed him, it is not in the record.[5] While he was a chaplain at Camp Sheridan in Montgomery, Alabama, trouble broke out between the residents and Ohio Negro soldiers, forcing the resignation of the Montgomery chief of police, but again Tittle's response is unknown. While in France, as we do know, Tittle's association with black troops elicited from him patronizing, though not hostile, comments. Although there is some indication that he touched occasionally on the race ques- tion during his Ohio pastorates, we may not presume that because he was caught up in the new spirit of reform the fate of the Negro there- fore greatly concerned him. It is one of the ironies of American history that the Progressive Era—an age that saw many cancerous social growths undergo surgery—coincided with the crest of the wave of racism. Many Progressive reformers were either indifferent to the Negro's plight or actually hostile to his aspirations. No longer could the southern black lift his eyes to northern liberals for help. By 1900 the ashes of the old

ciety, 1922), I, 375, gives the figure of 10,000. The 1900 United States Census places the number of Negroes at 4,253 of a total population of 38,258.

2. Author's interview with Miss Carrie Clarke and Mrs. Robert S. Shaw (the former Nell Clarke), Springfield, Ohio, June 15, 1960, and pictures in their pos- session of Tittle's third-grade class and high-school graduating class. See also Mier and Rudwick, "Early Boycotts," p. 746.

3. Author's interview with Stern Tittle, Thomasville, Ga., April 18-19, 1960.

4. See Harold H. Lentz, *A History of Wittenberg College (1845-1945)* (Spring- field, Ohio: The Wittenberg Press, 1946), p. 78, and *The Wittenberger*, XXX (October 28, 1903), 31, 34.

5. *Nashville Christian Advocate*, LXVII (March 29, 1906), 7.

abolitionist fervor were cool, and "enlightened" Yankees now acquiesced tolerantly in the South's solution to its peculiar problem. Many Social Gospel prophets expressed concern for the fate of the Negro,[6] but mostly this was a chord struck softly and rarely.

There is, therefore, insufficient evidence to state precisely when and why Tittle came to the realization of the enormity of America's caste system. All we may do is examine the evidence as it begins to gather after his arrival at First Church in 1918.

III

To begin with, Tittle sought from the pulpit to further racial justice. An examination of his sermons demonstrates that here was *not* merely a topic to which once a year he perfunctorily turned on Race Relations Sunday nor dismissed casually with condescending references to Booker T. Washington, George Washington Carver, or perhaps Joe Louis. Rather, in sermon after sermon he hammered out the conviction "that of all modern devils, and their name is legion, there is none which more urgently needs to be exorcised than does this lingering prejudice which people of one race feel toward people of another."[7] Most especially must it be exorcised from the heart of the Anglo-Saxon, for he is "peculiarly susceptible to race prejudice" and "this dread disease assumes in him its most virulent form."[8] One of Tittle's favorite axioms held that a better test of a person's Christianity than having him recite the Apostles' Creed is to observe the way he pronounces two words, the word "Negro" and the word "servant."[9] As early as 1921 he proclaimed that Christianity "regards each man, not as a member of some particular race or nation, but as a member of the human family to whom God is Father. It holds that a man is sacred in the eyes of God, not in virtue of the fact that he is a white man, or an Englishman, but just in virtue of the fact that he is a man." If Christians really believed that, how long would lynchings continue to take place? "Lord God of all races, all nations, open our eyes! 'If the whole body were an eye, where were the hearing? If the

6. I am aware that almost all published studies of Protestantism and the Negro assert that the Social Gospel ministers of the Progressive Era were indifferent to the race question, but one of my students at the University of North Carolina, Mr. Ralph Luker, has examined closely the record and finds a greater concern than is generally realized.

7. "Christianity and Race Relations," typed MS, a sermon preached February 24, 1935.

8. *Christian Stewardship in the World Today,* an address delivered before the United Stewardship Council in Philadelphia in 1943 (pamphlet).

9. *The Religion of the Spirit* (New York and Cincinnati, Ohio: Abingdon Press, 1928), pp. 255-56.

whole were hearing, where were the smelling? But now hath God set the members each one of them in the body, even as it pleased him.' "[10]

Not content with general exhortations to banish hatred with love, Tittle called for the abolition of all Jim Crow beliefs and practices: ghettos, restrictive covenants, segregated schools, unequal opportunities in employment, and "all other mechanisms whereby we have denied to a racial minority rights and privileges that we claim for ourselves."[11] What may a Christian do? Well, he may begin by conferring upon Negroes the simple, decent word "Mr." or "Mrs." or "Miss" and cease using such words as "nigger," "darky," and "coon." And he may cease telling allegedly funny jokes at the expense of the Negro.[12] Also he may reflect as to why Negroes are excluded or only grudgingly admitted into his university. He may inquire as to conditions regarding the use by Negro students of swimming pools.[13]

In his last Christmas sermon, Tittle declared:
Obviously, we cannot as one lone individual put an end to race prejudice everywhere upon earth. But we can put an end to it so far as we are concerned. We can treat a colored person as a person and not as a colored person, if you know what I mean. If the one seat left in a crowded bus is beside one occupied by a Negro, we need not stand up. We can sit down. If a Negro boy of fine character and of no little intellectual and athletic distinction is bid by a chapter of our college fraternity, we need not object. We can send a telegram of congratulation to the chapter that had the courage and the good sense to bid this boy. If a fine Negro family desires to locate, own property in our neighborhood, we need not violate the United States Supreme Court decision outlawing . . . racial restrictive covenants. We can seek a reasonable protection of property values by some such agreement as that proposed in Chicago by the Oakland Kenwood Property Owners' Association in which the deciding factor is not race or color but is the acceptance of responsibility on the part of white and black for the material and social well-being of the community.[14]

On July 4, 1948, Tittle appropriately preached a sermon on "The Problem of Freedom." He asked who among his congregation, had he

10. *What Must the Church Do to Be Saved?* (New York and Cincinnati, Ohio: Abingdon Press, 1921), pp. 163-64.
11. "The Sacredness of Life," *The First Church Pulpit*, Vol. VIII, No. 2, a sermon preached September 23, 1945.
12. "Love Thy Neighbor," typed MS, a sermon preached September 26, 1943.
13. *Christians in an Unchristian Society* (New York: Association Press, 1922), p. 19.
14. "The Day After Christmas," recording of a sermon preached December 26, 1948.

lived in Nazi Germany, would have protested Hitler's rule knowing that
the price might be imprisonment in a concentration camp? And who
was "sticking his neck out" to protest the "denial to Negro Americans
of the right to vote and the right to equal opportunity in housing,
employment, education, and medical service?" Tittle observed that
when he guided a resolution through the General Conference calling for
a "non-segregated church and a non-segregated society," he received a
number of letters "so unreasoning, so steeped in prejudice, so bitter and
violent that anyone reading them could hardly escape the thought, Here,
alas! is a mentality more compatible with Hitlerism than with democracy. The writers of these letters would feel entirely at home in a
society that sanctioned the doctrines and policies of Nazism. If such
persons should come to a majority among us, this nation would be
ripe for dictatorship."[15] Earlier, long before the era of sit-ins, Tittle
wondered what would happen if a group of students, Negro and white,
in the hope of removing the color bar, should undertake to eat together
in a restaurant from which Negroes are excluded. One consequence
might be a letter censuring this ungentlemanly behavior from "all the
good bishops, clergy and other pious and good men of the present and
past ages!"[16]

Tittle, of course, on scores of instances branded lynching as the sin
it was, but it is a fair guess that no First Church parishioner ever participated in such a barbarity.[17] Nevertheless, Tittle made his people
aware of their responsibility for acts of violence. "The citizen who draws
the line at lynching," he warned, "but who himself approves the
exclusion of Negroes on the ground of color from hotels, theatres, bathing beaches, who himself approves discrimination on the grounds of
race or color is not as guilty when it comes to a lynching as those
directly responsible for the lynching; no, but by his attitude and conduct
he helps to create a social environment in which lynching is always a
dread possibility."[18]

In sermons too numerous to mention Tittle hammered home the
point that modern science and scholarship affirm with Christianity that

15. "The Problem of Freedom," *The First Church Pulpit,* Vol. X, No. 2,
a sermon preached July 4, 1948.
16. "The Goodness We Need," *The First Church Pulpit,* Vol. IX, No. 8, a
sermon preached January 12, 1947.
17. However, Reinhold Niebuhr once observed, "If there were a drunken orgy
somewhere, I would bet ten to one a church member was not in it. That is
long odds, but on the whole I would assume a church member was not in it.
But if there were a lynching I would bet ten to one a church member was in it."
18. "The Christian Man in an Unchristian World," typed MS, a sermon
preached July 13, 1947.

no group of men is inherently superior or inferior to any other group, citing with devastating authority the evidence of anthropology, sociology, biology, psychology, and genetics. He also drew upon history to demonstrate that culture is not the result of race and that over the centuries peoples once deemed barbaric now in their new pride deem themselves superior. "Racial prejudice," he insisted, "is not instinctive; it is acquired. It is a social, not a biological, inheritance. Children are not born prejudiced; they have prejudice thrust upon them."[19] Tittle recognized that prejudiced people were often in flight from themselves. "If you are ignorant, even illiterate; if you are lazy, shiftless, incompetent, and unproductive; if your reputation among your neighbors is none too good, nevertheless, if you are a white person, you can gain a sense of superiority, not by doing anything worthy of note, but merely by telling yourself that you are better than a Negro—any Negro."[20] And what a pathetic sense of inferiority was revealed in the statement to him made by a white man: "I was fourteen years old before I knowed that I was better than a nigger."[21] On rare instances, Tittle alluded to the sexual fears undergirding segregation, fears that pictured the American Negro male as a kind of a walking phallic symbol, as James Baldwin phrased it. The question "Do you want your daughter to marry a Negro?" Tittle maintained in an oversimplification "has nothing to do with the question of decent housing, of fair employment practices, of educational opportunity, of equality before the law, of the right to vote, of personal security against lynching and against outrageous abuse of police power."[22] Tittle was not blind to the psychological wounds inflicted by segregation. To be excluded from hotels, restaurants, theaters, and bathing beaches, to live in blighted ghettos where the mortality rate far exceeds that in white communities, to be banned from the white public schools, to be placed under quota at even the most enlightened universities, to be refused admission to a hospital, to be denied membership in labor unions, to have jobs closed to you, to be told that your blood is not wanted to save wounded soldiers, most bitter of all, to be a Christian yet unable to worship in most Christian churches—these are such violations of human dignity as to shrivel the spirit of any man. "Supposing a man is born black," said Tittle. "What that means in present-day

19. *Christians in an Unchristian Society,* p. 19.
20. "In the Presence of Difficulty," *The First Church Pulpit,* Vol. VI, No. 10, a sermon preached November 21, 1943.
21. *Jesus After Nineteen Centuries* (New York and Cincinnati, Ohio: Abingdon Press, 1932), p. 165.
22. "Fellowship In Christ," *The Revival Pulpit,* Vol. II, No. 2 (February, 1945), 45.

America no one with a white skin knows or can know; and certainly no one with a white skin may sit in judgment upon anyone with a black skin who gives way to bitterness or to despair. Any white man, however, might well stand hat in hand before any black man who does accept himself."[23]

Tittle was a great preacher in part because it was impossible to hear him preach and remain unaware of modern America's racial disorder and its mockery of God's design.

IV

Tittle also sought to further racial justice through historic and characteristically American channels of protest and pressure. He wrote his congressman and others high and low in public office, signed petitions, contributed considerable sums to worthy causes, and joined voluntary societies. He was one of the founders and first president of the Chicago Council Against Racial and Religious Discrimination, and also was a member of the Inter-racial Commission of Greater Chicago.

Should the Red Cross segregate Negro blood in blood banks? Not if Tittle could help it! Was the electric chair to claim the Scottsboro boys as its victims? Not while Tittle could wield a pen! Did the National Association for the Advancement of Colored People, the American Civil Liberties Union, the Fellowship of Reconciliation, and other groups championing the Negro merit financial support? Of course! Should the Phi Kappa Psi chapter at Amherst, which admitted a Negro lad, be congratulated? "Bully for you!" flashed Tittle. Was it necessary to nudge Illinois congressmen to vote for federal antilynching legislation? Well, a telegram might be in order! Should the United States Congress and the Illinois legislature enact fair employment practices bills? Naturally! Did the Daughters of the American Revolution find it impossible to extend the facilities of Constitution Hall to Marian Anderson? In that case, the girls deserved a firm sermonic spanking, a chastisement the girls, including First Church Daughters, did not take lying down.[24] Tittle's concern is illustrated in a letter of inquiry he once wrote involving the Negro laborer under NRA: "What is being done about this situation? What could be done? What could I do personally? When you have time to do so, I would be glad to hear from you."[25]

23. "Self-Respect," *The First Church Pulpit*, Vol. VIII, No. 14, a sermon preached March 17, 1946.

24. The material in this paragraph is found scattered throughout the Tittle Collection and also throughout the news columns of the Evanston press.

25. Letter from Tittle to Paul Hutchinson, November 13, 1933.

V

Tittle's concern was not confined to the plight of Negroes in the South or even in Chicago's South Side; he was deeply implicated in their fate in that most crucial community of all, Evanston. Only a few months after his arrival in Evanston, First Church held a reception for returned Negro doughboys. Tittle compared their bravery to that of the Massachusetts 54th Regiment, under the command of Colonel Robert Gould Shaw, which distinguished itself during the Civil War, concluding, "These men, so willing to fight for democracy, surely deserve all the blessings of it and an equal chance to share in the opportunities offered by it."[26] In 1919 in Evanston it was by no means clear the chance would be proffered. The following year Tittle addressed a large audience at an outdoor community rally. "I have been told," he began, "that there are both Catholics and Protestants present here this evening. I should be happy to know that there were also Jews and Gentiles, and it would please me to see a larger number of the colored people of the community here with us."[27] In 1920 in Evanston it was by no means clear that the colored people would ever mingle—or be permitted to do so—in large numbers with other citizens.

Although Evanston was known nationally as an affluent, exclusive, and, in 1920, even elegant North Shore suburb, its Negro population, tightly jammed on the west side (away from Lake Michigan, naturally) was sizable. The 1920 census showed 2,522 Negroes in a total population of 37,234. Within five years, according to the estimates of the Evanston press, the Negro citizenry had doubled, accounting for about one-tenth of the total. At the time of Tittle's death, some 7,000 Negroes lived in the city of 73,000. Something of the community's attitude during the early years of Tittle's ministry is illustrated by a 1926 *Evanston Review* editorial: "Evanston has always leaned backward in its effort to treat its colored citizens white. But it has hardly treated its lawless blacks white, for no white group could ever have piled up such a record of law breaking and continued to live in this man's town."[28] That is to say, no Negro was ever lynched in Evanston and no riot ever gutted the Negro neighborhood. The blacks were not ordered to leave town at sundown. The high school was integrated and to some extent the grade schools, though most Negroes in the grades were concentrated in their own schools. On the other hand, Evanston was in truth a white man's town. Restaurants would not serve Negroes, theaters would not accept

26. *Evanston News-Index,* April 4, 1919, p. 1.
27. *Ibid.,* August 9, 1920, p. 1.
28. August 5, 1926, p. 1.

their patronage, the doors of the Evanston hospital were closed to them, the waters of Lake Michigan, save only for one beach, were denied to them, and most of the "better" stores did not welcome them. Moreover, on occasion Ku Klux Klan handbills were circulated, it was charged that the police were brutal in their handling of Negro criminals, and carloads of white boys as a lark raced through the Negro neighborhood shouting obscenities. Altogether, if in the 1920's and even 1930's Evanston was not a "bad" town for the black man, and it was not, then there could hardly be a sharper indictment of the prevailing caste system in the North.[29]

In 1933 a journalist sketched the career of Tittle pointing out that he occupied a solid place in the affections of Evanston's Negroes. "He supports their projects, attends their meetings, speaks to them at times as the only white man in the gathering, and has constructed upon this theme [of racial justice] a number of challenging and straight-hitting sermons."[30] For this concern, Tittle was of course reprimanded. "Does it occur to you," wrote one citizen, "that you . . . in the name of Christ and Humanity are stirring up a race riot in the city of Evanston and that when it breaks out you will be the sorriest of the lot because you, with the highest of motives, have been one of the main causes of it."[31] Other communications were more earthy.

Tittle engaged in panel discussions on the race question, urged the election in 1931 of a Negro alderman to the City Council, advocated fairness in the administration of public welfare, served on a commission to study low-cost housing for Negroes, protested the refusal of restaurants to serve Negroes, and in 1948 urged the hotels of Evanston to register Negro delegates to the annual convention of Baha'is of the United States and Canada. "It is high time," he informed the hotel managements, "that we Americans demonstrate to the world that a free society can assure to all its members equality of opportunity and just and courteous treatment."[32]

Furthermore, Tittle was twice elected president of the Inter-Racial Council of Evanston. Established in 1924 as the Inter-Racial Cooperative Council, the agency resulted from efforts of a group of First Church women to provide a community house for colored girls. In 1929 Negro members were added and its program was broadened to include Negro

29. For many of the statements in this paragraph I have drawn on my own boyhood memories.
30. Roland E. Wolseley, "Ernest Fremont Tittle," *World Unity*, XIII (December, 1933), 165.
31. Letter from Mrs. Clinton Merrick to Tittle, undated.
32. *Evanston Review*, undated clipping in Tittle Collection.

housing, education, and employment and indeed all matters of racial justice. As Tittle said, the aim of the council was to regard the Negro as a person rather than a race. Many of the white leaders in the council were First Church members and most of its meetings seem to have taken place in the First Church parish house.[33] In 1935 it was rumored that the Negro members of the council represented only the middle-class business and professional Negro population and that in return for a promised housing project they agreed to use their influence to limit the influx of poor Negroes into Evanston.[34] The truth of this charge is unknown, but it underscores the fact that from the perspective of the 1960's the efforts of the council do not seem very militant. Yet, as the members had good reason to know, in that earlier age they seemed to be dangerous agitators in the eyes of many Evanstonians.

Unquestionably, the most serious flaw in Evanston's claim to be a civilized community in the 1920's lay in the fact that a sick or injured or even dying black had no place to go save a mean little house with eight beds and an ill-equipped and ill-staffed operating room in the basement. The shack could not even pretend to the name "hospital." Yet such it was called. It is little wonder that the mortality rate of the Negro was double that of the white. As Tittle thundered to the whites, "You have a hospital for your dogs and cats, but not for your Negro brethren."[35] As early as 1923 Tittle placed the execrable situation before the First Church Official Board, urging that a community organization be formed to take action.[36] He attempted to arouse his congregation in a sermon: "If we sit by in satisfaction because of our sound financial position and great plant and fail to take a leading part in the effort to fill the crying need of our Negro fellow-townsmen, would not Jesus Christ have classified us with the Priest and Pharisee?"[37] The Inter-Racial Council entered the campaign. Finally, a Community Hospital Association of Evanston was chartered, and in 1930 a little Community Hospital was opened for Negroes. For the next fifteen years this modest structure, with its mere eighteen beds, was the only certain haven for Negro emergency cases in a 1,600-square-mile area between Chi-

33. The Evanston press carried a number of items covering the activities of the group.

34. See *Evanston News-Index*, February 16, 1935, p. 2.

35. Author's interview with Mr. and Mrs. Roscoe Page, Evanston, Ill., August 10, 1959.

36. Minutes of the Official Board, First Church, April 2, 1923.

37. "On Caring for People," quoted in letter from J. P. Margeson to First Church Finance Committee, November 5, 1945, in Scrapbook of the Official Board, First Church.

cago's mid-North Side and Waukegan, an area in which 15,000 Negroes lived—and died.[38] Not until 1945 was a great campaign organized to raise $200,000 to enlarge and modernize Community Hospital, Tittle serving as honorary chairman. First Church contributed generously as it had over the years for the maintenance of the hospital. Tittle's role was important, perhaps even crucial, but the man who labored hardest on behalf of the sick and injured black population of Evanston was Clyde D. Foster. Significantly, he was a First Church member.

In 1919 most of Evanston was segregated. In 1949 most of Evanston —its movies, restaurants, shops, beaches, schools, even Evanston Hospital —was not. It would be fatuous to claim this transformation to be an outward manifestation of the death of racial pride in men's hearts. Indeed, perhaps only those who remember Evanston as it was in its segregated days can appreciate the magnitude of the change. One hopes that Tittle's tired heart was gladdened to see before his death the passing of much of the discrimination that had grieved him during his thirty-one years in Evanston.

VI

Tittle also sought to further racial justice through his role as denominational leader. "We do not despair because the clouds of race prejudice apparently lower more darkly than ever," confided the fraternal delegate from the Colored Methodist Episcopal Church to the 1900 Northern General Conference. "Nor are we discouraged because conditions seem to grow more desperate. God still lives."[39] Another Negro also addressed the 1900 General Conference: "We wish to say what has been said for us and by us, that we are *loyal*. We are at home. We are not going anywhere. We will peaceably wait in our own Church until the Church, seeing and admitting our needs from every standpoint, they grant us what we need. . . . We contend for a principle, and, if we die without the sight, we will report to God that we were faithful over a few things. We believe Methodism will study, reason, pray and work itself out of any condition for the glory of God. We will not frustrate her purpose by running, but will hold our ground world without end. Amen."[40] At the first General Conference of Southern Methodism in the twentieth century the fraternal delegate from the Colored Methodist Episcopal Church said: "We, as well-raised children, delight to look on the great-

38. *Disease Knows No Color Line,* a pamphlet published by the Community Hospital Building Fund in 1945.
39. *The Daily Christian Advocate,* Methodist Episcopal Church, May 23, 1900, p. 300.
40. *Ibid.,* May 26, 1900, p. 339.

ness of our parent." He asked only one boon: "And that is, wherever, whether in town or city, you are strong and we are striving to house our people, please give us attention, and remember it is your little black child out of doors and asks for help." There followed "hearty applause" and "the most unbounded good humor" and a prayer that "our sable brethren" be "strong workers for truth and righteousness."[41] What did Tittle attempt to do in the subsequent half-century to make such black obsequiousness unthinkable and such unthinking white arrogance impossible in the relations between the black and white sons of Wesley? Our story of necessity will center on Tittle, but perhaps some illumination will also be shed on the broader subject of modern Methodism and the Negro.

At virtually every Rock River Annual Conference, the journals reveal, Tittle addressed himself to the race question, in reports, resolutions, and proposed memorials to the General Conference. Of course, the early statements called for justice and equality rather than explicit integration, but they may not therefore be dismissed as innocuous. In the context of the times, they were blunt, passionate indictments of America's racial practices. In 1941 he successfully presented a resolution: "God, who has made himself known to us in Christ, recognizes no man-made distinction of race, nation, color or class. The United States, from the days of the founding fathers, has been committed in principle to the ideal of equal opportunity for all citizens. We earnestly appeal of the Government of the United States to remove every discrimination against Negroes in the armed forces of the nation. With equal earnestness, we appeal to all Methodists who may be either employers of labor or members of labor unions to exert their influence to the end that discrimination against Negroes may be removed from all the industries of the nation."[42] By the mid-1940's the old words "justice" and "equality" now carried an unequivocal integrationist meaning. Years before *Brown v Board of Education* Tittle realized that separation of the races could never add up to equality, no matter how much money was poured into Negro facilities.

Tittle was permitted to live only long enough to attend three meetings of the North Central Jurisdictional Conference, but as chairman of the Committee on the State of the Church, Social Service, and Temperance he alerted Methodism at this jurisdictional level to the demoniac

41. *The Daily Christian Advocate,* Methodist Episcopal Church, South, May 22, 1902, p. 5.
42. *Minutes* of the Rock River Annual Conference (1941), p. 26.

nature of America's caste system. More significant, of course, was Tittle's General Conference role.

He attended his first General Conference in 1928 and was a member, though not chairman, of the important Committee on the State of the Church. As chairman of the Rock River delegation he presented four memorials; none of them dealt with the race issue. The report of the Committee on the State of the Church, adopted unanimously, reaffirmed Methodism's historic position on the oneness of humanity and denied the prejudiced assumption that some races are born to superiority and others to inferiority. It called for equal political rights, confessed shame over lynchings and supported federal preventative legislation, and closed in the hope of happier race relations in the near future.[43] The conference also reaffirmed the famous "Social Creed of the Churches," which asked for the "elimination of racial discrimination" and the "same protection and rights for all races."[44] Furthermore, for the first time in the history of American Methodism a Negro bishop, Robert E. Jones, presided at a session, and the delegates by rising vote gave thanks for his courtesy and skill.[45] Compared to the time the delegates devoted to the prohibition issue and considering the desperate plight of the American Negro, it is clear that Northern Methodism in 1928 underestimated the urgency of the race question.

The Methodist Episcopal Church held its 1932 quadrennium at Atlantic City. The Negro delegates, including the two Negro bishops (but not, apparently, all the Orientals) suffered embarrassment in the matter of accommodations, riding freight elevators in the convention building and themselves being required to reside at a hotel on a side street. This discrimination gave point to the fraternal inquiry of Bishop Randall Carter of the Colored Methodist Episcopal Church: must the American Negro "always be living on a knife's edge"?[46]

The Episcopal Address contained the usual condemnations of lynching, discrimination, and prejudiced attitudes. Tittle's Committee on the State of the Church (he was not yet chairman) carried the usual statements opposing "all forms of race discrimination," denouncing lynching as "inhuman, irrational, and thoroughly criminal," and requesting that "our Church shall operate all its Boards, Commissions, official groups, and institutions without discrimination against any person on account of

43. *The Daily Christian Advocate,* Methodist Episcopal Church, May 22, 1928, p. 471.
44. *Ibid.,* May 17, 1928, p. 382.
45. *Ibid.,* May 26, 1928, p. 579.
46. *Ibid.,* May 14, 1932, p. 305.

either race or nation."[47] The conference failed to approve Memorial No. 823 to create a Commission on Race Relations.[48] Indeed, it accomplished little, being racked by the episcopacy question, frustrated over the failure of prohibition, and bewildered by the depression.

On the sixth day of the dispirited conference, Tittle, striding purposefully to the platform, handed a statement to the secretary. It read: "I wish to offer a resolution: Whereas: 'There cannot be Greek and Jew, circumcision and uncircumcision; barbarian, Scythian, bondsman, freeman, but Christ is all in all'; therefore, Be it resolved: that the General Conference of the Methodist Episcopal Church shall hereafter meet only in cities where hotels, sufficient in number to accommodate its Delegates, shall in writing agree to meet the following conditions: (1) No segregation of specific groups in room assignments. (2) No discrimination against any delegates in the use of hotel entrances, lobbies, elevators, dining rooms and other hotel services or facilities. (3) Specific instruction of hotel employees by the hotel authorities regarding the interracial character of the conference and the treatment of all Delegates with equal courtesy."

The conference snapped to attention, tingling with excitement, and on that warm Saturday morning even dozing delegates were alerted by loud cheers and half a hundred shouts of "Mr. Chairman!" Joseph J. Shy, the first man recognized, moved to refer the resolution to a committee, which would have meant the kiss of death. "I do not think it is necessary to refer this perfectly Christian expression of conviction," countered Harold P. Sloan. If the resolution were passed, observed another, it would be impossible to hold another session of the General Conference within the boundaries of the United States. It would delay for generations union with the Southern Church, warned another. The chairman of the Commission on Entertainment pouted that the resolution was an implied criticism of his Atlantic City arrangements. But Bishop McConnell (who happily was the presiding officer that morning), amid shouts of "No!" "No!" gaveled him out of order, called for a vote, and the resolution easily carried.

Tittle spoke only briefly during the debate: "I believe that even under those conditions we can discover cities who would be glad to entertain us. I believe that if no city under those conditions would be willing to entertain us, it would be better for us not to meet and that

47. *Ibid.*, May 24, 1932, pp. 594-95; *Journal* of the General Conference of the Methodist Episcopal Church (1932), p. 170.
48. *The Daily Christian Advocate*, Methodist Episcopal Church, May 25, 1932, p. 642.

our refusal to meet would advance the Kingdom of God as much as our meeting under present conditions."[49]

The resolution represented prayerful and prolonged thought. It was signed by the Rock River delegation and had been discussed and agreed to two years earlier at a meeting of the Rock River Conference.[50] Prior to that fateful Saturday morning in Atlantic City, Bishop Wilbur P. Thirkield, a staunch and much-scarred friend of the Negro, had placed in Tittle's hands information concerning discriminatory treatment at past General Conferences.[51] The bishops themselves had provided a precedent for Tittle's resolution when in 1926, after two Negro bishops and their wives had been excluded from a social gathering in a Washington, D.C., hotel, they unanimously resolved not to accept future invitations unless all were included. As Bishop McConnell remarked, if the bishops could not secure desegregated facilities, then they did not need banquets.[52] In any case, Tittle followed a bold course in taking the resolution to the floor for immediate passage (or defeat) rather than referring it to a committee for probable burial.

Reaction to the resolution was immediate and widespread. The *New York Times, Literary Digest,* and other leading newspapers and journals gave it prominent attention, including a few overseas publications. Much of the secular press predicted that it would bring to an end the unification movement between Northern and Southern Methodism. Reunion, editorialized the *Abilene (Texas) Reporter,* "is now more remote than ever—in fact, impossible." "This action shows what a waste of time it is to even discuss a consolidation of these two great branches of the Methodist Church," commented the *Grand Junction (Colorado) Sentinel.* This resolution, averred the *Jackson (Mississippi) News,* cuts off "forever all hope of organic union between the Northern and Southern branches of the Methodist Church, which will not cause any heartbreaks among members of that faith in the Southern states." The *Pikeston (Colorado) Standard* philosophized: "This is all right. We would like to see a fat white brother and a fat black brother put to bed together in summer time. Vice versa with the sisters."[53]

The Methodist press was not nearly so discouraged—or at least masked its fears. Most Methodist editors, Northern and Southern,

49. *Ibid.,* May 9, 1932, p. 142; *New York Christian Advocate,* CVII (July 14, 1932), 526.

50. *Minutes* of the Rock River Annual Conference (1930), p. 15.

51. *New York Christian Advocate,* CVII (July 14, 1932), 758.

52. *Zion's Herald,* CIV (May 26, 1926), 652; David M. Reimers, *White Protestantism and the Negro* (New York: Oxford University Press, 1965), p. 105.

53. All quotations are taken from newspaper clippings in the Tittle Collection.

believed the resolution to be a stumbling block, but that the movement toward unification would proceed. As J. M. Rowland of the *Richmond Christian Advocate* calmly reminded his readers, "They were protecting their colored delegates and not rebuking the Southern Methodists."[54]

Some of the delegates who voted for the resolution, according to the conversations heard along the Boardwalk, later criticized Tittle for raising such a delicate issue. "Why," they said, "we might as well reconcile ourselves to meeting in tents somewhere next time. You can't find a city big enough to take care of the General Conference which will ever promise, let alone fulfill the promise, to make no discrimination on account of race or color."[55] Tittle himself reported to a colleague: "My General Conference resolution, which on the day I presented it was passed by an almost unanimous vote, was afterward keenly resented by some of the men who had voted for it and by most of our bishops! Indeed, I was told that an attempt would be made to reconsider the action that was taken. As you know, no such attempt was made, but the fact remains that many of the brethren, including our 'spiritual leaders,' did get terribly cold feet. However, the resolution stands and will, I hope, be productive of great good. From all over the country I have received letters, both commendatory and condemnatory. The latter have in some cases been positively vile—so vile that I have not allowed my wife to read them."[56]

There were in fact many condemnatory letters. "I've always been a Methodist, wrote a New York correspondent, "but never again will I set foot into a Methodist Church. Anyone, or any Church, that tells me that I must 'chin' around with a bunch of Damned, lousey Negroes in order to get to Heaven is crazy. If Heaven is filled with Negroes, Hell will be a Paradise." Intentionally or not, the writer of this letter observed proprieties by capitalizing "Negroes."[57] Another writer with the curious name of "Earnest Piffle" informed Tittle that the resolution would result in a "mismated and damnable intermixture of the races, the worst evil on earth, a plain defiance of such Providence as there may be."[58] A Virginia cavalier wrote: "We hope *your sister marries the* biggest *blackest* nigger in your congregation and brings home a house full of kinky head inky *black children* for you to raise as your own. Why dont you preach in a negro church and let the white folks have a

54. Quoted in *Literary Digest*, CXIII (May 28, 1932), 18.
55. *Northwestern Christian Advocate*, LXXXIV (May 28, 1936), 507.
56. Letter from Tittle to A. R. Meade, June 14, 1932.
57. Letter from Harry G. Fuller to Tittle, June 12, 1932.
58. Letter from Earnest Piffle to Tittle, undated.

WHITE preacher? Don't come to Virginia though."⁵⁹ "When a flock of blue birds meet with a flock of black birds," patiently explained a sophisticated New Yorker, "they do not stop and chatter or eat with each other but respectfully keep to their own kind and attend to their own business."⁶⁰

Other letters, restrained and polite, attempted in a reasonable manner to demonstrate to Tittle that the Negro, a loyal and contented soul when left undisturbed by Yankee agitators, was not now, never had been, and never would be the white man's equal. Word for word they echoed the biological, biblical, historical, and sociological arguments advanced in the antebellum South to defend slavery.

But these letters were matched by those cheering Tittle on. Negro leaders, such as George E. Haynes of the Federal Council's Commission on Race Relations, said Tittle's action sent "an electric spark" through all the friends of racial justice.⁶¹ Negro groups, such as the NAACP and the Chicago Ministers Association of the African Methodist Episcopal Church, wrote in recognition of the brave deed. Obviously untutored black people penned touching notes of gratitude. Churchmen in Africa and India also sent communications.

The most poignant letters were those few from Southern white preachers that were congratulatory. In spidery script a retired Baptist minister in Virginia honored Tittle on his "startling victory for inclusive Christian decency and fellowship. Give us 500 years, and we Southern Baptists and Methodists may catch up with you."⁶² An old Texas Methodist who expected soon to be in "New Jerusalem" closed his communication: "May God bless you in preaching salvation through Jesus Christ Our Lord, and also bless your efforts to have church organizations cherish and manifest the brotherly love of Him by 'whose stripes we are healed.' The Recording Angle [*sic*] simply notes that this man was washed in the Blood of the Lamb without reference to race or complexion."⁶³

Though some Methodists were embittered by Tittle's resolution, though opposition to unification stiffened momentarily, most shared the sentiments expressed by Southern Methodism's great champion of union, Bishop John M. Moore, to Bishop McDowell: "Of course we shall go

59. Unsigned, undated letter mailed from Richmond, Va., to Tittle.
60. Letter from J. A. Webb to Tittle, May 8, 1932.
61. Letter from George E. Haynes to Tittle, May 13, 1932.
62. Letter from W. R. L. Smith to Tittle, June 9, 1932.
63. Letter from J. S. McCaughan to Tittle, May 30, 1932.

on—Union must be consummated. We can only hope a wisdom that comprehends all conditions will prevail."[64]

The next General Conference met in Columbus, Ohio, in 1936. The meeting was fully integrated "And No Riot Ensued," as the *Northwestern Christian Advocate* joyfully headlined.[65] Indeed, the Negro delegates prepared a resolution commending Columbus for making good on its promise. The "courteous treatment and kindly consideration" "were all the more appreciated because they were marked by genuine good will and unspoiled by anything that had the appearance of mere condescension or patronage."[66] Tittle was of course delighted, not only for the sake of the Negroes, but because a number of white people, including waitresses and bellhops, had learned something from the experience.[67]

Nevertheless the Negro issue shadowed the conference, for this meeting was to vote on a Plan of Union with Southern Methodism and the Methodist Protestant Church, and the place of the Negro in this proposed unification created the most critical tensions. Though differences of polity and theology were real, the evidence is overwhelming that race was the major roadblock to reunion. Tittle's own position prior to Columbus is ambiguous. As we know, he was deeply committed to breaking down the institutional barriers separating Christians and dreamed that one day the Body of Christ would cease to be broken. At Atlantic City in 1932 he had spent a "very pleasant" evening with Bishop Moore and Bishop Waldorf discussing "means of bringing about closer cooperation and eventual union between the two churches." One suggestion Tittle acted on was to invite a Southern minister to address the Rock River Annual Conference.[68] And in turn he accepted in 1934 an invitation to talk before a Southern Methodist meeting in Nashville.

In 1933 Tittle stated: "Under no circumstances would I personally become associated with the Methodist Episcopal Church, South."[69] By 1935, however, he could "say without hesitancy that in my judgment the Methodist Episcopal Church, South, is now making a truly extraordinary progress in the direction of what you and I regard as essential Christianity. Indeed, I cannot think of any other denomination that

64. Letter from John M. Moore to William F. McDowell, May 13, 1932. Apparently McDowell, Tittle's old mentor and friend, had passed the letter on to Tittle, and this explains its presence in the Tittle Collection.

65. *Northwestern Christian Advocate,* LXXXIV (May 28, 1936), 507-8. See also *New York Christian Advocate,* CXI (June 4, 1936), 532.

66. *The Daily Christian Advocate,* Methodist Episcopal Church, May 20, 1936, p. 542.

67. *Evanston Daily News-Index,* May 20, 1936, p. 7.

68. Letter from Tittle to Gilbert Stansell, July 19, 1932.

69. Letter from Tittle to James Brett Kenna, September 5, 1933.

seems to me to be progressing more rapidly. It appears to have a growing number of truly noble and significant leaders; a fact of which I was made aware when last year I spoke in Nashville. . . ." Yet in concluding the letter he said: "My own mind is still open as regards the desirability of the proposed plan of union. I cannot but believe that union is desirable, provided only it can be achieved without the surrender of anything that is essentially Christian."[70] And only two months before the Columbus Conference he confessed, "More than I can say I deplore the fact that my own mind is as yet unclear as to the desirability of the present plan of unifying the three Methodist bodies."[71]

It is understandable that Tittle should be troubled, desiring, as he did, Christian unity, and also racial integration. The proposed Plan of Union provided for a General Conference, meeting quadrennially, and for six new jurisdictional conferences, bringing into one church an estimated 99 percent of all white Methodists and 15 percent of all Negro Methodists in the United States. Five of the jurisdictional conferences were based on geography (Northeastern, Southeastern, North Central, South Central, and Western), and one on color (Central); that is, about 95 percent of the Negroes in the new Church—The Methodist Church—some 318,000 of 325,000 were to be placed in the Central Jurisdiction. The new arrangement can be defended. Negroes had been segregated in the old Northern Church, having separate local congregations, separate Negro Annual Conferences, a separate Negro *Christian Advocate*, and two Negro bishops elected by separate ballots from which the votes for white ministers were excluded. Under the new plan Negroes would serve on an unsegregated and equal basis in the General Conference and on all national boards and commissions; indeed they would have more than their proportionate share of representatives. At the national level white Southern leaders would now associate closely with fellow Methodist Negro leaders. It was also claimed that Negro churches could easily be transferred into predominantly white conferences after union, and that rigid segregation was not being written into the constitution. Finally, it is true that the two Negro members of the commission drafting the Plan of Union, the able Bishop Robert E. Jones and President Willis J. King of Gammon Seminary, gave their endorsement. Yet the stark fact of the Central Jurisdiction seared the consciences of some whites and humiliated the souls of most blacks.

The transcript of the tense two-hour debate at Columbus on the Plan of Union makes fascinating reading. Bishop Hughes presided with abso-

70. Letter from Tittle to J. R. Caffyn, October 7, 1935.
71. Letter from Tittle to Miss Juanita E. Jackson, March 2, 1936.

lute fairness, even permitting the opponents one more speaker than the proponents. Bishop McDowell introduced the plan not as a perfected piece of ecclesiasticism or mechanical or legalistic skill, but as the best sixty-five fallible men could devise, a plan looking more toward the future than toward the past. Bishop Hughes stepped down from the chair to speak that day for the union: the Commissioners (he pleaded) did not feel that they had been appointed to reform Methodism, but rather to unite its three branches. The problem was not to introduce new features, but rather to heal old divisions. We were seeking (he concluded) a Methodist merger and were willing to let Methodist reformations wait upon the prayerful judgment of the future church.

Lewis O. Hartman of Massachusetts and editor of the influential *Zion's Herald*, perhaps with Whittier's *Ichabod* ringing in his memory, was the first to rise and speak in opposition. The debate was on, the speakers alternating pro and con. Among those gaining the floor were five Negroes: two in favor of the plan, three in opposition. George Lewis, a tall Tennessee Negro, relieved the tension when recognized by Bishop Hughes and asked, "Are you against it?" by replying as he moved toward the platform, "World without end!" President David D. Jones of Bennett College also spoke in opposition, telling the story of being informed by a kindly white lady of her inspired interpretation of the Biblical passage, "In my Father's house there are many mansions." That means, she sweetly explained to President Jones, that in heaven Negroes would have a lovely mansion. "It is going to be separate, and not quite as nice as ours, but it is going to be lovely."

Midway in the proceedings Tittle was recognized. "I may truthfully say," he began, "that never in my life have I wanted as much as now to support an organizational plan before the church in which it has been my privilege to serve for more than a quarter of a century." He then stated the central issue as he saw it. "All our other jurisdictions are geographic. This is racial. If that is not a concession to race prejudice, what is it? To be sure, by segregating Negroes in a Negro Conference we give them political opportunities which they would not possess as minority groups within our white conferences; but we take away from them the experience of Christian brotherhood which in my judgment, is far more important than is political opportunity." He continued by deploring the effort of the proposed action on young people and on colored people in mission lands. He concluded: "For every other feature of the plan I am prepared to vote. I wish it were not necessary to vote 'yea' or 'nay.' If we could make this one reservation I would be voting with all my mind and all my heart. As it is, my belief is that we should wait another quadrennium, if necessary two quadrenniums, when I fully believe we can have union without compromise; and in that case we will have a church which the living Christ can use, I profoundly believe as he may use no other now in existence." Alas, the proposed plan "does, I think, undeniedly make a concession to race prejudice [which] would, if adopted, present a church which the Christ could not use without considerable embarrassment." It is the memory of men who were present at Columbus that Tittle's was the strongest speech against the plan.

Soon a standing vote was taken. The plan passed, 407 to 83. Of the 47 Negro delegates present, 36 demurred. As the conference stood spontaneously to sing, "We're Marching to Zion," many of the blacks remained seated, their eyes swelling with tears.[72]

The reader must decide for himself how he would have voted had he been a delegate. In my judgment, in this grave debate there are no villains. It is impossible to say if, as Tittle believed, unification would have come in one, two, or twenty quadrenniums without some major concessions to Southern Methodism on the question of race. It must be said unequivocally, however, that it was possible to favor the Plan of Union as submitted without being a racist. Many good men, many color-blind men, including Tittle's hero, Bishop McConnell, supported it.

Yet several points stand out in sharp relief. First, most (but not all) Negroes were in opposition. In a caucus of 44 Negro delegates held before the debate began, 33 agreed to "protest in a mild, but manly way against this Plan." Months later when the plan was submitted to the nineteen Negro Annual Conferences of the Methodist Episcopal Church for ratification, the vote was heavily negative: 583 ministers for, 823 against; 253 laymen for, 477 against.[73] One Negro spokesman declared, "If the Methodist Church really dared to be Christian, would it humiliate thousands of its most loyal members by forcing them into a Jim Crow jurisdiction?"[74] And Roy Wilkins of the NAACP penned the bitter words: "We hope God has the Methodists in mind and that He will give compassionate attention to their special needs. They separated a hundred years ago over slavery. Now they have got back together again with old wounds fairly well healed, and with the persistent black man roped off into a separate conference where he will be happy riding

72. *The Daily Christian Advocate*, Methodist Episcopal Church, May 5, 1936, pp. 83-92; *Christian Century* LIII (May 20, 1936), 741.
73. *Zion's Herald*, CXV (May 12, 1937), 586.
74. *Ibid.*, CXVI (June 22, 1938), 816.

to Glory on a sort of jim crow car. We trust that if heaven is truly one great unsegregated family, God will not induct the American Methodists in too great numbers, or too rapidly, into a society that would shock them, perhaps, beyond hope of salvation."[75] During the debate David Jones had said it all in one blunt sentence: "Everyone knows the Plan is segregation, and segregation in the ugliest way, because it is couched in such pious terms."[76]

A second point is that Southern Methodists, despite the opposition of Bishops Collins Denny and Warren Candler, did not view the jurisdictional arrangement with alarm. "We are in this Plan, brethren," declared the speaker closing the debate at the 1938 Southern Methodist General Conference, "preserving every essential ideal that we have in the South on the Negro question."[77] And years later the editor of the *Alabama Christian Advocate* confessed, "It is an open secret that there never would have been any unification, so far as the Methodist Episcopal Church, South, is concerned, if some such arrangement as this had not been adopted."[78]

Thirdly, Tittle was unquestionably right in the belief that the compromise was less acceptable to younger Methodists, white and Negro, than to their fathers. The National Council of Methodist Youth, itself interracial, memorialized Methodism to "take no action on the unification of Methodism which will write into the law of the church this unchristian principle of segregation."[79] And subsequent decades disclosed that the Central Jurisdiction was an arrangement that the coming generation of Methodism could not live with. The Women's Missionary Council of Southern Methodism in 1937 stated the essence of the matter: "As a temporary expedient, the proposed plan may or may not be advisable, but as making for a permanent division within the Christian Church in America, we know that it falls far short of Jesus' ideal for the Kingdom."[80]

75. Quoted in Dwight W. Culver, *Negro Segregation in the Methodist Church* (New Haven, Conn.: Yale University Press, 1953), p. 100.
76. *The Daily Christian Advocate,* Methodist Episcopal Church, May 5, 1936, p. 87.
77. *The Daily Christian Advocate,* Methodist Episcopal Church, South, May 2, 1938, p. 62.
78. Quoted in *Zion's Herald,* CXXIX (January 31, 1951), 103.
79. See the booklets published by the National Council of Methodist Youth: *Being Christian in Times Like This* (Chicago, n.d.); Miron Morrill (ed.), *Methodist Youth Council* (Chicago, 1934); Miron Morrill (ed.), *The National Council Meets Again* (Chicago, 1936); and *New York Christian Advocate,* CXI (September 24, 1936), 928-29.
80. Quoted in *Information Service,* XVI (April 3, 1937).

The Plan of Union was of course ratified by the necessary number of Annual Conferences; even Tittle's Rock River Conference gave its endorsement by a vote of 194 to 3.[81] Tittle continued to term the Central Jurisdiction a "somewhat amazing example of segregation"[82] and a "somewhat amazing example of Jim Crow-ism."[83] Yet he desired a united Methodism, praised the Columbus meeting for its accomplishments, and held in high regard the growing minority of Southern Methodist prophets, "a gallant crew, engaged in a most difficult task and rendering a magnificent service."[84] Perhaps out of the great debate Tittle came to achieve a new understanding of what St. Augustine called "the misery of these necessities." At the great Uniting Conference of 1939, when Bishop John M. Moore called for those in opposition to the Declaration of Union to stand and raise his right hand not a single individual stirred. Bishop James H. Straughn exalted, "It was over; it was done! The Methodists are one united people! The Uniting Conference was and still is the prophetic testimony of the unity and the solidarity of the Methodist Church. It was an unforgettable experience. . . . Dissent was a sacrilege. It was a bath of love."[85]

In 1944 the Negro question again seriously occupied the attention of the General Conference of a now united Methodism.[86] Meeting in Kansas City, the conference subjected Negro delegates to shabby treatment regarding sleeping and eating accommodations, the color line being sharply drawn by hotels and restaurants. Many Negroes, including the bishops, stayed in private homes,[87] and one delegate bitterly remembered that he wandered the streets in search of a meal, finally finding food in the only place open to him, a saloon. In anger and humiliation, the Negroes were driven to make formal protest, selecting Matthew S. Davage to be their spokesman. Before the protest could be presented, however, Bishop Oxnam, as secretary of the Council of Bishops, made offi-

81. *Minutes* of the Rock River Annual Conference (1936), p. 28. Later the Rock River Conference voted to memorialize the General Conference to remove the Central Jurisdiction.

82. "The Methodist Ideal for the Church," *Highroad*, VII (March, 1948), 32-33.

83. "The Methodist Ideal for the Church," *The First Church Pulpit*, Vol. IX, No. 13, a sermon preached October 19, 1947.

84. Letter from Tittle to E. Fay Campbell, June 2, 1944.

85. James H. Straughn, *Inside Methodist Union* (Nashville, Tenn.: The Methodist Publishing House, 1958), p. 124.

86. The 1940 General Conference heard resolutions and reports (including those drafted by Tittle) dealing with race relations, but the question did not *rack* the conference.

87. Authors' interviews with Bishop Alexander P. Shaw, Denver, Col., May 2, 1960, and with M. L. Harris, Denver, Col., May 1, 1960.

cial apology, assuring the conference that the Committee on Entertainment was taking all steps possible to rectify the situation and hoping that those who had suffered would not think the action "too little too late." Davage withheld the protest and instead expressed appreciation for the conference's concern.[88] An improvised dining area was set up in the rear of the auditorium, and though the food was miserable Tittle and Glenna and a few other whites made a special effort to eat there to indicate it was not intended to be for Negroes alone.[89]

As chairman of the Committee on the State of the Church Tittle presented a resolution urging that hereafter meetings be held "in places where entertainment can be provided without distinction on the basis of race." On the floor, however, a Mississippi delegate successfully watered down the resolution to read that meetings be held "only in places where adequate and suitable entertainment can be provided for all delegates and representatives of the Church."[90]

Tittle also presented the report of the Committee on the State of the Church which held that "no group is inherently superior or inferior to any other, and none is above any other beloved of God." The report condemned discrimination, injustice, and inequality in all areas of life, though it did not use the word "segregation." It further declared: "We look to the ultimate elimination of racial discrimination within The Methodist Church. Accordingly we ask the Council of Bishops to create forthwith a commission to consider afresh the relations of all races included in the membership of The Methodist Church and to report to the General Conference of 1948."[91]

Tittle liked to relate this incident: "At the 1944 General Conference of The Methodist Church a friend of mine, minister of a church south of the Mason-Dixon Line, made a speech on the race issue in which he took the position that there must be no discrimination on the grounds of race or color; there must be an unsegregated church and an unsegregated society. When he returned to his seat a prominent lay member of his delegation said to him: 'Well, doctor, I do not know how many votes for the episcopacy you had before you stood up to speak. I do know how many you have now. You haven't got one.' This was not the

88. *The Daily Christian Advocate,* The Methodist Church, May 2, 1944, p. 74.
89. Author's interview with Glenna Myers Tittle, Evanston, Ill., July 27, 1959.
90. *The Daily Christian Advocate,* The Methodist Church, May 3, 1944, pp. 110-11, 162; *Zion's Herald,* CXXII (May 17, 1944), 311; *Christian Century,* LXI (May 17, 1944), 631.
91. *The Daily Christian Advocate,* The Methodist Church, May 3, 1944, pp. 107-8.

case. At the following Jurisdictional Conference my friend got 24 votes for the episcopacy, and needed only some 300 more to be elected!"[92]

The 1948 General Conference met in Boston unmarred by ugly racial incident. Once again Tittle was unanimously elected chairman of the Committee on the State of the Church. He presented for acceptance the fact-finding report of the Commission to Consider the Relation of All Races in The Methodist Church, authorized by the 1944 General Conference, though he had not been a member of the commission.[93] He also presented the statement on "The Christian Church and Race" of the Committee on the State of the Church. It was specific and hard-hitting, the most explicitly integrationist position yet advanced at a General Conference. "The principle of racial discrimination is in clear violation of the Christian belief in the fatherhood of God, the botherhood of man, and the Kingdom of God, the proclamation of which in word and life is our gospel. We therefore have no choice but to denote it as unchristian and to renounce it as evil. *This we do without equivocation.*" The practice of racial discrimination is "evil, being the prolific mother of injustice, dissension, and division in any society which practices it. Yet toleration of this practice, in some form or other, is as old as the Christian Church itself, and is coextensive with the history of the United States. Consequently thoughtful persons will know that it cannot be removed by a resolution. Neither will it be removed without real determination by significant parts of the Church and the nation. Hence we, as Christians, must address ourselves with patience and perseverance to the infinitely complicated task of removing racial discrimination, root and branch, from our common life, both in the Church and in the nation in which we live." Among other things, discrimination must be ended in all Methodist agencies, hospitals, schools, seminaries. Every Methodist and every Methodist church, conference, and institution must accept the achievement of full fellowship in our churches as a vital responsibility. The report closed, "We are not unmindful of the difficulties to which we summon The Methodist Church in this matter. For we are of all races and nations. Yet we are a frontier church! We therefore summon The Methodist Church once more to take up her position on a frontier."[94]

92. "In the Prophetic Succession," *The First Church Pulpit,* Vol. X, No. 2, a Garrett baccalaureate sermon preached June 12, 1949; "What Do We Want?" *The First Church Pulpit,* Vol. VII, No. 7, a sermon preached September 17, 1944. 1944.
93. *The Daily Christian Advocate,* The Methodist Church, May 6, 1948, p. 243.
94. *Ibid.,* May 7, 1948, pp. 276-77.

A Georgia delegate offered an extensive list of debilitating amendments, pleading that the report as presented implied the elimination of the Central jurisdiction and served only to raise more trouble and add more burdens. "Let's do things so that old feuds may be forgotten, that old wounds may be healed forever. Let's not be forever aggravating and tormenting and raising a problem," he concluded amidst applause. Tittle met the challenge:

> This problem is not a sectional problem; it is the problem of preaching the Christian gospel. I have lived for thirty years in a very conservative community, a community in which there is a vast concentration of wealth. I might in any one of those thirty years have said to myself: This is no time to preach certain aspects of the gospel. The preaching of such a gospel would stir up too much trouble in this parish. Had I done so, I would, sir, in my own opinion have been recreant to my calling as a minister of Jesus Christ. [Applause] We will never Crusade for Christ and His Church unless occasionally—if I may use a popular phrase—we stick our necks out. The unwillingness of ministers and laymen to stick their necks out in the name of Christ is defeating the ends that the Christian Church came into being to serve. [Applause] We preach the Cross of Christ; we sing about the Cross of Christ. There are times, my friends, when we have to take up His Cross in the sense of a little personal risk.[95]

The report was adopted. As always, Tittle received letters of gratitude for his leadership from Negroes and whites. And letters of criticism. Fifteen months later he died. The issue lived—and lives today.

VII

Shortly after his return from Boston, Tittle received a tormented letter from a white Methodist pastor in Louisiana. "We become like an island of loneliness in an infinite sea," the correspondent said of the little band of southern liberals. "And we cry out in our anguish: 'Does the church really mean what it says? Or were these merely fine words uttered in the security of Mechanics' Hall in Boston to be politely forgotten for another four years in Evanston and Ponchatoula?' " When the local newspaper carried a vicious editorial on race, the writer continued, he answered by calling attention to Methodism's position as set forth in Tittle's 1948 report. "Since then I have been showered with abuse and bitter criticism. I received just yesterday a letter of extreme bitterness calling me a 'nigger lover' (which I guess I am) and asking me if I wanted my wife to be raped by a 'nigger.' I now have several families

95. *Ibid.*, May 10, 1948, pp. 442-43.

staying away from church expressly because of the letter I wrote to the editor. I have some too who are calling fairly loudly for a new preacher. And, if the pattern follows, when our conference meets, I will be moved and in my place will be sent a pusillanimous pacifier who will never mention the subject and will seek to bring the divided units together." What is the local preacher to do if when he sticks his neck out it is certain to be chopped off?[96]

This letter stabs to the heart of Methodism's most signal failure in the area of race relations. When the letter was written, only about one hundred of the more than twenty thousand "white" Methodist pastoral charges in the United States were integrated with even one Negro member. First Church, Evanston, was not among the tiny minority of integrated local parishes.

It is true that in First Church Negroes utilized the parish house, attended conferences, spoke before various societies, participated in social affairs and worship services, and occasionally preached from the pulpit —and they were made to feel warmly welcome.[97] It is also true that Tittle fervently hoped that Negroes would become members and not merely guests. Yet "The Cathedral of Methodism" remained a membership of whites.

In 1933 the charge was circulated that a Negro woman was refused membership. This Tittle branded as "absolutely and libelously" false,[98] and a group of First Church officials signed a statement nailing the lie to the mast.[99] Two years later Mrs. Elizabeth Dilling whipped up hysteria by spotlighting the fact that black students had participated in a dance for Northwestern students in Great Hall under the sponsorship of the First Church Young People's Fellowship. As we know, Tittle was under intense pressure from the "patriots" at this time, and though he did not recant his views, his statements in private letters were excessively prudent. For example, he informed one individual that his 1932 General Conference resolution was not a "social equality plank."[100] This is

96. Letter from Edwin L. Brock to Tittle, August 15, 1948.
97. Letter from Clarence A. Bacote to author, March 8, 1960, who cited his own memories and those of other Negroes, including Dr. Rufus Clement and Bishop J. W. E. Bowen; author's interviews with Glenna Myers Tittle, Evanston, Ill., July 27, 1959, Raymond C. Wieboldt, Evanston, Ill., August 6, 1959, and James Alton James, Evanston, Ill., July 23, 1960; Minutes of the Official Board, First Church; and numerous items in the *First Church Review* and Evanston press. In several informal personal conversations, Professor Bacote confirmed his admiration for Tittle.
98. Letter from Tittle to Jesse Rudkin, March 7, 1933.
99. Letter from W. D. Schermerhorn, George A. Burcham, Edwin E. Voigt, Bruce H. Corzine, and Bernice B. Wolseley to W. J. Sherman, April 17, 1933.
100. Letter from Tittle to Mrs. Paul Douglas, May 7, 1935.

a narrow truth, but not the whole truth, for all the evidence proves that he believed in social as well as political, economic, and legal equality. To another individual he said, "I do not believe in intermarriage between the white race and black."[101] Yet again his entire life is testimony to the conviction that the Kingdom of God is a kingdom without caste, and that one day skin color would cease to make any difference whatsoever in even the most intimate of relationships, marriage.

It is necessary now to make a hard observation. The Christian Negro is himself guilty of idolatry. His church is his chief joy, in part because it is so definitely and completely his. He, too, has placed large value on the preservation of his institutional church and the powers, prerogatives, and prestige that a segregated church affords. He, too, cries, "Peace, peace," because the price of protest seems so painful. The important 1948 statement on "The Christian Church and Race" was written by Tittle and Harold A. Bosley. When Tittle died, Bosley became pastor of First Church. Ironically, as late as 1961, after a decade of assault on the walls of segregation, only four Negroes had elected to become members of First Church, and they were all drawn from the academic community. "For a while," related Dr. Bosley, "it seemed we would have some Negro professional people, too, but the Negro churches made it so hot for them they could not join! This is segregation in reverse!"[102]

VIII

On Tittle's death the Negro citizens of America in numerous communications expressed their admiration for "Dr. Tittle, faithful servant of God and mankind." It is altogether fitting that one of his last acts was to will his library to a Negro seminary.[103] Yet how absurd that in 1949 there still remained separated training for men of different color called to the work of God. "O Lord, have mercy upon us, miserable offenders."[104]

101. Letter from Tittle to Andrew J. Pruitt, November 26, 1935.
102. Letter from Harold A. Bosley to author, April 24, 1961. I suppose a Negro in turn might ask of Dr. Bosley, "Well, how many parishioners of your church left to join one of Evanston's black congregations?"
103. Letter from M. S. Davage, writing for Dr. Harry V. Richardson, president of Gammon Theological Seminary, to John M. Tittle, August 30, 1949.
104. I am prepared to admit that today my integrationist position is widely deemed old-fashioned and even reactionary, yet I cannot believe that black separatism is either a sound short-term strategy or a worthy long-range goal.

14. ECONOMIC JUSTICE

I

In 1921 Tittle addressed a ministerial conference in Minnesota. The *Minneapolis Daily News* carried his picture on the front page with the caption: "Millionaires' Pastor Says Welfare of Man Must Be First Concern of Industry, Rev. E. F. Tittle, Head of Wealthiest M. E. Congregation in World, Expresses Radical Views." Excerpts from the address followed, in which Tittle called for a Christianized social order, the substitution of the service motive for the profit motive, a just wage, and a larger voice by labor in the management of industry.[1] This little news item mirrors much of the history of Methodism's social concern in the last years of the nineteenth and opening decades of the twentieth century.

In the nineteenth century Methodism moved from sect to church—indeed, the largest and most muscular Protestant church in the nation—yet even as Methodists swelled with pride at this attainment of power and prestige they realized that Methodism was no longer the denominational home of the working masses, particularly as immigrant laborers increasingly manned the factories, mines, and mills of the industrial North. The middle-class nature of Northern Methodism at the turn of the century is rather conclusively demonstrated in the composition of the 1904 General Conference: "Of laymen, there were 55 merchants, 39 lawyers, 34 educators, 27 physicians, 20 bankers, 15 manufacturers, 12 judges, 9 capitalists; 7 each of clerks, contractors, farmers and real

1. September 22, 1921, p. 1, clipping in Tittle Collection.

estate agents; 6 insurance agents; 5 each of railroad officials, editors and mechanics; 3 stock and fruit growers, 2 business managers of church papers, 1 each of local preachers, State governors, architects, mining operators, students, revenue collectors, undertakers, nurserymen, and 32 miscellaneous and unknown."[2] As men who had struggled and survived in the Spencerian jungle of the Gilded Age and who now occupied the skilled blue-collar jobs and the managerial white-collar positions and, indeed, the seats in corporate board rooms, it was natural that they should look at questions of economic ethics through the eyes of the middle-class bourgeoisie.

Though Wesley preached to the Kingswood colliers and captured the enthusiasm of the poorer classes in England, Methodism even in its formative years was guided by men of the middle class. Though Methodist circuit riders won the hearts of American frontiersmen, the great revivals cannot be compared to the earlier radical religious movements capturing the European and English peasantry, for however poor the American farmer, he was considered—and considered himself—middle class. In sum, Methodism had been from its inception more middle class than anything else. Nevertheless, at the turn of the century it was more completely bourgeois in its composition and values than at any time in its history and more totally cut off from the urban industrial masses.

"My associates have come to look upon the church and the ministry as the apologists and defenders of the wrong committed against the interests of the people," declared Samuel Gompers of the American Federation of Labor. And Warren S. Stone, president of the Brotherhood of Locomotive Engineers, growled: "You want to know what labor thinks of the church. I tell you, very frankly, that labor does not think very much of the church, because the church does not think very much of labor." Even more bluntly, an old miner snarled, "The preacher points your eyes to heaven, and then the boss picks your pocket." And another grizzled veteran of the coal pits vowed, "I have to bow and scrape to the company all week, and by God, when I come to Sunday, I'll not have any damn boss telling me how to believe the Bible." The estrangement of the workers was not complete. Many immigrants remained in the church. When a racking textile strike broke out in Passaic, New Jersey, with the strikers victims of much brutality, a congressional investigation was called for by the local clergy: Katolicky sokol, Slovak Catholic sokol, Slovak Evangelical Union of America, St.

2. *The Daily Christian Advocate,* Methodist Episcopal Church, May 4, 1904, p. 5.

Vladimir Russian Orthodox Society, Marie S.S. dei miracoli Italian Catholic Church, Ascension Ukrainian Church. The *Christian Century* commented: "Here is the church, intervening at last in an industrial situation which has compelled the attention of the nation. But what church?"[3] It was not, obviously, the Methodist Church—or any other prestigious Protestant denomination rooted in the American past. Moreover, even as the established denominations were being drained of their working-class members—or more accurately, as the working-class members rose to middle-class status—the ranks of the Holiness, Pentecostal, and Adventist sects swelled. Thus, religion continued to be a consolation (if not an opiate) for many of the proletarian masses, but it was not often a consolation found in the sanctuaries of middle-class Methodism.

The sources of Methodist expression at the turn of the century reveal a deep, even desperate, awareness of labor's alienation. And a mighty effort was made to close the gulf. Almost all the points in the famous "Social Creed of Methodism" of 1908 centered on righting the wrongs suffered by the workers. The Methodist Federation for Social Service, in its early years, was far more implicated in the question of economic justice than in either racial justice or a warless world. Innumerable General Conference resolutions and Episcopal Addresses as well as Methodist press editorials and articles dealt with the exploitation of labor. Here and there Methodist clergymen investigated industrial conditions and supported strikes. Through a host of measures—home missions, social service, settlement houses, institutional churches, even a few labor churches—Methodism reached out its hand to the "toiling masses" (a phrase then much used), especially to the immigrants in the great industrial centers. Will Herberg characterized all this as the efforts of "morally sensitive middle-class people striving to do something for the 'underprivileged.' The spirit of *noblesse oblige* and Christian charity are curiously compounded in this concern, but there is little trace either of the evangelical fervor or of the movement from within the people themselves that won the continent for Christianity."[4] Measured by the statistics of conversion, Herberg is unquestionably correct. Methodism strained and brought forth a mouse. But if the church exists to serve the low and the lost rather than to fatten its membership rolls, then what does it matter if this great effort resulted in but few conversions

3. Quoted in Donald B. Meyer, *The Protestant Search for Political Realism, 1919-1941* (Berkeley and Los Angeles: University of California Press, 1960), p. 100.

4. *Protestant—Catholic—Jew* (Garden City, N.Y.: Doubleday & Company, 1955), p. 120.

of workers to the Methodist denomination? In any case, when in 1921 Tittle championed the rights of labor he was expressing a conviction widespread in the Methodist ministry. But the fact that he was talking about, not to, industrial workers, and that he was merely talking, further illuminates the distance between the Methodist Church and the labor community.

The Minnesota news item reveals a second facet of Methodism's response to the challenge of the industrialized and urban new century. Tittle was a preacher. A company of Protestant ministers and at least a platoon of Methodist clergymen forsook the pulpit to become professional social workers, labor organizers, Socialist party politicos, reform journalists, peripatetic gadflys in the cause of economic justice. The church's response to labor's fate may not be measured without reference to such "Fools-for-Christ" as A. J. Muste, such hard-headed and warm-hearted crusaders as Will W. Alexander, such passionate political evange-lists as Norman Thomas, and such labor organizers and union func-tionaries as Paul Blanshard, William Fincke, Albert Coyle, and Homer Martin. In an effort to understand their role, it is helpful to recall the parable of the "yeast" in the Gospels. It is necessary to look beyond pulpit utterances, denominational resolutions, church press editorials and the other formal evidences of religious opinion. These men in some cases withdrew from the institutional church in frustration, even dis-gust, but even when they judged the church unfaithful to Christ they remained faithful to his imperative: "of how much more value is a man than a sheep." They may have abandoned the official church, but did not—could not—cut the religious roots of their idealism.

The defections from the ministry were not inconsiderable, but Robert T. Handy is correct in stating: "Though the social gospel did call for action and did encourage responsible participation in phil-anthropic and political causes for the righting of social wrongs, its leaders were not so much activists as they were preachers, proclaimers, and educators. They sought to change men's views and attitudes, to win them to a new religio-social faith. The movement was strong in the pulpit and on the platform, and in the seminaries."[5] As a preacher, Tittle dealt in the coin of the spoken and written word, and though the coin was often debased by popular pulpiteers, it was the currency of the Social Gospel and, in fact, of Progressivism generally. Alert the Ameri-can public, educate the American public, proclaim to them the Word

5. *The Social Gospel in America, 1870-1920* (New York: Oxford University Press, 1966), p. 11.

of God and the findings of the new social engineers, and somehow economic injustice would be banished from society.

The news story touches a third aspect of the larger scene. Tittle was perhaps a rarity in being dubbed a "Millionaires' Pastor," but there was nothing eye-blinkingly unique in the pastor of a middle-class congregation expressing "radical views"—that is, if the term "radical" is taken with a liberal sprinkling of salt. The social Christianity of the early twentieth century was not a revolutionary attack on bourgeois society launched by the disinherited, but rather a reforming effort from within supported by Christians of means and rank; it was sheltered not in rural meeting houses or store-front "tabernacles," but rather in the larger, respectable urban and suburban parishes. It is not mere happenstance that the Social Gospel and Progressivism should flower at the same moment in American history; in fact, the relationship between the two movements is intimate. Progressivism, we are told, was not an uprising of the dispossessed industrial masses nor was it simply a continuation of the angry agrarian Populist protest. On the contrary, Progressivism was a middle-class movement arising in a period of relative prosperity and drawing support mostly from well-educated, economically well-off, old-stock Americans in whose hands as merchants, editors, lawyers, professors, and clergymen the reins of power and prestige traditionally had rested. As the old order passed, these men were made anxious by their loss of status, suffering a reduction less in income than in outlook, and they sought assurance of their continued social worth. Moreover, Progressivism was born of idealism as well as anxiety. The Progressives spoke in highly moral language. The entire movement was permeated with moral urgency. Unregenerate doers of evil would be toppled from the thrones in a great crusade led by an enlightened, educated, righteous elite. With Teddy Roosevelt they sang "Onward, Christian Soldiers," and stood at Armageddon to do battle for the Lord. And they were confident, holding as they did an evolutionary view of history and a hopeful view of malleable man, that society could be made, and was indeed becoming, sweeter and fairer.[6] The appeal of social Christianity was to the same elements in society that responded to the leadership of Roosevelt and Wilson. It is instructive that the "Social Creed of Methodism" of 1908 and the Bull Moose party platform of 1912 are virtually interchangeable. The Social Gospel in its agencies staffed by professionals, fact-finding studies, institutional outreach to the urban poor,

6. I am aware that not all historians are in agreement with this interpretation of Progressivism, if, in fact, there was such a thing as a Progressive movement. It would require a small book to summarize the conflicting interpretations.

and search for an orderly, rational, efficient solution to society's problems
was the religious counterpart to the hard—or scientific—side of Progressivism. In its faith in exhortation and revelation, the Social Gospel
was the religious counterpart to the soft—or moralistic—side of Progressivism. In either case, the witness of both the Progressives and
Social Gospelites was blurred by their general identification with and
acceptance of the American Way of Life. The critique of both was
blunted because they stood within, rather than outside, the American
consensus. And though both exposed and condemned the surface ills in
American society, neither penetrated to the sickness at the very heart
of that culture.

When in his Minnesota address Tittle admonished that labor *"be
given* a voice in the management of industry" he provided a hint to a
fourth facet of social Christianity in the early twentieth century. It was
not much aware of the nature of power; it did not possess a theology of
politics. As Donald Meyer and other students have discerned, the Social
Gospel had a tendency to "solve" problems of tactics by dissolving them
in good will. To evangelize and convert power rather than to bring
countervailing power against it seemed the essence of strategy. Thus, if
the possessors of power—the middle- and upper-class congregations of
America—could be presented with the vision of the Kingdom of God
and informed of the ethics of the Jesus of history and enlightened with
the findings of the sciences, then a cooperative commonwealth would be
ushered in, in which labor and capital shared in the great enterprise of
social justice. "When the spirit of Christ shall pervade the hearts of
individuals and when his law of love to God and man shall dominate
human society," read a report to the 1908 General Conference of
Northern Methodism, "then the evils which vex our civilization will
disappear."[7] It is not that the Social Gospelites expected the state to
wither away. They were not anarchists who believed the state to be an
enemy of freedom and justice. On the contrary, most champions of
social Christianity held an unreservedly optimistic view of the state.
They were as eager to grant the state control over the economic areas
of life as over such moral areas as liquor, prostitution, gambling, and
lurid literature. The state and the churches were allies in "Christianiz-
ing the Social Order" because the Social Gospel mind conceived of the
state in a platonic sense, transcending class interests and personal ambitions, a redeemed part of a society itself in the process of conversion.

Finally, the fact that in the news item the expressions by Tittle could

7. *The Daily Christian Advocate,* Methodist Episcopal Church, May 23, 1908,
p. 8.

be termed "radical" suggests the economic conservatism regnant in the 1920's. The decade was one of revolutionary intellectual and cultural change. It was even one of astonishing economic growth and innovation, including what was euphemistically called "welfare capitalism." But without entering into the great debate over the fate of Progressivism after World War I, we may say that even the mildest suggestions of economic reform were branded "bolshevistic" by much of the business community—and in the 1920's the business community knew its most prestigious hour.

II

In the second half of the twentieth century in the United States, in political, academic, and even religious circles, a slick, hard-nosed *Realpolitik*, which liked to compare itself favorably with the woolly minded idealism, soft-headed utopianism, and mushy moralism of the preceding generation of reformers, became fashionable. As I have suggested, the social Christianity of the early twentieth century was deeply flawed by illusions concerning the nature of social institutions and, indeed, of man. Yet we may be thankful that there were men such as Ernest Fremont Tittle in the Protestant pulpit in the "Golden Twenties" who continued to thunder against the idolatrous worship of the "bitch goddess—Success"; who continued to scourge the new kings of capitalism who "beat my people to pieces, and grind the faces of the poor"; who continued to warn the pious that (in Rauschenbusch's dictum) "We rarely sin against God alone"; and who proclaimed the vision of a coming kingdom of justice and love.

In sermons, addresses, and books Tittle repeatedly asserted that Christendom is not Christian, and that in the United States the "rule of gold" prevailed. Under this rule, labor suffered a "terrible loss of personality in huge mills and mines and factories," being reduced to a "part of a plant, a bit of human machinery, a means of production." "What the world to-day imperatively needs is some form of industrial democracy in which personality may be recovered."[8] Civilization would remain "semi-pagan" until men were persuaded to surrender the profit motive and risk the service motive.[9] Throughout the decade Tittle's Rock River Annual Conference had much to say about "unjust and intolerable" labor conditions, calling for minimum-wage, maximum-hour, and social-

8. *What Must the Church Do to Be Saved?* (New York and Cincinnati, Ohio: Abingdon Press, 1921), pp. 113-14, 161-62.
9. *The Religion of the Spirit* (New York and Cincinnati, Ohio: Abingdon Press, 1928), pp. 89, 306ff.

security legislation, and also for a federal child-labor amendment. Labor's right to organize and bargain collectively was recognized. When that right is denied, justifiable strikes follow. The present industrial system, built upon selfishness, is "as economically unsound as it is ethically unchristian." And for Tittle, "selfishness" was not a blemish of character but a theological concept, the very essence of sin. "An industry which cannot pay a living wage should be re-organized or passed out of existence."[10] Tittle did not attend his first General Conference until 1928, but in that year as a member of the Committee on the State of the Church he helped prepare a report (adopted by the Conference) critical of capitalism's exploitation of labor and of capitalism's emphasis on profits and the sanctity of private property.

I do not wish to magnify the significance of these expressions. The old parson who termed denominational resolutions the most harmless form of amusement ever devised by the human mind was issuing more than a pleasantry. And there is wisdom as well as wit in the advice of a young minister who when asked what a denominational social service commission might do for the common good, replied that they resign in a body as a protest against churches passing resolutions and doing nothing else. Moreover, it is well known that social service reports often represented only the opinions of the committee chairman and were accepted by the conservative majority in order to preserve harmony, with a tacit understanding that they would be forgotten after the meeting adjourned. Yet we also know that some of the reports engendered bitter debate and that once passed Tittle would quote them from the pulpit in order to place the Church's official position on public record. In any case, it is clear that Methodists in Rock River Annual Conference and General Conference were not left in doubt as to the economic injustices disfiguring the American landscape in the alleged "Era of Wonderful Nonsense," nor were they permitted to forsake the prewar questing spirit and relax into corpulency and contentment merely because President Harding "boviated" in the White House for more than two years and President Coolidge napped along the quiet Potomac for almost six years.

Tittle engaged in a continuing critique of a society that could boast of its wealth even as it doomed, through no fault of their own, millions of its citizens to poverty. Although the businessman and his janissaries in public office, editorial office, classroom, and pulpit could pronounce the perfection of America, great segments of the population (including

10. See the *Minutes* of the Rock River Annual Conference for the entire decade 1919-29.

frantically struggling little entrepreneurs) lived on the far side of paradise. Tittle, of course, could not but have been familiar with the sententious pronouncements of Harding and Coolidge, Mellon and Hoover, Babson and Barton, the NAM, and even William Green's AFL, all extolling the golden affluence of the "New Era." Tittle's response was akin to Mr. Dooley's observation: "I know histhry isn't thrue, Hinnissy, because it ain't like what I see ivery day in Halstead street."

Tittle continued to plead, "Let Christianity Again Become Revolutionary."[11] He continued to preach the hard truth, with facts and figures, that destitution was pervasive in the United States.[12] He identified Bruce Barton's best-selling biography of Jesus, *The Man Nobody Knows,* as the (unintended) blasphemy it was. He advised Methodist youth that they were living in "one of those momentous periods in human history in which an old order dies and a new order struggles to be born." Therefore he was willing to suspend judgment on events in Russia, saying: "If that old Russia, with its horrible serfdom, its political and ecclesiastical autocracy, its cowardly and stupid censorship, its continuous miscarriage of Justice and brutal persecutions—if that old Russia could have remained unshaken, would it not have become increasingly difficult for thoughtful persons to believe in God?"[13] When in 1925 a Students' Interdenominational Conference was held in First Church, though the press discerned a mood of radicalism and rebellion, Tittle dryly observed that the "middle aged fellows" (such as Niebuhr and himself) were in fact far more progressive than the young people.[14] He petitioned for the release of World War I political prisioners and for such "victims of injustice" as Mooney and Billings (though apparently he never commented publicly on the Sacco-Vanzetti case). He was of course an ardent member of the American Civil Liberties Union. In at least one instance he stood by the workers in a local strike, helping to quash the indictments issued against the strike leaders.[15] He once urged a national conference of clergymen to recognize the rights of church janitors and office employees to join unions. And no man held more strongly the conviction that the church should set an example in its own employment policies, not excluding the treatment of preachers.

Tittle was associated with and spoke before the Fellowship for a

11. *Christian Century,* XLI (April 3, 1924), 430-32.
12. See "Our Daily Bread," typed MS, a sermon preached March 18, 1928.
13. "In a Transition Period," *Epworth Herald,* XXXIV (July 21, 1923), 4.
14. *Evanston Review,* January 21, 1926, p. 1; *Evanston News-Index,* December 30, 1925, p. 1, and December 31, 1925, p. 1.
15. See letter from Worth M. Tippy to Tittle, April 21, 1924.

Christian Social Order, a group organized in 1921 by Sherwood Eddy, Kirby Page, and Reinhold Niebuhr to secure social justice.[16] He was a member of the Fellowship of Reconciliation, a pacifist organization that believed a warless world could be realized only if poverty, injustice, exploitation, and racial pride were first ameliorated. For most in the Fellowship, this meant the destruction of capitalism, that breeder of war and injustice. He was a member of the League for Industrial Democracy, a hard-hitting defender of labor and critic of capitalism. And, of course, he was a member of the Methodist Federation for Social Service, Methodism's true gadfly in the twenties. He contributed financially to its support and repeatedly defended it from attack, inside and outside the church. And the attacks were fierce and continuing, centering on the leadership of Harry F. Ward (not yet a Marxist) and most especially his sympathetic efforts to understand the Russian revolution and his opposition to management's vaunted (and spurious) open-shop, "American Plan" campaign. The Federation sponsored two conferences on Christianity and the Economic Order in 1922 and 1926. Significantly, they were held in Evanston, Tittle acting as chairman of the local arrangements. These were notable meetings, attended by several hundred leading churchmen, with Bishop McConnell presiding on both occasions. The temper of the delegates was critical, and in 1926 extremely so. The immorality of the economic order was not merely questioned, it was assumed. Capitalism was accused of destroying freedom, justice, and fraternity.[17] As mentioned earlier, in 1928 Tittle voted for Norman Thomas. Hoover, the victor, declared in his triumphant acceptance address: "We in America today are nearer to the final triumph over poverty than ever before in the history of any land. . . ." At least one Protestant clergymen—two if Thomas is counted—demurred.

III

As it turned out, Hoover was mistaken. For some churchmen, the depression was attributed to the "Providence of God"—to use the wording of the Southern Baptist Convention. "The nations that forget God," the Convention continued, "shall not prosper."[18] Poverty was just punishment for a prodigal people. The land was reaping a bitter har-

16. See *Evanston News-Index*, February 17, 1923, p. 1.

17. There is a good study of the Federation: Milton John Huber, "A History of the Methodist Federation for Social Action" (Ph.D. dissertation, Boston University, 1949). However, I made an independent investigation of Federation sources.

18. *Annual of the Southern Baptist Convention*, 1932, pp. 86-87.

vest, the seeds of which were sown in the sinful twenties. If an angry God unleashed the depression, only an appeased God would lift the yoke. Hence economic recovery waited upon a religious revival. But the revival never materialized. A people shorn of their wealth did not turn to God.

For other churchmen, the depression was a herald of the last days and men could but wait in trembling expectation; or if their theology was Kierkegaardian or Barthian rather than chiliast, they remained above the "housekeeping chores" of politics, leaving social reform to "busybodies who suffer from a lack of humor" in order to proceed with the main business of the self's confrontation with God.

Some churchmen, such as Gerald L. K. Smith and Gerald Winrod, embraced a crypto-fascism, convinced that America's economic health had been poisoned by a Communist-Jewish virus. Others, such as Harry F. Ward, spoke the language of Marx and extolled the Soviet Union as the world's last, best hope while America staggered like a blinded Samson chained to the millstone of capitalism, though more often than not the clerical "fellow travelers" were really utopian socialists rather than Marxian communists and they represented a liberal heresy rather than a challenge to liberalism.

A small but articulate and extremely influential band of churchmen led by Reinhold Niebuhr became in the early 1930's Christian Marxists. Not Communist party members, not innocents duped into following the party line, not uncritical of the repressive aspects of Soviet society or unaware of the utopian elements in the Marxist vision, they sought to do justice to the best insights of historic Christianity and the Marxian dialectic, believing that the "Christian Church should recognize the essential conflict between Christianity and the ethics of capitalistic individualism" and believing also that the "evolutionary optimism of current liberal Christianity is unrealistic."[19]

A much larger element representing the mainstream of Protestant liberalism saw in President Franklin D. Roosevelt's New Deal the embodiment of the social justice for which the churches had been laboring since the days of Teddy Roosevelt. As New Deal act after act was passed it almost seemed as though the president was ticking off for enshrinement into law the "Social Creed of Methodism" and the Federal Council's "Social Ideals of the Churches." Indeed, Dr. Albert W. Beaven, president of the Federal Council, informed the representatives

19. For a more extended discussion of the Fellowship of Socialist Christians, see Robert Moats Miller, *American Protestantism and Social Issues, 1919-1939* (Chapel Hill: The University of North Carolina Press, 1958), pp. 93-94.

gathered on December 8, 1933, to celebrate the twenty-fifth anniversary of the council's founding: "We rejoice in the many ways in which President Roosevelt's program for recovery embodies Christian social ideals for which the churches have long contended, and call upon our people for the most whole-souled and unselfish support of all those cooperative enterprises of goodwill by which, under the President's inspiring leadership, we hope to achieve the better tomorrow."[20] Among those in the audience who applauded was Franklin D. Roosevelt, who had accepted the invitation to deliver the keynote address.

Still other churchmen remained rooted to a conservative persuasion, viewing That Man in the White House a threat to American liberties and the New Deal a betrayal of American individualism. In truth, probably a majority of Protestant clergymen continued to find their political home in the Republican party. In 1936, 21,606 ministers replied to the question asked by the *Literary Digest*: "Do you *now* approve the acts and policies of the Roosevelt New Deal to date?" Some 70.22 per cent, or 15,172, replied "no."[21] "For the moment," wrote the perceptive John C. Bennett in 1939, "one of the hardest facts to face is that the success of the most promising political forces in American life [the New Deal] must be in spite of the opposition of the majority of the members of the Protestant churches."[22]

Let us now attempt to place Tittle on this continuum of Protestantism's political response to the challenge of the depression—a response, as we have seen, ranging from those who were washed in the blood of the Marxian lamb to those who would raise up a man on horseback—a Mussolini or Hitler—to save America through fascism.

Inaugurated in March, Herbert Hoover's ordeal began only months later when in October the Great Bull Market disintegrated. Tittle had much to say in his sermons about the depression, but not once did he publicly criticize Hoover's leadership. The things that the Hoover administration did to rescue the nation and the things left undone were not mentioned in the First Church pulpit.[23] Yet Tittle could not have been totally impressed by Hoover's efforts to combat the depression, however humane and even bold were these efforts compared to the

20. Albert W. Beaven, "The Spirit and Service of the Federal Council," Federal Council of Churches *Annual Report,* 1933, p. 20.
21. February 22, 1936, p. 8. A poll by this magazine in 1934 on the same subject revealed 13,513 clergymen in favor of the New Deal and 11,346 in opposition.
22. *Christian Century,* LVI (February 8, 1939), 181.
23. That is, Hoover's domestic policies did not receive comment; his foreign policies did.

inaction of earlier depression presidents and measured by the canons of laissez-faire orthodoxy. In June, 1932, he replied to an inquiry that "under no circumstances will I vote the Republican ticket!"[24] And in November he proceeded to again vote for Norman Thomas after joining with thirty-two Methodist ministers in penning an appeal on behalf of the candidacy of Thomas.[25] It is helpful to an understanding of the Methodist social passion to recall that in 1932 few Methodist liberals voted for either Thomas *or* Roosevelt. Just before the election, a group of Methodist ministers, including Daniel L. Marsh, Fred B. Fisher, Frank Mason North, Ralph W. Sockman, Lynn Harold Hough, Arlo A. Brown, Ralph E. Dieffendorfer, and Bishop Edwin Holt Hughes, announced their support of Hoover, for "no mind, in Washington or elsewhere, has towered above his in an effort to meet these problems with courage, with sympathy, with sanity, with understanding, and with infinite patience."[26] In October a straw poll was taken of the Rock River Annual Conference ministers: eighty-six intended to vote for Hoover, fourteen for Thomas, but none for Roosevelt. Patently FDR before taking office was distrusted in the Methodist world, and though the *Chicago Tribune* branded the Rock River Conference as socialistic, only a minority followed Tittle's example in voting for Thomas.

As Tittle had virtually nothing to say from the pulpit about specific measures of the Hoover administration, so he almost never mentioned specific New Deal acts. However, in private letters he was enthusiastic in his praise of Roosevelt's early leadership. In 1934 he wrote a young disciple: "Personally I feel very much encouraged over the way American society appears now to be moving under the Roosevelt direction. Not only are we getting more social control of business, industry and finance that I supposed we could get in so short a time but also and even more significantly a new attitude of mind, a new sense of social responsibility, a new outlook on life. So I, for one, am carrying on with high hopes and mounting enthusiasm."[27] And to the president he reported, "Please allow me to say that I approve and applaud your several acts of real statesmanship."[28]

In expressing this admiration Tittle stood with the majority wing of Social Gospel reformism, especially as reflected in the leadership of the

24. Letter from Tittle to James McCurrach, June 27, 1932.
25. Numbered among these gentlemen were Frank Kingdom, Halford Luccock, Edgar S. Brightman, Harris Franklin Rall, Dan B. Brummitt, James Yard, Robert J. Tucker, Paul Hutchinson, and Wade C. Barclay.
26. *Christian Century,* XXXIX (October 19, 1932), 1285.
27. Letter from Tittle to Robert Hamill, January 23, 1934.
28. Letter from Tittle to The President of the United States, May 22, 1933.

Federal Council of Churches. The New Deal, it was originally believed, heralded the dawning of a new day. But it was not long before many were disenchanted. Somehow the free-wheeling, pragmatic, power-oriented, and sharply limited New Deal reforms seemed to fall miserably short of the Social Gospel ideal of a cooperative commonwealth. And so while lauding Roosevelt's reform measures, Tittle continued to cherish the socialist dream, voting once again for Norman Thomas in 1936. After that date, Roosevelt's foreign policies so completely estranged Tittle that by 1940 he was unalterably opposed to continuing Roosevelt in the White House.

In 1934 Kirby Page, in association with a group of noted church leaders representing ten different Protestant denominations and the Jewish faith, sent out a questionnaire to 100,499 clergymen. Replies from 20,870 were received. Approximately half the questions concerned foreign affairs. Then the questionnaire turned to such economic matters as drastic limitations on wealth and income, labor unions, social security, banking regulation. Finally the clergymen were asked to choose between two economic systems: capitalism embodying the attribute of "rugged individualism" or a co-operative commonwealth in which the service motive predominates. Only 5 percent favored capitalism, suggesting the meaninglessness of the question. The ministers were then asked which political system they believed would best bring about the establishment of this "cooperative commonwealth." Approximately 51 percent answered "drastically reformed capitalism" and 28 percent (or 5,879) selected socialism as "represented by the Socialist Party of America, or by a new and more inclusive socialistic alignment, in which the present Socialist Party would be included." Socialist opinion among Methodists (34 percent) ran higher than in any other denomination. Fascism, as in Italy, was favored by 111 respondents; communism, as in Soviet Russia and as represented by the Communist Party of the United States, by 123.[29] Tittle participated in the poll, confiding that his answers "were all as radical as the questionnaire would allow, excepting only in the last case, where I voted for the Norman Thomas variety of socialism instead of communism."[30] He was joined in his endorsement of socialism by such Methodist friends as Paul Hutchinson, Halford Luccock, and Bishop McConnell.

Additional evidence reveals Tittle's commitment to the evolutionary socialism represented by the party of Debs and Thomas. "I have just

29. See Kirby Page, "20,870 Clergymen on War and Economic Justice," *World Tomorrow*, XVII (May 10, 1934), 222-56.
30. Letter from Tittle to Robert Hamill, January 23, 1934.

learned that you refused the Republican nomination for Governor of Indiana because of the wet plank in the party platform," he informed Arthur Sapp. "I am writing to say, Bully for you! The Republican party is hopeless anyhow. I am hoping that you will become a good Socialist, in which case I will vote for you as President in case we can persuade Norman Thomas to withdraw. But seriously, I am awfully proud of you, old fellow, and want you to know it."[31] On another occasion he wrote a colleague: "Hail and hurrah! Hail to you. Hurrah not only for you but for a Methodist Episcopal Church which allows its minister to become a candidate on the Socialist ticket for a place in the state legislature. Seriously, I am very proud of you, and with all my heart I rejoice in the noble adventure in which you are engaged."[32] Why, then, did Tittle not join the Socialist party? Many ministers did.[33] He supplied his own answer: "My one only reason for not joining the Socialist Party (I subscribe to its budget) is my belief that *in order* to preach effectively the gospel of the kingdom of God I must keep myself free from any suspicion of political partisanship, so that when I appeal for a new social and economic order I will appear to my people to be speaking in the name of Christ, not in the name of any political candidate or party."[34]

We have seen that only rarely did Tittle in his sermons refer to specific measures of relief, recovery, and reform of the Hoover and Roosevelt administrations; and not once did he voice from the pulpit support of a particular political party or candidate. But he did not take a Christian Science attitude toward the economic sickness in the land. He looked squarely at the physical and psychic toil exacted by the depression. It was real, not, as some alleged, merely the fanciful imaginings of "bleeding heart" liberals or the excuses of society's deadbeats or the propaganda of Communists. In sermon after sermon Tittle described the hellish reality of unemployment, bread lines, Hoovervilles, hunger riots, Okies, scavenged garbage dumps, youths riding the rails, broken morale, blighted dreams. Though most First Church members felt the lash of the depression and some were beaten to their knees, it is probably true that the majority were sheltered from the utter destitution visited upon laborers in the industrial centers and the small farmers. But they

31. Letter from Tittle to Arthur Sapp, July 21, 1932.
32. Letter from Tittle to Andrew Juvinall, November 6, 1934.
33. See Miller, *American Protestantism and Social Issues,* chap. vii, for evidence supporting this statement, based in part on an examination of the records of the Socialist party at Duke University.
34. Letter from Tittle to William Kroll, April 30, 1934.

could not long have worshipped in Tittle's church unaware that millions of their fellow citizens were ill-fed, ill-clad, and ill-housed.

"The Bible speaks of days of judgment," Tittle thundered. "Almost beyond doubt ours is one of them. An old order has been condemned, the order that produced the World War and is now producing world-wide unemployment. Unless we are fools or cowards we shall not be content with this old order; and even though we ourselves were willing to tolerate it a moral universe might not be. The choice which appears to lie before us is whether we shall allow ourselves to drift into revolution, anarchy and chaos, or whether we shall dare to believe in the possibility of a new and nobler social order and proceed at whatever personal cost to bring it to pass."[35] Again: "An era of selfish profit-seeking has come to a tragic end in a world-wide catastrophe. Like physical lust, selfish competition appears to carry within itself the seeds of its own destruction. It now remains to be seen whether our present capitalist system can survive. It is, however, practically certain that it cannot survive unless it is made to serve not only the fancied interests of the few but the real needs of all."[36] And again: "There are some among us who believe that the capitalistic system is doomed, that with or without a violent revolution it will presently collapse through inherent weakness. I for my part am not so sure about that, but I am sure about this: If the capitalistic system is to survive it must be made to serve . . . not only the interests of the few but the welfare of all. It must produce with reference to ascertained needs; and the power which is placed in its hands by labor-saving machinery and improved technologies it must be willing to use and to learn how to use for the benefit of all."[37]

In sum, on scores of instances Tittle held rugged individualism or, as he termed it, irresponsible egoism,[38] responsible for the depression. Moreover, he despaired of securing any substantial disarmament in the present capitalistic order, an order based "upon reckless and unregulated competition for private gain"; which is to say, he despaired of international peace as long as the old economic order prevailed. Armaments are but the outward, visible sign of an inner strife—a strife engendered when men selfishly, recklessly pursue private gain.[39] Tittle clearly favored the establishment of some sort of socialized society—a co-opera-

35. *We Need Religion* (New York: Henry Holt & Co., 1931), p. 31.
36. *Jesus After Nineteen Centuries* (New York and Cincinnati, Ohio: Abingdon Press, 1932), pp. 157-58.
37. *We Need Religion*, p. 29.
38. *A Way to Life* (New York: Henry Holt & Co., 1935), p. 110.
39. *Christians in an Unchristian Society* (New York: Association Press, 1940), p. 23.

tive commonwealth, to employ a favorite term of the day—but his socialism was undogmatic and unprogrammatic. Moreover, he was unwilling to employ violence or to sacrifice democratic liberties to usher in the new order. This of course opened him to the charge of "irrelevant moralism" and brought him into sharp debate with the Christian Marxists.

Tittle's heightened concern in the depression decade in economic justice is revealed not only in his sermons, but also in the statements of the Rock River Annual Conference, statements, as we know, often emanating from his pen and defended by his voice. Declared the Conference: "We cannot hold any order as Christian which is organized upon the principle of competition, which appeals to the motive of selfish profit, and which makes of our economic order a system of warfare between individual and individual, class and class, one business organization and another, one nation and another. The Kingdom of God cannot be built upon the poverty of the many and absurd and cruel wealth of the few. From the viewpoint of citizenship we of America know that the democracy for which our fathers died may be destroyed by the inhuman and un-Christian monopoly of great wealth." Therefore, "we hail with delight the promise of a new order in which natural resources and the principal means of production and distribution shall be brought under some form of intelligent control and operated with a view to the common good."

Throughout the decade Rock River Methodists addressed themselves to specific measures. The state of Illinois and the United States Congress must take immediate and bold relief action to succor the unemployed, for private charity was unequal to the task. Unemployment, sickness, and old-age insurance was imperative. Labor's right to organize and bargain collectively was championed, but labor unions were admonished to end the color line and also to recognize "their obligation to the working class as a whole, especially as to the organization of the weaker and more exploited groups." The Methodist Book Concern was petitioned to practice the principle of collective bargaining in its own operations. The WPA was not deemed a dole. The Supreme Court was praised for upholding the National Labor Relations Act. "We welcome the National Industrial Recovery Act, not because we look upon it as a panacea for all our ills, but because we see in it the possible beginning of a planned economy." Minimum-wage, maximum-hour, and child-labor legislation was endorsed.

Moreover, every meeting delivered a strong statement on civil liberties, reprobating "the method of repression and the denial of such rights whether found in the autocratic communism of Russia, the autocratic fascism of Italy, or in this country in the misuse of authority or in those misguided attempts, not infrequently in the name of patriotism, which alike contravene our Constitution and tend to promote violence. Especially do we condemn any effort to limit the prophetic freedom of the pulpit or the private rights of the preacher as a citizen in the line of his political preference." The teachers' oath movement was characterized as ill-advised; dangerous, too, was the "persistent effort of certain newspapers to mislead their readers by inciting unwarranted fears of the Communist menace." Perhaps this was a pointed reference to those Chicago papers which zeroed in on Tittle. And it is possible that First Church was in the minds of the delegates when they deplored "the attempt to suppress free speech and free discussion . . . recently witnessed in connection with well-known young people's organizations. This attempt at intimidation on the part of certain self-appointed vigilantes is, in our opinion, an un-American spirit masquerading in the guise of patriotism."[40]

Common sense dictates the diluting of these astringent resolutions and reports. We know that in their political behavior not many members of the Rock River Conference actually "went socialist." Yet it would be unfair to the memory of Tittle and his progressive comrades to assume that it was all a charade. Many of the sessions were stormy. Many of the debates were angry. The conservative wing of the conference did not meekly submit to being placed on record as critics of capitalism. And sometimes they were successful in beating back liberal proposals. Regarding the 1934 session, the *Christian Century* reported: "Another amendment . . . offered by Dr. Ernest F. Tittle of Evanston, scarcely less socialistic in its outlook, was adopted by a large majority, in spite of bitter opposition, led chiefly by Charles O. Loucks, president of the laymen's conference."[41] We may begin to comprehend how bruising was the battle when it is remembered that Mr. Loucks, a skilled lawyer, was a leading Evanston citizen.

Tittle was, of course, under intense fire in Evanston in the 1930's, but he was not the only minister to return from a Rock River meeting to "face the music" at home from a conservative congregation. And many of the younger ones wrote Tittle of their troubles, whereupon he would flash some such note as this: "Perhaps you will allow me, as an old codger, who has himself been in difficulties aplenty, to urge you to

40. See the *Minutes* of the Rock River Annual Conference for the entire decade.
41. LI (October 17, 1934), 1319.

keep a cool head, a smiling countenance, and an undisturbed heart. God, I find, has a way of taking care of men who are eager to serve him, and He will, I am sure, take care of you."[42] Apparently God sometimes failed to inform Methodist bishops and their cabinets of how he wished his servants cared for—and the servants were overwhelmed with bitterness. The point can be made without adornment by simply quoting a letter to Tittle dated November 21, 1939:

Dear Dr. Tittle:

When I wanted to see you back in October, I was in a very much upset state of mind. Since then I have somewhat recovered my balance . . . .

As you may have heard, I am very much hurt by the treatment accorded by the Bishop and His Cabinate at the last Annual Conference. They bragged that they would send [the writer's name] where he "can't lead labor parades" (the words of one D.S.) and I guess they have accomplished their purpose. As my wife's health is broken, there is not much to do about it now. But I shall not forget either their unfair actions or the ease with which my "friends" found excuses for their actions. I am now back where I started fifteen years ago, a little church, a little parish, a little salary and no great crusade for broken humanity. The people of my parish are nice middle class folks and I must play chaplain to a dying class in a dying order. Even in my dreams I am rebellious.

Rightly, I think, my wife chids me and seeks to show me how in-evitable it all was. I knew it with my mind but the experience is almost too bitter. Of course we are trying to make the best of it till something can be done. She is loyal and that means a lot.

And at long last the social movement within the churches has turned out to be a failure. It is not a fellowship of kindred spirits in my opinion ready to sacrifice for each other but a mere collection of individuals, each insisting on his own "jot and tittle" of the social gospel law. Even those who make no pretence of a social view-point do not even so much as think this mutual aid is necessary. All with one accord manufacture excuses why it would be well for thus and so to happen. And thus they salve their conscience and continue the merry game of grab. There is, in my opinion, as much politics in an Annual Conference as there is in the machines that run City Hall of Chicago, only the former goes on under the pious cloak of religion. I love a political fight. But give me a good clean knock-down-and-drag-out kind such as it is to be found anywhere except within the "sacred" walls of the ecclesiastical institutions of religion.

Before I close I wish to thank you for your intervention with the Bishop on my behalf. Even though the Bishop may have

42. Letter from Tittle to Howard Buxton, November 3, 1938.

fooled you as to the nature of his intentions toward me, you were not to blame for what happened. You may be interested to know that so far as I have been able to learn no one else even so much as spoke to the Bishop about me. . . . Everyone else pretty well left the sinking ship. And I hope that by now you, too, see how the Bishop fooled you in the way in which my case was to be handled.[43]

On reflection, perhaps this letter is as revealing of some liberals as it is of some bishops and their "Cabinates."

Tittle traveled to the 1932 General Conference in Atlantic City as chairman of the Rock River delegation and member of the Committee on the State of the Church. He returned feeling "bruised and disgusted"—as did many delegates. The *Christian Century* correspondent termed it a "conference of depression; negative, unadventurous, even timorous. It has been responsive to every note of fear, cold to every plea for daring, and bold only in its determination to retrench wherever a salary could be cut, a service curtailed or an agency of the church discontinued."[44] The following week the correspondent packed his bags, concluding that the Conference had flickered out in futility. An agonizing nineteen ballots were required to elect only two bishops. Criticism of the episcopacy was rampant. The failure of prohibition haunted the assemblage. Full ministerial status to women was denied. Enterprise after enterprise was set adrift because of lack of funds. When at the close of one session a bishop-elect pronounced the Aaronic benediction, ending "and give thee peace," one discouraged delegate was heard to murmur under his breath, "Without expense to the general conference expense fund!"[45]

Nevertheless, it cannot be maintained that the conference was completely blind to the nation's social problems. The Episcopal Address sounded a call to take up arms against the sea of troubles. The industrial practices of the past decade were blamed for the appalling paradox of bursting granaries and starving people, banks bulging with money and ghastly poverty, idle machinery and idle men anxious to work, mountains of coal and children freezing, cotton piled high in warehouses and millions thinly clad. "Industry has as a rule given labor a grudging, insufficient wage, keeping it down by child exploitation, by suppression of legitimate organizations, and by other expedients, while at the same time huge fortunes have been amassed for the favored owners of the

43. I think it would be uncharitable to identify the author. He was well known in the Chicago area for his crusading passion.
44. IXL (June 1, 1932), 713.
45. *Ibid.*, p. 714.

resources of production. To-day the burden is without conscience shifted to the worker who, after giving his labor for miserable financial results, is turned off to starve or beg. Thus, the machine, which might have been used to lift the load of poverty from the backs of all the people, has been used selfishly for the benefit of the few." The Kingdom of God cannot be built upon the poverty of the many and the absurd and cruel wealth of the few. As the senior bishop read these blunt passages, the delegates burst into applause.[46]

Moreover, Tittle introduced a resolution that the conference send a delegation to Washington to personally petition the president and Congress to institute immediate federal relief, private charity and state relief funds now being reduced almost to starvation level. Tittle defended the resolution, saying:

> There are sections of our country that need Federal relief. I live in one of them. I live on the edge of a city which has had corrupt politics, but that is bye the bye. The fact is that millions of people in our part of the world are on the dizzy edge of starvation, and the question is death. You and I have been living here for several weeks in hotels along a boardwalk that is famous. We have had plenty to eat. I beg of you in the closing hour of this Conference not to take an action which would lead people outside the Christian Church to point to the amount that we have spent here on ourselves and then say, "Before they adjourned they refused to do one thing that they might have done to persuade the Federal Government in cases where it is needed to provide relief on conditions which the Government itself would lay down."[47]

Bishops McDowell, Hughes, and McConnell were soon off to Washington to place Tittle's petition before the Hoover administration. Moreover, the conference adopted reports of the Committee on the State of the Church terming the depression "both a spur and a rebuke to the Christian Church," noting the poverty that existed in the midst of plenty, and calling for the "replacement of our present policy of unplanned, competitive industrialism with a planned industrial economy, which aims definitely at economic security for all."[48]

46. *Journal of the General Conference of the Methodist Episcopal Church,* 1932, pp. 171-74; *The Daily Christian Advocate,* Methodist Episcopal Church, May 4, 1932, p. 57.

47. *The Daily Christian Advocate,* Methodist Episcopal Church, May 26, 1932, p. 678.

48. *Journal of the General Conference of the Methodist Episcopal Church,* 1932, pp. 652-55; *The Daily Christian Advocate,* Methodist Episcopal Church, May 20, 1932, pp. 444-45 and May 24, 1932, pp. 594, 678.

In the 1930's an anticapitalist temper in fact infused a significant and articulate minority within American Methodism. Increasingly pulpits rang with jeremiads in denunciation of the "fat cats" whose greed had brought on these lean years. Increasingly Annual Conferences, such as the New York East, pronounced that "the twenty-five months of strenuous effort under the New Deal to reform the system has only proved that it is beyond reform. The conviction grows, therefore, that capitalism must be discarded and a planned Christian economy established. . . . The tenderness with which the sacred cow of private profits has been protected, while suffering has been indescribably inhuman, indicts both the intelligence and the character of our nation."[49] The Methodist Federation for Social Service tacked sharply and dangerously to the Left. In 1932 Chicago Methodists organized a Christian Social Action Movement predicated on the assumption that capitalism was doomed and that the economic aims of the Socialist party most nearly coincided with the principles of Christianity. The National Council of Methodist Youth, formed in 1934, chided the New Deal for its pusillanimity, declaring: "We endorse socialism, as being at present, the most workable political expression of Christian social ideals. Essentially socialism, as we define it, is the theory of government based on the principles of public ownership and democratic control of natural resources, public utilities, and all basic and essential industries for public use instead of for private profit."[50] Indeed, throughout the land Methodist young people "renounced" capitalism and pledged themselves to the building of an economic order based on co-operation and unselfishness, holding "the possession of wealth is unbecoming a Christian."[51]

Vastly disturbed, Methodist businessmen formed such groups as the Conference of Methodist Laymen to check the spread of radicalism and to reorient the pulpit along personal rather than social lines. "We are going to demand a settlement of the status of the Communist-influenced Methodist Federation for Social Service, and of clergymen and church officials who use their positions to preach Socialism and Communism," the businessmen announced.[52] Greatly exercised, Methodist churchmen such as the Reverend Rembert Gilman Smith published warnings entitled *Moscow Over Methodism* and *Methodist Reds* and organized the Meth-

49. *New York Times,* May 14, 1935, p. 21.
50. Miron A. Morrill (ed.), *Methodist Youth Council* (Chicago: National Council of Methodist Youth, 1934), p. 178.
51. Theodore Graebner, *The Business Man and the Church: An Economic Study* (Clinton, S. C.: n.p., 1942), p. 10. See also *Northwestern Christian Advocate,* LXXXII (September 27, 1934), 798.
52. *Social Questions Bulletin,* May, 1936, p. 2.

odist League Against Communism, Fascism, and Unpatriotic Pacifism to combat radicalism in general and the Methodist Federation for Social Service in particular—or, to use Smith's nomenclature, the "Marxist Federation for Social Strife." And of course the Hearst press and the *Chicago Tribune,* the American Legion and the Liberty League, and a host of other patriotic societies entered the lists to splinter lances with the subverters of true Americanism and true Wesleyanism. "Rid the M.E. Church of 'Red' Incubus," was the title of a typical exposé.

It was anticipated that at the 1936 General Conference there would be a "show down" between conservatives and liberals. The religious press headlined "The Coming Battle At Columbus." The conference was likened to a gladiatorial grapple from which it was possible for only one of the contestants to emerge alive. When it was all over, many observers characterized the conference as a smashing defeat for the liberals, and if they were not quite exterminated, at the very least they were forced to beat a severe retreat. There is truth in this evaluation, but it is not the whole truth. A Negro quartet opened a conference session with the song, "Keep in the Middle of the Road."[53] The selection was, if not providential, certainly appropriate. Tittle was not a member of the Committee on the State of the Church and therefore its long report need not be quoted. Deliberately designed to be "The Peace Pact of Methodism," the report reviewed the terrible suffering caused by the depression, listing fourteen specific evils in American economic life ranging from unemployment through inequality of income to tenant farming. Solutions were suggested, including demisocialism, co-operatives, and "enlightened" capitalism, but whatever the solution Methodists were pledged to work within the democratic form and to resist both the totalitarianism of communism and fascism.[54] Thus, though the 1936 conference did retreat from its 1932 utterances, it was hardly pushed back as far as the conservative trenches. Significantly, Tittle himself believed the statements on economic justice "fine and significant"[55] and characterized the conference as outstanding.[56]

Of course, the unofficial nature of the Methodist Federation for Social Service was pointedly emphasized, but on the other hand the conservatives did not succeed in denying to it the name Methodist nor were

53. *The Daily Christian Advocate,* Methodist Episcopal Church, May 18, 1936, p. 456.

54. *Journal of the General Conference of the Methodist Episcopal Church,* 1936, pp. 513-19.

55. Letter from Tittle to Harry W. Knowles, June 9, 1936.

56. *Evanston Daily News-Index,* May 20, 1936, p. 7.

they able to replace it with a more tractable official social-service commission.

Nevertheless, when the Board of Bishops in the closing sessions voted to replace Bishop Edgar Blake with Bishop Edna Leonard as the head of the Board of Education and when the conservative Leonard proceeded to purge the board of its liberal members, particularly two young social-ists, Owen Geer and Blaine Kirkpatrick, Tittle was outraged. "It is, of course, a thousand pities that the reactionary members of the Board of Bishops threw their monkey wrench into the 'peace pact' between the liberal and conservative groups," he wrote a friend. "However, the end is not yet, and I still have hope that we shall be able to retain the great services of Kirkpatrick and Geer. In any case, we shall not take this regrettable action lying down."[57] The following day Tittle wrote Dr. Frederick C. Eiselen, corresponding secretary of the Board of Education: "It is a vast pity that our conservative brethren are now attempting to throw a monkey wrench into the 'peace pact' which was made at Colum-bus. The liberals among us who went away in high hope that we had found a Way in which the whole church could move on toward the City of God are now being led to suspect that we were cruelly tricked. What a pity! What a vast pity! This terrible, although apparently well grounded, suspicion simply must now be removed, as it only can be by the retention of these two men, who have become human symbols of a point of view, an outlook on life, which at least a large and significant minority within the church considers to be Christian."[58] By the fall of the year Tittle still recalled the "skulduggery practiced by our reaction-ary bishops at the close of the General Conference," but he now believed the youth movement in the Board of Education to be in good hands. "As a matter of fact," he estimated, "Heil Bollinger is almost if not quite as radical as either Kirkpatrick or Geer. But the question of per-manent personnel remains to be answered and it behooves all right-minded Methodists to maintain an everlasting vigilance."[59]

Tittle pursued the dream of economic justice in ways additional to proclaiming God's judgment from the pulpit and seeking to place Meth-odism on record through Annual and General Conference action. For one thing, First Church during the depression offered a varied program to minister to the physical needs and broken morale of Evanston's citi-zens. For another, Tittle sought to advise his parishioners on specific economic problems. For a third, Tittle wrote a bundle of letters urging

57. Letter from Tittle to Harry W. Knowles, June 9, 1936.
58. Letter from Tittle to Frederick C. Eiselen, June 10, 1936.
59. Letter from Tittle to Amy Blanche Greene, September 14, 1936.

his representatives in the Illinois State Legislature and the United States Congress to support a particular economic measure or to oppose a retrogressive one. He signed a petition and communicated personally with the governor of California to secure the release of Mooney and Billings and contributed funds to succor southern sharecroppers and imprisoned tenant-farmer leaders. He wrote in commendation of the La Follettee Civil Liberties Committee and in condemnation of the House Committee on Un-American Activities. Occasionally he signaled his sympathy for strikers in a labor dispute and he voiced protest of the 1937 Memorial Day Massacre on Chicago's South Side during the Republic Steel strike.

Tittle continued to support with his name and purse the League for Industrial Democracy, serving on its Board of Directors in the early thirties. His involvement in the American Civil Liberties Union remained intense. He had a tenuous relationship with the newly formed National Religion and Labor Foundation, contributing monthly to the Foundation's journal, *Economic Justice*, a list of recent books on social problems. He was concerned in the formation in 1932 of the Christian Social Action Movement, composed mostly of Methodist clergymen committed to socialism. In 1936 he gave encouragement to the organization of the Laymen's Religious Movement, an unofficial group of Methodist laymen committed to the social implications of Christianity and whose leadership was drawn in part from First Church members. As Tittle explained to Bishop James C. Baker, this group would more clearly and adequately represent Methodist lay sentiment than the conservative Conference of Methodist Laymen, just formed and also partially drawn from the First Church membership. Tittle importuned Bishop Baker to cooperate by naming a "half a dozen men on the Pacific coast who in your judgment would be sympathetic toward a movement which aims to be liberal rather than either radical or reactionary."[60] It is significant that the 1,012 delegates to the first meeting in 1934 of the National Council of Methodist Youth assembled in First Church. Their criticism of capitalism was unequivocal; their endorsement of socialism unqualified. Naturally Tittle came under heavy fire for housing the Methodist "Young Turks," but in fact he had contributed to their mood of rebellion.[61] The Methodist Federation for Social Service also continued to warrant his support, but no longer without qualification.

60. Letter from Tittle to Bishop James C. Baker, December 23, 1935.
61. See his message to the National Council, "What Can You Do?" *Epworth Herald*, XLV (September 1, 1934), 3, 26.

For these utterances and activities the charge of radicalism was hurled at Tittle by conservatives within and without the church; and, as we know, in the 1930's he had to fight for his very ministerial life against an imposing army of patriots. It is revealing of the temper of the depression decade to learn that even as Tittle battled with the conservative foe, he received cannonading from the Left. In the thirties the old gulf between liberalism and radicalism widened dangerously and the ancient debate between evolutionary and revolutionary change took on a heightened urgency. Violence was now a living option as it had not been in the Prosperity Decade or the Progressive Era. Writing to a colleague in 1931, Tittle warned that any attempt to defend the existing order actually increased the chances of violence because it would give the disinherited the impression "that those of us who are responsible for a deplorable situation are either hopelessly blind or hopelessly callous." He utterly repudiated "any so-called religion which, in a time like this, is able to offer nothing more hopeful than pious exhortations to desperately situated people to put their trust in the powers that be."[62] But though he scored the hollowness of "pious exhortations," he did not agree with the growing band of Christian radicals who sanctioned violence to effect social justice. As he wrote a leader of the Methodist Youth Council: "It may be true, as you say, that the liberal is in for a tough time, but, I, who am one, and not ashamed of it, do not despair. Liberalism, after all, is primarily an attitude of mind which is concerned to know the facts, whatever they may be, and to build upon them its theories and hopes. Furthermore, it puts its trust in the spirit, not in the sword, which is also to say that it takes the long view of human development and is willing to be patient in order to be profound. When all is said and done, it is more radical than any radicalism, so-called, which is prepared to use violence and coercion in order to secure immediate results which, however, cannot hope to be permanent in as much as they do not affect the inner life of man."[63]

Tittle was wholehearted in his admiration for the principles and activities of the American Civil Liberties Union. He was long a member and served on the advisory board of the Chicago branch. Sometimes the local unit met in First Church; such a meeting in 1933 touched off the famous "Dilling Incident" which almost resulted in Tittle's being driven from Evanston. Freedom of speech and freedom of assembly were not even to be denied to those who if in power would themselves suppress these rights. When Earl Browder, Communist party candidate for

62. Letter from Tittle to C. A. Elliott, September 23, 1931.
63. Letter from Tittle to Miron A. Morrill, March 8, 1935.

the presidency in 1936, was forbidden to give an address in Terre Haute, Tittle informed the Methodist Women's Home Missionary Society that free speech is recognized in most places in America, "but hardly at Terre Haute, Indiana, not to mention points further west." He further warned that various patriotic societies claiming to act in the name of true Americanism are actually "trampling underfoot every great American tradition."[64] When in that year also the Communist party candidate for the governor of Illinois was taunted and jeered by American Legionnaires as he attempted to address an audience in the First Congregational Church in neighboring Oak Park, Tittle presented a resolution, unanimously passed, to the Evanston Ministerial Association upholding the right of the Oak Park church to open its doors to speakers of every ideological persuasion.[65] Yet at one point Tittle took issue with the position of the ACLU, especially its national chairman, Harry F. Ward, who believed that freedom of speech should be tolerated even when the speaker advocated assassination. "I disagree with him and have said so," Tittle explained. "Furthermore, through Doctor Reinhold Niebuhr . . . I am attempting to have Ward modify his position. However, the American Civil Liberties Union is rendering so great a service to the cause of free speech in these United States that I am continuing my membership in it."[66]

During the thirties a Socialist Ministers' Fellowship was formed composed of "followers of Jesus engaged in full time religious work" who desired to band together to attack the capitalist system and to establish a new social order based on the principles of socialism. To join the Fellowship one had to become a "member of some political party committed to the 'principle of Socialism.' " In June, 1934, the group met in Evanston. Several speakers characterized the New Deal as fascistic. Dr. James Yard, formerly director of religious education at Northwestern and Tittle's friend, averred that "the hope of the future for religion lies in socialist ministers and others who take the side of true religion in the class struggle." William Galatsky advocated communism rather than "pussyfooting" socialism. Carl Haessler informed the delegates that "the socialist is like a Christian Scientist when the surgeon knows a caesarian operation is necessary." But again Tittle drew the line. Any new social order to be truly new and truly redemptive must be born free from violence, he argued. And though the conference adopted statements maintaining that many good Christians in America had joined the Com-

64. *Evanston Daily News-Index,* October 10, 1936, p. 1.
65. *Ibid.,* September 28, p. 2, and September 30, 1936, p. 1.
66. Letter from Tittle to Carl C. Morgan, November 21, 1931.

munist party and that under communism religion might have a better opportunity to develop than under capitalism, the majority of the members, following Tittle's leadership, condemned the use of violence in the class struggle.[67]

The question of violence racked and then split a much larger and more influential organization, the Fellowship of Reconciliation. Born during the First World War in England in protest to the madness engulfing Europe, it became the leading society of liberal Christian idealists. Pacifistic, believing the ethic of love sufficient to the overcoming of evil and the creation of a warless world, it increasingly became concerned with economic justice, and by the thirties the majority of its membership embraced socialism. In late 1932 key leaders argued that loyalty to the absolute principle of pacifism in the class struggle was unrealistic. The beneficiaries of the status quo could not be dislodged by exhortations of kindliness and love. Therefore those who sought a better society must choose between more violence and less violence, for to deny to the workers the weapons of force was to doom the revolution. Neutrality in the class struggle is not neutrality at all, for in practice it strengthens the vested interests who have only to defend what they already possess. Justice is more fundamental than peace because it is a prior condition to peace. Hence the duty of pacifists is to support revolutionary change even if it involves the use of violence. What about those who would not personally participate in armed social conflict, but who would serve as noncombatants in the ranks of the proletariat? This position, believed Niebuhr, speaking for the Christian Marxists, "represents an abortive effort to maintain personal purity while holding an organic relation to a social movement which is bound to result in some degree of violence in the day of crisis." After a tense debate at Swarthmore College in October, 1933, the executive committee of the FOR mailed out a questionnaire to the more than six thousand members. Though the questionnaire was detailed, the results can be summarized by stating that 90 percent believed the Fellowship should "hold to non-violence in the class war as well as in international war." Included in the dissenting minority was J. B. Matthews, the leading advocate of militancy in the class struggle. (Ironically, Mr. Matthews later recanted and was relentless in his "exposure" of "Reds" within and without Methodism.) The Fellowship's national council then voted to accept Matthews's resignation as secretary. The additional resignations of some fifty-three members followed, including those of Roger Bald-

67. *Socialist Ministers Conference Proceedings* (n.p., n.d.), a pamphlet.

win and Reinhold Niebuhr. In a famous article, "Why I Leave the F.O.R.," Niebuhr accused the majority of ethical perfectionism which revealed "the failure of liberal Protestantism to recognize the coercive character of political and economic life."[68] Tittle, of course, was not persuaded by Niebuhr's "realism." It did not really matter at the time because the New Deal forestalled the predicted violent encounter between the defenders of a dying capitalism and the proletarian bearers of the new socialist order. But within a few years the great debate was to be renewed, this time in the context of man's most violent enterprise, war. Tittle learned in 1933-34 in the FOR split who was to be his— and pacifism's—most formidable critic as the international crisis edged closer to total war. That man's name was Niebuhr.

Meanwhile, Tittle was much concerned by a development within his own denominational home. Formed in 1907, the Methodist Federation for Social Service was more the creation than the creator of the emergent social consciousness arising within Methodism, taking as its purposes to "deepen within the church the sense of social obligation and opportunity, to study social problems from the Christian point of view, and to promote social service in the spirit of Jesus Christ."[69] The founders were Frank Mason North, Herbert Welch, Elbert R. Zaring, and Harry F. Ward. In time most of the Methodist prophets were associated with it. Although always maintaining an unofficial relationship to the Methodist Episcopal Church it was looked upon, as the 1912 General Conference stated, as the executive agency to rally the forces of the church in support of social thought and action. Bishop McConnell, president of the Federation in the twenties and thirties, described its purpose in more homely terms: that of raising disturbing quesions— ahead of time. The Federation's unofficial status gave it the freedom necessary to pursue unfettered a prophetic role; the respect and support received from the church provided needed funds and prestige. It quickly became the most influential organization of its type within American Protestantism.

Always critical of the abuses of capitalism and in the 1920's viewing

68. *Christian Century,* LI (January 3, 1934), 18. Actually Niebuhr resigned from a position of leadership but he stayed on as a member of the FOR. Although I have made an independent study of the Fellowship of Reconciliation, including an examination of files of its journals, *World Tomorrow* and *Fellowship,* and although I have read a number of secondary accounts, by far the best analysis of the 1933-34 split is in Earl Charles Chatfield, Jr., "Pacifism and American Life, 1914 to 1944" (Ph.D. dissertation, Vanderbilt University, 1965), pp. 522ff.

69. *The Daily Christian Advocate,* Methodist Episcopal Church, May 16, 1908, p. 8.

the "Russian experiment" with sympathy and hope, in 1932, the Federation cut to the far Left, equating capitalism with fascism, the New Jerusalem with Soviet Russia. Miss Winifred Chappell and Harry F. Ward, co-leaders of the Federation, pressed the society into the ranks of the proletariat in the all-out class war. The New Deal was dismissed as a tinkering intended perhaps to keep some of the victims of the profit system from actually starving, but being quite incapable of staying the death of capitalism, though under Roosevelt the nation would first pass through the hell of fascism before the final proletarian triumph. The Socialist party under Thomas was considered much too conservative and mild-mannered to perform the historic mission of slaying capitalism. In 1932 Miss Chappell, a Methodist deaconess whose radical views were rooted in deep religious idealism, publicly announced her support of Earl Browder—and waited expectantly for the approaching revolution. In that year Ward returned after nearly a year's travel in Russia, convinced that that Communist state was the world's last, best hope. "Ward was the burning mystic, the pure mystic, in whom the logic of absolute vision burned away all but itself."[70] In Stalin's Russia he found the final form of the Absolute.

Inasmuch as fascism was already upon the nation, Ward argued, "If its reign is to be shortened, if its repressive political and cultural aspects are to be prevented, a union of all the forces that have declared themselves against the profit motive is imperative."[71] And so in 1934 the Executive Committee voted to affiliate with the American League Against War and Fascism and this action was upheld by the Regional Conferences. The decision cost the Federation heavily in membership and beyond question the affiliation was a tribute to Ward's adroit leadership rather than a true reflection of majority opinion of the membership. It also cost the Federation the confidence of many Methodist liberals, for the American League Against War and Fascism was suspected—and correctly so—of being an instrument in the Communist's United Front strategy. As it happened, in 1934 Ward had become national chairman of the American League Against War and Fascism.

In 1930 Tittle contributed $200 to the support of the Federation; in 1935 he contributed only $6. This reduction was due in part to his own straitened finances, but also to a sense of unease. He was sending a check, he explained to Ward, "notwithstanding the fact that the Bulletin appears to be going in the direction of Russia, a direction in which I personally cannot whole-heartedly go. As I have told you before, I

70. Meyer, *Protestants Search for Political Realism*, p. 201.
71. *Social Questions Bulletin*, XXIV (December, 1934).

am sincerely and thoroughly opposed to the use of violence and coercion as a means of securing needed social reform. Which leads me to be far more patient than the Bulletin is with the present administration at Washington, critical though I am of many of its attitudes and policies. However, there is no other organization in Methodism that is equipped to render any such fact-finding service as that which the Federation is now offering. I am, therefore, glad to make this small contribution, and I am genuinely sorry that it cannot be larger."[72] Tittle believed it a blunder for the Federation to affiliate with the American League Against War and Fascism. He himself repeatedly turned down invitations to become a member, indeed, an honorary member. He warned his friends, especially younger radicals, that the United Front was a booby trap.[73] By the end of the decade, though he was on the advisory committee of the Rock River branch of the Federation, he felt compelled to write: "I am hoping that you will yourself see why I cannot conscientiously accept membership on the National Committee of the Federation. I intend to remain a member of it and to contribute to it the amount which I have been giving in recent years." Nevertheless, he concluded, the Federation's stand on violence "is one which I simply cannot bring myself to endorse."[74]

Thirteen years after Tittle's death Harry F. Ward could call to mind only two conversations with Tittle: "In one he [Tittle] was disturbed by my criticism of the growing aesthetic tendency in Methodism which he was then helping to develop. In the other he was much worried about my activities and statements in the movement against war and fascism and for peace and democracy, showing an emotional anti-communism that made it impossible for me to convince him that I was not turning communist."[75] Ward repeatedly denied that he was ever a member of the Communist party, and we may believe him. Few American Methodists were more perceptive in discerning and more courageous in exposing the demoniac attributes of capitalism than Ward. But few American Methodists were so blind to the demoniac attributes of Stalin's Russia or so willing to sacrifice the individual to an ideal. Although

72. Letter from Tittle to Harry F. Ward, March 8, 1935.

73. Letters from Tittle to Robert Hamill, December 17, 1935; George A. Coe, November 13, 1934; Frank A. Horne, April 6, 1936; E. Jasinski, June 14, 1938. Bishop Oxnam also warned, "The united front is a dangerous gift horse." *New York Christian Advocate,* CX (October 17, 1935), 924.

74. Letter from Tittle to Charles C. Webber, October 25, 1939.

75. Letter from Harry F. Ward to author, December 15, 1962. For an exceptionally favorable assessment of Ward—an assessment I do not wholly share— see Robert H. Craig, "An Introduction to the Life and Thought of Harry F. Ward," *Union Seminary Quarterly Review,* XXIV (Summer, 1969), 331-56.

Ward was allegedly the "realist" and Tittle the "idealist," actually Ward's total commitment to the ideal classless state made him a True Believer, far removed from the reality of events in either Russia or the United States.

In 1932 Tittle confessed to a correspondent that he was a socialist, hastily adding, "I am not, however, a Communist, inasmuch as I violently disbelieve in the use of violence as a means of securing social change."[76] Tittle's aversion to violence did not blind him to "the challenge of Soviet Russia, where children in public schools are being told that there is no God but that a far better world than their fathers knew is possible, is, indeed, even now in the making, and that in the making of it they themselves may have an important and thrilling part. However much one may quarrel, as I personally do, with some of the methods which Russia is employing to reach her goal—violence and compulsion, bureaucracy and the denial of liberty, dogmatism, atheism and anti-religion—one cannot but approve and applaud the goal itself—a new civilization based upon intelligent planning and unselfish cooperation for the common goal; a new opportunity, a new hope and happiness, a more abundant life for all the sons of man."[77] In the Wilkin Lectures Tittle again expressed praise for the purposefulness of the Soviet society, its spirit of heroic self-sacrifice, and its vision of a new civilization, concluding that in many areas of the world communism carried far greater appeal than an "emasculated Christianity."[78]

But Tittle never subordinated means to ends. "Russia, I frankly admit, presents a tough question to a pacifist," he observed to a friend in 1934. "But what is the answer? Is it not too soon to say? Russia *may* through violence and coercion produce a type of mind which will guarantee the permanent success of a radical experiment. But if she does so, it will be the first time in history, so far as my knowledge goes, that such a result has been accomplished. Hitherto violence has secured immediate but no permanent results."[79] By the following year Tittle was prepared to render a judgment—and it was a critical one. Acknowledging certain unquestioned gains, Tittle then cited the "permanent and odious system of terrorism and espionage," the "decimation of the intelligentsia through secret arrests and punishments and most unconvincing 'sabotage' trials," the liquidation of the kulaks as a class, the subjugation of the peasantry, and the state-organized famines.[80] In 1938

76. Letter from Tittle to Quentin Ogren, November 15, 1932.
77. "Wishful Thinking," typed MS, a sermon preached probably in 1932.
78. *We Need Religion,* pp. 10, 30.
79. Letter from Tittle to Vernon Van Dyke, June 4, 1934.
80. *Way to Life,* pp. 155-58.

Tittle informed the readers of the *Christian Century*, "Today in Russia a god is being made of the proletariat, in whose service all things are considered justifiable, including the suppression of freedom, forced labor, liquidation and a revolting spy system."[81] And in 1940 he remarked dryly concerning the Marxian dialectic, "As a substitute for God it has, I should think, a fairly big job on its hands!"[82]

In 1931 the *Christian Register*, a Unitarian journal, said editorially: "No one who studies the religious press steadily and carefully can doubt that American Protestantism has gone over in its sympathy to the Russian experiment and the basic idea of the Russian philosophy. . . . These ministers, true to the traditions of the prophets, are aware of the moral evil beneath our economic and social order, and are satisfied that Russia's fundamental principle of a non-profit making and cooperative commonwealth is true to the teachings of Jesus and square with the pretensions and professions of all the churches. . . ."[83] At the conclusion of the decade, after the disenchantment of the Berlin-Moscow Pact, John Haynes Holmes spoke for many of those Protestant churchmen who once had celebrated the Soviet noble experiment: "I am sick over this business as though I saw my father drunk and my daughter on the street. And all the more, since I feel that I have deceived myself as well as been deceived."[84]

Though Tittle never cried for a Holy War against Red Russia, though he was himself cited before the House Un-American Activities Committee as a suspected "Red,"[85] though he was widely characterized in conservative circles as a "fellow traveler," the fact is his illusions about communism were few. This is not to say, however, that he believed that class consciousness was invariably baneful. "In so far as it serves to unite the unprivileged and disinherited in a persistent demand for social and economic conditions which might yield to all of their fellows, including present-day possessors of wealth and power, a more abundant life, class consciousness is altogether good and greatly to be desired."[86] Nor did he see much hope in appeals from the privileged to the unprivileged to refrain from the use of violence. "When men are driven to desperation, that plea is unavailing. And there is, alas, the all

81. LV (November 9, 1938), 1366.
82. *Christians in an Unchristian Society*, p. 9.
83. (October 8, 1931), pp. 772-73.
84. Quoted in Eugene Lyons, *The Red Decade* (Indianapolis, Ind., and New York: The Bobbs-Merrill Company, 1941), p. 355.
85. Ralph Lord Roy, *Communism and the Churches* (New York: Harcourt, Brace & Co., 1960), p. 240.
86. *Jesus After Nineteen Centuries*, pp. 79-80.

too just retort, 'Do not you yourselves resort to violence when it seems to you that there is no other way to protect your own interests?' The situation will not be saved by any amount of moralizing, not by any counter threat; for men who may argue, not without reason, that they have nothing to lose but their chains, will not be disposed to hold back through fear of consequences."[87] But if the proletariat cannot be gulled or bullied into docility, on neither Christian nor pragmatic grounds does this sanction violence in the class war. Men do not gather grapes from thorns or figs from thistles, and neither do they build utopias on bloodshed.[88] Moreover, it is an illusion to "persistently idealize the unfortunate and the oppressed, attributing to them virtues which very few human beings belonging to any social group appear to possess," because then one is "accordingly unprepared for the history-repeating fact that under-dogs behave very much like upper-dogs the moment power is placed in their hands."[89] "Even a classless society," he observed elsewhere, "would have to reckon with the fact that 'every new generation is a fresh invasion of savages.' "[90]

Tittle understood that the Kingdom of God stands for a reality that transcends any possible achievement on earth. Even so, he thought men must strive endlessly for an approximation to it: "To be sure, we have here no 'continuing city,' as the New Testament reminds us and modern science flatly informs us. But surely it does not follow that we should permit such cities as we do have to become and remain corrupt. Granted that earth can never be heaven, it hardly follows that we should allow it to become hell."[91]

IV

The war came and with it a measure of general prosperity, though in a relative sense the gulf between the "haves" and the "have nots" was not appreciably closed. Franklin D. Roosevelt's New Deal was continued under President Truman's Fair Deal and legislative measures once deemed "socialistic" were accepted matter-of-factly by all save Old Guard Republicans, though massive numbers of citizens remained ill-fed, ill-clad, ill-housed, their poverty masked by a surface glitter of affluence. In the 1940's Tittle's concern with economic justice continued, but the depression-spurred intensity of the 1930's was somewhat muted.

87. *Ibid.*, p. 78.
88. *Ibid.*, pp. 76-77.
89. *We Need Religion*, pp. 12-13.
90. *Christians in an Unchristian Society*, p. 15.
91. *Ibid.*, pp. 15-16.

In his sermons he continued to hold before the eyes of his people the vision of a co-operative commonwealth and to open their eyes to the unconscionable gulf between that vision and the American reality. In Annual and General and now Jurisdictional Conference he continued to pen reports and defend resolutions bearing on economic matters. In his personal politics, he voted for Norman Thomas in 1944, and in 1948. Congressmen and Illinois legislators continued to receive letters from him. And as in earlier decades, Tittle offered his mediation services in strikes.

The leadership of the Methodist Federation for Social Service (after 1947 the Methodist Federation for Social Action) remained a thorny issue—and a stormy one at the 1944 and 1948 General Conferences. (At long last, in 1952 the Conference voted to order the Federation to drop the word "Methodist" from its name.) As Tittle had had doubts about Harry F. Ward, his successor as executive secretary, the Reverend Jack McMichael, also incurred distrust because of his high-handedness and extremely leftist convictions. Nevertheless, Tittle did not break completely with the Federation; perhaps his memories of its old gallantry and prophecy would not permit him to make the final divorce.

The American Civil Liberties Union remained close to his now tiring heart. Indeed, in 1944-45 he helped form a new Chicago branch to succeed the one ousted by the national organization because of tainted leadership. From first to last, Tittle was a champion of civil liberties, and we may be certain that had he lived only a year or so longer he would have been deeply involved in the McCarthy hysteria.

Perhaps it is permissible to feel a sense of relief that death called him before the madness of the early 1950's. And perhaps it is well that he did not live to see the United States go to war in Korea—the fourth war since his birth in 1885.

15. WAR AND PEACE

I

An American boy born in 1885, as was Tittle, might well have had a father, uncles, and older brothers who fought in the last Indian wars or in Cuba in the "splendid little war" with Spain or in the Philippines subduing the insurrectionist Aguinaldo or in China rescuing Christians from the wrath of the Fists of Righteous Harmony or in the Caribbean re-establishing order in various "banana republics." He himself perhaps took lives pursuing Villa in Mexico with Pershing's punitive expedition, or in France during Wilson's Great Crusade, and there was an outside gamble with death when American forces intervened in revolution-torn Russia. In the 1920's Nicaragua provided yet another battle ground. In the 1930's perhaps his son volunteered to fight with the loyalists in Spain or with the Flying Tigers in China. Before December 7, 1941, the son might have sent Hitler's submariners to cold North Atlantic graves while serving on Roosevelt's destroyers. After Pearl Harbor the opportunities to kill multiplied. If the son survived the Second World War perhaps it was only to be recalled into service in 1950 to engage in the task of slaughtering North Koreans and Chinese rather than Germans, Italians, and Japanese. Then, for his son, the grandson of the American born in 1885, Vietnam presented a seemingly open-ended opportunity to fight a new foe.

Yet the vast majority of Americans were singed but slightly by this record of violence. For one thing, their land was spared bombing and invasion. For another, in comparison with the bloodlettings of other peoples, American casualties were "acceptable." For a third, wars seemingly brought excitement and purpose to drab and aimless lives—and prosperity to the nation. "War is essentially the health of the State," said Randolph Bourne. Moreover, most American citizens were patriotic and idealistic, believing in the concept of the "just war" and holding with their presidents that only those not afraid to die are fit to live, that the right is more precious than the peace, that it is better to die fighting on one's feet than to live on one's knees, and that it is better to be dead than Red. As to the future, in a thought process explainable by psychiatrists, almost all mid-twentieth-century Americans embraced the reassuring mid-nineteeth-century words of James Russell Lowell: "I take great comfort in God. I think he is considerably amused with us sometimes, but that he likes us on the whole, and would not let us get to the match-box so carelessly as he does, unless he knew the frame of his universe was fireproof."

Ernest Fremont Tittle did not share, in an age of cobalt matches, this confidence that God would never permit men to ignite an apocalyptic fire, but he did know the nonchalance born of a perfect faith in God: "At all times God reigns: we have the option of doing his righteous and loving will, or meeting disaster. The eternal kingdom of God is beyond the confusions of history. It may never be made fully manifest on earth."[1] But this trans-historical perspective did not for Tittle lead to a "realistic" acceptance of sinful man's inhumanity to sinful man or to a fatalistic resignation to the inevitability of war. Precisely because God is not mocked, men must choose between nonviolence or nonexistence, for as Leo Szilard stated, "The problem which the bomb poses to the world cannot be solved except by abolishing war, and nothing less will do." For thirty years Tittle pursued the destruction of war with the megalomaniacal passion of an Ahab. Fascism, Nazism, communism, tyranny of every stripe, and aggression of every form were evil, but war itself was the supreme sin, the first and the last enemy of mankind. No other issue so completely dominated Tittle's sermons and prayers, his public utterances and activities, his waking thoughts and restless dreams. "I have talked so much about peace," he once ruefully confessed to his assistant, "that my people are about ready to go to war."[2] And unlike a battalion of peacemakers, he did not recant his pacifism after Pearl Harbor. "Yes, I am still a damn pacifist" was the standard reply to the

1. Tittle, "Implications of the Christian Faith for a Just and Enduring Peace," *When Hostilities Cease: Address and Findings of the Exploratory Conference on the Bases of a Just and Enduring Peace, Chicago Temple, May 27-30, 1941* (Chicago: The Methodist Church, 1941), p. 104.
2. Author's interview with Kenneth F. Thompson, Wilmette, Ill., August 6, 1959.

repeated queries.[3] Bishop Paul Jones's aphorism, "A pacifist between wars is like a prohibitionist between drinks," was not coined with Tittle in mind.

Before attempting to delineate Tittle's commitment to a warless world, I am compelled to make a personal confession. Without entering into the whole question of historical relativism and subjectivism, I am bound to say that as I write these words I am in essential argreement with C. Wright Mills: "We are at a curious juncture in the history of human insanity; in the name of realism, men are quite mad, and precisely what they call utopian is now the condition of human survival." Unless some radical transformation is wrought in the lives of men and their institutions (I do not mean that they must obtain perfection), it is entirely possible that we historians or our students will be at our typewriters cooly, rationally, "realistically" describing the irrelevancy of pacifism even as the war to end all wars and all human life breaks out. What used to be the question was whether men would continue waging wars as they always had or whether they would make a seemingly utopian dream of a world without war come true. Now, with the survival of man at stake, what used to be a dream has become a necessity. As a *New Yorker* editor said, "We can no longer emulate those who cry 'Victory or death!' because in our time victory *is* death."

II

America, as a whole, had been pushed and kicked into the First World War, from incident to incident.[4] For most Americans, war was reluctantly declared against Germany in order to vindicate the nation's rights and honor, and only after the decision to intervene because of the submarine issue did Wilson seek to consecrate the war as a selfless moral crusade on behalf of humanity. As we know, the pre-1917 Social Gospel was infused with a strong pacifist strain, and for America's pacifist idealists it was a psychological necessity to see the war in the most lofty moral light. Men such as Tittle had to believe the welfare of mankind was at stake, for only then could they reconcile themselves to the employment of violence. And so when Tittle volunteered for "Y" work in France he did so confident of achieving as a consequence of the crusade a world made safe for democracy. Not surprisingly, the idealists with the brightest hopes ran the gravest peril of dark disenchantment once the returns were in. It has been said that the more noble war seems the

3. Author's interview with Mrs. Bernice Wolseley, Evanston, Ill., July 13, 1960.

4. Robert E. Osgood, *Ideals and Self-Interest in America's Foreign Relations* (Chicago and London: University of Chicago Press, 1953), p. 256.

more it fastens itself on honorable men, but it is psychologically truer to say the more noble the man the more he is *compelled* to believe war honorable.

Tittle returned from France in December 1918, less innocent to be sure, but not cynical and (despite his later statements to the contrary) not yet a pacifist. He advocated magnanimity toward the defeated enemy. Lasting peace could not be built on the spirit of revenge, for "just as certainly as hate breeds hate and murder breeds murder, just so certainly shall the cry, 'God destroy Germany,' now, beget the cry, 'God save us from Germany,' later on."[5] The harsh Treaty of Versailles, therefore, was a betrayal of the Fourteen Points and carried the seeds of future wars. It was a "peace which does, indeed, pass all understanding."[6]

Tittle's new awareness of the monstrousness of modern war did not in 1919-20 lead him to advocate America's withdrawal from the violent world. To the contrary, in sermon, article, address, and debate he pronounced the death of the old isolation. "We are living today in a vastly different world from the world of Washington and the patriot fathers. . . . A mad Serbian shoots an Austrian prince, and as an indirect result of this mad act American boys lie dead at Chateau Thierry. We are now living in a world where war in Europe means worry in America, and may mean war for America at any time."[7] Tittle therefore held imperative American membership in the League of Nations. On Sunday morning, March 2, 1919, he preached a sermon on "Christianity and the Proposed League of Nations" to a packed First Church congregation. At the conclusion he read a resolution to be telegraphed to the United States Senate placing the members of First Church on record in favor of the League, and when the question was put before the congregation "practically everybody in the great auditorium voted in its favor."[8] Tittle's fervent endorsement of the League of Nations was shared by American Methodism in general. Northern Methodists in 1916 had called upon the United States to take the lead in the establishment of a league or federation of nations, and in 1919 the bishops of the Methodist Episcopal Church urged acceptance of Wilson's plan. The bishops repeated their plea for a "real and effective" League at the 1920 General Conference. The conference greeted the utterance warmly and ordered

5. *Evanston News-Index,* January 8, 1919, p. 1.
6. *What Must the Church Do to Be Saved?* (New York and Cincinnati, Ohio: Abingdon Press, 1921), p. 133.
7. *Ibid.*
8. *Evanston News-Index,* March 3, 1919, p. 1.

the message transmitted to the president and the Senate. Earlier the Board of Foreign Missions expressed approval of the League. At least twenty-nine Northern Annual Conferences endorsed the League either with or without reservations, but by 1920 the number had dropped to seven and by 1921 to four. Ministers preached sermons, signed petitions, and co-operated with the Federal Council of Churches, the Church Peace Union, and the World Alliance for International Friendship Through the Churches in bringing pressure to bear on the Senate. One petition alone carried the names of 4,019 Methodist clergymen. Southern spokesmen such as Bishop John M. Moore were on record affirmatively although the first postwar General Conference of Southern Methodism did not meet until 1922 and hence did not speak on the League fight. Bishop Hughes declared he did not know of a single Northern Methodist minister who opposed American membership. The Methodist press did its part. The *New York Christian Advocate*, commenting on the defeat of the League, suggested that America change its motto from "In God We Trust" to "Ourselves Alone." The *Northwestern Christian Advocate* termed the League the "most profoundly significant document ever penned by man" and held it was "destined to more profoundly affect the course of human history than any one act since the sacrifice of Christ." "Blind fatuity," "blatant selfishness," "partisan narrowness" were some of the terms employed by the *Nashville Christian Advocate* to characterize opponents of the League. *Zion's Herald* and the *Methodist Review* added their support, and the *Arkansas Methodist* was proud to announce that one of its pro-League editorials had been printed in the *Congressional Record*.[9]

Tittle was grateful to President Wilson for bringing the League into being but the Treaty of Versailles as a whole he deemed a betrayal of Wilsonian idealism. In this estimate of the treaty Tittle was in agreement with such liberal religious journals as the *Christian Century* and the *World Tomorrow* and such liberal churchmen as John Haynes Holmes and Bishop McConnell, the latter averring that "in the treaty itself are the seeds of about as many wars as we can count" and "because of its manifest social injustice, and denial of the things we went to war for, is an abomination that smells unto heaven."[10] This was also the judgment of a host of secular liberals including Villard of

9. This paragraph was borrowed from my "Social Attitudes of American Methodists, 1919-1929," *Religion In Life*, XXVII (Spring, 1958), 185-86 and my *American Protestantism and Social Issues, 1919-1939* (Chapel Hill: The University of North Carolina Press, 1958), pp. 317-24.

10. *The Daily Christian Advocate*, Methodist Episcopal Church, May 13, 1920, p. 242.

the *Nation* and Croly of the *New Republic* and of the band of progressive-isolationists led by La Follette, Borah, Norris, and Johnson. However, unlike these men (and unlike conservative nationalists such as Lodge) Tittle did not spike American membership in the League of Nations. He advocated neither a return to the old splendid isolation nor a new sullen withdrawal from the world—nor would he have the United States impose its will on the world unilaterally. Indeed, if his words truly reveal his attitude, he was prepared for his nation to participate in a program of collective security. Ultimately Tittle accepted the Treaty of Versailles with all its faults because American adherence to the League promised to provide an "ultimate corrective" (in Wilson's words) for temporary injustice.

Although Tittle was not yet a pacifist, it is permissible to wonder if in supporting the League with sanctions he really thought through the consequences of United States membership. As Robert E. Osgood pointed out, "American enthusiasm for a league was, in large part, enthusiasm for a world in which the nation could escape a recurrence of its present involvement in the toils of world politics. To this extent the desire for a league arose from the very sentiments that made acceptance of new international commitments unlikely."[11] That is, many of the "internationalists" supported the League not as an assumption of new responsibilities but as a magical formula that would free the United States from the obligation of foreign wars, the League being, in Bourne's biting words, "a palpable apocalyptic myth, like the syndicalists' myth of the 'general strike.'" Tittle supported the League because he believed it "the one last hope of civilization," the surest instrument "to secure justice and maintain peace."[12] The League "would result in the end of war for all time."[13] When in later years the League failed to maintain peace it would become necessary for Tittle to make a hard decision: was a Christian *ever* justified in drawing the sword to secure justice? If his answer was to be no, what then becomes of the concept of collective security, a concept he embraced in 1919-20?

III

America had known a vigorous peace movement before 1914, though obviously not nearly sufficient in strength to maintain unbroken peace in the nineteenth century or deter intervention in the Great War. The very

11. *Ideals and Self-Interest*, p. 280.
12. *Christianity and the Proposed League of Nations*, a sermon preached March 2, 1919 (pamphlet).
13. *Evanston News-Index*, January 27, 1919, p. 1.

horror of the Great War, however, served as a spur to a resurgent peace crusade in the 1920's. By the end of the decade there had been established some twelve hundred organizations for the study of international affairs and perhaps two hundred peace societies. Some of these were richly endowed, handsomely domiciled, and expertly staffed, such as the Carnegie Endowment for International Peace, the World Peace Foundation, the Church Peace Union, the Women's International League for Peace and Freedom, the National Council for Prevention of War, the World Alliance for International Friendship Through the Churches, the American Friends Service Committee, and the Department of International Justice and Goodwill of the Federal Council. Although many of these organizations were technically secular, it is nonetheless true that the leadership of the peace movement was deeply religious, that ministers provided the most committed crusaders in the cause, that church members were the most numerous peace workers, and that Protestant denominations were the most effective agencies through which the peace advocates reached public opinion. The peace lovers (a term perhaps sufficiently imprecise to embrace the amorphous nature of the antiwar movement, or sentiment) sought disarmament, repudiation of sole German guilt for World War I, a cancellation of reparations and war debts, recognition of Soviet Russia, constitutional protection of conscientious objectors and release from prison of those convicted during wartime, entrance into the World Court, qualified or unqualified entrance into the League of Nations, the outlawry of war, the abolition of military training in schools, removal of trade barriers, the end of colonialism and imperialism, the muting of nationalism—in sum, they sought to insure peace by establishing the conditions of peace.

Time was to reveal the conditional, prudential, even conservative nature of the great majority of the peace lovers of the 1920's. But a small minority of pacifists provided the cutting edge of the crusade, following the plumb line of pacifism straight and true to Pearl Harbor— and beyond. "They were the evangelists of the peace movement. Like Paul on the road to Damascus each had seen a sign and heard a call."[14] They marched under many banners and their strategies took many names: nonresistance, nonviolence, passive resistance, civil disobedience, nonviolent resistance, Gandhian *Satyagraha*. But they shared one common outlook: that human affairs can be settled by nonviolent means, by arbitration, mediation, conciliation, reconciliation—finally, sacrificial love. And it is pacifism, the renunciation of all organized violence and

14. Robert H. Ferrell, *Peace in Their Time* (New Haven, Conn.: Yale University Press, 1952), p. 26.

a commitment to a way of life "that taketh away the occasion of all wars," that Tittle came to embrace.

Before the twentieth century pacifism had largely been the passion of the historic peace sects—the Brethren, the Quakers, the Mennonites —but after the Great War it came to be the faith of a galaxy of Protestant leaders. Indeed, American Protestantism, save for the Protestant Episcopal Church, the Lutherans, and the Southern Baptists, was swept by an intense antiwar fervor, and no major denomination was more unqualified in its dedication to a warless world or more deeply penetrated by the thrust of pacifism than Northern Methodism. Thus if Tittle's pacifism in the 1920's is to be comprehended, it must be placed in the context of the times, when it may almost be said that pacifism was the "party line" of liberal Protestantism and when millions held with Dorothy Detzer that "life seemed to open up a new pathway to peace."

It is revealing that the peace movement of the 1920's was essentially middle class, embracing many of the groups that had supported prewar progressivism and Social Gospelism: clergymen, professors, journalists, professional women, students, political spokesmen for midwestern agrarianism. If in America the Socialist party was too weak[15] and labor unions both too weak and too conservative to provide the peacemakers with leadership, it is nonetheless true that almost invariably a commitment to world peace was coupled with a devotion to domestic reform. The peacemakers believed that war grew in the soil of economic and social injustice and that of necessity a warless world must be a world freed from poverty and exploitation and from class and caste barriers. Those major denominations most devoted to Social Gospel reformism were also the most concerned with the peace crusade. Clergymen of the major denominations who embraced pacifism were generally liberal in their political and economic views—and in their theology, too. It cannot be emphasized too strongly that in the 1920's pacifism was an integral and important element in both religious and secular liberalism. It was not until the period immediately preceding Pearl Harbor that liberal pacifists found themselves being joined by conservative isolationists (including spokesmen for powerful business groups) in common opposition to President Roosevelt's interventionist foreign policies.

It is well known that the Great War bequeathed a legacy of disillusionment and many Americans sought to retire from the world "as a jilted bride to a convent." Led to believe that American intervention

15. Of course Eugene V. Debs had opposed America's entry into the First World War and Norman Thomas was a gallant and consistent opponent of war.

would end war once for all and cherishing the hope of first a peace without victory and then a peace without end, their idealistic expectations were shattered by the hard realities of the Versailles settlement. The failure of the peace meant the failure of the Great War and the failure of the Great War meant the futility of all wars. The folly of intervention could be compensated only if America firmly resolved never again to be played for a sucker. "About all that America got out of Europe was its army," growled one citizen; "unless it be prohibition and influenza," added another.

As early as 1920 Germany's sole guilt for causing the war, an indictment written into the Treaty of Versailles, was being challenged by scholars, thanks to the unprecedented availability of sources; and as Warren I. Cohen has pointed out,[16] once the equal guilt of the Allies was "established," the moral case for America's intervention broke down. Soon novelists, playwrights, and poets were stripping the war of all glory, scholars and journalists were exposing the "truth" about Allied propaganda, and the sinister role of the "merchants of death" was unveiled. Debunking became a common pastime among liberals, reflecting a kind of inverted idealism. Liberal after liberal stepped forward to confess his guilt for baptizing the war as holy, the pages of such journals as the *New Republic* and the *Nation* becoming "an historical Wailing Wall where the penitent revisionists lamented their sins and sought forgiveness."[17] The result often was a sullen and peevish isolationism typified by the remark of one of the Lost Generation's sophisticated heroes, George Jean Nathan: "If all the Armenians were to be killed tomorrow and if half of Russia were to starve to death the day after, it would not matter to me in the least. . . . For all I care the rest of the world may go to hell at today's sunset."

But just as not all liberals said farewell to reform in the 1920's so not all liberals said farewell to the world. The extent and nature of American isolationism after the Senate's rejection of the treaty and League is a matter of much debate among historians. As we have just seen, for many disenchantment did take the form of isolationism. But for Tittle and a host of peacemakers the hope to end war in the world rested on America's greater participation in the affairs of the world. In this decade of peace, pacifism and isolationism were poles apart, for basic to pacifism is the conviction of the essential unity of all mankind overriding barriers of class, nation, and race. Pacifism cultivated an

16. *The American Revisionists: The Lessons of Intervention in World War I* (Chicago and London: University of Chicago Press, 1967), *passim*.
17. Osgood, *Ideals and Self-Interest*, p. 318.

internationalist frame of mind in order to counter nationalism, that breeder of chauvinism and militarism and hence war. Whether in the warring 1930s the pacifists and the isolationists would be pressured into an uneasy partnership was a question for the future.

What many commentators on the twenties fail to understand is that the postwar peace crusade was characterized by hope and optimism, not despair and cynicism. When Tittle and his fellow pacifists confessed their repentence they did not merely wring their hands; rather they translated their contrition into peace action. And it was action informed by a great sense of urgency precisely because the Great War had demonstrated how imperiled civilization was by war. Before 1914 there had been widespread confidence in the permanency of peace. For Tittle and others the war did not "prove" that men will always fight; rather it "proved" that men must either cease to fight or perish. Therefore it was imperative to labor all the harder for peace. And the hope was held that the labor would not prove vain because of a new affirmation of the social utility of pacifism. "Faith in the establishment of a just and peaceable Kingdom on this earth was not destroyed by the war; rather, the method of achieving it had been purified," writes John K. Nelson in his perceptive study of pacifism. "The confidence of the liberal Protestant pacifists in the social gospel, far from being shattered by the war experience, took on new meaning and courage because it was now felt that they had discovered their source of earlier weakness. In pacifism, not understood simply as a protest against war, but as an attitude to be applied to all the social relationships of life, they felt they had found the key to the Kingdom, the means to win the peace and realize the society in which all men would be brothers."[18]

This vision, possessed by Tittle, Fosdick, Sockman, and many liberal clergymen and informing the position of the major Protestant denominations, especially the Methodists, was not simply a modern adaptation of the doctrine of nonresistance of the historic pacifist sects. For these quietist fellowships, such as the Brethren and the Mennonites, nonresistance was a literal injunction of the New Testament and Jesus' command that evil should not be returned for evil, that the sword should be put away, that one should love and pray for one's enemies, that ultimately one must submit to but not participate in the violence of this world. Nonresistance abjures coercion as well as violence, for as the Mennonite Guy Hershberger observed, nonviolent resistance "is really a form of warfare, since its primary purpose is to bring about the submis-

---

18. *The Peace Prophets: American Pacifist Thought, 1919-1941* (Chapel Hill: The University of North Carolina Press, 1967), p. 47.

sion of the opposition through compulsion."[19] And Umphrey Lee argued that nonviolent resistance is "still a technique for overcoming a superior force, and has little more relation to the teachings of Jesus than the technique of war."[20] Absolute nonresistance is an assertion of individual conscience in obedience to religious authority, a perfectionist renunciation of the sinful world, and rather than seeking to Christianize the state, which must exercise coercion, its adherents live as patient pilgrims awaiting the reign of peace in another world. When ordered by the state to participate in carnal warfare, the nonresistant will refuse. He will instead obey his Savior and as his Savior submit if necessary to the Cross.[21]

The main body of post-1918 pacifism, however, was not world-renouncing, but world-affirming. Rather than negative, it was positive, seeking not simply peace—in the sense of the absence of war—but a new social order. Rather than individualistic, it was social, seeking not simply personal salvation, but the conversion of nations. Rather than quietist, it was active, even aggressive, in pursuing a program of educational, social, and political action. Rather than dualistic, with one standard for the pure Christian community and another for the coercive state, it held the state accountable to God and thus sought to impose a Christian ethic upon the state. Rather than having isolated individuals stand firm in their conscientious objection to military service after the outbreak of war, it hoped to create a "will to peace" among great masses of people everywhere making impossible the declaration of war in the first instance. Finally, although absolutely refusing to participate in or condone violence and war, the pacifists of the twenties, unlike the historic pacifist sects, would resist evil and ultimately overcome evil.

Thus, the new pacifism was at once a way of life, a program of social change, and a technique of social action. And increasingly the new pacifism was concerned with the distinction between nonresistance and nonviolent resistance and with the extent to which nonviolent coercion employed in the interests of justice might be ethical. War is invariably unredemptive. Violence is totally inconsistent with the law of love and

19. *War, Peace, and Nonresistance* (Scottdale, Pa.: The Herald Press, 1946), p. 1.

20. *The Historic Church and Modern Pacifism* (New York: Abingdon-Cokesbury Press, 1943), p. 217.

21. Both H. Richard Niebuhr and Reinhold Niebuhr held nonresistance to be a true reading of the New Testament and the true position of the early Christians. See H. Richard Niebuhr, "The Grace of Doing Nothing," *Christian Century* XLIX (March 23, 1932), 374, and Reinhold Niebuhr, *Christianity and Power Politics* (New York: Charles Scribner's Sons, 1940), pp. 10-11.

the moral order of the universe. But for Tittle and those Protestants committed to seek the establishment of the Kingdom of God on this war-torn planet, the ideal of nonresistance was inadequate. The forces in the world making for war must be resisted and overcome by a program of nonviolent action.

IV

"I can best state my own position with respect to war," Tittle wrote Walter Van Kirk, "by quoting the pledge which is taken by members of the English War Resisters League: 'War is a crime against humanity. I am therefore determined not to support or take part in any war, international or civil.'"[22] As a member of the League, Tittle made this pledge. It faithfully represents a conviction Tittle reached in the decade following Versailles. He came not simply to "favor" pacifism but to *be* a pacifist. Tittle's pacifism stemmed in part (but only in part) from his personal experiences in France. "Upon his soul the great war left its deep mark," observed Charles Clayton Morrison,[23] and Tittle himself repeatedly referred to this scarifying chapter in his life. His pacifism stemmed in part from his reading of history. The futility of war in the past was amply documented and the destructiveness of future wars seemed beyond debate. His pacifism stemmed in part from a sympathetic understanding of past men of peace and of such historic people of peace as the Quakers; indeed, he once described himself as a Quaker. And his pacifism also drew upon the contemporary example of Gandhi, who he believed "has done more to convince the world of the practicability of the Sermon on the Mount than have all the discourses that have been delivered in Christian churches for a generation."[24] But I am convinced, as are individuals who were close to him in Methodist peace work,[25] that ultimately and essentially Tittle's pacifism was theological in origin. War, for Tittle, was a violation of all that he understood to be the nature of God and His purposes for man. Like the Quakers, Tittle believed that pacifism is an obligation, not a promise. He could not

22. Letter from Tittle to Walter Van Kirk, December 27, 1933. For a slightly different wording of the pledge, see the splendid study by Earl Charles Chatfield, Jr., "Pacifism and American Life, 1914 to 1944" (Ph.D. dissertation, Vanderbilt University, 1965), p. 505. See also Walter Van Kirk, *Religion Renounces War* (Chicago and New York: Willett, Clark & Company, 1934), p. 21.

23. *The American Pulpit* (Chicago: Willett, Clark & Company, 1925), p. 342.

24. *The Religion of the Spirit* (New York and Cincinnati: Abingdon Press, 1928), p. 313.

25. For example, author's interviews with Daniel E. Taylor, Denver, Col., May 1, 1960, and Herman Will, Denver, Col., May 1, 1960.

guarantee that it would work, much less that it would be safe. He was only sure that it was for him the right understanding of the will of God.

Tittle's sermons in the twenties were permeated with the pacifist passion. He penned numerous articles on the subject. The four books bearing his name published between 1921 and 1931 make clear his anti-war attitude. He was also involved in many national and international movements designed primarily or tangentially to erase war from the world including the War Resisters League, the Fellowship of Reconciliation, the League for Industrial Democracy, the Committee on Militarism in Education, the National Council for Prevention of War, and the No War Movement. The Methodist Federation for Social Service, supported by Tittle, was antiwar in the twenties, standing for the "excommunication of war by the church, outlawry of war by the nations, and an honest consideration of what is the Christlike attitude for individual men and women who really propose to take and seriously win in a semi-pagan world."[26] Further, Tittle was on the Advisory Committee of the Federal Council's important National Study Conference on the Churches and World Peace, the third meeting convening in First Church. Under Tittle's leadership the Rock River Annual Conference adopted strong reports and resolutions in condemnation of war, both reflecting and molding the position of Northern Methodism's General Conference of 1924 and 1928. And Tittle was instrumental in the formation of the Methodist World Peace Commission. Until his death he was deeply involved in its labors, though only in 1948 did he succeed Ralph Sockman as chairman. Tittle had enormous admiration for the popular New York preacher who rightly won much fame through his radio sermons. "Doctor Sockman," Tittle once replied to an inquiry, "is all you think he is—a fine preacher and a fine man."[27] Although Sockman was a dedicated and forceful chairman thoroughout almost the entire period, Tittle was the stronger man on the Commission, and Sockman sensed this and deferred to him.[28]

Essential to the blunting of war was the muting of nationalism through the creation of a countervailing spirit of internationalism. Tittle often quoted Nurse Edith Cavell, "Patriotism is not enough." And once in a wrathful mood he added, "Certainly that bastard patriotism that goes

26. *Social Service Bulletin,* May 15, 1924.
27. Letter from Tittle to Edith Hubbart, July 9, 1942.
28. Author's interview with three former Commission members whose names perhaps should not be disclosed because of their close association with the late Dr. Sockman.

by the name of 100% Americanism is not enough."[29] Let Tittle's position not be misunderstood. For him, love of country was a normal and noble emotion: "He who loves not his home and country which he hath seen, how can he love humanity in general which he hath not seen?" The very word "Patriotism," "pater," he observed, suggests that natural and altogether proper love a man has for his home. Nevertheless, "The patriot who is concerned about the highest welfare of his country is by very virtue of the fact concerned about the highest welfare of all other countries, because he sees that in all its higher interests the world is one." Thus, who today "is disturbed by the fact that Shakespeare was an Englishman, or that Pasteur was a Frenchman, or that Dante was an Italian, or that Goethe was a German, or that Tolstoi was a Russian? Who today even recalls the fact that Jesus was a Jew? Such men do not belong to any one nation. They belong to all nations. All that they represent, all of imperishable worth and glory and inspiration, is today the common heritage of mankind." Nations are under a higher judgment. "A patriotism which pledges an uncritical allegiance to any government on the face of this earth may some day discover that it is standing in opposition to Almighty God." The idea that the state owes no allegiance to any authority beyond or above it is a modern and fatal concept. "To any man who is able to take a long view of the human situation it must be evident that this notion that the state is above the law will have to be repudiated if civilization is to endure." There is a higher sovereignty and when this certitude grips men they will have their state seek first not its own selfish interests and aggrandizement, but the universal good and glory of mankind.[30]

Tittle sought to advance internationalism by continuing to urge American membership in the League of Nations. For many Americans the League was not radical enough or pacifist enough or isolationist enough or revisionist enough, but for Tittle and most peacemakers in the twenties the alternative seemed to be either the flawed League or a heightened nationalism that would further cut off America from the world. Tittle's position on the League was generally that of Northern Methodism, and the 1924 and 1928 General Conferences in Episcopal Addresses, reports, and resolutions recommended American participation, as did the bulk of the Methodist press. Yet it cannot be said that Meth-

29. "The Moral and Religious Challenge of These Times," handwritten MS, undated.

30. For these statements, see "Patriotism" and "An Adequate National Defense," chaps. xiv and xv in *The Foolishness of Preaching* (New York: Henry Holt & Co., 1930).

odist enthusiasm for the League approached the intensity of that of 1919-20. Nationalists feared membership would geld American sovereignty and some pacifists feared the League was only a new and greater system of military alliances. (Significantly, the most influential liberal Protestant journal in the nation, the *Christian Century,* shared this latter fear.) Thus in 1922 a Rock River resolution endorsing the League passed by only the narrow margin of 89 to 85, and the following year a similar resolution was defeated. Nevertheless Tittle continued his support. America "ought not, and indeed cannot, refuse to participate in the tangled and troubled affairs of the world."[31] The League "is not a perfect instrument but one eager for spiritual enterprise knows the folly of waiting for perfect instruments."[32]

Urging membership of the United States in the World Court was almost a mark of enlightenment among the peacemakers, and Tittle did his part in many ways, even to writing every member of the Senate Foreign Relations Committee. The Northern bishops gave their "hearty endorsement" and the Northern General Conferences of 1924 and 1928 transmitted their affirmative wishes to the Senate in blunt language. Methodists participated in World Court Week and World Court Sunday and co-operated with the Federal Council in meeting with government leaders. "The World Court," editorialized the *New York Christian Advocate,* speaking for much of Methodism, "represents the most important effort yet made in all the history of the world to substitute legal machinery for brute force, to substitute law for war."[33]

No element in the peacemakers' program of the twenties now seems so utopian as the Kellogg-Briand Pact of 1928 in which the contracting parties—sixty-four nations including Germany, Japan, and Russia—renounced war as an instrument of policy and promised to settle all disputes among themselves by peaceful means. No provision was made for the use of force or coercive measures against violators of the pledge. Moreover, everyone understood that defensive wars did not come under the ban. We now know much about the origins of the Pact of Paris (as this multilateral renunciation of war is also called) that Tittle could not have known at the time, particularly the desire of the profane United States Secretary of State, Frank B. Kellogg, to avoid a commitment to France implicit in the astute Aristide Briand's proposed bilateral treaty. There was something (because there was so little of substance) in the pact for almost everyone—except Briand. To the internationalists such

31. *Minutes* of the Rock River Annual Conference (1922), p. 72.
32. *Ibid.* (1923), p. 67.
33. CI (December 30, 1926), 1751.

as Professor James T. Shotwell it was a way of bringing the United States into closer cooperation with the League of Nations, the first of many steps in building a systematic peace structure. To the isolationists such as Senator William O. Borah it re-enforced the position that the United States would not fight in foreign wars. To the idealists such as Salmon O. Levinson it seemed the fulfillment of his dream to outlaw war, though in fact the word "outlaw" did not appear in the document.

The 1928 General Conference of Northern Methodism in reports, resolutions, and the Episcopal Address heralded the negotiations leading to the pact, asserting that "as a Christian body, we 'renounce war as an instrument of national policy.' " Tittle's Rock River delegation presented a resolution commending Secretary Kellogg's "heroic, earnest and unprecedented stand in favor of the outlawry of war,"[34] being naturally quite unaware that Kellogg privately cursed the silly "——— ——— pacifists."[35] Earlier Northern Methodism had been extremely active in the movement to renounce war. A host of Annual Conferences, including Rock River, had supported the idea. The Methodist Peace Commission circulated a petition and secured ninety thousand signatures urging ratification of the pact. As early as 1924 the General Conference, in a detailed maneuver, checked the attitude of every candidate for Congress toward outlawry and ordered the information announced to each Methodist congregation, the political threat in this action being obvious. The Methodist Federation for Social Service, the Epworth League, and the Methodist press gave their endorsement, though it is evident that some Methodists followed Charles Clayton Morrison and Senator Borah in believing outlawry to be a substitute for the League and the World Court while others followed Professor Shotwell in believing the pact to be a step toward collective security.

Tittle's own assessment was somewhere between the cynical view that the pact was a mere "international kiss" and the wildly optimistic hope that with the signing "international war was banished from civilization."[36] When the pact was signed he was quite aware of the many loopholes, reservations, and crippling interpretations. They leave the world, he observed, "very much in the condition of a man who is trying to break a long-standing and exceedingly costly liquor habit, and who publicly renounces his right to drink whiskey except in case of snake

34. *The Daily Christian Advocate,* Methodist Episcopal Church, May 8, 1928, p. 184.
35. Quoted in Robert H. Ferrell, *American Diplomacy* (New York: W. W. Norton & Company, 1959), p. 331.
36. *Christian Century,* XLV (September 6, 1928), 1070.

bite, toothache, malaria, and abdominal cramp. The number of
stomach aches with which such a man may appear to be threatened is likely to prove astonishing to his friends!" "Nevertheless," he
continued, "the Pact of Paris is at least a step in the direction of a new
and more adequate kind of national defense. The governments which
have signed it have renounced aggressive war for selfish ends." They
have further promised to settle by pacific means all disputes. If these
governments mean what they say, there will be no need of defensive war
and no excuse for not beating their swords into plowshares. "For the
first time in history, war has been officially condemned as an instrument
of national policy and as a means of settling international disputes.
Whether or not this official condemnation shall turn out to be anything
more than a scrap of paper lies with the people of the world to say.
But they have at least a chance to say that the Pact of Paris shall be
taken seriously, and if they do say it, international war will be done away
with."[37]

Years before the signing of the Kellogg-Briand Pact, Tittle and much
of American Methodism had advocated the cause of disarmament. The
1924 General Conference of Northern Methodism rejoiced in the presumed brilliant success of the Washington Conference. Indeed, in 1920
Northern Methodists had urged the calling of a disarmament gathering
in the first instance. Further, in 1921 at least thirty-six Annual Conferences in the North endorsed the idea of a naval limitations conclave. In
the spring of 1921 a petition urging the president to call such a conference was signed by 4,950 Northern Methodist ministers and by 1,500
Southern Methodist clergymen. Methodists, along with other denominations, observed June 5, 1921, as Reduction of Armament Sunday, and
Sunday, November 6, was set aside as a day of prayer for the delegates
meeting in Washington. Sermons were preached, pamphlets published,
meetings held, officials button-holed, all to the end that the conference
might succeed. *Zion's Herald* knew that with the conference the "final
establishment of the kingdom of God on earth draws nearer"[38] and the
New York Christian Advocate characterized the Washington agreements
as marking "the longest step on the road to peace that has been taken
since civilization began."[39] Methodism gave comparable endorsement to
the naval disarmament conferences held at Geneva in 1927 and London
in 1930, the first being an utter failure and the second a very limited
success.

37. *Foolishness of Preaching*, pp. 221-23.
38. C (February 8, 1922), 163.
39. XCVII (February 16, 1922), 185.

It seemed to Tittle as to many peacemakers that the greatest hope for a warless world rested with the youth of the world. Tittle carried the message of peace to Northwestern and Garrett students, to campuses over the land, and to innumerable gatherings of young people meeting in First Church and elsewhere. Additionally, he was a member of the Committee on Militarism in Education, a major but ultimately vain effort on the part of the pacifists to eliminate military training in the schools. It knew the support of virtually every noted peacemaker and peace society and enjoyed the financial assistance of Oswald Garrison Villard. When, in October, 1940, Congress passed a peacetime conscription bill, the committee shortly disbanded.

Tittle guided reports through the Rock River Conference calling for the abolition of military training. More significant was his action at the 1928 General Conference. He introduced an amendment to the report of the Committee on the State of the Church in opposition to *all* military training in high school (rather than merely *compulsory* training) and to compulsory military training in colleges and universities. The amendment easily carried, one unconvinced delegate ruefully confessing, "I feel like a lone wolf upon the matter." As always, Tittle's contribution to the debate was factual, forceful, and earnest.[40]

Tittle's determination to create a "will to peace" led him down many paths in the twenties, though in some cases it was not until the thirties that he traveled the full distance. He examined the chaplaincy question and concluded that while the Church must continue to minister to the needs of soldiers and sailors, a chaplain should not be an officer subject to the commands of his military superiors. He sought for Methodist conscientious objectors the same exemptions enjoyed by members of the historic pacifist sects. Of course he protested the denial of citizenship to Professor Douglas Clyde Macintosh when that Canadian scholar could not promise in advance to bear arms in any and all future wars in which the United States might engage. And he anticipated later movements for the enactment of neutrality legislation.

The period between the Washington Conference of 1921 and the Japanese invasion of Manchuria in 1931, though a turbulent era, was yet a time of general international peace, and when the hopes of men of good will soared. It was also a time when it was possible to seek greater American participation in the world without having to face the immediate question of whether this desired diminishment of American isolationism and unilateralism might not result in heightening America's

40. *The Daily Christian Advocate,* Methodist Episcopal Church, May 16, 1928, p. 350, and May 22, 1928, pp. 466-67, 470.

chances of being drawn into a foreign war. That is to say, for a brief decade Tittle and the peacemakers knew the luxury of urging the United States to accept full membership in a world at peace without reckoning the dues that might be required to keep the peace. Moreover, if America joined the world and if the world stumbled from peace to war, what then? Was it possible and proper to be a member of the international club only in fair times, promptly resigning with the first rumble of thunder?

V

The period between 1931 and 1939 was a time when the world hung suspended between peace and war. For Tittle and the peacemakers the circle tightened. Was it possible to work collectively to keep war out of the world without committing America to involvement should war break out? And if the United States was unwilling to make such a commitment, how could peace be preserved in the world? Or rather, how could peace be preserved short of the total appeasement of ruthless, predatory rulers with the consequent sacrifice of freedom and democracy?

The crux of the dilemma was rooted in the objective facts of twentieth-century life. The world was contracting. The economic power and consequent potential military power of the United States was expanding. Short of turning back the technological clock and short of America's returning to a pastoral economy, there was no way to halt the globe's shrinkage or America's increasing influence. It is obvious, therefore, that every act by the United States relative to Europe and Asia was bound to be consequential. It is further evident that a decision *not* to act might also have fateful consequences. Things left undone as well as things done in Washington affected events in London, Paris, Berlin, Moscow, Peking, and Tokyo. This is not quite to accept the proposition of almost all scholars that it is impossible to insulate a great power against events outside its borders; rather, it is to insist that should a great power succeed in so doing, the results might be no less determinative on world developments than massive intervention.

Involved in the equation were factors of foreign trade and investments and domestic prosperity. By sealing itself from the outside world in a determined effort to escape the contagion of war, would America then reap the lesser material rewards of a second-class state and perhaps deepen the depression? Was not economic recovery contingent upon the stimulus of war preparations and trade with belligerents? Involved also were considerations of national honor and prestige. Surely for America to relinquish her traditional rights as a neutral and to surrender all responsibility for the fate of Europe and Asia would be to ask her citizens to redefine and scale down the meaning of "national greatness." Further, did not America's very survival depend on checking through collective action aggression across the seas, for if Nazism and Japanese imperialism triumphed in the 1930's, would not the United States, now standing alone, fall victim in the 1940's? And for idealistic Americans such as Tittle, there was an additional painful moral issue: should the United States take refuge in storm-cellar neutrality, ride out the struggle, and keep her hands unstained by blood? If she followed this course, could white hands cloak a conscience stricken by the fate of conquered peoples pinioned on Japanese bayonets and broken on Nazi swastikas?

"Ninety-nine Americans out of a hundred," estimated the *Christian Century* in 1935, "would today regard as an imbecile anyone who might suggest that, in the event of another European war, the United States should again participate in it." A year later a poll conducted by the American Institute of Public Opinion set the exact figure at 95 percent.[41] Isolationist sentiment in the United States reached its zenith in the 1930's. Never in the entire annals of American foreign relations was isolationism more passionately expounded or more vociferously defended. This was not because the isolationism of the thirties manifested a new spirit of unilaterialism in foreign affairs or a new determination to remain aloof from foreign quarrels. The American people had held these convictions since the days of the Founding Fathers. Rather, isolationism reached such a feverish intensity in the thirties exactly because a contracting world and an expanding American power rendered questionable its viability as a national posture even as the fearful nature of modern war was increasingly beyond question. In the nineteenth century isolationism was not much debated. It was deemed a "given" by the great majority of citizens. In the 1930's a sequence of events in Europe and Asia made isolationism at once less possible and more desirable. After about 1937, however, increasing numbers of citizens came to question even its desirability, believing it neither moral nor prudent to disengage from the task of halting aggression. At the same time, the isolationists, the great majority of whom were not pacifists, found common cause with the absolute opponents of war, while the pacifists, the great majority of whom were not isolationists, found themselves (unlike in the twenties) retreating back to unilaterialism, continentalism, and noninterventionism.

A fair number of scholars have probed the roots of twentieth-century

41. Manfred Jonas, *Isolationism in America, 1935-1941* (Ithaca, N. Y.: Cornell University Press, 1966), p. 1.

isolationism, especially in the interwar period, though their conclusions add up to something less than a consensus. One theory explains the strong isolationism of Middle Westerners on the geographic remoteness of their section. Another theory locates isolationism in the needs, desires, and value sytems of American agricultural society. Perhaps religious affiliation is a factor, we are told, with Roman Catholics and Lutherans, for example, being more isolationist than the population as a whole, and Episcopalians and Unitarians less. Allied to this thesis is an ethnic interpretation which finds isolationism predominant among German-Americans and Irish-Americans and also Italian-Americans. Perhaps, it has been suggested, political party allegiance holds the explanation. Indeed, isolationism has even been traced to emotional and psychological bases.

All these interpretations merit exploration, but neither singly nor collectively do they quite convey the varied motivations of the individuals who in the thirties came to be categorized as isolationists. It is true that the semiagrarian Middle West was a stronghold of isolationism, but it is a further fact that the even more fully agrarian South strongly supported interventionist measures. Moreover, many of the most articulate isolationists were residents of great cities, including New York, thereby, it would seem, vitiating the argument that isolationism is a rural phenomenon. It is true that conservatives, led by Herbert Hoover and Robert A. Taft, increasingly assumed a commanding position in opposition to interventionism, fearful that involvement in foreign war would spell death to America's free-enterprise system, already threatened by Roosevelt's New Deal. But liberals also were concerned about the impact of war on American society. War would mean the end of reform and the wreckage of the promise of creating a just, democratic, co-operative commonwealth. Thus old progressives such as Villard and socialists such as Thomas and pragmatic liberals such as Beard thundered warnings. Ironically, conservatives saw as a possible consequence of war a socialist dictatorship while liberals discerned on the horizon a fascist state, totalitarianism entering the backdoor of America as the United States engaged in total war to halt totalitarianism abroad. It is true that pacifists were eventually forced into alignment on many positions with unilateralists and continentalists, but it is false to conclude that nonviolence characterized all isolationists. To the contrary, the vast majority of isolationists were not pacifists; in fact, they often were ardent champions of military preparedness, being fully prepared to fight to uphold the Monroe Doctrine.

Some isolationists were idealists who believed the United States could best serve humanity by remaining an island of sanity in a world gone mad, standing ready to minister to the needs of a shell-shocked postwar globe. Others were quite prepared to permit the world to hang itself, cherishing the historic belief of American exceptionalism. Europeans and Asians have always and will always be at war, and self-interest dictated that America not take sides, now or in the future. A few sympathizers of the Soviet Union were pro tem isolationists, following the vagaries of the Communist party line, but for these fellow travelers isolationism was a tactical matter to be jettisoned on the will of Moscow. A very few rooted their isolationism in an admiration for Hitler or Mussolini. A much larger number, while acknowledging the depravity of Nazism, nonetheless viewed Germany as a shield against Russian expansion. To further muddy things, a considerable group were isolationist regarding Europe, but hawkish on America's Asian role.

As the thirties saw an articulation of isolationist conviction based on a variety of motives—idealistic, prudential, and selfishly nationalistic—so the decade witnessed a burgeoning antiwar passion. Opponents of war were found in all ranks of society, especially among socialists, liberals, churchmen, professors, students, journalists, novelists, educated women and spokesmen for farm organizations. Pacifism provided the cutting edge of the antiwar movement and it was from the ranks of the Protestant clergy, more than from any other group, that pacifism drew its life blood. The pacifists claimed that they were not isolationists at all, "save only with respect to war." With the breakdown of peace in Asia and Europe, this exception was to be everything.

Poll after poll in the 1930's revealed the increasing commitment of the Protestant clergy to pacifism. The most famous were those conducted by Kirby Page and associates in 1931 and 1934. Others were sponsored by religious journals and denominational and interdenominational agencies.[42] A remarkable number of the respondents recorded as their present purpose not to sanction or support or participate in any future war. To be sure, the percentage varied widely from denomination to denomination, and the pulpit was clearly more pacifist than the pew. Also, the *Iowa Legionnaire* accurately predicted that should a similar poll be taken "a week after Old Glory were fired upon" the high percentage of clerical pacifists would "shrink amazingly."[43] Another prediction was made by the *Pennsylvania Manufacturers' Journal*: "It is interesting, if not pleasant, to contemplate the number of telegraph poles that would be adorned by white cravats, re-enforced by hempen neck-

42. For the results of these numerous polls, see Miller, *American Protestantism and Social Issues*, pp. 337-39.
43. Quoted in *World Tomorrow*, XIV (June, 1931), 194.

ties, should another war be declared—which, may heaven forfend—to test the 'loyalty' of these anti-patriots. . . . The event of a war and the active participation of the clergy against national defense, to which so many have pledged themselves, would give us a brand new national sport: gunning for clergymen."[44]

However needful it is to discount opinion measured by polls, the fact is that the polls confirmed rather than contradicted a mass of evidence pointing to the pacifism of Protestant churchmen. Sermons, resolutions, petitions, pledges, church press editorials, the formation of denominational peace fellowships add up to the irrefutable conclusion that pacifism gripped a strong, articulate, and prestigious minority. Sometimes the professions of pacifism were contingent. Typical of the more restrained utterances was the 1933 declaration taken by the Young Men's Club of Broadway Tabernacle Church, New York:

> I have quietly considered what I would do if my nation should again be drawn into war.
> I am not taking a pledge, because I do not know what I would do when the heart of the war mood is upon the country. But in a mood of calm consideration I do today declare that I cannot reconcile the way of Christ with the practice of war.
> I do therefore set down my name to be kept in the record of my Church, so that it will be for me a reminder if war should come; and will be a solemn declaration to those who hold to this conviction in time of war that I believe them to be right; and I do desire with my whole mind and heart that I shall be among those who keep to this belief.
> I set down my name to make concrete my present thought upon the question of war, and declare my purpose to think and talk with others about it, that my belief in the Way of Christ shall become operative in this and in other questions which now confuse our thought and action.[45]

Sometimes the expressions of pacifism were unequivocal. In 1935 John Haynes Holmes, a towering figure in the antiwar crusade, led a group assembled in Judson Memorial Baptist Church in the litany:

> If war comes I will not fight;
> If war comes I will not enlist;
> If war comes I will not be conscripted;

44. Quoted in *ibid.*, p. 197. In this issue there appeared a letter to the editors from General Douglas MacArthur hoping that pacifist clergymen would cease attacking the national keepers of peace and turn their attention to the individual sinner and to ridding the country of crime.

45. *Federal Council Bulletin*, March, 1933, p. 10.

If war comes I will do nothing to support it;
If war comes I will do everything to oppose it,
So help me God![46]

Sometimes the expressions of pacifism were spelled out. In February, 1939, a group of one hundred notable ministers, including Tittle, met with Allan Knight Chalmers of the Broadway Tabernacle Church to prepare an "Affirmation of Christian Pacifist Faith." By June one thousand had signed. The lengthy statement is summarized in the following seven paragraphs:

> We believe that God is the Father of all mankind, that his will as revealed in Jesus Christ is universal love, and that Christ's gospel involves the faith that evil can be overcome only with good.
> We believe that in the cross is revealed God's way of dealing with wrongdoers, and that to this way all Christians are called.
> We believe that war, which attempts to overcome evil with more evil, is a denial of the way of the cross.
> We believe that the church is called to the way of the cross.
> We believe that when the state in the prosecution of war seeks to compel the denial of the gospel, the church must resist at any cost.
> We believe that God leads his church into new life through obedience of the individual believer in refusing war for Christ's sake.
> Therefore we proclaim to a world which is once again madly preparing for war that the gospel of God as revealed in Jesus Christ, which leaves us with no other choice but to refuse to sanction or participate in war, contains also its hope of redemption. We affirm our faith that the mission of the church today is to witness with singleness of heart, at whatever cost, to the power of good to overcome evil, of love to conquer hatred, of the cross to shatter the sword.[47]

With varying degrees of intensity almost all the major denominations joined the historic peace sects in declaring war on war, but no major denomination matched the fervor of the Methodists. The polls provide one source of documentation for this assertion. For instance, the famous Kirby Page questionnaire of 1934 showed the Methodists leading (78 percent) all other clergymen in holding that the churches should go on record as refusing to sanction or support any future war; and Methodists also led (72 percent) in stating their intention not to sanction or participate in any future war. Moreover, no other denomination matched

46. *Christian Century,* LII (May 29, 1935), 716.
47. *Ibid.,* LVI (March 15, 1939), 344.

Methodism's pacifist leadership: Tittle, Sockman, George Buttrick, Henry Hitt Crane, Ralph E. Diffendorfer, Georgia Harkness, Halford E. Luccock, Harold Bosley, Albert Day, E. Stanley Jones, Daniel Marsh, Harold Case, among many others. Further, the Methodist Commission on World Peace (the first denominational agency of its type) became virtually a pacifist body under the direction of Sockman and Tittle.

Methodist young people seemed consumed by pacifist idealism. The utterances emanating from the Methodist Youth Council could not have been more unequivocal, perhaps reflecting Kirby Page's admonition to the council that even if the United States were invaded, a true Christian could not take up arms.[48] Methodist seminarians shared this anti-war zeal. In 1931, according to the first Kirby Page poll, 81 percent of Boston University School of Theology students and 74 percent of Garrett students stated as their present purpose not to sanction any future war or participate as an armed combatant. Not even Epworth Leaguers were immune from the passion—or from antiwar indoctrination. Writing in the *Epworth Herald* of March 3, 1934, Miss Winifred Chappell, in a mood much like the militant spirit of resistance of the 1960's and employing logic not unlike that of Fathers Phillip and Daniel Berrigan, urged Methodist youth not simply to plead conscientious objection with consequent detention, but to enter the army or industry as deliberate saboteurs. "Stay out of jail—why thus separate yourself from the masses? Why thus let yourself be put out of the game? Accept the draft, take the drill, go into camps and onto the battlefield, or into the munitions factories and transportation work—but sabotage war preparations and war. Be agitators for sabotage. Down tools. . . . Spoil war materials and machinery." Patently Miss Chappell spoke for an infinitesimal minority. As the *New York Christian Advocate* in an editorial entitled, "For Conscienceless Objectors," observed, "No true friend of youth would suggest such a possibility. Nathan Hale is still more of a hero than Benedict Arnold."[49]

The permeation of Methodism by a near-pacifist spirit is further revealed in denominational papers, Sunday School materials, local congregational committees on world peace authorized by General Conference action, the formation of the Methodist Peace Fellowship, the leadership of Methodists in a host of nondenominational and secular peace groups, and the actions of Annual Conferences. Tittle's Rock River Conference branded war "the greatest social sin of modern times, a

48. Miron A. Morrill (ed.), *Methodist Youth Council* (Chicago: National Council of Methodist Youth, 1934), p. 45.
49. CIX (March 15, 1934), 243-44.

denial of the ideals of Christ, a violation of human personality, and a threat to civilization." Rock River also memorialized the General Conference to make it clear that the Methodist Episcopal Church, as an institution, formally dissociated itself from war and preparation for war, and supported any of its members whose conscience required them to be pacifists. However, despite Tittle's urging, Rock River Methodists refused to take the final step of resolving that no Christian under any circumstances could participate in war.[50]

The General Conference is of course the most authoritative expression of official Methodism, and the 1932 General Conference affirmed the strong antiwar stand of 1928, though it did not commit the church to the position of absolute pacifism. The 1936 General Conference edged Northern Methodism closer to a position of outright pacifism, declaring "that the Methodist Episcopal Church as an institution does not endorse, support or propose to participate in war," war being utterly destructive, a denial of the ideals of Christ, a violation of human personality, a threat to civilization, a sin.[51] The bishops in their Episcopal Address informed the "confessed militarist" of a bleak fact: "If he flees from Methodism because of our peace pronouncements, he will find that, feeling persecuted in our city, he has none other refuge within Protestantism."[52] The great Uniting Conference of 1939 adopted the position: "We believe that war is utterly destructive and is our greatest collective social sin and a denial of the ideals of Christ. We stand upon this ground, that the Methodist Church as an Institution cannot endorse war nor support or participate in it."[53]

Tittle played a crucial role in the formulation of these General Conference positions. Increasingly he came to believe that the word "pacifist" carried a freight of misunderstanding in the public mind, and increasingly he came to distinguish between nonresistance, negative and quietist, and nonviolent resistance, affirmative and active. Significantly, he read, admired, and much quoted Richard B. Gregg's influential *The Power of Non-Violence*, a militant, almost bellicose, assertion that Gandhi's nonviolent resistance could work to overcome evil and was a more Christlike way than the pacifism of other-worldly ascetics. On the eve of the outbreak of war in Europe, Tittle reviewed his position:

50. This last point was the subject of regular debate in the sessions of the 1930's.

51. *The Daily Christian Advocate,* Methodist Episcopal Church, May 15, 1936, pp. 378-79.

52. *Ibid.,* May 4, 1936, p. 67.

53. Walter G. Muelder, *Methodism and Society in the Twentieth Century* (New York and Nashville, Tenn.: Abingdon Press, 1961), p. 156.

In the present situation, I do not advocate a "do nothing" policy; nor do I believe in "selfish isolation." I believe that, now and always, evil should be resisted, but not with its own weapons. I believe that evil cannot be overcome with more evil but only with good. I believe that the means men use determine the ends they actually achieve. I believe that such ends as may be associated with the purpose of God in history cannot possibly be attained by means which involve hatred, lying and indiscriminate killing. If this is what it means to be a pacifist, then a pacifist I am. Of course, "there are values more important than life itself." It certainly is more important that truth should live, and freedom, justice, mercy and good will, than it is that I, or any other man, should live to a ripe and tottering old age. But none of these "values" can be preserved by war, which, as we now have super-abundant reason to know, tramples them, one and all, into the mire. Spiritual values can be preserved only by a regard for them, an unswerving loyalty to them, which the collective use of violence makes utterly impossible.[54]

On a thousand instances in the thirties Tittle decried the prideful nationalism that set nation against nation. On a thousand instances he held that the preservation of peace depended on the muting of nationalism and the flowering of internationalism. In the twenties the most hopeful existing instrumentality of internationalism was the League of Nations. In the thirties the almost magical promise of the League melted away until Tittle's disenchantment became total. As to a second instrumentality of internationalism, the World Court, it is perhaps enough to say that Tittle from the pulpit urged his congregation to wire the United States senators (as he himself did) calling them to vote American membership.[55] When, in 1935, the Senate refused to take this action, thanks in part to the opposition of Father Charles Coughlin, Will Rogers, and William Randolph Hearst, the *Christian Leader* editorialized: "We have to swallow the galling fact that the foreign policies of the United States are practically dictated by a sensational priest, a stuttering comedian and a cynical newspaper man."[56] Tittle, too, was angry, but by 1937 he was inclined to think American membership was unwise.

While debating at the 1936 General Conference the international economic situation, Tittle said: "We may sign petitions in behalf of peace, we may send representatives to disarmament conferences that meet and adjourn without disarmament, we may cry 'Peace, Peace,' but there will be no peace until there is economic justice." There are many

54. *Christian Century,* LVI (June 21, 1939), 796.
55. *Evanston News-Index,* January 28, 1935, p. 3.
56. February 9, 1935, p. 164.

causes of modern war, but "none so utterly important as this one."[57] Tittle's long standing belief in the economic roots of war hardened in the thirties into dogma. He was in essential agreement with Norman Thomas that if war came it would be between the House of Have and the House of Have Not; between what Kirby Page called the self-righteousness of the surfeited with the self-assertion of the frustrated. "A war between Britain-France-America and Germany-Italy-Japan would not be a war in behalf of the ideology and practice of democracy," Tittle asserted in 1938. "It would be merely a war of competing imperialisms for the lion's share of the markets and resources of the world. It would be a war between nations that 'have' and nations that 'have not,' the former determined to keep what they have, the latter to get what they want. Of course, the ideal of democracy would be used as propaganda, but it would have exactly no influence on the conduct of the war or on the making of 'peace.' "[58] Supporting Tittle's position, the editors of the *Northwestern Christian Advocate* declared, "It is easy to say the democracies of the world must unite against the autocracies, but only in cloud-cuckoo-land could the thing be done."[59]

Paul van Zeeland, former premier of Belgium, was commissioned by Great Britain and France to study international conditions. In his report of January, 1938, he urged the United States, Great Britain, France, Germany, and Italy to join in a pact of economic collaboration on specific items. Tittle clutched the straw of hope, saying of the van Zeeland suggestion: "Such an attempt and no other might confidently claim the support and approval of God."[60] Reinhold Niebuhr responded in a letter to the editors of the *Christian Century*.[61] "At its best," said Niebuhr, "the van Zeeland report is . . . a counsel of perfection which is completely irrelevant to the situation because the dictators would sign their abdication if they accepted it. At its worst the van Zeeland report is just one of the many efforts of the Chamberlain government to beguile Germany into partnership in the imperial business in order to overcome her threat of a rival imperialism." The dictators battened on the fact that they could "count on the moralistic illusions which have filled the so-called liberal world for generations. Is it really 'Christian,' is it God's will, never to call the bluff of a bully for fear that you might be involved in violence?" He concluded:

57. *The Daily Christian Advocate*, Methodist Episcopal Church, May 18, 1936, p. 461.
58. *Adult Student* (December, 1938), pp. 5-6, clipping in Tittle Collection.
59. LXXXVI (September 22, 1938), 967.
60. *Christian Century*, LV (November 30, 1938), 1462-65.
61. *Ibid.*, (December 14, 1938), pp. 1549-50.

On rereading my vehement tirade against my friend Tittle, I fear
that the lust of battle betrays me into passions which seem out of
accord with the opening sentence of my letter. I can only say
that for many years I have constantly held up Dr. Tittle as an
example of the kind of integrity and courage which saves the
church from futility. I should hate to be in a church which did
not include him in its ultimate communion. But the church
which he has set up will exclude many of us. For we are determined upon political policies for the saving of democratic civilization: boycott of Japan, lifting the embargo on Spain, etc., which
in his opinion are counter to God's will. Perhaps the only church
to which both groups could comfortably belong would be one in
which there was some knowledge of the defiance of God's will in
even the best of human intentions.

Tittle might have reminded Niebuhr of Niebuhr's earlier words:
"Another war will be suicidal to our civilization, and it will be caused
by the fact that the Western nations are maintaining a social system
which makes the kind of economic reciprocity upon which peace must
be based impossible. For this reason I will refuse any kind of participation in the next war."[62] Or of Niebuhr's words of 1935: "I do
not intend to participate in any war now in prospect. I take this position not on strictly pacifistic grounds, for I am not an absolutist, but
simply because I can see no good coming out of any of the wars confronting us. The position of Russia on the one hand and of Germany
on the other hand in any of these wars would not affect my decision."[63]

"I feel very strongly," Tittle wrote an associate in 1934, "that we
should continue the agitation for universal and total abolition of national
armies and navies and for the creation in their stead of an international
police force that would operate under a neutral authority, say the World
Court or the League of Nations."[64] He continued to hold, as he had in
the twenties, that armaments do not "buy" national security, that when
nations arm to the teeth world tensions become "unbearably high," that
the world "is nervous and afraid because it is armed," that there is no
analogy between a national army and a municipal police force, that
great military machines do not long remain idle, though their avowed
purpose is purely defensive, that it is insanity for the world to pour
billions of dollars into armaments while humanity goes unfed and un-
clothed, that the lines of Alfred Noyes were true:

62. Quoted in Van Kirk, *Religion Renounces War,* p. 23.
63. *Fellowship* (October, 1935), p. 13.
64. Letter from Tittle to Roger Shively, February 24, 1934.

Their dens are ankle deep
  With twisted knives; and in their sleep
They often cut themselves; they say
  That if you want to live in peace
The surest way is not to cease
  Collecting knives; and never a day
Can pass unless they buy a few.
  And, as their enemies buy them too,
They all avert the impending fray
  And starve their children and their wives
To buy the necessary knives.

And so in sermons, conference reports, petitions, and letters to Congress he sought to brake America's accelerating rearmament program, and to have America "lead the other nations of the world in a program for the progressive reduction of armaments."

In the thirties Tittle continued to pursue the eradication of militarism from the schools. At Rock River Annual Conferences and General Conferences he advocated, and in debate successfully defended, reports and resolutions calling for the end of all military training in civilian educational institutions, broadening the earlier opposition to all military training in high schools and compulsory military training in colleges and universities. He concurred with Norman Thomas, "If we mean business in our war against war we must dig out the R.O.T.C., root and branch—polo ponies, pretty girl colonels, snappy uniforms and all." Clearly the effort failed, despite a few victories in a few states. But it is further true that for a moment in the mid-thirties a substantial minority of American youth, mostly idealistic, articulate college students, were gripped by an antiwar fervor. Youth group after youth group resolved against and agitated against war. Pledging pacifism became *au courant* on campus after campus. Tens of thousands of students vowed never to bear arms. One poll of sixty-five colleges revealed 39 percent of the students holding a position of absolute pacifism. On April 12, 1935, sixty thousand students participated in a "strike" against war. The Oxford Union peace pledge crossed the Atlantic to enjoy a great vogue in America. Three hundred chapters of the Veterans of Future Wars were formed on college campuses, a sardonic society organized by Princeton undergraduates to enable prospective soldiers to collect their bonuses in advance. Vassar girls, unwilling to concede the superior imagination of boys, forthwith organized the Gold Star Mothers of Veterans of Future Wars. In 1938 a World Youth Congress met in Poughkeepsie and the representatives of an estimated forty million young people promised to work against war, though the promise was not a vow of absolute pacifism.

Tittle was not displeased at peace activities on the Northwestern campus. In 1933, for example, when the Naval ROTC unit passed in review before President Scott and a number of military and naval dignitaries, demonstrators also paraded with placards saying "Down with the R.O.T.C.," "Look at the Tender Hearted Sops in Uniform," and "We Are Against War and Against Northwestern University." "An attempt was made," reads the laconic newspaper account, "on the part of an unidentified woman to stop the demonstration by driving her car into the ranks of the marchers."[65] In 1936, one thousand Northwestern students staged a strike against war, President Scott addressing the demonstrators from the steps of Lunt Library with the mild words, "I'm glad to see a parade in the interests of peace. It's unanimous. Go to it."[66] The following year, such was the temper of the times, a mass student meeting to protest war, chaired by Tittle, was addressed by such speakers as a Wildcat football star and the former state commander of the American Legion![67] This student ferment seems less frivolous—in fact it seems deadly serious—when we remember that the overwhelming majority of those boys who marched in the peace demonstrations were in a few years to march off to war without a whimper. And if they survived, it was to sire sons who perhaps in the 1960's marched in peace demonstrations and then off to their deaths in Vietnam—or to prison or to expatriation in Canada or Sweden. (In 1970, following the Cambodian invasion and the Kent State tragedy, the Northwestern faculty finally voted to end credit for all NROTC courses without exception.)

In anticipation that should war come to America not a few Methodist young men would stand firm in their pacifist convictions, preparations were made to place about them the protective mantle of the church. In all Methodism, no man did more than Tittle to assure conscientious objectors that they would not be deserted in their hour of testing. As Tittle preached a "higher loyalty," so he felt an intense loyalty to those youngsters who responded by placing the Cross above the flag. Tittle's Rock River Conference memorialized the General Conference on behalf of the lads and the General Conference acted affirmatively. "We earnestly petition the government of the United States," stated Northern Methodism in both 1932 and 1936, "to grant to members of the Method-

65. *Evanston News-Index,* May 18, 1933, p. 1.
66. *Ibid.,* April 22, 1936, p. 1.
67. *Ibid.,* April 22, 1937, p. 1.

ist Episcopal Church who may be conscientious objectors to war the same exemption from military service as has long been granted to members of the Society of Friends and other similar religious organizations."[68] The 1939 Uniting Conference reaffirmed this position.

In almost all areas of peace and war the Christian Church could do little more than attempt to persuade the government to do this or that or refrain from doing thus and so. Tittle believed, however, that the Church could act decisively and unilaterally on at least one matter, that of the military chaplaincy. Rock River Methodists memorialized the General Conference "to order that henceforth no pastor of our denomination shall become a military chaplain; and further to ask the Federal Council of Churches to seek similar and united action on the part of other religious bodies. . . ."[69] During the ensuing debate, Tittle insisted that he did not advocate leaving "our boys without any spiritual shepherding in time of war nor in time of peace." His only intent was that chaplains "be appointed by the Church, be paid by the Church and be amenable to the Church and not to the military arm of the United States government."[70] The final statement adopted by the Conference was a restrained request to the Federal Council of Churches "to seek to find a method by which the spiritual ministry of the churches to the armed forces of the United States . . . may be performed by ministers appointed and supported by and amenable to the churches"[71]

By the mid-thirties events in Asia and Europe made painfully evident the accelerated disintegration of the Versailles and post-Versailles peace structure. American peacemakers responded with a great Emergency Peace Campaign designed to stave off war, and should war come to the world, to forestall America's entry, the very title of the effort revealing the peacemakers' sense of urgency. The Emergency Peace Campaign "was the most impressive effort in the history of the American peace movement."[72] For the two years, 1936-37, it dominated the peace movement.[73] This well-organized, well-financed crusade was not an indepen-

68. *The Daily Christian Advocate,* Methodist Episcopal Church, May 16, 1932, p. 334, and May 15, 1936, p. 379. Most major denominations adopted similar protective resolutions.

69. *Minutes* of the Rock River Annual Conference (1935), p. 16.

70. *The Daily Christian Advocate,* Methodist Episcopal Church, May 12, 1936, pp. 256-57.

71. *Discipline* of the Methodist Episcopal Church (1936), p. 663.

72. Chatfield, "Pacifism and American Life," p. 321.

73. Robert Edwin Bowers, "The American Peace Movement, 1933-1941" (Ph.D. dissertation, University of Wisconsin, 1947), p. 300. See also two additional dissertations: Doniver A. Lund, "The Peace Movement Among the Major American Protestant Churches, 1919-1939" (Ph.D. dissertation, University of

dent organization but a representative action group, enlisting the participation of many of the societies working for peace in America. Many prominent citizens were involved, including Eleanor Roosevelt, Admiral Richard Byrd, and Charles P. Taft. Clergymen, however, were the heart and the head of the Campaign, and the churches provided the working machinery. Ray Newton, Devere Allen, Kirby Page, and Harold E. Fey were key directors. John Haynes Holmes, Harry Emerson Fosdick, Sherwood Eddy, Albert Palmer, and in fact almost every pacifist minister in the land enlisted in the enterprise, almost three thousand of them serving as speakers without pay. The Emergency Peace Campaign was an expression of pacifism, the left wing of the peace movement, the last great effort of the pacifists, as distinct from isolationists, unilaterialists, and continentalists, to give leadership to the antiwar passion. The Campaign reached its climax on the twentieth anniversary of the American entrance into World War I. On April 6, 1937, its officers launched a mighty "No-Foreign-War-Crusade." For two intensive months every available resource was committed to the task of so arousing public opinion and so shaping public policy as to make impossible a repetition of 1917.

Tittle was deeply involved in this great peace drive. He was present at the organizational conference at Buck Hills, Pennsylvania, in December, 1935. He helped launch a local Evanston Emergency Peace Campaign Committee. Major rallies were held in First Church addressed by national peace leaders. Tittle himself volunteered to speak in Kansas City, St. Louis, and elsewhere under the auspices of the Campaign. He prepared a critique of his experiences for the guidance of Ray Newton, pointing out certain flaws in the organization of the Campaign, the most telling being that the people who attended his addresses were already dedicated to peace. The best way to reach the uncommitted, he believed, was through local speakers appearing at the regular meetings of luncheon clubs, service clubs, and chambers of commerce.[74] The final stages of the Campaign extended into 1938 under the direction of the National Peace Conference of the National Council for Prevention of War, still another enterprise enlisting Tittle's support.

Writing to an associate in 1934, Tittle stated that "in the event of

Nebraska, 1956) and Vernon Howard Holloway, "American Pacifism Between Two Wars, 1919-1941: An Analysis of Pacifist Groups and Doctrines in the United States" (Ph.D. dissertation, Yale University, 1949), summarized in "A Review of American Religious Pacifism," *Religion In Life*, XIX (Summer, 1950), 367-79.

74. Letter from Tittle to Ray Newton, November 3, 1936.

war I would urge that an absolute embargo be placed upon munitions and also upon loans. If we should allow ourselves to ship munitions to either of the contesting groups or to loan money to them, I very much fear that we would become involved again as in the case of 1917." Moreover, "I am personally agitating for an immediate transference of the manufacture of munitions from private hands to the hands of government. We simply must take private profit out of the manufacture of munitions."[75] In the mid-thirties Tittle's opinions were the common property of a majority of Americans. Intervention in the Great War was done at the behest of bankers and munition makers—"merchants of death"—abetted by the astute propaganda of the Allies. This popular view received scholarly support from such revisionist historians as Barnes, Millis, and Tansill. It was the theme of Seldes's *Iron, Blood, and Profits,* Engelbrecht's *One Hell of a Business,* Engelbrecht's and Hanighen's *Merchants of Death* (a Book-of-the-Month Club selection), Waldman's *Death and Profits,* Lewishohn's *The Profits of War,* Ponsonby's *Falsehood in Wartime,* and Lasswell's *Propaganda Technique in the World War.* A kind of revived muckraking gripped the American reading public, the Great War being the target of a thousand magazine and monograph exposés.

On April 23, 1934, Senator Gerald Prentice Nye of North Dakota was elected chairman of the Senate Committee Investigating the Munitions Industry. Though he had not coveted the assignment, though he was an unpretentious and uncomplicated midwesterner, though he shared committee leadership with such commanding figures as Senator Arthur H. Vandenberg and drew heavily on such investigative assistants as Alger Hiss and Stephen Raushenbush (the son of Walter Rauschenbusch who changed the spelling of the family name), Nye became the symbol of the movement to curb the "merchants of death." In the popular mind, the Nye committee was synonymous with the thesis that American entry into World War I was the work of wicked Wall Street bankers and sinister arms barons. We now know[76] that this famous Senate investigation committee originally had the backing of the Roosevelt administration, that it was not antibusiness and did not browbeat business witnesses, that it did not "prove" business was responsible for American intervention, and that actually it had little influence on the formulation

75. Letter from Tittle to Roger Shively, February 24, 1934.
76. See John E. Wiltz, *In Search of Peace: The Senate Munitions Inquiry, 1934-36* (Baton Rouge: Louisiana State University Press, 1963) and Wayne S. Cole, *Senator Gerald P. Nye and American Foreign Relations* (Minneapolis: University of Minnesota Press, 1962).

of administration policies. Yet after stripping away the more conspiratorial inferences falsely drawn from Senator Nye's investigations, there remained for many citizens (including Tittle) the hard conclusion that economic ties had drawn the United States into war on the side of the Allies, her customers, and debtors; and that if intervention were to be averted in a future war, America must remain scrupulously free from economic entanglements.

Tittle's library contained most of the studies "proving" the economic roots of American intervention in 1917. He had long believed in the economic interpretation of international rivalry. Therefore, the Nye committee's reports (and the press much exaggerated the findings) did not trigger Tittle's determination to keep America out of war by taking the profits out of war, but simply provided him with additional ammunition. In 1936 he wrote Nye, "Along with many thousands I rejoice in the noble service you are rendering in the cause of peace."[77] In 1937 the North Dakota senator spoke at First Church on the subject, "Preparedness for Peace."[78] The Rock River Annual Conference in its request to nationalize the arms industry specifically praised the Nye committee. The General Conference also lauded the committee's work and asked the federal government to "assume exclusive responsibility for the manufacture of munitions of all kinds."[79] In fact, the sources of Methodist opinion are replete with citations to the Nye committee, and despite the moderating findings of recent scholars, it is difficult to escape the conclusion that American public opinion was greatly influenced by the seeming support the committee gave to the "merchants of death" thesis. In fact, also, much in recent United States history suggests the continuing interrelationship between war and profits or, less narrowly but more dangerously, between war and general prosperity.

Closely attuned to the assumptions of the Nye committee, but not a consequence of the Senate investigations, were the Neutrality Acts of 1935, 1936, and 1937. The purpose of this legislation was to insure American neutrality if war broke out in the world by making it impossible for the United States to extend aid—arms, munitions, credits, or, at the president's discretion, other articles except on a "cash-and-carry" basis—to either belligerent. Additional provisions further restricted historic neutral rights, such as the traveling of American citizens on belligerent ships. Concerning these complicated acts one thing may be said with

77. Letter from Tittle to the Honorable Gerald P. Nye, September 11, 1936.
78. *Evanston Review*, June 3, 1937, p. 19.
79. *The Daily Christian Advocate,* Methodist Episcopal Church, May 15, 1936, p. 379.

certainty: the overwhelming majority of diplomatic historians judge them a failure and, moreover, doomed from the outset to fail. They were predicated on a devil theory of war and designed to exorcise this devil. They were predicated on a false reading of the events of 1914-17 and the drawing of a false parallel between those years and the 1930's. They flashed a green light to aggressor nations, signaling as they did America's intention to draw no distinction between attacker and attacked. Conversely, they weakened the resolve of the democracies to resist, because now no assistance from the New World could be expected. Their authors failed to consider that inevitably and rightly Americans would not remain neutral in a war between Germany-Italy and England-France or in the Far East between Japan and China. The "cash-and-carry" provision made possible continued war profits, merely placing the risks of the transaction on the belligerent with the money and ships to buy and fetch, and where was the morality or neutrality in such an arrangement? In sum, the neutrality legislation was a victory more for isolationism than for pacifism, though it was endorsed by the pacifists. It failed to keep peace in the world; ultimately it failed to keep America out of war.

What defense, if any, then, can be made for the endorsement of this neutrality legislation by Tittle and other pacifists who did not consider themselves morally neutral and who did not deem themselves isolationists? For one thing, far from being too extreme a break with historic neutral rights, they believed the laws were too limited; in their view, nothing less than a total and mandatory embargo of all trade with belligerents was necessary to keep America out of war. For a second thing, they held that the neutrality legislation was never really given a chance: it was not applied to the Sino-Japanese conflict, and after the fall of 1939 it was amended, indeed, gutted. Thirdly, Tittle and the pacifists had different (and as they believed, higher) concepts of national rights and national honor, and they were more prepared than other Americans to sacrifice the "traditional" prerogatives of a neutral. Fourthly, Tittle and the pacifists were willing to lose America's foreign commerce and accept, if necessary, depressed domestic conditions as a consequence of a tight embargo, for such a high price was not too much to pay for peace. Finally and most crucially, to Tittle and the pacifists war was murder. As was said at the time and affirmed by a handful of individuals in a later era, nothing justifies modern war—"neither Communism, Fascism, nationalism, tyranny, nor freedom; the conquest of the earth or the preservation of any way of life: nothing. Nothing in the world, however base or however good, or however theoretically admirable, can justify murder as an act of policy."[80]

Tittle stated in a 1937 sermon:

> What I have termed neutrality legislation, using the popular form of designation, is, of course, not a legislation which aims at neutrality. The word in this case is clearly a misnomer. This legislation is not seeking to keep us from doing anything in the interest of truth and right and freedom and democracy and peace. It is not even intended to keep us out of war in the extremely improbable contingency that we should find ourselves threatened with actual invasion. All it is intended to do is to keep us from engaging in a foreign war, whether for private profit or for any other reason whatsoever. If this legislation should turn out to be successful, it would not inevitably isolate us; it would isolate war. . . . If it were successful, it would enable us to maintain here on this continent at least one area of sanity and peace and so to be in a position, after the epidemic had run its awful course, to start movements for world recovery.[81]

And so Tittle wired his congressmen urging them to support the various neutrality bills. And he, together with other Methodist peacemakers, persuaded both the Rock River Annual Conference and the General Conference to adopt resolutions endorsing the neutrality acts.

As isolationists and pacifists joined in endorsement of the neutrality acts and successfully fought off amendment of the absolute arms embargo in the spring and summer of 1939, so they supported, though without success, the so-called Ludlow Amendment. An Indiana Democrat, Louis Ludlow, introduced in the House of Representatives in 1935, 1937, and 1938 a constitutional amendment providing that a declaration of extraterritorial war would have to be validated by a national referendum. Such a measure had been introduced in every Congress since 1922, reflecting the popular sentiment that wars are started by ambitious rulers in violation of the peaceful proclivities of the common people. Almost all historians agree with President Roosevelt that such a constitutional restriction was subversive of representative government, impractical in application, and disastrous to executive leadership, and they justify Roosevelt's pulling out all the stops to defeat the measure finally on January 10, 1938.

Tittle worked for the Ludlow Amendment by word, pen, and telegram. He was unable, however, to persuade either the Rock River Annual Conference or General Conference to give endorsement, and the

80. James Cameron as quoted in the *New Yorker*, February 24, 1968, p. 135.
81. "On Being Neutral," typed MS, a sermon preached May 30, 1937.

Methodist press was far from united in its attitude. The 1950s and 1960s have raised anew the momentous question: what, if any, checks are there on a president's power to bring the nation into war? What voice, if any, do the people possess to call a halt to risky foreign policies? The warnings of Tittle—and Charles A. Beard—seem less fatuous in light of Korea, Cuba, Vietnam, Laos, and Cambodia. If not the people, who, then, will restrain an executive branch having (in any substantive sense) unlimited authority in foreign affairs? Millions of citizens in the third quarter of the twentieth century are gripped by a sense of utter helplessness to determine whether they shall live in peace or die in war. However romantic the Ludlow Amendment, it was rooted in the people's disquietude over the loss of control of their own destinies.

Beginning with the Manchurian Incident in 1931, Asia and then Europe cascaded sickeningly into war: Mukden, Ethiopia, Spain, Marco Polo Bridge, Munich, the Berlin-Moscow Pact, Poland—but the searing events of the thirties are too burned into our collective memories to warrant even cursory review. What were Americans to do? Collective security and sanctions, whether applied by the League of Nations or not, lay in one direction. Mandatory neutrality and over-all embargo applied unilaterally by the United States lay in the opposite direction, and there was no way to follow both courses. "With Manchuria," writes Donald Meyer, "the peace movement began to sort itself out along the lines of its suppressed inner divisions."[82] Tittle was driven by events and his own convictions to support the latter course.

To be sure, he asked that the "conscience of mankind" voice its moral disapproval of aggression. He sought to moderate tensions by extending diplomatic recognition to Russia and terminating the discriminatory Japanese Exclusion Act, by lowering American tariffs and canceling European war debts, by withdrawing United States military and naval forces from the Far East and placing the Philippines under an "international guarantee of neutrality," by extending relief to the victims of war in China and Spain and opening America's doors to the victims of Hitler's fury, by protesting the bombing of Guernica and the rape of Nanking, by expressing "contrition for sins we ourselves have committed—we of the United States, of Great Britain, of France, and of Russia."

These things and others Tittle would do and have his country do. But he was unwilling—he was unable—to advocate or accept coercion, economic or military, unilateral or collective. To impose economic sanc-

82. *The Protestant Search for Political Realism, 1919-1941* (Berkeley and Los Angeles: University of California Press, 1960), p. 353.

tions against Japan or Germany or Italy, to join the democracies in an economic boycott of these aggressor nations, he argued, would not serve as an effective deterrent. Economic coercion would only heighten bitterness and frustration and feed the fires of aggression. As for the threat of military retaliation, this was not a viable option to anyone as deeply committed to pacifism as was Tittle. The way to help China, he insisted, was to help Japan, and thus remove the motives driving her to conquest. If the economic and emotional needs of the Japanese, German, and Italian people were fulfilled, they themselves would restrain their ambitious leaders. Ultimately, if these things failed to keep the peace, then it was to America's self-interest and to the entire world's long-range interest for the United States to remain neutral, refusing materials of war to any and all belligerents—Japan or China, Italy or Ethiopia, Franco or the Loyalists, or, if it came to the terrible eventuality, Germany or England. Only by remaining out of war could the United States serve her citizens and all humanity.

As Tittle followed the path of pacifism straight and true into 1939, increasing numbers of former peacemakers, led by Reinhold Niebuhr, came to the conviction that only collective coercion would secure the world from Japan's appetite and Hitler's wrath. "I am not a little disturbed by defections from the ranks of pacifism," Tittle wrote Roswell P. Barnes in January, 1939.[83] And as the ranks of the pacifists thinned and as the Roosevelt administration's foreign policies became ever less neutral, Tittle's admiration for the president evaporated. By the summer of 1939 he expressed in a thinly veiled sermon reference a fear shared by both pacifist liberals and isolationist conservatives: "And what if some day an American president, desiring not only a third term but a fourth and a fifth, should decide upon a foreign war as a means of consolidating support for his administration at home?"[84] In 1940, of course, for the first time in the history of the republic a president was elected for a third term. By then Europe was aflame and the great debate over American neutrality had entered its final stage.

VI

At three o'clock on Friday morning, September 1, 1939, President Roosevelt was awakened by a phone call from Ambassador William C. Bullitt in Paris informing him that Germany had invaded Poland. At 10:30 in the morning the president held a special press conference at which he stated his belief that the United States could and would remain

83. Letter from Tittle to Roswell P. Barnes, January 20, 1939.
84. "The Church and the State," typed MS, a sermon preached July 2, 1939.

at peace. He then conferred with Secretary of State Hull and, with Hull's concurrence, decided to call Congress into special session within a short time to revise America's neutrality legislation in order to permit supplies to flow to England and France. The tension thereby established on September 1 between the objectives of keeping the peace and aiding the Allies was to heighten for the next twenty-seven months. Not until December 7, 1941, did release come—release borne on the fins of Japanese bombs at Oahu. During this agonizing period the energies of Tittle and the peacemakers were in five major areas of concern: how to bring an end to the war in Asia and Europe; how to aid the victims of war; how to keep America out of war; how to prepare for the care of conscientious objectors should America be drawn into war; and how to plan for the postwar world.

On September 24, 1939, the first Sunday after returning from his vacation, Tittle mounted the pulpit to preach on "The Church in a World at War." The United States must not again be stampeded into a "Great Crusade." Rather, "in the name of Christ, let the church now demand a peace without victory. . . ." How might this be done? Well, America "might initiate and continue a conference of neutral nations to discover ways and means to bring the war to an end."[85] For two years Tittle cherished the hope that somehow the neutral nations could persuade the belligerents to sit down at a conference table and negotiate a peace without victory. This hope was expressed in sermons, articles, and letters to the president and embodied in the reports of the Methodist World Peace Commission and Rock River and General Conference resolutions. A new organization was formed, the Churchmen's Campaign for Peace Through Mediation, sponsored by the Ministers' No War Committee, and of course Tittle was active in it. Niebuhr flayed Tittle's hopes as utopian, saying that most of Europe's neutral nations were shivering little mice waiting for the cat to pounce. Churchill defied Hitler to do his worst. The Roosevelt administration increasingly committed the United States to aiding the Allies. In the end, the Wilsonian plea, "peace without victory," again fell on ears deafened by the thunder of battle. The idea of a negotiated peace under the sponsorship of neutral nations may very well have been a hopeless one, but we will never know with absolute certainty, for beyond a few ceremonial gestures it was never given a chance. Churchill and Hitler at the same conference table staggers the imagination, but is "realism" an adequate term to

85. "The Church in a World at War," *The First Church Pulpit*, Vol. III, No. 1, a sermon preached September 24, 1939.

describe what was done to achieve the "unconditional surrender" of the enemy?

While the work for a negotiated peace went on, millions of men, women, and children were being chewed up in the maw of war, and Tittle anguished over their fate. He was active in various agencies to bring relief to China, and First Church specifically and Methodism generally gave generously. He repeatedly sought to widen America's doors to the victims of Nazi oppression, most especially Jews, and this became the official position of Methodism at the 1940 General Conference. It must be said here that neither the English government nor the Roosevelt Administration did all those things that might have been done to save European Jewry. (The record of our ally, Stalin, is too infamous to merit comment.) The evidence mounts that indifference and then, after the outbreak of hostilities, military considerations—the defeat of the Axis with a minimum of Allied casualties—dominated the thinking at No. 10 Downing Street and 1600 Pennsylvania Avenue. Military necessity decreed the obliteration bombing of Dresden, Hamburg, and Berlin. And military necessity decreed that Jews must die unaided lest the aid somehow shore up the German military machine. Hitler's genocide design provided the least unambigious justification for going to war against him. If anything gave World War II a moral basis it was Germany's monstrous "final solution." Yet six million European Jews were not saved by England and the United States; and it is increasingly clear that England and the United States were unwilling to jeopardize victory by ransoming the prey in Hitler's slaughterhouses.[86] It is frequently charged that pacifism had no answer to Auschwitz and Belsen. But for the overwhelming majority of the Jews who passed through their gates, Churchill's and Roosevelt's answer came too late, for by 1945 the inmates had been rendered into soap and lampshades. Certainly to have saved the Jews would have meant the payment of blackmail to Hitler. And if paid, the blackmail may have strengthened Germany for war, then prolonged the war, and cost the lives of English and American soldiers. But if all is subordinated to victory, then the pacifist indictment of modern war becomes increasingly convincing. It is true that after 1942 Hitler increasingly blocked the exits, but in the crucial years from

86. See Arthur D. Morse, *While Six Million Died: A Chronicle of American Apathy* (New York: Random House, 1967) and David S. Wyman, *Paper Walls: America and the Refugee Crisis, 1938-1941* (Amherst: University of Massachusetts Press, 1968) and Henry L. Feingold, *The Politics of Rescue: The Roosevelt Administration and the Holocaust, 1938-1945* (New Brunswick, N. J.: Rutgers University Press, 1970).

1938 to 1941 Jews were less locked in the Third Reich than they were locked out of Great Britain and the United States.

On November 10, 1940, Tittle preached a sermon, "Should Europe's Hungry Be Fed?"[87] Published in the *Christian Century* and *Zion's Herald*, it came to the attention of the National Committee on Food for the Small Democracies, headed by Herbert Hoover, an organization whose purpose it was to stay mass starvation in Poland, Finland, Belgium, Luxemburg, Holland, Norway, and Greece. The National Committee mailed the sermon with a covering letter by Albert W. Palmer, president of the Chicago Theological Seminary, a fellow pacifist and Tittle's friend, to sixty thousand ministers. The National Committee advocated the following program. In essence, the countries whose people were to be fed would carry the needed food in their own ships and pay for it with their own money. The German government would have to agree to allow free passage of relief ships, to take none of their cargoes for its own use, to take none of the domestic produce of the peoples being relieved, and to give to the international relief commission full control of distribution and inspection. The British government would have to agree to allow the free passage of relief ships as long as Germany's guarantees were fulfilled and no longer. In the event of Germany's failure to live up to its agreement, the British would be free to reinstitute a blockade of all shipping. The arrival of relief ships would be so timed as to prevent any accumulation of food, so that the amount on hand at any time would make no appreciable difference in favor of Germany if the German government should in any way violate its agreement.

Mr. Hoover has described how the plan was killed by the British government and the Roosevelt administration.[88] To the charge that the feeding of the peoples in these small nations would strengthen Germany, Mr. Hoover explained patiently and repeatedly that this simply was not so. Meanwhile American churchmen took sides, public statements appearing in the *New York Times* and elsewhere. The most vehement clerical critic of the plan and of Tittle's sermon was Henry Pitney Van Dusen of Union Theological Seminary. "Men cry for freedom and are given bread," he thundered. Nothing, however humanitarian, must weaken the British war effort or dull the recognition that American

87. *The First Church Pulpit,* Vol. IV, No. 2.
88. *An American Epic* (Chicago: Henry Regnery Co., 1964), IV, 1-73. See also William M. Tuttle, Jr., "Aid-to-the-Allies Short-of-War versus American Intervention, 1940: A Reappraisal of William Allen White's Leadership," *Journal of American History,* LVI (March, 1970), 844ff.

security demanded Hitler's defeat. Meanwhile, also, Palmer and Tittle were receiving dozens of letters from clergymen. Many of the correspondents endorsed the relief program, but a clear majority were in opposition. "I suggest that you send a copy of Dr. Tittle's sermon. . . . to Hitler," wrote a Methodist minister. "I am sure that of all the persons on earth who might agree with it, it would be that tyrant." A Presbyterian insisted, "The only way to save our people from starvation is to rescue them by force of arms." "The sermon has a touch of . . . sentimental mushiness," charged a third, "and your plan would give people full stomachs but it would strengthen the possibility of a Hitler victory which as President Roosevelt rightly says means slavery." If the responses received by Palmer and Tittle were in any way representative, it is clear that by late 1940 a significant element of the Protestant ministry was prepared to go to the limit in support of England.[89]

Tittle had already given his answer to the critics of the program in the concluding words of the controversial sermon:

> The motives of men are sometimes better than their arguments. What are the opponents of this relief plan really concerned to say? Is it not something like this: Civilization, today, is in grave peril. It is threatened with utter destruction by the forces of reaction, tyranny, and cruelty. It must, at any cost to the present generation, be preserved. If we oppose this plan, it is not because we are lacking in human sympathy. It is because we are convinced that no ordeal, however, terrible, is too great a price to pay for the defeat of barbarism and the preservation of civilization.
>
> But what does it mean to preserve civilization? It surely means (among other things) to keep alive in the world a high regard for human life, a deep sense of responsibility for the welfare of other human beings, an unrelenting demand for human decency. These are surely essential to a humane and civilized culture. And these, I submit, are not safeguarded but are, to the contrary, terribly imperiled by the deliberate killing of innocent aged persons and women and children, even though the killing be done slowly with a food blockade and done in the name of "civilization."
>
> Belief that civilization can be saved by the destruction of millions of innocent people is, of course, the ancient belief that evil can be overcome with more evil. Once again we are being asked to do evil that good may come. But in the light of human experience, including our own during and after the first World War, we are now bound to ask, Would good come if we should

89. For some reason, Palmer turned over to Tittle the letters he received and they are in the Tittle Collection. All quotations are taken from letters in the Collection. Tittle's older son, John, was active in support of the plan.

consent to such outrageous evil as is involved in a deliberate decision to let millions of innocent people die? Surely, we now have reason enough to believe that when you do evil that good may come, what you actually get is not the good you seek but the evil you do.

Tittle and the peacemakers largely failed in their efforts to provide succor for the victims of war as they totally failed to effect a negotiated peace. And as the months passed it became increasingly evident that they were to fail in their purpose of keeping the United States out of war. "What a majority of the American people want," wrote Freda Kirchwey in the *Nation*, "is to be as unneutral as possible without getting into war." Poll after poll revealed increasing numbers of Americans willing to risk war with Hitler by aiding the Allies rather than sealing off assistance and chancing a German triumph. After the fall of France the fear of an Axis victory heightened, until by early 1941 68 percent of all Americans favored all-out aid even at the risk of war. The figure remained nearly constant until Pearl Harbor. Poll after poll also disclosed growing public support of tightening economic pressure against Japan in the hope of deterring her expansion in Asia. Moreover, most of the great measures of preparedness and assistance to the Allies, such as Lend Lease, were fully debated and finally enacted in accordance with the American democratic legislative process. In the years 1939-41 America became, in FDR's stirring phrase, "the great arsenal of democracy," and it did so with the concurrence of the majority of citizens as their will was revealed in polls and at the polls, in debate and congressional action. The ranks of pacifism and isolationism thinned as the administration's posture toward Japan and Germany hardened because fewer and fewer Americans could remain morally neutral toward Japan and China, and Germany and England, and also because fewer and fewer continued to believe the Western Hemisphere impregnable from attack should Hitler win control of the Atlantic and Africa and should Japan conquer China, southeast Asia, and the western Pacific. Though Roosevelt was less than candid, it is simply not credible that he hungered for war (for whatever reason) or that he imposed on the American people policies contrary to the majority will. In sum, Roosevelt wanted what a majority of the American people wanted: to be "as unneutral as possible without getting into war."

Before examining Tittle's position in the twenty-seven months preceding Pearl Harbor, several additional observations must be made. Athough informed citizens were aware that "all aid short of war" carried the risk of war, at no time did their president warn them concerning the actual extent of the risk. Of course they were alerted to the possibility of war, but it is not Monday morning quarterbacking to assert that the United States pursued policies that made war probable, indeed, as Tittle and others cautioned at the time, made war virtually certain. Roosevelt knew the danger to be graver than he ever intimated publicly. Before December 7, 1941, fewer than 25 percent of the American people (according to the polls) favored a shooting war. Surely Roosevelt's measures "short of war" would have been less popular if the American people had been told the full truth: that the distance between war and "short of war" was a matter of inches rather than miles.

Then too the polls never asked a question centering on what in fact transpired: "Do you favor pursuing unneutral policies which probably will result in war with Japan and Germany simultaneously?" Yet, there were those, including Tittle, who discerned that this would be the precise consequence of America's policies.

Also, how many Americans would have assumed the responsibility of ridding the world of aggressors (that is, Japan, Germany, and Italy) and saving the free world (that is, England and France and also Chaing Kai-shek's China and Stalin's Russia) if they could have forseen the cold and hot wars of the 1950's and 1960's? Again, this is not a matter of 20-20 hindsight, for at the time not a few voices warned that to intervene would be to repeat 1917 and continue down an endless road of "perpetual war for perpetual peace."

These observations could be—and were—made by isolationists who were not necessarily pacifists. But Tittle and the pacifists grounded their critique not in isolationism, continentalism, American exceptionalism, prudence, or a realistic amorality. Rather, for the pacifists war was the ultimate enemy. To do evil that good may come, to slaughter Italians to save Ethiopia, Spanish rebels to save Loyalist Spain, Japanese to save China, Russians to save Finland, Germans to save Russia and France and England was to mock the God revealed in Jesus Christ. The pacifists stood unalterably opposed to going to war to "save" "democracy" "civilization," even "Christianity." They did not believe that these deeply cherished values could be saved by the mass murder that is modern war. Significantly, although nonpacifist isolationists were of increasing importance in the movement to keep America out of war, within the peace movement itself the pacifists became of more commanding importance.

It is impossible here to trace the measures taken, beginning with the repeal of the arms embargo in November, 1939, to make America "the great arsenal of democracy" and it is hardly necessary to chart in detail

Tittle's efforts to brake this downward careening course (as Tittle believed) into war. Month by month, step by step, Tittle singly or jointly with others communicated his dissent to congressmen, the secretary of state, the president. He protested initial emasculation of the neutrality legislation shortly after the outbreak of the European war. The sale of so-called surplus stocks of war materials to private firms to be resold to belligerent states he found "shocking," and he so informed Roosevelt, Hull, and Senators Lucas and Slattary. The Destroyer-Bases Agreement was an unneutral and illegal transaction. The Burke-Wadsworth conscription bill was characterized as "a deadly blow at liberties which Americans have had and cherished since the foundation of this republic. It would radically change the whole character of our society, which, under its operation, would cease to be a society of free men."[90] He continued to question the build-up of the armed forces and he continued to urge a constitutional amendment providing for a national war referendum.

As the months passed, his suspicions of Roosevelt deepened. "I, too, fear that President Roosevelt is attempting to place us on the road to war" and similar expressions appeared with increasing frequency in his correspondence.[91] On the eve of the 1940 election Tittle wrote a Korean Christian leader: "The situation in the United States is now rapidly worsening. It looks as if we were getting ready to intervene in Europe, despite the fact that the great majority of us . . . are wholly unwilling to do so. It also looks as if we were, ourselves, heading for dictatorship under President Roosevelt who is almost daily, now, seizing more power and who seems to be in the way of getting what he very much wants, namely, an army of conscripts. I have, myself, lost all confidence in his judgment, if not in his integrity, and I consider that he is now the greatest menace we have to face."[92]

Manifestly Tittle opposed Roosevelt's third term. And though he urged upon the Republican party an "unequivocal anti-war plank" because "only on that issue can Republicans win,"[93] in the end he again voted for Norman Thomas. He did so reluctantly, because war was now the overriding issue and he feared that should the Socialist candidate be

90. *Evanston Review,* August 1, 1940, p. 7. This statement was signed by Tittle and seventy-five Chicago-area clergymen. It was also the conviction of the Methodist Peace Commission and the First Church Peace Committee.

91. Letter from Tittle to E. Gut Cutschall, May 24, 1940.

92. Letter from Tittle to Hyunghi Lew, September 4, 1940. The Reverend Mr. Lew's church in Seoul was supported by First Church contributions.

93. Wire from Tittle to Resolutions Committee, Republican National Committee, June 19, 1940.

decisively defeated, this would "convey a totally wrong impression as to the attitude of the American people toward war and peace."[94]

Early in 1941 Tittle made the flat accusation, "We have sold the New Deal for a mess of international power-politics."[95] The Lend-Lease act of March stripped away the last pretense of neutrality. Tittle informed all Illinois senators and representatives of his "conviction that this bill, if passed, will almost certainly lead us into war both in Europe and in Asia. It undoubtedly will mean the loss of our democracy, with but little chance in our lifetime of getting it back."[96] Senator Burton K. Wheeler termed Lend-Lease the New Deal's "Triple-A foreign policy to plow under every fourth American boy." An angry president told reporters, "That really is the rottenest thing that has been said in public life in my generation."[97] Admitting that Wheeler hit below the belt and admitting that Tittle's prediction about the "loss of democracy" was extreme, both men were essentially correct that Lend-Lease meant more than the possibility of war, it meant the probability of war. Yet, when queried by a reporter whether the bill would not lead to war, the president replied emphatically, "No, not a bit of it."[98] That really is one of the most disingenuous things said in public life in Roosevelt's generation. When in June Germany invaded Russia, Roosevelt moved, though slowly, to make Stalin eligible to receive Lend-Lease materials, eliciting Senator Robert Taft's dry remark, "Apparently we are to follow Bundles for Britain with Packages for Petrograd."

Tittle petitioned against the extension of the draft. He protested "the sending of United States troops to Iceland without the knowledge or consent of Congress."[99] He earnestly hoped the president would not "under any circumstances, authorize the convoy by American war vessels of shipments to Great Britain or to any of her allies."[100] When Fiorello La Guardia, director of the Office of Civilian Defense, designated Sunday, November 16, as "Freedom Day" and sent out a canned sermon and covering letter to every church and synagogue in the country, Tittle remonstrated. The sermon itself was "quite unobjectionable," but Tittle believed the intent of the communication was the "mobilization of the

94. Letter from Tittle to A. J. Muste, January 26, 1940.
95. Letter from Tittle to Edgar H. Webster, February 24, 1941.
96. Identical letter from Tittle to all Illinois senators and representatives, January 28, 1941.
97. See Selig Adler, *The Uncertain Giant: 1921-1941; American Foreign Policy Between the Wars* (New York: The Macmillan Co., 1965), pp. 247ff.
98. *Ibid.* See also Warren F. Kimball, *The Most Unsordid Act: Lend-Lease, 1939-1941* (Baltimore: The Johns Hopkins Press, 1969).
99. Letter from Tittle to President Franklin D. Roosevelt, July 8, 1941.
100. Letter from Tittle to President Franklin D. Roosevelt, April 25, 1941.

churches behind the foreign policy of the present administration," an attempt to make the Church "merely a propagandistic agency for the state."[101] Perhaps the large rat Tittle smelled was only a small mouse, but the La Guardia idea was widely deplored by churchmen—and by laymen, too, if the anger of the First Church congregation is any barometer.

In the final months of 1941, United States destroyers on convoy duty in the North Atlantic clashed with German U-boats, American commanders received "shoot-on-sight" orders, American merchantmen were armed and freed from neutrality legislation restrictions to transport any type of goods anywhere in the world under the protection of naval escort, and the not surprising result was an undeclared naval war in which American destroyers and freighters and German submarines were sunk. Tittle, increasingly dismayed and angry, could only protest, often in petitions signed with other ministers, these actions "leading the United States into shooting war."

Yet full war finally came not in the North Atlantic but at Pearl Harbor. An ambitious Japan, stung but not intimidated by American economic pressure, in an act at once mad and comprehensible, struck on Sunday morning, December 7. The war Tittle and the peacemakers had long feared was now here. If one believes that totalitarianism (that is, the special brand of Hitler, Mussolini, and Tojo) is the great foe, then the Roosevelt administration's gamble, though it failed, was worth taking. If one believes, as did Tittle, that war itself is mankind's great enemy, then the pacifists were the true realists in their awareness of the unacceptable penalty of losing the gamble.

In retrospect Tittle's position seems a forlorn one, the tides of intervention being irresistible. Yet, in September, 1939, the overwhelming majority of American citizens agreed with Senator Harry S. Truman's conviction, "The role of this great Republic is to save civilization; we must keep out of war."[102] The outbreak of the European war did not demoralize the American peacemakers. To the contrary, the very failure to keep war out of the world now permitted them to concentrate on the task of keeping the United States out of war, and because the peril was now patent, they had the attention of many individuals who formerly had deemed war too remote to fret about.

Certainly the official position of The Methodist Church did not leave Tittle cut off from his denomination. The Rock River Annual Conference adopted reports and resolutions urging the retention of the

101. Letter from Tittle to Judge Martin M. Gridley, November 18, 1941.
102. Quoted in Bowers, "The American Peace Movement," p. 404, n. 88.

neutrality laws, and in 1941 the conference accepted, after debate, a statement drafted by Tittle: "We deplore administrative actions that, step by step, are involving us in a shooting war, though undeclared, without giving the National Congress a chance to exercise its constitutional right in this matter and without regard for the predominant sentiment of the nation. We respectfully remind the President of his emphatic and repeated promise not to send our boys to war overseas. We believe that our nation can best serve mankind by abstaining from belligerent participation in present wars, by employing its immense resources for the constructive ministry of healing and rehabilitation and by associating itself with other nations, at the earliest possible moment, in earnest effort to rebuild the world on a foundation of justice and co-operation for the good of all."[103]

As chairman of the Committee on the State of the Church, Social Service and Temperance of the newly created North Central Jurisdictional Conference, Tittle influenced the statements adopted by that important regional body. "It is our sincere conviction that this nation should not become a belligerent in the present conflicts in Europe and Asia." "We believe . . . that the United States should take no step that inexorably leads to war. We deplore and condemn any action that may involve us in war without a declaration of war by the national Congress. We are unalterably opposed to the use of the armed forces of the nation outside the Western Hemisphere." "We are unalterably opposed to universal compulsory military service while the United States is at peace." Such were some of the utterances, drafted by Tittle, of the North Central Jurisdictional Conference in 1940.[104]

Tittle was also chairman in 1940 of the key General Conference Committee on the State of the Church, and the committee's statement on peace, which he wrote,[105] was adopted after spirited debate without amendment. To the extent that the statement called for the participation of America in many areas of international life, it was not isolationist. Nevertheless it firmly held that the United States "should remain out of the present conflicts in Europe and the Far East." The heart of the report reads: "Therefore, we stand upon this ground: the Methodist

103. *Minutes* of the Rock River Annual Conference (1941), pp. 83-84.
104. *Journal of the First Session of the North Central Jurisdictional Conference,* 1940, pp. 158-63.
105. In a private letter regarding the statement Tittle reported: "I may say to you privately that I myself wrote it and it, therefore, may be supposed to represent my own position. . . ." He added, however, that his personal position went even beyond that of the report, being that of pacifism. Letter from Tittle to Norman Riedesel, May 24, 1940.

Church, although making no attempt to bind the consciences of its individual members, will not officially endorse, support, or participate in war. We insist that the agencies of the Church shall not be used in preparation for war, but in the promulgation of peace. We insist that the buildings of the Church dedicated to the worship of God shall be used for that holy purpose, and not by any agency for the promotion of war."[106]

During the course of the debate over the report's adoption, Tittle asserted that if the United States tightened the economic screws on Japan alone, Japan would retaliate, and "almost certainly there would be incidents which the American people, in their present mood, would not tolerate." "In this connection," he continued,

> it is interesting to recall the prophecy of Sir Frederick White, who is director of the American Division of the British Ministry of Information. Sir Frederick White has predicted that if the United States goes into a second World War, it will be by way of the Far East. Twenty-odd years ago Mr. Wilson . . . said to the Congress of the United States, "It is a fearful thing to lead this great peaceful people into war." My friends, it is a fearful thing to lead the United States of America into war. It is a fearful thing by word now, or by act, to push the United States of America into war. If we should get into a war with Japan, inexorably we would be drawn into Asiatic power politics for generations to come, with very doubtful gains, in my judgment, to our Chinese friends. If we should be drawn into a second World War, the lights of civilization might be blown out and another Dark Age come upon us all.[107]

In addition to leading the Methodist peace forces in Rock River Annual Conference, North Central Jurisdictional Conference, and General Conference, Tittle, together with Ralph Sockman and Charles F. Boss, continued to lead the Methodist World Peace Commission, and it may be asserted without adornment or qualification that the Commission's position was pacifistic and almost identical to Tittle's. The Methodist National Youth Council looked to Tittle for leadership. Immediately following the invasion of Poland the council adopted a resolution, surely in accord with Tittle's convictions, that its members would "refuse to support or participate in any war in which the United States may engage."[108] Another Methodist agency supported by Tittle, the unofficial Federation for Social Service, adopted a position ultimately

106. *The Daily Christian Advocate*, The Methodist Church, May 7, 1940, pp. 461-63.
107. *Ibid.*, pp. 462-63.
108. *New York Times*, September 4, 1939, p. 7.

less pleasing to Tittle. Between September, 1939, and June, 1941, it insisted that the European war was a fascist power struggle in which America had no stake. However, when Hitler invaded Russia the Federation immediately advocated American intervention, for the war was now suddenly transformed into a contest between fascism and freedom.

Tittle further remained active in 1939-41 in a cluster of nondenominational peace societies. He served as vice-chairman of the National Council for Prevention of War and chairman of the Mid-West office of the Fellowship of Reconciliation. He was loyal to the old War Resisters League and extremely active in the new Pacifist Ministers' Fellowship, the midwestern branch usually meeting monthly in First Church with about fifty clergymen in attendance. The Ministers' No War Committee, formed in early 1941 with Albert W. Palmer as chairman, was a much larger organization dedicated to keeping America out of war. Its membership included virtually every leading Protestant churchman who had not, by 1941, defected from the ranks of pacifism. Tittle, of course, was up to his hips in its activities, as he was in an associated group with much the same personnel, the Churchmen's Campaign for Peace Through Mediation.

It was one thing for Tittle to work with other churchmen and pacifists to keep America out of war, and quite another to find himself aligned in common opposition to administration leadership with Communists (until June, 1941), Coughlinites, anti-Semites, isolationist Democrats, conservative Republicans, Roosevelt-haters, and even such old adversaries as Colonel Robert McCormick, publisher of the *Chicago Tribune*, and Mrs. Elizabeth Dilling, author (it will be remembered) of *The Red Network*. It was a strange and strained alliance. As we have repeatedly observed, pacifism and isolationism are poles apart, and though in the years 1939-41 both groups shared an apprehension of involvement in war and both criticized the steps progressively leading (as they believed) to intervention, so different were their fundamental assumptions that no true co-operation was possible.

The Keep America Out of War Congress was the last stand of the co-operating peace movement before Pearl Harbor. Formed in 1939 with John T. Flynn as national chairman, KAOW was a coalition of antiwar groups, not a pacifist organization. Pacifists cooperated with it as long as it was a congress rather than a membership organization, but by early 1941 such pacifist groups as the Fellowship of Reconciliation and the War Resisters League had withdrawn from it, although they still participated in specific projects. For a season Tittle gave his support. For one thing, on September 29, 1939, he spoke at the Belasco theatre in

Washington before a mass meeting of representatives of all "Keep America Out of War affiliates, the purpose being to prevent revision of the neutrality laws. For another, he introduced Flynn to wealthy First Church members for the purpose of soliciting financial support. And in October, 1939, Tittle and Flynn shared the platform at an "Evanston Town Meeting Against War." Tittle never was a commanding figure in the Keep America Out of War Congress, but it is clear from his correspondence with Flynn, as well as from his deeds, that he wished the organization success. In the last analysis, however, Flynn and other KAOW leaders were too conservative, too isolationist, and too concerned with America's military defenses to win the total commitment of Tittle and the pacifists.

This judgment applies with double force to the most famous of all organizations engaged in the struggle to preserve American neutrality in the crucial years of 1940-41, the America First Committee. Formed in September, 1940, to counter the effective propaganda of the Committee to Defend America by Aiding the Allies, America First rapidly boasted 450 chapters (including one in Evanston) and a membership of over 800,000, approximately two-thirds of whom lived within a three-hundred-mile radius of Chicago, the organization's headquarters. General Robert E. Wood, chairman of the board of Sears, Roebuck and Company, was national chairman. R. Douglas Stuart, Jr., the twenty-four-year-old law student son of the first vice-president of the Quaker Oats Company, was national director, and it was he who conceived the idea of a great noninterventionist coalition. Although America First enlisted many famous Americans from all walks of life, most notably, perhaps, Charles A. Lindbergh, from first to last it was the servant of conservative business elements.

Although the original policy of barring pacifists from membership was reversed and although the America First Committee supplied several peace groups, including the Ministers' No War Committee, with sums of money, pacifists had very little to do with this conservative, isolationist, patriotic, even chauvinistic body. It is, therefore, understandable that Tittle was not a member and had no correspondence with its leaders. (Albert W. Palmer, the one prominent pacifist clergyman on the national committee, quickly resigned because of the committee's endorsement of strong military preparations.) [109]

The limited participation of pacifists in the Keep America Out of War Congress and the almost total noninvolvement of pacifists in the

109. See Wayne S. Cole, *America First: The Battle Against Intervention, 1940-1941* (Madison: University of Wisconsin Press, 1953), *passim*.

America First Committee suggests a larger truth. In the battle against intervention, pacifist leadership did not dominate as it had dominated the peace movement of the mid-thirties. Until December 7, 1941, there were unquestionably millions of Americans who wished to remain isolated from the wars in Asia and Europe, but only a fraction of them were absolute opponents of all war. Pacifists and isolationists tended to follow parallel courses, both hoping to lead to the single goal of maintaining the peace of America, but so different was the rationale of their neutralism that full co-operation was impossible. Historians have discerned fully the correlation between isolationism and conservativism and between isolationism and agrarian progressivism, but they have not, perhaps, quite comprehended that the so-called isolationism of men such as Tittle was really a matter of theology, and in fact, was not isolationism at all.

The battle against intervention was lost. Tittle anticipated that it might be, and so he made preparations for the day when his country would be at war. Between December 4, 1940, and February 5, 1941, the *Christian Century* ran a series of articles by ten Christian leaders on the general subject, "If America Enters the War—What Shall I Do?" Tittle's statement, the last in the series, merits extended quotation, the heart being these words:

> I am now convinced that war, being, as the Oxford Conference said, "a defiance of the righteousness of God as revealed in Jesus Christ and him crucified," cannot serve the ends of freedom and justice but is certain to defeat them. So, if the United States becomes a belligerent in Europe or in Asia, I shall undertake to contribute in some way to the good of my country, but I shall not "support" the war. The present war in Europe is not only a clash of imperialism; it is also a conflict of ideologies and ways of life. There is now far more at stake than there was in 1917. Prussianism threatened the world with whips; Hitlerism threatens it with scorpions. It is now all-essential to the welfare and progress of humanity that Hitlerism be overcome. On this point American Christians are agreed. The point on which they are not agreed is the means by which Hitlerism *can be* overcome. Christian pacifists do not proclaim that tyranny is better than war; they proclaim that tyranny cannot be overcome by war.

On numerous occasions Tittle returned to the theme of how a Christian might resist aggression. His answer was always the advocacy of a resolute nonviolent resistance. Nonviolent resistance, a steadfast refusal to return evil with evil, was admittedly dangerous. Undoubtedly it would mean arrests, torture, executions, and "perhaps even massacres of women and children." But the hope of the world was to follow the example of Jesus in the first century and Gandhi in the twentieth century. Believing as he did, it was only natural that he should rejoice when a young man, after sober meditation, came to the personal position of pacifism. Tittle received many pleas for guidance from troubled lads concerning the proper course for a Christian pacifist to follow, and his answer was neither draft resistance nor draft evasion. Rather, the draftee should register when called upon to do so and at that time state the fact that he feels bound to abstain from war and from training for war. Tittle wrote a number of letters to the authorities testifying that young men whom he knew were bona fide conscientious objectors, and he and his assistants also appeared in court to bear witness for them. Moreover, First Church formed a Laymen's Board for Conscientious Objectors, a subcommittee of the Committee on World Peace, to interview members of the congregation who were pacifists, carefully probe their sincerity, enroll their names, and then, when the government conducted its examinations, stand up for them. In Evanston young men pleading conscientious objection to war were given an exceedingly searching and rigorous questioning by the authorities, and they needed all possible preparation and support.

On April 1, 1940, the First Church Official Board recognizing that there is no common judgment among Christians concerning what a Christian should do when his country becomes involved in war, declared "that those Christians within our membership, in however small a minority, who feel bound, in the name of Christ, to abstain from any war and to employ only nonviolent means of resisting evil, and who are now organized as a body of conscientious objectors, should have a rightful place within the fellowship of the church and be permitted to use facilities of the church, under the rules of the church."[110] Thus, the ruling body of First Church gave official recognition to and support of the First Church Christian Pacifist Fellowship, formed on January 1, and composed of First Church members and affiliate members only. Meeting twice a month, the Fellowship raised money for overseas relief, worked for the betterment of race relations and other humane causes, and sustained each other in their pacifism. Significantly the Fellowship survived Pearl Harbor, in 1942 numbering about eighty members, seventeen of whom were in Civilian Public Service Camps.[111]

Thus it was that in the twenty-seven months between the invasion of

110. Minutes of the Official Board, First Church, April 1, 1940.
111. Letter from Tittle to Walter S. Coffman, December 28, 1942, copy sent to author, June 6, 1960.

Poland and the Pearl Harbor strike, Tittle worked to bring about a negotiated peace in Europe and Asia, to succor the victims of war, to keep America out of war, to prepare for the protection of conscientious objectors should war come, and to maintain the transnational fellowship of the Christian Church. Tittle also was intensely engaged in planning for the postwar world. He had much to say about the matter in his sermons. Many forums, sometimes involving experts of national distinction, were held under First Church auspices. On March 30, 1940, he was invited by the Commission to Study the Organization of Peace to speak over the network of the Columbia Broadcasting System. In the address he stressed that any realistic attempt to organize the postwar world for peace involves the surrender of the "claim of absolute national sovereignty" and the more equitable redistribution of the world's wealth.[112] Tittle displayed a fleeting interest in a group founded by Clarence K. Streit, author of the once-famous *Union Now*, the Interdemocracy Federal Unionists, soon rechristened Federal Union, Inc., but Streit's plan was too exclusively Anglo-Saxon to win Tittle's lasting support.

Tittle's energies were most fully devoted to the Federal Council's famous Commission on a Just and Durable Peace, under the chairmanship of John Foster Dulles. As we earlier learned (in Chapter 11), Tittle was on the Committee of Direction and was responsible for drafting the well-known Delaware statement on the church and the economic order. The Methodist Peace Commission worked closely with the Federal Council's Commission, and in May, 1941, an important Exploratory Conference on the Bases of a Just and Enduring Peace was held in Chicago. Bishop Oxnam served as convener, Dulles addressed the group, and Tittle was made chairman of the Commission on Christian Faith. The report of the conference, *When Hostilities Cease*, was widely circulated and studied by American Methodists, Tittle having penned the statement, "Implications of the Christian Faith for a Just and Enduring Peace." In general even before the American entry into the war, Tittle, Methodism, and American Protestantism were committed to the establishment of a co-operative world community, the surrender of major attributes of national sovereignty, the freer flow of goods between nations, the co-ordination of monetary systems, the end of colonialism, the muting of militarism, and other efforts for economic equalization

112. *Peaceful Change*, a radio address delivered March 30, 1940 (pamphlet). See also Robert A. Divine, *Second Chance: The Triumph of Internationalism During World War II* (New York: Atheneum Publishers, 1967), p. 36.

and cultural understanding so that men, with the help of God, might live on a basis of justice, fellowship, and co-operation.

Meanwhile, during these twenty-seven months when America hung suspended between peace and war, Japan continued to apply the flame to China's already blistered flesh, and then aggressively pressed south-westward into Indochina. In Europe the countries of Denmark, Norway, Belgium, the Netherlands, Luxemburg, and France suffered invasion, defeat, and Nazi occupation, while in southern Europe Rumania, Hungary, and Bulgaria became Axis satellites and Yugoslavia and Greece Axis victims. Britain gallantly resisted Göring's Luftwaffe with "blood, toil, tears, and sweat"—and Spitfires and Hurricanes—but it seemed incredible that England alone could long endure. Then, in June, 1941, Hitler turned on Russia, storming victoriously toward Moscow, and by autumn the capitulation of the Slav to the Teuton appeared certain.

In the terrible spring of 1941, Maude Royden, an English pacifist during the First World War and long an inspiration to Tittle and the American peacemakers, found her pacifist faith melted by the flames of Britain's bombed cities, and she sent a stern command to her old comrades, the pacifists safe in America, "Do not preach to us. Pray for us if you can. If you cannot, let us alone. We are doing what we can."[113] And in the United States Reinhold Niebuhr stung the pacifists with the scorpion words: "Will the moralists who think that it would be a simple matter to make peace with Hitler if we only called an economic conference and promised to allocate raw materials, please be quiet while we weep?"[114] "If modern churches were to symbolize their true faith," Niebuhr wrote in unvarnished reference to the liberalism and pacifism exemplified by Tittle, "they would take the crucifix from their altars and substitute the three little monkeys who counsel men to 'speak no evil, hear no evil, see no evil.' "[115]

In the very month that France fell, Tittle assessed for a Methodist missionary the temper of America: "The situation in the United States is rapidly worsening. In consequence of the president's war-and-panic mongering, growing numbers of people are losing their heads, and it now looks as if we might be edged into the war despite the fact, revealed in every recent poll, that nine Americans out of ten are exceedingly anxious to stay out of it. University faculties, one after another, are becoming prowar, although there is in each of them a respectable minority that is keeping its head. The churches, so far, are keeping their heads, although

113. *Christian Century*, LVII (April 16, 1941), 523.
114. *Radical Religion*, V (Summer, 1940), 1-2.
115. *Christianity and Power Politics*, pp. 33-34.

452 / *The Life of Ernest Fremont Tittle*

a number of outstanding clergymen are vociferously advocating all methods short of war. It seems incredible that we should be preparing to do it again. One can only hope that there will be, in any case, a strong Christian minority that will stand out against the universal madness."[116] Among those "outstanding clergymen" urging immediate intervention on the side of England or willing to risk war by extending all necessary aid to England were Henry Sloane Coffin, Henry Pitney Van Dusen, Sherwood Eddy, Episcopal Bishops Henry Knox Sherrill, William Manning, and Henry Hobson, Methodist Bishops James Cannon, G. Bromley Oxnam, and Francis J. McConnell (how this wrenched Tittle's heart!), and John A. Mackay, John Bennett, Douglas Horton, John R. Mott, William Adams Brown, Justin Wroe Nixon, Robert E. Speer, Francis Miller, Christian F. Reisner, and many, many others, including after June, 1941, Harry F. Ward and those whose position on intervention followed the fortunes of the Soviet Union. Interventionist churchmen were not only numerous but also the most prestigious and powerful in American Protestantism. And in the years immediately ahead their careers prospered and their reputations soared. Ministers such as Tittle who remained loyal to their pacifist convictions did not become outcasts in the 1940's and 1950's, but rarely did they know commanding positions in the seminary, theological, and ecclesiastical world.

Interventionist churchmen sought to influence the editorial policies of denominational journals, the declarations of denominational assemblies, and the positions of denominational agencies—as they had every right to do. They placed their signatures to petitions to inform the Roosevelt administration of their support. They formed new committees such as the Interfaith Committee for Aid to the Democracies and the Fight for Freedom Committee and the Friends of Democracy, Inc. They joined such new secular groups as William Allen White's famous Committee to Defend America by Aiding the Allies. They also endeavored with success to direct the attitudes of such established peace societies as the Church Peace Union and the World Peace Foundation.

Reinhold Niebuhr was the most incisive critic of pacifism and the most persuasive advocate of aid to the Allies in all Protestantism; indeed, excepting only the president, perhaps no individual in all America did more to shape the opinion of the educated classes than he. George F. Kennan was not alone in terming Niebuhr "the father of us all." On February 10, 1941, the first issue of a biweekly journal, *Christianity and Crisis*, appeared; it was edited by Niebuhr and founded by a group of

116. Letter from Tittle to T. T. Brumbaugh, June 11, 1940.

noted churchmen under his leadership. The specific purpose of the new journal was to expose the perfectionism and utopianism of the Christian pacifists and to enlist the churches in the fight for freedom against tyranny. The introductory circular made its stand clear: "In the conflicts in Europe and Asia, ethical issues are at stake which claim the sympathy and support of American Christians. . . . When men or nations must choose between two great evils, the choice of the lesser evil becomes their duty. We hold that the halting of totalitarian aggression is prerequisite to world peace and order."[117]

What can be said concerning this great debate between Niebuhr and his fellow interventionists and Tittle and his fellow pacifistic noninterventionists?

First, for every published article or book about Tittle or Fosdick, Muste, Holmes, Chalmers, Palmer, Day, Page or other Christian pacifists, there are one hundred dealing with Niebuhr and his thought. In fact, perhaps less has been published about all of the pacifists of the period combined[118] than about this single individual, pacifism's severest critic—and by "severest" I mean not the most savage but the most penetrating and therefore the most devastating. It is proper that Niebuhr be the subject of extensive examination, such is the range of his thought, the brilliance of his mind, the depth of his faith, the passion of his polemics, the arresting quality of his style, and, indeed, the sheer bulk of his writing. Above all, such was his influence on an entire generation of American (and British and European) intellectuals, secular as well as religious, that to know Niebuhr is to gain some understanding of the thought of an era. Yet to fairly judge a debate it is necessary to hear the arguments of both sides, and not many scholars have troubled to listen carefully to what the pacifists were saying.

Second, almost all scholars, whether diplomatic historians, political scientists, or theologians, have concluded that Niebuhr completely demolished the case for pacifism. His "realism" became almost the party line of the new breed of intellectuals who came to occupy the seats of prestige in the 1940's, 1950's, and 1960's.

Third, scholars make much of the fact that Tittle and the pacifists found themselves in the unlovely company of Nazi sympathizers, anti-Semites, Anglophobes, economic reactionaries, political right-wingers,

117. Quoted in Paul A. Carter, *The Decline and Revival of the Social Gospel: Social and Political Liberalism in American Protestant Churches, 1920-1940* (Ithaca, N. Y.: Cornell University Press, 1956), p. 215.
118. Happily, with the passing of each year this statement becomes less and less true.

isolationist moral eunuchs indifferent to the fate of any human being not a U.S. citizen, and, for a season, Communists. To this presumably devastating observation, it may be replied that it requires a courageous man to take the position demanded by his principles when that position associates him with unpopular groups he himself loathes. Moreover, the guilt-by-association tactic cuts with a double edge. If the pacifist case against intervention can be thrown out because nonintervention was also the position of America First and the *Chicago Tribune* and the pro-Nazi Bund, then logically the Niebuhrian cause for intervention is tainted by the support given by such frenetic Episcopal Anglophiles as Manning and Hobson, such conservatives as Christian F. Reisner, such power-hungry ecclesiastics as Bishop James Cannon, such Fundamentalists as much of the Southern Baptist clergy. Ironically the churchmen most favorable to intervention were High Church Anglicans, neo-orthodox theologians centered in eastern seminaries (especially Union in New York), and southern Fundamentalists. Further, among the interventionists were all those who cynically sought war in order to profit financially and all those neurotic war lovers driven by sadistic or masochistic compulsions. The point is—and it is a point to be driven firmly home—that Niebuhr, too, found himself in unlovely company, that of Tories, jingoists, and profiteers and, after June, 1941, Communists and other unsavory citizens.

Fourth, opponents of the Roosevelt administration's foreign policies were subjected to much personal abuse. The debate was naturally bitter because the issue was so fundamental, a life and death matter for the participants involved, and for their sons, their nation, and Western civilization. Though ugly charges were hurled at Roosevelt, at Jews, at all interventionists, for Tittle, as for Hoover, Beard, Taft, Nye, Villard, Holmes, Muste, Lindbergh (and his wife), and for all those who sought to thwart the administration, the consequences of opposition were heavy. "Coward," "fascist," "Jew-killer," "Hitler-lover"—these were the terms one could expect to be called in private and in public if one believed, for whatever reason, America should remain out of war.[119] The fury of the interventionists is understandable, but the brutish accusations they poured on those who disagreed with them—especially the unfair charge of anti-Semitism—ring discordantly, coming as they do, from the champions of humane, civilized values.

Fifth, a central charge of the Niebuhrians was the immorality of the

119. See, in addition to the biographies of these men, Mark Lincoln Chadwick, *The Hawks of World War II* (Chapel Hill: The University of North Carolina Press, 1968), *passim*.

noninterventionists who would purchase America's peace and security with the blood of brave Chinese, British, French, and Russian soldiers. It was this hidden lovelessness of the neutralist position that unfailingly triggered Niebuhr's polemic vehemence. "Proclaiming love, demanding love, anticipating love, the effect of neutralism was to sanction division and isolation," writes Donald Meyer in summarizing Niebuhr's critique. "The neutralists could not identify themselves with the other men because of the image they held of themselves and that, concomitantly, was true because they could not find in themselves the needs and the weaknesses of other men."[120] Yet Niebuhr never called for outright intervention, nor before Pearl Harbor did the Roosevelt administration request that war be declared on Hitler, Mussolini, or Imperial Japan. It may be argued that "all measures short of war" was the most immoral of all positions. If the "war against tyranny" was in fact "our" war, then the United States should have flung itself into the crusade, openly, fully, committing without measure the lives of American boys. As it was, Niebuhr (and the Roosevelt administration) asked only that the American people be the "arsenal of democracy." And just what sacrifice was involved in sending "Bundles to Britain"? Allied soldiers might now be armed with American weapons, but no American blood was to mingle with theirs. No Americans would be expected to kill or be killed. No devastation would come to American cities. The defeat of Hitler could be accomplished, the American public was assured by President Roosevelt, by no greater sacrifice than the lending and leasing of materials. Americans would experience the thrill and delicious pride of having participated in a great moral struggle to defeat tyranny without having suffered or directly inflicted suffering. Whatever may be said in defense of the "realism" of this position, surely it has nothing to commend it as a morally superior policy. To repeat, if the Roosevelt administration believed the fate of civilization hinged on the outcome of the war, then the American people should have been asked to give their lives in this great cause. Yet the president repeatedly assured the voters that the United States would not be drawn into war. And repeatedly in 1940 and 1941 Niebuhr maintained that America ought not and need not actively enter the war.[121] It may be added that as late as 1938 Niebuhr was terming the defense budget of the United States the worst piece of militarism in modern history and the American naval program the most

120. *Protestant Search for Political Realism*, p. 396.
121. See, for example, *Radical Religion*, V (Summer, 1940), 5-7; *Christianity and Society*, VI (Spring, 1941), 4-5; *ibid.* (Winter, 1941), pp. 1-3.

unjustified piece of military expansion in a world full of such madness.[122]
Only in the world of Alice in Wonderland can this be characterized as
"realism," that is, considering Niebuhr's position only a year or two later.

Furthermore, just who were the utopians and who were the realists
from 1939 to 1941? It is ironic that the so-called realists such as Niebuhr kept insisting that America's unneutral policies need not lead to
war, surely a utopian hope, while the so-called utopians such as Tittle
realistically assessed the high odds against the gamble of assisting the
Allies without being drawn into war.

Finally in the great debate, the Niebuhrians spoke of the sacrifices
necessary to be endured, but only rarely did they recognize what the
defenders of democracy would be called on to inflict in order to defeat
the enemy. Much was said about the rape of Nanking, the bombing of
Rotterdam, Coventry, London, the obliteration of Lidice, the strafing of
refugees, the hanging of civilian hostages, the bayoneting of prisoners,
and the whole, obscene documented record of atrocities committed by
the enemy. Much was said about sacrifice and suffering. But the interventionists did not say that in this war we would inflict wholesale death
on the civilian populations of Dresden, Hamburg, and Berlin and Tokyo,
Hiroshima, and Nagasaki and a hundred other cities, including those of
our allies; that in order to win *we* would shoot prisoners, rape women,
level villages, and betray friendly agents into the hands of the Gestapo
—but surely it is unnecessary to review all that *we* did in the name of
victory. It may be asserted again that Tittle and the idealists were the
true realists in their understanding of the demoniac nature of modern
war. The Niebuhrians extolled stout-hearted resistance to tyranny but
neglected to spell out this noble phrase in terms of the hundreds of
thousands of German, Italian, and Japanese old men, pregnant women,
youths and infants whom *we* blinded, scalded, boiled, flayed, buried
alive, disemboweled, eviscerated.

Bitter as was the debate over intervention, divided as was American
Protestantism, the message of the Oxford Conference was not totally
forgotten by either Niebuhr or Tittle: the Church must manifestly be
the Church; the fellowship of prayer must at all costs remain unbroken;
the Church should honor its members' conscientious decisions, whether
they are led to participate in or to abstain from war; the Body of Christ
must not be broken by national boundaries, not even in wartime.[123]

122. See Miller, *American Protestantism and Social Issues*, p. 337.
123. See Tittle, "Christian Fellowship in Time of Crisis," *The First Church
Pulpit*, Vol. III, No. 3, a sermon preached June 16, 1940. In Tittle's correspondence, the strongest personal criticism of Niebuhr is the warning to Albert W.

VII

The great debate suddenly ended on December 7, 1941. The following Sunday Tittle spoke from the First Church pulpit the words:

> Among ourselves, though we have not all seen eye to eye on the war issue, there has been a fellowship in Christ through which God has blessed us and enabled us to contribute to the good of others. What, then, are we now called to do? *We cannot deny the faith that is in us, to which heretofore we have borne witness. That would be cowardice, betrayal of trust, and indeed, spiritual suicide.* Surely we are called to be loyal to what we believe to be the will of God revealed in Jesus Christ. In ways we may take in loyalty to the will of God as we understand it, we are called to resist evil, to serve and make sacrifices for our nation, to seek justice, freedom, and peace for all men. Also, we are surely called to maintain our fellowship in Christ on the basis of a common devotion. We are called to pray for one another and for the Christian church throughout all the world; that in this crisis it may indeed be the church, the body of Christ, seeking to heal the hurt of the world through the reconciliation of men to God and to one another.[124]

Within months Tittle was receiving letters branding him a "Nazi neurotic," a "spineless man," a "hypochrondriac and coward all through." A penciled notation on one such envelope read: "Filed at Mrs. Tittle's request; not seen by Dr. Tittle. B. W." However, far more significant than these inevitable and truly neurotic expressions of wartime hysteria was the assessment of the First Church situation made by Tittle one year after Pearl Harbor, in the conclusion to a letter to a friend: "I may add that, according to the testimony of some of our laymen, we have never had such unity as now exists in First Church, notwithstanding the fact that both of its ministers are, and are known to be, pacifists."[125] There could hardly be a warmer tribute to First Church members than this grateful acknowledgment of their continuing loyalty to their veteran pastor. And there could hardly be a truer measure of Tittle's courage than his continuing loyalty to pacifism. For he did not recant. Immediately following the outbreak of war, *Newsweek* and *Time* requested from him a statement for publication. He replied that the Christian church should not bless or promote this or any war but should

Palmer, who was shortly to debate with Niebuhr, that "Niebuhr is inclined to be merciless." Letter from Tittle to Albert W. Palmer, August 25, 1942.

124. "The Need for Spiritual Adventure," *The First Church Pulpit*, Vol. **IV**, No. 7, a sermon preached December 14, 1941. Italics in original.

125. Letter from Tittle to Walter S. Coffman, December 28, 1942, copy sent to author, June 6, 1960.

seek, in ways that are consistent with its basic convictions, to resist evil, to serve the nation in which it is placed, and to contribute to the good of humanity.

But what, specifically and concretely, did this statement mean? For one thing, it did *not* mean that First Church boys who volunteered for the colors or that servicemen stationed in the Chicago area would be denied support. As we have seen in Chapter 5, First Church ministered magnificently to her own soldiers and sailors, and also to the thousands of lads in blue and khaki in training at Northwestern, Great Lakes, Fort Sheridan, and elsewhere in northern Illinois. Few, if any, churches in all the nation had a more comprehensive program than First Church to succor servicemen. On the other hand, the young men of the First Church congregation who could not in conscience bear arms were not set adrift. The First Church Pacifist Fellowship carried on, sustaining those members who pleaded conscientious objection and consequently served their country in Civilian Public Service Camps. An Official Board committee continued to investigate the sincerity of those claiming pacifism, in some instances denying its approval. But if a lad survived the stiff screening, he could be assured that his church would represent him when he appeared before the government examiners.

Tittle made clear that it was not his intent to obstruct the war effort.[126] Nevertheless, he did not feel personally able to buy war bonds,[127] and it was his conviction that First Church not invest its money in war bonds.[128] The broad formula adopted by First Church was that life-giving functions were permissible, life-destroying ones were not. Thus, the Red Cross was granted use of the Community House to collect blood, but bond drives and recruiting were banned.[129]

Inevitably the question of a roll of honor had to be faced. Should recognition be accorded only those First Church young men in military service, or should the roll also include the names of conscientious objectors serving in Civilian Public Service Camps? Tittle solicited the advice of Harry Emerson Fosdick, consulted his own conscience, and finally persuaded the Official Board to inscribe these words on a plaque hung in the narthex: "This tablet is erected in recognition of members of this parish who are serving the nation in various ways. We pray for them in our hearts and in their behalf we request the prayers of those who wor-

126. Letter from Tittle to Hillis C. Culver, December 26, 1941.
127. Letter from Tittle to Forest E. Dudley, May 27, 1942.
128. Letter from Tittle to Norman E. Richardson, April 9, 1943.
129. Author's interview with Mrs. Bernice Wolseley, Evanston, Ill., July 13, 1960.

ship here." It was a controversial question, but not, significantly, a racking one. The debate was earnest, but not fatal to First Church unity.[130]

Meanwhile, what was the wartime witness of The Methodist Church, a denomination, as we know, historically the most distinctively American and fervently patriotic of all major Protestant bodies, yet also the one most deeply permeated by pacifism in the pre–Pearl Harbor years? Shortly after the outbreak of hostilities, the Council of Bishops issued a message to American Methodists, declaring: "Our country has stood, always and unequivocally, for the democratic way, and therefore the clash was inevitable. . . . There can be no peace in the world until the totalitarian threat against the liberties of all freedom-loving people is thoroughly eradicated. Our duty, as American citizens, is clear. . . . The Methodists of America will loyally support our President and nation. We roundly condemn the processes of war even while accepting the awful alternative, not of our making, forced upon us by the selfishness and the perversity of men. From a measure of the guilt of this, none of us is free."[131] The final sentences indicate a long journey in the church's thinking since World War I. There was not to be again the total identification of flag and cross, the absolutized vision of the war as a holy crusade, the hounding of pacifists as traitors. Albert Day in Pasadena, Henry Hitt Crane in Detroit, Harold Case in Scranton, Tittle in Evanston—these and other pacifists preachers were not driven from their Methodist pulpits, as surely would have been their fate in 1917-18. Indeed, when in 1944 First Church sought a new associate pastor, Tittle was free to seek a man who was "preferably (although not necessarily) a pacifist."[132]

Nevertheless a close examination of Annual Conference pronouncements during World War II discloses much backtracking from the near-pacifism of the thirties.[133] Tittle's Rock River Conference held its first wartime meeting in June, 1942, with First Church as host to the assembly. Tittle presented the report of the Commission on World Peace, which reaffirmed the 1940 General Conference statement that "The

130. See Minutes of the Official Board, First Church, November 2, 1942; letter from Tittle to Fosdick, September 29, 1942, and letter from Fosdick to Tittle, September 30, 1942; letter from Eugene Durham to author, undated; author's interview with Mr. and Mrs. Roscoe Page, Evanston, Ill., August 10, 1959, who helped draft the inscription and who had one son in the Navy and another in a Public Service Camp.
131. Quoted in Muelder, *Methodism and Society*, p. 182.
132. Letter from Tittle to Hiel D. Bollinger, January 18, 1944.
133. The examination was made by James W. Gladden and his findings are summarized in Muelder, *Methodism and Society*, pp. 183-184.

Methodist Church, although making no attempt to bind the consciences of its individual members, will not officially endorse, support, or participate in war." After extended debate, the report was adopted. Then the Reverend Olin Clark Jones offered from the floor a resolution that said in part: "We believe that who wins in this struggle makes a difference to the cause of human freedom, and to the kind of peace which follows afterwards." The conference stirred, Tittle demurred, and the resolution was tabled overnight. Tittle and Jones worked on a compromise statement, and the following morning Tittle presented for the conference's acceptance the measure:

> The function of the Church is different from that of the state. The state has resting upon it the necessity to render a political judgment in respect of war. This necessity rests also upon individuals who are members both of the state and of the Church. This we recognize. Further, we are deeply aware of the values that are involved in this present struggle and of its momentous consequences for the future of mankind. But human judgments are fallible. Hence it is the peculiar function and duty of the Church to direct the minds of men toward God. . . . Let the Church minister in every possible way to the relief of human distress. Let it undergird the faith of the people. To those who remain behind and those at the front under fire, let it declare anew the Christian faith that behind all this struggle by man God still reigns and cares and strives for a better world. Let it remember in prayer the chosen leaders of the nation and commit its youth, wherever they may go, to the protection and guidance of God.[134]

This Rock River occurrence foreshadowed the momentous 1944 General Conference division over the proper relationship of the Methodist Church to the Second World War, "as deep a rift as any that has occurred on a social issue since unification."[135]

On Wednesday, May 3, Bishop A. Frank Smith announced, "We now come to Report No. 8 of the Committee on State of the Church." Then suddenly the storm broke, and what had been, according to an observer, a "quiet, orderly, leisurely sewing-circle session came to life." Tittle, as chairman of the committee, presented the report on "The Church in Time of War." It was a reaffirmation of the 1940 General Conference position: The Methodist Church will not officially endorse, support, or participate in war, and the agencies of the Church shall not

134. *Minutes* of the Rock River Annual Conference (1942), pp. 17-18; *Evanston Review*, July 2, 1942, p. 44.
135. Muelder, *Methodism and Society*, p. 184.

be used in preparation for war, nor shall the buildings of the Church be used for the promotion of war. Two additional paragraphs recognized that the United States was now, unlike in 1940, at war. They read:

> The Church cannot be indifferent to the issues at stake in the present conflict. It is deeply concerned in the human values in jeopardy and in the ultimate effect of the conflict upon the cause of justice, freedom, and brotherhood. As a corporate body seeking to declare the will of God, it must express its moral judgment and use its moral force against tyranny, aggression, persecution, and all forms of political dictatorship and totalitarianism which run counter to our Christian belief in the worth and dignity of every individual.
>
> We call upon the Church to pray for the welfare of those in the armed forces, for the maintenance of their Christian faith and ideals and their safe return to our homes and churches, if this be possible. Believing that God has a stake in the victory of peace with justice in the present conflict, we commend our cause to Him, praying "Thy Kingdom come, Thy will be done."

The report presented by Tittle voiced the position of the majority of the Committee on State of the Church. A determined minority of the members of this key committee, however, had caucused, drafted a minority report, and come to the session hoping to win conference endorsement of their substitute. The stage was set for what observers agree to be one of the most brilliant debates in the annals of Methodism. The division in the committee had come about largely because of the independence of mind and flinty character of one man, Charles C. Parlin. Later to emerge as perhaps the outstanding layman in all American Methodism, this New York lawyer was then a freshman General Conference delegate and a junior member of the Committee on State of the Church. Days earlier Tittle, Henry Hitt Crane, and Albert Edward Day had presented to the committee for its approval a draft reaffirming the 1940 position. Parlin, however, began to question the triumvirate, probing—and as a lawyer, probing deeply—for their interpretation of portions of the report. It soon became clear that other members of the committee had reservations, and they welcomed Parlin's leadership, forming a minority section of the Committee on State of the Church. A minority report was drafted, largely the work of two noted critics of pacifism, Umphrey Lee and Lynn Harold Hough, to be substituted for Tittle's majority report. (Lee and Hough were not members of the committee signing the minority report, however.)

On that fateful Wednesday when the two reports were submitted to the governing body of Methodism it was agreed, by suspension of rules, to permit one leader and five supporting speakers for each report. There was to be no applause. Tittle, of course, spoke first for the majority report, followed by Crane, Day, Glenn James, Edmund Heinsohn, and Mrs. Frank Wright, the mother of a conscientious objector, a 4-F, and a sailor. Parlin, of course, presented the minority report with Hough giving the most brilliant of the five supporting addresses. Amendments were proposed and accepted by both sides permitting the use of church buildings by "agencies of mercy and healing such as the Red Cross" and endorsing the provision of chaplains for the "ministering in the Name of Christ to those engaged in military service."

At the conclusion of the debate, when Tittle and Parlin and the others were physically and emotionally drained, the Tittle forces moved that the vote to substitute the minority report for the majority report be taken by orders, that is by separate vote of the clergy and lay delegates. Parlin believed this an unusual and unfair parliamentary maneuver designed to enable the pacifist clergy to block the will of the majority of all delegates. But the separate balloting was sustained. The vote was taken and after an agonizing delay because of adjournment, Secretary Estes announced the results: 203 laymen voted for the minority report and 131 voted against it; 170 ministers voted in favor and 169 against (with one defective ballot and one delegate not voting). Tittle, crushed, attempted to move for reconsideration, but the motion died for lack of a second. By a margin of one vote, therefore, the Methodist Church officially declared:

> In this country we are sending over a million young men from Methodist homes to participate in the conflict. God himself has a stake in the struggle, and he will uphold them as they fight forces destructive of the moral life of men. In Christ's name we ask for the blessing of God upon the men in the armed forces, and we pray for victory. We repudiate the theory that a state, even though imperfect in itself, must not fight against intolerable wrongs.
>
> While we respect the individual conscience of those who believe that they cannot condone the use of force, and staunchly will defend them on this issue, we cannot accept their position as the defining position of the Christian Church. We are well within the Christian position when we assert the necessity of the use of military forces to resist aggression which would overthrow every right which is held sacred by civilized men.

Several days later Tittle introduced a resolution, seconded by Parlin, that was accepted without debate and amidst applause, which branded war in general and looked toward an era of permanent peace.[136]

It is necessary to say several things about this wartime General Conference action. In the first place, although the secular press headlined, "Methodists Favor War," such an interpretation is a plain misreading of the Parlin report adopted by the conference. It is not a jingoistic statement; it does not glorify war; it does not call for the damnation of the enemy. Not a single speaker for the minority report may be fairly characterized as a war hawk. In the debate, there was no spread-eagleism, flag-waving, or patriotic bombast. The significant point is not the narrow repudiation of Tittle's report, but rather that the statement adopted was itself far different from the frenzied denominational proclamations of 1917-18.

Secondly, the vote by orders clearly underscored what was already well known; namely, that the clergy was more fully committed to the pacifist passion than the laity.

Thirdly, pacifism was not in fact the issue in the debate. As Tittle explained, his "report did not deal with the duty of the *state* in time of war, or, for that matter, with the duty of the individual citizen. What it undertook to say was that the Church, as the institution which represents in history the things that Jesus Christ stood for, should not *bless* war. It should, of course, give its blessing to those of its members who are serving in the armed forces, but it should not give moral or spiritual sanction to activities which most of them find morally revolting."[137] During the debate itself Tittle drove home the conviction that though war might become the only possible course of action in a given historical situation, the Church cannot pray for military victory, though victory may be recognized by Christians as a necessity if a better world is to be built. All that the Church can pray for is that the will of God may be done in the situation. Only by retaining its sense of transcending any earthly order or nation can the Church be the Church in time of war, and only if the Church retains thus its integrity can it be a really effective agent of God in leading men and nations away from war and into peace.

In the fourth place, the vote was close. Tittle repeatedly observed

136. My account of the 1944 General Conference is based on several sources, by far the two most important being *The Daily Christian Advocate,* The Methodist Church, May 3-8, 1944, and an extended personal interview with Charles C. Parlin, Denver, Col., May 1, 1960.

137. Letter from Tittle to Shy Banks, June 2, 1944.

that one clerical vote "would have defeated the attempt of what I still think was a *minority* to have the Church repudiate the position it took four years ago."[138] In the weeks following the conference he received many letters praising him for his stand, including some from delegates who now regretted they had voted for the Parlin report. Moreover, Tittle found some comfort in the fact that the important North Eastern Jurisdictional Conference, comprising New York, Pennsylvania, and New England, refused by a vote of 114 to 92 to endorse the action of the General Conference; and several Annual Conferences, including Rock River, reaffirmed the old 1940 position.[139] Surely, however, Tittle found most moving letters from lads in the service. A Marine pilot on duty in the Central Pacific wrote in criticism of the General Conference vote: "I would rather kill an enemy knowing that the Church does not approve of it, but will overlook it as something that under the circumstances could not be helped, than for the Church to say 'kill him, kill him, we as Methodists think it right in this case.' "[140]

Finally, what does this debate reveal about Tittle the man, his sensitivity to rejection, his pride if not his stubborness, his rationalization of hard tactics in a fight? Daniel A. Poling once characterized Tittle as a "pacifist who was at once militant and combative" who "fought with all the weapons in his hand, and they were many." But, Poling added, he was a "gracious, sincere and fearless Christian."[141] Poling's observation complements H. Stuart Hughes's generalization: "A longing for harmony, a passionate advocacy of peace, may well emerge from the sublimation of deep-seated aggression. I doubt whether there has ever been a strenuous pacifist who has not been fascinated by war and violence."

In Parlin's estimation, Tittle (and Day and Crane) did not originally afford all the members of the Committee on State of the Church adequate opportunity to study and reflect on the report. In Parlin's estimation, the motion to vote by orders was devious and the move to reconsider unsporting. Moreover, after the defeat Tittle was bitter, brusquely rejecting Parlin's gesture of reconciliation, although Albert Day breakfasted with Parlin the next morning and was most pleasant. Parlin then wrote Tittle assuring him of Parlin's continued respect. The letter went unanswered. Happily, however, the story does not end there. As it happened, Parlin had a son living in Chicago who fell in love with

138. Letter from Tittle to Mrs. Emma C. Kennett, June 13, 1944.
139. Letter from Tittle to F. Nelson Underwood, June 27, 1944.
140. Letter from Lt. D. L. Rousch to his father, May 18, 1944. The father sent a copy to Tittle.
141. Poling's review of *A Mighty Fortress* (New York: Harper & Brothers, 1949) in the *Christian Herald,* September, 1950, clipping in Tittle Collection.

a Northwestern co-ed. The girl, however, was a Roman Catholic, and the young lovers "went through the tortures of the damned" attempting to reconcile their religious differences. In time they turned to Tittle for advice. He gave them heartfelt counsel. Ultimately they were married by Tittle in First Church with the blessing of the bride's parents and "have lived happily ever after." For helping to make possible the marriage of his son to the girl of his heart, Parlin gratefully acknowledged a debt to Tittle "he could never repay."

Perhaps Poling was right. Tittle was at once a combative champion of pacifism and a gracious Christian.

More than sixteen million American men answered their country's call to the colors and more than a million of these young lions came from Methodist homes. But what of those Americans who could not bring themselves to kill another human being even though that person marched under the brutal banner of the swastika or Rising Sun? Though the statistics are incomplete, there were possibly 100,000 objectors to war of military age. This is only an infinitesimal fraction of the more than 34,000,000 registrants—not more than 0.30 of 1 percent.[142] Yet the fate of this handful was to Tittle a matter of conscience, and in his concern Tittle was the conscience of Methodism.

A large number of these objectors to war, at least 25,000, served as noncombatants in the army and navy; this kind of duty was elected especially by Seventh-Day Adventists. More than 5,000 of these objectors to war went to prison, either because they refused to register or because their objection was based on political grounds inadmissible under the law, and of these many were Jehovah's Witnesses. Some 11,868 objectors reported for alternative service work under the Civilian Public Service, a program proposed by the historic peace churches, endorsed by the Federal Council of Churches and the major denominations, and rather warmly accepted by the Selective Service Administration, "glad to have the churches shoulder responsibility for the conduct

142. Mulford Q. Sibley and Philip E. Jacob, *Conscription of Conscience: The American State and the Conscientious Objector, 1940-1947* (Ithaca, N. Y.: Cornell University Press, 1952), p. 84. The Selective Service System estimated that a total of 72,000 eligible registrants claimed Conscientious Objection status. Sibley and Jacob make a plausible case that this figure is too low and suggest the number be revised upward to about 100,000. Lawrence S. Wittner, *Rebels Against War: The American Peace Movement, 1941-1960* (New York: Columbia University Press, 1969), p. 41, gives this breakdown: 25,000 men classified I-A-O (noncombatant); 6,086 C.O.'s imprisoned; 11,887 classified IV-E (alternative service). Wittner further states that of the 10,022,367 males ordered to report for induction, the government classified as C.O.'s 42,973, or 0.42 of 1 per cent.

of persons who could, with infinite firmness, say 'No' to every military demand."[143] In the Public Service Camps these almost 12,000 men toiled more than eight million man-days of work, tilling the soil, making roads, fighting forest fires, caring for the mentally ill, acting as "guinea pigs" for medical research. If the government had paid for this labor at the same rate as for its Army, it would have spent over $18,000,000. As it was, the C.O.'s were obliged to work for nothing, while they, their families, and the churches voluntarily contributed or raised $7,202,000 for their maintenance. The historic peace churches furnished the central core of the CPS "brotherhood," but of the 15 percent composed of major Protestant denominations, the Methodists supplied by far the largest segment, 941.[144]

In their 1944 Episcopal Address the bishops declared for the Methodist Church "its purpose to defend those of our number who cannot in good conscience participate in war. We will not be driven from that position by hysteria which always develops in time of struggle. The principles of democracy and the teaching of the Christian religion accord to men freedom of conscience. The conscientious refusal to bear arms is for some persons a natural expression of their desire for peace on earth. To all members of The Methodist Church who as conscientious objectors seek exemption from military service the church must continue to give its moral protection."[145] The General Conference, with Tittle as ramrod, emphatically reaffirmed its 1940 declaration: "We ask and claim exemption from all forms of military preparation or service for all conscientious objectors who may be members of The Methodist Church."[146]

The Methodist Commission on World Peace was represented on the National Service Board for Religious Objectors, a co-ordinating agency set up by the Friends to aid and protect pacifists. Bishop Oxnam was chairman of the Federal Council's Committee on the Conscientious Objector, another watchdog and ministering agency. The Methodist Commission on World Peace further appointed a full-time secretary-chaplain for work with Methodist C.O.'s, and Methodist ministers near CPS camps visited and counseled with the men. Although the small pacifist sects supported about half the cost of the Civilian Public Service Camps, Methodism acknowledged a "debt of honor" and contributed

143. Wittner, *Rebels Against War*, p. 122.
144. Muelder, *Methodism and Society*, p. 194. Sibley and Jacob, however, give for the Methodists the figure of 673.
145. *The Daily Christian Advocate*, The Methodist Church, April 27, 1944, pp. 30-31.
146. *Ibid.*, May 6, 1944, p. 167.

$425,000, with the Commission on World Peace being officially author-ized to solicit in the name of Methodism.

What specifically did Tittle do on behalf of the young pacifists who in the words of Justice Holmes took the Sermon on the Mount more seriously than the rest of us? For one thing, he contributed to the main-tenance of his son, William, who labored in Public Service Camps in Michigan and Montana, and he sheltered his son's wife and child dur-ing Bill's painful absence. (John Tittle, being older and the father of three children, was not forced to choose between military service and Civilian Public Service.) For another, Tittle gave generously to the peace sects to assist in their work, and at least twice he posted bond for C.O.'s. He also visited camps to counsel the lonely and often bitter young idealists.

He encouraged the First Church membership to honor its pledges to stand by its lads of conscience. The First Church Pacifist Fellowship by June, 1945, had contributed more than $6,000 to the Civilian Public Service Fund. He saw to it the Rock River Annual Conference was not forgetful. "Members of churches within the bounds of this Conference," he reported in 1945, "who are now serving in Civilian Public Service Camps have incurred for their support in these camps an indebtedness of $29,410. . . . This indebtedness, unless otherwise cared for, must be assumed by the three historic peace churches—the Mennonites, the Church of the Brethren, and the Society of Friends. We think it should be regarded by us as a debt of honor, and we ask the appropriate apportioning body to provide for its liquidation by spreading the amount —$29,410—among the churches of the Conference. . . ."[147] He also pleaded with the North Central Jurisdictional Conference to contribute to the support of C.O.'s.

Much as he honored those who refused to bear arms, Tittle was well aware of the dissension in many of the CPS camps, the bitterness between different groups of pacifists, the proud and defiant spirit of many of the resisters, with some of the younger radicals scoring the "Pacifist Establishment" for its docile co-operation with the government. Life in these camps was lonely and monotonous, the work sometimes trivial, the supervision often stupid though rarely brutal. Yet, Tittle insisted, those C.O.'s who were forever complaining do not sufficiently realize "how much progress has been made during the last twenty-five years in popular understanding of the pacifist position, which is also to say that they do not sufficiently appreciate the significance of govern-

147. *Minutes* of the Rock River Annual Conference (1945), p. 53.

mental provision of an alternative to military service."[148] Tittle was "convinced that the men in the Civilian Public Service Camps, *if they demonstrate by their lives the validity of their position,* will be used of God to lighten the darkness, to relieve the suffering, and to improve the conditions of the world."[149]

Before Pearl Harbor American Methodism officially had recorded its conviction that chaplains be withdrawn from the military system and that they be supported by and responsible to the Church. Yet when the war came the old arrangement prevailed. Ultimately, some fifteen hundred Methodist ministers served as chaplains, constituting the largest single Protestant group. They were recruited and screened by the Commission on Chaplains, an agency operating under the Council of Bishops. A chaplaincy was no sinecure, demanding as it did enormous toil and inflicting much loneliness and peril. It is symbolic that Bishop Adna W. Leonard, chairman of the Commission on Chaplains, died in a plane crash while visiting American troops in Iceland. Tittle's own reservations about the chaplaincy remained. "As to whether you should apply for a chaplaincy only you can decide," he replied to an inquiry in 1942. "For my own part, I feel unable to take any part in the war effort, and I am convinced that a chaplaincy does involve a man, willy-nilly, in the prosecution of war. This I feel bound to suppose in view of my own experiences during the First World War, in which I served as a Y.M.C.A. secretary at the front."[150]

In late March, 1944, Brigadier General Robert H. Dunlop addressed a communication to Samuel McCrea Cavert, general secretary of the Federal Council of Churches: "Your letter of 16 March 1944, addressed to the President, concerning your inquiry relative to the bombing of enemy territory, has been referred to the War Department for reply. You may be assured it is not the policy of the War Department to deliberately subject entire communities to wanton destruction and every effort is made to confine bombing attacks strictly to military objectives and that any military operations will be predicated solely upon military necessity. However, so long as Axis controlled cities remain a vital military significance and are utilized as transportation and strategic focal points of the Nazi military machine, it will be incumbent upon the Allies

148. Letter from Tittle to Jack Phillips, February 9, 1943. Phillips had written Tittle not to gripe, but to state that he was finding happiness in his C.P.S. work, quite in contrast to the angry tone of some letters.
149. Letter from Tittle to F. Nelson Underwood, June 27, 1944. Italics in original.
150. Letter from Tittle to G. MacDonald Jones, January 15, 1942.

War and Peace / 469

to seek out these objectives and achieve their destruction in order to avoid an unnecessary sacrifice of lives of our soldiers."[151]

Surely it is unnecessary to review the large body of literature dealing with the Allied bombing of Europe and the American bombing of Japan, its justification, its effectiveness, its contribution to the shortening of the war and thus its saving of Allied lives and, as some argue, of enemy lives as well, in order to assert the irrefutable: namely, that Britain and the United States did in fact "deliberately subject entire communities to wanton destruction" in the name of "military necessity"; that every effort was *not* made "to confine bombing attacks strictly to military objectives"; and that our acceptance of massive, indiscriminate bombing of men, women, and children in Vietnam and our anticipation that should World War III break out entire populations will be annihilated by bombing is directly traceable to a bombing strategy first approved by Winston S. Churchill, Franklin D. Roosevelt, and Harry S. Truman.

Early in 1944 Dr. Cosmo Gordon Lang, former Archbishop of Canterbury, and the Rt. Rev. George K. A. Bell, Bishop of Chichester, protested in the House of Lords the Allied indiscriminate bombing of German cities. On February 20 Tittle joined with fourteen Canadian and American churchmen in cabling Lord Lang the following message: "The appeal of Chichester and yourself in House of Lords against Allied policy of blotting out whole German cities and nonmilitary areas is welcomed by many American churchmen. Obliteration of historic cities and incineration of masses of civilian victims does violence to professed war aims and standards of Christian faith. Deeply grateful for your courageous stand."[152] Two weeks later the journal of the Fellowship of Reconciliation, *Fellowship,* published as a supplement to its regular March issue an article by Vera Brittain entitled, "Massacre by Bombing," a wrathful, eloquent indictment of Allied bombing strategy, an indictment especially forceful because it was penned by an English citizen who had herself endured German bombing. As a foreword to the article there was an appeal to end obliteration bombing signed on March 5 by twenty-eight American clergymen, including Tittle and fellow Methodists Sockman, Crane, and E. Stanley Jones. The appeal read in part: "Christian people should be moved to examine themselves concerning their participation in this carnival of death—even though they be thousands of miles away. Here, surely, there is a call for

151. Copy of letter from Brigadier General Robert H. Dunlop to Samuel McCrea Cavert in Tittle Collection. The copy is undated, but the letter must have been written in late March.

152. The statement with the signatures is in the Tittle Collection.

repentance; that we have not acquainted ourselves with the verities and realities of what is being done in our name in Europe; and surely Christian obligation calls upon us to pray incessantly to God that He in His own way may bid the winds and waves of war be still."[153] The appeal and the Brittain article, coming as they did hard on the heels of the Lang and Bell protest in the House of Lords, touched off what Harry Emerson Fosdick termed "an outburst of vitriolic denunciation"; and Miss Brittain estimated she was condemned in two hundred articles. The *New York Times'* story stimulated a heavy reader response. The letters ran fifty to one in opposition to the protest, Bishop Oxnam being one of the many American churchmen favoring the continuation of the Allied bombing policy. Of course, the relentless logic of "military necessity" prevailed, and the skies—or more precisely the Allies—continued to rain death over Europe. Inevitably Tittle was sprinkled with accusations of "traitor" and "big mouth meddler." He explained his protest to a young disciple: "It will not, probably, serve to change the policy that calls for the indiscriminate killing of men, women, and children, but . . . the Christian conscience imperatively demands that this protest be made."[154] Incidentally, Tittle in July, 1944, also protested the German robot bombing of England.

In time Germany surrendered. We will leave it to the experts, who have debated the matter in painstaking studies, to determine if Tittle was right or wrong in his belief that obliteration bombing would not hasten the end of the European war. It is, however, my conviction that even if it could be proved that the bombing of cities such as Dresden contributed measurably to the defeat of Germany, such a strategy is still an atrocity.

On August 6, 1945, a uranium atomic bomb, "Little Boy," was dropped over the inhabitants of Hiroshima. Three days later the people of Nagasaki received the visit of "Fat Man," a plutonium atomic bomb. There was no true debate and hence no real "great agonizing decision" concerning the employment of these new bombs. Civilians of Japan, as earlier those of Germany, had long been decreed fair targets. In six months of fire bombing, accelerating with the Tokyo raid on the night of March 9/10 that cremated seventy thousand men, women, and children, civilian casualties were more than twice as great as total Japanese

153. The statement with the signatures is in the Tittle Collection.
154. Letter from Tittle to Robert Hamill, April 3, 1944. The generalizations concerning the churches and bombing made by George E. Hopkins, "Bombing and the American Conscience During World War II," *The Historian,* XXVIII (May, 1966), 451-73, are not, in my opinion, sound.

military casualties in forty-four months of war. The concept of obliteration bombing had long been accepted by American leaders and acceptable to the American people, and therefore the last step on the ghastly road to Hiroshima was not, save for a few scientists, an agonizing one to take, especially since it was honestly believed that the use of the new bombs would bring a quick end to the war and save hundreds of thousands of American and Japanese lives. (The much-debated question concerning whether Hiroshima and Nagasaki were intended as warnings to Soviet Russia need not concern us here.) We may agree that President Truman and his advisers were not moral monsters and that the bombs were not dropped in a spirit of vengeance, just as we may continue to believe that Churchill and Roosevelt saw no alternative to razing Dresden, Hamburg, Berlin, and other Nazi cities. But we further hold with Tittle and thirty-three other churchmen that the use of the atomic bombs "against an already virtually beaten foe will have to receive judgment before God and the conscience of humankind."[155] Revealingly, the first time Tittle was in the pulpit after Hiroshima he preached on the words of Deuteronomy 30:19: "I have set before thee life and death, the blessing and the curse: therefore choose life." For Tittle, the "bomb that was dropped on Hiroshima was no different in moral principle from the bombs unleashed over Nanking, over Barcelona, over Rotterdam, London, Berlin." Nevertheless, the action was appalling, "for that single blinding flash which obliterated Hiroshima revealed the depths to which mankind had descended in recent years." The "destruction of civilization, if not of all life on this planet, is now a stark possibility."[156] As we know, Tittle was the only "working minister" on the Federal Council's famous Commission on the Relation of the Church to the War in the Light of the Christian Faith. In its 1944 report the "massacre of civilian populations" was declared "morally unjustifiable," though some members defended as necessary the bombing of civilian areas. In its 1946 report on *Atomic Warfare and the Christian Faith* the decision to use the bomb was termed "morally indefensible," Americans having "sinned grievously against the laws of God and against the people of Japan."[157]

Tittle sought to mitigate the horrors of the war by continuing to urge that food be sent, under carefully controlled conditions, to the

155. The statement with the signatures is in the Tittle Collection.
156. *That You May Live,* a sermon preached September 16, 1945 (pamphlet).
157. For an extended discussion of the Federal Council's reports and of the entire question, see Robert C. Batchelder, *The Irreversible Decision, 1939-1950* (Boston: Houghton Mifflin Company, 1962). I do not share Batchelder's conclusions.

starving children in the occupied countries of Europe. And he had a hand in the 1944 General Conference petition to the president and secretary of state to accept America's "heavy responsibility for the first and worst victims of totalitarian tyranny, the Jewish people, who now have no refuge."

Tittle also did what he could to see that civil liberties in the United States were not washed away by a tidal wave of hysteria, as was the case in 1917-18. Though he acted in many areas, undoubtedly his greatest concern was for the Japanese-Americans. "Is it too late, even now," he asked President Roosevelt, "to abandon the policy of mass evacuation of Japanese from their homes on the Pacific coast and to substitute for it a policy of selective evacuation, that is, provision for examination of Japanese-Americans so that those whose record is above suspicion may be left in their homes? This, I am convinced, would be approved and applauded by many Americans who are profoundly disturbed by the treatment that is now being accorded a people whose members, for the most part, are loyal and devoted to this country."[158] He remained in contact with Japanese-American churchmen, and they were grateful for his "calmness of spirit and good-will."[159] Moreover, he extended aid and protection to Evanston's few Japanese, and during the war perhaps five Japanese families joined First Church.[160] In the larger scene, of course, Tittle's efforts were ineffectual in preventing what he rightly termed a cruel, unjust, unchristian, un-American, and unnecessary policy.[161]

Even as the war raged, Tittle helped prepare for a "just and durable peace" in sermons, addresses, articles, correspondence, and leadership in Rock River, North Central Jurisdictional, and General Conference sessions. He participated fully in Methodism's great Crusade for a New World Order and continued to give direction to the Methodist Commission on World Peace. Moreover, as we know, he was a member of the Federal Council's Commission to Study the Bases of a Just and Durable Peace and was in attendance at all its important meetings from Delaware in 1942 to Cleveland in 1945, as he also spoke throughout the Middle West under the auspices of the Christian Mission on World Order, sponsored by the Commission.

158. Letter from Tittle to the Honorable Franklin D. Roosevelt, April 3, 1943.
159. Letter from Sozaburo Watauobe to Tittle, February 6, 1942. The letterhead is The Japanese Union Church, Los Angeles.
160. Author's interview with Glenna Myers Tittle, Evanston, Ill., July 31, 1959.
161. "God Meant It for Good," typed MS, a sermon preached November 18, 1945.

VIII

Only four years passed between the bombing of Hiroshima and Tittle's death. During these years mankind first confronted the awful possibility of a final death by its own hand. Could faith in God possibly be sustained in a post-Hiroshima age? "Yes!" Tittle affirmed.

> The believer in providence is . . . not confronted with any-thing new in principle. The end of human existence on earth was regarded by the early Christians as near at hand; by modern Christians as far in the future. But long before Hiroshima the modern Christian did entertain the idea and expectation of an eventual end of man on earth, so that what is new in the present situation is not the possibility of a last generation but the possi-bility—sobering enough I grant—that *ours* may be the last gener-ation. This, to be sure, is not all that is new in the present situation. There is the dread possibility that the end may come not from the action of cosmic forces but as a consequence of human sin and folly; not as a stage in the outworking of the divine purpose but as a fatal defiance of the will of God.
> But would there be even in that outcome anything new in principle? Any philosophy of history that takes serious account of human freedom must reckon with the possibility of man-made catastrophe. The present possibility of a world-destroying catas-trophe, so far from presenting anything new in principle, is, as it seems to me, but the ultimate meaning of the saying: "Be not deceived; God is not mocked: for whatsoever a man soweth, that shall he also reap."
> The believer in providence may hold fast the faith that God is the Ruler of the world—yes, and that he is the Lord of History, seeing that history on the Christian view is not limited to this passing world but will have its consummation in the eternal Kingdom of God.[162]

The conviction that the Lord of History shall rule for ever and ever did not for Tittle result in a fatalistic indifference to the prospects of a nuclear holocaust. The United States, he predicted in 1945, would have sole possession of the atomic bomb for only two or three years, five at the most.[163] There is no military defense against atomic bombs and none is to be expected.[164] Nothing in history encourages the hope that the destructiveness of new instruments of warfare will keep nations from going to war, or that nations at war will abstain from using any weapon they have to their own advantage.[165] Therefore, the United States

162. *Christian Century*, LXIII (May 1, 1946), 556.
163. *That You May Live*, a sermon preached September 16, 1945 (pamphlet).
164. *Ways To Peace*, a sermon preached November 9, 1947 (pamphlet).
165. *That You May Live*, a sermon preached September 16, 1945 (pamphlet).

should halt all manufacture of atomic bombs and take the initiative in seeking to place atomic energy under international control, a control to be made effective through international inspection.[166]

Robert W. Tucker has observed pointedly that the measure of one's moral sensitivity and humanitarian sentiment is not determined simply by the degree to which one publicly anguishes over the horrible prospects of nuclear war.[167] But Tittle was not simply a "nuclear pacifist," and though there is much that is annoyingly simplistic in his reading of the origins of the Cold War, his witness to peace long antedated Hiroshima. If he could not bring himself to justify World War II in the name of anti-Nazism, is it to be wondered that he refused to risk World War III in the name of anticommunism? From the perspective of statesmen and diplomats, Tittle and his ilk possessed no power and hence no responsibility for making the awful decisions affecting the life and death of the United States. Perhaps a politics of pacifism is an impossibility. Perhaps no responsible political leader holding office has the moral right to place the welfare of mankind above the survival of his own nation. Tittle could only reply that the God revealed in Jesus Christ would not be deceived by any explanation, rationalization, or justification for the infliction of nuclear death on whole populations of women and children. It was Tittle's task to remind American statesmen that nations as well as individuals do not have death to fear, but God. Tittle believed that only if nations freely gave up their own lives, that is, their lives as totally independent, totally sovereign, egocentric nation-states, could there be any hope of permanently staying a third and possibly last world war.[168] In this belief, Tittle was joined by official Methodism and virtually all of the major Protestant denominations.

It is scarcely necessary to point out the utopianism in Tittle's views on world government. He minimized self-interest in the conduct of international affairs. He minimized the powerful thrust of nationalism in the emerging nations. He minimized the difficulty of gaining any sort of consensus on abstract principles of international conduct. And despite references to an international police force, he never quite saw that principles were never self-enforcing; that is, he minimized the place of power in the new supergovernment. "We must bring the world as a whole under a system of international law," he declared in 1946 to the

166. *Ibid.; Christian Century,* LXIII (May 1, 1946), 556; *Minutes* of Rock River Annual Conference (1946), p. 50, and (1947) p. 59, and (1948), p. 72.

167. *The Just War* (Baltimore, Md.: Johns Hopkins Press, 1960), *passim.* See also Paul Ramsey, *The Just War: Force and Political Responsibility* (New York: Charles Scribner's Sons, 1968), *passim.*

168. "God and the Nations," typed MS, a sermon preached October 24, 1948.

graduating class at Ohio Wesleyan.[169] But just how in the late 1940's was agreement to be reached in the drafting of this "system of international law"? And if somehow achieved, just how was this law to be enforced? In November, 1950, Secretary of State Dean Acheson informed a Washington audience: "Instead of wholeness, we get fragmentation, if those who have a keen sense of our moral obligations do not also think responsibly—that is, if they do not confront themselves with the actual conditions with which we must deal in the world, if they do not begin with the actual, available alternatives from which choices must be made. Moral guidance is not effective if it directs itself to ideal, but unavailable solutions. Morality, if it is not to be divorced from the practical world of action, must inform itself and relate itself to things as they are. The exercise of responsibility involves making real choices in a real world, which rarely affords the luxury of ideal conditions."[170]

Acheson's admonition might have been uttered with pacifists such as Tittle in mind. And Tittle could only have replied: "My commission is to proclaim the word of God and the word of God is a word of judgment on 'things as they are.' It is my business to confront the 'practical world of action,' a world of rival nationalisms now armed with Doomsday weapons, with the vision of a world community of peace and justice, love and law." Of course responsible statesmen (such as Secretary of State Acheson) must "begin with the actual, available alternatives," but Tittle was right that if realistic statesmanship failed fundamentally to restructure the world order, a postthermonuclear-war world might render statesmen and diplomats as irrelevant as preachers were usually deemed to be in the post-Hiroshima world.

The overriding political fact of the immediate post-Hiroshima world was the sharpening tension between the United States and Russia and the critical question was whether war between the two giants would erupt before statesmanship could begin even to work on blunting the tension. The origins of the Cold War are fearfully complex and controversial and Tittle's understanding was too simplistic. Yet even in retrospect, possessing as we do facts denied to him, it is permissible to say that in the larger issues he was essentially correct.

Only weeks before his death, he asked of his people: "Is it the will of God that we shall resist blind hatred and hysteria in relation to

169. *Evanston Review*, July 11, 1946, p. 19.
170. Quoted in Norman A. Graebner, "Dean G. Acheson," *American Secretaries of State in the Twentieth Century*, ed. Norman Graebner (New York: McGraw-Hill Book Co., 1961), p. 269.

Russia? Is it the will of God that we shall try to get along with Russia? Getting along with Russia does not necessarily mean endorsement of communism; nor does it mean appeasement. It means the determination to keep open as long as possible the channels of communication, and the determination to abstain, even in the face of extreme provocation, from vituperative language and hostile acts. It means the resolve to do all that is humanly possible to avoid a rupture that might conceivably issue in the destruction of the present world civilization, if not of mankind upon earth."[171] Tittle was quite aware of the terrorism and tyranny in Stalin's Russia, and he was not blind to Russian expansionism. Nevertheless he personally and the 1948 General Conference officially declared intolerable the suggestion of a "preventive war." Russia's behavior in some measure was dictated by fear of America. Relentlessly Tittle listed those things the United States had done or left undone to justify Soviet fears. He did not succumb to the new "imperialism of righteousness." Neither the present rulers of Russia, he observed in 1948, "nor the present rulers of the United States can properly be cast for the role of world saviour. It is not up to us to save the world. We ourselves are in need of salvation from passions and ambitions that have brought the world to the edge of the abyss and are now threatening to push it over."[172]

Tittle's last words to the 1948 General Conference of The Methodist Church were a reaffirmation of his persuasion that war is a defiance of the righteousness of God as revealed in Jesus Christ and Him crucified and that man's only earthly security is in obedience to the God and Father of our Lord Jesus Christ who has "made of one blood all nations of men for to dwell on all the face of the earth."

171. *Mighty Fortress*, pp. 140-41.
172. "Our Part in Rebuilding the World," typed MS, a sermon preached April 11, 1948.

16. A FAITH THAT
COULD NOT BE SHAKEN

I

Ernest Fremont Tittle's name is not found among the galaxy of twentieth-century theological giants, nor should it be. He was a preacher —and a Methodist preacher at that—not a theologian or philosopher or formal scholar. Christian theology is the record of a continuous conversation carried on within the Church and between the Church and the world in which it lives. Though participating in the conversation, Tittle contributed little of originality or profundity. His voice was heard but faintly in the House of Theology and Philosophy where the Barths, Tillichs, Niebuhrs, James's, Whiteheads, Bubers, Bultmanns, Brunners, and Teilhard de Chardins resided. Since Tittle penned no major theological treatise, it is unnecessary to submit his theological thought to intensive examination. Such a book-length enterprise would be unfair to Tittle, who did not count himself in the succession of Church savants.

Nevertheless, how shall we think of God, how does He reveal Himself, what is His will and Word, what is man's nature and what is man's destiny were questions much meditated by Tittle, and the gospel Tittle preached on Sunday morning grew from intensely worked theological soil. Tittle the preacher, Tittle the prophet, indeed, Tittle the pastor, may not be divorced from the man who in hard study searched out the Word and in sustained prayer awaited the Word to be spoken. "In recent years," he related in 1939, "an overwhelming recognition of the world's needs—and of my own—has led me to re-examine the grounds for Christian belief in God. It also has led me to study the Christian faith experimentally, not merely intellectually—for homiletical purposes.

Yet like many another who, walking in darkness, has finally seen a great light, I am convinced that such assurance as I now have was graciously given me by God himself, so that I can only wonder and be thankful."[1]

How Tittle thought of God, man, and history reveals much of the theological travail of modern American Protestantism precisely because he was not a formal scholar and precisely because his thought was not profoundly original. Historians attempting to reconstruct the intellectual life of Protestantism and who concentrate on texts studied at Union, Harvard, Yale, and Princeton to the neglect of the message actually preached from the nation's pulpits are likely to reach conclusions truly "other worldly." Therefore, while freely acknowledging that Tittle was not a new Copernicus of the theological world, a brief commentary on his thought illuminates both his own pulpit ministry and the fluctuating theological weather of a stormy era.

Sunday after Sunday the preacher mounts the pulpit and from the pews the congregation looks up in expectation of being fed the Word. We are commanded to be faithful, not to be relevant. The command is true. It is a command, however, less difficult for theologians to honor than preachers. Theologians who are faithful need not cease writing if a sightless generation finds their works irrelevant. The written word lives after the writer dies. There is always the hope some future generation will discover and read his faithful words. Moreover, the theologian need not trouble overmuch about the relevancy of his message (at least beyond the confines of his seminary or seminar room) because his position is independent of the people's judgment. He can afford to be faithful. A preacher who would also be a prophet may not pay for relevancy with the coin of unfaithfulness, for then he would be a popular pulpit prince, perhaps, but certainly a false prophet. Yet unless a gospel can be preached, with what does the preacher feed his famished flock? And if the flock finds the gospel irrelevant, will they not soon scatter? Of course, certain celebrated theologians have insisted on just this point —the institutional church should shut its doors and preachers should stop talking about God. This is understandable, considering (as Sidney E. Mead observed) that many modern theologians appear to belong to the highly abstract and conveniently "invisible" church whose fulfillments are "beyond history" and not of this world. But Tittle refused to go out of business. He continued to search for words to preach that were at once faithful and relevant, and grateful thousands of men and women who worshiped in First Church believed he found the true

1. *Christian Century,* LVI (June 21, 1939), 795.

words. Prestigious spokesmen in the second half of the twentieth century are fond of contrasting the faithfulness of the once rejected Sören Kierkegaard with the popularity of certain unfaithful purveyors of piety. Tittle's life reminds us, however, that preaching on Sunday morning in a formal worship service conducted in a Gothic sanctuary of an institutional church to an upper-middle-class congregation need not be a sign, after all, of the death of Christianity.

Tittle was raised in a Methodist home, educated at a Methodist college, trained at a Methodist seminary, and in his career served none but Methodist pastorates. The untheological character of Methodism is notorious and Wilhelm Pauck is only one of many scholars to impute the alleged general theological indifference of American Protestantism to Methodism's example and influence.[2] What scholars have asserted, popular writers have echoed, *Life* magazine expressing the prevailing opinion that John Wesley paid "small attention to the fine points of theology" and that the Methodist approach to matters of doctrine was and still is "casual."[3] Methodists themselves are fond of citing Wesley's indifference to creedal orthodoxy, quoting his statements: "Is thy heart herein as my heart? If it be, give me thy hand" and "Orthodoxy, or right opinions, is, at best, but a very slender part of religion, if it can be allowed to be any part at all."[4] In 1944 the Methodist bishops declared as Methodist bishops had been declaring for a century and a half: "The Methodist insistence has not been so much upon opinion as upon life. Its distinguishing mark is not so much what men believe, as what they are, what they experience, how they act. The unique traditions of Methodism are, therefore, to be sought in patterns of action rather than systems of dogma."[5] This stress on life and experience over doctrine and dogma is well summed up in the reply Nels F. S. Ferré received in answer to his question of what was the rock-bottom truth with most Methodists: "Brother, when an honest-to-goodness Methodist tells you that he has had an experience, you don't argue with him."[6]

2. "Theology in the Life of Contemporary American Protestantism," *Religion and Culture: Essays in Honor of Paul Tillich,* ed. Walter Leibrecht (New York: Harper & Brothers, 1959), pp. 273ff.
3. November 10, 1947, p. 113.
4. Quoted in S. Paul Schilling (ed.), *Methodism and Society in Theological Perspective* (New York and Nashville, Tenn.: Abingdon Press, 1960), p. 25. The first quotation is usually given: "Is thy heart as my heart? Then give me thy hand."
5. *Journal of the General Conference of The Methodist Church,* 1944, p. 155.
6. "God Can be Experienced," in *Methodism,* ed. William K. Anderson (Cincinnati, Ohio, and Delaware, Ohio: The Methodist Publishing House, 1957), p. 116.

It is true that nineteenth-century Methodism developed a "folk theology" dangerously drained of normative content, that no strict doctrinal test is required for admission to church membership, and that the Articles of Religion fall short of being a full body of dogma. It is further true that American Methodism has produced less than a legion of theological giants and that denominational heresy hunts have been infrequent because heresy can only exist where orthodoxy is meticulously defined. In sum, it is true that Methodism historically has subordinated creeds to deeds, correct doctrine to Christian living, ritual to righteousness, theological speculation to individual experience.

Yet, although such observations are true, they do not represent the whole truth. Church historians, perhaps most especially Sydney E. Ahlstrom, are coming to recognize the large and impressive theological achievement of American Protestantism, an achievement not confined to the intellectual labors of the New England Puritans. Methodist historians, perhaps most especially Leland Howard Scott, William J. McCutcheon, Frederick A. Norwood, and S. Paul Schilling, in searching the past have rediscovered a rich theological heritage that had been partially obscured by secular historians who equated evangelicalism with anti-intellectualism. Methodist spokesmen themselves also contributed to the veiling when they equated Calvinism with barren scholasticism.

In addressing Methodism's concern for theology, so much depends on one's understanding of the term. Is theology the tinder-dry preoccupation of hair-splitters? Is it to be considered only technically as the scientific ordering of the faith a church confesses and teaches? May it be defined (in the words of Jules Michelet) as the science of befuddling oneself systematically? In truth, theology "moves out from the religious acceptances of a community or a person and moves toward momentous questions of life and death, goodness and truth, time and eternity. The most difficult problems of nature, man, and God come within its purview. Theology deals with the human situation in its totality, historical and cosmic. It reflects man's ultimate concerns, and seeks to speak the truth about ultimate reality. It demands a grappling with virtually all of the philosopher's traditional problems, calls for a historical grasp of the church's long involvement with the major issues, requires an understanding of contemporary science, art, and culture, and presupposes an understanding of the nature and situation of the men it addresses. Indeed, its scope is almost boundless."[7]

7. Sydney E. Ahlstrom, *Theology in America: The Major Protestant Voices from Puritanism to Neo-Orthodoxy* (Indianapolis, Ind., and New York: The Bobbs-Merrill Company, 1967), pp. 12-13.

Accepting this inclusive definition of Professor Ahlstrom's, it is clear that Methodism has not been totally indifferent to theology. Wesley himself specifically repudiated "speculative latitudinarianism." As he further asserted, "Indifference to all opinions" is "the spawn of hell." The genuine Christian is not a man of "muddy understanding" whose mind is "all a mist." Rather, "he is steadily fixed in his religious principles, in what he believes to be the truth as it is in Jesus."[8] Wesley's followers in America also asserted that the people called Methodists must surely hold and firmly believe the great Christian truths, for a faith to be lived must first be believed. The noble Episcopalian, Phillips Brooks, in counseling the divinity students at Yale, expressed well the Methodist understanding of theology: "Preach doctrine, preach all the doctrine that you know, and learn forever more and more; but preach it always, not that men may believe it, but that men may be saved by believing it."[9]

II

Tittle's understanding of theology was essentially Methodistic. Early in his First Church ministry, he asked, "Where shall the supreme emphasis of modern Christianity be placed? Upon doctrine, or upon spirit? Upon organization, or upon life?" "What is Christianity fundamentally? Is Christianity, fundamentally, a set of doctrine to be believed? Or is Christianity, fundamentally, a kind of life to be lived?" He answered that "important as is the nature of a man's belief, even more important is the character of his life; that neither individuals nor society will ever be saved by mere subscription to theological dogmas, but only by a radical change of heart."[10]

Religion, said Tittle, is the experience of God, theology the attempt to explain that experience.[11] He frequently expanded the theme, once setting forth the difference between theology and religion in these words: "Theology has to do with belief, one's theory of the world and life, one's intellectual view of God. Religion, which of course involves belief, is, however, something vastly more than a theory of the universe, a bare intellectual view of God. Religion, as has been said, is a relationship to God that makes a profound difference in the life of the man who has it. The difference between theology and religion is the difference between theory and practice, the difference, let us say, between the

8. Quoted in Schilling, *Methodism and Society,* pp. 31-32.
9. Quoted in *ibid.,* p. 42.
10. *First Church Review,* II (June, 1925), 1-5, 11.
11. Unidentified newspaper clipping, September 10, 1922, in Tittle Collection.

science of aeronautics and actual flight in an airplane. And as in the latter case so in the former, there is but one way to bridge that difference, and that is an adventurous act of trust. A man must take his chance. There comes a time in the life of every human individual when he can make no further progress in religious experience, when, indeed, he can hardly hope to retain the religious faith he now has, unless in some concrete way he dares to act upon it. If a man believes that God is, then let him not go on fearing and worrying as though God were dead and he had nothing to depend upon save his own human resources. If a man believes that there is a God, then in heaven's name let him trust God and have no fear save only the proper and necessary fear of failing to carry out God's plan for his life."[12] Repeatedly he hammered home the points: Faith is not an intellectual attitude, but a volitional one; theological systems have their day and cease to be for they are but broken lights of eternal truth; religions of authority harden into creeds and creeds fetter and divide men, resulting in a loveless legalism, inquisitions, and spiritual timidity; ecclesiastical dogmatism and political autocracy go hand in hand. Let us then, he challenged the young seminarians of Drew, "throw overboard a considerable number of so-called, 'religious beliefs' and then sail valiantly in quest of truth and righteousness and a better world."[13]

In one of his earliest published articles, Tittle wrote that the "final test by which all men must stand or fall will be not an intellectual or creedal test, but a moral and religious test." In that same article, however, he acknowledged it "a matter of very considerable importance what a man's creed is. . . . For what a man believes will eventually influence what he does. His creed will determine his deed. . . . What one really believes will influence his whole life."[14] And as the years passed, particularly in the last two decades of his life, Tittle's awareness of the theological foundations of the Christian faith deepened. In 1931 he made an evaluation that was to some degree a confession:

> For a generation now religious liberalism, certainly in this country, has been characterized at once by the presence of moral conviction and the absence of religious certitude. It has possessed the prophet's passion for righteousness but it has lacked the prophet's sureness of God. For a time it pooh-poohed historic creeds. It saw no use for any creed. It considered itself to be

12. "Paths To the Presence of God," typed MS, a sermon preached May 17, 1936.
13. "What Kind of Christianity Is Needed?" typed MS, a Founder's Day Address delivered at Drew, undated but probably 1920.
14. *Methodist Review*, XCIX (November, 1917), 866-74.

above the theological battle. It said that what mattered was not a man's belief about Deity but a man's attitude toward Duty. His conception of God might be ever so vague, his belief in God ever so unsure; after all what did it matter so long as he saw clearly the need of industrial justice and of international peace. Presently however religious liberalism began to suspect that its early attitude was a bit sophomoric; that a creed is just as much of an intellectual necessity as a back bone is a physical necessity; that an idealist certainly is seriously handicapped if he has only a vague conception of God and pitifully handicapped if he cannot believe there is a God. . . . Today, religious liberalism in this country is fully awake to the fact that it is by no means above the theological battle, that it must fight its way through skepticism and flabby thinking to a conception of God which is at once intellectually respectable, emotionally fortifying and morally stimulating. Meanwhile it must somehow recover its faith in the existence of God by deepening its experience of the presence of God."[15]

In 1931 also Tittle said that Fundamentalism at least is always earnest and sometimes passionate, "whereas Modernism took excess pride in its intellectual respectability, its practitioners praying: 'I thank Thee, O God, that I am not as these pious, unenlightened fundamentalists; I do not believe in any such pre-scientific and absurd notion as the resurrection of the body and a virgin birth: scientifically and philosophically I am up to date.' "[16]

At the very end of the thirties Tittle made a more explicit confession: "For many years I was in revolt against what I took to be a more or less conscious attempt to make theological belief, or ecclesiastical activity, serve as a substitute for moral obedience. "Why call ye me, Lord, Lord, and do not the things which I say?' was the theme, if not actually the text, of many a sermon. Moreover, I was greatly concerned to maintain, as I still am, that the Christian ethic is relevant to every relation of man to man. Hence, much time was spent saying, Yes, to the question, Is Christianity practicable? and in urging that Christianity be practiced in daily life. My preaching, consequently, was mostly of the ethical type. To be sure, there were occasional sermons on God. But such sermons do not necessarily bespeak a God-centered ministry; and I more than suspect that much of my preaching, including some of those occasional sermons on God, left the congregation religiously unfed."[17] Ultimately Tittle came to see that "the Christian ethic derives

15. "The Divine Initiative," typed MS, a sermon preached September 27, 1931.
16. *The Religion We Need*, a sermon preached January 25, 1931 (pamphlet).
17. *Christian Century*, LVI (June 21, 1939), 795.

from the Christian faith and cannot long live without it; let Christian faith be denied and repudiated and the Christian ethic will not long survive. . . ." Yet he never abandoned the conviction that "a creed is something to live by and that the livable portions of it are the ones to be urged upon oneself and others. The doctrine of the virgin birth cannot be lived, the doctrine of the love of God can be. Moreover, action, in the way of belief, is bound to lead to some conclusions as to the value of the belief. I am myself prepared to suppose that a man who for twenty years should live the doctrine of the love of God, would have no doubt that a God who is loving exists. John Dewey's thesis that we learn by doing is certainly relevant to the religious life."[18] Belief, then, was based upon Christian experience rather than exclusively upon any external dogmatic authority.

As we have seen, it was Tittle's responsibility as a working minister to find a preachable gospel with which to confront his congregation Sunday after Sunday, and to present it in language intelligible to laymen so that they might decide for or against it. Preachers are accused of being vendors of popular piety, tenderizing and diluting the tough fare prepared by theologians, and doubtless the indictment is often well founded. The other side of the coin is to remember that the preacher has the greater obligation to be comprehensible and relevant without sacrificing faithfulness. We have seen also that as a Methodist Tittle was challenged to reconcile faith and order with life and work, and that he attempted to walk the line between theological indifferentism and sterile dogmatism, and that as he grew older he discovered an increasing harmony between doctrine and experience.

III

A consideration of enormous importance in assessing the theological foundations of Tittle's preaching is that he lived in a time when the theological foundations of Christianity were being severely shaken. "Fifty years ago," remembered Harry Emerson Fosdick in 1935, that is to say, in 1885, the year of Tittle's birth, "a boy, seven years of age, was crying himself to sleep at night in terror lest, dying, he should go to hell, and his solicitous mother, out of all patience with the fearful teachings which brought such apparitions of the mind, was trying in vain to comfort him. That boy is preaching to you today and you may be sure that to him the achievements of Christian modernism in the last half century seem not only important but indispensable."[19] Fosdick

18. Letter from Tittle to G. W. Stewart, February 2, 1940.
19. *Christian Century*, LII (December 4, 1935), 1549.

uttered these words in his famous sermon, "Beyond Modernism," a tribute to the liberal and liberating theology of the late nineteenth and early twentieth century associated with the great German scholars Schleiermacher and Ritschl and in America with Borden Parker Bowne, William Newton Clarke, Walter Rauschenbusch, William Adams Brown, Washington Gladden, George A. Gordan, Albert G. Knudson, Henry Churchill King, Edgar S. Brightman, Shailer Mathews, Lyman Abbott, Harris Franklin Rall, Fosdick himself, and others. Modernism, Fosdick affirmed, had fought a necessary battle with a militant, obscurantist Fundamentalism which had sought to preserve the "fundamentals" of Christian orthodoxy and the principle of Scriptural infallibility from the encroachments of modern science and scholarship; and Fundamentalism had sought also (or been used) to preserve the economic and political status quo. But, Fosdick continued, it was now time to go "beyond Modernism," to confront and challenge twentieth-century culture with a deeper, sterner faith.

In that year, 1935, American Protestantism was already listening to the unfamiliar and terrible words of judgment of Reinhold and H. Richard Niebuhr and from across the ocean of Emil Brunner and Karl Barth. At the time of Tittle's death in 1949 still other voices were commanding attention: Paul Tillich, Nikolai Berdyaev, Martin Buber, Rudolph Bultmann, to cite only four men of awesome influence in the history of modern religious thought.

Tittle's reading lists and library holdings disclose that he made a valiant endeavor to keep abreast of contemporary theology and philosophy, European as well as American. He was not intellectually lazy. He wrestled in the solitude of his study with subtle minds. Nor was he an intellectual coward. He exposed his own theological convictions to the challenge of antithetical ideas. The task was formidable. Surely we must sympathize with every working minister who, nurtured on Bowne,[20] Clarke,[21] and James,[22] was then forced into encounters with linguistic analysis, dialetical theology, demythologization, and existentialism. Tittle died an early death, but the distance between the cordial Christian evolutionism of Henry Ward Beecher and the Biblical literalism of Dwight L. Moody of Tittle's youth and Niebuhr's dialectics, Tillich's

20. The Methodist Borden Parker Bowne's personal idealism was almost the official philosophy of American Methodism for nearly a half-century.

21. In his early career Tittle pronounced William Newton Clarke, a Baptist, America's greatest theologian. Clarke's theology had its sources in the Bible centered in Christ and evangelical Christian experience. For Tittle's assessment, see the *Columbus Evening Dispatch*, April 6, 1918, p. 5.

22. William James was clearly one of Tittle's heroes.

existentialism, and Bultmann's demythologizing is very far indeed; perhaps no further, however, than the distance between the charge up San Juan Hill and the nuclear death rained down on Hiroshima. Tittle is usually categorized as an evangelical liberal, and that strain of modern American theology has not so much been characterized by scholars as it has been caricatured.[23] We shall now attempt to see how in fact Tittle thought of God, man, and history, and how Tittle's thought clashed or merged with Fundamentalism, Modernism, neo-orthodoxy, existentialism, and what has been called the post-Christian secularity associated with Dietrich Bonhoeffer and those younger theologians of the 1960's who praised *The Secular City* and announced (again) "the death of God."

IV

How did Tittle think of God? For modern secular man the concept of "God" has become problematic. God is dead or missing in action or has become silent or become eclipsed or edged out of the world. This is not a fact about God, such as the honest old atheists asserted, but about people's experiences of God. God is absent from their lives and is therefore unreal. He may *once* have lived. He may *once* have reigned. But twentieth-century man need no longer reckon with God. Perhaps He has only slipped over the hill for a time. Perhaps He will break His silence and one day speak again. Perhaps, however, He is really gone.

Tittle agreed that many of the gods men once worshipped no longer lived. He agreed that the Christian Church over the centuries had set up conceptions of God unbelievable to modern man. And he agreed that modern man did not see or hear God and acted as though He were dead. But, for Tittle, God lived. If men did not see Him, it was because of the scales encrusting their eyes; if men did not hear Him, it was because they willed to listen to other voices. The restless anxiety of twentieth-century man is a consequence of his living apart from God. The demoniac history of the modern era is evidence not that God is obsolete, but of the consequences of men mocking Him.

Tittle was not much concerned to argue the question of God's existence; the old-line "proofs" were irrelevant. Intelligent people were no longer interested in the "argument from design" or other theistic deductions drawn from logic.[24] In this, Tittle was a child of the early

23. My favorite critique of this caricature is William R. Hutchinson's witty and incisive essay, "Liberal Protestantism and the 'End of American Innocence,'" *American Quarterly,* XV (Summer, 1963), 126-39.

24. See "The Christian Idea of God," *The First Church Pulpit,* Vol. II, No. 1, a sermon preached October 24, 1937.

twentieth-century Christocentric liberalism, holding with his hero William Newton Clarke, "Not that God is, but what God is, is the first point in Christian doctrine."[25] On a thousand instances Tittle affirmed, "We can bet our life that there is a God and that God is love."[26] On a thousand instances he advised, act *now* as though God lived, leap *now* from unfaith to faith, love thy neighbor and serve him *now*, for if you wait for prior proof of God's existence it is *you* who will not have lived. Tittle once suggested to some fraternity boys, instead of holding endless "bull sessions" debating the existence of God, why not proceed to act as though He lived, and perhaps in the action God would be encountered, as for example by striving to eliminate racial prejudice on their own campus.[27]

Writing in 1933, Tittle ticked off some of the gods created by man in man's image:

> It seems to be natural, if not inevitable, that human beings should think of Reality in terms of the dominant factor in their environment. Ancient man, living in a world of autocrats and slaves, pictured his God as an omnipotent, capricious tyrant. Medieval man, living in a world of feudal lords and serfs, pictures his God as a mighty potentate of a feudalistic character. When, after the Protestant Reformation, western society lost its unity, the birth of nationalism influenced men's conception of Reality to such an extent that a British sea captain, when being pursued by a Dutch man-of-war, felt sure that the wind would change in his favor, for, said he, God cannot desert a fellow countryman. The appearance of political democracy likewise registered itself in a congenial conception of Reality. The monarch of the skies was shorn of much of his power and made responsible to some extent to the wishes of his subjects. Men who refused to submit to taxation without representation refused also to submit to damnation without explanation. Today, once more, the dominant factor in man's environment is influencing his conception of Reality. A machine-made civilization is producing a mechanistic theory of life and the world. In some quarters we are being told that man himself is but a highly complicated machine, differing from other machines in degree but not in kind; able, to be sure, to reproduce himself and to some extent to repair himself when he gets out of

25. Quoted in H. Shelton Smith, Robert T. Handy, Lefferts A. Loetscher, *American Christianity: An Historical Interpretation with Representative Documents* (New York: Charles Scribner's Sons, 1963), II, 27.

26. See for example, "On Betting Your Life," typed MS, a sermon preached September 28, 1947. "Religion is betting your life that there is a God," is a phrase of Donald Hankey's often quoted by Tittle.

27. *The Foolishness of Preaching* (New York: Henry Holt & Co., 1930), p. 46.

order, but possessing no more of real freedom than is possessed by an automobile. Some, indeed, would have it that we must think of the universe itself as a kind of infinite machine."[28]

For Tittle, the God who lives was not a tribal deity, the god of battles, the Yahweh of the Old Testament, concerned with the fate only of His chosen people.[29]

For Tittle, the God who lives was not an Apocalyptic Judge waiting in the heavens to do his ultimate vengeance. Tittle remembered that in his youth Christians lived in terror of such a God. From pulpits throughout the land, mothers were told that unbaptized babies would suffer forever the torments of hell; fathers were told that for prodigal sons who died "out of Christ" there was no hope throughout all the unending future; parents were told that their child who drowned while swimming on Sunday had incurred the Almighty's wrath and suffered His retribution.[30] The liberal theology that emerged at the turn of the century was a reaction to the intellectual obsolescence of the old ortho-doxy, but almost equally important, it was a rejection of a theology of terror. A God who caused little children to cry themselves to sleep at night for fear of Him and of His hell was an offense to Tittle's moral sense—and he rejoiced in the death of such a God.

For Tittle, the God who lives is not the Deist's watchmaker who made His watch (the universe), set it a-going, and had "nothing to do with it save wind it up every twenty-four hours and repair it when it gets out of order." Laplace's announcement that he had searched the heavens with his telescope and found no trace of God would in the twentieth century cause little consternation. And why should it, asked Tittle, for modern men know "that the universe is not the snug little three-story affair which the ancients supposed it to be (heaven above, earth beneath, and water under the earth); that it is, in fact, a galaxy of universes, every one of which is unimaginably vast."[31] Elsewhere Tittle said, "No intelligent person today thinks of God as being 'up there.' The modern mind finds itself driven to think of God as immi-nent in the world process and does not stand, as it were, outside the world in the manner of a carpenter working on a house."[32] But if God is not "up there" or "out there," where is He? It does not much help

28. *Ibid.*, pp. 140-41.

29. *Ibid.*, p. 36; *What Must the Church Do to Be Saved?*, p. 55.

30. *What Must the Church Do to Be Saved?*, p. 51.

31. *Where Is God?*, a sermon preached January 15, 1933 (pamphlet).

32. "The Problem of Loneliness," *The First Church Pulpit*, Vol. VI, No. 9, a sermon preached October 31, 1943.

to be told that He is everywhere. Such a "statement leaves us cold; for a God who is declared to be everywhere appears to be nowhere in a form which the mind can grasp or the heart respond to. He appears to be as impersonal as a map, as vague as the fourth dimension, as unapproachable as infinity."[33]

For Tittle, the God who lives is not the Efficient Executive portrayed by Bruce Barton. He is not the kindly Man Upstairs portrayed by hawkers of peace of mind. He is not a Cosmic Bellhop waiting for men to whistle for His services. And he is not a kind of Oblong Blur murkily perceived by the more feckless Modernists. It is important to recognize that evangelical liberals such as Fosdick and Tittle found these conceptions of God as blasphemous as did Barth and Niebuhr. "The jolly good fellow conception of God," declared Tittle in 1930, "is just about the most sentimental and superficial idea that has been set afloat in modern thinking. If God is love it will not be well with anybody He condemns."[34] And with what assurance can one pray, "What is Thy will, O Thou Kind-of-an-oblong-blur"?[35] Time and again Tittle censored liberal Protestantism for being "anaemic with but little power over the hearts of men."[36]

For Tittle, the God who lives is not the "wholly other" of Karl Barth, the radically transcendent God of neo-orthodoxy. Tittle read Barth and paid him high tribute: "Karl Barth, as perhaps no other man in our time, has uttered with conviction that greatest of all words—God. And it is, indeed, no small sensation—or comfort—to discover that in this skeptical, floundering, discouraged world there is a man of profound learning and first-rate intelligence who, literally, has no doubts concerning God; for whom, on the contrary, God is the one, great dependable reality!"[37] In private letters, too, Tittle honored the great European theologian, "with whom I partly, but not wholly, agree!"[38] Yet, while acknowledging the deepening correctives of neo-orthodoxy, Tittle remained essentially an unrepentent liberal. In his 1932 Lyman Beecher Lectures Tittle mentioned Barth's theology, concluding, however, that a metaphysical dogma divorced from history and resting upon sheer external authority could be expected to function only in some mechanical

33. *Where Is God?*, a sermon preached January 15, 1933 (pamphlet).
34. *Foolishness of Preaching*, p. 97.
35. "On Trusting God," *The First Church Pulpit*, Vol. II, No. 2, a sermon preached October 31, 1937.
36. *Jesus After Nineteen Centuries* (New York and Cincinnati, Ohio: Abingdon Press, 1932), p. 124.
37. *Discovery and Revelation*, a sermon preached April 29, 1934 (pamphlet).
38. Letter from Tittle to Kenneth T. Whitby, December 17, 1948.

or miraculous fashion.[39] In his Ayer Lectures three years later Tittle presented a reasoned and sympathetic analysis of Barth, but again rejected Barth's transcendent God of "sheer mysterious power" and the "absolute discontinuity" Barth draws between God and man.[40] Tittle could not bring himself to believe in a God who played hide-and-seek with man, "of necessity a one-sided affair in which man is forever seeking and God is forever hiding Himself."[41] "It is," Tittle wrote in 1939, "I think, a travesty of Christianity to assert that the God of Christian faith is but transcendent and incalculable power. Moreover, such an assertion may be the expression not so much of confident faith as a secret and sickening doubt. (I do not say that it necessarily is but only that it may be.) Desperately wanting to believe in a God who is more than a match for intrenched and triumphant evil, and being none too sure that there is such a God, one may nervously proclaim the transcendence of God in terms of sheer otherness and arbitrary, unlimited power."[42] On another occasion Tittle quoted approvingly Canon Raven's biting description of neo-orthodoxy as "an inverted Pharisaism that prides itself on its own damnation, exalts Satan as lord of the earth, and thanks God for the good news of original sin."[43] Without exception, those individuals closest to Tittle agree that he listened attentively to the voices of "crisis theology" and that his own preaching deepened in the crisis decades of the 1930's and 1940's, but that to the end he remained in the tradition of evangelical liberalism.[44] A story told of old Father Taylor, the famous Methodist chaplain of the Mariners' House of the Boston Port Society, is to the point. Discussing the doctrine of God with a prominent Boston Calvinist, Father Taylor finally growled, "Well, as far as I can see, you and I are in perfect agreement. There is only this minor difference between us; the Being whom you call God I call my Devil!"[45] On more than one instance Tittle could only say of

39. *Jesus After Nineteen Centuries*, pp. 23-25, 140.
40. *A Way To Life* (New York: Henry Holt & Co., 1935), pp. 20-25.
41. "The Christian Idea of God," *The First Church Pulpit*, Vol. II, No. 1, a sermon preached October 24, 1937.
42. *Christian Century*, LVI (June 21, 1939), 796.
43. "The Message of the Church in the Post-War World," typed MS, a convocation sermon preached at Garrett Biblical Institute, October 10, 1944.
44. Author's interviews with Dr. and Mrs. Harris Franklin Rall, Evanston, Ill., August 24, 1959; Mrs. Bernice Wolseley, Evanston, Ill., July 13, 1960; Bishop Ralph Magee, Evanston, Ill., August 31, 1959; Paul Schlipp, Evanston, Ill., August 27, 1959; Horace G. Smith, Evanston, Ill., August 17, 1959; Joseph Thomas, Evanston, Ill., July 29, 1959; Kenneth F. Thompson, Wilmette, Ill., August 6, 1959; Glenna Myers Tittle, Evanston, Ill., July 31, 1959.
45. Quoted in Willard L. Sperry, "Liberalism and Neo-Orthodoxy," *Religion in Life*, XVI (Summer, 1947), 326.

the theology of Barth, Niebuhr, and Tillich (I am quite aware of the oversimplification of lumping these independent minds together): "Whatever it is, if carried to its logical conclusion, it would no longer be Christianity." Most Methodists, at least as late as the year of Tittle's death, concurred. Tittle's Methodist theological mentors, most especially Rall, McConnell, Knudson, and Edgar S. Brightman, resisted the gulf (as they saw it) neo-orthodoxy drew between God's radical transcendence and man's utter corruption.[46]

How, then, *did* Tittle think of God? Early in his First Church ministry Tittle drafted "A Personal Confession of Faith," beginning with the statement: "I believe in God. I believe that God is a personal power, infinitely greater than man, who evermore is making for good: for personal righteousness and social justice, for beauty, brotherhood, co-operation, and peace."[47] Late in his ministry he wrote a friend, "The Power behind the universe is a personal will, Christlike in character, making for good."[48] Repeatedly he asserted (borrowing from Haeckel) that the central question of all life is: "Is the universe friendly to man?" Repeatedly he replied (borrowing from Matthew Arnold) that "there is a Power not ourselves that makes for righteousness." And no quotation appears more frequently in his sermons than the words of Deuteronomy often cited by William James, "The eternal God is thy dwelling place, and underneath are the everlasting arms."[49]

For Tittle, the God who lives is a personal being. In a sermon appropriately entitled, "On Trusting God," he said:

Now, it is one of the glories of the Christian idea of God that it

46. For the limited penetration of American Methodism by neo-orthodoxy, see William J. McCutcheon, "Barth and the Methodist Masses," *Christian Advocate,* VI (November 8, 1962), 7-8; William J. McCutcheon, "Praxis: 'America Must Listen,'" *Church History,* XXXII (December, 1963), 452-72; William J. McCutcheon, "American Methodist Thought and Theology, 1919-60," in *The History of American Methodism,* ed. Emory Bucke (New York and Nashville, Tenn.: Abingdon Press, 1964), chap. xxx; William J. McCutcheon, "Theology of the Methodist Episcopal Church in the Interwar Period (1919-1939)" (Ph.D. dissertation, Yale Divinity School, 1960); Schilling, *Methodism and Society, passim.* For background, see Leland Howard Scott, "Methodist Theology in the Nineteenth Century." (Ph.D. dissertation, Yale University, 1954). For a working bibliography of Methodist thought, see Frederick A. Norwood, "Methodist Historical Studies, 1930-1959," *Church History,* XXXVII (December, 1959), 391-417 and XXXIX (March, 1960), 74-88.

47. *A Personal Confession of Faith,* pamphlet published by First Church, undated. Internal evidence suggests the credo was written in the 1920's.

48. Letter from Tittle to Thomas H. West, May 14, 1945.

49. These utterances appear so frequently in Tittle's preaching that it is unnecessary to provide specific citations.

can be lived. The Christian idea of God does not leave you with a bare abstraction of which you can form no definite idea, toward which you can take no attitude, about which you can feel nothing save, perhaps, a kind of awe, such as a dog may be supposed to feel when it bays at the moon. Nor does this Christian idea of God leave you with an impersonal process which, to be sure, you may study—and trust if you can—but with which you can have no personal relation. Tell me that God is the Absolute, the Unconditioned, the Timeless, the Eternal, and I may listen to you unmoved. Your words do not convey to me any impression of God such as might lead me to give three cheers or, more restrainedly, to say, "Here am I, Lord; send me." Or if you tell me that God is a kind of cosmic energy which creates and sustains the world, still I may feel unmoved to act differently than I am now acting. What could I do for or with "a kind of cosmic energy" save submit to it with as much grace as possible, even though it should appear (from my point of view) to be turning out things evil as well as good? But what if you should tell me that God is a personal spirit, Christlike in character, who is persistently and powerfully making for good?[50]

Again: "The question of supreme importance for us men and women is, of course, the question concerning God—whether the Power behind the universe is oblivious to us and our fate or is a personal being to whom we may cry, 'Abba, Father!' in the conviction that He knows and cares what happens to us, that he desires and seeks our highest good, and that He is adequate to every human situation. Is God an impersonal principle or force that merely accounts for the world as it is? Or is He a personal will, active in history making for good?"[51] Tittle's people were assured that the "Creator of the universe is aware of our existence, concerned with our welfare, and responsive to our call. The God of our faith is a personal being whom we may address as our Father in heaven."[52]

The God comprehended by Tittle was not absolute in the sense that He is wholly other. Being limited in His power from His prior decision to create man with freedom, He must live within this limitation. "Some things God cannot prevent in a world where men and women are given the power of choice. He cannot prevent the misuse of freedom."[53] We may not expect God to act contrary to His own nature as revealed in Christ; we may not pray for Him to suspend natural law so that we may

50. "On Trusting God," *The First Church Pulpit,* Vol. II, No. 2, a sermon preached October 31, 1937.

51. "Good News for the World," typed MS, a sermon preached June 18, 1944.

52. "The God of Our Faith," *Methodist Layman,* VIII (July, 1948), 1-6.

53. *A Mighty Fortress* (New York: Harper & Brothers, 1949), p. 111.

escape the consequences of our misuse of freedom.[54] "God will never do anything that is not Christlike: He never will be vindictive, unmerciful, unforgiving, or unkind. As the New Testament put it, 'If we are faithless, he remains faithful; for he cannot be untrue to himself.'" Because we are free we are free to sin, and in the resulting chaos not even God can save us from the consequences. "God will not undertake to save us from folly and its consequences by resorting to methods of coercion which would rob us of our manhood—every chance we now have to achieve goodness and greatness—and reduce us to the status of trained animals, whose performances are controlled by promises of food and threats of the lash."[55]

Though not totalitarian, neither was the God Tittle worshipped impotent. Men and nations are under His judgment—and not easily is He mocked. We are punished by our sins, not for them. The eternal God is our refuge, but He is not our escape from the consequences of our folly. These certitudes were stated by Tittle in scores of sermons. "We have God to fear in that we cannot hope to sin against truth and right and love and get away with it," were among the last words Tittle uttered from the First Church pulpit.[56] "If we *could* do evil year after year and get away with it," Tittle argued, "this would mean that the universe was completely indifferent to moral values and considerations. It would make mock of the belief that there is a God of righteousness and love."[57] God created us and gave us freedom, which we abuse, but God cares too much for us to let us do evil with impunity. God sets before us life or death; we must choose.[58]

Tittle was both a product of nineteenth-century theological liberalism and, in chastened form, one of its strongest proponents in the opening half of the twentieth century. The essence of this liberalism is the spirit of freedom. The freedom to search out God's truths in every area of life and learning and the freedom to accept every fresh revelation of His truth to man. Tittle's God was not "the Great Unknown," the passive object of an endless and hopeless quest; nor was He like Egypt's sphinx, silent, inscrutable, inactive.[59] Further, Tittle could not believe that only in one period of history did God speak directly to men and that only in

54. "Providence and the Individual," *Methodist Layman*, V (May, 1945), 1-6.
55. "On Trusting God," *The First Church Pulpit*, Vol. II, No. 2, a sermon preached October 31, 1937.
56. *Mighty Fortress*, p. 94.
57. "Providence and the Individual," *Methodist Layman*, V (May, 1945), 1-6.
58. "On Trusting God," *The First Church Pulpit*, Vol. II, No. 2, a sermon preached October 31, 1937.
59. *Discovery and Revelation*, a sermon preached April 29, 1934 (pamphlet).

the Bible could the authentic word of God be found and that after this supreme self-disclosure He retired into permanent hiding.

For one thing, Tittle was concerned that religion come to terms with the findings of modern science and scholarship. All too often Modernists conceived this to mean the accommodation if not capitulation of Christianity to scientism. For the older biblical infallibility a new final authority of science was substituted. The truth about God was to be discovered in the study of geology and astronomy, anthropology and sociology, psychology and linguistics, archaeology and physics, biology and zoology. Early in his ministry, in an era of heresy trials, anti-evolution laws, textbook censorship, and the hounding from the pulpit of liberal preachers by aggressive Fundamentalists, Tittle sought to demonstrate that there could be no warfare of science and religion when science and religion met in common devotion to truth, since all truth is ultimately one. Revelation that is purely arbitrary must give way to reason. Cherished myths, if proved by science and scholarship to be myths, must be discarded. The demand for miracles, "startling, law-defying stunts," as a condition of belief is an attribute of intellectual and spiritual immaturity.[60] As for the evolutionary hypothesis, that stumbling block to millions of the faithful, Tittle's favorite (but hardly original) device was to quote the lines of W. H. Carruth ("Each in His Own Tongue," 1909):

> A fire-mist and a planet
>   A crystal and a cell,
> A jellyfish and a saurian,
>   And caves where the cavemen dwell;
> Then a sense of law and beauty,
>   And a face turned from the
>   clod—
> Some call it Evolution,
>   And others call it God.

Tittle's preaching, especially in the Ohio years and in the 1920's at First Church, endeavored to adjust Christian faith to the modern intellect so that a man could be a Christian without throwing his mind away. Before smiling too condescendingly, it would be well to recall Henry Sloane Coffin's comment: "The younger men who now so freely castigate liberalism have never had to fight, as their fathers did, for the

60. *Can We Believe in Miracles?*, a sermon preached October 6, 1929 (pamphlet).

right to believe and to say the things they now take for granted."[61] Scores of individuals have testified in gratitude that Tittle set forth the Christian faith in terms that did not insult their intelligence, and that without his persuasive mediation of reason and revelation they would have left the church rather than jettison their minds. Some, of course, did leave the church, that is First Church, in anger over Tittle's apostasy from the "fundamentals" of the true faith. Indeed, as we know, he was branded as an "Anti-Christian."

Yet, though Tittle always welcomed new truths revealed by science and scholarship, he never maintained that the Christian faith rested alone on intellectual demonstration, and he never accepted Shailer Mathew's definition of Modernism as "the use of the methods of modern science to find, state and use the permanent and central values of inherited orthodoxy in meeting the needs of the modern world."[62] That is to say, Tittle never handed over to science final authority in matters of faith and he never was under the illusion that the scientific method could disclose the final truth about God. Tittle belonged less to the school of scientific modernism of Mathews and Henry Nelson Wieman with its interest in discovering general religious affirmations based on a "scientific world view" than to the school of evangelical liberalism of Rauschenbusch and Fosdick with its concern to relate the Christian faith in terms convincing to modern man. Both schools were called by the same term, "Modernism." It is a term historians use, and of necessity must continue to use, much as they would like to throw it out because of its ambiguity.

Tittle was not a Biblical literalist. He accepted the historical-critical method in the study of the Bible, and consequently he rejected the cherished Protestant belief of Scriptural inerrancy. No longer was it possible to read the Bible as an infallible scientific textbook or as an objective history of the ancient world. No longer was it possible to believe that "the human writers of the Bible were merely pens held in the hand of the Almighty, so that every word of the Old and New Testaments was a veritable word of God, fully representative of his thought and purpose."[63] Tittle was one of those charged by the Fundamentalists with laying impious hands on the sacred citadel of divine authority.

61. Quoted in Georgia Harkness, "The Theology of Dr. Rall," *Wesleyan Quarterly Review,* II (August, 1965), 143.

62. Quoted in Smith, *American Christianity,* II, 240.

63. *Discovery and Revelation,* pamphlet reprint of sermon preached April 29, 1934.

The charge is a misunderstanding of Tittle and, indeed, of most liberals. Tittle gave the Bible profound study. His sermons and prayers are steeped in the language of the Bible. In his later ministry almost always he preached from a Scriptural text. He urged his parishioners to practice a regular reading of the Bible. For Tittle, the Bible remained the divine revelation of the Word of God: God's supreme disclosure of Himself and of His authentic will for men. The Bible proclaims the deeds of God and records the experience of men who faithfully respond to Him. It is a book, said Tittle, "about God—what God is like, what God has done, what God is now doing and abundantly able to do for mankind."[64] Its truths are timeless. "After thousands of years the Twenty-third Psalm is still on millions of lips. Isaiah still is a living voice, as is also Saint Paul. And amid the breaking up of empires that are creations of human pride and greed, still speaks that supreme voice which said: 'I am the Way, the Truth, and the Life.' "[65]

In the Bible God reveals Himself through the history and experience of ancient Israel. To be sure, God's revelation of Himself is not limited to any one people or to any one period. He has not left any people without a witness to His reality and goodness, as the Bible itself declares. Nevertheless, "God was able through the history and experience of this uniquely gifted people to give to the world an incomparable revelation of Himself culminating in His supreme self-disclosure in Jesus Christ."[66] The Bible is the Word of God for the second reason that "God makes continued use of it to bring home to men the demands of His righteousness and the availability of His mercy. Reading the Bible you . . . find yourself confronted with God. Words written long ago by some prophet or psalmist or evangelist may of a sudden become God's word to you. A man opens the Bible and begins to read, and often, if not always, the passage that he is reading exposes his secret sin, stabs his conscience broad awake, calls him to repentance. Or, in a different case, he comes upon a passage that quiets his fears, brings him courage and comfort, enables him for the work he has to do."[67] Tittle was convinced that God speaks to us all in great literature, poetry, drama, and philosophy, but that no other literature "approaches the Bible as the Word of God to men."[68] A historical-critical approach to the Bible, therefore, did not for

64. "By All Means Celebrate Christmas," typed MS, a sermon preached December 24, 1939.

65. On Reading the Bible," *The First Church Pulpit*, Vol. VI, No. 12, a sermon preached December 5, 1943.

66. *Ibid.*

67. *Ibid.*

68. *Ibid.*

Tittle destroy its authority. To the contrary, because it was no longer necessary tortuously to explain away discrepancies or to swallow prescientific and unhistorical passages, it was possible to see more clearly God's revelation of Himself.

Divine imminence was a central belief of religious liberalism and Tittle, too, held that God speaks to men in the beauty of nature, in the moral order of the universe, in the evolutionary progression of history, and in great human souls—Socrates, Gautama, Confucius, Gandhi, as well as the Christian saints and martyrs. Early in his ministry he rather too frequently talked about finding God in the beauty of a sunset or in the poetry of Robert Browning or in the laboratory where truth is being discovered. As for history, "Through all the long, slow, costly process, will you not be able to discover the footprints of a living, loving, advancing God?"[69] This is an immanentism that borders on pantheism and is characteristic mostly of Tittle's early preaching. Yet he never swung to the other extreme of neo-orthodoxy's radically transcendent God. To the end Tittle believed that through the love of one's neighbor and in that love we meet God; that God calls man to be His partner in creating a better world; that God has a purpose He is working out in human history, though time and again men frustrate that purpose; that God sustains the moral order of the universe, though men continually violate that order and break themselves. God dwells in the world, works through it, cares what happens in it, shares its anguish and knows its joy. In the midst of a world at war, Tittle affirmed:

God works through conscience which, unless it is persistently stifled, cries out against sham and cowardice, injustice and cruelty. He works through the revelation of truth and through the appeal of love and sympathy. He works through consecrated individuals who, being responsive to His leading, gain new and important insights. He works through prophetic minorities who think and live ahead of their time. He works through great numbers of "ordinary" people who desire to do good in the world and who in their relations to others are just, merciful, and kind. He works through institutions that have no selfish ends to serve but are devoted to the welfare of the people. In a distinctive and most important way He works through the Church, which is the bearer of the Christian faith and tradition, which gives people the opportunity of worship, and which (at its best) ministers to their deepest needs. Above all, He works through His blessed Son, Jesus Christ our Lord, bringing home to men in

69. *The Religion of the Spirit* (New York and Cincinnati, Ohio: Abingdon Press, 1928), 128.

various ways the truth about the world and life which was made
manifest in him.[70]

V

At the very heart of evangelical liberalism, that is, at the very center
of Tittle's preaching, stood Jesus Christ. The man of Nazareth was not
simply a religious teacher of unparalleled purity and spirituality.
Through him, as through no one else in all history, God spoke and God
acted. In the life, teachings, death, and resurrection of Jesus Christ
there was revealed to men the surest clue to the nature of God and the
clearest example of what God called men to be. Fairly early in his
First Church ministry Tittle wrote that Christianity does not say that
Jesus is God, but rather "that Jesus was so much like God that he could
with perfect propriety and profound truth declare, 'He that hath seen
me hath seen the Father.' "[71] Seven years later he elaborated: "Contrary
to much popular thought, Christian faith has never asserted that Jesus
of Nazareth was God, the creative source and final goal of the world
and life. Certainly there is more in the God of the universe than ever
did or could appear in any human individual having a human body and
a human mind and all the limitations which inevitably go with these.
Christian faith never has equated Jesus of Nazareth and God the Father
Almighty. It has, however, confidently affirmed that in Jesus of Nazareth
the Almighty God expressed Himself with a fullness never seen or heard
before. To be sure, there had been other revelations of God in history,
in nature, in great and good individuals, and in human experience of
various kinds; but in Jesus the innermost thought and being of God
achieved, at long last, a complete and marvelous utterance."[72] A year
before his death Tittle preached these words:

> Christianity does not teach that Jesus was God. The historic
> phrase "the divinity of Christ," whatever else it may mean, does
> not signify that the Jesus of history was the God of the universe.
> In the New Testament, Jesus appears as a man among men. He
> knows hunger and thirst, grows weary and sleeps, confesses ignor-
> ance, asks questions, exhibits surprise, and is "in all points tempted
> like we are." He lays no claim to moral perfection, but to one
> who has addressed him as "Good teacher" he replies, "Why do you
> call me good? No one is good but God alone." Nor does he
> claim to be self-sufficient. He professes himself dependent on his

70. "The Eternal Refuge," *The First Church Pulpit*, Vol. V., No. 1, a sermon
preached September 20, 1942.
71. *Foolishness of Preaching*, p. 83.
72. "The Christian Idea of God," *The First Church Pulpit*, Vol. II, No. 1, a
sermon preached October 24, 1937.

Father in heaven, and seeks through prayer to attain understanding of the will of God and strength and courage to do it. In the New Testament the real manhood of Jesus is never questioned. Nor is it questioned in orthodox Christianity. What Christianity affirms concerning Jesus is that in him the eternal God entered fully into human life, to make himself known to us men and to work for our good. This conviction Christianity has set forth in various ways. It has said with Saint Paul: "God was in Christ reconciling the world unto himself." It has said with the author of the Fourth Gospel: "The word became flesh and dwelt among us full of grace and truth; we have beheld his glory, glory as of the only Son from the Father." It has said in the language of the Nicene Creed: "I believe in one God, the Father Almighty, maker of heaven and earth, and in one Lord, Jesus Christ, the only begotten Son of God—God of God, Light of Light, very God of very God . . . being of one substance with the Father by whom all things were made." In setting forth its faith about Jesus, Christianity uses the thought forms of a given age, as of course it must do if it is to be understood—a fact to be remembered when you come upon formulations of Christian faith that are no longer meaningful, or, indeed, intelligible to anyone untrained in theology. What is all-important here is not a particular form of words, but simply the faith, however stated, that in Jesus of Nazareth the eternal God drew near, to make himself known to us men and to work for our good.[73]

Tittle kept abreast of Biblical scholarship. He was quite aware that the New Testament's picture of Jesus could not be a photograph. Of course Jesus believed that people could be possessed of demons. Of course Jesus shared with his Jewish contemporaries a "strange apocalyptic hope."[74] "Let it plainly and boldly be said that in some respects Jesus does belong to the first century, not the twentieth."[75] Yet to the end Tittle insisted on the essential creditability of the Gospel accounts, and that through these accounts Jesus could be known. "Christianity is a historical religion," Tittle claimed, "not a religion based on general ideas about the world and life. It is founded upon fact—the fact of Christ and the religious experience of the early church—and claims to set forth an act of redemption which God has achieved for us men."[76] Jesus had never heard of Marx, Darwin, Freud, or Einstein, but "the awful suffering that may come of man's stupidity and of man's inhumanity to

73. "The Place of Christ in Christianity," *The First Church Pulpit*, Vol. IX, No. 17, a sermon preached March 14, 1948.
74. *Jesus After Nineteen Centuries*, p. 27; "The Living Christ," typed MS, a sermon preached May 3, 1936.
75. *Jesus After Nineteen Centuries*, pp. 26-27.
76. *The Gospel According to Luke* (New York: Harper & Brothers, 1951), p. .1

man" was as known to him as it is to us.[77] The miraculous elements in the Biblical story are not crucial. "What is important is the fact of Christ—his life and teachings, his love and devotion, his sacrifice and amazing triumph—not the mode of his coming into the world. On any view of his birth, it is possible to hold the faith: 'God was in Christ, reconciling the world unto himself.' "[78]

Tittle was leery of substituting for the word "Jesus" the more churchly title, "Our blessed Lord," for then "you *may* subtly pass from history to dogma, from a historic personality who made revolutionary ethical demands to a purely conventional confession which makes no demands that may not easily be met by a man who has money invested in whiskey or munitions." There were also perils in the phrase "the great Galilean," for then one "may go on to speak or write in a vague, sentimental fashion about the duty of being kind, yet feel under no compulsion whatsoever to face up to the full ethical demand of a life lived in the faith and spirit of Jesus."[79] The real question is not whether Jesus is Godlike but whether God is Christlike.[80]

Tittle acknowledged the presence in Jesus of something profoundly "numinous," agreeing with Horace Bushnell that "Christ differs from us, not in degree, but in kind."[81] Yet Tittle insisted on the real humanity of Jesus. To deny the humanity of Jesus is to lose his relevance for ordinary mortals. "If you tell me that Jesus was not human in the same sense in which I myself am human, must I not reply to you in something like dismay: 'You have taken away the Captain of my soul. I had hoped that some day I might become pure enough and brave enough to follow him. I had even dared to hope that some day I might become like him. But if the category to which I belong is essentially different from the category to which he belongs, I can no more hope to follow him than a plowhorse may hope to soar after an eagle; I can no more hope to become like him than a blade of grass may hope to resemble a sequoia.' "[82]

Does the death of Jesus represent a sacrifice made to propitiate an offended God? Is it the will of an inexorable creditor, demanding the payment of the last pound of flesh or the judgment of an eternal judge pronouncing the penalty decreed by an abstract justice?[83] No, "For

77. "The Living Christ," typed MS, a sermon preached May 3, 1936.
78. *Gospel According to Luke*, p. 4.
79. *The Wonder of Jesus*, a sermon preached December 24, 1933 (pamphlet).
80. *Ibid.*, p. 18.
81. Quoted in Smith, *American Christianity*, II, 262.
82. *Religion of the Spirit*, p. 32.
83. *If God Is Like Christ*, undated sermon (pamphlet).

Christianity the cross of Christ is the revelation of a love at the heart of the world that cares enough for us men and women to suffer and die in our behalf. And for Christianity God's love to us is the basic, all-compelling reason why we should love one another."[84] The uniqueness of Calvary was in Christ, not in the cross. The cross remains a "perpetual reminder of the awful odds which human faith is sometimes obliged to pay."[85] In Tittle's view, Jesus did everything he could to avoid martyrdom, short of renouncing his mission. He submitted to crucifixion only because doing otherwise would have meant deserting his followers and betraying his cause. Jesus did not in the first place come to die; he died as a consequence of living a life wholly committed to doing God's will.[86]

The resurrection of Christ may be accepted as fact, believed Tittle. Apart from it there is no accounting for the Christian Church. Without the resurrection, Christianity is an illusion. Tittle, however, broke from the dogma of Christ's physical resurrection, arguing that the true faith does not require adherence to the belief that Christ after his death appeared in a body of flesh and blood. Patently, to Tittle the major portions of the Apostles' Creed were a stumbling block. A reviewer of *The Gospel According to Luke* claimed that Tittle "doesn't like that business about the glorified Lord eating a boiled fish" and that Tittle merely "holds that somehow or other there was some sort or other of a resurrection, whatever can be understood by that word."[87] Among the last words preached by Tittle are these: "If Christ was indeed raised from the dead, then life is not meaningless and futile but has set before it an end, a goal, a triumph in which the human spirit can rejoice." The worst that life may inflict can be faced "without dismay by those for whom human history is the outworking of divine purpose, a purpose of good which cannot be worked out fully amid the accidents and tragedies of earth but which will have its consummation in the eternal kingdom of God."[88]

The parallel between how Tittle thought of Jesus in the 1920's, 1930's, and 1940's with what the younger theologians of the 1960's seem to be saying must not be pressed too hard, but certain similarities are interesting. Jesus is the man for others. His real humanity speaks to us today. We must shape our lives by the example of his life as we know him from the Gospels. We should stop talking about transcendence and talk about involvement. The proper focus of a restored religion is

84. *Mighty Fortress*, p. 155.
85. *Foolishness of Preaching*, pp. 286-87.
86. *Gospel According to Luke*, pp. 247ff.
87. *Cresset*, February, 1952, clipping in Tittle Collection.
88. *Mighty Fortress*, p. 105.

already available; its name is Jesus. We are summoned to follow Jesus as the exemplar and paradigm of conduct—which means, for today, total commitment to the love and service of our fellow man. Christianity is to be understood in the ethical terms of sacrifice, suffering, service. If we want to know about Jesus, then get involved in the suffering of others, get hurt in the ordeal of service. If we want to encounter God, then live a "worldly" life and so participate in the suffering of God. Not where I breathe, but where I love, I live. The place to be—the place of Christ—is in the city with both the needy neighbor and the enemy. "To be a Christian," says Bonhoeffer, "does not mean to be religious in a particular way, to cultivate some particular form of asceticism (as a sinner, a penitent or a saint), but to be a man. It is not some religious act which makes a Christian what he is, but participation in the suffering of God in the life of the world."[89]

The old evangelical liberals comprehended that it is in the human life of Jesus that the Word is revealed to men in its fullness. And they understood, too, the pertinency of the life and teachings of Jesus to this world at this moment, for as Tittle asked, "If it is not in this world that we are to love our enemies, in what world are we to love them?"[90] Token involvement in life would not suffice. "Nothing," said Tittle, "is more characteristic of respectability than its habit of limited concern."[91]

VI

How did Tittle think of man? Writing on the eve of the Second World War, he affirmed:

> Recent events have disclosed depths of evil in the human heart which surely forbid a facile optimism as to the immediate future of the human race. Yet I cannot go with those who, in revolt against a superficial optimism, are now proclaiming a dogmatic pessimism. If man is but an accidental product of a cosmic process that is without meaning and goal then, in view of his present predicament, there may indeed be occasion for despair. But if man, as Christian faith maintains, is at least potentially a son of God, it is then not merely a question of what he is at the moment; it is also a question of what, by the grace of God, he can hope to become. Jesus viewed human beings in the light of

89. I have made what I think to be a valiant attempt and know to be a vain attempt to "keep up" with what the theologians of the 1960's seem to be saying. It should be unnecessary here to append a bibliographical essay. The writings of Dietrich Bonhoeffer, executed by the Nazis in 1945, did not become well known in America until after Tittle's death.
90. "A Word That Jesus Made Unforgettable," typed MS, a sermon preached February 16, 1941.
91. *Foolishness of Preaching*, p. 114.

their possibilities. His followers should not be content to view them merely in the light of their present cruelties and stupidities. And they certainly should not attempt to set limits to the grace of God. Man, no doubt, is a sinner in need of redemption. Yet the most significant fact about him is not, I think, his tendency to sin but rather his capacity to respond to the redeeming love of God. "Be not deceived: neither fornicators, nor idolaters, nor adulterers, nor effeminate, nor abusers of themselves with men, nor theives, nor covetous, nor drunkards, nor evilers, nor extortioners, shall inherit the kingdom of God. And such were some of you: but ye were washed, but ye were sanctified, but ye were justified in the name of the Lord Jesus Christ, and in the Spirit of our God." For me, the second part of this statement appears more significant than the first.[92]

Nothing was more characteristic of the liberal theology with which Tittle was associated than its high estimate of human nature, centering in belief in the worth of each person as a child of God. "Reverence for personality," "dignity of the individual," "sacredness of human life" were phrases worn almost smooth by repeated handling, and the text, "Of how much more worth is a man than a sheep," was oft-cited. This profound conviction, drawn from the belief that man bore in his being the stamp of the eternal, the *imago Dei*, and from the example of Jesus' loving concern for all persons, undergirded liberalism's social passion. Any economic system based on the exploitation of men's bodies, any caste system based on the violation of men's personalities, any political system based on the expendability of human life was a defiance of God's will and God's Word as revealed in Jesus Christ. Yet it was on precisely this question of human nature that neo-orthodoxy found liberalism most vulnerable and, in fact, un-Biblical. Man has entirely too good an opinion of himself. Chronically sinful man is unable to know a wholly transcendent God in any way or to approach Him the least bit, except as God chooses to make himself known to man and to approach man. God so chooses, being constantly faithful to incorrigibly rebellious man, but the bridge between sovereign God and wretched man is forged by God alone. It is pretentious of man to assume he can reason or will himself from sin to unsin; it is utopian of man to assume the Kingdom of God can be established in history; it is fatuous of man to assume that history is redemptive. Injustice, violence, catastrophe are not simply mistakes, results of ignorance or cultural lag, or the work of peculiarly wicked individuals, but rather are bound into the very existence of the self. Natural man is not innately good and inherently perfectable, wait-

92. *Christian Century*, LVI (June 21, 1939), 796-97.

ing only for social engineering and scientific planning (and moralistic preaching) to work their wonders. Even if the Barths and Niebuhrs had never spoken a single thundering word, the blithe confidence in man held by much of turn-of-the-century liberalism could not have been long sustained in the twentieth century—save only by the most shallow and/or blind liberals. (That such a shallow and/or blind liberalism partially lived on even after the chastening lessons of depression, totalitarianism, total war, and cold war has been documented in many withering articles and books.)

Tittle was not such a liberal, nor were many of Methodism's leaders. His (and their) position mediated between a one-sided, Pelagian stress on human goodness and freedom and an equally one-sided, Calvinistic, deterministic conception of divine sovereignty. Man's nature is neither so good that he can avoid sin by his own unassisted will nor so corrupt that he has lost all freedom. He has real freedom of choice, and so can accept or reject the divine grace, but this freedom is itself not an inherent capacity, but a gift of God.[93]

As we know, Tittle readily accepted the evolutionary hypothesis, as did almost the entire educated ministry of his generation, and though the hypothesis confounded the orthodox view of man's creation, for Tittle Darwin was not a racking question. Late in his ministry Tittle said: "Christianity has no quarrel with evolution. The evolutionary view, that man had a lowly origin, has, after all, nothing on the biblical view that 'God formed man out of the dust of the ground'—which ought to satisfy the most thorough-going evolutionist! But Christianity insists that man *is* a creation of God, and not the chance product of a blind process. Furthermore, Christianity believes that man is made in the spiritual image of God."[94] Thus, though accepting evolution, Tittle unwaveringly insisted that man came into being as a result of God's creative action.

Tittle repeatedly, tirelessly, vigorously rejected the naturalistic view, so commanding in American literature in the opening decades of the twentieth century, and in the sciences and social sciences, and not the least in Freudian psychology, that man is an animal and nothing more, differing from brute creation only by having a superior brain; a view that reduced man to a tiny lump of impure carbon and water, a creature as helpless to control his destiny as a sick fly clinging to the wind-

93. Schilling, *Methodism and Society*, p. 116.
94. "Man as Christianity Sees Him," *The First Church Pulpit*, Vol. IX, No. 15, a sermon preached February 29, 1948.

ward side of Mount Everest. Rather, argued Tittle, man is a marvelous mixture of dust and divinity.[95]

Unacceptable also to Tittle was a totally anthropocentric view of the human situation. That man is alone in a universe unaware of his existence is a heroic posture. The Bertrand Russells have noble aspirations for man, and if man is the sole custodian of his ideals, at least humanism is not lacking in idealism. Yet in humanism there is much posturing. In light of the demoniac events of the modern era, how damning it is to pronounce that man is the measure of all things; and how presumptuous it is to say that man may (or will) pull himself up by his own bootstraps. "A religion which begins by denying the existence of God and affirming the sufficiency of man," said Tittle, ends by denying the significance of man and affirming the futility of life."[96] Contrary to the fashionable indictment, the evangelical liberals were not unaware of man's flawed nature. Man knows only too well, observed Tittle in words reminiscent of Freud as well as of Lincoln, what it means to be "a house divided against itself."[97] No serious Christian thinker has ever supposed that man is a completely rational creature. The most intelligent of men are possessed by an inordinate love of self. "Nor does Christianity suppose that all man needs for the realization of his true destiny is a good education, that is the illusion of modern humanism; or that all he needs is a favorable social environment, that is the illusion of communism. Christianity is far too realistic to believe either of these things. Christianity knows that highly educated people, and people living in the suburbs of Chicago, such as Evanston and those north of us, may be swept off their feet completely by the irrational forces of fear and pride and prejudice and selfishness." "Yesterday there were many among us," Tittle remembered, "especially in our own country, who had no doubt of man's ability to solve his problems by his own efforts alone. He would conquer poverty. He would end war. He would rid himself of diseases of the body and disorders of the mind. By increasing mastery of his glands he would even rid himself of moral ills. . . . But this confident expectation of yesterday has been shattered by events. The fact is that man is never a completely rational animal who only needs to see what is true and right, who if he sees what he ought to do can be depended upon to go straightway and do it. Man's

95. *A World That Cannot Be Shaken* (New York and London: Harper & Brothers, 1933), p. 23.

96. *Living in History,* a sermon preached May 11, 1930 (pamphlet).

97. "The Meaning and Way of Salvation," *The First Church Pulpit,* Vol. IX, No. 18, a sermon preached March 21, 1948.

reason is not only limited by his finitude; it is corrupted and distorted by his egoism, his unholy love of self."[98] On another occasion Tittle said: "Our modern notion that human nature is inherently good and needs only to be released from social imprisonments and psychological inhibitions is proving to be almost if not quite as false as was that medieval notion which held that human nature is inherently bad and needs everlastingly to be repressed. . . . The fact of the matter appears to be that human nature is neither inherently good nor inherently bad but inherently indeterminate, containing the possibility of both good and evil—of good so good that it deserves to be called divine and of evil so evil that it can only be called devilish."[99] Tittle often returned to the theme of the plasticity of human nature. If human nature is fixed, there is very little hope for you or me—a fact, he added wryly, "which may not trouble us very much but is likely to prove a distinct disappointment to those who are obliged to live with us!"[100]

Sin involves a rupture of man's fellowship with God. For Tittle, this broken relationship was far less a consequence of man's sins of the flesh than those of the spirit. Pride and self-centeredness were more perilous to the soul than concupiscence or gluttony. It is revealing that Tittle devoted few sermons to such subjects as prohibition but many to Pharisaism.

However much Tittle repudiated the Niebuhrian and also the Nietzschean view of man, it is interesting that he, too, saw man as a free being. "Take away from human beings all power of choice, force them to think what is true and do what is right," Tittle believed, "and you will have a world in which there are no sinners; you will also have a world in which there are no saints. Speaking for myself, I would rather live in a world in which there are a lot of sinners and a few saints than in a world all of whose inhabitants, however intellectually and morally correct, were, after all, nothing more than plastic puppets manipulated by celestial strings."[101] Life is tragic because man is at once a son of God and a sinner who has misused the freedom God gave him.[102] And again: "Human beings are entrusted with a measure of freedom, as they

98. "The Church and Human Salvation," typed MS, a sermon preached October 19, 1941.
99. "The Practice of Morality and the Celebration of Religion," typed MS, a sermon preached November 15, 1931.
100. "God and Human Nature," typed MS, a sermon preached February 10, 1935.
101. *Religion of the Spirit,* p. 60.
102. "The Christian View of Tragedy," typed MS, a lecture delivered at Ohio Wesleyan, April, 1940.

must be if they are to be men and not robots. They can, therefore, do evil. But, as God lives, they cannot get away with it."[103] Tittle repudiated the doctrine of original sin. Rather, he said, every man is his own Adam; sin originates from nothing besides man's own corrupted will, though a man broken by social conditions—by poverty, oppression, exploitation, ignorance—is less free than other men to will to escape the bondage of sin. As we know, one of the lasting glories of the Social Gospel was its dawning recognition that men are damned by social conditions, that we sin by syndicate, that we rarely sin against God alone.

Is it God's will for men to escape from the bondage of sin? To this question, Tittle repeatedly gave a good Methodist answer. Christians live by faith, not by existential anxiety. It is permissible to believe in man not because we overestimate him but because we do not underestimate what God can do with him. It does not add to God's glory to diminish man. The supreme value ascribed to persons is not inherent in human nature as such, but rooted in man's relation to God. The dignity of man is rooted in the destiny to which God has called him. To set man and God radically against each other is to deny that God can really enter human life. It is true that man cannot save himself, but it is contrary to the New Testament to say that God saves men either contrary to or in absence of human volition. Man's redemption is not achieved by his being saved from this world, but in being saved in this world. As Tittle (and Methodism) saw it, men are made new in Christ Jesus. It is God's purpose that men be blessed, that they grow in grace and stature, that they become perfect in love. Those who see God, as Nels Ferré states, are a people who are clean unto the Lord. They are pruned trees which bear much fruit; they bear the fruit of the spirit. Nothing short of perfection, affirmed Wesley, Christlikeness in thought, word, and deed, can measure God's loving purposes for us. Faith in the Christian sense, said Tittle endlessly, is not mere intellectual assent to certain theological dogmas. It "calls for a momentous decision—the decision to have done once and for all with selfish aims and purposes and to commit oneself fully to God. . . ."[104] Men *desperately* need to be saved. The "good news which Christianity brought to the world was the proclamation of God's marvelous action for the salvation of men. 'God was in Christ reconciling the world unto himself.' "[105]

103. "A Hopeful View of History," typed MS, undated.
104. "The Meaning and the Way of Salvation," *The First Church Pulpit,* Vol. IX, No. 18, a sermon preached March 21, 1948.
105. "Can Human Being Be Made Over?" *The First Church Pulpit,* Vol. IV, No. 8, a sermon preached September 28, 1941.

Man cannot save himself by a mere act of will any more than a man can stop trembling from fright merely by telling himself that he ought not be afraid.[106] "Positive thinking" will not save us, as surely the events of the twentieth century demonstrate. But the good news of the Gospel is that God can save us if we will turn to Him in penitence and trust, not only in the sense of pardoning our offenses but even in the sense of creating within us a new mind and a new heart.[107]

Yet not even God can save us against our will. "God cannot bring us into right relation with himself unless and until we repent of our sins. And here it is necessary that we should see clear, very clear indeed. If the final reality with which we have to deal is Christ-like in character, then the sins we have to repent of in order to be in right relation with God are not only profanity, drunkenness, and sexual immorality, but also greed and selfishness and pettymindedness, all hate and uncharitableness, including the spreading of gossip, and snobbery, racial prejudice, contempt of others, and the treatment of others merely as tools for the production of a comfort and a culture in which they themselves have no chance to share. These all are sins in the sight of God, and we shall have to repent of them if we are to have life and have it abundantly."[108] In an early credo Tittle penned words to which he clung throughout his life: "I believe that the methods of God are 'judgment' and 'redemption.' There is in the universe a moral order which man, in his ignorance or selfishness, may disregard, but not with impunity. Soon or late, 'the wages of sin is death,' the price of greed and injustice is catastrophe. That is the judgment of God upon all iniquity—a judgment which serves to discipline and educate the race. But hand in hand with judgment comes redemption—the revelation of truth, the inspiration of beauty, the healing and heartening of love. Human lives are changed, they know not always how, and through transformed lives the world itself is transformed. . . ."[109]

VII

"Whenever I see a Methodist," reported a Washington statesman, "I say to myself, 'There goes a man who really believes that some day the world is going to begin to live happily ever afterward.'" There is

106. Letter from Tittle to Thomas H. West, May 14, 1945.
107. "Can Human Beings Be Made Over?" *The First Church Pulpit*, Vol. IV, No. 8, a sermon preached September 28, 1941.
108. "The Meaning and the Way of Salvation," *The First Church Pulpit*, Vol. IX, No. 18, a sermon preached March 21, 1948.
109. *A Personal Confession of Faith*, pamphlet published by First Church, undated. Internal evidence suggests the credo was written in the 1920's.

a story that early in the century a YMCA secretary closed a prayer on the positive note, "Cheer up, God, we are coming to help you!" And Rufus Jones tells of admiring a Quaker farmer's handsome lands, saying "You and God certainly have worked wonders together with this property." To which the farmer replied, "You should have seen the place when God was working it alone." These oft-quoted little anecdotes are supposed to reveal the anthropocentricity and utopianism of Social Gospel liberalism with its (alleged) faith in inevitable progress, its confidence in human goodness, its view of God and man as co-partners (with God as the junior partner) in the establishment of the Kingdom of God in history. Certainly Social Gospel liberalism at its shallowest did see history as redemptive, squeezing out sin, overcoming and resolving the contradictions and ambiguities of the human enterprise; and if progress was not quite automatic, surely the future would hold more of cosmos than chaos. Certainly some old liberals said with Lyman Abbott, "what Jesus was, humanity is becoming." Certainly some Modernists thought their labors and sacrifices contributed directly to the building of the Kingdom, not the eternal transcendent Kingdom of Augustine or the eschatological Kingdom of early Christianity, but the glorious reign of love on earth, and that this grand consummation would take place if not next year, at least the year after.

Anyone who has dipped into the record will recognize an element of validity in this description of early twentieth-century Protestant liberalism; yet anyone who has studied what Rauschenbusch, Fosdick, and Tittle actually said will discern a lot of straw in this "liberal man." Tittle had much to say about the Christian interpretation of history, much to say about the Kingdom of God, and much to say about man's role in the cosmic drama. Early in his ministry, in particular, Tittle's preaching was laced with illusions about the past and utopian expectations of the future. But by 1939 he had arrived at the following position, one far removed, to be sure, from that of neo-orthodoxy, but surely one far less simplistic than neo-orthodoxy charged:

> The Kingdom of God I take to be the complete and perfect rule of God, not externally imposed but inwardly accepted by human beings who feel bound and glad to live in a relationship of love to God and to one another. Such a condition, as I now see, is a religious and moral absolute that can never be fully realized in history. This apprehension, I frankly confess, came to me first as a shock; but I now recognize very great value in it. The Kingdom of God, viewed as an absolute, may serve as an ideal by which to judge every social order that has appeared or may ever appear in history. It may serve as a check upon human

pride, including the pride of the social reformer. It may serve as a source of divine discontent with any social achievement, reminding human idealists that even "the best of social orders" falls short of embodying the complete and perfect rule of God. It may greatly serve to prevent what in our time has all too often occurred—the ascription of a divine sanction to social programs and panaceas that reflect the "wisdom" of men but not, as it presently appears, the wisdom of God.

To say that the Kingdom of God can never fully come on earth is not to say that proximate goals in history may rightly be denied and betrayed by an otherworldliness that abandons its historic task and leaves the future of man on earth in the hands of political and economic barbarism. In my view, God himself is working in history for the salvation of individuals and, *therefore*, for the salvation of the "world" itself—those political institutions, social customs, and economic practices that so largely condition the spiritual development of men. On any other view, I can see no meaning in the prayer: "Thy kingdom come. Thy will be done on earth as it is in heaven."

In history, God, I believe, is making for righteousness and will not tolerate unrighteousness; he is making for justice and will not stand for injustice; he is making for brotherhood, "increasing interdependence and cooperation in the world." Certain it is that we moderns are not being permitted to live securely behind our national and racial barriers. We are discovering that the wages of greed is war, at once loathsome and futile; that the reward of selfishness and injustice is economic disaster. Held back by historic fears and hates and also by hope of private gain, we nevertheless are being moved, by forces stronger than ourselves, to extend our horizon and to have some regard for the rights and needs of our fellow men all the world around.

The Kingdom of God is the gift of God, as is life itself and all that supports it. But God in history works through men. When it comes to the achievement of a historic justice and peace, God is necessarily dependent upon human cooperation. In history, there are things which not even God can do until men consent to work with him, not against him. Hence, the imperative need for the church to confront the world, including a half-pagan Christiandom, with the religious and moral demands of the Kingdom of God.[110]

Tittle never—not even in his early, most hopeful years—advanced a belief in automatic, inevitable progress. The "absurdity of that idea is now being proclaimed on every continent and on every sea."[111] Indeed, none of the great spokesmen of Protestant liberalism ever held that man

110. *Christian Century*, LVI (June 21, 1939), p. 797.
111. "The Unfinished Task," *The First Church Pulpit*, Vol. V, No. 8, a sermon preached May 30, 1943.

was effortlessly riding an evolutionary escalator. "The kingdom of God is always but coming," said Rauschenbusch. The goal of history is a "flying goal, an ever new heaven, an ever new earth," said Tittle.[112] Tittle accepted the predictions of science that one day the earth would cool off, leaving the silence of death; that one day the earth will be covered with ice, as its poles are now. That is, long before Hiroshima Tittle accepted the possibility of the absolute death of all life on earth.

What Tittle obdurately did refuse to accept was the meaninglessness of history or the absolute helplessness of man, that man's struggle for life was nothing more than "a trouble of ants in the gleam of a million million suns." "Granted that earth can never be heaven," he once said, "it hardly follows we should allow it to become hell."[113] Again: "But even though on the plane of history man will never succeed in creating a perfect society, it does not follow that his attempt to do so is vain, for attempting to do so he brings out the best in himself. And what is more, according to Christianity the purpose of God is not confined to the plane of history; the purpose of God is not exhausted in the ebb and flow of earthly tides or historical processes."[114] Tittle wacked the Niebuhrians for their (alleged) "dogmatic pessimism," who appear to stand and pray thus with themselves, "God, I thank Thee that I am not as the rest of men—stupid optimists, would-be reformers, social gospelers— or even as this pacifist. Twice in the week I wrote an article proving that there is no hope for the world."[115]

On many occasions, Tittle affirmed the Kingdom of God is both "among you" and "within you," and that it cannot be a social order unless it is first within men's hearts.[116] The Kingdom of God *is*, and "what is required of us is that we shall apprehend it and desire it and receive it."[117] The Kingdom of God is both future and present, and some people even now are entering into it—"not the self-righteous, to be sure, nor the cynical and unbelieving, but the truly humble and penitent, including publicans and harlots."[118] Among the final words to come from Tittle's pen were these: "We do not know what the future

112. "A Protestant View of Religion," *World Tomorrow*, XVI (March 29, 1933), 307-8.
113. *Christians in an Unchristian Society* (New York: Association Press, 1940), pp. 15-16.
114. "Inner Satisfactions of Christian Living," typed MS, a sermon preached January 19, 1936.
115. "The Triumph of God," typed MS, a sermon preached March 28, 1940.
116. *Gospel According to Luke*, p. 187.
117. "Will the New Paganism Win?" *Current Religious Thought* (May, 1941), p. 28.
118. *Gospel According to Luke*, pp. 113-14.

holds for mankind upon earth. But if it be true that in Jesus of Nazareth the eternal God entered into human life, then something beyond man, a superhuman purpose and power, is now at work in the world; and we may be entirely sure that God's purpose of good is ultimately beyond defeat."[119]

In a postneo-orthodox and postexistentialist age, it is of some interest to hear American Protestant theologians in the 1960's proclaiming: "The Kingdom of God, concentrated in the life of Jesus of Nazareth, remains the fullest possible disclosure of the partnership of God and man in history."[120] And: "*In* his free, creative, responsible work man discovers what it means to be related to God who is also at work and calls man to be his partner."[121]

This brings us to a final element in Tittle's theology. The Kingdom of God is not of this world only. "It cannot be, for it is not confined in men and women who are loyal to God at any one moment in history. It includes the faithful dead as well as those who today are seeking to know and to do the will of God. Those in every generation who put others above self, who lived for ends too great to be realized in their own lifetime, who in some cases laid down their lives that those who should come after them might have life and have it abundantly—those all are included in the kingdom of God, which is at once in history and beyond history."[122] Christianity refuses to believe that bodily death means final frustration. "In this world there is frustration enough! Millions of people never have a chance to know life at its fullest and best. Little children incinerated in air raids, young girls raped and killed, mere boys still in their teens mowed down by machine guns or shell fire, underprivileged multitudes living all their days in shabby houses, on mean streets, in blighted neighborhoods, without helping influence of any kind whatever—these have little or no chance in this world to come to fullness of life. But they will be given a chance, if the God of Christian faith exists. The God of Jesus Christ has a purpose which he is working out in human life. He is seeking to bring us men and women into fellowship with himself, that, coming to see as he sees and to care as he cares, we may develop and express the best that is in us and experience

119. *Ibid.*, p. 11.
120. Harvey Cox, *The Secular City*, rev. ed. (New York: Macmillan, 1966), p. 97. See also Melvin L. Vulgamore, "The Social Gospel Old and New: Walter Rauschenbusch and Harvey Cox," *Religion In Life*, XXXVI (Winter, 1967), 516-33.
121. Charles C. West, "What It Means To Be Secular," in Daniel Callahan (ed.), *The Secular City Debate* (New York: Macmillan Company, 1966), p. 61.
122. "Our Eternal Home," typed MS, a sermon preached June 25, 1944.

a joy and peace surpassing all our dreams. This purpose cannot be worked out fully amid the accidents and catastrophes of history. But if not in this present world, then in a world where hunger and poverty and fetid slums and obliteration bombing shall be no more men will be given a chance to come into fellowship with God and, so, to experience life at its fullest and best."[123] Tittle was persuaded that nothing, not even death, shall be able to separate us from the love of God. On the last Sunday of his life he stood before the people of First Church and spoke the comforting words: "It is the Christian faith that there is no situation in which God is not present with saving help. The presence of God does not necessarily mean deliverance from bodily injury or death. But for any man or woman who turns to God in time of need it means deliverance from fear and despair; it means the power to triumph over disaster, to go down, if one must, with all flags flying and the confident hope of the resurrection and the life everlasting. . . . And when his work on earth is done, the servant of God may with entire confidence say in the spirit of his Lord: 'Father, into thy hands I commit my spirit.' "[124]

* * *

It was beastly hot in Evanston that summer of 1949. On the last Sunday in July Tittle ended his summer preaching. Nineteen hundred worshippers in sanctuary and chapel heard him utter his final words from the First Church pulpit. These words, providentially said some, were on "Hope." It had been a demanding spring. His appointment book for the fall was already crowded with engagements. His twice-wounded heart cried for rest. Soon he would be off to the North Woods to catch a few fish, "so that they may learn to be more careful next time." But first there was a duty to perform. For three years he had toiled on the Saint Luke volume, a task he found enormously arduous, and at long last the end was in sight. A few additional days of sweat and the book would be completed; he would be freed from the bondage of his hot study. For two days he worked steadily. On the third morning at 10:30, Wednesday, August 3, the summons came. Tittle died as he wished, quickly and while "in harness."

Friday afternoon in the First Church sanctuary there were no flowers except the customary altar vases, no candles except the usual altar candles, no casket. At four o'clock the great organ pealed out modern Methodism's glorious hymn of service, North's "Where Cross the Crowded Ways of Life." And then Bach's "Jesu, Joy of Man's Desir-

123. *Gospel According To Luke*, p. 221.
124. *Mighty Fortress*, pp. 175-76.

ing," Isaac Watts's "Jesus Shall Reign," and Lane's "All Hail the Power of Jesus' Name."

The chancel choir entered in processional, singing Luther's hymn of dauntless Protestantism, "A Mighty Fortress Is Our God."

A prayer and passages from the Scriptures read by the assistant minister, Kenneth F. Thompson: "Lord, thou hast been our dwelling place in all generations. . . ."; "God is our refuge and strength, a very present help in trouble. . . ."; "The Lord is my shepherd: I shall not want. . . ."; "The Spirit of man is the candle of the Lord. . . ."; "Let us now praise famous men, and our fathers that begat us. . . ."; "There be of them that have left a name behind them that their praises might be reported. . . ."; "We know that in everything God works for good with those who love Him, who are called according to his purpose. . . ."; "In nothing be anxious; but in everything by prayer and supplication with thinksgiving let your requests be made known unto God. . . ."; "For our light affliction, which is for the moment, worketh for us more and more exceedingly an eternal weight of glory; while we look not at the things which are seen, but at the things which are not seen: for the things which are seen are temporal; the things which are unseen are eternal. . . ."; "But someone will say, how are the dead raised? And with what manner of body do they come? . . ."; "And I saw a new heaven and a new earth; for the first heaven and the first earth were passed away. . . ."; "Jesus said: 'Let not your hearts be troubled: ye believe in God, believe also in me. In my Father's house are many mansions: if it were not so, I would have told you. I go to prepare a place for you. And if I go and prepare a place for you I will come again, and receive you unto myself; that where I am, there ye may be also. I will not leave you desolate; I come unto you. I am the way, the truth, and the life: no man cometh unto the Father, but by me. Peace I leave with you, my peace I give unto you. Let not your heart be troubled neither let it be afraid."

Prayers by the assistant minister, Joe Thomas. The name of Ernest Fremont Tittle is mentioned but once.

The congregation joins in saying the Lord's Prayer.

The Benediction: "The peace of God which passeth all understanding. . . ."

The Recessional Hymn: "O God our help in ages past."

For sixty-three years Ernest Fremont Tittle as preacher and pastor, citizen and friend, husband and father, had labored and prayed to make this earth, man's temporal home, a more sheltering, less contingent abode.

A NOTE ON SOURCES

This note has been written on the assumption that many readers will not require a formal bibliography and that those interested in knowing the research supporting the volume will find in the footnotes adequate indication. I should like to set forth here only a few clarifying observations, beginning with the general one that I have been engaged in the study of American Protestantism since 1950 and in the specific preparation of this biography since 1958 and in the teaching of United States history for two decades, and that it is impossible for me to compartmentalize my research and reading (and mulling) into Tittle and non-Tittle categories. Inevitably, then, material for this study has been drawn in a willy-nilly fashion from my other researches, my classes and seminars, and my general reading.

The Tittle Collection is very full and very rich, containing as it does virtually everything Tittle wrote after 1918 including manuscript drafts of sermons, articles, addresses and also his appointment books, account books, scrapbooks, reading lists, and much additional material relating to his ministry and private life. The special strength of the collection are the thousands of letters he received and the carbon copies of the hundreds of letters he sent—and copies were made of even the briefest of notes dealing with the most minor subjects. The Tittle family to their enduring credit did not withhold a single item from my examination, and to my knowledge the collection has been spared even the slightest family censorship; that is, there was no winnowing of Tittle's files after his death. The collection is flawed in two major respects: it contains no diary or autobiographical reflections and it is thin on the early, pre-First Church years. The collection was first examined over the period of two summers in the home of John M. Tittle where it had been placed after Tittle's death. Then, in answer to my plea, John Tittle, with extraordinary understanding, permitted the collection to be temporarily housed at the University of North Carolina where I had convenient access to it. The collection will now be permanently deposited in the Garrett Theological Seminary Library, Evanston, Illinois, for unrestricted use by qualified researchers. Dr. Tittle's extensive personal library, willed to Gammon Theological Seminary, was examined in the limited manner explained in the text. All of Dr. Tittle's published books and many of his published articles and printed sermons are cited by title in the footnotes. It seems to me that no useful purpose would be served by listing here every title, particularly since such a listing would require many pages.

If the Tittle Collection provided the bricks for the construction of the biography, oral interviews served as mortar. Almost one hundred individuals shared their memories with me, some of them in brief, informal chats, but most of them in scheduled interviews extending over several hours and entire mornings, afternoons, or evenings—indeed, in a few instances over several days. In my judgment oral testimony if evaluated with the historians' customary critical caution is a valid and valuable source, especially when that testimony can be checked by cross-examination and against the written record or the oral testimony of others. My most serious reservation concerning evidence obtained in interviews is that people who agree to testify are more inclined to say favorable rather than critical things, and that in the case of Tittle far more witnesses took the stand for the defense than for the prosecution.

In response to petitions placed in the religious and secular press and in reply to specific letters of inquiry, many individuals wrote to me about their association with Tittle. The value of this source is diminished by the fact that almost all the correspondents were warm admirers of Tittle. This, of course, is a tribute to Tittle, but it also suggests that most people, knowing that we have the dead at our mercy, chose to be merciful.

Tittle's boyhood and early Ohio pastorates was an unexplored country and there was no alternative but to go to Springfield, Delaware, Dayton, and Columbus and personally walk the terrain. It was slow, tedious, contingent work, but thanks to the generous cooperation of many individuals—former Tittle neighbors, schoolmates, and parishioners, municipal clerks and librarians, Wittenberg College and Ohio Wesleyan University officers, and parish secretaries and parsons—it was possible to know the young Tittle. I found the files of the *Springfield Daily News, Dayton Daily News, Columbus Evening Dispatch* (all available on microfilm), and the *Delaware Daily Gazette* indispensable in reconstructing the external events of these early years.

The records of the First Methodist Church, Evanston, are voluminous, completely filling a large basement room. I was given a key to the room and absolute freedom to examine anything and everything in it. This handsome gesture on the part of the First Church authorities reflects the broad and free spirit of this great congregation. Among such a vast archival richness, especially valuable were the Minutes of the Official Board, the Scrapbook of the Official Board, and the files of the *First Church Review* and worship service bulletins.

For the Evanston scene, files of the *Evanston News-Index* (after April, 1935, the *Evanston Daily News-Index*) and the *Evanston Review* were crucial, and well worth the months required to scrutinize them page by page. The *Chicago Tribune* was examined only for selected periods of crisis. I am grateful to the librarians of Northwestern, Garret, and the Evanston Public Library for directing me to additional materials dealing with the two schools and the community. I was raised on the North Shore and I suspect that this experience has at once both blurred and sharpened my view of the Evanston scene, paradoxical as this may seem.

Every student of American religious history understands that the standard offical sources of Methodism are the quadrennially published *Doctrines and Discipline*, the *Journal of the General Conference*, and the *Daily Christian Advocate*. I examined these three sources for the Methodist Episcopal Church since the 1900 General Conference, for the Methodist Episcopal Church, South, since the 1898 General Conference, and for The Methodist Church since the great 1939 Uniting Conference. Although the *Discipline* and the *Journal* are authoritative, the *Daily Christian Advocate* alone carries the General Conference debates and is therefore the most helpful. The *Journal and Year Book of the Rock River Annual Conference* (1918-1949) and the *Journal of the North Central Jurisdictional Conference* (1940, 1944, and 1948) were invaluable in assessing Tittle's leadership at these critical levels. I have long believed the Methodist press to be a source of supreme importance, and my understanding of American Methodism is derived in goodly measure from a reading of the twentieth-century files of the *New York Christian Advocate*, the *Nashville Christian Advocate*, the *Northwestern Christian Advocate*, *Zion's Herald*, the *Arkansas Methodist*, the *Methodist Review*, the *Epworth Herald*, *Social Questions Bulletin*, *Social Service Bulletin*, *Religion in Life*, and, more recently and less systematically, *The Pastor* and *Motive*. Periodical research is a slow game but worth the candle. Additional Methodist sources, such as the records of the Methodist Federation for Social Service, the Methodist Youth Council, the Methodist Peace Commission, and Methodist Sunday School materials are cited where appropriate in the footnotes.

For Methodism's relationship to other Protestant denominations, I drew where appropriate on my earlier work, *American Protestantism and Social Issues, 1919-1939*. Interested readers may wish to consult the bibliography in that volume, since it includes a variety of church and secular sources, both primary and secondary.

Of the dozen sketches of Tittle, Paul Hutchinson's "Portrait of a Preacher" is by far the most perceptive. (Most of the other sketches are cited in the footnotes.) The single extended examination of Tittle is Harold Arthur Brack's unpublished dissertation, "Ernest Fremont Tittle's Theory and Practice of Preaching," a work of such a different intention from my own effort that no comparisons need be made.

Only a handful of private papers were examined, the most significant being the James Cannon, Jr., Papers at Duke University, the Edwin McNeill Poteat Papers at the University of North Carolina, and the

Charles Brent Papers at the Library of Congress. This requires some explanation. For one thing, the papers of most key individuals in Tittle's career, such as Bishop Francis J. McConnell, have simply disappeared. For another, most of the limited number of collections that have survived, such as the Devere Allen Papers, contain little or nothing from Tittle. Above all, because Tittle kept carbon copies of the letters he sent as well as preserving those he received, the collections of men with whom he corresponded become of lessened importance. (For inexplicable reasons I was denied access to the Bishop G. Bromley Oxnam papers in the Library of Congress. The papers of such towering churchmen as Harry Emerson Fosdick and Reinhold Niebuhr are not yet available.)

In conclusion, I found this a tough book to research. Tittle's concerns were at once appropriately and appallingly ranging, from liturgy and psalmody to philosophy and theology to racism and civil liberties to socialism and pacifism to ecclesiology and eschatology. I trust the footnotes suggest the enforced breadth of my reading. To list here the specific items would be a hopelessly long enterprise and an unconscionably pretentious one.

R. M. M.

INDEX

A

Abbott, Lyman, 25, 181, 485, 509

Addams, Jane, 224, 227

African Methodist Episcopal Church, 269, 349

Alcoholics Anonymous, 304-5

Allinson, Brent Dow, 213-14, 216, 218, 219

America First Committee, 447, 448

American Civil Liberties Union, 224, 226, 228, 339, 369, 385, 386, 387, 395

American Friends Service Committee, 226, 402

American League Against War and Fascism, 390, 391

American Legion, 211, 213-14, 215, 216, 219, 224, 225, 226, 229, 319, 383, 387, 426

American Liberty League, 232, 237, 383

American Protective Association, 309, 314, 317

American Protective League, 229

American Vigilance Intelligence Federation, 224

Anderson, William F., 49, 51, 57, 58, 59, 281, 303, 316

Anti-Saloon League, 302, 304, 306

Anti-Semitism, 226, 312, 314, 319, 324-28, 330, 436, 446, 453, 454

B

Baker, James C., 208, 239, 285, 385

Baldwin, James, 333, 338

Barth, Karl, 477, 485, 489-90, 491, 504

Bashford, James Whitford, 21, 22, 33

Beecher, Henry Ward, 25, 180, 188, 485

Berdyaev, Nikolai, 485

Blake, Edgar, 283, 284, 285, 384

Blanchard, Paul, 212, 364

Bombing, Allied and American, 436, 456, 468-71, 473-74

Bonhoeffer, Dietrich, 325, 486, 502

Borders, Karl, 224

Bowne, Borden Parker, 38, 40-41, 275, 485

Brittain, Vera, 469, 470

Broad Street Methodist Episcopal Church, Columbus, Ohio, 51, 52, 57-58, 68

Brooks, Phillips, 24-25, 84, 106, 163, 196, 481

Browder, Earl, 386-87, 390

Brown, Arlo Ayres, 41, 274, 373

Brown, Hugh Elmer, 270

Brunner, Emil, 477, 485

Buber, Martin, 176, 477, 485

Bultmann, Rudolf, 477, 485, 486

Buttz, Henry Anson, 37-38

G

Gammon Theological Seminary. *See* Interdenominational Theological Center

Garland Fund, 226, 229

Garrett Biblical Institute (Garrett Theological Seminary), 39, 56, 67, 88, 164, 183, 211, 212, 215, 219, 233, 246-47, 263-64, 297, 420

Gladden, Washington, 22, 25, 40, 53, 63, 161, 202, 300, 485

Gompers, Samuel: criticizes church, 362

H

Haessler, Carl, 228, 387

Helm, Wilbur, 233, 236

Henschen, Henry S., 236

Higher Criticism, 22, 40, 41, 48

Hoffman, John Washington, 50, 51

Holmes, John Haynes, 393, 400, 418-19, 428, 453, 454

Hough, Lynn Harold, 41, 51, 274, 316, 461-62; supports Hoover, 373

House Committee on Un-American Activities, 385, 393

Hughes, Edwin Holt, 91, 222, 277, 281, 316, 381, 400; supports Plan of Union, 351-52; supports Hoover, 373

Hutchinson, Paul, 11-12, 13, 19, 21, 45, 51, 92, 94, 170-71, 195, 198, 201, 233, 280, 374

I

Immigration, 9, 262, 298, 299, 320, 328, 330, 361, 362, 363; and prohibition, 301; hostility to, 310-13, 322; and anti-Semitism, 324-25

Interchurch World Movement, 244

Interdenominational Theological Center, 196, 351

Inter-racial Commission of Greater Chicago, 339

Inter-Racial Cooperative Council, 341-42

Isolationism (Isolationists), 63, 399, 404-5, 411, 413, 415-17, 431, 432, 439, 440, 446, 448, 454

J

James, James Alton, 56, 94, 233, 273, 287, 291

James, William, 26, 485, 491

Japanese-Americans: evacuation of, 472

Japanese Exclusion Act, 433

Jefferson, Charles E., 64, 198

Jones, Robert E., 345, 351

Jung, Harry A., 224, 227, 229, 236

K

Keep America Out of War Congress, 446-47

Kellogg-Briand Pact, 410-12

King, Willis J., 351

Knights of Labor, 8

Ku Klux Klan, 163, 211, 225, 234, 267, 308-319, 330, 341

L

Labor, 8, 182, 300, 312, 313, 361-64, 367-68, 369, 370. *See also* Strikes

Laymen's Missionary Movement, 24

Laymen's Religious Movement, 385

League for Industrial Democracy, 224, 226, 230, 370, 385, 408

League of Nations, 74, 399-401, 409-10, 411, 422, 424, 433

Lee, Umphrey, 461

Leonard, Adna W., 284, 384, 468

Lewis, Edwin, 41

Luccock, Halford E., 94, 137, 172, 235, 374, 420

Ludlow Amendment, 432-33

Lutkin, Peter Christian, 94, 153-54

M

McConnell, Francis J., 94, 220, 240, 273, 283, 285, 370, 381, 389, 491; denounces Ku Klux Klan, 316; opposes Al Smith, 321-22; opposes segregation, 346, 347; supports Plan of Union, 353; endorses socialism, 374; attacks Versailles Treaty, 400; urges intervention in World War II, 452

McDowell, William Fraser, 47, 50, 56, 57, 58, 222, 268, 281, 285, 349, 381; introduces Plan of Union, 352

Magee, J. Ralph, 277, 278

Methodism (Methodists), 19-20, 29, 35-36, 51-52; and theological conflict, 40-41; and World War I, 61-63, 66-68, 81; and morality, 121, 254, 307; conduct of services of, 148-52; music of, 152-53; and pacifism, 218-19, 405, 411, 412, 419-21, 430, 433; and Negroes, 225, 344-60;